THE
VICTORIAN
RAILWAY

JACK SIMMONS

THE VICTORIAN RAILWAY

with 60 illustrations

*The smoothly-gliding engine, whisking as many passengers
along as would have filled the old coaches for a week, unlocking
the country for miles, and bringing parties within a few hours
of each other who had formerly been separated by days.*

R. S. Surtees (1860)

Thames & Hudson

Designed by Liz Rudderham

First published in the United Kingdom in 1991 by Thames & Hudson Ltd,
181A High Holborn, London WC1V 7QX

www.thamesandhudson.com

© 1991 Jack Simmons
First paperback edition with corrections 1995
Reprinted 2009

British Library Cataloguing-in-Publication Data
A catalogue record for this book is available from the British Library

ISBN 978-0-500-28810-8

Printed and bound in China by SNP Leefung Printers Limited

CONTENTS

LIST OF TABLES

A NOTE ON SOME POINTS OF USAGE

In the spelling of place-names the general rule followed here has been to accept the practice established on the railways themselves in the Victorian age. The names of places that had passenger stations are spelt as in the *Railway Clearing House Handbook of Railway Stations,* 1904 (reprinted in 1970); Bartholomew's *Survey Gazetteer of the British Isles* (1904 edition) has been the authority for the rest. As a necessary consequence, all Welsh place-names appear here in an anglicized form: e.g. Carnarvon.

Similarly, counties are referred to throughout as they were in 1914, not in the form they have come to assume under the Local Government Act of 1972. The expression 'the City' refers to the City of London, usually in its corporate capacity. A simple conversion table in respect of currency is given below.

The term 'Regulation Acts' is used as a generic description of all the ten Acts passed, with slightly different titles, for the regulation of railways between 1840 and 1893.

MONEY CONVERSION TABLE

Table of £ s. d./£ p equivalents

£	s.	d.	£p	£	s.	d.	£p
		1d.	½		6s.		30p
		2d.	1p		7s.		35p
		3d.	1p		8s.		40p
		4d.	1½p		9s.		45p
		5d.	2p		10s.		50p
		6d.	2½p		11s.		55p
		7d.	3p		12s.		60p
		8d.	3p		13s.		65p
		9d.	4p		14s.		70p
		10d.	4p		15s.		75p
		11d.	4½p		16s.		80p
		12d. (1s.)	5p		17s.		85p
	2s.		10p		18s.		90p
	3s.		15p		19s.		95p
	4s.		20p		20s. (£)		100p
	5s.		25p				

To

Michael and Elspeth Robbins

PREFACE

This book sets out to present the mechanically-worked railway through the eyes and minds of those who watched it between 1830 and 1914; to consider some of the changes it produced in their habits of looking and thinking and feeling; to indicate what they noticed, here and there what they missed or ignored.

It also discusses what the railway did. It has been, in my opinion, too much treated on its own, as a piece of mechanism, a device. Of those who have written broadly of the Victorian age, only Clapham gave what may be called adequate attention to the part the railway played in it, and even his excellent account is limited because he was writing an *Economic History of Modern Britain*. Railways did many things that lay outside his scope in that book, and no one has assigned them their place in the general life of the age. This book tries to show them in their context.

The first six chapters are concerned with the impact the railway made on the Victorians' eyes; now and then on their ears and noses too. To ordinary people, not experts, the physical impression they made was strongest, and that arose most powerfully from the structures created to carry the railway itself and from the machines required for its working. So structures and machines are examined here first, with some attention in Chapter 4 to the men who were responsible for what was done, appraising them both as technicians and as artists. Their work evoked a response among artists of another kind, who recorded it in drawings and paintings, and presently in the new medium of photography. This is examined in Chapter 5.

However, the railway also wrought a good deal of damage in its construction, both to the landscape it passed across and to the towns it entered. As early as the 1860s that came to be dubbed 'vandalism'. It raised for the first time a broad issue that we can recognize very well today: the conflicting claims of material advantage and of the protection of the environment – an environment especially vulnerable in an island so small, containing so large a population.

The second part of the book deals more with the Victorians' minds than with their eyes, examining some of the things the railway did to enlarge their experience of life. It looks first at the impression the railway made on language, and then on the literature of a very productive age; an uneven impression, here and there deep and powerful, at other points perfunctory. Its services in disseminating written matter come next: in the acceleration and cheapening of the posts, the development of the telegraph, the circulation of newspapers and their sale on station platforms, creating unselfconsciously what grew into national networks of bookshops. Railway companies did not undertake all this business solely for the benefit of others. They needed to communicate with the public on their own account. To that end they used advertising, in many different shapes. Their premises and vehicles carried a great many advertisements put out by other commercial undertakings too. Most of all this was crude, some of it hideous, and that brought the railway companies a good deal of odium. At the same time they were arousing hostility for other, more important reasons, which expressed itself in Parliament. This persuaded some of their abler managers that they must try to communicate with their customers, and so with the country as a whole, more effectively and imaginatively than they had done in the past. At the turn of the century we can perceive in them a stirring of the concept not merely of publicity but of public relations.

In Chapters 12 and 13 I examine the contribution the railway made to the use of leisure; the leisure that many people came to be granted or to win for themselves through a reduction in the hours of work, accompanied by a rise in the real rates of pay. Those advantages arrived slowly and irregularly – being conferred on one large class of Victorian workers, domestic servants, scarcely at all. Yet they went further in Britain than they did anywhere on the mainland of Europe before 1914. The British railways had much to offer to those who secured these benefits, particularly through the excursion train, carrying a large number of people for a day out at the cheapest fares that seemed likely to bring in an adequate return. No other railways adopted this device with anything like the same energy or enthusiasm as those in Britain.

As soon as their ordinary passenger traffic had come to be worked with regularity on a national system, the railways set themselves to attract business from all those who wished to make holidays of any kind; not British travellers alone, but foreign visitors as well. The leading figure in that movement, in Britain and in the world at large, the first to perceive what railways might do to this end, was an Englishman of genius: Thomas Cook.

The railway was designed to promote the movement of men and women, and of every sort of goods. This book is concerned chiefly with the men and women. The railway conferred on them a new freedom to move: in the course of their daily employment; in search of employment itself; on personal business, within the family or between friends; for the pursuit of any kind of interest or pleasure. The Victorians accepted this freedom with both hands. The number of railway journeys they took became startlingly greater, per head of the population, than it was anywhere else. My concluding chapters offer some explanations of this remarkable mobility and discuss certain of the results that flowed from it, in the Victorian age itself and beyond, down to our own time.

This is not in any sense a history of the Victorian railways. I have treated some of the matters discussed in it – their civil and mechanical engineering, for instance, their part in the development of holiday resorts – more fully in two earlier works, *The Railway in England and Wales* and *The Railway in Town and Country*. I hope this book may be read in conjunction with them, assisted by some cross-reference in its notes. The framework here is different from theirs, however, in that they dealt only with England and Wales, whereas this one concerns itself with Scotland also, with the whole island of Great Britain.

This book has been a long time in preparation. A good many people have assisted me in my work on it, some of them over many years.

I am glad to acknowledge the services I have received from a number of institutions: Bristol University Library (especially George Maby), the British Library, the Ironbridge Gorge Museum (especially David de Haan, John Powell, and Michael Vanns), Leicester University Library, the National Railway Museum (Phil Atkins, John Coiley, Beverley Cole, John Edgington), the Public Record Office, the Science Museum, the Scottish National Portrait Gallery (Sara Stevenson), the Scottish Record Office (George Barbour).

I am also grateful to friends who answered questions and read drafts of chapters, drawing attention to things I might otherwise have missed: Theo Barker, Gordon Biddle, David Brooke, Philip Collins, Alfred Heinimann, John Hume, David Jeffreys, George Ottley, Ken Phillipps, Roger Taylor, and David Treffry. My greatest debt is glanced at in the dedication of the book.

Leicester   *J. S.*
21 February 1990

I

IMAGES

This book is concerned largely with the impression made by the railway on habits of seeing, thinking, and feeling. To understand them, we have to rid ourselves of much preconception. The railway does certain things today, and we assume it will continue to do them. It is only when it fails, through an accident perhaps or a strike, that we think of it specially, or on those uncommon occasions when it offers some new service or proposes to withdraw a well-established one. As for seeing the railway, that is a faculty almost forgotten now, except when it is treated in some television programme; forgotten most of all through the disappearance of the steam locomotive, with the noises and the clouds of smoke it emitted, drawing attention insistently to its presence. There is little to distinguish a railway, at first glance, from a motorway, beyond the rails and the large size of the units conveyed on it. Most people think of the railway as something achieved and finite. They are almost unaware of it.

To the Victorians all this was different. They saw the railway arrive, evolve, expand. 'A new world of inventions – of railways and of telegraphs – has grown up around us, which we cannot help seeing': Bagehot selected those in 1867 as the most obvious examples he could offer of the progress of 'physical knowledge' in his own time.[1] H. G. Wells went further. If a symbol was needed to characterize the nineteenth century, he said, looking backwards in 1902, it would be 'almost inevitably ... a steam engine running upon a railway'.[2]

Although the Liverpool & Manchester was the most startling of all railways, the number of those who saw it, in spite of its fame, was not very large, and only a few of them were articulate. Nevertheless, accounts of its working soon spread, addressed not only to sophisticated audiences in the great cities but to country people also.[3] It was a commonplace among early travellers on the line that the journey, made at a speed of 20 mph and more, called up the idea of flight, most of all in crossing the spongy tracts that gave the engineers so much trouble when the line was being constructed. But what struck nearly all these early passengers most was the shock and speed of meeting a train coming in the opposite direction. The American Emerson expressed the sensation vividly: 'Strange it was to meet the return cars; to see a load of timber, six or seven masts, dart by you like a trout'.[4]

Some good descriptions came from those who were furthest removed from anything to do with railways; perhaps the best of all the very well known one from a young actress, Fanny Kemble, who enjoyed the special advantage of travelling on the engine, where she was under the attentive eye of George Stephenson himself.[5] Here is another, by a French priest, struggling with the

[13]

difficulties of an unmechanical mind trying to describe a machine and to do that in the English language:

> I took my passage to Manchester on that truly astonishing Machine called Steam Coach. Fancy a bulky machine composed of two very large carriages joined together on a same line, the whole occupying in length a span of about 50 ft, each carriage divided by boards in three *compartiments* or partitions, each partition containing six passengers facing each other, and very comfortably seated on arm chairs. Thus each carriage contains eighteen passengers and the five together ninety, independent of four persons destined to feed the steam, and who go on at the rate of about twenty-five miles an hour. The steam is compressed within so narrow a compass that the place where it is lodged is scarcely to be perceived, and were it not for the thick wittish [whitish] smoke which comes out from the large tube placed to the end of the machine which attests the existence of the Gaz below, one would fancy to be drawn by any faery or other invisible or other supernatural agent.[6]

The most celebrated description in English of any railway being built is Dickens's in *Dombey and Son*.[7] There he depicts the upheaval created by the London & Birmingham Railway as it was being driven through Camden Town in London, the destruction of Staggs's Gardens. This brilliant description in words happens to be matched by a meticulous presentation of the scene, to *Ill. 1* the eye, in John Bourne's delicate and precise record. No such conjunction, at this level of art, ever occurred again, in Britain or anywhere else.

The construction of a railway began with the arrival of the first projectors and engineers, looking for alternative routes that the line might take. Their arrival often led to conflicts with landowners and farmers. The antipathy between the engineers and the country people was natural and strong, and it was well described by George Eliot, looking back forty years afterwards to what she had seen and heard as a girl in Warwickshire.[8] By intelligent engineers too. Here is one of them, recounting what he had observed in Hertfordshire in 1834:

> One or two strange faces appeared in the town [Watford], and men in leathern leggings, dragging a long chain, and attended by one or two country labourers armed with bill-hooks, were remarked as trespassing in the most unwarrantable manner over pasture land, standing crops, copse and cover; actually cutting gaps in the hedges through which they climbed and dragged the land-chain. Then would follow another intruder, bearing a telescope set on three legs, which he erected with the most perfect coolness wherever he thought fit, peering through it at a long white staff, marked with unintelligible hieroglyphics, which was borne by another labourer, and moved or held stationary in accordance with a mysterious code of telegraphic signals made by the hand.

The farmers, naturally indignant, ordered these intruders from their
fields. The engineers, for such they were, took but little notice. The
farmers proceeded to threats. The ringleader of the invaders produced a
red book, folded in an oblong form, from the voluminous pocket of his
velveteen jacket, and offered it to the irate farmer as a sedative, informing
him that it was the Act of Parliament by authority of which he was
acting . . . One thing alone remained for them [the farmers] to do . . . they
would shoot the intruders. But the latter calmly replied that that was no
business of theirs, and the farmers did not draw trigger.[9]

Although similar conflicts of interest had arisen over the acquisition of land
for the building of some canals (the power of compulsory purchase was equally
resented there),[10] none of them were as fierce as these, over the building of
railways.[11]

When railways got to work they might inspire satisfaction; astonishment
and reverence; bewilderment; fear, in some people intense dislike. There were
those who took to travelling by train without the least difficulty. A country
gentleman – Scott's friend J. B. S. Morritt of Rokeby – could write in calm
commendation of his first journey, from Birmingham to Liverpool on the
Grand Junction Railway in 1838; amazed by the speed, which yet was 'so
deceptive that even when done it seems quite unaccountable'; attained so
smoothly at 28 mph that he had 'felt more dizzy when whirled along by four
horses at the rate of ten or eleven miles in the hour'. Though the 'spattering
and rattle' of the train were tiresome, he found it 'perfectly practicable to
read, and still easier to sleep in the carriage'.[12]

As for reverence, John Bright always kept the impression made on him by
the first train he ever saw, at Rochdale in 1839. 'It was a new thing', he said
many years afterwards, 'and I think the power, the speed and the grandeur
of these great locomotive engines can never grow old, and that we can never
regard them without wonder and without admiration'.[13]

Many simple people, when they first saw them at work, were terrified by
them. In 1841 a Wiltshire clergyman took his parish clerk, William Hinton,
to watch the passage of one of the first trains along the Great Western main
line between Wootton Bassett and Chippenham. They stood on the edge of a
cutting.

Presently our ears were assailed by the gruff snort of the engine as it
laboured up the severest and sharpest gradient on the whole line from
London. As soon as it attained to the highest point strange palpitating
throbs burst from the throat of the chimney, preceded by the shrill scream
of the whistle, followed by a frenzied w-h-i-s-h and then an impetuous
rush down the incline at sixty miles an hour. The novelty of the sight,
the strangeness of the sounds, the marvellous velocity with which engine,
tender, carriages, and trucks disappeared, the dense columns of sulphurous
smoke, were altogether too much for the reason of my simple dominie
[Hinton], and he fell prostrate on the bank-side as if he had been smitten

by a thunderbolt! When he had recovered his feet, his brain still reeled, his tongue clove to the roof of his mouth, and he stood aghast, unutterable amazement stamped upon his face. It must have been quite five minutes before he could speak, and when he did it was in the tone of a Jeremiah. 'Well, Sir, that was a sight to have seen; but one I never care to see again! How much longer shall knowledge be allowed to go on increasing?'[14]

Exclamations of this sort continue to be recorded, far down into the Victorian age. Martha Vickery, travelling from Ilminster to Bridgwater in 1855, fortunately had her comments noted down in her rich Somerset dialect: 'the devil himself was a drawin of em [the carriages] – the vire an the smoake comm'd out o an and on they went the Lord knows where'. She preferred to return home by canal boat and on foot. Here is a poor woman at Thame in 1864, hopelessly muddled by the complications of travelling to see her daughter at Aylesbury, changing at the wrong place and finding herself back at Thame, to be forwarded by the kindly stationmaster under the charge of the guard.[15]

The fear the railway inspired in many travellers was natural enough, arising from the turmoil of the stations and the complexity of the arrangements there, the loud and sudden noises made by the engines and trains, the dizzy heights at which some lines were carried over river-valleys,[16] and the alarming, unlighted passage through tunnels.[17] These things might discompose even very strong men, like Nelson's Hardy,[18] and women as tough as old Lady Holland. Yet she, having been a 'vituperator' against railways, was brought to express satisfaction with her first journey on any of them, after Brunel had taken her down from London to Chippenham in his own carriage, holding her hand all the way.[19] The coachmaster Edward Sherman, lamenting the decline of his business, said in 1839 that his passengers were then largely 'timid people', nervous of travelling by train, but he added: 'Daily we find that many people who would not have gone [by railway] for any consideration go now'.[20]

Some people nevertheless retained an unconquerable distaste for railways. Here the Duke of Wellington's attitude is worth attention. In 1827 he travelled behind a locomotive (a 'steam elephant') on the Marquess of Londonderry's private colliery railway near Sunderland.[21] The next train journey he made was at the opening of the Liverpool & Manchester Railway; a miserable occasion, with Huskisson's accident and the Duke's fiercely hostile reception in Manchester. In public life he took a responsible line towards railways, urging closer regulation of them by government in 1838, and seeking to persuade Gladstone to require the companies to run cheap third-class trains on Sundays as well as on week-days.[22] When it came to planning a railway to run near his own country house in Hampshire, he at first insisted that no station should be opened at less than five miles' distance and then accepted one much nearer, at his neighbours' request.[23] His personal dislike for railway travelling remained with him, however. He went habitually in his own carriage, mounted on a flat truck, preferring that arrangement to a journey in 'a public conveyance in which one may be quite certain of having worse company than in any stage coach, without the chance of relief at short distance'. But then he was the most famous man in England. If, at a station, he had to obey a call of nature, he would be 'followed by one of these well-dressed mobs as a hunted animal is by the hounds, till he is forced again in his carriage'.[24] What he valued above all was privacy, which the railway destroyed.

Such feelings were fed in a new form as accidents increased and grew more terrible. The novelist Peacock always thought with apprehension of high-pressure steam, of boiler explosions on locomotives and steamships.[25] That form of disaster proved much less destructive of human life than Peacock expected.[26] But many other dangers hung over Victorian travellers. On solitary journeys in enclosed compartments rich men might be murdered, and anyone might find himself shut in with a lunatic, or a smallpox patient.[27] It was not until the 1890s that an effective system of communication between passengers and train crews won general acceptance. The danger of fire was appallingly displayed in the wreck of the Irish Mail at Abergele in 1868;[28] a risk intensified by the use of gas for lighting in carriages and cooking in dining-cars, proclaimed in frightful accidents in 1910–13.[29]

The only leading Victorian writer who was in a serious railway accident was Dickens, at Staplehurst in 1865,[30] but his words tell us very little of the accident itself. We get some clear accounts from passengers who were not professional writers at all. The accident at Abbot's Ripton in 1876, a collision between two expresses and a coal train occurring in a heavy snowstorm, was described by Lord Colville of Culross. He escaped by a hair's breadth – two young men sitting opposite him in the same compartment disappeared, and their bodies were subsequently found buried beneath six others; but his own nerve was strong, and he was able to recount his experience plainly.[31]

From 1841 onwards railway accidents were investigated by the Board of Trade through inspectors, whose reports were published as government papers. Publicity like this had not been given to coach accidents. No accurate comparison could be made then between the mortality rate on roads and on railways; but in 1851 John Francis was asserting that the likelihood of death or injury to a traveller by train was very much less than to one who went by coach.[32] The Stockton & Darlington Railway never killed a passenger.[33] The same record could be claimed by the two pioneer underground railways, the Metropolitan and the District, neither of which was responsible for the death of a single passenger while it was worked by steam (1863–1905). After 1880 the Victorians generally came to recognize railway travel as a wonderfully safe mode of locomotion.

There were moments when the railways suddenly shone out, in long-remembered achievements or episodes of operation. They were for example admired and beloved – very rightly – for the services they rendered in snowstorms, when they alone were able to convey passengers or food supplies or coal with anything like regularity.[34] Their feats of moving people in enormous numbers were occasionally noticed and applauded: at holiday times, for instance, when they took excursionists to the seaside in hundreds of thousands. At the turn of the century they put that capacity at the disposal of the State. The London & South Western company conveyed nearly all the troops to the South African War in 1899–1902 through its own port of Southampton: a rehearsal for the much vaster undertaking, managed by the same company at the same port, in 1914–18.

There was among the railways' operations one that was particularly impressive: the conveyance of royal and other great persons. Such journeys became very frequent: the Prince of Wales remarked in 1873 that he travelled by train at least once or twice in every week of his life.[35] The Queen's journeys between Windsor and Balmoral were usually made overnight, and the passage of her train was little noticed: but the banks of the cutting at Ferryhill Junction, south of Aberdeen, were filled with people watching the immutable ceremonial. Here the train coming up from the south was handed over from one company to another, the blue engines of the Caledonian Railway replaced by the green ones of the Great North of Scotland; a special form of the changing of the guard. When there were State guests to be received – the Emperor of the French or the President of the Republic, William II of Germany or the Tsar of Russia – they all travelled by railways in the most handsomely-appointed trains the companies could provide. The splendour was sometimes muted: for Queen Victoria's funeral journey in 1901, and for Edward VII's nine years later, when the train carried nine reigning sovereigns down to Windsor from Paddington.[36]

Ill. 25   These journeys had to be managed with exact precision, with every care for safety,[37] and with the dignity expected of a State routine. Here the railways became part of a consummately-arranged ceremonial; carrying their own responsibilities, managing them independently of the State.[38]

Such spectacles were infrequent, however, and the railways' ordinary work had nothing to do with pageantry. They came to be accepted as the instruments of a necessary public service, durable even to permanence. Their first projectors would have been content with that. When Edward Pease gave George Stephenson his instructions for laying out the Stockton & Darlington Railway, he said: 'It is to be borne in mind that this is for a great public way and to remain as long as any coal in the district remains.'[39] Half a century later, another writer looked back and observed truly enough: 'We, who accept with as little gratitude as wonder the marvellous results of our railway system – who complain of the slightest delay or inconvenience, and in whose estimate the slightest casual annoyance outweighs a thousand continuous and unspeakable benefits – find it difficult, if we even try, to realise the enormous difficulties of the first beginning and the early progress'.[40]

2
STRUCTURES

The Track and its Bed · Tunnels and Underground Railways ·
Bridges and Viaducts · Passenger Stations ·
Hotels · Goods Stations and Warehouses · Engine-Sheds
and Signal-Boxes · Housing

This chapter concerns itself first with the infrastructure of the railways, and then with the great range of buildings their work called for. In 1914 there were still a fair number of people in Britain who had never travelled by train, but there were very few, except those living in western Sutherland or the Hebrides, who had never seen a railway, its embankments and bridges, even in the distance. Nearly all of them could recognize at least a few of the railways' structures. However little their purpose may have been understood, they were a familiar sight.

The Track and its Bed

The pre-mechanical railways had seldom called for any works of magnitude. The greatest of them were the Causey Arch in Co. Durham and the Rumney Railway's long viaduct at Risca in Monmouthshire.[1] Railways of this sort generally took the surface of the ground. The embankment over 20 ft high, buttressed with a double stone retaining wall, on Lord Elgin's railway in Fife was on a line expensively laid out.[2] When locomotives were introduced, the works necessarily became heavier. The weight on their wheels was much greater than any imposed, by railway or road, before. The track had to be strengthened to bear it. Iron rails weighing about 25 lb to the yard sufficed in 1800. By 1835 the Liverpool & Manchester company had settled on 75 lb as a standard.

The structures carrying the railway had to be not only stronger, but broader too. Before 1825 most lines were single, except at passing-places.[3] The Stockton & Darlington and all its successors expecting any large traffic were laid out for two lines. Four were contemplated as early as 1831, by Vignoles for a railway he was planning from Liverpool to Leeds. James Walker's Leeds & Selby Railway (opened in 1834) was actually built with earthworks and bridges wide enough to take four tracks from the start, though no more than two were laid down.[4]

The works had therefore to be much bulkier, standing out in the landscape more starkly than any canal or road. The few large masonry bridges built for

Ill. 10 single lines of railway, like the noble Treffry viaduct at Luxulyan in Cornwall or the Leaderfoot viaduct on the Tweed below Melrose, achieved an elegance rare among railway bridges of any kind. Moreover, roads were usable, given a sufficient supply of horses, on inclines far steeper than any that could be negotiated by locomotives. Gradients of 1 in 18–20 were accepted on main roads in the 1820s.[5] The steepest on any main line of railway laid out in the following decade were at 1 in 36–8, and Locke was severely criticized for taking the West Coast line to Scotland over gradients as stiff as 1 in 74 instead of easing them by deviation or tunnelling.

In pursuit of a course as level as possible, railways usually traversed stretches of low-lying country by embankments and bridges, which made their passage much more obtrusive. With embankments this could be avoided, in some measure, by planting them with trees. Some landowners insisted on such cladding as a prior condition of the sale of their property.[6] It might not be merely a sop to them. The roots of the trees strengthened the embankments themselves. At the turn of the century the Great Western company planted some of its new lines with firs, aliens in the countryside they traversed – between Banbury and Bicester, in Gloucestershire and in Somerset.

Ills. 2,8 Cuttings through hills were powerfully impressive. The 'Cowran cut' on the Newcastle & Carlisle line was – it remains – a truly magnificent piece of engineering, a mile long and reaching a maximum depth of 110 ft. There came to be others much longer: $2\frac{1}{2}$ miles at Weybridge on the London & Southampton line, for example, almost three miles at Winchburgh on the Edinburgh & Glasgow.

These works were constructed by the power of men and animals, aided by the use of explosives and the force of gravity. In the making of an average British railway, through fairly easy country, something like fifteen cubic yards of spoil had to be shifted for each foot of line that was built. On the London & Brighton and the Manchester & Leeds Railways the quantity was twice as great.[7]

The six-mile line between Folkestone and Dover, completed in 1844, epitomised these achievements. It began with the tall Foord viaduct, inland from Folkestone. Eastwards lay a tumbled mass of chalk down, pierced by four tunnels. There would have been a fifth if the engineer, William Cubitt, had not decided (with excellent advice from the chief inspector of railways) to blast Round Down Cliff entirely away with dynamite, so that it crumbled quickly and quietly into the sea. The line emerged from Shakespeare's Cliff

Ill. 5 tunnel straight on to the foreshore at Dover and was then carried on a wooden trestle viaduct along the top of the beach.

In the United States, where labour was scarcer and much more expensive than in Britain, steam-powered excavators were employed very early. One of them, imported across the Atlantic, was used in 1834 in the construction of the Eastern Counties Railway.[8] But more than thirty years went by before such equipment as that – heavy in capital cost, though a cheapener of labour – began to make its way in Britain.[9]

By that time almost every element in the railway had become much larger than it was in 1830–50. At the end of the century 500 tons of metal were being used in every mile of double track, compared with 110 tons on the Liverpool & Manchester line.[10] Embankments and bridges had in addition to support the weight of the timber sleepers (each one over 150 lb) and the ballast, which might be broken stone, rubble, gravel, slag from furnaces, or shingle from the sea-beach. The rails were now made of steel, not of iron,[11] and were much longer, reducing the shocks set up by rail-joints on the springs of engines and vehicles, and easing the passengers' ride. The 15-ft length of the rails of the 1840s was soon trebled, and 60-ft rails were coming in at the end of the century. As early as 1866 F. W. Webb experimented with a continuously-welded steel rail two miles long.[12]

The structures the railways erected to carry their lines in the later Victorian age grew immensely ponderous: plain and solid, the solidity emphasized by the materials generally used, dark blue bricks, iron and steel customarily painted dark grey or black. All this was exemplified in the additional works required when the great railways doubled the capacity of long sections of their main lines out of London, providing four tracks instead of two. They took some of these tracks by slightly different routes from those originally laid down, in order to ease gradients. The new and old lines did not always run parallel, and the over-bridges needed to span them sometimes took on contorted shapes; notably on the Midland Railway north of Hendon, and at Souldrop (Bedfordshire), where one bridge, built in 1884, spanned two sets of tracks at entirely different levels.[13] Here brickwork became almost plastic.

The Great Central's extension line from Nottinghamshire to London represented a distillation of the engineering experience of the previous seventy years. Forty-three mechanical excavators were used in its construction, and about as many steam cranes. Nevertheless, 3000 men were engaged continuously in 1896–8 on the last section, two miles long, at the London end. As a work of engineering, the line was most creditable to those who designed and made it, to the engineers, to the contractors, and to the men they employed; all partners in the making of this, the last trunk railway to be built in Britain.

Tunnels and Underground Railways

The art of tunnelling had long been practised by military men, and by miners in pursuit of coal and salt, lead and tin. It was taken to a higher level by canal builders.[14] The first canal tunnel in Britain was Brindley's at Harecastle in Staffordshire on the Trent & Mersey Canal, 1880 yd long, completed in 1777. This was followed by others even longer; longest of all the Standedge through the Pennines (5456 yd, 1811). No British railway tunnel equalled that one in length until 1886.

The Canterbury & Whitstable and Liverpool & Manchester Railways required considerable tunnels in 1830, on steep gradients. The traffic through them was at first worked by cable haulage, not by locomotives. That avoided one evidently serious problem, the ventilation that would be necessary if locomotives passed through the tunnels, emitting smoke. Before the year 1830 was out, however, another railway was setting itself – like these two, under the Stephensons – to the construction of a tunnel in which locomotives could be used. This was the Leicester & Swannington, penetrating a hill at Glenfield. Here the tunnel was level throughout the whole of its length. Ventilation was provided by means of ten circular shafts. The directors of the company were anxious lest intruders should walk in and out, so they guarded one entrance with a 'tunnel house', occupied by staff, and shut the other up entirely at night by a gate.[15]

The interiors of these great structures could be glimpsed by travellers only where daylight penetrated down into them through exceptionally large shafts, as at Kilsby on the London & Birmingham line and at Higham on the South Eastern. Their magnitude could be proclaimed, however, by treating their entrances monumentally. A sequence of splendid portals was provided by Brunel for the tunnels on the Great Western line. Each was freely treated in its own manner, ranging from Romanesque and Gothic at the western end to classical nobility at Middle Hill and Box.[16] They were matched by some of those on the Stephensons' lines: at Milford (North Midland) and Littleborough (Manchester & Leeds), at Bangor on the Chester & Holyhead, where one catches a whiff of the Egyptian. Among the numerous Gothic tunnel mouths Thomas Grainger's on the Leeds & Thirsk Railway may be mentioned, and the southern face, powerful and menacing, of Hawkshaw's Beacon Hill tunnel at Halifax.

Here and there a portal might reveal that the form of construction behind it was of some exceptional kind, owing to the geology of the hills it pierced. The short Toadmoor tunnel on the North Midland line at Ambergate was a

Ill. 5 flattened ellipse. The one that penetrated Shakespeare's Cliff at Dover comprised two separate bores, shaped like the naves of French Gothic cathedrals, tall, slender, and coming to a sharply-pointed apex: Cubitt's device for reducing the pressure exerted on the crowns of the arches by the treacherous shifting chalk.

The tunnels through the Pennines were very difficult to make. The first to be completed, at Littleborough north of Rochdale, took $3\frac{1}{2}$ years (1837–41); that at Woodhead, between Manchester and Sheffield, more than six. The men who worked at Woodhead lived in appalling conditions, investigated by people with a social conscience in Manchester, influenced by Edwin Chadwick, their findings presented to a Commons Committee on Railway Labourers in 1846.[17] The number of men employed here seems never to have exceeded 1500 at one time. Wages were high, but even so labour proved hard to recruit. The men lived out on the high moorland in rough huts, their stone walls unmortared; 'filthy dens' they were called by John Roberton, a surgeon who visited the site. They were paid only once in nine weeks ('to preclude their indulgence in hebdomadal excesses'),[18] and the only shop available to them was kept by one of the contractors. However, Roberton and Chadwick met with a cogent reply to their attack from the contractor principally involved, Thomas Nicholson.[19] Chadwick, as usual, marred his case by exaggeration and vituperative rhetoric. Nicholson was not called before the Committee.

Two of the Pennine tunnels (Charlestown and Chorley) had to be abandoned altogether and the lines built differently. The Sough tunnel between Blackburn and Bolton gave great trouble, during construction and afterwards. Moreover, its whole bed had to be lowered in 1874, to accommodate larger rolling stock.[20]

The longest of all British tunnels lay not in the Pennines but in the south: the Severn tunnel, authorized in 1872 and finished only in 1886. After $6\frac{1}{2}$ years' work no more than five shafts had been sunk, and two miles of small heading driven. Then, in October 1879, the Great Spring burst into one of the headings, and it and all the works connected with it were totally flooded. The Great Western directors considered abandoning the enterprise altogether but determined to go on, led by their chairman Gooch. Hawkshaw, who had been the consultant engineer, now took over the whole responsibility. The credit for the achievement was due above all to these two men, together with a third: the contractor Thomas Walker, who wrote an admirable account of the whole undertaking, unique in British engineering literature.[21] The tunnel had its own heroes: notably diver Lambert, who at his third attempt succeeded in closing a door in the workings that had been left open by the men fleeing when the Great Spring burst in.[22] In October 1883, as a result of a tidal wave, a night shift of eighty-three men was imprisoned in the tunnel, watching the water rise until it was only 8 ft from the crown of the arch under which they were huddling. They were extricated with very great difficulty. The whole work was a triumph of pertinacity and courage, on the part of everyone who was engaged in it.[23]

Another sort of tunnelling became important from the Mid-Victorian age onwards: the driving of urban railways beneath the streets.

The Metropolitan Railway in London was a shallow line, most of it built on the 'cut-and-cover' principle: i.e. an open cutting was first made, and it was then roofed over. For most of its course it followed the line of the streets.[24] The interruption of traffic while it was being built (the streets had to be entirely closed, except to pedestrians, a section at a time) and the discomfort caused to the occupants of the adjoining houses, which were all shored up, were very considerable.[25] The passage of the railway through a honeycomb of sewers and gas-pipes was a daunting task. It was largely owing to the resource and indomitable confidence of the chief engineer, John Fowler, that the work was carried through to a successful opening on 10 May 1863.

The same resolve infused Fowler's continuations of the line as they nosed their way to form a circle underneath London, not completed until 1884. Being almost wholly subterranean, their merits could seldom be seen and appreciated by the traveller. But one complex piece of engineering was visible to the west of Farringdon Street station: what came to be called 'the gridiron', completed in 1868, to allow the passage of two pairs of railway lines, one above the other, beneath road bridges. No British railways, it may be added, were built under more constricting limitations – legislative, financial, and technical – than these in London.[26]

In 1870 a railway was completed in a small iron tube under the Thames. It was a mechanical failure, though the tunnel came to be used by foot passengers until 1894. This 'Tower Subway' was an innovator in several important respects. It was all built in a true tunnel, 50–60 ft below the ground and water level, not in a cutting covered over; the tunnel, driven through by means of an iron shield,[27] was lined with cast-iron rings; the railway was reached from the streets by hydraulic lifts; and its cars were moved not by steam locomotives, as on the other underground lines, but by means of wire ropes attached to stationary engines. Some of its lessons were applied to the City & South London Railway, opened in 1890: the first electrically-operated underground railway in the world, and the first railway to work successfully in a deep-level tube. This line was a commercial failure, which discouraged further projects for the moment. However, a whole network of tube railways was constructed underneath central London in 1898–1907. By 1914 it comprised a system nearly 40 miles long.

Meanwhile other underground railways were appearing in the provinces. The Mersey Railway, under the river from Liverpool to Birkenhead, was opened in 1886. It was bankrupt from 1887 to 1900 and did not begin to pay its way until it had been electrified in 1903. Glasgow came to have three such lines, completed in 1886–96. Two were worked by steam. The third, the Glasgow & District Subway, was a circular railway $6\frac{1}{2}$ miles long, passing twice underneath the Clyde; built partly by cut-and-cover and partly in tube. It was worked by cable and established itself quietly. But it did not become profitable until the abandonment of cable traction for electricity in 1935.[28]

All these Glasgow railways were hit hard by the new competition brought by electric trams in 1898–1902. The London railways suffered likewise. Only one of the tubes paid: the simple Waterloo & City, providing a shuttle service over a distance of two miles. The rest had to fight electric trams and then motor buses, and there was not enough revenue to provide an adequate living for all the competitors. But this financial failure was not, in any important sense, owing to failures of construction. The engineers, most notably J. H. Greathead and Sir Benjamin Baker, had done their work well.

These London railways set an example followed across the world. By 1914 six other great cities had electrically-worked underground railways: Budapest, Paris, Berlin, and Hamburg; New York and Philadelphia in the United States. Dissatisfaction was repeatedly expressed at the end of the Victorian age with the performance of British railways in comparison with those elsewhere. Acworth observed in 1899 that 'the tide of progress seems to have reached high-water mark, if not to be actually receding'.[29] He makes no mention whatever of the electrically-operated underground lines in London; two of them actually at work when he wrote those words, a third nearly finished, and others under construction. The bold experiment they displayed, and their resolution in the face of most discouraging difficulties, were in the true heroic spirit of the 1830s and 1840s. But out of sight, they remained out of mind. The only full accounts of the London underground railways, their construction and working, were written by Germans.[30] The Victorians themselves ungratefully disregarded them.[31]

Bridges and Viaducts

Bridges and viaducts* were the most numerous of the railways' works of civil engineering, and the most widely admired. They were constructed of every available material: stone, brick, timber, iron, steel, concrete.

Thomas Harrison's Grosvenor bridge at Chester had demonstrated in 1827 the grace and power attainable by a road bridge in a single 200-ft span: a design adopted in order to leave the river it crossed clear of any obstruction from intermediate supports. No stone railway bridge in Britain ever came quite to equal that width. But then the weight and the stresses that the railway and its traffic placed on any arch were very much greater. In 1839 Brunel began to show what the railway might do in this direction, in the two 128-ft spans of his Maidenhead bridge. Nine years later John Miller produced the railways' counterpart to the Grosvenor bridge, in the Ballochmyle viaduct in   *Ill. 9* Ayrshire, with a central span 181 ft wide and 164 ft high, constructed entirely of stone. For half a century it remained the greatest masonry arch on any railway in the world. These two bridges were masterpieces in the boldness of their conception, in the excellence of their craftsmanship, and – no less – in their visual distinction. The leap of the one at Maidenhead is superb; the strength and elegance in Miller's structure unforgettable, seen from the valley below, its strength tempered by the architectural treatment of the tapering piers and the deep incision of the masonry.

Miller was here carrying on the long and distinguished tradition of stone bridge-building in Scotland, adapting it to a new purpose. That country had little timber suitable for building, and the varieties of brick it produced were all rough; none of them could stand comparison with those of south-eastern England. Hence the Scottish railways built few timber bridges – only two of any great size, at Marykirk and Stonehaven;[32] when they used brick it was commonly as a filling, and faced with stone. Towards the end of the nineteenth century they responded with enthusiasm to the opportunities presented by iron and steel, exemplified in the great bridge spanning the Forth; and between Fort William and Mallaig they employed concrete more boldly in the 1890s than any other railway had yet done in Europe. But the main material used by all railways in Scotland remained stone to the end of the Victorian age. The last long masonry viaduct, of any kind, built in Great Britain was that crossing the River Nairn on the western side of Culloden Moor. It was

---

*Strictly, a 'bridge' denoted a work of a single main span. Humphry Repton coined the word 'viaduct', by analogy with 'aqueduct', in 1816 (OED) to describe a roadway carried on many arches. The railways used the words interchangeably; the great viaducts crossing the Tweed, the Forth, and the Tay were always known as bridges.

completed in 1898, to the plans of the Highland company's engineer, Murdoch Paterson, and faced in a deep red sandstone throughout. Anyone who appreciates fine masonry, good stone excellently handled, will get much pleasure from a tour of Scotland, looking at its great railway bridges (some of them disused) today.[33]

In early years, everywhere in the island, the railways' structures were mostly built of local materials. The Penshaw stone that went into the Victoria bridge, south of Sunderland, was quarried only $1\frac{1}{2}$ miles away.[34] The red bricks used by Brunel for his bridges over the Thames at Basildon and Moulsford were made in those parishes.[35] The railways soon became enormous consumers of bricks; the Kilsby tunnel is said to have called for 36 million.[36] Though many new brickworks were opened up close to the lines, the engineers had often to look far afield for what they needed. They came to use one special sort of bricks very extensively, most of them made in a single district: the Staffordshire blues, which were noted for their strength and their resistance to water. Their first appearance in any large railway structure seems to have been in 1840, when Vignoles chose them as a facing material for the Midland Counties viaduct at Rugby.

All the great British railway engineers used timber for bridges somewhere on their lines. George Stephenson accepted it on the Whitby & Pickering (where traction was to be by horses), Robert on the Chester & Holyhead. Cubitt turned to it, either alone or in conjunction with brick and iron, on the South Eastern and the Great Northern. Laminated timber, developed on the basis of the work of Wiebeking in Germany, appeared in some important railway bridges in England in 1839–46: first on the Newcastle & North Shields line and then east of Manchester.

The great exponent of the use of timber for railway bridges was Brunel.[37]
Ill. 6 He mistrusted cast iron as a structural material, and wrought iron was expensive.[38] Iron stays were sometimes used in his timber viaducts, and the wooden deck carrying the trains might rest on masonry or brick piers. The longest, those at Newport and Landore on the South Wales Railway, crossed navigable rivers. The tallest was at St Pinnock in Cornwall (151 ft). The aggregate length of all the forty-two timber bridges between Plymouth, Penzance, and Falmouth was just on six miles.[39]

These bridges were exposed to obvious danger from fire. The Newport viaduct was burnt down before it was brought into use, the central span being then replaced in iron. The timbers needed watchful maintenance, and a good many sections of them had to be replaced.[40] But the bridges were low in capital cost. If those on the Cornwall Railway had been built of any other material, the line would certainly have been opened a good deal later than 1859. After careful trials of preservatives, and with experience in handling it, the yellow pine Brunel used was a material he could trust. No serious accident ever befell any of the Cornish bridges that was attributable to defects in its timber construction.

In the very large bridges erected in 1849–59 iron eclipsed all other materials.

Only two were of masonry or brick: Robert Stephenson's Royal Border bridge at Berwick and Thomas Bouch's Hownes Gill viaduct in Co. Durham.

The earliest railway bridge to be built wholly of metal seems to have been one on a line into Carron Works in Scotland, completed in 1810, followed in the next year by another at Robertstown, near Aberdare in South Wales.[41] The first careful effort to design an iron bridge in a form specially suited to a railway was for one carrying the Stockton & Darlington line over the River Gaunless, for which George Stephenson and the Newcastle ironfounders John and Isaac Burrell were jointly responsible.[42]

The earliest great iron bridge in Britain built to carry locomotive-hauled trains was Robert Stephenson's High Level bridge at Newcastle, completed in 1849. As a structure it was conservative, comprising six bow-string spans of cast iron, with wrought-iron ties.[43] The upper deck took three railway tracks (this was the first important bridge in Britain to be designed for more than two), the lower carried a road with footways either side.

At the same time Stephenson was closely engaged on two great bridges in north Wales, completed in 1848–50, one at Conway, the other crossing the Menai Strait. Here there were rectangular tubes, through which the trains ran, constructed entirely of wrought iron in spans from 230 ft to 460 ft long. No girders comparable in length with these had ever been made before. At the Britannia bridge the four biggest tubes had to be raised to 100 ft, on the Admiralty's insistence, clear above the shipping in the Strait.[44] This was one of the outstanding iron constructions of the nineteenth century, its girders the ancestors of all the steel plate girders that are used today.

Ill. 4

Brunel also designed a pair of big iron bridges, at Chepstow (1852) and Saltash (1859). Both of them used the suspension principle, in ways never seen before. The trains ran across them in the open, on a wrought-iron deck kept secure and steady by trusses joined to rounded tubes above. The Chepstow bridge looked an oddity, its superstructure extending over only half its length, but this asymmetry arose from the curious site at which it was built, a mud-flat facing a high cliff across the Wye.[45] The second bridge, over the Tamar at Saltash, was a far greater proposition. Again a clear height of 100 ft above the water was required. The two central spans were each 455 ft long.

A notable contrast is to be seen between these two pairs of iron bridges. It can be summarized thus:

TABLE 1

FOUR IRON BRIDGES, 1848–59

	Date of opening	Length (ft)	Final cost
Conway	1848–9	413	£145,700
Chepstow	1852–3	600	77,000
Britannia	1850	1800	674,000
Saltash	1859	2200	225,000

Sources: P.S.A. Berridge, *The Girder Bridge* (1969) 48, 61;
P.E. Baughan *The Chester and Holyhead Railway* (1972), 135.

Some explanations are called for here. The price of iron when the Chepstow bridge was built was exceptionally low.[46] The first three of these bridges all carried a double track. The cost of the Saltash bridge was reduced by £100,000 through restricting it to one track only, in order to meet the Cornwall Railway's financial difficulties. On the other hand that bridge, including its approach on the west side, was substantially longer than the Britannia. It seems fair to say that in each case, with the smaller and the larger works, Brunel's cost about half as much as Stephenson's. Berridge attributes the difference to the much tighter control that Brunel kept over his work.[47] But it must also be remembered that Stephenson's work preceded Brunel's and that Brunel therefore had the great benefit of his friend's experience.

Three other iron railway bridges achieved distinction too at the same time. They were very light lattice structures: the Crumlin viaduct in Monmouthshire and those at Belah (Westmorland) and Deepdale (Co. Durham), all completed in 1857–61. These bridges reached a much greater height than Stephenson's and Brunel's, at Crumlin 200 ft. All carried double track on a timber deck,[48] resting on iron lattice girders and columns. The whole of this ironwork was prefabricated, which had an astonishing effect on the speed of construction. Belah, 1040 ft long, with 16 spans, was built in four months. The cost of these three works was less than one-tenth, per foot, of the cost of the Stephenson bridges, a quarter of Brunel's. They all had a century of useful life and were demolished in 1962–4 solely because the lines they carried were closed. The designer of the first of these structures was T. W. Kennard, in consultation with Charles Liddell. The two northern ones were due to Thomas Bouch. They should redound to his honour as some offset to the obloquy he subsequently incurred through the failure of his bridge over the Tay.

The lines these three bridges carried all dealt principally in mineral traffic. They were not required to withstand the strains that heavy locomotives, running at high speed, would have imposed on them. Only one structure of this type was ever built on any British line carrying express trains, the Meldon viaduct on the London & South Western line between Exeter and Plymouth (1874), and in crossing that there was a speed limit of 20 mph. Some bridges of this sort gave rise to anxiety, however: the Staithes viaduct north of Whitby, completed in 1875, had to be strengthened with two sets of additional girders in 1883.[49]

All iron girder bridges came under suspicion after the Tay bridge disaster in 1879. That was brought about by the failure to test the design of the structure adequately against the force of the wind, which blew with a well-known violence down the river, by the scandalously bad manufacture of the iron used in it, and by the poor maintenance of the bridge while it was in service.[50] All these defects were remedied in the second Tay bridge, an immensely solid construction of iron and stone. But prejudice against all-metal structures was strengthened in 1881 by the demolition of forty-five of the iron arches of the Solway viaduct through the action of ice-floes in the water it spanned. And two serious accidents occurred, in 1883 and 1891, through the failure of cast-iron under-bridges, at Inverythan in Aberdeenshire and Norwood Junction in south London.[51]

When the Tay bridge collapsed its designer Bouch was already building an even bigger work to cross the Firth of Forth. The task was at once taken away from him, and in 1882 its execution was entrusted to Sir John Fowler and Benjamin Baker. They had worked together on a succession of plans for bridging the estuary of the Severn. Their first, in 1864, had been designed to include a single span of 1000 ft. Soon afterwards a new possibility had begun to appear: to construct bridges of this kind wholly or partly in steel. 'With steel', W. H. Barlow had prophesied firmly in 1873, 'we shall be enabled to cross openings which are absolutely impracticable in iron'.[52] Fowler and Baker recommended that their bridge over the Forth should be built of steel, with two central spans each 1710 ft long. This thinking was very bold, but it prevailed.

The preparation now was meticulous. Baker made the essential calculations and experiments concerned with wind pressure in 1883. The contractor, William Arrol, was much more than adequate to his task. 'Which was the greater achievement, it is hard to say' (the words are an engineer's); 'the preparation of hundreds of detail drawings and calculations in their Westminster office and the superintendence and continuous control over the entire operation of building the bridge, by the engineers; or the carrying out of the actual work on site. Both were stupendous undertakings, with the reputation of the whole industry at stake'.[53] Under the sure direction of these three men the bridge was completed in 1890, and the national disgrace arising from the catastrophe on the Tay was more than retrieved. It demonstrated to the world the skill, the vision, and the tenacity still found in British railway engineering.[54]

Ills. 12,13

Another new material was now beginning to be used in railway bridges: concrete.

Mass concrete had gone into the foundation work of railway bridges (on the London & Greenwich, for example, in the 1830s), as well as of sea-walls and docks. Fowler was among the engineers interested in the material. Under his direction the Metropolitan District Railway erected a bridge of concrete near Gloucester Road station in 1867 (perhaps the first arched bridge ever built in that material anywhere), and four years later made the walls of its carriage repair shops at West Brompton entirely of concrete too.[55] The first concrete bridges on British railways that achieved a lasting success appeared, almost simultaneously, on the Lanarkshire & Dumbartonshire and the West Highland Extension lines in Scotland between 1892 and 1901 and in south-western England, on those to Bude, Lyme Regis, and Calstock (1898–1908). The last of this series, the Calstock viaduct in Cornwall (1908), deserves special mention as a great rarity: a structure faced with concrete blocks, not masked by any rendering, that can truly be called beautiful.

There is not much evidence of the participation of architects in the building of railway bridges, except those of the Chester & Holyhead line. A railway company might consult one occasionally. We can be pretty certain, for instance, that William Livock drew out the Lichfield Drive bridge on the Trent Valley Railway:[56] plainly an architect's job, with its quotations from the buildings on the Earl of Lichfield's estate at Shugborough. But that was an exceptional case.

On the Chester & Holyhead line there was work that demanded an architect insistently: at Chester, at the passage of the railway immediately past Conway Castle, and at the crossing of the Menai Strait. Robert Stephenson worked here with Francis Thompson, as he had before on the North Midland Railway and in the eastern counties.

Thompson was versatile, well read, and willing to accept necessities. The Gothic style was virtually imposed on him at Conway, to harmonize with the medieval castle and walls. His original design clad the tubes with a lightly-patterned Gothic decoration, which was discarded on grounds of expense. This left the tubes to stand exposed, uncompromisingly stark and ponderous.[57] The masonry of the bridge, however, remained elegant, all the external work in limestone from the Great Orme's Head and from Penmon in Anglesey.

In the Britannia bridge engineer and architect achieved a true and satisfying collaboration. The bridge could not emulate the lightness and grace of Telford's road bridge, within view only a mile away: it had necessarily to be much bulkier, to support the loads it was designed to carry. But here, crossing this broad arm of the sea, its two enormous tubes could be set in an appropriate framework, designed without any restrictions. The towers had originally been intended to provide for suspension chains, which were later discarded. That determined their height. The Egyptian tapering was not functional, it was the architect's inspiration. The masonry, again from Penmon, was magnificent: in just proportion to the iron of the tubes (patterned only with vertical ribbing), the right counterpoint to them. And the entrances, guarded by John Thomas's lions, were properly monumental.

The fire of 1970, necessitating the reconstruction we see now, ruined one of the master-works of the Early Victorian age.

At Saltash Brunel worked with no architect. Masonry here played a smaller part, though a very important one to anybody who looked up at the bridge from the Cornish waterfront, where the granite piers of the approach viaduct on its curve, slim and amazingly tall, were – and still are – unforgettable. Modern architectural critics have either ignored the metal bridge or written it down. The arches of this one, Pevsner remarks in his *Cornwall* (1951), are 'by no means elegant'; 'not a handsome, but a safe and sound solution' is his patronizing summary. There would have been plenty of Victorians to disagree with him. Two years after the bridge was opened, it was photographed by George Washington Wilson from Aberdeen.[58] He responded to the impression that the bridge made at close quarters from below. But he also had the imagination to go out on the water to take the high spans from a distance, *Ill. 11* with the hulk of a wooden warship lying in front of them. His picture was a tribute both to the poetry of the bridge and to the triumph of iron; perfectly

[30]

timed, for at that moment the ironclad HMS *Warrior* was close to completion, which swept wooden warships away.

The aesthetics of the Forth bridge were variously assessed by the Victorians. William Morris dismissed it as 'the supremest expression of all ugliness'. Alfred Waterhouse, on the other hand, said this to Fowler when he had seen it completed: 'The simple directness of purpose with which it does its work is splendid, and invests your vast monument with a kind of beauty of its own, differing though it certainly does from all other beautiful things I have ever seen'.[59] That was a striking tribute, paid by an architect to an engineer.

Passenger Stations

The earliest railways made little of their passenger stations. The Stockton & Darlington at first had none at all. Its passenger business was insignificant, and handled for some time by contractors, using horse-drawn coaches. Passengers were booked by the company's agents at their own premises in the terminal towns, and at Stockton the coaches started out from inns on the quay.[60] On the Liverpool & Manchester Railway, at its opening, there were 'stations' for handling passengers at the termini, but no others at all; only recognized stopping-places, usually at level crossings, where passengers might perhaps find shelter in the gatekeeper's hut.[61] The company did however commission plans from John Foster the younger, architect to the Corporation of Liverpool, for a number of its works. With his partner John Stewart he designed the roof (and perhaps the remainder) of Crown Street station; and his firm may also have designed the buildings of the first terminus in Manchester, on Liverpool Road.[62] When the company's Lime Street station came to be built in Liverpool he designed a handsome facade for it, paid for jointly by the company and the Corporation.

On the other short railways of the 1830s the engineers managed the whole of this business themselves. James Walker was responsible for the Leeds & Selby's modest termini, Vignoles for the North Union one at Preston.[63] Many stations were no more than makeshifts. The first at Hartlepool (1840) was 'the poop of an old Dutch galliot.... Its cabins housed the booking clerk and stationmaster'.[64]

The trunk railways pursued differing policies in this matter. The Great Western employed no architect whatever, entrusting all its works to its engineer, Brunel. At the western end of the line he displayed the range of his eclectic taste: in the quiet approach to Bath from the east through Sydney Gardens, where he took the railway through a curved trough of elegant masonry; in the station there, which had a Gothic train-shed but a Jacobean building outside; and at Bristol, where his passenger station was Gothic all through.

So the Great Western Railway directors secured such architectural flourishes as they wanted from their own engineer. Those of the Grand Junction wanted no flourishes at all. Their engineer Joseph Locke made its works plain and strong, and the station buildings on the line were at first minimal. This railway prided itself on the economy with which it was built. And justly.

The London & Birmingham, on the other hand, commissioned Philip Hardwick, one of the best-known architects of the day, to provide it with two passenger terminals. His design for the entrance to the London station at Euston Square took the form of a Doric portico,* flanked with two pairs of pavilions and standing, when it was completed in 1838, on the north side of a large open space. It was neither a necessity nor a convenience. It was a gesture. Here, at the edge of the capital city, stood a gateway to the Kingdom beyond, constructed of adamantine Bramley Fall sandstone and symbolizing everything that the railway represented. Why should Hardwick have elected to express that by means derived from Athens in the fifth century BC? And after seeing his design, why should the directors of the London & Birmingham Railway – business men, not dilettanti – have spent, in the end, some £30,000 on it? Pevsner accounts for the decision convincingly:

> While the functionalist must...call it [the Euston portico] a sham, it receives its ultimate justification from its evocative quality...Styles were chosen for what they would evoke. Robert Stephenson's railway all the way from London to Birmingham, at a break-neck speed of up to 30 mph, was considered one of the greatest achievements of the human mind. Hence only the greatest of all architectural styles could express it.[65]

Hardwick's other terminal building, at Birmingham (Curzon Street), was smaller, and it accommodated substantial offices. Architects designed the facades and forebuildings of most of the principal stations opened down to 1842: Tite at Nine Elms in London, at Southampton and Gosport; Mocatta at Brighton; Parsons at Leicester (Campbell Street); Collie at Glasgow (Bridge Street). But the accommodation that lay behind these outward-facing structures was kept firmly in the hands of the engineers. That became the common practice. In 1849 for example the second Liverpool (Lime Street) station had a roof with the unprecedented span of 154 ft, designed by Richard Turner (of the Palm House at Kew), while the whole external work was in the hands of the architect, Tite.[66]

There were exceptions, tending both ways. The architect John Dobson seems to have been responsible for the beautiful and innovative train-shed at Newcastle (1850), as well as for the forebuilding.[67] Another architect, Lewis Cubitt, designed the whole station at King's Cross (1852). This was the most completely functional concept ever carried out for any large passenger station in the Victorian age: a pair of arched iron-and-glass train sheds, ribbed in timber, expressing themselves to the world through two large semi-circular windows; constructed of London stock brick, with the barest minimum of

---

*It must surely be called that. 'The Euston Arch' is a misnomer. An 'arch' is generally understood to be curved; every line in this gateway was rectangular.

dressings. The only external decoration was a small Italianate turret, and even that was useful, for it contained a clock.

The engineer Brunel bore the whole responsibility for the permanent terminus at Paddington, completed in 1854, though he did invite his friend Matthew Digby Wyatt to become his '*Assistant* for the ornamental details'. He saw the station as a work both of engineering and of architecture. His sketches of different ideas for the train-shed, as a huge enclosure of space, make that plain.[68] But as he told Wyatt, 'for *detail* of ornamentation I neither have time nor knowledge';[69] and he recognized that here that kind of detail was going to be important. We can almost sense his feeling as a comment on King's Cross, where the interior was very bare, lacking all enrichment of moulding and colour. Enrichment was just what he sought, and what Wyatt supplied.[70]

Architects might contribute to the design of small wayside stations too. On some lines hardly any attention was paid to the passengers' needs. At Moreton-on-Lugg, for example, on the Shrewsbury & Hereford Railway, opened in 1852, the station comprised the hollow trunk of a withered tree.[71] The Newcastle & Carlisle Railway was the first to erect a series of permanent buildings for wayside stations; plain stone structures, three of them completed by 1836.[72] The first extensive commission of this kind given to an architect was for the London & Southampton Railway, opened in 1838–40. Here William Tite founded the largest railway practice developed by any Victorian architect, extending over thirty years and reaching out from England into Scotland and France.[73] A certain coarseness appears in his work; but he was an excellent man of business and drove his buildings through efficiently, collaborating frequently with Locke, a no less efficient engineer. He appears at his best at Micheldever (Hants), a shapely Georgian building surrounded with a simple iron canopy and achieving real distinction in its flint flushwork.

Ill. 16

Ill. 17

David Mocatta used standard materials in his thirteen stations for the London & Brighton Railway (1839–41). He gave careful thought to evolving designs that should be economical, functionally sound, and comfortable for passengers. His roofed-in platforms, for example, protected them well against wind, being furnished either with alcoves or with screens at each end.[74]

Francis Thompson, on the other hand, seized every chance he could to provide variety in the stations and other railway buildings he designed. He worked in association with one engineer only, Robert Stephenson, except at a brief moment, when he gave some assistance to Brunel.[75] At Derby and Chester his task was confined to providing the facades and the accommodation for the passengers and the companies' servants. The passenger traffic at Derby was to be handled – so Stephenson had decided – at one very lengthy platform. Thompson clad this and the company's offices in a brick facade, with stone dressings, a fifth of a mile long. At Chester he gave an even longer front vertical emphasis by means of two towers. Each of these stations stood on the outer rim of its town, with new streets cut to reach it. Each confronted the traveller not with a classical portico or an Italianate house but with a true railway building.

Ills. 14,15

On the North Midland line, for which he worked in 1839–41, all Thompson's stations were different externally, and inside they were laid out to different plans. Here he came to treat the company and its passengers to a theme (the railway) with twenty-five variations. He used every possible material: brick, stucco, the stones that were locally available; wood very sparingly. At Ambergate he turned impressively to the Jacobean; at Chesterfield he chose Gothic; Eckington was a delightful Italianate fantasy. Between Chester and Holyhead (where there was little money to spend), all Thompson's stations were similar, in a classical tradition. Even there, however, no two were identical.

After the completion of the Britannia bridge Thompson vanishes from sight. His last appearance on any railway seems to be late in 1850, with a design he prepared for the architectural work at New Street station, Birmingham; adjudged by two sensible engineers 'most handsome and elegant, but quite out of the question for a railway station in these times'.[76] 'These times', of sharp economy following on the wasteful expenditure of the previous years, must have displeased him, and he apparently retired altogether, to live on quietly in London until he died in 1871.[77]

Few of the architects who designed buildings for railway companies concentrated their attention wholly on railway work.[78] Thompson was one. So it seems were J. W. Livock, whose work was done mainly for lines connected with the London & North Western Railway, and H. A. Hunt, much employed by the Eastern Counties and the North Staffordshire. But Mocatta produced designs for works very different from the railways – a synagogue, for example, a fever hospital, and a great house in the Azores. G. T. Andrews, who did excellent work for George Hudson on his railways in Yorkshire until the end of Hudson's regime in 1849, was also responsible for nine churches there in 1834–55.[79] Even at the time of their most rapid expansion, the railways seldom offered enough work to provide a living for an architect. The North Midland company paid Thompson an annual salary of £1000; but that lasted for three years only.

The organization of railways changed rapidly in the later 1840s, giving much less encouragement to architects than to engineers. Once standard designs and plans had been laid down, for use over large systems, the architect's role came to be principally that of supervising erection, and on many railways he became a quite subordinate officer, hardly named in public, within the engineer's department. On some small railways everything was designed by the engineer, and where he secured a number of commissions in succession he could transfer his expertise from one to another. The activity of one of these men, William Clarke, has now been traced,[80] in the design of twenty-four stations on a series of lines (at length merged into the Great Western Railway), opened in 1873–97.

Seven new terminal stations were opened in London in 1860–75. All of them except the wretched Holborn Viaduct had train-sheds of iron and glass. The most elegant roof was perhaps Fowler's for the Chatham company's station at Victoria, a pair of shallow ellipses graced by light and delicate ironwork. The most spectacular was Barlow's at St Pancras, where the 240-ft span of the train shed was the widest yet seen in a railway station anywhere. It was not however a piece of competitive sensationalism. Barlow's lucid exposition of the rationale of the whole design, in its inter-related parts, should be read.[81] It is a masterly, a majestic performance.

These stations varied considerably in the traffic they were designed to carry. Only one of them, St Pancras, was intended primarily for long-distance trains; at the others suburban business preponderated. All were served by the new underground railways as they came into use.[82] Every one of the seven – again excepting St Pancras – was cramped for space. The Great Eastern company had already spent well over £300,000 on the purchase of land for Liverpool Street and the short new railway approach to it before the building of the station began. The price of the extensions from London Bridge to Charing Cross and Cannon Street seems to have been about £4 million, or at the rate of £2 million a mile.[83] Within the stations the use of every square yard of space had to be minutely considered. At Cannon Street John Wolfe Barry, who had been a resident engineer under Hawkshaw in its construction, subsequently allowed that 'the platform area ... is probably minimal'.[84]

It was fortunate for the streetscape that hotels provided the fore-buildings of most of these stations. The two stations at Victoria had no facades at all and were among the public shames of London. Their sheds rose up starkly behind clusters of ignoble wooden buildings, mostly single-storied, accompanied by squalid hoardings of advertisements.[85] This disgrace remained (there was then no planning authority) until in the reign of Edward VII the companies at last erected the frontages that had been lacking for over forty years.

Nearly all the London terminal stations came to be enlarged. At King's Cross the work was shabbily done, at Euston it was unimpressive; but a decent addition to Paddington was under way when war broke out in 1914. A few very extensive reconstructions were undertaken after 1875: at Glasgow, Edinburgh, and Aberdeen; at Liverpool (Exchange) and Manchester (Victoria) and at the Midland station at Sheffield;[86] at the great junctions of York and Crewe; at Waterloo station in London. But though these all represented welcome improvements – including, at Glasgow Queen Street, an exceedingly fine elliptical roof to the train shed, designed by the engineer James Carswell (1877) – only Glasgow Central and Waterloo were on a scale to match the Hauptbahnhöfe of Germany and Switzerland and the Union Terminals of the United States. And none of them whatever commanded a physical presence in its city in any way comparable with that of the stations in Frankfurt or Leipzig, with the Central station in Naples or the Union Terminal in St Louis.

By the 1870s Bridge Street station, Glasgow, used by the Caledonian Railway on the south bank of the Clyde, had become entirely inadequate for its traffic, and the company determined to extend its lines into a new Central station across the river. It was opened in 1879 and at once proved too small. By 1897 a great enlargement became imperative. Under the direction of the company's imaginative and dynamic chief engineer, D. A. Matheson, the work was driven through in 1901–6.

The area the building occupied was trebled, by lengthening the platforms towards the river and by broadening its outer end, giving on to a vast new bridge that – together with the old one by its side – brought thirteen tracks across the river. The station's ground-plan resulted from the economics of land-purchase on a prime urban site, densely built-up; already confined at its head by the Caledonian Hotel, which was to be left untouched, as the station's familiar and dignified facade to the city. The shape of the site was turned to advantage, however, by making the concourse a huge diagonal, each division of the company's traffic opening out of it to form a succession of varying spaces. The movement of the millions of passengers who used the station was made as easy as possible. Those entering from the front, off Gordon Street, had no stairs whatever to climb, and at the other two entrances the flights were short. Inside the station there were no steps at all. Observing 'the tendency of people to spread like pouring water and travel along the line of least resistance',[87] Matheson saw to it that all the surfaces they pressed on were curved. His architect James Miller made a graceful response to this directive. The severity of glass and steel and stone was tempered by panelled walls of dark wood, warm and rich. A very big train indicator was incorporated into them, which any passenger who could read at all could see at a distance, *read and understand*. As a device for communicating with the public, its modern electronic successor (insensitively placed, attempting to dominate the whole concourse) is a bungling affair by comparison.

Glasgow itself responded to this station, which became a general meeting-place, 'a substitute for George Square': a true centre of town life, as no London terminus ever was. Londoners were glad to make appointments to meet under the clock at Charing Cross or Victoria, but those were meeting-places only. There was no room at either station to circulate, to stand and converse. The Caledonian company provided a service of that sort in Glasgow: not entirely to its own advantage, for the Central station afforded hospitality to a great many thousands of people who were not passengers. But in doing so it became, perhaps more than any other British station, a treasured possession of its city.[88]

When the station building was completed, the traffic was still controlled by manually-operated signals and points. But a new installation was already under way, and in 1908 manual working gave place to a power-operated electro-pneumatic system, greatly in advance of that installed at any other British terminal station. This was the crown of the whole work. Glasgow Central was then beyond question the finest terminus in the island. Some people – not a few – consider that it retains that title today.

The London & South Western Railway secured powers to reconstruct Waterloo in 1899–1900. It sent its engineer, J. W. Jacomb-Hood, to the United States to examine some of the new stations there. The work, based on his well-considered plans, took over twenty years. The entire station except its northern unit (opened as recently as 1885) was demolished and replaced, on a site extended from 16 to $24\frac{1}{2}$ acres. The concourse behind the buffers could be truly called a circulating area: for, except at the height of the rush hours, passengers could move about with ease in that vast crescent. While the station was being rebuilt, it admitted its first electric trains: underground in 1900–6, on the surface in 1915–16. Delayed by war, the great task was not completed until 1922. As a work of engineering, guided by the practical skill of operating men, it could then stand comparison at most points with the best in Europe.

But such attempt as it made to present itself as a work of architecture failed. Its formal entrance was immensely pompous, up a broad flight of steps under an arch encrusted with thick decoration and placed askew, gazing glumly on to a road intended for departing cabs and taxis, with a railway viaduct beyond. The decoration was the work of J. R. Scott, who was 'chief architectural assistant' to the engineer. The station was almost unseen from the main street nearest to it and made no contribution whatever to the face of London.

A similar comment might have been passed, by a superficial observer, on the most numerous group of stations opened in London at the beginning of the twentieth century: those built for the tube railways. But that would have been unjust. The managers' task here was not easy. How could travellers be persuaded to go underground? The station buildings at street level must give them a sense of welcome. Though the colour schemes adopted for them were quiet, they achieved a distinctive character, soon strengthened by uniform signing. Underground, there was some standardization in the approaches to the platforms in the stations, and in their layout; but an engaging difference appeared too in the decoration applied to them. The prevailing tone of the coloured wall-tiles changed from one station to the next;[89] no mere quirk, but a useful aid to regular travellers in recognizing their destinations. The seventy-eight stations opened in these years (two-thirds of them designed by Leslie Green, a promising architect who died in 1908, aged thirty-three) present a series of solutions to some novel problems. No happier combination of unity with diversity was to be seen in any group of Victorian stations than the one so modestly realized by the tube railways in London in these years. Something more strongly imaginative followed under Pick and Holden from 1924 onwards. But the work of Green and his contemporaries opened the way to that famous achievement.

Hotels

The introduction and early development of the steam-worked railway coincided with the arrival in Britain of the purpose-built hotel.

The first hotel built to serve a railway was opened at Euston station in London by stages, beginning in September 1839.[90] It consisted of two buildings facing each other across the approach to the great portico. The construction and management of the hotel were undertaken not by the railway but by a separate company associated with it;[91] this work lay outside the purposes for which railway companies had been given powers in their Acts of Parliament.[92]

The next hotels to be opened in collaboration with railways were not at terminal stations but at important junctions: at Derby, Swindon, and Normanton (1838–42).[93] At Derby the hotel was a quite separate enterprise, and it remained so until the Midland company bought it in 1860.[94] The Swindon hotel was accommodated above the station itself and was let out on lease by the Great Western, together with the refreshment rooms below it.[95]

Another type of railway hotel now appeared. At Folkestone the South Eastern company opened the Pavilion Hotel in 1843, for travellers passing between trains and the steamers that ran to and from Boulogne. Presently it undertook to provide a similar establishment at Dover: the Lord Warden, designed for it by the architect Samuel Beazley and completed in 1854. Others followed for the same purpose, at Neyland (for passengers to and from Waterford) and at Harwich.

The building of such hotels as these encountered some opposition. The York licensed victuallers, for example, sent a memorial to the directors of the York & North Midland Railway, urging them to reconsider their decision to erect an hotel there at the station.[96] They argued that it represented an illegitimate extension of the company's business and pointed to the capital already invested in the city's hotels, inns, and public houses (which they put at not less than £170,000), asserting that the proposed one was undesirable and unnecessary. However, the railway company opened the hotel in 1853. Twenty-five years later it was replaced by another at the new station, vastly bigger. Something of what the memorialists feared did happen. One of the two principal coaching inns, the Black Swan, certainly declined; but that was due to the loss of its coaching business in general, not especially to the new hotel's competition, and it was not ruined.[97] The railway had simply created new business, which it shared with the community.

Late in the century a number of new hotels were opened that were intended to compete with those of the railway companies. The County at Newcastle, for example, looked over Neville Street at the station and the railway hotel that adjoined it; the Midland at Birmingham faced the London & North Western company's Queen's Hotel across Stephenson Street; the Metropole at Leeds lay almost opposite the Great Northern Hotel and the Queen's, which belonged to the Midland Railway. On the other hand there were several towns – Stoke-on-Trent, Preston, York – in which the railway hotel remained the only one of a high class built during the Victorian age.

In London, even though the Euston Hotel proved profitable, earning a steady 6% dividend for its shareholders, fifteen years passed before a second railway hotel was opened. Then two appeared in 1854, at King's Cross and Paddington.

The Great Northern at King's Cross was an eminently sensible job. It was designed by Lewis Cubitt, the architect of the station, from which it was entirely detached, standing to one side of it and screened from its noise by the substantial structure that contained the booking hall and the company's offices. A rectangular building in pale yellow brick, sparsely dressed in order to keep the costs down, would have been a mere block. The hotel was curved, which made it an attractive foil to the station. Its final cost is stated to have been £35,000.[98]

The Great Western Hotel at Paddington was bigger and cost almost £60,000.[99] Brunel did not design it. That, he agreed, called for an architect, and P. C. Hardwick was chosen. The French elements in its external decoration, noted by some historians of architecture, were less important than its scale. Sir John Summerson put the matter straight: 'the large hotel was the creation of the railway, and Paddington was the first'.[100]

A Metropolitan Hotel Company was launched in London in the following year, holding up the one at Paddington as a model for imitation,[101] and by 1862 a number had been built, unconnected with railways, notably the Westminster Palace and the Langham. Other railway companies set out to emulate the Great Northern and the Great Western. At Charing Cross and Cannon Street hotels formed integral parts of the station plans and were undertaken by companies associated with the South Eastern. Here the station buildings were both designed by the engineer, John Hawkshaw; the hotels, which formed their frontages to the streets, by the architect E. M. Barry. This *Ill. 20* arrangement was followed in the next railway hotel, the Midland Grand at St Pancras: perhaps the most spectacular Victorian hotel, of any kind, except the Grand at Scarborough.

It has been dismissed as 'a mere trade advertisement';[102] with some truth, yet ungenerously. The Midland company was late in reaching London and drew attention to its arrival there with a magnificent train-shed, accommodating an ambitious service of expresses. A large hotel at its terminus had formed part of the company's thinking while the station was being built, and a competition was held for its design in 1866, before traffic began.

Competition was very seldom adopted by railway companies as a device for choosing architects.[103] Their directors preferred unfettered freedom. The Midland board (advised by no assessors from the architectural profession) awarded this valuable trophy to Gilbert Scott, whose entry flouted the rules of the contest, being well above the size laid down as a maximum by the directors themselves. Although some of the other entrants complained, they had no remedy at law. Wealthy and brazen, the company and its architect went ahead without attending to them.[104]

The result was a huge building on an aggressively dominant site, high above the Euston Road, looking down (in both senses of that phrase) on the trim hotel at King's Cross. It was Gothic through and through, and richly loaded with Gothic ornament. Too richly perhaps, yet the decoration was good, and it was skilfully fused into the whole design. The materials were excellent throughout, the strong red brick calculated to make everything at King's Cross look anaemic.

As an hotel the Midland Grand made a good name for itself, and kept that.[105] The railway company extended its holdings until it had eight hotels, kept in its own hands under the management of William Towle, one of the most respected men in the British hotel business. He appreciated very well the principle enunciated in 1902 that 'hotels that run themselves...obey the laws of gravity and run downwards'.[106]

Three more railway hotels followed in London: at Holborn Viaduct (1877), Liverpool Street (1884), and Marylebone (1899). All were the work of architects. The Great Eastern Hotel at Liverpool Street, on an awkward site, was ingeniously planned by the younger Charles Barry and his son Charles Edward.[107] It had an assured City business *clientèle* and an international one also, of travellers to and from the Continent via Harwich. The Great Central Hotel formed a comically vast frontispiece to the diminutive Marylebone station.[108]

By this time railway companies had hotels in all the ten largest English provincial cities, except Bristol. In some there were two, competing with each other; Liverpool, with its American traffic, had three. The last of the series was in Manchester: the gross, enormous Midland Hotel of 1898.

Two more were still to come in Scotland: the North British and the Caledonian in Edinburgh, a pair of rivals at the opposite ends of Princes Street completed in 1902–3. The North British Hotel was a coarse-grained edifice; a true monument both of the vulgarization of Princes Street (then just beginning) and of a palace revolution in the railway, which had briefly seated a disreputable gang of vulgarians in power.[109]

It is happier to bring a consideration of the railways' city hotels to a conclusion in Glasgow, with the one that Rowand Anderson designed for the Caledonian company as part of its first Central station, completed in 1884. Large yet compact, quietly adorned, in scale with its neighbours, this building was a civilized contribution to the streetscape of the city.

The railways built or acquired hotels of three other kinds besides.

They felt their way cautiously into the business at seaside resorts. The first success in this field was achieved by the Stockton & Darlington company, with its Zetland Hotel at Saltburn, opened in 1863; part of the development of a wholly new seaside resort based on a branch railway. It did reasonably well.[110] In 1863–76 two railway hotels appeared at Hunstanton.[111] The Midland company added one at Morecambe to its chain. So far as I am aware no other railway built or purchased one in a seaside resort until the Great Eastern acquired the Felix at Felixstowe in 1920.

Four Scottish railways took up the notion of building hotels for golfers. The first was at Cruden Bay, south of Peterhead, where the Great North of Scotland opened an hotel in 1896, with its own golf-links, served by a new branch line, together with an electric tramway over the 600 yards from the station. The bay itself provided glorious sands; the hotel had good prospects for family business before it. All who went there spoke well of it, but the 'all' were far too few, and the enterprise proved an entire financial failure.[112] A light railway was built from the Highland main line to Dornoch, where the links were already well reputed, and an hotel was provided in conjunction with it, opened in 1904. The Glasgow & South Western undertook the construction of an ambitious hotel and golf-links at Turnberry on the Ayrshire coast, opened simultaneously with a light railway in 1906. This hotel succeeding, the Caledonian Railway set up a nominally independent company to go one better in the same business, at Gleneagles on its main line in Perthshire, in February 1914. But the war delayed its completion, and the hotel was not opened until 1924.

British railway companies helped to point the way to what has now become a considerable element in European hotel keeping. They were among the pioneers of the 'country-house hotel'. The Furness Railway bought the manor house at Furness Abbey in 1847 and converted it into an hotel.[113] The Chester & Holyhead company, at the instance of its chairman Peto, set out to build one on parkland it had acquired facing the Menai Strait. It was never finished, however, and the land was sold off in 1861.[114] In 1878 the Great Western Railway leased Tregenna Castle, outside St Ives in Cornwall, for the same purpose. It was a finely-situated house, high up overlooking the bay; a castle only in name, in reality a foursquare eighteenth-century mansion, easily adapted to make a comfortable hotel. The venture was successful, and the railway company bought up the lease of the estate in 1895.[115] The full potential of the country-house hotel came to be realized only with the development of motoring in the twentieth century. But the railways were already demonstrating the value of the idea in the nineteenth.

It is impossible to compute the total extent of the railway companies' hotel business in Britain with any precision. Before 1913 hotels made no separate appearance in the companies' annual returns. In that year the number owned by each company was given: ninety-two altogether in Great Britain, sixty-seven in England and Wales and twenty-five in Scotland.[116]

The railways were always cautious about making any public statements concerning the volume or value of this branch of their business. When shareholders occasionally asked questions about the profitability of their companies' hotels, they got vague answers. Even the directors' committees seem to have been little informed on this matter. The statements recorded in the minutes about the Great Northern Hotel at Leeds, for instance, in the 1870s were all unitemized and showed no more than that it paid its way without difficulty.[117] The companies seem however to have disclosed information to one another, and the Great Western records include some figures for the business of all of them in the years 1913–20.[118] In 1913 the gross receipts from railway hotels in Great Britain are put here at £3,197,307, the net receipts at £556,100. Capital expenditure is given only for the United Kingdom (£8,152,560, including Ireland, where the railway hotels numbered twenty-one).

Numerous questions remain unanswered. How many pubs did the railways own, as distinct from hotels? Was it indeed legal for them to own any? When the West Wickham & Hayes Railway purchased the Leather Bottle at Wickham Green in 1880, with a view to rebuilding it, two years' hesitation and argument ensued before the justices licensed the new tavern, renamed the Railway Hotel.[119] Why did the Cambrian Railways permit their power to acquire hotels at Pwllheli, Criccieth, and Harlech to lapse in 1908, but purchase the Queen's, Aberystwyth, five years later?[120] Why could the London & North Western and the Lancashire & Yorkshire companies make no more than £867 profit on average each year out of their finely-sited Park Hotel at Preston in 1908–13?[121]

The great strength of the British railway hotels lay in their reliability. They set a dependable standard of sound accommodation and decent service, at not unreasonable prices. We may allow the last word here to a German guide-book, Baedeker's *Great Britain*: 'the large hotels managed by the principal railway companies are generally excellent and may be safely selected in all cases of doubt'.[122]

Goods Stations and Warehouses

The Liverpool & Manchester Railway provided for freight traffic with separate stations in the two cities, together with warehouses. The warehouse at Manchester, for the storage of cotton, has been carefully investigated by R. S. Fitzgerald, who places it in the context of earlier buildings of its type, largely following the pattern set by canal warehouses.[123] It soon proved too small, and further buildings had to be added. By 1837 they were stated to cover an area of five acres, with a capacity of 4 million cubic ft.[124]

Some of the trunk railways entrusted the distribution of all the goods they carried to established road haulage contractors; others, like the Grand Junction, kept the business in their own hands. The London & Birmingham, and for a time its successor the London & North Western, made great use of Pickford's and Chaplin & Horne in London. At its big Camden goods terminal the contractors were allotted premises of their own.[125]

Ill. 22

These stations were the meeting-points of two forms of transport, by rail and road. At some of them three were involved, where the railway entered docks, as at Liverpool, or touched navigable water. The siting of the Great Western's original goods station at Bristol at a level 16 ft below the main line was adopted in order to allow easy transhipment to and from the Floating Harbour. The King's Cross goods station, when it was brought into use in 1852, was the most impressive structure of this kind yet erected in Britain. An arm of the Regent's Canal entered it. Here was a railway building designed for the quick interchange of traffic between all the modes of transport then in use. It was solidly built of brick with a glazed timber roof and timber platforms. Since steam locomotives did not usually come inside the building, the risk of fire from them was small.[126]

The Great Northern company threw itself into the business of carrying coal to London from Yorkshire.[127] The dirt that such traffic occasioned made it necessary to handle it separately from all other merchandise, and 'coal depots' came to be established near, but never within, the large sheds of the general goods stations.[128] At wayside stations coal was always handled in open-air yards, served by sidings.

The original goods stations in large towns soon grew inadequate for the steadily-growing traffic. The railways' reponse was to add other buildings to those they already had there, until each site held a disorderly clutch.[129] At least fifteen of the most important passenger stations in the country were rebuilt from 1875 onwards. But goods stations, however large or busy, were adapted to handle increased traffic by minor reconstructions and the squeezing of supplementary buildings on to their sites; not by replacing the outgrown buildings with any wholly new installations. The refurbishment of the larger passenger stations was a necessity imposed on companies by the force of competition. No such refurbishment was called for, from the same cause, at goods stations. It was natural therefore to neglect it, or at least to put it off.

Some companies came to use these sites for other purposes besides handling trains. They went on to establish wholesale markets there, for root vegetables for example, at which the goods brought up over their lines could be sold. One was set up at King's Cross (at first within the goods station, then in a separate building erected for it in 1864, at a cost of £40,000), followed later by others at St Pancras and Bishopsgate.[130]

The King's Cross goods station became, in the words of a retired officer of the Great Northern company, 'like most goods stations, something of a mosaic, additions and alterations having been made from time to time solely with regard to business, i.e. the convenient manipulation of the traffic'. But at the end of the century the company erected a wholly new building into which all the outward traffic was concentrated, the original one handling inward traffic only. This permitted the removal of the clerical staff from their previous cramped quarters into offices that were more comfortable and better equipped.[131] Here was the largest reform to be found at any of the old goods stations in London. The one at Paddington had remained without extension since it was built in the 1850s. The twelve broad-gauge tracks that entered the covered train-shed had then required it to be more than 30 ft wider than would have been necessary in one designed for the standard gauge; so as the broad gauge was gradually removed, down to 1892, some multiplication of tracks became possible. Nevertheless, what had been adequate in Brunel's day could hardly suffice forty years later.

That such stations were still made to work is attributable largely to the opening of smaller depots throughout Greater London. The Great Western had one in the City at Smithfield underneath the meat market; others at Poplar in the docks and at Brentford on the Thames upstream. The London & North Western reached its markets in south London by means of a series of depots, at Brompton, Clapham, Dulwich, and (jointly with the Midland) at Peckham Rye.

The North Western company also enjoyed another advantage in the large goods station it built, by arrangement with the North London Railway, underneath that company's Broad Street passenger terminus in the heart of the City, in 1865.[132] The goods station was at ground level. It was accessible easily from the streets; the wagons were conveyed down to it, and up again, by hydraulic lifts. The North London's passenger station was 60 ft above the ground. So passenger and goods traffic could be combined, one on top of the other, within a site of $2\frac{3}{4}$ acres. That space must surely have yielded a revenue unmatched by any similar plot elsewhere on the Victorian railway system.

The two-tier plan adopted here was not unique. At St Pancras the passenger station was designed to accommodate the beer traffic from Burton at ground level, underneath the platforms. At London Road, Manchester, the Broad Street arrangement had been anticipated by twenty years, wagons being raised to the level of the railway by a steam-worked crane. This station came to handle not much less than 2000 tons of goods on a normal day.[133]

Where the need arose, the companies spent freely on the complex installations needed for goods traffic. By 1880 the London & North Western had laid out well over £5 million on its goods stations and the lines associated with them in London, Liverpool, and Manchester alone;[134] the passenger station at St Pancras, including its monster hotel, had cost no more than £1 million.

The scale of the railways' operations of this kind is displayed most impressively in the huge warehouses they built to serve the textile industries of northern England. Here the raw materials were brought in, and the finished products dispatched across the world. To look at them now makes it easier for us to appreciate a little of what was involved in the railways' 'terminals' – the charges they made for handling and holding goods, over and above those for carrying them – and why they were high enough to form (whether reasonably or not) a main ground of complaint by traders in the 1880s and 1890s. These buildings were immensely strong, and many of them were partly or wholly of fireproof construction. Though architects had little or no hand in them, some were undoubtedly works of architecture.

It is sad that none of those in Manchester, which was *par excellence* the city of warehouses,[135] was especially distinguished. One of the last, that built by the Great Northern Railway on Deansgate in 1898, was indeed very large, but that was its chief claim to notice.[136] In Liverpool, on the other hand, there were at least two that were remarkable. The Cheshire Lines' warehouse at Brunswick Dock was truly a noble building. The Midland company's goods *Ill. 21* offices in Crosshall Street (1874) present a concave front of great assurance, enriched with splendid lettering, incised and gilded. Reilly adduced it as one of his proofs that 'architecture is not a matter of features but of proportion and expression'; and he went on to remark that this was to be reckoned 'one of the best buildings in the town'.[137] He was a good judge, and he did not throw such commendation about lightly.

The last range of goods depots to be built for the British railways before 1914 was that provided for the Great Central's London extension, completed in 1899. They comprised one very big one, at Marylebone in London; two of substantial size, at Nottingham and Leicester; and a series of smaller ones for the lesser stations on the line. At Marylebone the area allotted to goods traffic (including the coal yard and a wharf on the Regent's Canal) was considerably bigger than that assigned to passenger business;[138] and though space was reserved for one more island platform to be built later in the passenger station, enough land had been purchased to permit the coal yard to be more than doubled.[139] The dominant building here was the goods warehouse, measuring 390 ft × 262 ft; five stories high, and centrally heated. It cost nearly £300,000. Here, as at Nottingham and Leicester, the stations were equipped with Goliath 25-ton overhead cranes, electrically driven; the first appearance of this type, so it was said, in the country.

The railways' minor stations each comprised a small goods yard, served by a siding or two, a revolving hand-worked crane, a modest office and warehouse, and at some of them a cattle dock. The simple measured plan of the one at Daventry, given by Findlay, typifies the layout and the main equipment of these station buildings.[140] This one was of wood. Some were more substantial structures: the brick ones of the Midland Railway, for instance, specimens of which can still be seen (no longer used for goods traffic) at Irchester and Glendon (Northants.). We owe a debt to the Didcot Railway Centre for preserving a notable wooden transhipment shed of 1863, in which goods were removed from broad to standard-gauge wagons, and *vice versa*; and another to the North of England Open Air Museum at Beamish for reconstructing a village station goods yard. Here one can see, as nowhere else, a microcosm of the railways' rural traffic.

Engine-Sheds and Signal-Boxes

The railways erected many buildings for the construction, maintenance, and housing of their locomotives and rolling stock, and for the signalling equipment required for their operation.

Some of the largest of them were never seen by the public at all: the works in which the machines were built and repaired. These came to constitute whole quarters of railway towns, like Swindon and Crewe, where they were accessible only to the companies' servants. In old-established towns, Derby, Doncaster, or Edinburgh, the railways bought land on the edge of the built-up area, to allow them to extend in the future. The works themselves were usually walled in, except where they lay beside the railway lines. Where that happened, their privacy was tightly guarded. The iron foundry at Swindon showed a façade to the trains on the Great Western main line: a stone front boldly treated but, no less clearly, an outer boundary of a set of buildings that turned its back on the railway, the work in them carried on out of sight.[141] The companies' workshops might begin life impressively, as Bourne shows us in the repair shop at Swindon in the 1840s, a very ample timber building.[142]

But as time went on they became huge crowded halls of machinery.[143] The engineers' task was to design suitable halls, or to adapt old ones for new purposes.

The running-sheds serving locomotives in daily traffic and accommodating them at night were of two main types. One was rectangular: a plan adopted at Swindon in 1841, with a building nearly 500 ft long to house forty-eight engines.[144] By that time the alternative, polygonal plan had been demonstrated in two engine-sheds built in 1839–40, at Derby for the North Midland Railway and at Miles Platting for the Manchester & Leeds.[145] The building at Derby had sixteen sides. It was covered with a slated timber roof, resting on cast-iron columns, centred on a turntable serving sixteen tracks, and able to take thirty engines. This shed evidently proved satisfactory to Robert Stephenson, who was engineer to the company: for another of the kind was erected at Camden for the London & North Western Railway in 1847. It was designed by R. B. Dockray.[146] This was somewhat bigger, and circular. Hence it came to be called the Roundhouse; and that name was soon applied to all sheds of this type, with a central turntable, even when they were polygonal.

The Camden roundhouse attracted widespread notice. Rather surprisingly, Gilbert Scott gave it an architect's accolade in 1857.[147] When the Manchester Sheffield & Lincolnshire company erected its first works at Gorton, outside Manchester, in 1848, a circular locomotive running-shed was included in the complex of buildings. This was novel in two respects. The roof, of wrought-iron and glass, was supported on one central column only, which left the internal space free of all obstruction; and the turntable carried two tracks, side by side.[148] Several men had hands in the planning of these works: A. S. Jee, the company's engineer; Richard Peacock, its locomotive superintendent; and M. E. Hadfield, a Sheffield architect. Brees was quite specific on this matter.[149] Since he was himself addressing engineers, he was not likely to give an architect any undeserved credit. It seems that there was a real collaboration here.

The roundhouse plan was convenient, where the site was large enough, and suitable in shape; but it had the drawback common to all circular buildings, that it was not conveniently extendible. The Camden roundhouse ceased to be used for its original purpose in 1869. Where a very big engine-shed was called for, a rectangle came to be preferred. The North Eastern company built such a depot at Gateshead, in which there were five turntables, with eighteen roads for locomotives leading on to each. The Frenchman Perdonnet gave this arrangement special praise for its economy.[150]

On large, well-run railways engine-sheds came to be soundly built and equipped. That was only proper for structures designed to hold so many valuable pieces of machinery. (Towards the end of the century the average cost of a single locomotive when it was new was of the order of £2500.) On railways where economy reigned supreme, it was often exercised in a refusal to extend or improve these buildings, and in keeping them in use long after they ought to have been replaced.[151]

Their design had given rise to a passing flutter of interest, as the engineers played with the possibilities opened up by the installation of turntables inside them. Having reached their conclusions about that, they had no need to go beyond providing appropriate and economical structures. However, the provision could not be made to any single formula. Each shed needed some consideration on its own. The buildings varied greatly, in shape and above all in size. At the end of its separate life, in 1898, the South Eastern company had twenty-five running-sheds, to accommodate 413 engines. A third of the machines were concentrated into one only, at Bricklayers Arms in London. The remainder were dispersed over the system, 421 miles in length. Five of them held no more than a single locomotive apiece.[152]

The most ubiquitous of all the railways' buildings were their signal-boxes. In 1922 there were about 11,000 of them in Great Britain.[153] Their incidence was uneven. On systems serving large towns and industrial districts they might be very numerous, and at some big junctions, where the lines of several different companies converged: by 1900 there were some thirty within a two-mile radius of the station at Carlisle.[154] Their distribution can be indicated by means of a rough comparison between the numbers of those on the smaller systems. On the North Staffordshire Railway, the heart of which was a dense network serving the Potteries, there were in 1931 fifty stations and 134 signal-boxes. On the other hand in 1922 the rural Cambrian Railways had more boxes than stations (ninety-two to eighty-four), and on the Highland system the proportion was 154 to 126.[155]

The first rudimentary idea of the railway signal-box appears in the 1840s as a hut or cabin to shelter the men operating the signals. As the mechanism grew more complex, with the multiplication of lines and junctions and the gradual adoption of the electric telegraph for controlling them, this kind of accommodation also became more elaborate. A low raised platform at the foot of the signals was installed at Bricklayers Arms Junction about 1843. In the 1850s some such platforms came to be lifted up on stilts, to give the men occupying them a fuller view along the lines. The instruments growing more numerous, the whole platform space might be roofed in to make a room, fully glazed; called a signal-cabin, or a signal-box.[156]

These structures became almost infinitely various, in shape and size. They were purely utilitarian, and there was seldom any need to make them harmonize with their surroundings. They might do that unselfconsciously where they formed part of a group of station buildings or were designed along with them, as for instance on the West Highland line.[157] Some differed starkly from the buildings they adjoined; particularly where they towered up high above the rest, dominating them all. As long as mechanical signalling lasted, the signalman had to be able to keep an uninterrupted view of the line. It was provided for him most impressively in later days when his box was itself *Ill. 19* mounted on a gantry, usually quite separate from the station buildings.[158]

Decoration was allowed sparingly on these structures. A variety of barge-boards adorned the gables, most elegantly perhaps on the Bristol & Exeter and the Great Northern Railways.[159] Elaborate exterior designs were very rarely adopted, though surprisingly the Highland Railway put up four specially-adorned boxes at Inverness in 1898.[160] All signal-boxes were, however, essentially engineers' jobs: no more than housings for machinery and the men who worked it. As such, many of them displayed a seemliness, an instinctive decency of design and proportion and a blend of materials, that gave them a dignity of their own.

The boxes of two of the biggest companies came to be highly distinctive, for different reasons. The Midland was unique among them in refusing ever to purchase interlocking frames from private manufacturers. Its signal-boxes display an unbroken evolution from 1870 onwards.[161] They were all timber-built. The very biggest of them grew lumpish and ungainly, huge walls of wood.[162] Some however were built with the signalman's cabin 'oversailing', i.e. projecting outwards from the base that contained the machinery, and that gave them something like elegance.[163]

The London & North Western, convinced that it was paying too much to the manufacturers Saxby & Farmer, set up its own signalling department in 1873. Its signal-boxes developed to three main designs thereafter.[164] Most of them were built of bricks made in the company's works at Crewe. Some of the biggest were very tall, not only to provide for the signalman's view but also to accommodate increasingly elaborate machinery.[165] The last survivor of these giants is the Severn Bridge Junction box at Shrewsbury, built in 1903:[166] a huge fortress, as grim in its own fashion as the jail only a short distance away.

Leaving aside such monsters, nearly all the range and variety of these buildings can be observed in those designed for much smaller operations. The Great Eastern company's Type 7, which continued to be built by various contractors for forty years after its introduction in 1886, was very trim, especially perhaps in its timber version. The North British achieved an equal neatness in brick.[167] One of Saxby & Farmer's designs provided a hipped roof projecting over the windows on all sides. It was much found on the Brighton company's system, and also occasionally elsewhere.

On the Border Counties Railway, built in 1854–62 to run from Hexham into Scotland, most buildings (the signal-boxes included) were of stone – the only material available locally, in a district not easily reached by any form of transport until the railway itself was built. That was a rare practice. What made it rarer still was that the stone was dressed, to give it a smooth face. The masons here were simply carrying on the accepted local tradition. In signal-boxes, that refinement was bettered perhaps only once. When the Great North of Scotland company's Kittybrewster South box, on the edge of Aberdeen, was built in the 1870s it had to be raised very high, to give the signalman a clear view of the line, over an adjoining road bridge. The whole of the lofty plinth on which the box rested was built of granite, ashlared. Here again a local practice – a most distinguished one – was being faithfully observed.[168]

1 The London & Birmingham Railway burrows under Park St., Camden
Town. Drawing by John Bourne, 18 Sept. 1836

2 London & Birmingham Railway: construction of bridge over Tring
Cutting. Drawing by John Bourne

3 Great Western Railway: builders' work in progress. Sketch by
John Bourne, c. 1840

4 Floating of the second tube of the Britannia bridge crossing the Menai
Strait. Lithograph by George Hawkins, 1849

5 The South Eastern Railway carried along the beach at Dover on a timber
viaduct into Shakespeare's Cliff tunnel. Water-colour drawing
by George Childs, c. 1845

6 Coldrenick viaduct on the Cornwall Railway, between St Germans and Menheniot,
opened in 1859. Brunel's timber superstructure was rebuilt in brick in 1897

7 Wetheral viaduct, Newcastle & Carlisle Railway: arches completed 1834

8 The Stephensons' North Midland Railway (1840) was carried through
the town of Belper (Derbyshire) in a stone-lined trough, spanned by a series of
stone bridges, carrying streets across it. Lithograph, probably by S. Russell

9 The Ballochmyle viaduct, near Mauchline, Ayrshire. Oil painting by
D. O. Hill, 1849

10 The Treffry viaduct, in the Luxulyan valley in Cornwall, on its
completion in 1842. Oil painting, perhaps by Ambrose Johns

11 The Royal Albert bridge, Saltash (Cornwall), opened 1859. Photograph
by G. W. Wilson, 1861

12 The Forth bridge under construction. Photograph by G. W. Wilson, 1888

13 The Forth bridge soon after its opening in 1890. Photograph
by G. W. Wilson

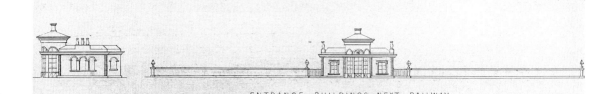

ENTRANCE BUILDINGS NEXT RAILWAY

14,15 Two of Francis Thompson's stations on the North Midland Railway:
Eckington (above), Swinton (below). Contemporary lithographs

16 A Tudor-style country station in red brick, with stone window-dressings:
Wye (South Eastern Railway), opened 1846. Anonymous water-colour drawing

17 Tite's frontage to Perth station (1848). Oil painting by James Fraser, 1883

18 Lodging house for engine-men built by the Lancashire & Yorkshire Railway at Blackpool.

19 The railway's approach to Charing Cross station, from the bridge over the Thames. Signalling installation by Saxby & Farmer

20 *Left* The Charing Cross Hotel (1864: architect E. M. Barry) formed the façade of the railway station, giving on to the Strand. Hawkshaw's train-shed lay behind. Photograph by G. W. Wilson

21 *Above* The Crosshall St. goods station and warehouse, Liverpool

22 *Below* Part of Pickford's depot at Camden Town, London & Birmingham Railway. Lithograph by Thomas Allom

23 Parliamentary train from Euston to Liverpool, 1859. Engraved from drawing by William M'Connell

24 Sketches by E. T. Lane of vehicles used in passenger service, c. 1848. No. 1 shows a London & North Western covered luggage van with a hooded shelter for the guard, his brake-handle in front of him. Nos. 2 and 3 (London & North Western and Midland) are of first-class carriages. Note the *coupé*, or half-compartment, in No. 2.

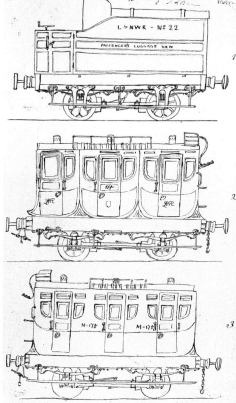

25 King Edward VII opened the second high-level bridge over the Tyne on
10 July 1906. Here he is crossing the original one, at the start of his return
journey southwards. North Eastern Atlantic engine,
London & North Western train

26 Midland Railway carriage, 1876: first and third-class accommodation only

27 *Gorgon*, one of Gooch's *Firefly* class for the broad-gauge Great Western
Railway, built in 1841. Water-colour drawing by E. T. Lane, 1849

OPPOSITE PAGE

28 No. 422, an engine of class C1 for the London Brighton & South Coast
Railway, built under Stroudley's direction at Brighton in 1882, standing on
the turntable at St Leonards. The high finish is striking: these machines were
designed only for ordinary freight service

29 A 'Skye Bogie' of the Highland Railway. These engines were designed
expressly for the long branch from Dingwall towards Skye. The bogies eased
the way round curves, and the small driving wheels aided hill-climbing

30 Another engine to meet special demands: one of the 0-6-2s that came to
be predominantly employed in the South Wales coalfield. This is one of the
last and most powerful varieties, class A, built for the Taff Vale Railway
in 1914

31 The first machine of the 'Star' class (4001, *Dog Star*), built under Churchward for heavy express work on the Great Western Railway in 1907

32 One of the largest and best British freight locomotives: the Great Central company's class 8K of 1911. More than 500 such engines were built to the government's orders for service abroad during the war of 1914–18

Further north still, the Highland Railway moved sluggishly with the introduction of interlocking and was forced to accelerate that process drastically by the Regulation Act of 1889. In 1890–4 Dutton & Co. supplied a number of the new boxes that were then called for. Some of them exemplified the simple timber box in its perfection;[169] perfection achieved by virtue of economy.

It is fitting to end this brief survey of signal-boxes, as structures, on that railway, for there they were prominent in a fashion that was all their own. Long stretches of its main line – north of Blair Atholl and again north of Helmsdale – passed through great tracts of uninhabited country. Its signal-boxes here stood up in the loneliest isolation. They were a fixed presence, proclaiming the passage of the railway, the telegraph, and all they brought with them, for many miles around.

Housing

In very early days the railways assumed a responsibility for housing some of the men they employed. From 1826 onwards certain companies found it convenient to establish their own works, for servicing locomotives and rolling stock, on sites that were almost or entirely virgin, away from towns: at Shildon, for instance, Wolverton, Crewe, and Swindon. If they were to attract the men they wanted there, and to keep them, it was not enough to rely on their lodging in the neighbourhood. So they came to create not merely new manufacturing works but new towns.[170]

At Crewe the architect John Cunningham of Liverpool was engaged by the Grand Junction company in 1842 'to superintend the whole of the buildings...the drainage also and any other matters connected with the buildings, cottages, and other erections'. For this work he was paid an annual salary of £300 for eight years. Though Locke, the engineer, laid out the ground-plan of what became the new town of Crewe and supervised the whole building of its locomotive works, Cunningham was responsible for the accommodation of the company's men there, in little red-brick terrace houses, set in streets laid out on a grid pattern. Something similar happened at Wolverton, though there we do not hear of the employment of any architect.[171]

The Great Western company managed the same business differently at Swindon. Its works there were erected on an almost empty site a mile away from the existing small town, and here also new houses were called for to accommodate the men employed in them. The company made the erection of the houses part of its contract with J. & C. Rigby, together with the building of the station, its refreshment rooms and hotel.[172] Three hundred cottages went up under this arrangement, laid out in eight parallel streets, with a good frontage in limestone (said to have come from the excavation of the Box tunnel)[173] and with brick outbuildings at the rear.[174] Architecturally this was among the best industrial settlements hitherto built in Britain. Another was erected close to the station at Derby, presenting a decent face of brickwork to people walking or driving into the town.

[65]

No railway company, however, continued for long to assume all such responsibilities as these. At Crewe the Grand Junction set out by letting its houses at economic rents, but when that policy proved unworkable, it reduced the rents and accepted the need to subsidize such building, and other similar building in the future. As the railway towns grew, speculative builders undertook to provide houses there.[175] In some of them house-building was undertaken entirely by this method: at Horwich and Eastleigh, for example, from the 1880s onwards.[176] At Inverurie, on the other hand, the Great North of Scotland company assumed the main financial responsibility for the whole of the very creditable settlement that grew up around the new works established north of the old town in 1898–1905.[177] The Glasgow & South Western company built a 'model village' at Corkerhill (near Bellahouston) for its men employed at the engine sheds there.[178]

There were other kinds of housing required for railwaymen, which the companies had to provide themselves. A man responsible for the gates at a level crossing clearly had to be sheltered. One placed in charge of a station (at least if it was of any importance) could scarcely perform his duties satisfactorily unless he lived on the spot.

The earliest clear records I have seen of houses to be built by a railway company relate to these two categories of its servants. They date from about 1835 and are contract drawings for the Grand Junction Railway, signed by Locke.[179] One of these buildings may be a crossing-keeper's cottage. It includes a waiting-room and has a projecting bay on the ground floor, to give a view up and down the line. The other is probably a stationmaster's house, having a dining-room and a kitchen, with two bedrooms above.

The accommodation provided for a stationmaster usually came to comprise a flat over the booking-office or other public entrance: as for instance in six stations of the Birmingham Wolverhampton & Dudley Railway (opened in 1854), for which J. R. McClean was the engineer.[180] Here there were three bedrooms, with kitchen, parlour, and closet. The flat might be at one end of the station building,[181] or below it if the railway was raised up on an embankment.[182] On the other hand, the stations designed by Mocatta for the Brighton Railway about 1840 had nearly all been single-storeyed, furnishing no accommodation of this kind whatever.[183] That practice was followed here and there for some time to come. In 1863, for example, a new stationmaster arriving to take up his post at Thame – a not unimportant little town – had to begin by finding himself a house, which he got for £8 a year.[184]

The railway companies provided a very considerable number of houses of other kinds besides these. When the Manchester Sheffield & Lincolnshire started to develop Grimsby as a fishing-port from the 1850s onwards, it found difficulty in persuading fishermen to come and live there and decided to build houses for men earning a range of different wages, letting them at rents yielding about 4% on their cost. The experiment succeeded, contributing to the growth of the fishing business at the port, from which the Sheffield company came to draw a large revenue.[185] This intelligent decision seems to have been due to the company's chairman, Watkin, who always showed some interest in the welfare of its servants and in the 1870s induced the board to embark on a policy of building houses for men stationed at lonely places on its system.[186]

The engineer John Wolfe Barry endorsed this policy: 'A company in good credit ought to be able to build houses more cheaply than other people, and can afford to let them to its servants at a lower rent than people who build houses merely for profit'.[187] Findlay, writing of the London & North Western, illustrates the need for them well by reference to the dangers arising from fog – an 'element which ... entails more anxiety upon those engaged in the management of a railway than all others put together'. The fog-signalmen, whose duty it was to place detonators on the rails at the feet of the signal-posts, might be called out at any hour of the day or night. Most of them were platelayers. Since they could not do their ordinary work during fog, they were now directed into this other duty. Great advantage accrued to the company from their living at places it selected, rather than in whatever houses they could find, scattered about in a rural neighbourhood. So it built cottages for these platelayers, close to stations or signal-posts where they might be needed when the emergency arose, proclaimed by an electric bell ringing in the ganger's house, worked from the signal-box. All the bricks, all the woodwork and ironwork used in them were made under the company's own care at Crewe, and the houses were erected by men in its employment. Let at weekly rents of three shillings or a little less, they produced an annual return of about 3.8% on the capital invested. They were kept in repair by the company; hence – Findlay's claim is surely justified – 'infinitely superior to the best accommodation which the men's small means would otherwise have enabled them to obtain'.[188]

In wild tracts of country, like the Highlands of Scotland, the erection of such cottages came to be treated as part of the building of the line itself, a pre-condition of its opening. The process can be seen in a photograph taken at Taynuilt in Argyllshire in 1880.[189] There the Callander & Oban company, though in constant financial difficulty, recognized the need by building a row of stone cottages at the same time as the nearby station.

Some of the railway companies' houses bore their initials on plaques: those of the Great North of England Railway, for instance, a few of which survive today beside the main line from York to Darlington. The Stockton & Darlington and London & Birmingham companies went further, to attach iron plates to those they owned, each bearing a number.[190] 'Railway Cottages' are still to be found on maps of the Ordnance Survey; as at Micheldever in Hampshire, on the road leading from the station to the village.

By the 1880s the London & North Western company provided its men with nearly 4000 houses altogether, the North Eastern with over 3000. In 1914 those numbers had been approximately doubled. The twelve largest companies then owned, between them, about 41,000.[191]

Such cottages as these met special needs in rural districts. But there came to be other needs, hardly less pressing. One example must suffice. In early days doubtless the drivers and firemen of locomotives could find lodgings without great difficulty. Where their running-sheds were in large towns, or in towns that the railway developed or dominated, like Derby or Carlisle, the quest would usually be an easy one. But as the system grew and its working became more complex an increasing number of such men were unable to reach their homes again at night. When their spell of duty ended at a distant place they might have to sleep there before returning next day. Lodgings available for one night only could not be easy to find, nor were they likely to be satisfactory. As early as 1867 the London & North Western built 'enginemen's barracks' for this purpose at Crewe, adding a second set thirty years later.[192] The Great Eastern provided dormitory accommodation at Stratford for men on these 'lodging turns', also purpose-built.[193] The Lancashire

Ill. 18 & Yorkshire erected a large block at Blackpool, partly to serve the needs of the enginemen who arrived there with excursion and other holiday trains, making their return home next day.[194]

Railways destroyed a great deal of housing as they forced their way into large towns, and even under the compulsion of the law they seldom built satisfactory accommodation for those they evicted.[195] But the housing that has been discussed here, erected at their own cost to fulfil their duty and interest as employers, also deserves remembrance.

3

MACHINERY

The Pursuit of Reliability · Economy and Safety ·
Divided Responsibilities · The Force of Competition ·
Traction 1870–1914 · The Control of Power

The preceding chapter has sketched the construction of the railways' road-bed and described some of their buildings, the framework within which their trains moved. Though horses by no means disappeared from the British railways (the twelve largest companies were still using some 26,000, mainly in cartage and shunting, in 1913),[1] the instruments that most characterized them in the eyes of the Victorians were their machines: locomotives and the vehicles they hauled, the devices that controlled their movement and, in normal service, ensured their safety.

The railway companies were bombarded with accounts of ingenious contrivances for improving their work. The directors of the Liverpool & Manchester gave patient attention to these proposals.[2] Some were directed towards the solution of important difficulties: Henry Booth's screw coupling, for example, which in conjunction with T. F. Bergin's spring buffing gear did away with the intolerable jerks and bangs that occurred every time a train started or stopped, as long as its vehicles were joined together only by loose chains.

Another man claimed to have put the idea of this coupling into Booth's mind: the stationmaster at Parkside, Abel Turton.[3] Booth must have been in constant discussion with the company's employees on the working of its trains, and Turton may well have suggested something of this sort to him. But it was Booth who produced the workable solution, so effective that it required no improvement.

'The proper credit of priority or invention is one of the greatest problems in preparing any history of technology': the remark comes from one of the best American practitioners of that art, as applied to railways.[4] When a new mechanical device is mentioned here, and the credit for it assigned to one man, he must be taken to be the effective inventor; not necessarily the man who had the original idea but the one who made the appliance work.

The brief survey of the railways' mechanical engineering that is now offered uses demand as the chief key to understanding development. What new needs had to be met successively, and why and when? The insistent question here will be not so much 'what *were* these machines?' as 'why were they what they were?'

The Pursuit of Reliability

Steam power had already become familiar before 1830 to those who lived in industrial districts, in the large towns or on the great river estuaries.[5] But it had not been applied to movement on land except in and around collieries, and there only on a small scale from 1812 onwards. That application was confined, in normal service, to the haulage of coal until in 1830 the Canterbury & Whitstable and Liverpool & Manchester Railways were opened, demonstrating the suitability of the steam locomotive to all kinds of traffic.

The Liverpool & Manchester changed the concept of speed in communication. It did so at a price, symbolized for many people in the harshly unpleasant behaviour of its machines, the loud, uncouth noises they made and the clouds of smoke they emitted – curbed however by Parliament's insistence that the steam engines employed should 'consume their own smoke'. That meant that they were obliged to burn coke, not coal, which diminished the nuisance but did not altogether remove it. Their machines made many enemies for the railways at first.

Most of the early locomotives of the Liverpool & Manchester company were built by Robert Stephenson's at Newcastle, and their designs incorporated improvements one after another. Their *Planet* of 1830 – already a great advance on *Rocket* – was superseded three years later by *Patentee*, a larger and stronger machine running not on four wheels but on six, set in a frame of more robust design.[6] This formed the basis of many of the engines put into service in the 1830s in France, Belgium, Germany, Italy, and Russia. In the United States there were at least thirty-five Stephenson-built locomotives; in 1843 there were eighty in Germany.[7] That firm had no monopoly in the business. Three of the earliest locomotives to run in America came from Foster Rastrick & Co. at Stourbridge; half of those built by Rothwell's of Bolton down to 1840 went abroad.[8] About forty firms seem to have manufactured locomotives in Great Britain in the 1830s.[9]

As the demand for these machines rose, the builders were hard put to it to fulfil orders, and some of them cut corners in order to do so. Their products were often delivered late, and then found faulty in design or materials, or both. In the next decade much of the export business of British locomotive builders disappeared. The Belgians, the French, the Germans, and the Americans now had manufacturers in their own countries to deal with. At home the main demands to be met were for punctual delivery and service. In the late 1830s some manufacturers were in serious arrears with production: Sharp Roberts, for example. Presently it became a not uncommon practice for them to deliver whatever machines they could spare, not in accordance with the orders they received.[10] Naturally, in this sellers' market, prices constantly rose. Edward Bury charged £700 for his first locomotive in 1830; by 1839 his price was £1250–1400. The Newcastle & Carlisle paid £1000 for its first one in 1835; within four years it was paying £1700.[11]

Some companies were dilatory in deciding what kinds of machines they wanted for working their traffic. They were warned plainly in 1839 that they would find certain builders committed for years ahead.[12] More serious, in some cases neither the directors nor their officers assessed correctly the articles they wished to buy for their work. That is to be observed, in an extreme form, on the Great Western Railway. Nineteen locomotives were supplied to it in 1837–40 to specifications laid down by the company's engineer, Brunel. They came from six manufacturers, in ten different varieties.[13] The demands Brunel made of the machines needed for working his railway were unlike those of any other engineer. The railway itself was different, being laid out to the 7-ft gauge; and that had been adopted primarily to facilitate a great increase in the speed of trains. Brunel wished his engines to run faster than any that had yet been seen; not just for a few minutes down hill, but on the level in ordinary service.

Unfortunately his specifications rested on mistaken principles. Not one of these engines was successful; eight had been withdrawn from traffic before the end of 1840,[14] and the rest were rendered serviceable only by drastic reconstruction. The blame for this fiasco does not rest wholly on Brunel. Some of the engines were defective in their construction. Had the Great Western company depended wholly on them, its railway would have been unworkable. It was saved from ignominious disaster by the steady application of conventional experience.

In addition to the nineteen engines already mentioned, two had been ordered from Robert Stephenson's, developments of the *Patentee* design. The first delivered, *North Star*, was a complete success. It was the only reliable engine the railway had, until it was joined by a similar Stephenson machine seven months later. By this time the company had acquired a new officer, Daniel Gooch, charged with responsibility for its locomotives. His immediate task was to make the other hopelessly unsuitable engines work. Ten more like *North Star* were bought from Stephenson's, and Gooch also evolved his own *Ill. 27* designs, based on his experience with them but incorporating improvements. Over the next twenty-five years they served his company well.

The Great Western directors showed a large liberality, following the example set on the Liverpool & Manchester, in permitting outside observers to make tests on their line.[15] Dionysius Lardner – a tiresome scientific busybody at this stage of his life, though he afterwards proved himself capable of better things – was given special facilities by them. For Charles Babbage they did more. They lent him a second-class carriage to be fitted up with machinery he designed himself, for the measurement of the tractive force of locomotives and of the vibration set up as the carriage moved.[16] This provided part of the basis on which Gooch constructed a new, more elaborate testing vehicle in 1848, the first true dynamometer car.[17]

The Great Western's experiments did not stand alone. The Gauge Commissioners conducted tests, to weigh up the merits of the machines used respectively on the standard and broad gauges they were examining.[18] The comparison however could not be satisfactory because the tests had to be made on two separate stretches of railway, 200 miles apart. Still, one result emerged clearly from them: that the broad-gauge locomotives were superior to any of their rivals in the haulage of fast passenger trains. But that was no startling conclusion, for since May 1845 the best service offered on the broad gauge between London and Exeter had been faster than any other in the world.

Few railways yet made any clear distinction between the locomotives they employed in passenger and in goods services. The chief innovator in this matter was Edward Bury, who was locomotive superintendent of the London & Birmingham and furnished it with a stock of four-wheeled engines. Some, built for goods traffic, had all their wheels coupled, so as to apply the whole adhesive weight to the driving of the locomotive. On the rest they were uncoupled, with driving wheels of larger dimensions in the rear, enabling them to run more freely at the higher speeds required for passenger trains.

Bury's locomotives were simple, good in their workmanship, and all alike because they were supplied from his own works at Liverpool. When they proved too small he used them in pairs, or even three to a train. Although that practice meant a doubling or trebling of manpower, the wages paid to the footplate men were not yet high enough to make it uneconomic; but it was open to all the difficulties and dangers arising from multiple haulage. When the London & Birmingham company was merged into the London & North Western in 1846 Bury's appointment was terminated in favour of a new man (who was not also a manufacturer), the much more progressive J. E. McConnell.

By this time the tank engine, carrying its fuel and water on top of its wheels instead of needing a separate tender, had begun to be tried out. Such engines could be driven in either direction, without being turned round, and that commended them for use in short-distance traffic. They also proved particularly valuable on lines with heavy gradients, where the locomotive needed the greatest adhesive power, since the weight of the fuel and water in a tank engine was added to its own. Gooch turned out a pair of them in 1849, for service on the very steep South Devon Railway between Newton Abbot and Plymouth, and they succeeded admirably. Almost the whole traffic over that line, and on to Penzance, came to be worked by such engines until 1884. They were the ugliest machines Gooch ever designed, and among the best.[19]

The South Devon Railway had been laid out by Brunel for working by an entirely different mode of traction: the 'atmospheric system', employing pneumatic power to drive trains, transmitted through large pipes laid between the rails to pistons underneath the carriages. The plan was tried out on three railways in the British Isles in 1844–8.[20]

The elimination of the steam locomotive under this system greatly reduced the weight placed on the track, so enabling the rails to be lighter and cheaper. Since power was supplied externally, from stationary engines, there was no need for a machine that hauled its own fuel about with it. The journey became much more pleasant for the passengers: quieter, and freed from the engines' smoke. Those were important gains. But the technique failed because no means were discovered of keeping the propelling air within its pipe when the train was in motion. It had other serious drawbacks too, however, which were never removed. The tubes, rising higher than the tracks, made level crossings impossible. More important, there was difficulty wherever two lines diverged; no satisfactory mechanism was devised for switching the wind pressure from one pipe to another.[21] If such problems as these had been solved, the railways might have turned over to a system that had many of the merits later offered by electricity, and the steam locomotive would then have been partly or wholly abandoned. Here demand was defeated by an insufficient technology.

Much lively experimentation went on in the 1840s, and Britain found her own ways of solving the problems of handling her traffic. In express service Gooch's *Iron Duke* locomotives of 1847 displayed the virtues of the broad gauge at its best, though a general slowing-down of such trains in 1852 removed the urgency to build others of similar capacity. For traffic at the opposite end of the scale in speed, a goods engine running on six coupled wheels, the last pair behind the firebox, was coming to be preferred. The first such engines, having their frames and cylinders placed inside the wheels, came to be built for the Great Western and for several standard-gauge railways in 1846–8. Powerful and capable of much enlargement, this became the characteristic British freight locomotive, and remained so well into the twentieth century. The last machine of the kind was not built until 1948.

In the 1840s British railway companies began to turn, in increasing numbers, to building their own locomotives and rolling stock. The Stockton & Darlington and the Liverpool & Manchester Railways initiated the practice. The Grand Junction followed them, at Crewe in 1843, imitated in 1844–7 by six other companies.[22] By 1867 every large railway in Great Britain except the Highland and the Great North of Scotland supplied the locomotives it needed, wholly or partly, from its own workshops, and many of them built their own carriages and wagons too.

No other country in the world adopted this policy to anything like the same extent. Two or three of the French railways built some of their locomotives themselves. A few in the United States did likewise, but only one on a large scale, the Pennsylvania Railroad at Altoona; and those shops did not produce in quantity until after 1875.[23] Why did the British railways, in this matter, act differently?

A company that decided to build its own machines might hope to secure more uniform standards than it got from the manufacturers, and hence greater reliability. In 1840 Locke argued that if those who were responsible for repairing locomotives became closely acquainted with their defects in normal service they would be 'better able than others to guard against them, in the construction of new ones'.[24] Such a pooling of experience might be achieved within a railway company, but was unattainable by a manufacturer.

Some chairmen and managers supposed that by making their equipment themselves their companies would get it more cheaply. The Liverpool & Manchester did indeed procure each of the locomotives it built itself for £400 less than it would have had to pay to local manufacturers; but the real price of these machines was probably higher than the manufacturers', taking into account all the costs incurred in building them.[25] As time went on, the two largest railway companies did not swerve from their determination to become self-sufficient. The Great Western never had a locomotive built for it by a commercial manufacturer after 1866,[26] the London & North Western none between 1871 and 1916.[27] On the other hand the Midland looked outside whenever its own works at Derby were too busy to fulfil its orders.[28] The Manchester Sheffield & Lincolnshire and its successor the Great Central decided each case as it arose. In 1858-1914 they built 51.4% of their locomotives for themselves and bought 48.6% outside.[29]

Ill. 24   By 1850 the British locomotive had become an acceptably efficient machine. The development of the vehicles it hauled had been much less remarkable. The ordinary passenger carriage was still, at its best, a combination of three wooden stage-coach bodies, resting on a framework made partly or wholly of iron, and on four iron wheels. Six-wheeled carriages were used on the Great Western Railway from the beginning, and in 1845–8 it had a few that were built of iron throughout. It provided an eight-wheeled carriage for Queen Victoria in 1842, and several intended for ordinary service from 1847 onwards. Although the bogie, a four-wheeled swivelling truck, was a British invention,[30] it passed into use in passenger vehicles in the United States and Austria[31] long before it was employed for this purpose in Britain.

Ill. 23   Gladstone's Act of 1844 required that, in the trains run to convey passengers at a penny a mile, the carriages should be provided with seats and 'protected from the weather'. That did not of itself forbid the railways to continue to use open wagons, with or without seats, for third-class passengers by other trains (especially excursions), a practice that lingered on at least until the 1870s. But it provided a standard specification of the minimum comfort that passengers came to expect in ordinary service.

Goods wagons too remained for many years very little altered. The chief types of them used throughout the Victorian age had already appeared before 1840, attended by hardly any experiment. Open wagons, with varying capacities, were much the most numerous, descending directly from those used on the pre-mechanical railways for carrying coal. Several sorts of covered-in wagons appeared, including some reserved for special purposes such as the conveyance of salt,[32] together with cattle wagons, roofed, and open for ventilation near the top. Hardly any change was made in the design of those vehicles during the rest of the nineteenth century, apart from some strengthening of the frames and a few improvements to their brakes.

In other departments of railway work, however, changes in machinery were introduced during these years that were comparable in importance with those made in locomotives. One, minimal in size and cost, was the invention of a method of printing tickets and storing and issuing them in booking-offices, developed by Thomas Edmondson from 1838 onwards. He improved it until it passed into use on almost every railway in the country. His ticket also became a vital instrument in the hands of the Railway Clearing House, for the purpose of making up the complicated accounts of passenger journeys from one system to another.[33]

The most considerable improvements that arose from the adoption of new machinery, apart from those applied to locomotives, were in the signalling devices used for regulating traffic. That control was exercised at first by men using flags in the daytime and lamps after dark; an arrangement that remained adequate only so long as trains were infrequent and junctions few. Such simplicity of working soon grew rare in Britain, though it continued for a long time elsewhere.[34] In 1837 Newton Junction became the meeting-point of the two most important railways yet opened in Europe, the Liverpool & Manchester and the Grand Junction. The passage of trains there was regulated by fixed signals, the mechanism manually worked. Another junction was brought into use in 1839 at Corbett's Lane, the point at which the new London & Croydon Railway diverged from the London & Greenwich, and in the hours of darkness it came to be controlled by lights 'with powerful parabolic reflectors', operated by two men stationed within a small 'lighthouse'. The points controlling the divergent tracks were worked by a third man, using hand levers, outside. The 'lighthouse' soon became, in the railway's language, a 'signal-box'.

Fixed signals were soon adopted by the trunk railways. The Great Western and the London & Southampton companies, for instance, were using them by 1840. The semaphore seems to have been first applied to railways by Charles Hutton Gregory, engineer of the London & Croydon, in 1841. An entirely new instrument was then beginning to be adopted for the control of railway traffic: the electric telegraph.

In its origin the telegraph had nothing to do with electricity.[35] It was a device for transmitting messages, by means of semaphores manually worked, communicating from one hill-top to another; developed in the 1790s, first in France and then by the British Admiralty for sending messages between London and Portsmouth.[36] It passed a little into commercial use. The Liverpool Dock Company set up one, for instance, to send information from Holyhead about the progress of ships, in 1827.[37]

By that time experiments with electrical systems of transmission had been under way for some time in Britain, Denmark, and Germany.[38] They began to be taken further by Charles Wheatstone and William Fothergill Cooke in 1837, and Cooke demonstrated their apparatus to the directors of that company and the Grand Junction in a series of experiments on the line out of Euston. He persuaded Robert Stephenson of its value, but not the railway directors. Cooke then got into touch with Brunel and the Great Western company, who proved more receptive, and in 1839 the telegraph was brought into use for working the line between Paddington and West Drayton (13 miles). Next year it was applied to another railway, $3\frac{1}{2}$ miles long, the London & Blackwall, as an essential element in its cable traction. The Great Western soon ceased using the device for the operation of its trains. The London & Blackwall stuck to it;

and another line, the Yarmouth & Norwich (conventionally worked by locomotives) came to use it in 1844. As yet, however, railway managers generally fought shy of it.

The government played an important part in breaking their resistance down. The Regulation Act of 1844 required railways to permit the telegraph to be set up beside their lines wherever the Board of Trade requested it. That order was first implemented a year later when the telegraph was laid by the London & Southampton Railway over the 88 miles between London and Gosport, to meet the needs of the Admiralty for rapid communication between London and Portsmouth. The public were allowed to send their own messages by it, and the railway had an additional line, entirely under its own control.[39] In 1845–7 the telegraph was installed for the management of traffic through the Woodhead and Box tunnels. Its use spread very irregularly along railway lines. The London & North Western, for instance, began to install it in the 1840s and was signalling the whole line from London to Rugby by it in 1856; yet the telegraph was still not in use on the original Liverpool & Manchester line in 1859, nor on the very busy section between Manchester and Stockport in 1862.[40] Before long, however, the spread of new signalling systems made it necessary in practice for the telegraph to be made available on every railway in the country.

Even when successful mechanically, such inventions and improvements might not be taken up. When the railway companies investigated the total expense of adopting them – their manufacture and installation, the patent fees that often had to be paid for using them, the cost of their day-to-day working and maintenance – they sometimes grew alarmed. Although by the later 1850s the railways had achieved a more steady prosperity than in the 1840s, very few of them offered large dividends to their proprietors. In 1860 those declared by all the 127 companies that paid something were at the average rate of about 4.4%; and 121 more, which had raised some capital, paid nothing at all.[41] Though economy was pursued by some railways too far, it was a watchword enjoined on every one of them.

Economy and Safety

The main lines of the railway system of Great Britain, linking the chief cities, were almost all completed by 1850. In the years that followed, experiment went on, and in some important matters led to improvement. But the speed at which traffic moved, and the ordinary weight of trains, did not continue to increase so much as they had done in the 1830s and 1840s.

The distances covered by expresses without stopping grew greater. On the London & North Western Railway Ramsbottom's device for allowing water to be picked up by the engine *en route* was installed in 1860–1, permitting the Irish Mail trains to run non-stop from Chester to Holyhead (84 miles), and its use was extended by that company thereafter. No other railways adopted it for twenty-five years, and some managed even longer runs without it. The

Midland's first services out of St Pancras in 1868 included one that ran without stopping over the 98 miles from Kentish Town to Leicester. It was only then that any expresses came to run at schedules as fast as those of the Exeter trains of 1845–52. But by this time the loads were beginning to grow heavier, the demands on engines and track correspondingly more severe.

The most important advances made in the design of locomotives in these years were concerned with the fuel they used and the materials of which they were built.

Coke was an unsatisfactory fuel for them: it clinkered easily, for instance, and produced much abrasion in fireboxes. Experiments with devices to enable locomotives to burn coal and yet throw out little or no smoke had achieved a measure of success by 1841. But the apparatus required was complicated and troublesome, until on the Midland Railway a simple firebox was devised in 1859, with a brick fire-arch and a deflecting plate that improved the draught of air and the combustion of coal. Equipped thus, and given a careful fireman, the engine emitted very little smoke. The gradual adoption of this type of firebox produced notable economies. Coal was then not much more than half the price of coke, and engines with this new equipment burnt smaller quantities of fuel.

At just the same time steel began to enter into the construction of locomotives in Britain. The leader here was the German Alfred Krupp, who was producing steel tyres and axles for locomotives in his works at Essen in the 1850s. By 1859–64 at least eleven British railway companies are known to have been supplied with such tyres.[42] It is possible (though not proved) that they fractured more easily than tyres made of iron; but it is certain that they lasted in service very much longer and were more economical. That was what did most to determine the decision to adopt them in Britain, as it did in the United States, where steel had come to be used for all locomotive tyres by 1870.[43] The use of steel in axles moved more slowly in Britain.[44] Yorkshire iron was exceptionally reliable and its manufacture thoroughly understood. It was better than any iron to be found on the Continent except in Sweden. British engineers were understandably hesitant to abandon such a well-tried material. Where boilers were concerned, many of them felt the same, and it was not until the late 1880s that steel could be said to be replacing wrought iron in those used in Great Britain.[45]

In the 1850s and 1860s, while serious improvement in the design of locomotives steadily continued, very little change appeared in the carriages used by passengers in ordinary service and none in the vehicles used in freight traffic. Some attention was given to improving the suspension of carriages.[46] Richard Mansell's wheels, each made of sixteen segments of teak with a boss and tyre of wrought iron, were patented in 1848 and passed into use, at first on his own South Eastern Railway and then gradually on others; on the Great Northern for example in 1861. The Great Western continued to fit the much noisier spoked wheels and began to experiment tentatively with Mansell's only in 1866. Eight years later more than half its standard-gauge passenger carriages and vans were equipped with them, but less than 7% of those running on the broad gauge.[47]

Some improvements were made in these years in the lighting and heating of railway carriages. The first lighting provided had been by pot lamps in the roof, which gave a feeble glow; one was often made to serve two compartments. Passengers who wished to read in trains after dark were obliged to take their own lamps with them.[48] Experiments soon began to be conducted with gas lighting. The first companies to adopt it for all their carriages, the North London and the Metropolitan, did so in 1862–3.[49] Elsewhere the change came very slowly. The London & North Western still lighted half its carriages by oil, half by gas, in 1890. When the Great Western took over a batch of companies in South Wales in 1922 it inherited from them, even then, five passenger carriages that had never had any lighting at all.[50]

Since no heating apparatus had been introduced into any of the minute interiors of horse-drawn coaches, railway passengers were not moved to ask for it. On some railways, Lardner records in 1850 that 'a heater is placed in cold weather in first-class carriages under the feet of the passengers';[51] but he says no more. The French began to offer something of the sort in trains soon after that: tin cans containing hot water.[52] The Great Western began to provide such 'footwarmers' in 1856, the London & South Western two years later, both companies making a small charge for them and supplying them to first-class passengers only.[53] On most railways they soon came to be available to all who chose to pay for them – though the Lancashire & Yorkshire company declined to supply them to third-class passengers until 1891.[54]

So the comfort of railway travelling increased a little in these years. Considered as a machine, however, the railway carriage remained in one respect thoroughly unsatisfactory. On a stage-coach, in an emergency, a passenger could put his head out of the window and hail the guard or driver, with a fair expectation of being heard. But the vehicle in which a railway passenger travelled offered him no means of communicating with those who were in charge of the train. In 1847 the Great Western company decided to affix iron seats to the backs of locomotive tenders, facing towards the train, and to station in them 'travelling porters', to observe that all was well. A passenger in trouble might then, if he was lucky, attract the porter's attention. Not surprisingly, this duty was much resented by the men it was imposed on. They nicknamed the seats (which were tall and hooded) 'iron coffins'. In 1853 Porter Bull was had up before the board and charged with writing the words 'Coffin No. 2' on his seat, as someone had noticed at Swindon. The directors refused to 'permit any such misconduct' and dismissed him from their service.[55]

Other solutions to this problem were pursued on the Continent: electric communication between guard and driver on the Paris–Orleans Railway, which was said to have failed; the use of a cord, in force on some German and Dutch lines. Parliament repeatedly demanded that the railway companies should find an acceptable device; the companies replied only that they had not succeeded in doing so. A spectacular murder in 1860 led the French

[78]

government to institute an investigation into the matter by three engineers. They dismissed any idea of communication between passengers and railwaymen. Instead they supported the practice established in Belgium, of requiring the guards to patrol the trains by means of outside footboards. As engineers they had nothing whatever to contribute.

When in 1864 the Commons called once again for advice on this matter from the Board of Trade, they received a very useful paper from H. W. Tyler, one of the senior inspecting officers, which arrived at a positive recommendation. He reviewed all the practices employed in Britain and abroad. When he came to the Belgian one he stressed the risks for the men themselves. The Belgians admitted that, on average, one fatal accident occurred every year to a man performing this duty. The British railway system was nearly twelve times as extensive. Would it be satisfactory, he asked, to accept ten or more fatalities annually from this cause, together with numerous injuries? The solution he favoured was a system devised for the London & South Western Railway by W. H. Preece, giving the passengers a communication, by means of electric bells, with the guard and the engine-driver.[56]

Tyler had now shifted the discussion in Britain decisively away from administration to engineering. Preece's system did not find enough favour to be adopted. The Regulation Act of 1868, nevertheless, required the railway companies to provide, on every passenger train running more than twenty miles without stopping, 'such efficient means of communication between the passengers and the servants of the company in charge of the train as the Board of Trade may approve', imposing a fine on any passenger abusing the apparatus.[57] Next year the Board approved a system devised by T. E. Harrison, chief engineer of the North Eastern. Unfortunately it turned out defective in practice, and approval had to be rescinded in 1873. Various systems then continued in use, none of which was sanctioned by the Board. All were therefore employed illegally, but the Board could not prosecute. In this strange fashion the problem was left, unsolved, for many years.

In some other matters concerned with the safety of railway working notable advances were achieved in the 1850s and 1860s. The extension of the telegraph made possible the acceptance of the 'block system' of signalling, which imposed an interval of space (not of time, as hitherto) between each train and its successor. From 1855 onwards this principle came to be extended, in conjunction with the telegraph, to long stretches of main line, such as the southern end of the London & North Western's, between Euston and Rugby.[58] At the same time experiments were being made with devices to control signals and points together, in such a way as to prevent their movements from conflicting; applied successfully in 1856–60 by John Saxby and then, in an improved form, by Austin Chambers.[59] This 'interlocking' machinery represented a most important step towards security of operation.

Such mechanisms, as installed on different railways, showed widely different degrees of efficiency. Some, which were prone to failure, might well be greater causes of danger than the older, more primitive manual methods had been, as appeared with dreadful clarity in the Clayton Tunnel accident in 1861.[60] The engineers and the running men continued to pursue further improvement: so effectively that what was a good, progressive system might soon become an unacceptable relic of the past. The London & North Western's block system had become out of date, overtaken by a better version of it, within ten years.

Its great weakness was that, in order to secure flexibility in working the traffic, the signalman could allow a driver to move cautiously into a section still occupied by a preceding train. The principle of the space interval was then broken. It soon became clear that safety could be achieved only by a strict adherence to the rule that two trains must not be in one section together. The North Western system came to be known as 'permissive', the more rigid one as 'absolute'. A thirty-years' struggle lay ahead, waged tirelessly by the inspectors, supported by the clearest possible evidence, to persuade the recalcitrant companies (the North Western was only one among many) to abandon the permissive block system for the stricter alternative.

Divided Responsibilities

The changes just described were all part of a general, slow-moving process by which the practices of the British railways, in the use of their machinery, became increasingly subject to the surveillance of the government.

In Great Britain the railway system was promoted, paid for, and managed by private companies. They were subject in certain matters – chiefly concerned with safety – to the supervision of civil servants. But it was supervision, not control. In 1840 the Board of Trade was authorized to inspect lines of railway before they were opened, and two years later to prevent the opening of any new line judged by the inspecting officer to be so badly built or equipped that its working would be dangerous to the public. There was no appeal to the courts against this prohibition. It was a piece of delegated legislation,[61] and subsequent extensions of the Board's powers over railways were at times objected to as such.[62]

Some companies flagrantly disregarded these rulings. The final portion of the West Midland Railway, from Malvern Wells to Shelwick Junction, was opened in 1861 without the Board's authority; so was the Metropolitan District's line from Blackfriars to Mansion House in 1871.[63] Some companies undertook to make changes required by the Board's inspectors, and then dishonoured their promises: in 1865–6, for instance, the Blyth & Tyne and the Exeter & Crediton.[64] Reporting on an accident on the Metropolitan Railway in 1871, the inspector William Yolland pointed out that the strict signalling arrangements accepted by the company at its opening in 1863 had been changed for others much looser, without any reference to the Board. He doubted whether 'such a state of things between railway companies on the one hand and the Board of Trade acting on behalf of the public on the other should be allowed to continue to exist'.[65]

The companies often grumbled at the Board's interference, and occasionally their complaints boiled up into open warfare. For a time, Allport of the Midland company made it a practice to reply pertinaciously to one inspector's report after another.[66] Some railway engineers and managers evinced great contempt for the inspectors. Brunel included them in his comprehensive detestation of government officials of every kind.[67] More surprisingly perhaps, T. E. Harrison, the wise and widely experienced engineer of the North Eastern company, said much the same.[68] Watkin pursued them with virulence; as one might expect, from his intense irritability and from the numerous accidents incurred by his company the Manchester Sheffield & Lincolnshire, in the later 1870s and the 1880s. In 1875 Edward Ross, the company's secretary, instructed by the directors of whom Watkin was the chairman, told the Board of Trade that it considered the report of Tyler on the Staddlethorpe accident as due to personal malice.[69]

In 1872 Richard Moon, chairman of the London & North Western Railway, told its shareholders that 'he believed the Board of Trade were as responsible for railway accidents as the railway companies were. It was a divided management, with all the responsibility on one side only. The Board of Trade insisted on signals and other works, which involved a large expenditure on the companies'. Reporting on an accident at Coventry, Tyler rejoined by pointing out that

> the passenger lines of the company near the site of it have been left for a series of years without any means of protection either by a stationary signalman, or by safety-points.... Is the Board of Trade responsible, on the one hand, for such an accident – occurring from the want of apparatus which it constantly recommends the company to adopt? Is not the Board of Trade justified, on the other hand, in insisting, as far as it has the power to do so, on the application of appliances necessary for safety, even though they 'involve a large expenditure on the companies'?[70]

Ever since 1840 the companies had been required to make returns of accidents occurring on their lines, and the Board had sent its officers to investigate those that seemed to call for its attention. But that power was made mandatory only in 1871. Even then the Board could not oblige the companies to change their practices.

Up to this time there had been only two occasions on which Parliament had interfered directly with the operation of railways: in 1846, when it had prescribed the gauges to which railways might be built in Britain in the future; and in 1868, when it obliged the companies to provide means of communication between passengers and train crews. These interventions were both unhappy. The Gauge Act was a confession of failure, for it established two gauges, not a single national one, on the basis of a geographical division to which it had itself to allow exceptions. The 'means of communication' approved by the Board of Trade under the Act of 1868 had proved unenforceable.

Railways were controlled very differently in France. There too they were owned by private companies. But those companies' shareholders were guaranteed a dividend by the State, and it was usually a much higher one than British shareholders received.[71] One of the prices paid for that guarantee was that the State controlled their management and working. It did so through a body of civil servants (there were 800 of them in the 1880s)[72] collectively called *le Contrôle de l'Etat*, which had power to regulate the companies' practice minutely: the timetables of their trains, for example, their fares and their rates. The ultimate responsibility for management and services differed likewise. In France it rested on the government and on the *Contrôle*. In Britain it did not rest on the Board of Trade, nor on the government, though Parliament had the overriding right to pass what legislation it chose.

Very important results followed from this British arrangement, affecting the attitudes taken up by the Board of Trade and its inspectors towards the running of the railways. The inspectors' own work and their predecessors' came in time to form a substantial body of experience. As new safety precautions were devised and perfected, they felt justified in recommending those they believed in. They also had things to say about locomotives, about the materials used in making their boilers and axles and tyres, about the suitability of particular types of engine for the duties to which they were assigned. They persistently criticized the working of engines tender-first as a source of danger. Several of them disapproved of the use of tank engines to haul fast trains and said so, with growing insistence, from 1866 to 1912.

But once having put their opinions on these matters, with the reasoning behind them, on public record, the inspectors' responsibility ended. When accidents occurred that appeared to be due to neglecting what they said it was the companies that bore the blame. The companies and their shareholders too were always liable to be hurt in their pockets by claims for compensation on behalf of those killed or injured.

This apportionment of responsibility had a rationale of its own. The British railways had been set up as commercial enterprises, not at all as instruments of the State. In 1867, when the Government had the opportunity to consider purchasing them, it declined to do so, on the advice of a Royal Commission. For another twenty years the powers of the companies remained limited only by the restrictions placed on them by general laws and by their own special Acts. In the end, no matter what the companies thought or said, the advice of the Board of Trade's inspectors came to prevail; but in prevailing it altered the balance of power between the companies and the government.

The Force of Competition

The railway companies in Britain had long been in some degree competitive with one another. The principle might be disguised, even disowned as something hardly reputable. 'I would not be connected with any line which was competing with an existing line' said Hudson to a Parliamentary Committee in 1844.[73] 'The public have never permanently benefited from competition between different lines of railway', Samuel Laing of the Board of

Trade remarked at the same time, predicting that in due course the main railway communications of Britain would be 'parcelled out into six or eight great systems', each a regional monopoly.[74] Samuel Smiles remarked five years later that competition between railway companies would 'be found to be in the end a mere delusion.... its effects on railway property are too onerous to allow it to be persevered in'.[75]

Those views did not command unqualified assent, however. Peel for example – a careful observer of all commercial practice – was making a distinction as early as 1844 between competitive lines running closely parallel with one another, which he condemned, and the development of alternative lines serving different districts *en route*, say between London and Manchester, which he thought might be desirable.[76] In the 1850s and 1860s such alternative lines appeared from London to Scotland, as well as to Birmingham, Manchester, Exeter, and Dover, the last two being shorter than the old routes they competed with. That consideration was so weighty that within six weeks of the opening of the second line to Dover the South Eastern company began to move towards securing powers to shorten its own roundabout route,[77] and did so by about 15% in 1868.

In 1870 there were competitive services between London and seven of the ten largest provincial cities in England and Wales, besides the three largest in Scotland. Outside London there was competition between Nottingham and Leeds, Liverpool and Hull, Edinburgh and Glasgow. Over shorter distances, and especially in suburban services, competition was to be seen everywhere: from London to St Albans for instance, and to Windsor; from Birmingham to Wolverhampton, Manchester to Buxton, Leeds to Bradford. The orthodoxy of the 1840s had proved false.

In the last thirty years of the nineteenth century, under the pressure of competition, the speed of British express trains grew notably faster. But at the same time their weight also increased mightily. Between 1870 and 1887 the weight of the 10 o'clock Scotch express out of Euston more than doubled, from 123 tons behind the engine's tender to 268.[78]

In 1893 new trains were provided for the corresponding afternoon service, in which access to dining-cars and to lavatories was provided for all passengers by means of side corridors, extending from one end of the train to the other.[79] Only one train of this description had ever been seen in Britain before, put on by the Great Western company in the previous year, but it lacked dining-cars. The practice established itself, and soon came to be accepted by all companies running long-distance expresses.

Sleeping cars, which had been provided in Britain since the 1870s, grew steadily heavier as more elaborate comforts were added to them. They were a luxury that cost the companies a good deal: not much less than £2000 each[80] for a vehicle that weighed about 40 tons and carried as a rule no more than eleven first-class passengers, who paid a supplementary fare of five shillings each. So every sleeping car represented nearly 4 tons of deadweight to be hauled, per passenger carried, even when it was full; more still for every berth that was vacant.[81] By the early twentieth century six trains of this sort were running to Scotland every night by the three routes that competed for the traffic, as well as five to Ireland, by Holyhead, Fleetwood, Heysham, and Stranraer. From Paris to Marseilles there were two such services nightly, and the sleeping-car supplement, over a distance half as long again as from London to Edinburgh, was twenty-four times as large: about £6.

The accommodation used by poorer passengers now grew more comfortable too, and in consequence heavier. That began to become prominent in the 1870s, owing principally to the fateful decisions of the Midland Railway: first, to open all its trains, expresses included, to third-class passengers, and secondly to discontinue second class altogether throughout its system. These will be discussed later as commercial and social policies. Here we must look at some of the consequences they entailed in the handling of the company's traffic.

The first of them went into force at very short notice on 1 April 1872. Though tenders had been accepted on 6 February from three outside manufacturers for 275 new third-class and composite carriages, none of them could be ready before the summer.[82] When the second change was made, which took effect on 1 January 1875, second-class carriages could be simply re-labelled third, and wooden seats on the existing thirds upholstered, to bring them nearer to the standard of the seconds. But a substantial new construction programme then already lay ahead, to meet the impending demands of the company's new route to Scotland, by the Settle & Carlisle line.[83] After some

Ill. 26   experiment, a series of vehicles emerged in 1875–6 that formed the prototypes of the British main-line carriage of the later Victorian age.

They were twice as long as the vehicles of the past; carried on eight or twelve wheels, against four or six, with the wheels arranged in pairs of swivelling bogies. Other eight-wheeled carriages were already in service in Britain, but bogies were used in hardly any of them. In accordance with the Midland company's evident intentions, its fine new carriages were designed to carry first and third-class passengers alike. Soon they were coming out in substantial numbers: 150 of them, for instance, in 1878–9.[84]

The long vehicle, carried on bogies, brought a very great improvement in the passengers' comfort. Just how great, only those who have travelled in a four or six-wheeled carriage in a fast train can realize today. The hard riding of the older vehicles now gave place to a much smoother and quieter motion, and the bogies took curves more easily, with equal safety.

But no other railway was quick to follow the Midland's example. Four-wheeled carriages were still being put into service on the East Coast line to Scotland in 1878.[85] In the same year the Lancashire & Yorkshire abandoned the construction of four-wheeled carriages altogether, and it turned out bogie vehicles from 1884 onwards, by which time the South Western was doing likewise.[86] The Great Western and North Western were also building eight-wheeled carriages then, but they were not mounted on bogies until 1888 and 1893 respectively.[87] Bogie carriages were not built for any Scottish railway company until after 1890.[88]

Even the Midland carriages were unsatisfactory, however, in some important ways.

They were heated solely by footwarmers: a defect that looks strange on this railway, for it had already been operating Pullman cars since 1874, and they were heated by hot-water radiators in the American manner. But the difficulties involved in applying a heating system to carriages divided into compartments were considerable.[89] Although some British railways had experimented with devices for heating trains since the 1850s,[90] none of them was thought to succeed. The Caledonian company installed an acceptable heating system in some of its Glasgow suburban trains in the later 1880s,[91] but in British main-line services no provision of the kind seems to have been made before 1893.[92]

The Midland carriages of the 1870s were at first very meagrely lighted, by a single oil lamp in each compartment; its Pullman cars better, by paraffin lamps with Argand burners. Though an experiment with gas lighting was approved in 1876, it was not thought satisfactory. Gas was fitted into the carriages in the Midland's suburban services that ran side by side with the Metropolitan's – almost of necessity, for that company had used gas from its first opening.[93] Elsewhere, the Midland did not turn to it permanently until the early 1890s.

Another illuminant was by that time available, electricity: first used for this purpose anywhere by the London Brighton & South Coast Railway in 1881.[94] But though the Midland experimented with it in the late 1880s and considered it again in 1900, it did not adopt it until 1921.[95] Some other companies acted firmly in a different way: the London Tilbury & Southend, North Staffordshire, and Great North of Scotland moved straight in the late 1890s from oil to electric lighting, never using gas at all.[96] Most, however, found electric lighting costly to fit and maintain; undependable too until J. Stone's system, with a dynamo driven by a belt off a carriage axle, proved itself in the final years of the century.

Some companies spoke uneasily of their own policies here. They wished to make plain to the public that they were not refusing to install new equipment merely on account of its cost. Findlay's tone in 1889 is distinctly defensive:

> It must not be supposed that the London & North Western company, in their endeavours to secure an improved system of lighting their passenger carriages, have overlooked the question of electric lighting, or that they have been oblivious of the experiments which have been made in this direction upon various railways, but chiefly upon the southern lines. They are, on the contrary, perfectly alive to the fact that in all probability the electric light is the light of the future for railway carriages, as for most other purposes; and they have not been behindhand in making experiments with it on their own account.[97]

The Midland carriages of the 1870s were also defective, as we should now think, in that they were not provided with lavatories.[98] The Pullman cars running on the same railway had them, but then their standards were

American. Though such things were known on the Continent,[99] no British carriages in ordinary service were equipped with them until 1882, when they were made available to a few first-class passengers on the Great Northern Railway. The Midland began to provide them also for third-class passengers in the following year.[100]

This amenity of travelling had a mixed reception. Medical men were a little alarmed by the discharge of the effluent; but the precautions taken in the design of the appliances soon rendered their fears unnecessary. Some otherwise sensible persons declared that lavatories were uncalled for, even in trains that ran for a long time without stopping, and sneered at those who wished to have them. Foxwell burst out: 'Poor souls, their invalid condition cannot stand the strain of these long breaks without a stop – or a "lavatory"'. Acworth took occasion to refer to 'gentlemen who are so delicately nurtured that it makes them uncomfortable to hear that other people are deprived of access to a lavatory for three whole hours'.[101] Such comments were however ignored by the companies, very properly. The larger ones set themselves to provide lavatory accommodation for all classes of passengers. The London & North Western turned out 700 vehicles so equipped in the 1890s; over 1600 more in 1900–14.[102] All this was done at a heavy cost, since a pair of lavatories squeezed into a carriage virtually displaced one compartment. The loss might be reduced by offering access to the lavatories from a limited number of compartments only; it remained a substantial consideration.

By the early years of the twentieth century a new bogie carriage, purchased from a manufacturer, might be expected to be priced at about £1900.[103] It is perhaps possible to say that in 1914 it cost, in very rough terms, £50 to provide a long-distance passenger with his seat, and that when he occupied it he carried some 1500 lb of deadweight with him as he travelled. Forty years earlier, when the Midland was estimating the expenditure to be incurred on its first bogie vehicles, that seat cost a little over £15, and the passenger carried 900 lb with him.[104]

In short-distance and suburban traffic the competitive principle did not stimulate the provision of better carriages to the same extent. Two of the most notoriously intense competitors in this business, the South Eastern and the London Chatham & Dover companies, were both also notorious for the badness of the accommodation they offered; their neighbour the London Brighton & South Coast, which competed with them too, was not in this respect much better. Purpose-built suburban trains, their vehicles close-coupled together in fixed sets, became widely accepted in the 1870s. A strikingly luxurious version appeared on the Cheshire Lines in 1881, composed of twelve-wheelers for the Manchester–Liverpool express services; greatly superior to any vehicles afforded on either of the rival routes. But nothing like them was seen again until the early years of the twentieth century, when the Caledonian and Glasgow & South Western companies built sets of twelve-wheeled vehicles for their bitterly competitive services along the Clyde coast.

The vehicles provided for the conveyance of freight showed no comparable development. Of those owned by the companies in 1913, 79% were uncovered open wagons,[105] exactly the same in principle as those that had been running sixty years earlier. Their frames were now of metal rather than of wood; a fair number, particularly of those used in mineral traffic, had metal bodies too; they were provided with spring buffers. The chief difference in them was that they had grown larger. In 1913 only 5.3% of these open wagons had a capacity of less than 8 tons.[106] Over the past twenty-five years some railways had been gingerly making experiments with much larger vehicles running on eight wheels and carrying 30 tons or more.

The open wagon was not predominant in any other country. The British trains were loose-coupled, chains alone serving to link the wagons together; continuous brakes were fitted to only a few express goods trains. Moreover, a large number of the vehicles running in freight trains did not belong to the railway companies at all. They bore in very large letters the names of other owners: collieries and coal merchants, brickmakers, co-operative societies, municipal corporations.

A foreign visitor who was alert enough to observe all that would have had in his hands most of the explanations of the peculiar character of the vehicles used for the carriage of freight in Britain. They differed from those elsewhere mainly because they had to meet different demands, put forward by the railways' customers.

Leaving couplings and brakes to the end of this chapter, let us consider the Victorian open wagons as a device for handling the railways' traffic. The units of freight they carried were small, partly because much of British industrial and commercial business was organized on a small scale and partly too because consignors expected a quick service, which discouraged delay in waiting for the accumulation of enough freight to fill large wagons.[107] Moreover, many of the private owners' railways, over which their wagons had to travel in order to reach the main lines, were sharply curved, which necessitated a vehicle with a short wheelbase.

The high speed at which freight traffic moved in Britain was widely remarked on. The American engineer Dorsey observed in 1885 that the freight trains ran at about 25 mph, much faster than those in his own country. He considered this an extravagance in operation, commending the handling of fast freight by 'express companies' (independent of the railways) instead.[108] At the same time James Grierson, general manager of the Great Western Railway, set out carefully the different expectations and legal requirements that the railways had to meet in conveying freight traffic in a number of Continental countries and he showed that the British services, which normally provided overnight delivery, were much quicker than those afforded elsewhere.[109] As the speed of transit grew greater, shopkeepers took advantage of it by ordering goods in smaller quantities at a time.[110] What was wanted was a small unit of carriage, moving at high speed. Within the island, nearly the whole of the densely-concentrated population, of manufacturing industry and of coal production, was concentrated within a maximum span of 400 miles, from the Thames and the Welsh Valleys to the Clyde. It was 700 miles from Lille to Marseilles, over 500 from Hamburg to Munich: distances much greater than a French or German freight train would cover in a single night.

The use of private owners' wagons was widely condemned, but it proved impossible to eradicate. They were a frequent cause of accidents, from being brought on to the main railway system in bad repair. As early as 1873 Tyler predicted that the railway companies would have to acquire all the wagons running on their lines, and urged that they should set about the purchase 'with as little delay as possible'.[111] Two large companies addressed themselves to this task: the Midland in 1881, followed by the Caledonian. But though they made some progress, they did not ultimately succeed.[112] In 1911 there were still some 650,000 of these vehicles, nearly half the total of all those that ran over British railways. The capital invested in them represented some £20 million, divided among 4000 owners, large and small.[113]

The companies had almost no power to require improvements in the construction or equipment of these wagons. While, from the 1850s onwards, oil gradually replaced grease as the lubricant used by the railways in the axle-boxes of their wagons,[114] many private owners declined to incur the expense of making the change. The same consideration was one of the obstacles in the way of fitting ordinary freight trains with continuous brakes. Despite strenuous and intelligent efforts on the part of the Railway Clearing House to benefit both the companies and the owners by securing agreements on such matters as these,[115] very little progress was made in settling them satisfactorily before 1914. Or for long afterwards. The number of private owners' wagons remained much the same in 1937; there were still 317,000 of them in 1953, half of which were lubricated by grease and lacked continuous brakes.[116]

It would be wrong however to suggest that no changes appeared in the handling of freight by the British railway companies in the years before 1914. New needs had to be provided for, which called for new machines. Paraffin came to require special vehicles of its own, and at the turn of the century the railways began to carry petroleum, in the service of the internal combustion engine. From that it was a short step to the conveyance of motor cars. In 1904–14 the Midland company built 146 vans for this traffic.[117] The spread of the demand for frozen meat obliged the railways to find satisfactory means of carrying it. Experiments with refrigerated vehicles began in 1874. Five years later the Great Western and Midland companies took to building substantial numbers of vans specially for the purpose.[118]

Some large-capacity wagons, mounted on bogies, were built in quantity for use in particular services: by the Lancashire & Yorkshire Railway, for instance, in 1901–5 for the conveyance of large single loads brought by ships from the Continent into Goole.[119] But few of the men closely concerned with the practical business of running railways in Britain were convinced at this time that such large vehicles ought to be widely used there. Theorists might deride 'our toy trucks', and paper demonstrations could be prepared of the savings that might accrue from abandoning them.[120] But even the North Eastern company, which set out to adopt the practice most enthusiastically, had to admit some of the difficulties it raised, and to conclude that the best results in ordinary traffic would be gained by a resolute enlargement of the traditional type of open wagon, running on four wheels, to take a load of 20 tons. That may be said to represent the most progressive British policy in 1914.[121]

Some railways were able to increase very substantially the size of the chief freight trains they ran. Those trains could not travel much faster in safety unless they were fitted with continuous brakes; but if they could be made longer and heavier the number of them could be reduced, easing the movement of trains as a whole and economizing in staff. Most of the large companies followed that practice, which demanded the provision of more powerful locomotives to haul the trains.

Traction 1870–1914

Between 1847 and 1870 the British locomotive displayed no striking increase in size or power. Its main design altered very little. The companies' systems were growing larger, and machines of proved worth could be sent to work all over them. Standardization appeared conspicuously. It was now indeed that the largest construction of a single locomotive type ever undertaken by a Victorian railway company was carried through: 943 goods engines of the DX class, identical in nearly all details, were built by the London & North Western Railway at Crewe, to the design of John Ramsbottom, in 1858–74. Here was mass production on a scale later associated with the United States.

Although competitive services multiplied in the 1860s they did not make a large immediate demand for locomotives of any new kind. Some meritorious ones appeared: two groups – quite different – for the Southern and Northern Divisions of the London & North Western, for example; Cudworth's 'Mail' engines on the South Eastern. These were all 2-2-2 machines,* with a pair of large single driving wheels, flanked by smaller ones at each end. In 1870 the Great Northern Railway produced a 4-2-2 engine carried in front on a bogie, the driving wheels having the very large diameter of 8 ft. By the mid-1870s, however, only the Great Northern and the Great Western Railways were using locomotives with single driving wheels consistently in their fastest services. Other railways had come to prefer theirs to have four wheels coupled, because that reduced the weight placed on a single axle and seemed to afford better adhesion to the machine when working uphill.

The 4-4-0 engine with a leading bogie was now introduced into Britain. It was pioneered chiefly in Scotland, most notably in a type designed for the North British Railway by Dugald Drummond in 1876 to work fairly heavy trains over the very difficult 'Waverley' route between Edinburgh and Carlisle: the ancestor of a long series of admirable express engines of the same sort,

---

*This notation gives the number of leading wheels, followed by the driving and then by the trailing wheels.

successively enlarged and improved, built for the Caledonian and London & South Western Railways down to 1912.

Here was what became the most characteristic type of late-Victorian express engine, the 4-4-0 with 6 ft 6 in or 7 ft driving wheels and 18 in or 19 in cylinders, placed inside the frames. Such machines were built before 1900 for every large railway company in the country except the London & North Western. They met all the chief demands made on them, being simple, robust, free-running, and competent hill-climbers with moderate loads. In the 1890s the normal price of such a locomotive, from a commercial manufacturer, was £2500–3000.[122]

Ill. 28 In freight traffic the 0-6-0 machine of the 1840s continued to be built in very large numbers for almost every British railway, with an increasing distinction between engines used in general goods service and those intended primarily for hauling mineral trains. The revenue from mineral traffic represented over 40% of the whole receipts from freight in the 1870s and 1880s; by 1913 it exceeded 50%. So such special provision was entirely justified. Mineral engines had smaller wheels, which gave them greater power, though they could run only at a lower speed. F. W. Webb's machines of this kind – 500 of them in all – slogged along on the London & North Western for very many years. Ahrons considered they were 'probably the simplest and cheapest locomotives ever made in this country'.[123]

Ill. 29 The extension of the system, and its increasing complexity, produced demands for locomotives to be employed wholly in certain specialized services. Tank engines of one design, for example, were employed exclusively on the circle and the other underground railways associated with it in London throughout the years of steam working from 1864 to 1905.[124] The tank engine was also used very extensively in South Wales. Seven local companies contended for the traffic there in 1913. Of the 641 locomotives they then owned, 559 were of this description.[125] Moreover, the majority of these tank engines were of one wheel arrangement, the 0-6-2, which formed a regional peculiarity.

Ill. 30 Machines of this kind had a relatively short rigid wheelbase, the small trailing wheels being made flexible to aid the negotiation of the sharp curves in which all these lines abounded; they accommodated good-sized water tanks and coal bunkers; a high proportion of their weight rested on their coupled wheels, giving them good adhesion. They proved equally successful with the mineral traffic that was the chief business of these railways and in passenger service.

One important change in design was adopted in these years on some British railways, extensively tried, and then abandoned: the principle of compounding, in which the locomotive's steam was used twice over, first at a high pressure and then at a lower one. This was intended to produce, among other improvements, a saving in the consumption of fuel. Anatole Mallet took out his first patent for this kind of engine in France in 1874. Five years later Webb experimented with Mallet's system, and then went on to devise his own, applying it to nine different types of locomotive intended for express passenger and freight service. They seem to have used less coal than comparable engines;

but the published figures do not demonstrate the amount of that economy with any scientific exactitude. What is certain is that in express service only sixty out of the 180 compound engines Webb produced performed satisfactorily – only ten of them really well; the rest proved sluggish, and some of them feeble.

Two other British companies – no more – built compound engines in any substantial numbers, the North Eastern and the Midland. They proved more steadily reliable than the North Western's. But the North Eastern turned them out in quantity only over a short period (1886–90), and the Midland never had more than forty-five, built in 1901–9.[126] Only one compound engine was ever commissioned by a Scottish railway company.

It was remarked at the time, with some disapproval, that Britain abandoned compounding just when it was proving itself best on the Continent, notably in France. For this difference of practice there were several reasons. Coal was abundant in Britain, and cheap: so a device intended primarily to reduce coal consumption was less attractive than it was for example in France or Austria. Moreover, a compound engine was dearer to build, from its greater complexity, more complicated to drive and to maintain in good order.[127]

Compounding proved a blind alley in Britain. But the engineers found themselves pressed urgently after 1890 to provide locomotives that were both faster and more powerful, in order to handle rapidly-increasing loads. A more powerful locomotive was nearly always a heavier one, and that required careful consideration of the maximum weight it imposed on a single axle. For this reason the ten-wheeled express engine – 'Atlantic' (4-4-2) or 4-6-0 – was now widely adopted. The 4-6-0 began to demonstrate its full capabilities on the North Eastern and Great Western Railways in 1899–1902, rather tentatively, and then with conviction on the Caledonian and Great Western from 1906 onwards. The Great Western's were of two types. They formed part of a much larger locomotive building programme; the most ambitious and the most completely achieved that was devised for any British railway before 1914.

The plan was laid down by G. J. Churchward in 1901.[128] He was then chief assistant to William Dean, the company's locomotive superintendent. But Dean was in failing health, and Churchward could look ahead with confidence to succeeding him, as he did eighteen months later. His programme provided for six types of locomotive, designed for all the chief duties on the railway, with as many common elements as possible. It was fully implemented, but not as a pattern intended to be followed rigidly. Its author never supposed that these six types would suffice; he himself made additions to them in later years. When it came to working them out in detail, he was careful to inquire what practices were being followed by French, German, and American railways in the matters under consideration. Churchward swam in the main stream of railway engineering.

Almost immediately after he succeeded Dean he secured his board's agreement to pay for the building of a French compound Atlantic engine, followed by two others in 1905, in order to compare them in running with those of the Great Western. The trials were carefully conducted, and showed that for most purposes the company's non-compound ('simple') engines suited its work best. In these comparisons, the compound engines did not prove more economical in coal-burning. But wherever the French machines showed a clear superiority, the lessons they taught were applied to Churchward's own designs. Notably in one matter. The French engines were beautifully built ('a watchmaker's job', Churchward called them)[129] and their parts were most accurately balanced, to produce a perfection of smooth riding. This was attributable mainly to their four cylinders, and to the divided drive into them from the two coupled axles.

By 1907 Churchward had made up his mind. There would be no more compound engines on the Great Western Railway. His original programme of 1901 had included a 4-6-0 type with two cylinders, already at work in growing numbers with conspicuous success. He would now have a four-cylinder 4-6-0, incorporating what he thought were the most valuable elements in the French engines. Sixty-one of these machines were built down to 1914, the *Ill. 31* 'Star' class.[130] From 1910 onwards, after careful experiments had been made, each was equipped with a superheater: a device recently developed, mainly in America and Germany, for raising the temperature of the engine's steam, producing important economies in coal consumption. These were the outstanding British express engines of their time.

Churchward's heavy mineral locomotive was equally successful; also a ten-wheeled machine, to the 2-8-0 arrangement. The first appeared in 1903; the last were being built when the second World War began. Eight-coupled engines now came to be used by every large company except the Midland and the North British. The Great Central's class 8K 2-8-0, which began to *Ill. 32* come out in 1911, was adopted by the Government in 1916 as a standard type for military service abroad. It has been rightly characterized as 'the British idea of simplicity and reliability developed to the utmost possible in a main-line locomotive'.[131]

Such engines as these were far more powerful than those used for heavy freight traffic in the nineteenth century. They were designed to meet a pressing need. That traffic continued to increase, almost without interruption. Could it be handled in a smaller number of larger units, which would free the tracks for occupation by other trains, especially passenger trains?

It could, and with a marked economy. In 1900–12[132] the total tonnage of freight conveyed by the British railways *increased* by 22.3%, while the number of miles travelled by their freight trains *decreased* by 16.2%. The achievement of some of the best companies was impressive indeed. On the North Eastern the decrease in mileage was twice as great as the national average, the increase in tonnage half as great again.[133] Or to put that in another way: whereas before these changes began – say, in 1888 – twelve freight trains had been run daily over the line from York to Newcastle, by 1912 the increased traffic was accommodated in only eight.[134] Hence, apart from any other consideration, the wages paid to thirty-six men for handling those trains had now to be paid to only twenty-four – and the wages bill of the company's locomotive department on account of train operation had increased since 1888 by 53%.[135]

The development of passenger traffic in Britain in these years was totally different. The mileage of trains was not reduced, it was increased by 18%: yet the increase in the number of passenger journeys was a third less than that in the tonnage of freight conveyed. The receipts from the two branches of traffic rose by almost exactly the same percentage. So the same rate of profit was to be had from a freight service reduced in mileage as from a passenger service lavishly increased.

Though all departments concerned with the companies' freight business contributed to this result, it was due primarily to the traffic managers and the locomotive men. It certainly arose in considerable measure from the new machines that their engineers provided. But admirable as many of them turned out to be in service, they represented no new technology.

One alternative source of power was now being used with success: electricity. Experiments with applying it to railways go back in Britain to 1837–42. A Scottish manufacturing chemist, Robert Davidson, was then at work on the production of an electromagnetic locomotive. He built a carriage for the conveyance of two people, powered in this way, which ran on a railway at an exhibition in Aberdeen in 1840. This was followed by a 6-ton battery-worked locomotive named *Galvani*, demonstrated on the Edinburgh & Glasgow Railway in September 1842. It does not seem to have got beyond a speed of about 4 mph. The experiment was not taken further.[136] However, the notion that electricity might be used, in some form, in railway haulage was not lost sight of. The South Eastern company entered into a contract with a patent agent to use electrically-driven machines devised by Floris Nollet, a Belgian engineer, in 1850.[137] Two years later John Herapath was confidently predicting the successful application of electricity to railway traction.[138] But he was before his time. Nothing came of these and other efforts of the same sort until after 1870, when Gramme's dynamo offered an alternative to the battery as a source of power. The first electric locomotive that performed its work successfully was demonstrated on a small scale – almost as a toy – in Berlin in 1879. Electric tramways made their appearance at Brighton, in Northern Ireland, at Blackpool and Ryde in 1883–5: creditable experiments, yet small beer compared with the extensive systems that were soon afterwards developed in the United States, largely through the genius of Frank Sprague – 3000 miles of them in 1891. In the previous December, however, Britain had taken the lead in a new direction, with the opening of the first electrically-driven underground railway: the first electric *railway* indeed in Europe.

This was the City & South London.[139] As a tunnelling achievement, the pioneer of all tube railways, it has already been discussed. Mechanically, it was a portent too. The directors resolved to adopt electricity as its motive power, in preference to cable haulage, when the line was already under construction. It was a courageous decision, and it gave Britain a distinguished place in the story of the advance of electric traction across the world.

The first locomotives were supplied by Mather & Platt of Salford (who took a contract for the working of the line) in consultation with the company's engineers Greathead and Basil Mott. They were ponderous, noisy, and slow, but they did their job and their design was somewhat improved in their successors. An experiment was made in 1894 with putting the motors into the trains. It was not judged successful, however, and the traffic continued to be handled by separate locomotives until 1907.

By that time a big system of underground railways had come into being in London, electrically powered throughout; all of it in tube except the original steam-worked Metropolitan and District lines, which went over to electricity in 1905.[140] The first electrically-worked elevated railway ever built had also *Ill. 49* appeared in Britain, at Liverpool, and a firm beginning had been made with the conversion of some suburban surface lines, at Liverpool again and at Newcastle. A number of established companies had taken powers to work their systems electrically, notably the Brighton, which altered its South London line accordingly in 1909 and then began to consider the idea of electrifying its main line, even its whole system.

But the work remained bedevilled by arguments about alternating or direct current and about equipment – should it be with overhead cables or with additional rails beside the tracks? Some companies were deterred by the capital expenditure involved. The Great Eastern, which had perhaps the most urgent need of the improvements electricity could bring, in order to move its exceptionally dense traffic in London, dismissed electrification on that account.[141] The Midland accepted a statutory duty to electrify the London Tilbury & Southend line when it bought it up in 1912, without any serious counting of the cost. It obtained a plan for the purpose in 1913 from the firm of Merz & McClellan, put it away and did nothing.[142] The North Eastern company, having made a clear success of its electrification on the north bank of the Tyne, sheered away five years later from extending it along the opposite side of the river to South Shields.[143]

Although some further progress was made on railways in and around London, by the end of 1913 electric traction had been applied to hardly more than 250 miles of railway in England;[144] to none as yet in Wales or Scotland. On the London underground system it represented a great, an exemplary achievement. Elsewhere it seemed hardly more than a token operation. Some people wrote down the effort that had been made as disappointing. The Royal Commission on London Traffic did that, for example, in 1905, with a bland disregard for the capital costs involved.[145] The companies' refusal to spend money on ambitious schemes of electrification – in a country so rich in the coal that kept its steam trains going – was defensible. Yet their inaction here was bound to be criticized. Looking at the success of the electric tramways and of the internal combustion engine in its various applications, some people were now beginning to ask if the railways had had their day. Even observers highly sympathetic to them admitted that possibility. Edwin Pratt, for example, wrote in 1912: 'The question that really arises here is, not whether electricity is likely to supersede steam for long-distance as well as for short-distance rail traffic, but whether the railways themselves are likely to be superseded, sharing the same fate as that which they caused to fall on the stage coach and, more or less, on the canal barge'.[146]

The Control of Power

During the thirty years before 1914, while British trains grew heavier, and the passenger expresses came to run faster, the number of accidents diminished. It remained, on annual average, well below the number that had occurred in the 1870s; and that on a system still growing in length – by 30% in 1880–1914.

This impressive achievement reflected a change in public policy. The alarmingly high accident rate in the years before 1880 had evoked strong demands for government intervention, which became more compelling as each year went by. The case for that intervention was constantly fortified by the inspectors' discussion of accidents and of the devices that would, or might, have prevented them. Under their pressure, backed by public opinion, certain appliances, seen to be essential in working the railways' traffic safely, were made compulsory under the Regulation Act of 1889.

The terrible accident on the Great Northern Railway of Ireland at Armagh in June of that year had arisen primarily from the inadequacy of the brakes with which the carriages were provided. That was so clear that, without waiting for the inspector's report, the Government announced that it was going to force the companies to use brakes that the Board of Trade considered efficient; and it showed it meant business by pushing the Bill through at exceptional speed, to become law within twelve weeks of the accident.

Experiments to devise a brake that was 'continuous' – i.e. one applicable effectively and smoothly to every vehicle in a train at once – had already been under way for over thirty years. The North London company was a leader here, though it discarded seven varieties of brake before it made its choice.[147] The East Lancashire and its neighbour the Lancashire & Yorkshire used different systems, invented by men in their own service, James Newall and Charles Fay. By about 1860 all passenger trains on the lines of these two companies (merged into one in 1859) were fitted with a continuous brake of one pattern or the other.[148] Brakes operated by chains were adopted by the London & North Western and the Metropolitan companies in 1868–9.[149] The Metropolitan abandoned this mechanism about seven years later; but the London & North Western clung to its chains until every other large company was using brakes that were much more efficient.

In 1869 the American George Westinghouse had designed a brake of a quite new sort, and two years later he appeared in Britain eager to make agreements for its use. Some companies consented to try it: the Caledonian, Midland, and North Eastern, for instance, in 1871–4. Other contrivances were being experimented with at the same time, and in 1875 the Royal Commission on

Railway Accidents, then sitting, proposed that trials should be made of a number of them, on trains of different companies. They were held at Newark in June of that year, testing eight different systems, without any clear result.[150]

But two things were now plain, and publicly known. A list of demands had been drawn up by the inspectors, all of which a brake must meet before it could be considered efficient; and the choice lay, broadly, between two systems. In the minds of the companies there was another consideration, never proclaimed: what would each of these systems cost, to install and maintain, and what licensing fees would be payable for its use?

The demands were essentially four. The brake must be (1) continuous; (2) used in everyday working, not in an emergency alone; (3) instantaneous in action; and (4) applied automatically if any part of the train became detached from the remainder. The continuous principle enabled the brakes to bring the train to a halt in less than half the distance needed with brakes actuated in any other way.[151] If the third and fourth of these demands were met, any want of skill or diligence on the part of the driver or guard was counteracted, and if the train broke the machinery took charge, wresting control from them immediately.

Westinghouse's appliance was actuated by air pressure, its rivals by creating a vacuum. Both systems proved reliable. The mechanism of the vacuum brake was simpler. The air brake was more expensive, but it was somewhat quicker in action. Neither system had therefore a clear superiority over the other; and that afforded many excuses for delay in adopting one of them. Westinghouse marketed his air brake with what was thought in Britain to be American importunity, and that antagonized some of those he sought to deal with.[152] The Act of 1889 did not require the companies to agree on a uniform system. Of the larger ones seven (the Brighton, Chatham, Great Eastern, North Eastern, Caledonian, North British, and Great North of Scotland) adopted the air brake and stuck to it, the rest using some form of vacuum brake.

This was unfortunate. In face of the general consensus of opinion, in Europe and America, in favour of the air brake, we may say that in Britain most of the companies fitted the continuous brake in its inferior form; and all engines and vehicles working from railways employing one type of brake to those that employed the other – all running, for example, in expresses on the two principal lines from London to Scotland – had to be 'dual fitted', to accommodate both.

One valuable consequence of the adoption of continuous brakes, in whatever form, was that it opened up the way at last to ending the arguments about systems of communication between passengers and train crews. A device could now be fitted to each carriage, allowing passengers, in an emergency, to apply the brakes themselves, by means of a chain, cord, or handle. Yet mechanisms of that sort were not adopted rapidly. The Board of Trade retained the power to require the use of a system it approved, but after the fiasco of 1873 it hesitated to act, beyond setting up a departmental committee to discuss the matter with the companies. The Railway Clearing House also sought to secure some agreement among them. But though accidents and outrages occurred that could have been prevented if an effective device had been in use, none was so widely shocking as to call imperiously for action.

The cynicism of the companies in this matter is exemplified by some words written by David Deuchars, superintendent of the line on the North British Railway. In 1897 he reported to his general manager, John Conacher, that the chain communication provided on its carriages had 'not proved a success, and is not reliable'. Yet in the face of long experience he went on to state his opinion that 'the companies should continue to resist any demand of the Board [of Trade] to provide some complicated or expensive mode of making communication'.[153] For him the passengers' safety counted for much less than the saving of money. The Board's committee reported in 1898, revealing a diversity of practices, efficient and inefficient, still.[154] It was not until the opening years of the twentieth century that passengers on most railways in Britain came to be adequately protected against such dangers.

The compulsion to fit continuous brakes applied only to trains in passenger service. Nearly all the vehicles in them belonged to the companies. In freight trains there were large numbers of private owners' wagons, and no government of that time would contemplate taking powers to require the re-equipment of those wagons or, if they were unsuited to that, their destruction and replacement. So the large majority of freight trains continued to run loose-coupled, with no more than a hand-brake fitted to each wagon. Continuous brakes were provided on some of the companies' vehicles running in express freight service, but that was done on a small scale, and slowly. On the Great Western it did not even begin until 1903.[155] Except on the stretches of line where separate tracks were reserved for freight traffic (as for instance over nearly the whole 55 miles from Wellingborough to Trent on the Midland Railway, put in during the years 1873–93), the slow loose-coupled trains had to occupy the same lines as the continuously-braked expresses. That this antiquated and dangerous system worked with a high degree of safety down to 1914 and for many years longer was due to the efficiency of the companies' signalling arrangements and the care of the men operating them.

Although the merits of the block system of signalling had come to be generally recognized in the 1860s, not all railways were prepared to adopt it. Whereas the Bristol & Exeter company (far from a pioneer in most improvements) went over to it completely in 1865–7, it was unknown anywhere on the Manchester Sheffield & Lincolnshire until 1869.[156] The stock excuse given for tardiness of that kind was that block working actually increased danger through encouraging enginemen to rely on it, diminishing their own vigilance. But any sensible person could point out that the lives of the enginemen themselves, at the head of the train, were usually most at risk, for they were commonly the first to suffer in a collision or a derailment.[157]

By 1872 the block system had been applied or was being introduced, on the absolute principle, to 44% of the lines in Great Britain. Seven years later that 44% had become 73%.[158] Much of this improvement was carried through at the instance of the companies' managers, in the face of opposition from their directors, voiced by chairmen at shareholders' meetings. There was some play-acting here. The job had to be done. But it cost a good deal of money, which came out of the companies' profits and affected the dividends they paid. The chairmen answered for the dividends to the shareholders. It naturally helped them to say that such items of expenditure had been forced upon them by the government and its meddlesome officials.

One chairman exceeded all others in the vehemence of his comments here: Moon of the London & North Western, in whom it revealed monomania, was perhaps even a sign of senility. His diatribes wearied everyone – not least some of his own officers, who on other counts respected him. 'We never failed to hear from the chairman', wrote Neele with reference to the year 1885, 'that these mechanical appliances were all inducements to inattention on the part of the signalmen and drivers.'[159]

By the end of 1888, 91% of the whole length of railway in Great Britain was worked on the absolute block system. In Ireland (then still part of the United Kingdom) the proportion of the system on which block-working was installed was no more than 21%. Among the powers placed in the hands of the Board of Trade by the Regulation Act that followed was that of requiring every company that had not already adopted the absolute block system completely to do so within a period of time it was to appoint. By 1895 virtually the whole railway system of the Kingdom – Ireland included – was worked on that principle, or by some other means approved by the Board. The long task was done.

The interlocking of points and signals, to prevent conflict between them, went back to 1856. The inspectors recommended this mechanism strongly for use at junctions from that time onwards. Here too they met with a stiff resistance from some of the companies' managers, notably James Allport of the Midland. But the Board was as determined as they were, and in 1866, after a particularly tough battle over the arrangements for the Midland's new Aston curve at Birmingham, the company gave way, its Traffic Committee resolving that the Board should be told 'that such requirements are against the conviction of the Midland directors and officers and that they must decline to be held responsible for their adoption'. It was a futile cry from the last ditch, a recognition of defeat.[160]

The inspectors were now sure of their ground and pressed on. Tyler, the most statesmanlike of them, pointed out in 1872 that though much progress had been made with the provision of interlocking, it was not yet installed at some very important junctions, where it was acutely needed, instancing York, Preston, Swindon, and Gloucester; and two months later he appended to his report on an accident at Kirtlebridge on the Caledonian Railway a list of 'a few of the worst accidents which have occurred on railways from defective signal and point arrangements and the want of interlocking' – twenty-six of them, over the preceding five years.[161]

In 1873 a Regulation Act required of each company a return of the mileage of its line worked on the block system and with interlocked points and signals.

This must have had some effect on the rogue companies. Watkin's Manchester Sheffield & Lincolnshire installed what seems to have been its very first piece of interlocking that September. By 1880 it appeared that 82% of the connections on passenger-carrying lines in England and Wales were interlocked, 64% in Scotland. This had called for a very large construction of new machinery. The Midland Railway stood for some time alone in making all its signalling equipment itself. Allport was convinced that the commercial manufacturers overcharged for their work. Some other companies moved cautiously into the business: the Great Western and the South Eastern for instance in the 1860s, the London & North Western (having formed the same opinion as Allport) in 1873.[162]

There came to be nine important firms engaged in this manufacture. Five of them were established before 1869; the other four followed in 1876–94.[163] The same sort of difficulties were apt to arise here, with the rapid extension of the system and the mounting demand for more elaborate equipment, as had troubled the railways in their quest for locomotives in the 1830s and 1840s. In 1873 the quality of Saxby & Farmer's machinery supplied to the London & North Western Railway came under severe criticism: 'it should not have been taken over in such a state', wrote the inspector who was reporting on an accident at Dudley.[164]

The demand for reliability, in design and manufacture and operation, was heard on all hands now within the railway companies themselves, coming from their servants and their managers alike. In 1873 North Eastern engine drivers petitioned the locomotive superintendent, Edward Fletcher, to get the working of the block system made regular and efficient: a bold step then, but they were right in trusting him, and he saw to it that the job was done.[165] Three years later the Abbot's Ripton accident, which was caused partly by the failure of a signal to move to 'danger' when its action was clogged by snow, led the Great Northern company to approve a change of mechanical practice: in future the normal position of its signals would be at 'danger', and if when at 'all right' or 'caution' a wire should break, the arm would revert to 'danger' automatically.[166] This application of what is now called the 'fail-safe' principle was soon adopted by most other companies in Britain.

In the last quarter of the century electric power came to play an increasingly important part in the railways' safety precautions. The principle of interlocking was enlarged in 1875 when the first installation of 'lock-and-block' apparatus was made on the London Chatham & Dover Railway, ensuring the agreement of the signals with the telegraph instruments. Experiments were then soon in progress with electrical devices operated by the locomotive's pressure on the rails, conveying an indication of its position to the signalman: 'track-circuiting'. The signalman's most valuable instrument was still his eyes. His box and the signals themselves were sited with care, to give him the clearest possible vision of the stretch of track he controlled. But that vision could not always be complete – where the line ran into a tunnel, for instance, or into a deep curved cutting. Track-circuiting supplemented and counter-checked the signalman's eyes. It was brought into use in the tunnels outside King's Cross station in 1894. The Great Western company began to install it in 1907, the London & North Western four years later.[167]

The central idea represented by track-circuiting was capable of being applied more widely. It could, to some extent, eliminate the signalman himself. The Liverpool Overhead Railway was signalled throughout its length, from its opening in 1893, on an electrically-controlled system that required manual working only at the two terminal stations.[168] In 1903–6, in the course of turning over to electric traction, the Metropolitan District Railway re-signalled its lines on a system based on track-circuits, dispensing with signalmen and their boxes except at junctions and a few other control points.[169]

Meanwhile electricity had come to be applied, in another form, to much larger and more complicated signalling installations. In 1899, almost simultaneously, the North Western and Great Eastern companies brought into use new systems, at Crewe and at Spitalfields in east London, in which the whole power placed in the hands of the signalmen was exerted electrically.[170] In 1901–5 the South Western and the North Eastern turned over to power-operated signalling on substantial stretches of their main lines. In 1908 the whole large installation controlling traffic at Glasgow Central station became power-operated.

At the same time the Great Western company was experimenting with another electrically-worked device, designed to convey intelligence automatically not to the signalman but to the driver. By means of a ramp installed between the rails and a shoe fitted underneath the engine, making contact with it, a bell rang in the cab to indicate that the next distant signal was at 'all right'; but if the distant signal was at 'danger', or if there was a failure of any kind, an electric circuit on the engine itself actuated a siren in the cab until the driver switched it off.[171] Audible signals had been tried out many times in the past. This was the first that entirely succeeded. Installed on the Henley branch in 1906, its use was extended to the main line from Paddington to Reading in 1908–10. It opened up the way to much more comprehensive systems of automatic train control, applied in later years.

Electricity contributed to the working of country branches, as well as of main lines and big junctions. The operation of single lines presented difficulties of its own and very evident dangers, proclaimed in two atrocious head-on collisions in 1874–6, at Norwich and Radstock. Careful controls had been established to prevent such disasters, but they proved ineffective. The working of these lines was no minor problem: 42% of the mileage of line in Great Britain was still single in 1874. The admirable signal engineer Edward Tyer set himself to devise a new mechanism, under which a driver might proceed through a single-line section only when he held a tablet authorizing him to do so; the machine issuing the tablet being electrically interlocked with another at the far end of the section, from which a second tablet could not be released until the one he held had been inserted into it. This system, with the variants that followed it, proved fully effective.

Occasional anxiety might still be felt over the consequences of a fault in the electrical supply, though that could usually be provided against by making the mechanism fail safe. But whereas in the Mid-Victorian age the railway companies had spent money on new signalling devices with great reluctance, by the beginning of the twentieth century they had come to approach such things in a different spirit. Their wage bills were troubling them greatly. The automation now put before them offered the opportunity of reducing the number of men employed to work their lines; an opportunity to which they devoted serious attention.[172]

The process of automation advanced, over the whole field of the railways' work, very irregularly. They employed machines everywhere: more and more of them, from massive overhead cranes and the biggest locomotives to the typewriters that some of them came to use in their offices in the 1890s.[173] But though new machines and improved versions of old ones might bring increased efficiency, they did not always produce any direct economy in manpower. A steam locomotive had required a crew of two men in 1830. In 1914 it was capable of much more work, reducing expenditure in other directions. But in one respect the machine was unchanged. It required a crew of two men still.

4
PRACTITIONERS

Professional Organization · The Early Leaders ·
Withdrawals and Failures · Consultancy and Partnership ·
Chief Engineers · Contractors · Subordinates ·
The Railway Profession

The two preceding chapters have offered a brief account of the equipment the railways worked with, as it evolved in the Victorian age. The names of those associated with particular techniques or practices have sometimes been mentioned, but very little has been said of them as men. The railways' equipment was not produced by impersonal forces, however. Though a hurricane on the Tay and ice-floes in the Solway revealed the defects of long iron bridges in 1879–81, it was the engineers who had to find the means of withstanding those furious pressures in the future.

Let us now take stock of some of them and of the architects, of the contractors who built to the engineers' specifications, and the assistants working under their direction to get the railways under way and keep them going, choosing as far as possible men who left records of their work themselves and can therefore speak of it to us directly now.

Professional Organization

Very few of the pioneer builders of railways in the 1830s were what we should call professional men. The professions themselves, of engineer and architect, were still struggling for public recognition. By the late eighteenth century engineering in Britain had separated into two divisions. The older of them was the military, institutionalized by the establishment of the Corps of Royal Engineers in 1787. Military engineers were not concerned with fortification only. They also built roads and bridges, and here their work overlapped with that of men called 'civil engineers' (civil as distinct from military), who were all in private practice. There was no body of government engineers in Britain comparable with the Ponts et Chaussées in France. The civil engineers established their own Institution in London in 1818, with Thomas Telford as its President.

Telford's life exemplifies the emergence of the civil engineering profession and some of its ramifications. He had begun as a stonemason's apprentice. Presently he set out to become an architect, designing churches built at Bridgnorth and Madeley in Shropshire in 1792. But in the following year he accepted a post with the managing body of the Ellesmere Canal Company as 'General Agent, Surveyor, Engineer, Architect, and Overlooker of the Canal and Clerk to the Committee and the Sub-Committees when appointed'.[1] Defined thus, that one man's task comprehended the duties that would now be undertaken by four, belonging to separate, well-organized professions – a land agent, a civil engineer, an architect, and a quantity surveyor; and it included the responsibility for the clerical work too. Nor was this for some minor undertaking. Telford wrote of it as 'the greatest work, I believe, that is now in hand in this Kingdom'. Considering that it came to include the Pontcysyllte and Chirk aqueducts, that claim was justified. He began to direct his mind henceforward, so he tells us, 'solely to Civil Engineering'.[2]

The scope of engineering now grew to embrace all appliances designed to ease and accelerate the performance of the tasks involved in mining, manufacture, and transport. Those who understood these machines and led the way in their improvement did not aspire to be considered gentlemen, after the fashion of some civil engineers. At their head were eminent men like James Watt and Jesse Ramsden the 'philosophical instrument maker'. But they were 'mechanics', trusted and respected, and generally contented to remain so. When the Institution of Civil Engineers was established, its members thought of such men as mechanics only, some of them using the word by this time with an inflection of disdain, and gave them little encouragement. With the development of railways the mechanics came into their kingdom, and in 1847 they set up their professional body in turn, the Institution of Mechanical Engineers.[3]

So British engineering had now three branches: military, civil, and mechanical. Presently the increasing complexity of mechanical engineering led to further division, with bodies of electrical, mining, locomotive, and signal engineers, founded in 1871–1911. The Institute of Engineers and Shipbuilders in Scotland dates from 1857. Engineers were not required to be members of any of these bodies before they could practise. There was no system of licensing.

Confusion frequently arose between what was done for railway companies by engineers and by architects. The two big laminated timber bridges on the Newcastle & North Shields Railway were designed not by the company's engineer Robert Nicholson but by its architects, John and Benjamin Green. The Institution of Civil Engineers recognized that: it listened to a paper on the bridges by Benjamin and published a summary of it in its own *Proceedings*.[4]

The architects also sought to establish a corporate identity as a profession. The Institute of British Architects (it became the Royal Institute in 1866) was set up in 1835; the Architectural Institute of Scotland in 1850. Here too there was no licensing. A man could become an architect merely by calling himself that. He might, like Mr Pecksniff, be a brazen fraud.

The promoters of a railway naturally tended to look to men in their own locality for advice of any kind when they needed it. The directors of the Stockton & Darlington, though they trusted their engineer George Stephenson, felt they wanted an architect to design the bridge for carrying the line over the River Skerne at Darlington, within sight of passing traffic on the Great North Road. They engaged Ignatius Bonomi for the purpose, who had been practising in the county since 1810. No railway seems ever to have employed an architect before.[5] In later days an architect often came to be included within the department of the railway company's engineer as a permanent, though subordinate, member of his staff; but he did not rank among the company's chief officers.

No railway, mechanically operated and in public use, was ever constructed without the services of an engineer; but many were carried through successfully without calling for an architect at all. That is not to depreciate the contribution architects made to railways. Here and there it was very striking. But it was the engineer's duty to make the railway work. Where an architect was employed, he had to meet the engineer's requirements in all matters of that sort. They were overriding, mandatory.

The Early Leaders

A few of the early railways were laid down by civil engineers already well known for their work on canals and roads: George Overton for example was responsible for the Penydarren Tramroad, William Jessop for the Surrey Iron Railway and the Kilmarnock & Troon. Telford himself surveyed a line for a railway, 125 miles long, from Glasgow to Berwick in 1810. It was designed to be worked by horses, and by gravity on inclined planes. Locomotives were not yet ready to be considered. When they were, Telford allowed them some merit, but he never laid out a railway for them.[6]

With a single exception, none of the engineers who were well recognized professionally before 1830 made any notable contribution to the mechanically-operated railway in England and Wales. The Rennie family, who regarded themselves as the leading engineers of the time, were defeated whenever they touched it. An egregious snobbery was entailed on them all, like a Habsburg lip. They were maladroit in their negotiations with promoters, which lost them the Liverpool & Manchester and the London & Brighton Railways, two great prizes. The account Sir John Rennie gives of his railway work in his *Autobiography* is a curiosity of literature: a narrative of unbroken failure, set out in detail with smiling complacency. At one point he lists twelve railways projected in 1844. 'I had my full share of them', he says:[7] only that share did not include any responsibility for their execution.

Some other civil engineers did however undertake work for the new railways. Jesse Hartley acted as consultant to the Liverpool & Manchester company. He gave valuable advice and aid to George Stephenson; he was probably responsible for both the Rainhill bridge and the Sankey viaduct.[8] He was also the engineer of the Manchester & Bolton Railway, built in 1833–8. The handling of masonry that immortalized him in the Liverpool docks was apparent here too.[9] James Walker, who was primarily a water engineer, worked for railways with varying success. He acted with J. U. Rastrick as a judge at the Rainhill trials and he carried through admirably the railway from Leeds to Hull, opened in two sections in 1834–40. He also laid out the Furness Railway in 1841–3. Having succeeded Telford as President of the Institution of Civil Engineers, he often reported on the railway plans of other men. But he left no strong mark on railways himself.

That cannot be said of William Cubitt. He had begun life as a millwright and had made a reputation in canal and dock undertakings. Though he drove through two railways only, they were among the boldest and best of all: the South Eastern and the Great Northern. But Cubitt was the only established civil engineer who took a really important share in the construction of the early English railway system.

In Scotland it was different. There a single pair of civil engineers laid down more than two-thirds of all the railways commissioned in 1824–38. They were Thomas Grainger and John Miller, who were partners, though in a very limited sense: for each of them attended to his own commissions, and they hardly ever worked jointly. Grainger was a civil engineer and surveyor of the traditional kind, who moved into railway work in the Monklands in the 1820s. Miller, eleven years younger, set out to be a lawyer but threw that business up, was trained as an engineer under Grainger and became his partner in 1825.[10] Though Grainger's practice came to extend as far southwards as Yorkshire, Miller confined himself to Scotland. There he left a noble monument behind him in the Edinburgh & Glasgow Railway and the Glasgow Dumfries *Ill. 35* & Carlisle: great works worthy to be compared with Telford's roads.

The older civil engineering, then, made a limited contribution to the British railway system as a whole; but the contribution of military engineers was much smaller. Indeed only one of them made any mark here: G. T. Landmann, who had been a Royal Engineer from 1795 to 1824 and was engaged to lay down two short railways, the London & Greenwich and the Preston & Wyre.

The greatest share of British railway engineering fell to men whose experience had been in collieries and ironworking: most notably George Stephenson and his son. It was those two great men who demonstrated the railways' full potential, turning them from an adjunct to coal mines into a new instrument of transport for all sorts of freight, for passengers, and for mails. In laying down their lines they brought together a band of young men who served under them. They appeared to have formed a clique, which was looked on jealously by those who did not belong to it; with suspicion too by some railway directors, who thought they were trying to create a monopoly, both in the construction of railways and in the manufacture of their equipment.[11] In the 1830s there were some grounds for this supposition, but they were quickly removed as the execution of one trunk line after another fell into the hands of men outside the group. The South Eastern went to Cubitt, the Eastern Counties to Braithwaite, the Brighton line to Rastrick (well experienced already as a mechanical engineer), and the Great Western to Brunel.

Among all the chief pioneers Brunel stood out as an alien. He was the son of a French refugee from the Revolution, who had settled in London and become an outstanding civil engineer, largely immersed in the construction of the Thames Tunnel. The younger Brunel was highly educated, passing two years in France when the wars were over, partly as an apprentice under one of the greatest of all watch-makers, Louis Bréguet. He was long frustrated in his search for employment. Having won the competition for the Clifton bridge at Bristol, he had to see the scheme laid aside – 'so many irons and none of them hot', he wrote in 1832.[12] But next year his luck changed, when he was appointed engineer of the Great Western Railway. He was then twenty-seven.

He had already firm opinions on what railways could and should be. He took all the experience of the past and moulded it into a plan for a railway of a new sort: designed for high speed, with track laid down to a gauge nearly half as broad again as the accepted one, equipped and appointed on a corresponding scale. Very soon it grew to be something more ambitious still. His railway from London to Bristol was to be the first stage in a journey to New York, continued in a steamship he designed himself.

But Brunel's imaginative vision was linked to a meticulous attention to detail in every part of the work he was entrusted with. He could admit mistakes and recognize the capacity of others to remedy them. His friendship with Robert Stephenson – a different kind of man altogether, undeviatingly *Ill. 34* pragmatic where his own cast of mind was speculative – was based on a deep mutual regard, and it does equal honour to them both.

Brunel always stood alone. He never took any partner. He had able assistants, who carried on his work after his death, devoted to his memory. Endlessly fertile in ideas, admired, feared, derided, he went his own way. His influence was less than the Stephensons'. What they founded was not a clique but a school: a school of practice and experience that quickly permeated the whole island and reached out across the world.

Some 6000 miles of railway were completed in Great Britain in 1830–50; more than a third of it under the direction of the two Stephensons, Joseph Locke, and Brunel. The wonder of the achievement was never adequately expressed at the time. It was a theme for a great prose epic, which nobody wrote. We cannot easily recover the intensity of this effort or measure its full magnitude now. Still, we have records of the work, kept by engineers themselves, their collaborators and assistants, affording us some insight into the way it was done. A few continuous accounts survive, in notebooks and diaries. Among diaries the most extensive and valuable – at least according to our present knowledge – are those kept by Rastrick, Vignoles, and T. L. Gooch.[13]

Rastrick's extend from 1805 to 1853.[14] They afford a brief day-by-day record of his work, not only on railways but on canals and other engineering enterprises too. They are particularly valuable for their account of the building of the London & Brighton Railway. His other papers include a very detailed valuation and calculations of cost for the Birmingham & Liverpool Railway (later the Grand Junction) in 1830–3:[15] a good example of this kind of document, which was prepared for every well-planned railway. Very few such records survive now. The notes Rastrick kept as a judge at the Rainhill trials in 1829 have been printed and discussed by Dendy Marshall.[16]

Vignoles' diary – drawn upon in both the biographies written by his descendants[17] – was kept with few substantial intervals from 1830 to 1862, and evidently written up either day by day or at very frequent intervals. So it affords us a detailed view of the normal round of an ambitious railway engineer. Let us consider two parts of it: one from a time when he was seeking employment, the other when he was heavily engaged on a formidable task.

Vignoles came into railway engineering late, having been a soldier, and his start there on the Liverpool & Manchester line was unhappy, but he carried through the St Helens and the Dublin & Kingstown Railways successfully in 1833–4. In 1834–5 he was involved in five railway schemes in Britain, as well as others in Germany and Cuba.[18] His diary shows us some of this work close up: three days, for example, trying to instruct a KC in the principles of railway-building, to enable him to cross-examine Brunel – three days entirely wasted;[19] a spell of continuous surveying on the Midland Counties line in the autumn of 1835.[20] He records the fees agreed on for his work, details his expenses, and occasionally notes the speed at which he moved – on 22 August 1834, for instance, from London to Manchester by the 'Telegraph' coach, 186 miles in $17\frac{3}{4}$ hours including stops, saluted as 'capital travelling!'[21]

The most difficult railway commission Vignoles undertook in Britain was the Sheffield Ashton & Manchester line, which was to bore through the Pennines in a tunnel three miles long. We can see his attention to it day by day, to the obstacles as they appeared and the means of overcoming them: from the erection of houses for the navvies (too few and too late, as it soon appeared) to repeated experiments with a steam-worked boring machine.[22] But the diary reveals something else too: the great volume of Vignoles' work on other projects at the same time, including lines in Ireland and in Germany, several dock schemes and one for a suspension bridge at Oporto.[23] He is also away in Paris for three weeks, called into consultation over the railway to Versailles in 1839.[24] No one seems to have suggested that he neglected his duty on the Sheffield–Manchester line, but he repeatedly demanded that the company should leave the responsibility for its engineering works solely with him, and the multiplicity of his engagements may well have been one of the reasons why he fell foul of the directors. His resignation in November 1839 might have been avoided if there had been confidence between them. An unprejudiced reader of his diary can appreciate that there were faults on both sides.

The work on each of the projects in which Vignoles is engaged is entered up here separately, in a rapid cursory hand, day by day; the clear-headed man muddled none of it. We have no other presentation of the business of a railway engineer in large practice that is as comprehensive as this diary, so resolutely maintained.

T. L. Gooch's diary[25] reads more smoothly, as a methodical narrative. He has a good deal to say about personal matters, about his religion and amusements for example, and his diary comes to form an interesting self-portrait.

He worked on the difficult Manchester & Leeds Railway as resident engineer under George Stephenson and was associated with Robert Stephenson and G. P. Bidder as engineer of the Trent Valley and North Staffordshire lines. He was never in charge of any company's main line as engineer, from planning to completion. He had – his diary shows it – the gift of working easily with others, and enjoying that. He was unambitious, never a *prima donna*; one of the most reliable railway engineers of the 1840s. Moreover, he was absolutely straightforward; as soon as he detected some chicanery in the dealings of the Manchester & Leeds directors with him, he sent in his resignation.[26] But his selfless devotion to his work undermined his health, and in 1851 he retired from practice at the age of forty-two. When he recovered, he never returned to railway engineering. He had made well over £40,000, a more than adequate competence, and he lived on quietly until 1882.

The greatest value of Gooch's diary to us is that he was *not* a chief engineer. He was little concerned with the politics of the board-room; his business was to get his railways built. He stood closer to the job than many chief engineers did, and he drove it through with a steadily efficient concentration. No important failure of any kind can be attributed to him. What we see in this diary is the engineer as executant, at his best.

Some long and valuable commentaries on railway work, seen at first hand, are also to be found in the diaries of men who were not responsible for executing any of it yet had nevertheless for a longer or shorter time much to do with them. The one kept by the surveyor Edward Ryde is referred to elsewhere. Another calls for brief discussion at this point.

The diary of Charles Pasley, inspector-general of railways at the Board of Trade from 1841 to 1846, has been well analysed.[27] He had seen long service with the Royal Engineers before he was drawn into railway work. Though he was then already past the age of sixty, he entered on his new task with energy and enthusiasm. That is apparent from his diary,[28] corroborated by the comments of some of those who watched him in the course of his inspections.[29] Pasley had to learn much about railways as he went along, and critics who were on the watch for his mistakes were sometimes able to crow when they found one; *Punch* turned the meticulousness of his reports on accidents into a source of merriment.[30] But he was tough and determined, and he worked on: to be dismissed on a revision of the government arrangements for dealing with railways in 1846. The Prime Minister, Russell, recognized his distinction as 'an officer both of invention and ability to instruct others' but remarked that he had not 'given satisfaction to the public'.[31] He had shown himself shrewd, untiring, and incorruptible. No wonder the public (i.e. the railway chairmen and managers) disliked him.

I know of only one diary kept by a director of a railway company and devoted to the work he undertook for it: that of the Quaker Samuel Priestman, who joined the board of the York & North Midland Railway in 1850 and immediately began a day-by-day record of what he did in its service, in attendance at meetings, discussions outside the board-room, and visits of inspection.[32] The diary covers three years in all. It shows very well the normal round of duties that a conscientious director (not a mere fee-taker) performed.

Withdrawals and Failures

T. L. Gooch stood by no means alone in his decision to retire from railway engineering at an early age. The pressure of work on these men in 1830–50 was greater than at any time afterwards, when railway building was not going ahead so fast and a good many aids had come into use that eased labour. Outstanding among them were the extension of the railway system itself and of the telegraph that went with it. We cannot wonder that other engineers, even if they had not suffered in health like Gooch, decided to retire. In 1850 Frederick Swanwick, also a Stephenson man, did likewise; so did the Scotsman John Miller.[33] These two lived on, occupied in other ways, until 1885 and 1883 respectively. A number of able young men, attracted into railway work by the opportunities it afforded in 1844–5, left it and made reputations in quite other fields: Alfred Russel Wallace, for instance, John Tyndall, Herbert Spencer, George Grove.

We can also note several men who failed to make their way as railway engineers, or who made a name and then lost it. Francis Giles was edged out of office on the Newcastle & Carlisle Railway in 1834 because his engagements were too numerous to allow him to attend properly to the company's work, and then on the London & Southampton three years later, for the same reason and also for his incompetent organization.[34] He was not, however, an incompetent engineer: his railway bridges over the Eden in Cumbria are a fine memorial to him still. Thomas Storey was obliged to resign his post as engineer to the Great North of England Railway owing to the manifest imperfections of the bridges built to his orders.[35] The curious case of Francis Whishaw seems to be of the same sort. He had been articled to James Walker and had worked as an assistant under Gooch on the Manchester & Leeds Railway, but he lost his post there for some uncertain reason. He made his name, and keeps it today, as the author of two books, *An Analysis of Railways* (1837) and *The Railways of Great Britain and Ireland* (1840). He served as secretary of the Society of Arts in 1842–5 and took on some railway work thereafter. But he died in the Marylebone workhouse, aged fifty-two, in 1856.[36]

One other man, who made more noise than any of those three, must be added to this list: W. S. Moorsom. He was busily engaged in seeking work from 1835 to his death in 1863, and his name appears frequently in prospectuses. But most of his lines did not get built, or were built under the direction of other men. He carried through only three in Great Britain: the Birmingham & Gloucester, the Southampton & Dorchester, and the little Ringwood Christchurch & Bournemouth, all to a reasonably satisfactory result. But his methods were slovenly,[37] and it seems likely that his reputation got round among those concerned with railway building.

These were civil engineers. Similar fates might befall the men whose work lay with machines. One of them, John Gray, is important, and the close of his career obscure. He entered the service of the Liverpool & Manchester company in 1832. When he came to work on its engines, he gave serious attention to mechanical methods of reducing their consumption of coke and evolved a new valve-gear, designed partly to serve this purpose, in 1838.[38] Next year he went on to become locomotive superintendent of the Hull & Selby Railway. There he set himself firmly to the design of locomotives. He and Daniel Gooch were almost the first of the railway companies' own officers to do that. Hackworth had drawn up plans for locomotives for the Stockton & Darlington in the 1820s, and built them, but those used by other companies in the 1830s had been wholly or largely designed by the manufacturers. Gray paid special attention to the balancing of his engines and to strengthening their frames; he raised the boiler pressures in them by about 25%; and he entirely rejected the received doctrine that the centre of gravity of locomotives must be kept as low as possible. In later years his views on that matter came to be accepted. He moved in 1845 to become locomotive superintendent of the London & Brighton Railway and designed twelve express engines that were the prototypes from which the celebrated *Jenny Lind* machines evolved.[39] But he left the company in 1847[40] and then vanishes from sight. We know he was alive eight years later, when he took legal action to defend a patent. Why did he leave Brighton? There is some hint that he caused delays by fidgeting about with the design of his machines, in pursuit of perfection; but it is a hint, no more. How did he occupy himself afterwards? Modern writers on locomotive history are agreed that his thought was original and valuable, reaching out well into the future.[41]

Gray's fate reminds us of the insecurity that was an element in the careers of these men. Dismissal, on little notice or none and without any compensation, hung over all railwaymen, senior officers included, both in the early days and for long afterwards. The North British company got rid of five successive locomotive superintendents (not always without reason) in 1851–75.[42]

Consultancy and Partnership

Some railway engineers, with good experience gained in the conventional way, slipped into free-lance consultancy. G. P. Bidder, a very able man, hardly ever served one railway company alone for more than a year at a time, preferring to work with several, to join with other engineers, and to give external advice and opinions.[43] Arrangements of this kind were open to the objection that they might divide responsibility. Brunel set his face very early against accepting any such appointments. In 1836 he was asked by the committee of a Plymouth & Exeter Railway, then being formed, to become its 'consulting engineer', yoked in that office with Robert Stephenson. He explained his refusal courteously:

The selection of the general line of country . . . is in fact that which principally calls into operation the judgment of the engineer; the determining afterwards of two or more lines which have been selected and surveyed is comparatively easy, and very often hardly requires a professional opinion, and the mere preparing of the estimates (when the nature of the works is determined upon) is quite a mechanical and subordinate operation.

By the arrangement here suggested, supposing Mr Stephenson and myself or any other acted as consultant engineer, the company would not obtain that individual responsibility which alone can secure to them the best advice; and they might become seriously embarrassed by differing opinions. . . . My advice would be that one person on whom the company may be disposed to place their ultimate reliance should have the sole control over the parties he may select to assist him in exploring the country, and consequently he would be responsible for the result.

Six weeks later the committee asked Brunel to undertake 'the general superintendence of the survey of the country for the proposed line' on his own, and he then agreed.[44] The plan was carried into effect long afterwards as the South Devon Railway.

None of the other leading railway engineers took so rigid a line in this matter. In 1847 Robert Stephenson was consulting engineer to six companies.[45] Three of them had their main lines open by that time, so his function there must have been chiefly as standing counsel. For the other three he acted in just the way Brunel disapproved of, jointly with other men.

In the later Victorian age the consultant engineer became a well-recognized figure in railway practice. The great majority of the lines built from the 1860s onwards either were branches of existing railways, laid out by the main companies' engineers, or were promoted by nominally independent companies, locally based, associated with the established ones whose lines they joined. The directors of a local railway might engage an engineer of their own, but the larger company would wish to make sure that the line was well planned, since sooner or later it would probably buy up the smaller undertaking itself. Under these conditions there was much to be said for associating a consultant, appointed by the larger company, with the engineer of the other. W. R. Galbraith is an outstanding example of a highly competent engineer who acted in this way all over the West Country, in collaboration with the London & South Western company, and widely in Scotland too.[46]

A change in the organization of the engineers' business also began to become prominent in these years. At first they had almost all been adamant on remaining individually in control. Locke broke with this practice when he took John Errington into partnership early in the 1840s. He himself was then heavily employed outside as well as inside England, his commitments extending from Aberdeen to Rouen. He engaged a French associate to look after the construction of the Paris & Rouen Railway. Errington had already proved himself as one of Locke's assistants, but he was eligible for a more important role on another ground also: he was a natural diplomat, patient and persuasive, and that made him an invaluable colleague. Locke's abilities were first-class, and he was an excellent man of business. 'He may be termed the Commercial Engineer', wrote R. B. Dockray on his death, 'one who made the money go as far as possible.'[47] But he seems to have lacked the personal charm exercised by Robert Stephenson and Brunel. A trusted partner, rather different in personality, might do better than he could himself. To say that this became Errington's chief contribution to the partnership ought not to imply that he was incompetent as a practising engineer – though that assertion was always liable to be made by anyone whom these two defeated in a competition for employment: by Joseph Mitchell, for instance, disappointed by them of becoming engineer to the Scottish Central Railway in 1844.[48]

In the later Victorian age the firm of partners became characteristic. Blyth & Westland made a name for themselves by their extensive railway work in Scotland, notably their reconstruction of Waverley station in Edinburgh. Simpson & Wilson were the engineers of the West Highland Extension line. John Fowler had taken Benjamin Baker into partnership in 1875. On the Forth bridge their responsibilities were divided, Fowler dealing mainly with the unusually extensive approaches to the bridge and Baker with the bridge itself.

Arrangements of this kind became more desirable as the complexities of all engineering work grew greater, owing not only to the emergence of new devices, techniques, and methods but also to the increasingly tight controls imposed by government and to the difficulties of finding capital for large works. All the London tube railways opened in 1900–7 had to be financed to some degree internationally.

Chief Engineers

Each large railway company employed a chief engineer – a civil engineer – with a substantial department of his own. He was usually one of its most powerful officers. That might be due to merit and experience, as for instance with W. H. Barlow and his successor J. S. Crossley on the Midland Railway. Inferior men sometimes sought to establish themselves by mere obstreperousness. The chairman of the South Eastern company once took occasion to warn its surveyor, Edward Ryde, that he must 'humour' the engineer (Peter Ashcroft, whom the chairman evidently considered a self-important mediocrity). 'If you do not', he said, 'you may as well get a bull in a china shop.' The surveyor noted the remark with contempt as 'the South Eastern chairman's opinion of their engineer in 1858'.[49]

The last survivor among the outstanding chief engineers was T. E. Harrison of the North Eastern. He died in office, just before his eightieth birthday, in 1888. He was exceptional in that he was not only an engineer but experienced also in the conduct of general business. As a young man he had worked for a year in an accountant's office. Long afterwards he put that among 'the most useful experiences of his life'. When George Hudson collapsed in 1849 Harrison took a powerful part in helping the York Newcastle & Berwick Railway to pull through its difficulties. He then went on to propose that the company should unite with the York & North Midland and the Leeds Northern, to form one large organization. He served as general manager of the three companies while the Bill went through to create the North Eastern Railway in 1854 and then reverted, at his own instance, to the office of chief engineer.[50]

He was perhaps the last chief engineer of a big British railway company who interested himself in every branch of his art and science. As a young man he had patented designs for locomotives, which were partly adopted in two built for Brunel. They failed; but they showed an appreciation, like Brunel's own, of the defects of the existing machines and explored ways of overcoming them.[51] In his later years he concerned himself much with brakes, in strong support of the Westinghouse air brake against its rivals. His iron bridges commanded much respect, notably his swing bridges at Goole and Naburn in Yorkshire, and he was known for his careful attention to the design of stations. He was in constant request as an arbitrator in matters concerning railways, including their disputes with the Post Office, where his grasp of accountancy proved its value. Harrison must be reckoned one of the great all-rounders of British railway history.[52]

Ill. 36

The chief civil engineer was always apt to be criticized as an expansionist, forever looking for more work to aggrandize himself and his department. But after 1850 the large extensions of the railway system more usually arose from empire-building chairmen: from such men as Richard Hodgson of the North British, who sought to make his company a monopolist in the border country between England and Scotland, and Edward Watkin, whose rapacious and ill-considered ambitions reached out in the 1870s and 1880s to embrace Blackpool and Le Tréport.[53] They might come from other officers too. It was for example Ryde who proposed the very important extension of the South Eastern company's line from London Bridge to Charing Cross in 1857. His authorship of the project was publicly acknowledged on its completion six years later.[54]

As might be expected, there were many struggles for power within the companies between their chief officers. The uneasy relations between civil and mechanical engineers that became apparent in the early nineteenth century carried themselves forward into the twentieth. Some of the companies' locomotive superintendents sought to achieve parity of status (and of salary too, as they might expect) by securing the title 'chief mechanical engineer', which implied that they enjoyed a completely separate power. The new title was accorded for the first time to J. A. F. Aspinall on his appointment to the Lancashire & Yorkshire Railway in 1886: surprisingly, for he was a very young man (only thirty-five), and not an aggressive bargainer for position. It was adopted by six other companies in 1902–14 – only one of them in Scotland, the Glasgow & South Western. On the North Western and Great Western ambitious mechanical engineers fought long and fierce battles with general managers: Webb with Frederick Harrison, Churchward with J. C. Inglis (who had himself been a civil engineer).[55] Such enmities might be exposed by the civil engineer's refusal to accept locomotives for service on lines in his charge owing to the excessive weight they were alleged to place on the track, as on the Highland Railway in 1914–15: a situation that surely ought not to have arisen if there had been adequate discussion between the two departments before the engines were laid down.[56] Rivalries between chief officers were of course common in such organizations, of every kind. Here they must have been exacerbated by revisions of salary and by the differing practices of the boards in allowing direct access to themselves, on the part of chief officers, as a matter of right, or insisting that all their business should be filtered to them through their general managers.

Contractors

When the portrait of an engineer was painted, the artist sometimes included, in the background, a representation of one of his most famous works. At the Institution of Civil Engineers, George Stephenson was depicted standing on a rocky hillock with a train behind on the Liverpool & Manchester line, crossing Chat Moss. It may be assumed that he consented to the choice of that subject to symbolize his achievement at its highest.

Yet the expedient on which the success at Chat Moss had depended – floating the railway on a raft of tree-trunks and wooden frames, covered with heather and brushwood – was due not to Stephenson but to the contractor Robert Stannard, who had worked on the Moss before. Stephenson's own method of carrying the line over the morass had failed. Stannard persuaded him, with difficulty, to try this alternative plan. Stephenson displayed an unconquerable perseverance – 'his stubbornness beat the bog'; but it was Stannard who showed him the way to his final success.[57]

Again: the passenger who skims up from the south towards Peterborough today at 100 mph and more, if he turns to think of the construction of the Great Northern Railway, blesses Cubitt for the racing track that he gave it, running for over seven miles north of Huntingdon, dead straight and nearly level, mostly on a high embankment. No easier railway travelling is to be had in Britain. But this stretch of line had to be laid across the western edge of Whittlesea Mere, which was then undrained and in some parts so treacherous that anyone standing on it could 'shake an acre of it together'. Brassey, the contractor, saw no way of overcoming this obstacle until he was introduced at Cambridge to the resident engineer of the Middle Level Drain, Stephen Ballard, who told him what he thought should be done. Thereupon he took Ballard on to his staff and entrusted him with the whole of this section of the work. Drainage was undertaken with the aid of one of the new 'portable steam engines' of Clayton & Shuttleworth, scarcely used before in railway construction. The line and its bridges were gradually built up on deep-sunk rafts (100 acres of faggot-wood were cut down to make them), and the task was accomplished without delaying the completion of the railway. Though Cubitt had the responsibility for the whole line he left the difficulties of carrying out this awkward part of it to the contractor and the resident engineer (his own son Joseph), and they owed the solution of this problem entirely to Ballard.[58] Cubitt had been called on to become the company's engineer late in the preparation of its final plans, inheriting them from Locke. The line from London to York was, when it came to Parliament in 1844, 186 miles long, together with 142 miles of branches: very much the largest railway scheme ever considered seriously in Britain as a single unit.[59] No survey could in these circumstances have been meticulously accurate, under any engineer. It was inevitable that the solutions to many such difficulties should have been found, not by the chief engineer but by those who had the actual task of constructing the way and works.

Contractors sometimes appear in railway history as sinister figures, their minds set on nothing but making a profit in the shortest time; the enemies of directors, shareholders, engineers and other officers, alike.[60] Such contractors did exist – William Ranger on the Great Western, for instance[61] – and their number much increased during and after the Mania of the 1840s; but they are not a fair sample of these men as a whole. When disputes arose between companies and contractors, the faults might lie with either party. We may sympathize with the prudent contractor who began his work for the notoriously indigent East Anglian Railway by locking up a load of rails and twenty-seven of its carriages in a shed, as security in case he was not paid.[62] Brunel, in his large way, saw the chief engineer as 'umpire' between the railway company and its contractors.[63]

Ballard's contribution to the crossing of that Huntingdonshire fenland is a shining example, but only one of many. Another thing is worth noticing about him too. He had begun as an engineer, in canal and drainage works. Under Brassey he came into contracting, and a contractor he then remained.[64] As an engineer-contractor he stood by no means alone.[65]

Only a few contractors found biographers.[66] The greatest of all these men was Thomas Brassey, and the biography accorded to him was the earliest and the best. Unfortunately no one attempted to write any full life of Peto. Since the proceedings arising out of his bankruptcy in 1867 extended over more than thirty years,[67] the welter of conflicting testimony they produced renders it impossible to compile any satisfactory account of his enormous operations, except in a very limited and partial form, now.

Most of those who contracted for railway work in the early days were small men. Brassey alone among them had been regularly to school. Their written papers must have been almost entirely confined to the accounts they had to render. I am not aware of the existence of a diary kept by any of these men before 1870. We have one from a contractor on the Scotswood Newburn & Wylam Railway, compiled while it was being built in 1872–5;[68] bare and brief, limited to recording the amount of work done each day, with notes of the weather as it affected the men employed, and not much more.

No large established contractor set his face against railway building, like some civil engineers, or was shut out of it. Here there *was* some transfer of experience. Brassey and Peto had both been involved in general building before they got their first railway contracts; George Burge had worked with Telford. The Nowell family, who began as stonemasons at Dewsbury, went on to build for at least twenty railway companies.[69] Such men had much to contribute to the execution of the railway works they undertook. Some contractors failed. Some made modest profits and retired on them.[70] A few acquired great fortunes and advertised their success. Peto began his elaborate reconstruction of Somerleyton Hall in Suffolk in 1844 to the designs of John Thomas, who went on to do a similar job for Peto's partner E. L. Betts at Preston Park in Kent (where the result 'could hardly be drearier').[71] Brassey, on the other hand, never had a country house at all.

For a short time such contractors as these were treated as men of great power. Trollope remarked in 1856 that they had more 'to say towards the ruling of the country' than any 'sporting marquess'.[72] When the nationalization of railways was under discussion in 1865 Bagehot, writing in the *Economist*, said he thought it was desirable to transfer the business of running the railways '*to* men like railway contractors *from* men like railway directors: to those who know by experience the two contrasted classes we need say no more'.[73] But public confidence in railway contractors was undermined by the revelations that followed the financial crisis of 1866, and they then came to be suspected and vilified. Beyond their deserts. They had contributed a great deal to the making of the railway system,[74] and they had more to contribute in the future; the Scotsmen Aird, Arrol, and McAlpine outstanding among them.

Subordinates

It is difficult to assess the work done by the railway engineers who carried through minor tasks or remained residents and assistants under the leading men without attaining any substantial responsibility of their own. A few wrote reminiscences of their employment, some of them long afterwards, like Herbert Spencer.[75] Some kept diaries, for a longer or shorter time;[76] some preserved letters they received, or copies of those they wrote themselves. Let us look briefly at a number of documents of this kind.

The diary kept by R. B. Dockray is of great interest. He had worked on the London & Birmingham Railway from 1832 onwards and continued with its successor the London & North Western until his health compelled him to resign, at the age of forty-one, in 1852. He was in charge of the building of several branch lines and of important works undertaken for the railway at Camden Town in London. Only a part of his diary is known to survive. A number of the entries for 1850 bear interestingly on the state of lines at the time of their opening. He has a good deal to say of engineers and other railway men he meets – of Charles Fox's 'imagination and malevolence', of Watkin's 'dirty work', of the cleverness and cunning of McConnell; these men's faults contrasting strongly with the virtues of Robert Stephenson, whom he revered. He is at his best in matters to do with permanent way: the diary for 1860 concludes with a copy of an able memorandum he submitted to the North Western board comparing different types of rail.[77]

Then a letter-book: a very early one, of 1838–9, kept by William Johnstone while he was serving as resident engineer for the construction of the Glasgow Paisley Kilmarnock & Ayr Railway under John Miller, to whom a number of the letters are addressed. They show Johnstone contending, for example, with serious difficulties in securing an adequate supply of the right kinds of stone, especially the blocks on which the rails were to be laid. Most of it was to come from the Isle of Arran, being shipped across to Troon, but deliveries were constantly late. Other stones specified by Miller proved hard or impossible to get. Might one be used from Dumbarton in place of the unobtainable Bell Rock on the east coast?

Johnstone was twenty-seven when these letters begin, assigned to the work from Miller's Edinburgh office. He stands out in them as a careful, hard-working, able man. He was something more than a sound technician. Two of his letters[78] for example give an account of a town's meeting at Newton-on-Ayr, showing very clearly the reasons why the plans for carrying the railway through the place were thought objectionable. The company's directors took him over from Miller, making him resident engineer for the whole line when it was opened in 1840. Five months later he became general manager of the railway, and he was continued in that office by its successor, the Glasgow & South Western. He had moved from engineering into administration, and there he stayed. He died, just after his retirement, in 1876.

I am not acquainted with any personal record of this kind, written by a minor engineer, extending over the same length as the diaries kept by Vignoles and Bidder, by Pasley and Ryde, or in the field of mechanical engineering as those of David Joy.[79] But among family papers, whether in private hands or in record offices, there may well be some that are comparable in interest with T. L. Gooch's and Dockray's. I hope that future historians of railways will discover them.

A few working railwaymen did attempt to record the daily routine of their lives. One wishes there had been more.[80] Yet how could that be expected, when many were illiterate and most – apart from those in clerical work – found writing very laborious, on top of a hard day's work? A permanent-way inspector on the North British Railway (his name is unknown) kept a diary for seven months in 1848, which has survived.[81] His beat extended from Dunbar to Berwick; an anxious responsibility, for this section of the line had been seriously damaged by heavy rain, undermining structures badly built, in 1846.[82] His simple account gives a good impression of the conscientious performance of routine duty falling on a man in his position, and it is interesting for the attention he pays to signalling and the telegraph. A senior official of the Lancashire & Yorkshire Railway (his identification presents difficulties) kept a record of his daily work, informative though impersonal, in 1851.[83]

Finally we must remember Hubert Simmons, whose published account of his life as a junior employee and then a stationmaster on the Great Western Railway appeared in two small volumes at Reading in 1879–80.[84] He was a man with a chip on his shoulder. Having left the company's service, and producing his book anonymously (indicating the persons mentioned in it by the old-fashioned device of making small alterations in their names), he gives free expression to his thoughts about what he had seen. He is cantankerous, sprightly, here and there genuinely comic, unreliable in factual details and in most personal judgments; yet he presents a vigorous account of a life as it was actually lived.

The Railway Profession

By the end of the nineteenth century railway engineers formed collectively a substantial element in the whole engineering profession. No serious effort was made, however, to set up an institution for railway engineers alone.[85] Perhaps this was a pity. A corporate body concerned wholly with railway matters, including both engineers and administrators, might well have benefited the railways themselves, becoming a forum for the general consideration of policies and for useful argument about them, improving the standards of the thinking and practice of all these men.

On the other hand, British engineering undoubtedly suffered from the divisions within it, the snobberies and resentments they reflected and made worse. The profession could never speak with one voice, even when that was most desirable: as for instance in discussions about training and education. Nor, divided like this, was it well placed to negotiate on equal terms with contiguous professions that were, or seemed to be, better organized. The railway engineers refused to create a separate enclave for themselves, at a time when they could certainly have done so if they had wished, choosing instead to associate with other engineers of all kinds. Nor did they ever subsequently form cliques of their own. It was a decent, peaceable decision.

These engineers and managers went on their way quietly by themselves, though without any parade of isolation. Their subordinates, of all ranks, did the same. The railway profession as a whole became an inward-looking unit, over 600,000 strong by 1913, forming about 4.5% of the occupied male population;[86] a body of self-contained specialists within British society. Though large numbers of people were acquainted with individual railwaymen whom they met in daily business, and often held them in respect and affection as persons, the railway profession made little mark as such. Few of its members amassed large fortunes, which would have drawn attention to themselves when their wills came to be published after they died. Few had any public honours paid to them.

It is true that some railway contractors became very rich. Brassey's will was proved at £3,200,000 in 1871.[87] That was the second largest personal estate that had then been bequeathed by any British citizen, and it arose principally from railway work, in Britain and abroad. Only three other contractors, much concerned with British railway business before the first World War, left over £1 million: George Wythes (d. 1887), Sir Walter Scott (d. 1910), and Sir John Aird (d. 1911). One other man much identified with railways, and one only, died a millionaire, George Carr Glyn, and he was a banker as well. Daniel Gooch left £670,000, but that does not appear to have been made primarily out of railway engineering. Robert Stephenson and Locke left £350–400,000, Hawkshaw and Henry Robertson about £200,000 each. Among the mechanical engineers Webb stands out, with his £212,000 in 1906.

These were all of course very large sums of money, multipliable by more than thirty to arrive at a modern equivalent; and moreover, at least until 1894, death duties were negligible. But, in the general scale of Victorian commercial and industrial wealth, these fortunes were not (apart from Brassey's) outstanding; far less impressive than many of those made in shipowning and shipbuilding, in brewing and some of the textile industries.

The public estimate of these men accorded with the scale of the money they amassed. Glyn was made a peer, Moon a baronet.[88] The first railway manager to be knighted was James Allport of the Midland Railway, in 1884 (four years after he retired), followed by Fenton of the South Eastern, Oakley of the Great Northern, Findlay of the London & North Western, and then a few others. To these names may be added those of Charles Pasley and Henry Tyler, knighted on their retirement as chief inspecting officers of railways at the Board of Trade in 1846 and 1877. George and Robert Stephenson both declined British knighthoods; so did Brassey. That honour was never conferred on any other railway engineer during the reign of Queen Victoria, or on any railway contractor save William Arrol at the completion of the Forth bridge.

5

THE ARTIST'S EYE

Early Prints and Drawings · Bourne and his Contemporaries ·
Paintings · Portraiture · Caricature · Photography ·
The Cinema · The End of the Age

Early Prints and Drawings

There are few satisfying pictures of the early, horse-worked railways. Of those we have, nearly all are illustrations of the rails, of the coal wagons they carried, and of details of equipment, engraved for publication in books dealing with the railways' technology. Some of them were skilfully executed: notably those in the Frenchman Gabriel Jars' *Voyages Métallurgiques* (1774–81). An elaborate engraving of 1750 by Anthony Walker showed Ralph Allen's wagonway at Bath in relation to his mansion, Prior Park, and a good water-colour drawing of the Causey Arch was made by J. Atkinson in 1804.[1] Railways figure incidentally in pictures of some of the large industrial undertakings that made use of them: the ironworks at Coalbrookdale[2] and Penydarren,[3] the Penrhyn slate quarries in North Wales.[4]

None of those pictures was produced with the sole purpose of showing a railway train, hauled by a locomotive. John Dobbin was perhaps the first to attempt that, when he watched the opening of the Stockton & Darlington Railway in 1825.[5] With the opening of the Liverpool & Manchester line in 1830, publishers soon started to offer pictures of the railway at work. Four important sets of views of it were produced in 1831: three in London from the well-known firm of Rudolf Ackermann, the fourth in Liverpool by I. Shaw, from his own drawings.[6] Ackermann's were issued in two separate series, of seven and six plates each, together with a pair of 'long prints', showing four complete trains. These are the most famous railway prints ever made, and they deserve their celebrity.

Five subjects were treated both in Ackermann's series and in Shaw's, all of them works of civil engineering: two at Liverpool – the Moorish Arch and the Olive Mount cutting; the skew bridge at Rainhill; the Sankey viaduct; and the crossing of Chat Moss. The same subjects figure freely among the cheap prints that were also issued at the time. These, with the longer of the two tunnels at Liverpool and the approach to the station at Manchester, were the works that were most evidently impressive.

Everything is of course depicted as new, the stonework unblackened by smoke. There is need for caution here, a caution that applies to all coloured prints. Though aquatints issued by good publishers like Ackermann were doubtless coloured to some instructions, lithographs and engravings were normally turned out in black and white line, to be tinted by print-sellers or to the orders of purchasers. Even the original colouring, where we can accept it as such, is by no means reliable. The bridge at Rainhill, for instance, is shown in Ackermann's print as between white and grey, with only a faint tinge of pink. It can still be seen today, unaltered and cleaned not long ago; built of a rich red sandstone.[7] The colouring has usually to be regarded as an artist's, designed to heighten contrasts and enliven them. As for the details of the mechanical contrivances the railway used, Ackermann's draughtsman T. T. Bury had little feeling for them (he was only nineteen when he made the first of these drawings, apprenticed as an architect to Pugin); his locomotives, in particular, are queer, waddling machines, too broad in the beam.[8] Perhaps Ackermann observed this deficiency. When he came to preparing his 'long prints' of trains, he turned instead to Shaw, who treated the engines a great deal better.

These prints must not be looked at as if they were photographs. They were the work of artists, whose eyes took in what they could but whose rendering of the things they saw was often defective because they had not understood them. Only a very few, whilst retaining their general sense of the pictorial, managed to delineate the apparatus of the railway at all convincingly.

The Liverpool & Manchester appears in early prints as a very plain piece of work, the Moorish Arch its sole flourish of extravagance. The deep-jointed masonry is strong and good, both in the bridges and in the retaining walls of the excavations. The Olive Mount cutting, on the descent to Liverpool, is awesome as it burrows through the rough-hewn solid rock. Anyone familiar with it today may think the artists have tried to render it more dramatic by exaggerating its depth. But the cutting is now twice as broad as it was then, having been widened to accommodate four tracks, and on measurement against the engine's chimney the proportions in Shaw's print appear to be right. For nine-tenths of its distance the railway ran through open country. Ackermann's prints of the view looking along the line eastwards from Liverpool and of Parkside station show us the careful arrangements made for running trains and a certain casual untidiness in everything else. The post-and-rail fencing for example is discontinuous, erected only where it might be necessary to prevent people from falling into a cutting. At Parkside the railway's pumps and water towers are encased in carefully-dressed stone; the railwayman's cottage adjoining them is a very rough structure indeed.[9]

So the Liverpool & Manchester Railway was portrayed by two observant artists, Bury and Shaw; and by other lesser men too, who had some things to add that they missed or had not thought worth recording.[10] Several valuable sets of prints came to be issued in the 1830s, depicting other railways, encouraged no doubt by the great success of Ackermann's pioneer venture.

Scotland was not to be left behind England here, and in 1831 the young David Octavius Hill, secretary of the Society of Artists in Edinburgh, produced a set of *Views of the Opening of the Glasgow & Garnkirk Railway*, beautifully composed as pictures and attesting careful observation; he could draw railway machines very well. Then came two other English series of 'views'; but they were views in a rather different sense, for both were primarily pictures of rural landscape, with the railway as an element in it. They were Dodgson's of the Whitby & Pickering Railway (1836) and Carmichael's of the Newcastle & Carlisle (1836–8).

G. H. Dodgson had been apprenticed to George Stephenson and worked under him on the line. The book for which his pictures were produced was called *The Scenery of the Whitby & Pickering Railway*, and he concentrated very happily on that. He had no machinery to bother with, for the railway was worked by horses. So while he depicted its little timber bridges with care he gave himself up chiefly to the splendid landscape it traversed, and the atmospheric effects to be observed there.[11] J. W. Carmichael was a young Newcastle artist (subsequently well known as a marine painter) with no knowledge of railways at all. He had the help of John Blackmore, the company's engineer, who supplied in words what technical commentary was required. His rendering of the crowded, lively scene at Hexham when the railway was opened there is attractive, and he set the Warden bridge, a wooden structure with abutments and piers of stone, effectively in a sharp light.

Bourne and his Contemporaries

By this time a new artist had begun work on a much larger enterprise, one of a pair that took the visual recording of railways to a level never achieved before, and seldom since.

John Cooke Bourne was a Londoner, of Staffordshire descent, and had been a pupil of the engraver John Pye.[12] He became interested in railways in 1836 when he looked at the London & Birmingham line under construction in Camden Town, half an hour's walk from his home. Fired by the excitement of what he saw – he was then twenty-two – he set himself to record it carefully.

Ills. 1, 2 Over the next three years he made an extensive series of drawings of the railway from end to end, sixty-nine of which survive.[13] He lithographed thirty-six of the drawings himself, and with the ready assistance of an antiquary and a publisher, John Britton and Charles Cheffins, these were put on sale by him in 1838–9 in association with Ackermann, Britton contributing a long introduction.

Most of the drawings were made in fine pencil, heightened by grey or sepia and Chinese white. Those that were published were issued without the addition of other colour; the varied colouring that appears on most copies of the individual prints to be seen today has been applied since. With this limited means Bourne achieved minute delicacy, combined with power; displayed in unison in his first batch of drawings, made in Camden Town in September 1836. This young man knew what he was doing; he had no need to play himself in. Five other drawings followed but only one of them was published. They show us the deep cutting past Park Village East and introduce us to the swarms of men actually engaged on the construction,[14] as well as to the crowd of spectators looking on at them at work. Bourne then takes us up to the railway's big depot above[15] and shows his mastery of the drawing of machines: from the largest ones – the accurate depiction of locomotives presented no difficulties to him – to the points in the track and the small pieces of equipment used by the men working on the line. So on to Primrose Hill, and out into the open country, to make short pauses at huge excavations and a longer one at Kilsby tunnel, the greatest single work on the line; then through Warwickshire, past Coventry (fine bridges here) to Birmingham.[16]

The publication of this set of lithographs appears not to have been a financial success. But Cheffins befriended Bourne loyally and encouraged him to go on to make another effort of the same kind, commemorating the Great Western Railway. From internal evidence it seems probable that he made some of the drawings (perhaps all) in 1840–1, directly after his work in publishing the London & Birmingham series was over; but though a few copies of the book were published in 1843, the main edition was held up until 1846.[17] The first work had been issued as *Drawings of the London & Birmingham Railway*. This one was called, more ambitiously, *The History and Description of the Great Western Railway*. Britton's long essay prefixed to the earlier publication had its counterpart in the second, written by a highly intelligent young engineer who had worked on the construction of the line, G. T. Clark.[18] Only one of Bourne's original drawings for this second work has survived, together with a number *Ill. 3* of sketches.[19]

The style of the pictures here is different. The delicacy of unadorned pencil-work has gone. The line is as firm and sharp as before, but now makes a broader effect. The countryside through which this railway ran was a more appealing one, crossing the watershed between the Thames and the Somerset Avon; and here the landscape is sometimes treated almost as elaborately as the railway. But it never takes over.

In this second book Bourne brings us face to face with the railway in service. At Swindon he conducts us inside the works to see the locomotives under repair. At Bristol he depicts the means of handling goods, passing between the railway and the waterway beneath it. And on the title-page of the book is a splendid demonstration of the steam engine's power, as *Acheron* bursts out of the Romanesque portal of No. 1 tunnel at Bristol. It is a wonder that the whole edition was not sold immediately on the strength of that picture alone. But this book succeeded in the market no better than the previous one.

So Bourne had to contemplate the failure of his two magnificent efforts. He seems to have turned away from railways almost entirely. Only two more drawings of them by him are known. For a time he earned money as an engraver – the engraver for example, but not the draughtsman, of a well-known print of the railway viaduct at Knaresborough. By 1848 he had become involved with Vignoles in recording the construction of the road bridge over the Dnieper at Kiev.[20] Back in England, and apparently assisted by a legacy, he survived until 1896. His death then passed quite unnoticed.

Bourne's experience of commercial failure as a railway artist was not unique. None of his contemporaries achieved any lasting success there; still less did any of them establish a permanent reputation that rested on his pictures of railways. Yet several of them produced work of considerable merit: drawings of which prints were made, some others that were never published at all.

Pictures of railways appeared now in works not specifically concerned with them; naturally, as their sounds and movement became a familiar incident of life. T. H. Hair, for example, depicted them at work in his *Sketches of the Coal Mines in Northumberland and Durham*, showing the staithes at which they delivered coal to the ships, the winding-house of the stationary engine that drew wagons up inclined planes, and one of the ancient Wylam locomotives hauling its coal train in the light of a murky evening, an embodiment of the crudest energy.[21]

The best known of the later prints devoted to railways are the twenty *Views on the Manchester & Leeds Railway*, drawn and lithographed by A. F.Tait, with a brief text by Edwin Butterworth, issued in 1845. These plates show careful observation – particularly those of the big iron bridges on the line; and the one of the south portal of the Summit tunnel at Littleborough is a strong and faithful representation of an exceptionally powerful piece of railway architecture.[22]

Something of Bourne's delicacy reappeared in the work of William Dawson of Exeter. He was an established topographical artist, and he gave his attention twice to the South Devon Railway, which began by adopting atmospheric traction. First he depicted it in an album of water-colour drawings with the title *South Devon Atmospheric Railway*, completed in 1846. He set about the task in an entirely original way. He drew a measured survey of the line from Exeter to Totnes, accompanied by a continuous delineation of both sides of the country through which it passed, mile by mile, and of the works of the railway itself; all in water-colour. It is, so far as I know, the only attempt ever made to depict a British railway in its entirety in drawings made to scale, as it was seen by the traveller passing along it. Engineers and cartographers could produce excellent plans and maps, but the recording of landscape was not their business. Here an artist contrived to fuse all these crafts together.

Plainly Dawson had an eye to publication. But the atmospheric system was abandoned on this line in 1848, after a year's trial, bringing great loss to the company's shareholders, and anything to do with it became unpopular in Devonshire. These drawings, which are now at the Institution of Civil Engineers, remain unpublished.

Although this must have caused him great disappointment, he did not turn his back on the South Devon line. In 1848 he portrayed it in a series of eight coloured lithographs, published by William Spreat of Exeter. These were views of the normal kind; but, delicately tinted, they had a quality of their own. He shows the line threading its way along the sea-coast and round the foothills of Dartmoor, to reach a climax at the Ivybridge viaduct. Seen from below, that looks – like all Brunel's timber bridges – fragile. But Dawson, like Brunel, knew just what he was about. The timber work and the web of iron ties between the piers are shown here exactly. The picture is an accurate statement, transfigured by the artist's vision.[23]

Another railway, which also had much to do with the sea, was being built at this time: the Chester & Holyhead. Its greatest works, the Conway and Britannia bridges, were in progress from 1845 to 1850, and their construction attracted several artists: S. Russell, for instance, a good craftsman; and George Hawkins, who stands among the best of them all. His pictures of the building of the bridges are, with Bourne's, the finest ever made in Britain that depict *Ill. 4* any works of this kind under construction. Hawkins attends meticulously to everything: the scaffolding, the stonework, the huge iron tubes and the raising of them, to stand 100 ft above the Menai Strait, with all the attendant human bustle below. His pictures are bathed in a calm, clear light, which helps to make every detail, the edge of every object he shows, more precise.

Nearly all these pictures of the 1830s and 1840s portray works of civil engineering. Some of the artists proved that they were competent to draw a locomotive or a train, but they hardly ever made that their main object. So far as we know none of them – except perhaps Dawson – had ever worked as an engineer.[24] They left the delineation of the railways' machinery to men who had the technical qualifications they lacked, some of whom (S. C. Brees, for example, and William Humber) were very respectable draughtsmen;[25] but they were addressing their fellow-engineers. We might have expected to find one set of good prints devoted to the railways' moving machines, the most striking part of their equipment, but there are none. All we have is a might-have-been, a torso, the work of a teen-age boy.

Edward Theophilus Lane came of a family of artists. Gainsborough was his great-uncle; his father was lithographer to the Queen. He was never trained as an artist himself. His bent lay towards engineering, and in 1847, at the age of seventeen, he became an apprentice at the Great Western Railway's works at Swindon. The excitement of what he saw going on around him there is apparent in his surviving sketchbooks, which include particulars of pieces of equipment that interested him and hasty notes and drawings of machines and *Ill. 24* vehicles, of the Great Western and other railways. These are jottings, no more. Presently he began to make careful drawings of locomotives, all to the same scale, seen in side elevation. There are, of a uniform size, twelve of them in *Ill. 27* water-colour. It looks as if he intended them to make an illustrated book (lithographed by his father?), comparable with the more general works on railways that have been spoken of here. But the series came to an end, uncompleted, in December 1849. He then caught typhus, and died in the following month, aged nineteen.[26]

His sketchbooks show us something of his natural talent as an artist, making serious professional notes yet touched with a boy's high spirits: here are knights in armour, one of them driving a railway engine, another on the top of its boiler, jousting with lances as if they were at a tournament. He was both an engineer and an artist in the making. Elaborate general-arrangement drawings of locomotives, tinted in order to show the parts of the machines clearly, are to be found, dating from the same time or a little earlier, and some of them are works of refinement.[27] But Lane's finished drawings are pictures of the exterior of the machines, as the man in the street saw them. The colouring here may be taken to be perfectly reliable. Lane had a special eye to that. His rough sketches of goods wagons are careful to indicate the colours in which the vehicles were painted. His work may claim to have a special fidelity to truth. Had he lived to complete it, he might have produced a set of prints comparable in quality with those discussed here.

All such publication came to an abrupt end in 1849–50, with the work of Dawson and Hawkins. Why?

By the late 1840s the railway had ceased to be an exciting novelty in Britain. It was an accepted fact of ordinary life; and not everyone thought it an agreeable fact. The boom in railway shares, and its collapse in 1847, made railways ridiculous, and hateful to those who had lost by it. Moreover, many of the artists whose work has been discussed here were very young when they produced it: Bury and Lane in their teens, Hill and Dodgson and Bourne all in their twenties. They had their way to make in the world, and they must have known – or been told by the publishers whose interest they tried to secure – that such prints as these enjoyed no great sale. Among all the sets that were issued as books, only Ackermann's of the Liverpool & Manchester went through any long series of reprints. The attention of these men soon moved to other subjects. Of the two who committed themselves most successfully to railways, Bourne abandoned them in despair and Hawkins died in 1852.

There was some call for little engravings to illustrate guide-books written for individual railways. From 1853 onwards it was met systematically by George Measom, an enterprising small publisher, who compiled a series of guides to railway systems, illustrated with numerous cheap steel engravings. Although some of these depict the railways themselves, their trains or stations or other works, the text relates mainly to the country traversed, purveying popular local history laced with shrewd (and sometimes entertaining) advertisement. They held their own for ten years and more. There were later series of railway guide-books too, of inferior interest, by R. K. Philp and others, and a number of companies came to produce guides of their own, illustrated photographically. But the railway itself seldom assumed any prominent place in these publications. Their purchasers were expected to take it for granted.

When the railways were new it had seemed worth trouble and expense to depict them with care, and display them handsomely. But only then. After that they became no more than a normal convenience of life. The years 1831–50 form the brief classical moment in British railway art.

Painting

So far as I know, the earliest extant oil painting of a railway is an attractive, simple work, apparently of the 1820s, showing the Surrey Iron Railway's wharf on the River Wandle with one of the horses that worked it, standing across the tracks, and his rider.[28] No part of the Liverpool & Manchester Railway seems to have attained the dignity of depiction in oils, at the time of its opening or for some years afterwards. Indeed, I am not aware of a single oil painting of any railway dating from the 1830s. The railway in motion was suited to the quick pencil sketch, which might without difficulty be translated into some kind of publishable print. There were of course painters of the day accustomed to depicting horses flying across the hunting field; but few of them could interest themselves in the flight of iron machinery, powered by steam.

It was an unconventional artist – the most unconventional, by far, in Britain – who first produced a great picture of a railway, with all its attributes: the iron and smoke of the engine hauling its train over a massive bridge.

Turner's 'Rain, Steam, and Speed' appeared at the Royal Academy in *Ill. 37* 1844. It sprang from an experience in the previous year, which happened to be recorded by a young woman, a stranger, who was in the same compartment with him and another old gentleman on a journey up from Somerset to Paddington. As Lady Simon, she became a friend of Ruskin's mother in later years, and she wrote down her recollection of the encounter for him.[29] Its truth to fact has been impugned, quite unjustly, owing to a mistake in the date of the railway's opening.[30] Read carefully, her account can I think be accepted as simply and straightforwardly accurate. It was a night train, travelling through a fearful storm up to Swindon. During the wait at Bristol, having tried to clear the window with his cuff, Turner let it down with the young lady's permission and leant out, watching the scene on the railway for nearly ten minutes; at her importunity he then allowed her too to see it for a moment. She found the drenching worth while. When the picture was first exhibited, she said to a bystander who condemned it as 'a ridiculous conglomeration': 'I was in the train that night, and it is perfectly and wonderfully true'.

The train is moving westwards across the bridge in the early morning light. The setting of the picture has nothing to do with Bristol, or with darkness– though the fire in the engine's belly may well have been one of the things Turner observed at night-time in Bristol; the sun glints on the brass sheathing of its haystack firebox. Turner regarded such machines themselves as repellent and stated that he had put this one into his picture 'to show what I can do even with an ugly subject'.[31] It has been rightly said that he 'was painting not a view of the Great Western Railway but an allegory of the forces of Nature, cast in the form of a landscape'.[32] He had depicted and commented on the Industrial Revolution in the past, in Coalbrookdale and at Newcastle.[33] This picture is, like most of Turner's later works, primarily a study of light. It was 'one of the great tributes of the Victorian age to steam',[34] and it displayed an intensity of vision that no painter ever devoted to a British railway again.

Perhaps the first ambitious oil paintings intended solely to depict a railway structure came from D. O. Hill in Scotland. The interest aroused in him by the Garnkirk line did not leave him. He knew the Edinburgh engineer John Miller, and they seem to have thought of collaborating in an illustrated book dealing with the Glasgow Dumfries & Carlisle Railway. If so, the idea was dropped. But, perhaps in connection with this project, Hill produced two large oil paintings of the Ballochmyle viaduct on that line, which pay a proper tribute to a magnificent work of engineering. Here the main arch, accurately depicted as high and wide beyond any other railway bridge, leaps across an Ayrshire river, portrayed with no less truth to nature as romantic.[35]

The passage of a train now sometimes formed an element in a landscape composition: for instance in a water-colour of Ely, perhaps by Edward Duncan, showing the cathedral towering up above trails of smoke, partly made by a railway engine.[36] David Cox's water-colour 'The Birmingham Express' (1849),[37] showing the distant train in the moonlight under a plume of smoke, certainly owes something to Turner, though not in the depiction of the train. Cox had a special purpose here: to show the contrast between the horse, symbolizing 'the old natural order of sublime power', and the smoke and fire of the train, representing the new.[38] Occasionally a painter set himself to commemorate some modern event, like the gay arrival of the Queen and Prince Albert at King's Cross on their way to the York races.[39] Some interest now comes to be shown in the railway as a carrier of people, the artists beginning to look inside the train, as Charles Rossiter did on a Brighton excursion.[40] Or they may use it as a setting for a story. Abraham Solomon's pair of paintings, 'First Class: the Meeting' and 'Second Class: the Parting', became famous directly they were exhibited at the Royal Academy in 1854, though the dictates of a ludicrous propriety obliged the artist to produce a different version of 'First Class' in the following year.[41] It was also in the 1850s that painters began to see the railway platform as the setting for anxious departures. Robert Collinson managed this well in 1855 in his 'Return to the Front', showing a soldier at Waterloo taking leave of the girl he loves on his way back to the Crimea.[42]

Such works as these form a prelude to the most famous (though not the best) of all railway paintings: 'The Railway Station' by W. P. Frith.

In 1851, 'weary of costume painting' as he said, Frith had turned to paint a scene from the modern world, in a picture called 'Life at the Seaside' – better known as 'Ramsgate Sands'. On its completion in 1854 he sold it for the high price of £1100 to a dealer, who in turn sold it to the Queen. His 'Derby Day' (1858) brought in a good deal more money, and in 1860 Frith determined to apply his abilities and experience to another picture, at first called just 'A Railway Station'. It was set at Paddington, and Frith was aided by photographs (taken in the open air) of a Great Western train.

The first pen-and-ink sketch of it, drawn out on the back of an envelope, survives,[43] and shows already much of the character of the finished work, nearly the whole of its 'plot': the detectives arresting the criminal, the foreigner in argument with his cabman, the agitated family hurrying to the train.[44] Frith offers a careful study of the station itself; nowhere else can we appreciate so well the original swirls of the tracery in the end windows, evolved by Brunel and Wyatt ten years before.[45]

Ill. 38

Ill. 39

Ill. 40

[128]

33 George Stephenson in later life: engraving
from a portrait by John Lucas

34 Robert Stephenson (left) and Brunel (right) at the final launching of the
Great Eastern steamship in Jan. 1858. They both died in the following year. In
the centre, Lord Alfred Paget

35 The Scottish engineer John Miller: engraved from a painting by A. C. Baird. The Almond viaduct on the Edinburgh & Glasgow Railway appears in the background

36 T. E. Harrison, chief engineer of the North Eastern Railway. Portrait by William Ouless

37 Turner's *Rain, Steam and Speed* (1844)

38 Robert Collinson's painting *Farewell to the Light Brigade*
Waterloo station, 1855

The first idea for the picture of the Railway Station by W. P. Frith

39 First sketch by W. P. Frith for *The Railway Station*

40 The finished picture (1862)

41 Anonymous caricature of 1832: the upper classes fleeing the
invasion of the people

42 One of the satirical drawings by C. A. S.
(see p.147)

He shows the Queen how to manage a Train.

He does an extraordinary number of Lines!!

He is crowned!! The world is at his feet.

43 Sketches of George Hudson by 'Alfred Crowquill'
(A. H. Forrester), 1849

MANNERS · AND · CVSTOMS · OF · Yᵉ ENGLYSHE · IN · 1849 ·   Nᵒ · 19 ·

A · RAYLWAYE · MEETYNGE.   EMOTYON · OF · Yᵉ ŞHAREHOLDERES AT Yᵃ ANNOVNCEMENTE OF A · DIVIDENDE OF · 2ᵈ ¼

44 Richard Doyle's depiction of a shareholders' meeting in *Punch* in 1849,
during the reaction from the Mania (17 *Punch* 32)

45 George Cruikshank foresees the extension of excursion trains overseas
in 1850

THE MODERN DICK TURPIN; OR, HIGHWAYMAN AND RAILWAYMAN.

Ghost of Turpin. "HO-HO, MR. DIRECTOR! DOING A BIT IN MY LINE, EH?"
Railway Director. "YOUR LINE? HA! HA! YOU WERE HANGED! WE ROB BY ACT OF PARLIAMENT!!!"

46 John Tenniel expressed his intense disapproval of railway directors
repeatedly in the cartoons he drew for *Punch*. The implication of this one is
that the Regulation Act of 1868, which had just then gone into force, would
serve to aid their maladministration and fraudulence. (55 *Punch* 70)

47 The earliest photograph of a railway scene that is at present known to exist. Taken by D. O. Hill and Robert Adamson in 1845, it is a general view of the town of Linlithgow, but the photographers have chosen to show the station prominently in the foreground. The waiting room can be seen on the far platform, the goods shed, a wagon, and the crane for transferring loads to and from road vehicles.

48 Down Great Western express passing Stoke Canon station, Devon, at speed in 1891. Photograph by A. J. Malan

49 An effort to treat an urban railway ornamentally: anonymous sketch for
the Liverpool Overhead Railway, perhaps of the 1870s

50 The building of the line from London Bridge to Charing Cross;
St Saviour's, Southwark (now the cathedral) in the background.
See p.166–67.

51 The Midland Railway crosses the Derbyshire Wye in Monsal Dale, giving
an impression of its intrusion very different from that
presented by Ruskin

52 A new line awaits its opening. A by-road passes beneath the Great
Central Railway's London extension near Grendon Underwood, Bucks.
Photograph by S. W. A. Newton. Note his care in depicting the details of the
post-and-rail fencing and the structure of the bridge

53 The earliest known British railway poster printed in several colours (red, white, and blue), and the earliest that depicts railway scenes realistically, not by means of printers' conventional dummies of trains. Produced for the South Eastern Railway about 1845

54 Norman Wilkinson's second poster for the London & North Western
Railway (1905), showing one of the company's ships crossing
Dublin Bay at dusk

55 Another spacious poster by the same artist for the same company (1911)

56 Poster by John Hassall for the London Underground railways (1908)

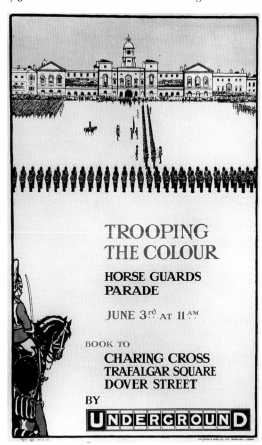

57 Clear, strong, alluring: C. Sharland, 1913

LONDON AND BIRMINGHAM

Newspaper and Advertising Office,

31, UNION-STREET, BIRMINGHAM,

AND 7, THAVIE'S INN, LONDON.

———

MESSRS. MANSELL AND CO.,

VENDERS OF EVERY DESCRIPTION OF DAILY AND WEEKLY
NEWSPAPERS,

Forward from the Office in London, Second Editions of the
Evening Papers, and from Birmingham, Daily Morning
Papers, which arrive early in the Afternoon, and are immediately posted or sent per parcel to Liverpool, Manchester, and all the intermediate Towns, the same day.

M. and Co. will have made such arrangements at the
opening of the London and Birmingham Railway, which
will enable them to dispatch Newspapers with the utmost
facility.

31, UNION-STREET, BIRMINGHAM.

58 The early days of the carriage of
newspapers by rail: advertisement from
*The Grand Junction, and the Liverpool and
Manchester Railway Companion* (publisher
J. Cornish, Birmingham, 1837)

59 W. H. Smith's bookstall at Crystal
Palace (High Level) station, 1907; the
date is supplied by items from the
newspaper bills

60 This membership certificate of a Great Eastern Railway pension fund,
designed about 1913, alludes to a number of its activities. The portraits are of
the chairman (Lord Claud Hamilton) and of the secretary of the fund,
G. Thurston. The armorial bearings assumed by the company include those
of the counties it served, with the City of London's in the centre

The picture was immensely successful. On seeing the earliest oil sketch the dealer Louis Victor Flatow agreed to buy it on its completion, paying Frith £4500 for it, a price Frith called 'one of the most exorbitant on record'. He went through some despondency as he worked – 'damped by the indifference of my artist friends', he noted at one point[46] – but he completed the picture in March 1862. Flatow then put it on exhibition for seven weeks, hanging on its own, when over 21,000 people paid to see it, and he sold engravings of it in large numbers.

'The Railway Station' was well remembered in later years. But it was never imitated. Whatever might be thought of the quality of his work, the effort that Frith had put into its painting stood out clearly enough, and nobody thought it worth while to depict a large crowd scene on a railway again. It brings to an end the main development of railway painting in the Victorian age, though that had an aftermath, of fresh interest, beginning in the 1880s. Other forms of graphic art now call for attention.

Portraiture

The portraits of the great pioneers of railways are seldom impressive. George Stephenson sat several times in his later years, but the painters were apt to treat him rather timidly, and they only hint at the ruggedness there must have been in his face. That can however be clearly detected in the one by H. P. Briggs.[47] There are fewer of his son Robert. George Richmond's crayon is a charming drawing, but slightly bland;[48] the photographs of him are more convincing. Brunel was treated with fuller insight by J. C. Horsley, who knew him well.[49] Gooch was fortunate twice, in a daguerreotype and in the rich formal portrait of him painted by Sir Francis Grant in 1872.[50] Some of these men were perhaps better commemorated by sculptors: E. H. Baily's statue of George Stephenson,[51] Marochetti's of Robert (still where it ought to be, at Euston), and Theed's of Henry Booth in St George's Hall, Liverpool.

Ill. 33

Ill. 34

Railway companies occasionally commissioned portraits of chairmen, either out of their own funds or by subscription. Works of this sort might be paid for by the companies' officers and servants, such as the portrait of Charles Russell, chairman of the Great Western Railway, painted by Grant in 1852 and hung behind the chairman's seat in the board-room at Paddington station. It came to take its place in folk-memory. When a servant of the company was summoned to attend a board meeting, either as a witness or as a delinquent, he was said to be 'going to see the picture'.[52]

A number of the large companies assembled collections of official portraits. The North Eastern directors made a special effort of this kind. In 1898 they decided to erect new offices for their headquarters at York, and they formed a collection of portraits of the company's chairmen for the board-room there. They secured representations of the eight chairmen of the company since its establishment by amalgamation in 1854 (six oil paintings and two photographs); the last of the line, Lord Knaresborough (1912–22), had his portrait added in due course. In addition there were portraits of a number of the company's chief officers, hanging in the adjacent ante-room. The moving spirit in this business was the aged Henry Tennant, who had been general manager from 1871 to 1891, became a director, and was joint deputy-chairman in 1905–10.

The portraits are still in their place today. British Rail has cared for them well. It has added a reproduction of a portrait of George Hudson (who would not have figured here with the approval of some of the other sitters) and published a useful account of the collection as a whole.[53] The pictures are nearly all the work of the well-known academic painters to whom official bodies customarily gave such commissions: Lowes Dickinson, William Ouless, Sir George Reid, R. G. Eves. They are dignified, extremely sober – even sombre – in their general tone, lightened only at one point by Tennant's venerable white beard. Taken together, they form a very good representation of the public face of a great railway company, which enjoyed high respect and usually deserved it.

Ill. 36   Tennant's portrait is memorable, but it is that of a patriarch. The outstanding representation in the whole series is surely Ouless's of T. E. Harrison, the company's chief engineer. His portrait in this collection, painted towards the end of his life, shows him well: a four-square powerful man, his hair untouched by grey but his face seared with lines, from the responsibilities he had carried. The picture is a noble commemoration of one professional man by another.

Caricature

As soon as the steam-worked railway began to carry passengers, it invoked hostility: from those who wished it to fail, who envied its wealth, feared its power, and resented the social changes it brought or threatened in the future. They ridiculed it by every means at their disposal, in words and in many sorts of caricature. Written satires must take their place with other literature later in this book; and the treatment here of satirical drawings needs to be read with reference to what is said there.

The Liverpool & Manchester Railway had the misfortune to invite one kind of attack immediately. What could show the dangers of steam traction better than the killing of an ex-Cabinet minister during the opening ceremony? Though the accident to Huskisson was not itself a seemly subject for caricature, it reverberated through the minds of all those who were nervous about railways and formed a good basis for demonstrating the dangers inherent in them. In 1831 two horrifying pictures appeared. One, 'Caught on the Railway', presented a Liverpool & Manchester locomotive relentlessly trampling down people in its path while its nonchalant driver and fireman read a newspaper. The other, 'The Inconveniences of a Blow-Up', illustrated what to many people seemed the most dreadful of all the dangers they would confront on a railway: the explosion of the engine's boiler.[54] As for social change, that was quickly seized on, in the displacement of horses and stage-coaches and all that

[146]

went with them[55] and in the invasion of select retreats by the common people, brought in by the railway. As early as 1832 the anticipated effects of one to serve Brighton were spelt out, in terms unflattering to everyone, the sufferers *Ill. 41* included. All these themes were repeated often in later years. The satire did not come only from professional artists. One set of ten spirited drawings depicting railway absurdities and disasters has survived, apparently from about *Ill. 42* 1840, signed only with tantalizing initials.[56] The Mania of 1844–7 was rich in absurdities that were good meat for caricaturists. They quickly pounced on their opportunities. But to make their satire generally intelligible they needed a popular image, a bull's-eye in the centre of the target; some institution or – much better – a single person. And when the speculation got going the right person was there, evidently in the thick of it: George Hudson.

Hudson has a place in the history of popular art. He was the first Englishman from the middle-class commercial world (neither a royal person nor a politician nor a naval or military commander) who was made by the caricaturists into a familiar image, recognizable at once. His physical characteristics rendered that an easy task. He was bulky and had an appetite for banquets; loud, coarse-spoken, overbearing. But those qualities alone would have made him no more than a windbag. He had others besides, and his tormentors knew it. They admired his ceaseless energy and perceived that his abilities made him formidable, even if some of them from the beginning set him down as a bad hat. However unwillingly, they found him engaging, which produced another spice thrown into the fun they had with him. He became a character, something more than a pasteboard figure of wickedness and cunning. And to crown it all, he himself enjoyed publicity, and appreciated what it could do for him. He was temperamentally good-natured, and wise enough to conceal resentment. What a triumphant performer Hudson might have made in certain kinds of television today!

He was helped by the nickname he acquired, The Railway King.[57] That enabled *Punch* to show him in 1845 holding a *levée*,[58] approached by peers and a dignitary of the Church on their knees. (The greedy persons who toadied to him were usually treated by the satirists a good deal more harshly than Hudson himself.)

The liveliest of the fireworks thrown at him on his fall was the set of drawings published in 1849 as *How he Reigned and How he Mizzled*, by Alfred Crowquill – *Ill. 43* i.e. Alfred Henry Forrester. The medium was well suited to its purpose: a set of pen-and-ink sketches, mere outlines and no more. They indicate Hudson's girth, his ponderous movements, and his nonchalant, irresponsible gesturing, more effectively than any other pictures.

Punch was now fastening firmly on the railways. Richard Doyle included two memorable scenes, of a shareholders' meeting and of Swindon refreshment *Ill. 44* room, in his delightful satire on 'The Manners and Customs of the English', published there in 1849–50.[59] One of the paper's artists, who worked for it from 1850 to 1901, took an unceasing interest in them from a special point of view. This was John Tenniel, remembered now pre-eminently as the illustrator of *Alice in Wonderland* and *Through the Looking-Glass*. He felt it as 'his mission to strike at fraud and corruption',[60] and he saw railways riddled with those two vices, as well as a cynical disregard for their passengers' safety and for the welfare of their own servants. In 1868 he treated the railway director as a highwayman;[61] in 1891 a railway company became a murderer, with Death gloating as a train approached a faulty bridge.[62] These are only two examples of Tenniel's constant watchfulness for what he thought of as the railways' criminal negligence.[63] *Punch* gave serious and unrelenting attention to their misdeeds, and very seldom commemorated their exploits.[64]

Ill. 46

Victorian Britain never threw up a pictorial satirist of genius, like Daumier. He fixed his eyes on railways too; but the contortions of his managers and of the victims of their callous incompetence confront us with a world of black comedy that is at a much higher level of creation.

Photography

Photography gradually came to play a part in the recording of the railways' work and in the depiction of their structures and machinery. They were not quick to make use of it themselves, and no strong demand for photographs of railway scenes and objects, for any purpose, became apparent before the 1880s. This rather slow development is largely to be explained in terms of the evolution of photographic techniques, the limitations they imposed on the kinds of pictures that could be produced, and the successive removal of them one by one.

Though the first photographs had been taken in France in the 1820s, and great improvements had been effected by 1839 in the processes and materials used in producing them, the practice of this new craft was expensive and very laborious at first, and that confined it to the wealthy. Daguerreotype pictures, on metal plates, became available in the 1840s, but they required a long exposure and suffered from the drawback that no copies could be made from them, each picture remaining unique. Fox Talbot had already offered a means of multiplying copies in 1839–41, from paper negatives; but from 1847 onwards the glass plate gained general acceptance.

Ill. 47

None of this new technology appeared specially or immediately applicable to railways. The earliest known photograph showing a railway scene is one of Linlithgow, with its station in the foreground, taken by D. O. Hill and Robert Adamson, probably in 1845.[65] Of about the same date is the famous daguerreotype of Daniel Gooch standing beside a model of a locomotive: one of his own early machines, of the *Fire Fly* class. It has traditionally been dated to 1845, and that must be about right.[66] The posture is stiff, as it had to be on account of the long exposure required. But here we can see the young man (he was not yet thirty) exactly as he was, sure of himself without arrogance or smugness. It is a quiet memorial of achievement.

In April 1847 we hear that Brunel was making use of daguerreotypes of engineering drawings to communicate instructions to railway projectors in

Austria and Italy.[67] Other engineers were now showing this interest too. Though Vignoles is not known to have employed photography in his work on railways, he used it extensively in the building of the Kiev road bridge, where his photographers were John Bourne and Roger Fenton, and he was himself a founding member of the Photographic Society of London in 1853.[68] From the early 1860s onwards John Fowler secured photographic records of the building of the underground railways for which he was engineer.[69]

Beyer Peacock of Manchester, a new firm of locomotive manufacturers that quickly became one of the most enterprising and successful in Britain, adopted in 1856 the practice of photographing each machine they made before it left the works. C. F. Beyer, the founder of the business, had himself experimented with daguerreotypes but now settled on Fox Talbot's methods for this purpose. He was looking to the market in foreign countries and used the photographs to advertise the firm's products. They were among the most elegant railway engines of their time, and he was fortunate in persuading a good photographer, James Mudd, to turn to this work, as a change from landscape and portraits.[70] Some other manufacturers of railway appliances followed the same practice. The Gloucester Wagon Company photographed all its products with care, placing a newly-painted board beside each vehicle, giving its particulars.[71]

Railway companies gradually came to appreciate the services that photography could render to them, and took one or more photographers on to their own staff. The London & North Western established a photographic department at Crewe Works in the mid-1870s.[72] The Midland appointed Thomas Scotton its official photographer in 1882, with his son as an assistant in the following year. They were employed on many tasks, photographing machines at Derby works, recording the condition of civil engineering structures, and taking pictures of accidents as soon as possible after they occurred, in order to provide some evidence that would be exact beyond dispute.[73]

At the same time some companies began to consider putting photographs inside their carriages, depicting scenes and places of interest on their systems. In 1884 Wilson Worsdell, locomotive and carriage superintendent of the Great Eastern Railway, commissioned a photographer, Payne Jennings, for this purpose.[74] Four years later the Lancashire & Yorkshire company experimentally fitted up one of its carriages with photographs of landscape.[75] The idea came to be generally accepted, the expenditure on it approved. In 1892–3 the Midland's photographers were heavily engaged in taking pictures all over the system, to meet this need.[76] Then in 1895 the Great Western Railway began to use coloured photographs supplied by the Photochrom company; within five years they had come to be placed in many of the carriages on that line.[77] Most of these pictures, though not all, were conventional views of the obvious. But, even so, they had something better to say to the passengers than the dismal and dirty metal advertisements they replaced. They may well have turned the minds of some of those who looked at them towards the idea of visiting Porlock or Ely or the Derbyshire Wye.

On their side, some commercial photographers were now offering pictures of what they considered outstanding railway structures, for sale to the public. G. W. Wilson had initiated this practice with fine photographs taken in Cornwall and his own Scotland in the early 1860s. Presently it was taken up by other large firms, like Frith's and Valentine's.

All this photography was confined to static scenes. But in the 1880s, with the introduction of more sensitive chemicals, it became possible to take satisfactory pictures of objects in motion; and since railway trains then moved faster across the ground than any other objects, they presented photographers with a challenge to their new techniques. It was not a challenge of much direct interest to the railways themselves, but it appealed to some amateurs. Let us look at one of them, A. H. Malan, vicar of Altarnun in Cornwall.

From about 1883 onwards, when he was just over thirty, he set himself to make some photographic records of locomotives and trains on Brunel's Great Western Railway, in the closing years of its operation on the broad gauge. He seems to have taken his summer holiday on the railway each year, at Newton Abbot perhaps or at Weston-super-Mare, though not east of Swindon. Among his surviving photographs[78] the earliest that are dated are of engines at rest, *Ill. 48* but the later ones extend to trains in motion, hauled by machines of the *Rover* class, the final version of Gooch's express engines of 1847. They show that the photography of trains running at speed was now being mastered.

Malan took great pains over his work. He was careful to note the atmospheric conditions at the times when his pictures were made, and any other details that might affect them specially. They were always carefully composed. He liked to photograph express trains on lines that were level, or nearly level, inland from Weston and in the vicinity of Exeter, where they would be travelling at about 60 mph; not where they were running fastest, towards the foot of the descent to Wellington, for there steam would be shut off and the plumes of white smoke that were an important element in his pictures would be absent. He accorded the same close attention to depicting the engines when they were standing still. Every detail of their bright copper and brass, their varnished paintwork, stands out. The broad-gauge railway cast a spell over many of those who saw it. No one recorded it more faithfully than this Cornish clergyman with his eyes, his mind, and his camera.

The photographic recording of lines of railway, under construction or newly finished, continued from its beginnings in the 1860s as commissions were given to photographers by engineers or contractors. In 1864–1901 photographs were taken of a number of railways in northern Scotland: the Highland, the Callander & Oban, the West Highland and its Extension.[79] The erection of the train-shed at St Pancras was photographically recorded in 1867–8.[80] In 1872 John Baylis, contractor for the line from Mansfield to Southwell, sent the Institution of Civil Engineers an album of photographs of its chief engineering works, taken by A. E. Cox of Nottingham, hoping it would show that 'the most *ordinary* of our railway works may be treated artistically by photographers', and adding that he intended to commission photographs of other lines too.[81] Frank Sutcliffe of Whitby took a number of pictures of the difficult construction of the line from his town northwards to Loftus between 1875 and 1881.[82]

Another commercial man tackled a similar task in the 1890s; similar, but a great deal more ambitious. S. W. A. Newton of Leicester, young then and excited by the building of the Sheffield company's extension to London, set himself to record as much as he could of the whole operation, as well as that of constructing the associated line from Northolt to Princes Risborough in 1901–6. Nothing less than the whole would satisfy him. The track and its bed, *Ill. 52* the structures that carried it and the machinery that eased the task of making them (especially the mechanical excavators), the trains that ran on it, the stations and warehouses, large and small: he looked at them carefully and recorded what he saw. But he turned his sharp eyes elsewhere too, particularly on to the men who were engaged in the work. He paid little attention to those at the top. It was the contractors' men, the navvies, who interested him most, the work they did, the way they did it, the lives they led. He took up with his camera the same task as Bourne had set himself with his pencil on the London & Birmingham and Great Western Railways seventy years before, and he performed it faithfully over almost exactly the same distances, but on a far larger scale. His work extended over ten years, Bourne's over less than three; about 1100 of his negatives survive, against less than 100 of Bourne's drawings and sketches.[83]

That is not a comparison of the quality of these two men's work, merely a statement about its scale. Newton's photographs are never in the top class of their age. (It would be no more sensible to suggest that Bourne drew as well as Ingres.) But they are honest work, directed by an observant eye, and some of his portraits of the men he watched are exceedingly good. They are not just records of fact, of the way in which craftsmen went about their tasks. They are informed by sympathy, and they evoke character.[84]

The great majority of the artists whose pictures have been mentioned were looking at the railway as one element in the scenes they portrayed; and they were making, in whatever medium, a single picture, or a series commissioned by an engineer or a contractor. Bourne, at the very beginning of the Victorian age, and Newton at its end stand apart. They set themselves to work, over long periods of time, to depict the creation of the railway on the ground and to comment on the men who, in the simplest physical terms, made it.

The Cinema

One branch of photography, as it began to emerge at the end of the Victorian age, was by its very nature specially well suited to railways. We have seen something of the effort made in the 1880s to produce a satisfactory still image of a moving object on a glass plate. Fresh experiments followed, in the attempt to achieve a 'moving picture' corresponding to the motion of life itself. In 1895 the brothers Auguste and Louis Lumière presented a successful programme of short films in Paris, which included a portrayal of the arrival of a train at La Ciotat station, not far from Toulon. It was a continuous scene 49 ft in length. These films were shown in London early in 1896, and in the course of that year another one was made in England, of the same length, also of the arrival of a train on its way to Watford. In Scotland in the following year, it seems for the first time, a camera was placed on the front of a locomotive, to make a film nearly six times as long entitled 'Railway Ride over the Tay Bridge'.[85] A number of similar films were made, mostly on the London & South Western Railway in Devonshire, in 1898–1900. Then in 1905 and 1911 came two much longer and more ambitious films of scenes on British railways, directed by the American Charles Urban. They showed the building of locomotives at Crewe and Swindon. These, and other films of industrial processes made at the time, were early 'documentaries'. They laid the foundations of distinguished work, for which Britain later became celebrated.

The railway companies in whose shops they were made were then sedulously promoting the holiday and tourist business, and someone concerned with publicity on the London & North Western was quick to seize on the motion picture as an instrument well adapted for use in it. Three substantial films were made on that railway's system. One, by Urban's company, depicted North Wales as 'The Land of Castles and Waterfalls', with scenes linked by shots taken from a train. The others, produced by the Kineto company and issued in 1909, were quite frankly advertisements, one more than 100 ft long.[86]

These were special efforts, and must have cost a good deal of money. But moving pictures were already growing to be accepted as a useful element in the ordinary plans of publicity that most railway companies were adopting. The Great Western was into this business by 1904 and co-operated in the making of two quite ambitious films shot in Cornwall in 1912.[87] In 1911 the Metropolitan included films in its comprehensive plans for advertising the attractions of the rural districts it served.[88]

Although these films were not of any high aesthetic merit, they displayed a successive mastery of new techniques and a quickly-advancing skill. They revealed something of the potential that the railway offered to the cinecamera in the future, preparing the way for the finished works of art that emerged in the years between the wars, crowned by *Night Mail*.

The railway took its place very early as a setting for scenes in film drama. These were numerous in the United States, and had grown almost commonplace there before 1914. In Britain there were fewer of them. One, however, shows us very plainly the changing popular attitude towards the railways themselves. A British serial with Lieut. Daring RN as its hero includes an episode 'Lieut. Daring and the Plans of the Minefields', in which there is a chase from London to Folkestone.[89] The villains pursuing him travel by train, but the glamorous hero wins by making use of all the other kinds of transport: bicycle, motor-cycle, car, and aeroplane. The railway has here become, by implication, the haunt of the wicked. For these cinema audiences in 1913, it had evidently also become slow.

The Close of the Age

Frith's 'Railway Station' had owed its success, in part, to the moment at which it was painted. In that as in everything else he showed a keen sense of the market. The market very soon declined. The railways then came under some public reprobation for what were, or were thought to be, their misdoings, and an artist with an eye to selling his picture would not be likely to choose any subject connected with them. When they next received attention it was from Frenchmen, who can have had little expectation of finding buyers for their pictures in England.

A number of French painters, notably Monet and Camille Pissarro, crossed the Channel during the Franco-Prussian war of 1870–1 and lived for some time in or near London. Monet paid attention to Turner during his stay there. He saw 'Rain, Steam, and Speed' at the National Gallery, and that may have influenced the pictures he painted later of the Gare St Lazare in Paris. When, on a series of visits to London in 1899–1904, he produced his splendid series of paintings of the Thames, the harsh solidity of the railway bridge at Charing Cross entered powerfully into some of them. It would certainly not have occurred to an English painter that *that* could ever have anything to do with poetry.[90]

Pissarro settled for a time in the London suburb of South Norwood, and while he was there he painted a scene on a railway.[91] The railway itself is depicted in it as carefully as anyone could ask for, signal and all; but the light in the sky and the engine's smoke are what nobody but an Impressionist could have set down. As Hamilton Ellis truly remarked, the Impressionists 'were never interested in the railway as a source of drama or incident; for them it remained a purely objective visual phenomenon'.[92]

Looked at beside such paintings as these, most English pictures of the time are inert. They include some more sad paintings on station platforms, the sadness genuine enough but the portrayal of them hardly poignant.[93] In this *genre* too the French could do rather better. James Tissot, who lived in England for more than ten years of his life, twice painted platform scenes there, showing middle-class ladies at Willesden Junction and Victoria;[94] still with little to say, but with an elegant way of saying it. The Irishman John O'Connor was more ambitious, and his painting of 1884 'From Pentonville, looking West – Evening (St Pancras Station)'[95] pays a fine tribute to the inspired outline of the hotel, standing up in the smoky light. Three years later he painted another London evening scene, of Ludgate Hill. Here he underplays the railway element, seizing on the curl of smoke from a train passing over the bridge, but making it and the bridge inconspicuous, to concentrate on St Paul's, rising up (improbably slender) behind. That bridge was an eyesore, but artists loved the smoke the engines puffed out as they crossed it: rendered best of all perhaps by the American photographer Alvin Langdon Coburn in his evocative picture of 1908.[96]

In the years just before 1914 a slight but perceptible fresh interest came to be taken in railways in Britain. In painting it was to be seen in the work of at least two members of the Camden Town Group, which established itself in 1911: Charles Ginner and Spencer Gore. In his 'Victoria Station, the Sunlit Square' (1913),[97] Ginner looked across from Grosvenor Gardens to the forecourt, warmed by a shaft of sunlight and enlivened by the new General motor-buses, in their scarlet; with the homely muddle of houses along the Wilton Road and the campanile of Westminster cathedral beyond.

Spencer Gore looked at the railways themselves, though not with any desire to romanticize them. Here is a viaduct on the North London Railway at Chalk Farm with telegraph posts and signals and a train moving along it (without any obtrusive smoke), taking its place beside the Regent's Canal and a factory.[98] And here is his cheerful and decorous view of the 'temporary' station at Letchworth, opened in 1905 to serve the new Garden City; standing in the Hertfordshire countryside, before the builders' invasion began.[99]

Some good artists were coming to be involved with railway companies through poster work, the foundation of an admirable partnership in the years between the wars. (See pp. 256–7.)

Looking back over the whole of the Victorian age, we are bound to note the absence of any artist who made a name for himself by his railway commissions and then concentrated on them for a long period of time. Yet the good tradition of marine painting continued, even when ships powered by sail had given place to coal-fired steamers. Railways had visual opportunities to offer, in the complicated geometry of their tracks for instance, and photographers in America perceived them: Alfred Stieglitz, for example.[100] In Germany one painter fixed his eyes and mind firmly on railways at the end of the nineteenth century. Hermann Plauer began painting them at Stuttgart in 1896 and continued to study them with devoted attention – small pieces of their equipment grew to fascinate him as they had fascinated Bourne sixty years before – until his death in 1911.[101] No similar work appeared in Britain.

That might be accounted for by arguing that the British people did not express themselves as freely and naturally in the graphic arts as, say, Frenchmen. It is quite true that a Frenchman's portrayal of any kind of event was likely to be more dramatic than an Englishman's: whether in representing a dreadful accident, like that on the Versailles railway in 1842,[102] or the rush for excursion trains in 1850.[103] And yet it was Britain that took the lead in the depiction of railways. The aquatints and lithographs made from English drawings in the 1830s set the pattern for the prints that were produced in Europe as railways appeared there, in one country after another. Moreover, the decline of interest in railways on the part of artists is to be noted also in the poets, the novelists, and the writers for the stage.

The true explanation must be sought elsewhere, in the changing habits of thought of people in Britain as they came to live with these machines – above all as they came to use them, more intensively than any other people in the world. Their special familiarity with railways bred, not indeed contempt for them but indifference.

[154]

6

THE RAILWAYS' VANDALISM

Types of Vandalism · Some Early Battles · Ancient Towns ·
The Beginnings of Protest · London · The Curbing of
Arrogance · The Railways and their own Buildings ·
A Retrospect

Types of Vandalism

The main lines of the British railway system were driven through at high speed with all the energy, the conviction and power of the Early Victorians, and with a full consciousness of what was at stake: among other things, some £200 million of capital invested in the early trunk lines alone. It was a ruthless affair. Opposition had to be fought, or bribed or persuaded into acquiescence; obstacles of every kind in the railways' path to be removed. In the process a good many amenities were impaired, and much was destroyed that was of beauty, of historical interest or antiquarian value. The only powerful group of people who protested at all frequently against the building of the early railways were landowners, anxious to preserve their estates from damage; and their protests were apt to appear merely self-interested, made with a view to bidding up the promoters into paying them higher compensation. Nevertheless, those promoters found themselves obliged to heed such protests, sometimes changing their plans in consequence. But another result emerged too. Some arguments of this kind stimulated a new consciousness of what was threatened, on the part of antiquaries, local councillors, and building developers. This is an early chapter in the history of the preservation movement; one in which government usually played little or no part, except as an ultimate arbiter. It was a battle of private interests and notions and ideals, and it prefigures a good many of the similar struggles of our own time.

The railway was, or could be, a vandal in four main ways. First, it destroyed or damaged residential property and the amenities that went with that. Second, in a broader sense, it interfered with and sometimes marred the landscape: the natural landscape, as in the Lake District or in Perthshire; the man-made parkland that had been shaped and cherished by the four generations immediately before the railway system began to develop. Third, it drove itself into and through towns and villages, sometimes disfiguring seemly streets and always carrying with it pollution. Finally, in the course of these operations the railway destroyed or injured or threatened historic buildings and sites lying on or close to its path. In the later years of the century railways forced many people to consider, more carefully than ever before, what they were prepared to sacrifice in the cause of material progress, indeed to ask themselves what 'progress' might really mean.

Of these four kinds of destruction I am concerned here chiefly with the last, with damage to historic buildings and archaeological sites, though I shall speak of others too, for none of them should be thought of in isolation from the rest. I have made no attempt to catalogue the whole of the damage that was done, or to discuss all the controversies that arose, proceeding only by way of example.[1]

Some Early Battles

The demolition of ancient buildings in the service of public improvement – particularly the improvement of transport – did not begin with the railways. Many towns in the eighteenth century had removed historic monuments in order to widen streets, or to straighten them. The High Cross at Bristol was taken down in 1733 as 'a ruinous and superstitious relic, which is at present a public nuisance'.[2] More fortunate than most monuments summarily removed in this way, it was dismantled with care and eventually re-erected at Stourhead. The City of London destroyed all its gates except Newgate in 1760. Provincial towns did the same, often in order to ease the passage of stage-coaches: Leicester for instance in 1774, Canterbury in 1781–91. Old bridges were demolished too, especially if they carried buildings that spanned their roadways, as at Chester and Bedford. The greatest of all exercises of that nature was the rebuilding of London Bridge in 1829–31. It set some precedents for what followed, in the making of railways.

The construction of the northern approach to the bridge involved the demolition of a Wren church (St Michael, Crooked Lane) and of Falstaff's Boar's Head Tavern in Eastcheap. In Southwark the first plan demanded the removal of the retrochoir of St Saviour's church (now Southwark cathedral). At this there was a very proper outcry from antiquaries, from churchmen, and from the vestry of the parish. The southern approach to the bridge was then replanned, to leave the retrochoir standing, though the bishop's chapel, an eastward extension of it, was destroyed. This demand for the retention of an ancient building threatened by a large street improvement had been almost wholly successful. Such victories, however, were most uncommon.

Although in many ways the building of the canals set patterns for the railways, in this matter they contributed little or nothing. Their course ran through open country or through modern industrial towns, where nothing lay in their path that anybody would have wished to protect. A few landowners were displeased by the sight of them, but that was all. One improvement in water transport, however, did raise an important question of this kind. The construction of St Katharine Dock, close to the Tower of London, required the demolition of St Katharine's Hospital in 1825, with its distinguished fifteenth-century chapel. However, the loudest protest here came not from antiquaries but from the occupants of the 1250 houses that were destroyed in order to allow the dock to be built.

The pre-mechanical railways were usually laid out with the easy concurrence of landlords, who could shape their course as they liked; and as long as their traffic was hauled by horses its passage was little more obtrusive than that on a road. With steam traction it was different. Lord Derby and Lord Sefton saw that and resisted the Liverpool & Manchester Railway accordingly. Their protests set an example attended to by other landowners elsewhere.

The next large railway to be undertaken, the Newcastle & Carlisle, had novel difficulties to face. It disarmed some opposition by proposing to work the whole of its 60-mile line by horse traction. Subsequently it secured consent to the use of locomotives from the owners of the land adjoining it – all except one, Charles Bacon Grey of Styford, near Corbridge. He secured an injunction against the company on this account when it began to use locomotives on his part of the line in 1835 and held out for six weeks, disorganizing all the traffic, until he was cajoled or bullyragged into accepting the violation he so much disliked.[3]

This railway was confronted by a famous antiquity. It cut through the course of Hadrian's Wall twice. But the engineers carefully avoided damage to any of the standing structure. At Greenhead the line was taken immediately east of a surviving piece of the Wall. Near Gilsland it passed right below Milecastle 48, again without damage to any visible remains.[4]

The first statutory protection to an ancient building threatened by a railway was given in 1833 to Berkhamsted castle. By the London & Birmingham's first Act[5] the company was forbidden to deviate – even within the limits usually allowed – from the authorized line where it passed by the castle; and it was also forbidden to erect any buildings, to dig earth, or to raise spoil banks at this point. Those provisions did not prove wholly effective. Then, or when the railway was widened, the line cut away part of the ditch of the castle and destroyed all traces of the approach to its barbican.[6] Still, the ruins of the castle buildings remain intact.

Further north on the same line, at Castlethorpe, the railway cut diagonally through another castle's outer defences and later established its station right on top of them.[7] Nearer to London, it drove through Grim's Dyke, a little north of where Hatch End station now stands.[8] Here a substantial diversion, through unfavourable ground, would have been needed in order to avoid the earthwork, and tunnelling beneath it would have been expensive. We cannot be surprised that it was cut through.

In the flush of their triumphant progress some railways demanded the right to demolish a building of any kind that stood in their way. The chairman of the London & Croydon company, John Moxon, enunciated this doctrine before a Commons Committee in 1839. Westminster Abbey? asked the chairman of the Committee, Lord Granville Somerset; Blenheim? Moxon, momentarily staggered, indicated that he would perhaps reprieve the abbey, but probably not the house.[9]

In the 1840s the question began to appear at its most difficult, and first in Scotland.

Two separate companies were formed to build railways entering Edinburgh, from the west and the east. The Edinburgh & Glasgow was opened in 1842. It ran to a terminus at the Haymarket, and wished to strike further east towards the centre of the city. This ambition was thwarted by the Proprietors of Princes Street, whose gardens (laid out recently at a cost, it was said, of £7000) the line would have to traverse. The Proprietors were indignant at the thought of the dirt and noise the railway would occasion, and backed by the Society of Antiquaries of Scotland they managed at first to stop its progress. But not for long. The company succeeded in a second application to Parliament for powers to build this extension. The cutting was to be shrouded behind an embankment, planted with trees and shrubs; but that was all the Act required.[10] Directly the line was opened in 1846 the insufficiency of this protection became obvious. Steam locomotives smoked, and sometimes shrieked, their way below Princes Street, at the foot of the castle rock.

Meanwhile the North British Railway, approaching from the east, was confronted by a venerable antiquity lying in its path. The railway had to tunnel under Calton Hill and emerge into the narrow valley between it and the Old Town. It needed a goods as well as a passenger station, and sought to acquire every inch of level ground. Part of this space was occupied by the Trinity Hospital, with its fine medieval church, one of the best of its kind left in Scotland. The company sought to purchase all these buildings and demolish them. The minister, the presbytery, and the town council agreed, whereupon a loud outcry arose. The Antiquaries protested to the government; but nothing could be done since the legal owners had agreed to sell, and the buildings were demolished in 1848. Plans were laid for the re-erection of the church elsewhere. All the stones were numbered and piled up, to await removal to another site. But the railway had paid £22,000, and the interested parties fell to squabbling over the division of this spoil. Squabbling led to litigation, lasting nearly twenty-five years; and by the time the wrangle was ended and the building of the new church could be undertaken many of the stones had vanished, transported we are told into 'suburban rockeries'. The remainder were duly re-used. If the railway company was the vandal here in the first instance, its guilt was surely much less than the guilt of those who should have been the church's guardians.[11]

Ancient Towns

The same company encountered an awkward antiquity at the other end of its line, the castle at Berwick-on-Tweed, which offered a convenient place for a station: high above the river at the point where a railway coming up from the south could be expected to bridge it. The ruins of the castle were extensive, and the station was planted on the site of the great hall, some of the outer walls and defences remaining intact. That did not destroy a notable fabric;

but anyone with a sense of history might feel that there was very gross insensibility in the siting of that station exactly where John Balliol had done homage to Edward I for the crown of Scotland. Though this might appear to be a Scottish revenge for a national humiliation, the North British Railway was dominated by English capital.

Other castles were maltreated by railways too: at Penrith, for instance, at Huntingdon and Clare. At Northampton a small station was established in the castle ruins in 1859. When it was enlarged in 1882, every vestige of the buildings was swept away but an arch and a fragment of one wall, which were re-erected in the road outside.[12]

Most early railways were content to remain beyond the built-up areas of towns. They often ran just outside the line of the medieval walls: at Canterbury and Winchester, Oxford and Norwich, Lancaster, Carlisle, and St Andrews. Small towns might be treated brutally: Flint for example, where the Chester & Holyhead Railway ran straight across the medieval town (on its thirteenth-century grid plan), separating the church from the castle.[13] But in the 1840s railways found themselves obliged to penetrate at least into corners of five famous historic towns: York, Chester, Conway, Shrewsbury, and Newcastle.[14]

The complex work at York has been dealt with elsewhere.[15] The York & North Midland Railway and its successor the North Eastern caused breaches to be made in the city walls to allow the passage of lines to the first permanent station, set up inside them in 1840. The piercing of the walls was managed well. The company had a good architect, G. T. Andrews, and he was required to design his arches to the satisfaction of the Yorkshire Philosophical Society, which represented the local antiquaries. The York City Council refused to permit another company to make a further breach in the walls in 1845.[16] The first permanent station was inserted into their south-east angle. Four-centred arches were cut in them by Andrews, bold and strong. As the traffic grew, the station became hopelessly cramped, until it had to be rebuilt on a different site, outside the walls, in 1872–7. This second station, the very large new hotel, and the adjoining railway lines, were placed on top of a Roman cemetery, which was excavated carefully before they were built. None of this can be fairly considered 'vandalism'. Much trouble was taken at every stage, and at every level of responsibility from Parliament to the navvies, to ensure that as little harm as possible was done to antiquities.

The second historic town that the railway penetrated was Chester, and there it inflicted no more than a slight flesh wound. The Chester & Holyhead Railway was authorized in 1844 to burrow beneath the north-eastern tip of the city walls – reasonably enough, for it would have been costly and awkward to take the line altogether outside them. The company's first Act required the walls to be preserved without interruption above the railway arches, jacked up if necessary to give sufficient headroom. The company was to pay for any damage the walls might suffer.[17] The railway's passage here was sometimes obtrusive to those who walked the walls in the days of smoke and steam. It is almost unnoticeable now.

[159]

In its course further westward the same line had to pass by the third of these towns, Conway. The conditions laid down for it at this point were more stringent than at Chester. They were designed to ensure that the new bridge should be as far as possible in harmony both with Telford's road bridge and with the castle behind, as well as to protect the town walls and the castle itself. Watchdogs were appointed in the Act to see that the work was carried out acceptably: the Commissioners of Woods and Forests and the Governor of the Castle.[18] At Conway a railway's architecture was required, for the first time in Britain, to meet an official anxiety to protect one of the principal antiquities in the island against possible 'vandalism'.

The work was in the hands of an engineer of the first rank, Robert Stephenson, and a good architect, Francis Thompson, working in collaboration. The railway ran through its tubular bridge, with a new castellated portal, right under the castle, a goods station directly beneath the walls, and a passenger station inside them; followed by a short tunnel under the north-western corner of the town.

Opinions on this work have varied, and vary still. Twenty years afterwards an engineer, William Pole, put his finger on one of the chief weaknesses of the bridge when he remarked that 'alterations subsequently introduced into the construction, and the omission of the ornamental parts to save expense, crippled the design', and that prompted a sombre generalization from him about the work going on around him when he wrote: 'The unfettered reign of private enterprise, which, under the dictatorship of the engineer, has of late so much prevailed in this country, has been no doubt a grand source of works of commercial utility, but it has doomed us to much bitter humiliation in matters of art and taste'.[19] On the other hand a distinguished modern authority on medieval building, Arnold Taylor, takes this view: 'Where there might so easily have been indiscriminate destruction, posterity can be grateful to the railway builders...for their skilful and considerate handling of the problem which the presence of the castle and walls at this particular spot posed for them'.[20]

In the fourth of these historic towns, Shrewsbury, Pevsner speaks of the railway's intrusion as 'callous',[21] and that is no bad word. The placing of the station, to occupy the neck of the peninsula on which the town stands, directly beneath the castle, is horrible. No outcry appears to have been raised in 1844–6, when the railway companies (four of them came to be concerned) sought powers to put the station where it is. A determined opposition might have forced them to site it in the empty land on the other side of the river, allowing the line going northwards to Chester to slip, almost unseen, through the narrow gully between the castle and the jail. That would however have required heavy expense in building up the ground to meet the dangers of flooding. Nothing of architectural or archaeological value seems to have been destroyed in the building of the station. Many of the houses demolished were ramshackle; several were brothels.[22] So it may well have been considered that the erection of a building that accommodated an important new public service and also removed such wretched property represented a piece of betterment.

The architect called on to design the façade of the station, Thomas Penson of Oswestry, produced a conventional essay in Early Victorian Tudor, distinguished only by a certain liveliness in the chimneys and by decent stonework. The London & North Western company's engineers subsequently treated it very badly. They rebuilt the long retaining wall of the forecourt that bordered the castle mound, immediately above, in a screaming vermilion brick, discordant with everything around it, most of all with the rich red sandstone of the castle. That remains an atrocity today.

When the railways came into Newcastle from north and south in 1847–9 they passed close to the castle and severed the keep visually from the town. Furthermore the Central station, built at this time, obliterated a stretch of the walls. Those things – the first particularly – did serious injury; one is bound to regret them still. Yet what else could have been done? If the line from the north had passed further away from the castle it would have destroyed the Jesus Hospital and impinged on the civic church of St. Nicholas (now the cathedral). Any realignment of the railway from the south would have moved the station unacceptably far from the centre of the town. Whereas at Shrewsbury there was an alternative site for the station, at Newcastle the course the railways took could hardly have been different. And if they damaged the town they also enriched it. The High Level bridge they built is a most remarkable work, the bridge over Dean Street a superb tall masonry structure; John Dobson's Central station a true civic building, one of the finest stations in Britain.

Such adornment of a town by a railway was not, alas, common. More often it did damage wherever it appeared, particularly where it thrust its iron bridges across streets: Foregate Street at Worcester, for example, or the High Streets of Leamington and Hungerford. At Derby the Great Northern Railway, crossing the noble Friargate in 1872, thought to atone for its intrusion by tricking out the ironwork of its bridge with meretricious decoration, which only emphasized the insult.

As railways were driven all over England much damage was done to sites that we should now consider archaeologically important. The prehistoric sites suffered most; little was then known about them, and the case for their protection often went unstated. Near the centre of Cheltenham a round barrow was destroyed to build a station in 1846.[23] The Lancaster & Carlisle Railway (opened in 1848) ran on a high embankment straight across a stone circle at Shap.[24] In 1857–8 the line from Blandford to Poole cut through Spetisbury Rings, an Iron-Age hill-fort.[25]

More respect was sometimes paid to Roman antiquities. When the Great Western Railway was being constructed between Bath and Bristol a mosaic pavement was found near Twerton. It was lifted, and preserved for years at Keynsham station.[26] Not far from Kendal a vigilant antiquary, Cornelius Nicholson, intervened to prevent some avoidable damage to a Roman site, though he afterwards allowed that the *agger* was 'nipped in between the railway and the turnpike road'.[27] Not all Roman sites were respected. An important railway junction was established at Normanton, near Wakefield, within a Roman camp.[28] Railways shaved the eastern wall of the fort at Richborough (Kent) and cut through the western edge of one at Ravenglass in Cumberland.

No ancient building could be thought safe if it stood in a railway's path. The remains of the hall and chapel of Tonbridge priory were demolished in 1840 for the passage of the South Eastern line.[29] Two medieval hospitals, at Oakham and Bradford-on-Avon, were destroyed in this way, though the chapel of the one at Oakham was spared.[30] As for the buildings of a later day, they often perished, though sometimes the railway itself might purchase them, putting them to incongruous use. The Red Hall at Bourne in Lincolnshire, a good Elizabethan building, was noted by Murray in 1890 as 'probably the only railway station in England that can boast of antiquity'.[31] The Eastern Counties Railway acquired a good house of Wren's time at Enfield and turned it into a station. It was used for that purpose from 1849 to 1872, when the Great Eastern company pulled it down, allowing part of the façade to be removed to the South Kensington Museum.[32] Sometimes an ancient building was bought by a railway, not used, and then demolished: the Old Hall at Ashton-under-Lyne, for instance; Hindley House, Acton.[33]

The Beginnings of Protest

In England the first important cases of the railways' assault upon antiquities that were widely noticed were at Lewes, Furness Abbey, and Dorchester.

The Brighton Lewes & Hastings Railway was permitted in 1844 to pass through the ruins of St Pancras Priory at Lewes, with its large and important church, the earliest Cluniac house in England. The results can still be seen today, coming in from Brighton on the train. The excavations revealed a substantial part of the foundations of the church and the monastic buildings; the line passed over the site of the high altar. This aroused a good deal of interest, in London as well as locally.[34] The discoveries led to the establishment of the Sussex Archaeological Society in 1848, with a view to the careful excavation and recording of similar discoveries in the future.[35]

The Furness Railway sought powers, also in 1844, to construct a line from Dalton to Barrow, at first passing right through the ruins of Furness Abbey and then altered so as to skirt them, uncomfortably close. This was vandalism indeed. The abbey itself was a major monument of Cistercian monasticism, and it stood in an exquisite site, of the kind dearest to that order, sequestered deep in the Vale of Nightshade. There was no outcry at the time, however. The ruins belonged to the Earl of Burlington (later seventh Duke of Devonshire), who was among the chief promoters of the railway. Wordsworth spoke of them as 'profane despoilers'. But that was all. By some people, however, the offence was not forgotten. Nathaniel Hawthorne noticed it with disgust in 1855. When Ruskin was offered the gold medal of the Royal Institute of

British Architects in 1874 he declined it, in protest against what he considered four public atrocities committed in his lifetime, one in Britain and three in Italy. The passage of the railway by Furness Abbey was the British one.[36]

Soon afterwards Dorchester was being approached by two railways, from the north and east. Both threatened Maumbury Rings, on the southern edge of the town. When the Act for the earlier of the two lines, the Wilts Somerset & Weymouth, was passed in 1845, there was loud protest, in which the leaders were the antiquary Charles Warne and William Barnes, the poet.[37] To some purpose. In 1846 the company was statutorily forbidden to deviate at all from its centre line as laid down on the plan, so as to approach any nearer to the antiquity.[38] Maumbury Rings is a monument of exceptional note; successively henge, amphitheatre, and Civil War fort. It also deserves recognition as the first antiquity to be saved from injury by a railway as the result of a protest made by local people, who were indignant at the threat to it; the first in Britain, probably the first anywhere.

At the same time protests began to be heard against the destruction not of antiquities but of amenities prized by outraged citizens, on broad public grounds. An outstanding case of this kind arose at Perth.

In 1844 a new company was projected, the Scottish Central, which proposed to build a large station on the South Inch, one of the two delightful open spaces by the Tay that are among the distinctions of the city. The approaches from the south and east were physically difficult, and this was a natural meeting-point of railways from those directions with one going on northwards to Aberdeen. An ample station could be erected here without any interference with existing structures. But the plan was fiercely opposed when it came before Parliament. As it happened a local artist, MacNeil MacLeay, had produced an oil painting of the South Inch in 1842; rich and delicate as a picture, and also truthful as a record. It was taken to London and exhibited to the Committee investigating the proposals. The railway company's case was supported by the Board of Trade in a report drawn up by its inspector, Capt. Coddington; but the Committee found against it. The citizens of Perth had won. The station was not built on the South Inch but on a site to the north- *Ill. 17* west of it, and the line approaching from the east was diverted to make its way past, and even through, existing buildings. The painting that took its part in this controversy now hangs in the city's Art Gallery.[39]

Railways had aroused antagonism very early by the passage they proposed to make through open landscape. Sensitive people were quickly shocked by that: the young John Stuart Mill for example, who wrote bitterly in 1836 of the line devised to run through the gorge of the Mole south of Leatherhead, on Robert Stephenson's proposed route from London to Brighton.[40] The first public statement on this matter, nationally heard, came from Wordsworth in 1844, when he attacked the Kendal & Windermere Railway scheme:

Is there no nook of English ground secure
From rash assault? ...

Those words were the call of a trumpet. Though his opposition to the railway was widely ridiculed at the time, the part of it that he specially objected to was never in fact built. The Lake District continued to be a stamping-ground of railway projectors. There and elsewhere they had to face resolute opponents, *Ill. 51* like Ruskin, who could command an extensive hearing.[41]

Not all those who objected to the railways' passage through an open landscape did so for purely aesthetic reasons. The Commissioners of Woods and Forests stopped lines being built across the Home Park at Windsor[42] and gave the Southampton & Dorchester company much trouble in negotiating a route through the New Forest.[43] They were acting as their duty required, in defence of the State property entrusted to them, and as custodians of the deer and other animals grazing there.

Some years later, in the Highlands of Scotland, there was another struggle to keep an extensive tract of distinguished landscape inviolate. When in 1860 the Inverness & Perth Junction Railway was launched, to build a line crossing the Grampians, the sixth Duke of Atholl was entirely hostile to it. Since it was to traverse his estates for no less than 24 miles northwards from Dunkeld, this was a very serious matter for the promoters. He was brought to admit that, as a through route, this railway would be useful to the public, though he declined to withdraw his opposition merely on the evidence afforded by plans. He agreed to have the line 'pointed out' to him by Joseph Mitchell, the engineer of the project. Mitchell drove out steadily with the Duke and Duchess looking at the projected railway, laid down for a length of several miles between small white flags. The Duke could then see which individual trees would have to be felled for its passage, the points at which the line might impinge on his park, and the measures that could be taken to minimize the damage it would cause.

Mitchell got his reward. In the face of these demonstrations, the Duke ceased to oppose the plan. Instead, it came to interest him, and he insisted on being conveyed over one part of it on a truck, even though he was already dying of cancer, just before the line was opened in September 1863.

The result of all this discussion was that a railway cutting through a series of rightly celebrated tracts of landscape – Birnam Wood, the Pass of Killiecrankie, and the park of Blair Castle – was managed with outstanding skill. It was delicately unobtrusive; but when it had to obtrude, its iron girder bridges were firm and bold. Here the railway was indeed no vandal. Mitchell had demonstrated that it could now tame itself.[44]

London

The London & Blackwall Railway, when it was extended to Fenchurch Street in 1841, cut through a section of London's Roman wall, $7\frac{1}{2}$ ft thick and 6–7 ft high.[45] Otherwise, the line made its timid way into the City without any disturbance of antiquities. Although in the 1840s a number of wildcat schemes appeared for building lines into the heart of London, such ideas were discouraged by the decision of Parliament in 1846 to prohibit railways entirely within a large tract of the whole city, stretching from Park Lane to Bishopsgate and from Euston to the Borough.[46] True, in 1853 the North Metropolitan Railway was granted powers to build a line within the northern limit of this territory; but that was to run underground. For the rest, the rule was maintained until 1858, when a new line was sanctioned to cross the river by Pimlico; the germ of the system at Victoria station today.

In the next year a much bolder bid was made, setting the rule of 1846 entirely aside, when the London Chatham & Dover company announced a plan for a railway bridging the Thames at Blackfriars, to run northwards through the City itself. The case, considered solely in terms of railway building, was a good one. The decision of 1846 had prevented any direct link between the northern and southern systems. The new scheme proposed to make use of the underground railway, then under construction, to form this link, so that traffic from the Great Western and the northern lines could be brought across the river for south-eastern England and for places on the Continent. The scheme also offered something useful to the City itself: a station built on the site of the Fleet Prison, long vacant and notoriously in need of what is now called 'redevelopment'. The Ward of Farringdon Without was one of the poorest parts of the City; the railway might help to give it some new life.

It was to run over Ludgate Hill by a bridge, passing straight across the front of St Paul's cathedral to anyone who looked at it westwards along Fleet Street. An attempt was made in the City both to welcome the railway and at the same time to ask that it should avoid causing this grave disfigurement. It gained little support.[47] As the plan was under discussion, outside Parliament and then in Committee there, it was occasionally criticized from this point of view. Very late in the day a proposal came forward to re-route the line, taking it under Ludgate Hill in a tunnel.[48] No one considered this plan seriously. The line was sanctioned in 1860 and opened in 1866. Then, too late, many Victorians realized the horror of what had been permitted. Here is the view of one of them: 'That viaduct has utterly spoiled one of the finest street views in the metropolis, and is one of the most unsightly objects ever constructed, in any such situation, anywhere in the world'.[49]

He was surely right. The bridge carried a heavy traffic, both passenger and goods, all of it worked by locomotives belching steam and smoke. Yet it quickly became an accepted part of the maelstrom of Ludgate Circus. When Sir William Treloar (son of one of the leading opponents of the construction of the line) came to write his history of Ludgate Hill in the 1880s, he remarked mildly that 'there were those who stood against the London Chatham & Dover's purchase of the Fleet Prison', without indicating why such people (his own father among them) had taken that stand.[50] Today, many of the trains having gone and all being electrically powered, they are not very noticeable. But the bridge is still there, as vulgar as ever.

This invasion of central London did not stand alone. In direct response to it the Chatham company's rival the South Eastern determined to undertake something similar itself: an extension of its line from London Bridge to cross the river by two new bridges, to a West-End terminus at Charing Cross and a City one on Cannon Street. These lines were brought into use in 1864–6.

The Cannon Street one involved the building of another ponderous iron bridge across the river to carry its tracks into a huge high-arched train-shed. The station displaced the surviving remains of the Steelyard of the Hanseatic League; its construction also led to the discovery, close to the mouth of the Wallbrook, of a group of large Roman buildings behind a wall 200 ft long.[51]

Ill. 50 South of the Thames, in Southwark and Lambeth, the railway wreaked havoc. It hemmed in St Saviour's – with the arm going off to Cannon Street, it clasped the church in on two sides – and then made its way at a high level westwards to Charing Cross. It had few antiquities to encounter here, but the defacing of the streetscape made sensitive observers gasp. One thing only may be said in extenuation. The injury the railway does to south London is much accentuated by its massive and hideous bridges. John Hawkshaw, the engineer who designed them, said something of interest about them in 1863:

> With regard to the Charing Cross line, I have made some bridges which I must say are ugly enough. But the law says that these bridges shall spring from the shop front on the one side to the shop front on the other without intermediate supports, and at a uniform height above the street. Then the requirements of the public with regard to preventing horses being killed give you another line ten feet above that. Those are the conditions you have to work upon. . . . I do not see how you are to produce architectural effect with such conditions. I think all attempts would be abortive, and therefore I have given it up. . . . Charing Cross terminus will be a handsome thing, which will not disgrace the metropolis. But girders cannot be adorned with any advantage.[52]

These lines damaged the face of south London irreparably. Their brutality was startling.[53] Proposals were heard in these years for elevated railways in London, running above streets, as in New York.[54] They were resisted with success, largely on the grounds of the disfigurement they would cause. A Londoner who is inclined to become smug on that point now should take a walk through Southwark under the shadow of this railway.

Still, there is much to be thankful for. The Thames Railway of 1864 proposed to construct a line on an iron viaduct down the middle of the river.[55] But it did not succeed. No other railways comparable with that or with those of the Chatham and the South Eastern companies were ever built into the heart of London. New lines indeed *were* built there; but they ran underground.

The first of them, the Metropolitan, opened in 1863, encountered no difficulties of the sort now under discussion. When it came to extending the system, precautions were taken. The Metropolitan District Railway was compelled to accept special conditions of construction within 200 ft of West-minster Abbey and was forbidden to destroy Tallow Chandlers' Hall without the consent of the Livery Company that owned it.[56] Inevitably in the course of the slow completion of the circular line through the City, some damage was caused to ancient monuments. About 70 ft of the Roman wall were removed in Trinity Place, north of Tower Hill, in 1882. In the previous year another stretch of it, including one of the bastions, had been destroyed close to America Square, to permit the line running into Fenchurch Street to be widened.[57]

In the 1860s a total of 219 Bills were brought forward for the construction of 882 miles of railway in London.[58] As the frenzy rose, and as the consequences of the plans already sanctioned came to be obvious to the eye, cries of alarm were raised. Not least by *Punch*, already at war with railway companies. In 1863 it suggested that St Paul's cathedral should be turned into a station: 'What else will it be fit for when every railway runs right into London?'[59] Next year it was warning its readers that a railway proposed to be cut through Kensington Gardens, 'the utmost conceivable atrocity of sordid vandalism', was no absurd fantasy but was actually being considered.[60] That was the first time *Punch* had used the word 'vandalism' in this connection. Next year it came in handy again, in a furious onslaught on the Great Western company for its proposal to construct new works for building carriages at Oxford. 'The Great Western Vandals at Oxford' is the heading of one of its most rumbustious assaults.[61]

It was time to resist the railways' demands, or at least to subject them to much closer scrutiny before they were granted.

The Curbing of Arrogance

A number of exemplary arrangements had by now been adopted to concede railways the passage they wished through stretches of public parkland, on terms that safeguarded the interests of those who enjoyed them. At Harrogate, for instance, in 1862 the Stray was crossed by the North Eastern Railway in a cutting (handsomely lined in stone) that hid the trains from sight.[62] Later, in 1879, the Midland company followed the same pattern in traversing Sutton Park, a much-prized tract of heathland adjoining Sutton Coldfield, north of Birmingham.

Where battles had to be fought, they did not all go in favour of the railways. One rumbled for twenty years over lines proposing to cross Epping Forest from Chingford to High Beech. Powers were given to the Great Eastern company to construct one in 1864, but they were not exercised, and when the proposal was revived in 1873 it was turned down: owing chiefly to the opposition of those who were determined to preserve what remained of the Forest, as a tract of open country accessible to those who lived in the neighbourhood and to visitors from the East End of London. Ten years later another attempt also failed, and that was final. Here we can see a well-developed 'preservationist' movement acting, as one of the same sort might now, in defence of a public amenity and winning its case.

Some promoters, however, were still set on taking their lines by routes that were likely to arouse similar opposition. The construction of any railway through the built-up area of a town – even if the line was a short one and the town not very distinguished – might now threaten serious damage to what we call the 'environment'. At Wrexham for instance a new railway, just over half a mile long, was authorized in 1886 to carry the Wrexham Mold & Connah's Quay line to a new station alluringly described as 'Central'. This did no substantial damage to the town: the land it crossed was either open and empty or occupied by breweries, which were closed or removed. In 1892–5, another railway was built to join it end-on, running to Ellesmere. Its trains then smoked their way across the streets of the southern part of the town, passing very close to its great church and demolishing numerous houses. Wrexham was a small place, however, and had no organized body of citizens to protect its interests.[63]

The closing years of the century present us with some plans for railway building that do indeed take away the breath.[64] At Norwich in 1882–3 the Lynn & Fakenham and the Eastern & Midlands Railways proposed to extend round the north side of the city to a terminus on King Street, and at the same time to link up with the Great Eastern by means of a line running straight across the Lower Close of the cathedral. The plan also included the driving of a railway across Mousehold Heath, a large open tract immediately outside the city, highly valued by its people. A hard fight was needed to get these proposals dropped.[65]

Again in 1883, we come upon what is surely the most remarkable of all such projects: for a new trunk line from London to Bristol, running over Salisbury Plain and straight across the avenue at Stonehenge.[66] The scheme failed, but only because the promoters did not make out their case for it as a desirable new railway.

Those were threats to antiquities. Others, no less alarming, continued to appear at the same time from railways wishing to violate natural landscape. One more scheme was brought forward in 1882 for a railway in the Lake District, from Buttermere to Braithwaite. In 1884 a railway sought to erect a brick bridge 80 ft high immediately over Aysgarth Force in Wensleydale. A leading figure in the hue and cry after that disgusting proposal was the novelist Ouida,[67] and it was defeated. However, six years later the Lancashire Derbyshire & East Coast Railway made this scheme into very small beer when it sought to drive the central part of its line, between Buxton and Chesterfield, across Monsal Dale on a viaduct nearly 300 ft high; and Parliament made no demur to sanctioning the atrocity.[68] That it was not in fact executed was due to the company's failure to raise the necessary money for building this part of its line.

To be fair to the railways, it must be recorded that their demolition of historic buildings was not always a matter for regret. Once at least it received a positive welcome.

The West Highland company secured powers in 1889 to build a railway from the Clyde to Fort William. It planned to reach its northern terminus straight through the Fort itself. That had been built in 1690, as a base for keeping the Highlands under the control of the London government; the order for the Massacre of Glencoe was signed in it in 1692. It now lay disused and empty. The government had sold it off, and the owner did not object to its demolition.

The railway company acted here with intelligent propriety. It avoided demolishing the Government House within the Fort and kept the Governor's Room (where the final order for the Massacre had been signed) intact. It also arranged for the gateway to the Fort to be dismantled and re-erected on the site at which the Cameron Highlanders had first been sworn in.

The removal of this historic building was surely advantageous: to the railway company, to Scotland, indeed to the United Kingdom. Few local people ever spoke of the place as Fort William; they called it 'the garrison' or 'the fort'. The Fort itself now disappeared, with all its hated associations; supplanted by a railway that has done much, during almost a century of life, to aid the town and the people of Lochaber in their hard struggle to maintain themselves.[69]

We have as yet come upon very few battles of the kind we are familiar with now, say in street-widening or property-development, where an antiquity stands in the way that must either be demolished or avoided, and where, through public opinion, the monument triumphs. One arose at Leicester in 1890.

The Manchester Sheffield & Lincolnshire company's first plans for its London extension involved taking the railway along the western edge of the old town. The centre line ran immediately under the windows of the castle, placing most of the castle precinct and the whole of the Roman Jewry Wall within the 'limits of deviation', so that the railway could if it chose destroy them. Local opposition was led by the town's Literary and Philosophical Society and the Leicestershire Architectural and Archaeological Society; and they secured the backing of the Borough Council. Opposition in Leicester soon generated opposition in London too.[70] The Bill failed to pass; rival railways and other interests were too strong for it. But when the Sheffield company secured the powers it was seeking in 1893, the course of the line was altered, to leave both Jewry Wall and castle intact. The company had given way. Protest had entirely succeeded.[71] More than that. The site now chosen for the station included the mosaic known as the Blackfriars Pavement, still *in situ*. The railway was now required to provide public access to it.[72] For many years it was to be inspected in its specially-built chamber, directly under the platform. This seems to be the first occasion on which official and unofficial bodies came together to resist a railway's threat to destroy an antiquity.

The story is continued in London. Tube railways were then being planned on a large scale. Their construction could yield archaeological finds of importance; though they ran deep down they could threaten buildings that stood above them. As far as finds were concerned, the Central London was required by Act of Parliament to preserve them and pass them to the Guildhall Museum.[73] In 1900 the London County Council went further, trying to get the principal railway companies to agree that in future all objects of archaeological interest found during railway construction in London should be handed over to it; but the request was not granted.[74] In other matters, however, the companies had to make concessions. Much trouble arose over Hawksmoor's church of St Mary Woolnoth when the City & South London Railway came to construct its station at the Bank, immediately beneath it, under powers given in 1895. Its demolition was proposed in 1897. That idea being abandoned, the church was closed for many years. The company had to pay large compensation for disturbance of its fabric. In the end the job was well done, and an entrance to the station was dexterously inserted close to the church. Here – given goodwill, patience, and ingenuity – a problem of this kind was solved: *solved*, not settled by some uneasy compromise. That is just what is sometimes achieved in similar cases today.

The Railways and their own Buildings

The last malpractice to be considered here was the least common, yet it was not without importance.

The railways erected many buildings of their own that called for enlargement or alteration, as the requirements of traffic changed. The simplest course then was to replace the old one completely by another, specially designed to meet the new needs. That entailed the demolition of a number of buildings that would be considered handsome today, deserving to be adapted rather than destroyed. Bridge Street station, Glasgow, and Campbell Street, Leicester, are examples. However, nobody could sensibly deny that the facilities afforded by the Central station in Glasgow and the new London Road station in Leicester were greatly superior to those provided before, for the railways and their customers alike.

The companies often sought to attract attention and bring business to themselves by loud and insensitive adornment. Two instances of that may be adduced, from Scarborough and Aberdeen.

G. T. Andrews designed a neat and dignified terminal station at Scarborough, opened in 1845. With railway services the resort prospered, and the station came to need enlargement. In the 1880s the North Eastern company decided that the building wanted a tower, to assert itself in the townscape. Furthermore, the tower ought to have a clock, and the Corporation egged the company on by agreeing to supply the gas required for illuminating its faces by night, free of charge. Andrews's well-mannered building now came to be surmounted by a grotesque erection, wholly out of keeping with it and all its surroundings. Topheavy and mis-shapen (docketed by Pevsner as 'wildly baroque'), it did two things: it told the time – very usefully; and it proclaimed the coarse thinking of its architect, William Bell.[75]

The city of Aberdeen owes its physical distinction to one thing first of all: its colour, the uniform tone of the grey and silver granite that pervades it. Excluding the medieval town at its northern tip, the whole of Aberdeen shows a rare harmony, with minor variations only, and those muted. In one important building, however, and one only, the harmony is broken. When the railway station came in for long-overdue reconstruction from 1913 onwards, the consortium of companies that owned it commissioned a new polygonal forebuilding, to jut out from the granite walls of the station. They allowed it to be executed under their engineer, J. A. Parker, in a pinkish-yellow sandstone. Cleaned not long ago, and therefore looking today much as it did when it was new, it shouts at everything near it, at the whole city itself. The design is restrained, and the proportions are right. But the colour is a disaster: remediable only over the years as a merciful pollution descends, to cover the building with a neutral grime.

One more case must be mentioned, of a different sort: the treatment accorded in the Victorian age to the first and greatest of all railway monuments, the Doric portico at Euston. Its grandeur was quite disproportionate to the accommodation provided for passengers behind it, hardly extended since the station was opened except by the addition of the Great Hall and of three new platforms in 1846–63.

In 1868 the Midland Railway arrived at its splendid St Pancras station, close by, and the opening of the Midland Grand Hotel there followed in 1873–6. The London & North Western company, with which it was in direct rivalry, now felt obliged to reconsider its whole unsatisfactory installation at Euston.

The approach to it from the Euston Road was greatly improved in 1870 when a drive was provided, graced by two lodges in Portland stone and making straight, between the two hotel buildings, for the portico: an admirable arrangement, much to the credit of J. B. Stansby, the company's architect.[76] But the hotel remained divided into two blocks, as before; and in 1878 a committee of directors adopted plans to link them at second-floor level by a corridor, crossing the approach road directly in front of the portico, and to provide additional offices at the foot of the portico itself. The committee was not unanimous, however. One of its five members, J. P. Bickersteth, voted against these proposals, arguing that the portico should be accorded the respect due to it by being removed altogether to stand close to the lodges on the Euston Road, thus freeing a large space for carefully-considered, not makeshift redevelopment. The company's officers were instructed to investigate the costs of this solution, and it was never heard of again.[77] The corridor was completed in 1881.

It is easy to ascribe what was done here to the company's 'parsimony'. Easy, and unjust. We have no means of knowing what the cost of removing the portico, with all the consequential changes, would have been; and times were not good in 1878–9. Nevertheless, this was an unhappy, a fatal decision. The building of the corridor struck the portico across its face and rendered it meaningless, for no one thereafter could see it properly or even imagine its original purpose. It now became visible only at very close quarters, and constituted nothing but a vast obstruction to movement. In consequence it was left neglected; decaying, uncleaned. After sixty more years, when a total rebuilding of the station was decided on, there was fresh talk of re-erecting the portico on the Euston Road. But by no contrivance could this monument have been brought into any satisfactory relation with the enormous block of building that was then contemplated. Standing on its own outside, it would have been only an elephantine joke. Something better might just possibly have been managed when the nationalized railways set about the reconstruction vigorously, on different lines, in 1959. But the portico was destroyed two years later.

The critical decision here was the one taken by the North Western company's directors in 1878. They were then urged to provide for the re-siting of the monument to a careful plan, which would have preserved it in some sensible relationship with the buildings behind it. They would neither accept that proposal nor face its clear alternative, to destroy the portico altogether, as an impediment to the railway's business. Both those policies must have appeared costly at the time; yet either would have produced great saving of cost in the future. Instead, the company remained as it were imprisoned in its own history, meeting its problem by a cheap, unsatisfactory compromise. Bickersteth alone tried to resist that, and he was over-ruled.

A Retrospect

New railway lines were still being constructed in Britain at the turn of the century, but none of them gave rise to a single argument of consequence comparable with those just mentioned. New roads did not begin to be built there, to meet the demands of the internal combustion engine, until the 1920s. The threats to buildings, monuments, and landscape went through a quite distinct phase, arising from railway work, in 1830–1900.

Some had succeeded; the vandals triumphed. Their memorials are with us still. One of them has even been accorded some protection of its own. The railway line across the Friargate bridge at Derby is now disused. The bridge is a listed monument, Grade II; and anyone bold enough to propose its removal would confront the angry protests of those who admire its loud ironwork and see it (truly enough, indeed) as a commemoration of the Derby firm that built it, Handyside's, at the zenith of its prosperity. Will it remain, though it now serves no useful purpose whatever, or will it one day be re-erected at enormous expense elsewhere, as London Bridge has been in Arizona?

The damage that the railway wrought was in some cases final, irreversible. Yet one may well end by being surprised that in such a huge burst of construction, uncontrolled by any local authorities' planning restrictions, the amount of serious damage was so relatively small. The Norwich and Stonehenge proposals were disgraceful and ought never to have been made. But they were defeated.

The word used here to comprehend all these plans and actions, 'vandalism', is an emotive one. The alteration, even the demolition, of an ancient structure in favour of a railway was sometimes necessary, in what may fairly be called a broad public interest – a kind of interest that a critic like Ruskin neither perceived nor allowed. Not all such relics of the past could be kept. Even in the nineteenth century, as the idea of 'preservation' developed, this truth became apparent. Late in the twentieth it looms up before us, larger and more oppressive with every year that goes by.[78]

The railway was not always a vandal. As we have seen in chapter 2, many of its own works and buildings achieved grandeur, sometimes refinement, so that they in turn adorned a town or a landscape. Moreover, it would be wrong to suggest that the philistinism sometimes shown by the British railways was unique. None of them can be said to have mutilated a notable antiquity as grossly, I think, as the railway was permitted to mutilate the medieval bridge at Orthez in the French foothills of the Pyrenees,[79] or the Pantaleonstor in Cologne.[80] Nor should we think today that we always do better than the Victorians did. The thrusting of the M5 motorway through the grounds of Clevedon Court in Somerset, not far from the very windows of the medieval house, was a piece of vandalism not excelled by anything the railways perpetrated. Perhaps as one drives past it the sight may cause one to sympathize a little with the landowners in their fights against the early railway promoters who wanted to cross their parks in a similar fashion.

Railways brought with them evident benefits to the country and opened up others, hitherto undreamt of. They also injured it, quite extensively in fact, and by intention – if they had not been curbed – much more.

7
LANGUAGE AND LITERACY

Railways made a clearly discernible mark on the English language, and English words and phrases describing them and their operations passed into other languages too. They engendered expressions of their own, necessary for describing new concepts, new practices and techniques. As time went on, some of these figured in the everyday speech of men and women who had nothing to do with railways. The large majority, however, remained technical terms, used by railwaymen and needing interpretation when laymen encountered them: forming an *argot* composed partly of expressions relating to machinery, partly of words and phrases describing operations, and partly of dialect – preponderantly, in early days, the dialect of Northumbria. Some of these words were inherited from older kinds of transport. The railway's 'guard', for example, was taken over from the coach, its 'cuttings' from the canals, its 'season tickets' from the steamboats.

The *argot* was used by managers and engineers and working men. But the railways also provided useful words and phrases for writers. That showed itself in the 1830s and 1840s, when their presence became an exciting novelty of life, visually striking and a stimulant to fresh thought. Over the next generation we can see the railways percolating into writers' minds. Transmitted thus, these words and phrases became fully accepted and absorbed. A number of them remain part of the furniture of our minds still.

Five Words

Let us start by considering the evolution of five words: rail, railway, station, train, locomotive.

'Rail' and 'railway' are the most important words of all in this language, for they describe what is completely distinctive in the thing itself. Locomotives ran on roads, as traction engines or steam rollers; we speak today of 'bus stations'; but without rails a railway does not exist.

The word 'rail' had long been used to denote a bar of wood. When parallel wooden bars were laid down to ease the passage of coal carts, it was natural to call them rails too, and that duly happened in Nottinghamshire in 1605–10.[1] But the entity they formed came more generally to be described as a waggon-way elsewhere.[2] That term was standard on Tyneside. It is in the West Midlands that 'railway' makes the first appearance that has so far been recorded, at Pensnett in Staffordshire in 1681. The alternative 'railroad' comes to be found in Shropshire in 1702.[3] The two words both established themselves, and were used indifferently. Athough in the nineteenth century 'railway' became normal in Britain and 'railroad' in America, that distinction was not rigid. The Denver South Park and Pacific Rail*way* company was incorporated in 1872, though on its reorganization in the following year it became a Rail*road*.[4] Some important American companies retained the title 'railway' – the Northern Pacific, for example, and the Atchison Topeka & Santa Fé. In England on the other hand, Ruskin (admittedly a writer who liked to use language with an old-fashioned turn) was still referring to 'railroads' in 1887.[5]

In the early nineteenth century 'railway' and 'railroad' were often used interchangeably with 'tramway' and 'tramroad', though they denoted different things. A tramway then was usually a plateway, L-shaped, on which wheels with flat treads like those used on roads could move; a railway came to signify one with a different kind of track that required the wheels to be flanged.[6] Most tramways were laid on or beside public roads; railways had separate roads of their own. Nevertheless the two terms were commonly confused. The early Acts of the Stockton & Darlington company refer to the undertaking as a 'railway or tramroad'. But the tramroad was already coming to be regarded as something inferior. Sending in an expense account to the promoters of the Taff Vale Railway in 1835, Brunel said he could not remember whether the undertaking was called a tramroad or a railroad company. He was no kind of snob, but he thought it tactful to add: 'I have dignified it with the latter appellation'.[7] The difference between the two things became much clearer with the development of the street tramway, for the conveyance of passengers in Britain from 1859 onwards.

The word 'station' was not used by the Stockton & Darlington company when its line was opened in 1825.[8] The Canterbury & Whitstable and the Liverpool & Manchester companies, on the other hand, had 'stations', so named from the beginning. Those at Liverpool (Crown Street and Edge Hill) and Manchester were expressly designed for the purpose, and they were the first railway stations, in the full sense of that term, in the world. The company never had any doubt what they were to be called. The card of invitation to the opening ceremony announced that 'the doors of the station in Crown Street, Liverpool, will be open at nine o'clock in the morning'.[9]

With few exceptions the other railways of the 1830s were on a much smaller scale. On the Leicester & Swannington (1832) the Leicester terminus was called, in canal language, a 'wharf'.[10] The Whitby & Pickering Railway (1836) had a 'depot' at Pickering.[11] Some effort was being made to establish that word then. In the following year one writer said firmly that a station was 'merely a starting or stopping place on a line of railway; where there are warehouses attached to a station, the whole is called a "depot" '.[12] This was something like the distinction that presently emerged in French between *station* and *gare*; but it did not maintain itself in English. By the time the first trunk lines came to be opened, in 1837-42, 'stations' was the standard word, whether for termini or for the minor stopping-places on the way, which were sometimes called 'road stations'.[13]

'Train' appears first in a compound phrase: a 'train of wagons', a 'train of carriages';[14] but railwaymen soon abridged it to the single word 'train', standing on its own.[15] Before long that word had passed into common use, appearing in a sketch of Marryat's in 1835 and in a hasty note by Dickens three years later.[16]

Finally, 'locomotive'. This word was slower to find general acceptance. Trevithick described his Penydarren machine of 1804 as a 'tram waggon' and as an 'engine'. Its successors remained 'engines' too, but adjectives came to be attached to them, to indicate their essential difference from stationary steam engines, namely that they moved with the loads they hauled. So they became 'locomotive engines', 'travelling engines', or 'movable engines'. 'Locomotive or self-moving engines' appear in the Edinburgh & Dalkeith company's Act of 1826.[17] The unwieldy 'locomotive engine' continued for some time to be the standard form, or else 'engine' alone. Who first used the word 'locomotive', as a noun? In 1828 it had begun to appear in the records of the Stockton & Darlington company.[18] Robert Stephenson used it in a letter written towards the close of that year, and again a year later.[19]

So the single word 'locomotive' had made its way into ordinary use with engineers by 1828–9. (The stationary engine, or 'permanent engine',[20] never became familiar enough to demand any similar abbreviation.) The contraction took time to establish itself. The diarist Creevey travelled behind a 'Loco Motive engine' in 1829, but spoke of the 'locomotive' that caused Huskisson's death in 1830.[21] By about 1850 writers on railways had generally adopted it.[22] The Board of Trade continued, however, to adhere to the more elaborate phrase; its inspectors, in their accident reports, normally used the shorter single word 'engines'. Parliamentary draftsmen went on writing 'locomotive engines', with one curious exception: they used the single word 'locomotives' to mean steam engines running on roads; regulated in what were entitled Locomotives Acts from 1861 onwards. The single word first crept into a railway statute in a schedule attached to the Railway Companies (Accounts and Returns) Act of 1911.[23]

There then are five basic words in the railways' language, all established and all but one in common use by 1850. Many more were current too, as we can see from reading the accident reports of the time. Stationmaster, signalman, ticket collectors, and porters all appear in a single sentence in one of them, in 1849.[24]

A New Vocabulary

The railways' vocabulary soon began to be noted freely by people unconnected with them.[25] Talking to Sir Walter Scott about the team of impecunious assistants he had formerly employed, Lockhart likened him to 'a locomotive engine on a railway . . . when a score of coal waggons are seen linking themselves to it the moment it gets the steam up'. At which Scott laughed and added 'but there was a cursed lot of dung carts too'.[26] That conversation seems to have taken place in 1831, Lockhart having lately had an article on railways through his hands for the *Quarterly Review*, which he edited.[27] When the single word 'locomotives' made its way with literary men, its meaning, as they used it, was not always the same. Sydney Smith, in the first of his letters to the press in 1842 to complain about the locking of railway carriage doors, spoke of being 'hermetically sealed in the "locomotives" ', i.e. the trains.[28]

The speculative mania of 1835–7 did much to make the idea of railways familiar. It now became important to a good many people to understand the words and phrases used in prospectuses and in engineers' reports because they were attracting general attention as investments. How were potential investors to interpret this language? The need was first met by Francis Whishaw in his *Analysis of Railways* (1837), examining eighty projects then before Parliament and advising investors about them. He included in it a 25-page glossary of these technical terms. A number of them belong to engineering alone, civil or mechanical: angle of repose, buffing apparatus, chair, kyanize. But some of the entries throw light on usage: the difference between various sorts of rail; the relationship of embankment to excavation. As railways came to attract more widespread interest, other similar vocabularies of technical terms were compiled, useful not only to investors but also to those who aspired to employment on them.[29] When the Mania was at its height in 1846 *Chambers' Journal* (which was addressed to the general reader) published an article entitled 'Phraseology of the Rail'. 'Among recent inventions', the author remarks, ' "the rail" has been peculiarly prolific of colloquialisms, many of which are so pat and appropriate that they are not unlikely in time to arrive at a classical distinction.' Here he makes an intelligent effort to take the new vocabulary on the wing.[30] Some of the phrases mentioned by him have become a permanent part of the language, almost unchanged: 'getting up the steam',[31] going 'off the rail'. On the other hand, 'shift the switches' has not maintained itself as a synonym for changing the subject in conversation. 'Railway speed', obsolete now, was already well established. *A Trip to Rome at Railway Speed* is the title of an account of a tour by Thomas Barlow published in 1836 – though none of it was in fact made by railway. Walter Bagehot was still using the phrase in 1874.[32] Such expressions multiplied as time went on. Those who had not run 'off the rails' might be said to be 'on the right lines'. It seems to have been the railway industry that introduced 'working to rule'.[33] In the Mid-Victorian age railways came to enter freely into literary metaphor. Their behaviour and devices were understood, vaguely or precisely, by educated people.

English Words in Foreign Languages

English words and phrases played a considerable part in the making of similar vocabularies in other languages. A number of the most important are indicated in Table 2, with their equivalents that came to establish themselves in Europe and North America.[34]

In French the process has been admirably studied by P. J. Wexler.[35] He shows that some words were taken over direct, almost unchanged: rail, viaduct, tender, wagon, for example. Some were never used in France at all, such as 'brake'.[36] Other French terms did battle with English ones, and eventually defeated them. *Chemin de fer* itself, for example. Although that phrase had been used as early as 1784,[37] some Frenchmen thought it would be better to lift the single word 'railway' from the English. There was even a periodical called *Le Railway*, published in 1845–6.[38] As in Britain, so in France, 'locomotive' did not secure acceptance immediately as a single word; it had a harder struggle there indeed, for in French other single words competed with it – *locomoteur* and *locomotrice*.[39]

TABLE 2

RAILWAY WORDS IN ENGLISH AND OTHER LANGUAGES

English	French	German	Italian	Spanish	American*
Carriage (coach)	Voiture	Personen-wagen	Carrozza	Coche	Car
Driver	Mécanicien	Lokomotive-führer	Maccinista	Maquinista	Engineer
Fireman) Stoker)	Chauffeur	Lokomotive-heizer	Fuochista	Fogonero	
Locomotive	Locomotive	Lokomotive	Locomotiva⟩	Locomotora	
Points	Aiguillage	Weiche	Scambio	Cambio	Switches
Rail	Rail	Schiene	Rotaia	Carril	
Railway⟩	Chemin de fer	Eisenbahn	Ferrovia	Ferrocarril	Railroad⟩
Rolling stock	Matériel roulant	Rollendes Material	Materiale rotabile	Material rodante	
Signal	Signal	Signal	Segnale	Señal	
Sleeper	Traverse	Schwelle	Traversa	Traviesa	Tie
Station	Gare) Station)	Bahnhof	Stazione	Estación	Depot
Tender	Tender	Tender	Tender	Ténder	
Train	Train	Zug	Treno	Tren	
Tunnel	Tunnel	Tunnel	Galleria	Túnel	
Wagon	Wagon	Wagen	Carro	Vagoń	

* Where different from English.

⟩ But see p. 179.

Some English technical expressions came to be permanently assimilated into French. In the excellent manual of railways produced by Lefèvre and Cerbelaud (both railway engineers) in 1888, we find for instance *tunnel, ferry-boat, ballast, compound* (applied to locomotives), and *block-system*.[40] All technical terms referring to machinery. The French felt no need to import any concerned with administration or management.

This traffic in language did not move entirely in one direction. If the French word *dépôt* was already in use in Britain in a military context before the railway seized on it, 'derail' was a new importation from France, adopted by Lardner almost as soon as it had been coined there.[41] The *coupé*, a half-compartment in a railway carriage, appeared in print in English in 1853[42] – though the accommodation itself had been provided in 1842 in Queen Adelaide's carriage on the London & Birmingham Railway. And the *buffet*, at stations and on trains, became acclimatized in Britain too.[43]

The Germans resisted the importation of foreign words, and in this case they were provided with a number of their own, for they had had railways for a longer time than the English. *Hund* and *Truhe* were ancient words to describe wagons, which were running on rails in coal mines in the sixteenth century.[44] *Weg*, a way, established itself as the word for the track on which they ran, presently joined by *Bahn*, a road. When the track came to be made partly or wholly of iron (a practice imported from England), it was called an English coal way, *ein englischer Kohlenweg*, and the fully-developed railway became an *Eisenbahn*, an iron road. *Bahnhof* was a new word, easily formed, for 'station'; and *Zug* (a procession, a file or column in military use) could be made to do duty for 'train'.

There was however one English word that the Germans did accept from the beginning. The locomotive became *Lokomotive* (or *Lok*), and was never anything else. But more than that. In every other widely used language in western Europe, whether Latin or Teutonic, the word for a steam engine running on rails was 'locomotive', or something very close to it (and its tender was a 'tender' everywhere too); with the unique refinement in Italian that the steam locomotive was *locomotiva*, the electric (and later diesel) one *locomotore*. The adoption of this term so widely is a striking tribute to the impression that the new machine made as an English device, a reminder that in most of these countries the first locomotive ever seen had been made in England.

Another English word also established itself early and became universal throughout Europe, with minor variations: signal. That too must be regarded as a tacit acknowledgment of the priority of invention.

One more language was closely concerned with steam railways from their beginning: the emergent American language. Similarities and distinctions appeared between the terms used in managing and working railways on the opposite sides of the Atlantic. The man who controlled the locomotive, on the move, was a 'driver' in Britain. But in the United States he was an 'engineer'.[45] (Might this have been, at least in the North, an instinctive recoil from association with the drivers of slaves?) His mate was, in both countries, a

[179]

'fireman', though in Britain he was also called a 'stoker'. A railway coach or carriage was for the Americans a 'car'; and when Pullman's vehicles were exported across the Atlantic in the 1870s they became 'Pullman cars' in England. So did their derivatives, for sleeping and dining. But not immediately, and on one great English railway there were never 'sleeping cars' at all. The London & North Western came to accept 'dining cars', but it still retained 'sleeping saloons' in 1914.

In England a tenacity in retaining an old word sometimes hindered the adoption of a new one from America that was demonstrably better. The English word 'goods', for example, was used in two different senses. In the companies' official returns it was applied to all traffic other than that in passengers, parcels, and mails; but it was often intended to mean general merchandise, as opposed to minerals, where it was desirable to indicate mineral traffic on its own.[46] What was wanted was a generic term, to serve when they were both added together. The Americans had such a term: 'freight'. That was regarded as an Americanism, on both sides of the Atlantic, during the nineteenth century.[47] But at the opening of the twentieth its value came to be appreciated by some English writers: the economist George Paish, for instance, was using it in this sense in 1902.[48] It made little headway in Britain, however, until after the first World War.[49]

Many of the prime English railway words found easy and immediate acceptance in America: the rails themselves, the locomotive and its tender, the rolling stock and the brakes with which the vehicles were fitted. On the other hand the 'sleepers' on which the rails rested in Britain[50] became 'ties' in the United States. The English guard was transformed into a conductor; and an American, interpreting the English system to his countrymen, had to say that that official 'rode in the tail caboose'.[51]

The Navvies' Language

We must now turn to look more closely at the language used by the men concerned with building and working railways in Britain, beginning with a brief account of the forms of speech that emerged among the navvies who undertook the physical labour of construction. They had a slang of their own – many indeed, for the words and phrases they used never came to form any fully coherent language: yet there was enough cohesion to produce some expressions that were generally understood among gangs working in different parts of the country.

Their name itself was an abbreviation of 'navigators', a term applied at least as early as 1775 to the men who worked on the canals and in common use by the 1830s.[52] As the men themselves grew famous in the following years, chiefly (though not with justice) for their drunkenness and violence, the word that described them itself sometimes became a term of abuse. At Tonbridge, for example, the trouble they caused when they were building the South

Eastern Railway in the early 1840s lodged itself in local memory. Half a century later the rough lads in the town were still being called 'navvies' by the boys of Tonbridge School, who sometimes fought them.[53] But not all navvies, by any means, were of that description. Their behaviour varied according to the way in which they were managed, and especially the way they were paid.

When the construction of railways was at its height in 1847, there seem to have been about 210,000 men employed up and down Great Britain in the manual labour of railway building.[54] Hamilton Ellis finely observed that they constituted a 'great army, which under other conditions might have carved out a great empire'.[55]

Whether they were violent or orderly, however, they certainly appeared to be a peculiar people, somewhat like gipsies and the boatmen on the canals.[56] They were a shifting population, moving constantly from one job to another, and their language became a mixture of dialects, reflecting their diverse origins: experienced men who had worked on the construction of canals and on drainage in Lincolnshire or Somerset; men from the Pennines; Scots and Irishmen, together with a few Belgians; in later days Cornish miners, adepts at tunnelling, thrown out of work at home in the 1860s.[57]

Very few people watched and listened carefully to these men at the time. Their most sympathetic observers were clergymen, 'missionaries',[58] and doctors. The men often worked in silence. Though they sometimes sang, their songs have almost all perished. They can never have had the compelling vitality of those that were heard as the American railways were built: 'In eighteen-hundred and sixty-one', 'Drill, ye tarriers, drill', and the rest. The only British navvies whose singing was particularly remarked on were Welsh, and their songs were hymns.[59] There must have been other songs, of a different sort, sung up and down the country. At any rate here is one – a jaunty little piece heard on the Dartmouth & Torbay Railway in 1858–9:[60]

> I'm a nipper and a tipper,
> I'm a navvy on the line.
> I get me five-and-twenty bob a week,
> Besides me overtime.
> Roast beef and boiled beef
> An' pudden made of eggs,
> An' in comes a navvy
> Wi' a fine pair o' legs!

He was a tipper, no doubt, because tipping was part of his work. Was he a nipper because he was small, or perhaps because he enjoyed a nip? The earliest modern use of 'overtime' given in the *Oxford English Dictionary* is just of this date; but the casual tone of the reference to it here makes it plain that the expression was already well established. Did the paying of overtime first become widely known from the practice of railway contractors, during the days of most urgent construction, against the clock?[61] As for wages, the navvies on this line might well boast of them, for they were over three times as large as what a farm-worker then got in that part of Devonshire.[62]

Much of the navvies' speech between themselves, as it has been recorded, was a rhyming slang. Here is a whole sentence in this jargon, recorded by a Northamptonshire clergyman. 'Now then, my china-plate [mate], out with your cherry-ripe [pipe], off with your steam-packet [jacket] and set your back and growl [trowel] again'.[63] The navvies bestowed nicknames on one another; when the men were inquired for they could often be found by means of them alone, not by those that legally belonged to them.[64] The names might be an inheritance from folklore. A navvy who was discovered to come from Wiltshire would be known as a moonraker, an appellation that enshrined a traditional joke at the expense of all Wiltshiremen.[65] On the other hand a 'mountain picker' was a descriptive nickname for a Welshman that had, it seems, no earlier ancestry.[66] A name of that kind might be a tribute of admiration for skill or daring. On a contract in Westmorland one navvy was known as 'Steeple Jack' from his extraordinary feats in the erection of scaffolding for viaducts.[67] The men sometimes named the quarters in their shanty towns with a mild sarcasm: Regent Street, Hanover Square, the Quadrant, and The Strand.[68] They also used a number of phrases that seem to have been widely current among them. When one said 'I shall jack up' he meant he was going to look for work elsewhere. If he left without paying what he owed for his lodgings he was said to have 'sloped his lodge'.[69]

As railway construction diminished, many of the navvies moved off to other public works – sewerage, reservoirs, high dams; others went abroad. They were always a quite separate body from those who maintained and worked the railways. Few of them ever passed into the companies' service. Their lingo remained private to themselves; its racy rhyming and punning answered to the special tasks they performed but not to the steady routine that settled down on railways at work. It was primarily a means of communication between working men, and between navvies and gangers – many of whom had themselves been navvies once.

A quick ear noted moreover that the slang in use among bricklayers was quite different. On railway contracts where they were employed side by side with navvies the phrases bandied about within each group could be clearly distinguished.[70] When that observation was made, in the late 1870s, railway navvies were a dwindling band in Britain. But they kept their individuality, their separate character, to the end.

The Language of Operation

The railways had to evolve a vocabulary consisting of technical terms for their equipment and also of terms needed for communication with their customers.

Before they ever began to carry passengers, the coaches had had their precise hours of departure and arrival, subject however to interruption, through storm or accident or human error. When railway services began, they were liable to disorganization from the same causes, and on occasion from mechanical failures as well. But gradually these vagaries grew fewer, and it came to be realized that trains were appointed to run at exactly fixed times, and that they normally did so. As the system developed in the 1840s the number of these fixed times up and down the country steadily increased. Important junctions appeared, at which converging trains were intended to connect with one another: Crewe, for instance, and Parkside in Lancashire. All this imposed rigidities on business and movement never imagined before. It was an evident necessity that the times should be clearly announced, and not at the stations alone. They were advertised in newspapers, but some people wished to refer to them more conveniently. A new contrivance was devised for this purpose, and it was called a 'time table'. These words were used by the London & Birmingham Railway in 1838[71] and then passed into general currency, soon hyphenated or amalgamated into one. Not all railway companies adopted 'timetables' immediately, however.[72] The Liverpool & Manchester preferred to issue a 'scheme of departures' (something more cautious, for it did not specify times of arrival) as late as 1843.[73] But 'timetables' steadily made their way, to become part of the railways' standard equipment. The word was sometimes applied strangely. The South Yorkshire Railway issued something called a 'timetable' in 1851; but it did not give the times of any trains and added, for the more thorough discouragement of passengers, 'no guarantee of punctuality'.[74]

The timetable brought with it another word, coined from a proper name: Bradshaw. George Bradshaw, a Manchester Quaker, started to produce his *Time Tables* in 1839. Their success was instant and complete. They never had any serious rival in presenting the times for the railway system of the United Kingdom as a whole. Other attempts of the same sort were made indeed, but none of them established itself,[75] whereas Bradshaw's *Railway Guide* was published, under successively varying titles, every month for 120 years.[76]

Its main drawback was that many people found it difficult or impossible to understand. In the early Victorian age the book was produced in a small format, on poor paper, in minute – here and there in minuscule – type, with notes appended wherever they could be fitted into a page, often running sideways or even upside-down. Some of its symbols and conventions were ambiguous, and the information given was frequently baffling. So 'Bradshaw' became a by-word for incomprehensibility. Dickens poked fun at it on this account, in 'A Narrative of Extraordinary Suffering' in 1851, ending up with the sufferer, demented, muttering the single word 'BRADSHAW'.[77] 'At what hour I shall get to Glasgow', wrote Trollope in 1869, 'I cannot learn without an amount of continued study of Bradshaw for which I have neither strength nor mental ability.'[78] This timetable was then called everywhere by its original compiler's name alone.[79] It made a figure in the music halls: a comic song, 'Bradshaw's Guide', was 'written, composed, and sung with unbounded applause by Fred Albert at the London and provincial concerts'.[80] A 'Guide to Bradshaw' ran through nine instalments of *Punch* in 1865: a well-directed satire, sometimes facetious but often funny still. It turns up again and again in conversations in fiction (best of all perhaps at the very end of Max Beerbohm's *Zuleika Dobson*)[81] and came to be regarded as one of the mysteries of its country. 'I've seen you with Bradshaw', exclaims an American to an Italian, teasing him for his confusion, in Henry James's *Golden Bowl*. 'It takes Anglo-Saxon blood.'[82]

So the timetable, and above all Bradshaw's indispensable compilation, made its way into the lives of the Victorians. It acted as an agent in the dissemination of standard time. The idea it represented came to be applied to purposes other than those of the railways. The 'timetable' soon penetrated the schools, to provide a neat means of organizing their lessons.[83] By 1858 it was being used to record the services of steamboats and the rise and fall of tides, as well as for furnishing 'a check upon the period of labour of workmen'.[84] Here the railway forged an instrument widely adaptable to the closer regulation of society at large.

The working of railways came to demand a good many special terms and phrases, intelligible to men at several grades of education, involving a fusion of the new language of technology with the familiar one of order and control. Something like a lingua franca thus grew up, which was never adequately recorded in the Victorian age. It has only recently begun to attract study.[85]

It was, and long remained, in part a matter of local speech. The pioneer railways ran over short distances, in isolation from one another. They called some of their component parts by different names in different tracts of the country. On Tyneside the railway itself was sometimes known as a 'wayleave', by a transference of the legal term for the grant of permission to lay down a railway across someone else's property.[86] The parapet of a bridge was called a 'battlement' in Lancashire.[87] In Northumberland and Durham, again, brake-levers were 'convoys'; in Shropshire they were 'jigs'.[88]

The local vocabulary was naturally drawn on by the steam-worked railways when they appeared. But such variants gradually fell out of use as railways ceased to be local concerns. When they came to be managed as larger units, they were worked in accordance with a standard language, established over the whole system.

In Scotland a fair number of terms were employed that were unknown in England. In pre-steam days the railway itself was sometimes called a 'cassey-way' – a causeway.[89] English companies divided their platelayers into 'gangs'; in Scotland in the 1840s they worked in 'squads'.[90] The Garnkirk & Glasgow Railway called points 'snecks', the old word used in Scottish coal-mines, and its pointsmen were 'sneckmen'.[91] North of the Border almost every stationmaster was known as an 'agent'.[92] On the Glasgow & South Western Railway vehicles were never coupled together, they were 'tied'. Its men had a special term for the violent, dangerous jerk that a freight train made when the three-link couplings of the wagons were suddenly pulled tight; they called it by an old word used by fishermen, a 'rug'.[93] Where notice had to be given at stations by passengers who wished trains to be stopped for them, it was required to be 'timeous' on the two northernmost Scottish railways (i.e. given in good time), and that word was retained in the Scottish Region timetables of British Rail until 1967.[94]

Railwaymen commonly used ordinary words in special senses. Acworth gives two telling examples:

> Most of us think we know what a bank is. To a railway man a bank is, in the first place, an incline...and, secondly, a platform when used not for passengers but for goods. The 'shipping' office at Broad Street station dispatches goods not to India and China, but to Manchester, and Leeds, and Birmingham.[95]

Sometimes an ordinary word was seized on by an outsider to describe a railway work or service, and then accepted, or even adopted, by the railway itself. 'Tube' is one such word, bestowed on the Central London Railway, the third deep-level underground line. The company announced that it was going to charge a uniform fare of twopence. On 30 July 1900, a month before its public opening, it was hailed in a newspaper headline as 'The Twopenny Tube'. The alliteration was attractive, and the phrase was widely adopted at once. At least by April 1901 the Central London was being referred to simply as 'The Tube', a word that is now current to describe all the deep-level lines in London.[96]

When a word was itself a novelty, it was apt to be misapplied by the men who used it. Sleepers that had been 'kyanized' (i.e. saturated in a solution of bicarbonate of mercury as a preservative, a process called after its inventor Dr Kyan) were said by the men working on the Manchester & Birmingham Railway to have been 'canonized'.[97]

The language used by the railway companies in their official notices, communicating with the public, was often obscure. There was the special difficulty that arose in Wales, not always helped by well-meant efforts at translation. 'List of booking. You passengers must be careful', ran a notice at one station in North Wales observed in 1875. 'For have them level money for ticket and to apply at once for asking tickets when will booking window open. No tickets to have after departure of the train.'[98]

That was a painstaking effort to solve a problem. In England the methods used to communicate with passengers were sometimes merely careless. In 1880 W. W. Skeat, the philologist, illustrated the South Eastern company's mode of addressing its customers, at Cannon Street and other stations, by means of this notice: 'Tickets once nipped and defaced at the barriers, and the passengers admitted to the platform, will have to be delivered up to the Company, in the event of the holders retiring from the platform without travelling, and cannot be recognised for re-admission'. 'Can anything be more slipshod?' he fairly inquired.[99]

In these communications the railways bore part of the responsibility for the increasing use of pompous jargon, well under way before 1914 and confronting us on all sides grotesquely now. Bradshaw came to exemplify it – though it

[185]

was merely publishing, of course, the instructions handed in by the companies themselves. 'Passengers desirous of commencing their journey at the station' – it is the Great Northern company addressing them in 1910.[100]

Railwaymen frequently bestowed nicknames on objects familiar to them. Many of these referred to the physical attributes of the machines they used. Stirling's large 0-4-4 tank engines on the Great Northern Railway were known as 'Wolves', from the distinctive bark they made;[101] a goods engine on the Midland & South Western Junction Railway, which was powerful and also had a turn of speed, was commonly called 'Galloping Alice'.[102] The huge 0-8-2 tank engines of the Lancashire & Yorkshire Railway were known as 'Little Egberts'. They were much loved by their crews for the reliable way in which they performed their duties (mainly of banking trains up inclines) and got their nickname from a celebrated troupe of performing elephants.[103] One engine had a private nickname all its own, acquired by its spectacular fate. This was no. 224 of the North British Railway, which fell with its whole train off the Tay Bridge in 1879. Thriftily salvaged from the bed of the river, it was repaired, put back into service, and lasted until 1919. The men referred to it as 'The Diver'.[104]

Nicknames might reflect some public discussion that was current when the thing to which they were applied was new. The noisy imperialist enthusiasm of the last quarter of the century fired some railwaymen. A Plymouth express put on by the Great Western company in 1879 was at once unofficially called the 'Zulu', from the war that was then being fought in South Africa.[105] The first large extension to the terminus at Waterloo, completed at the same time, was officially called the South Station. Unofficially it was known as 'Cyprus', alluding to the British annexation of the island in 1878. When the North Station followed in 1885 it became 'Khartoum', with reference to Gordon's death ten months before.

At least one installation got a wry nickname. At Norwood on the London Brighton & South Coast system there were 'Teetotal Sidings': so called, it appears, because trains often had to wait on them for a long time, and no comforting refreshment was to be had in the neighbourhood.[106]

Literacy and Self-Improvement

In his important discussion of literacy in Victorian England, R. K. Webb concluded – very tentatively – that in the 1840s, over the country as a whole, some 70% of the population could read.[107] He took a wide sample of evidence (including some from the Commons Committee on Railway Labourers in 1846) and set out a number of the difficulties that arise in using the information that is available.

From the beginning it was essential that some railway employees should be literate. Those who were responsible for taking money from passengers had to account for it in writing; guards and conductors who inspected tickets must be able to read them. On the other hand a platelayer could be instructed verbally by his ganger. In ranges of employment between those categories the practices of early companies varied.

I have not found any evidence concerning literacy among railway employees before 1837, when candidates for work – presumably in clerical posts – on the Great Western Railway, shortly before it opened, had to apply in their own handwriting.[108] In 1839–41 some public attention was given to the question whether literacy should be considered a necessary qualification for driving a train. Two Parliamentary Committees heard evidence on the matter from engineers. Entirely conflicting attitudes and policies then emerged. When Edward Bury was asked in 1839, as the superintendent of locomotives on the London & Birmingham Railway, how his drivers got 'sufficient practical knowledge' of their craft, he replied: 'we do not want them to have much; I would rather the men should not touch the engine themselves'.[109] To Bury the driver's job was to drive, and nothing else. The idea that the man could do that job better if he could read did not seem to him to need discussion. On the other hand in 1840 Charles Hutton Gregory – a trained civil engineer – defining the regulations for the appointment of drivers on the London & Croydon Railway, laid down that they 'must be able to read and write, and, if possible, understand the rudimental principles of mechanics'.[110] The Railway Department of the Board of Trade, which had lately been set up with Sir Frederic Smith from the Royal Engineers as its inspector-general, took the same view: 'There can be no doubt', it said in a report to Parliament in 1841, 'that an engine-driver should be able to read his instructions'.[111]

Two months later one of the greatest engineers then alive held this statement up to public ridicule. Giving evidence to the Committee of 1841, Brunel said not merely that it was unnecessary but that it was undesirable for engine-drivers to be literate. His statement closes with an engaging revelation concerning himself:[112]

> I would not give sixpence in hiring an engineman because of his knowing how to read and write. I believe that of the two the non-reading man is the best, and for this reason: I defy Sir Frederic Smith, or any person who has general information, and is in the habit of reading, to drive an engine.... It is impossible that a man that indulges in reading should make a good engine-driver; it requires a species of machine, an intelligent man, an honest man, a sober man, a steady man; but I would much rather not have a thinking man. I never dare drive an engine, although I always go upon the engine; because if I go upon a bit of the line without anything to attract my attention, I begin thinking of something else.

Brunel's attitude in this matter may fairly be called a quirk, unworthy of a man so large-minded and humorous. His words indicate no contempt for the drivers. The four qualities he listed as requisite in them are high qualities. That he should have feared a 'thinking' driver would be liable to fall into a reverie on the footplate, as he knew he would do himself, does not destroy the force of his statement that the railways needed men of that character. And, under his trusted colleague Daniel Gooch (who did not share the view he expressed here), the Great Western company got them.

In line with this disagreement, a diversity of practice grew up among railway companies in the 1840s. It is known that some drivers were illiterate because in accident reports, where their names had to be appended to statements, that was sometimes done by means of a mark instead of a signature. So we can tell that, for example, the Midland Counties and the North Union Railways employed illiterate drivers in 1842.[113] Much later, in 1856, when an express train on the Newport Abergavenny & Hereford Railway met with an accident, the inspecting officer took special occasion to remark that its driver (temporarily employed in that capacity, from a shortage of regular men) 'was unable to read or write and could not therefore make himself acquainted with the book of regulations'.[114]

'The book of regulations.' How could the railways' servants become familiar with it if they could not read? And how could those men be expected to understand some of the rules and instructions they were told to obey, when they were strangely worded? Some managers took time to learn the craft of expressing themselves simply, or perhaps never learnt it at all. In 1836 the Monkland & Kirkintilloch and the Ballochney Railways in Scotland laid it down in their by-laws that 'no owner or driver of any wagon shall apply water, grease, oil, or other unguent to the periphery of the wagon or carriage wheels, or to the surface of the rails'. The penalty for ignorance of the meaning of 'unguent' and 'periphery' could be as much as a fine of £5.[115] G. P. Neele quotes a London & North Western Railway notice of 1846:

> The fan or arm of the auxiliary signal at Cheddington, Leighton, Roade, Blisworth, and Weedon are repainting to a yellow colour which will be more discernible than green, the ground colour is obliged to be nearly red, the signal will, however, continue to be shown for the assistance of the drivers, although it is not intended they should stop thereat but come on as heretofore as far as the stationary post, when the policeman will tell them why the train has been stopped.

He remarks mildly: 'It is to be hoped that the drivers understood it'.[116] How could they? But what was to be done when the men had to receive written instructions and could not read them?[117] Some railway companies, recognizing that candidates for employment, otherwise suitable, might not be literate, allowed that in that case the rules they had to obey might be read over to them. This was provided for on the Liverpool & Manchester Railway in 1840;[118] and on a number of Scottish railways later in that decade the foremen of platelayers were enjoined to read out the rules to their men at least once a week.[119] The Bristol & Exeter still had a similar practice in 1864.[120] Its demise can be traced, as illiteracy grew less common, on the Great Western. A provision for reading over the rules, when necessary, was still in force at Swindon works about 1890; by 1904 a signature was being required from everyone employed there.[121]

The alternative practice, of making literacy an indispensable qualification for service, was adopted by some companies quite early: by the Southampton & Dorchester, for instance, in 1847.[122] In 1856 the London Brighton & South Coast company issued a questionnaire to its station staff concerning the history of their employment in its service. Of the eighty-seven returned forms[123] only one shows any notable irregularity of spelling, and it was submitted rather surprisingly by the assistant superintendent of London Bridge station. Nearly all the others are neatly written and well expressed. This branch of the railway service was clearly encouraging literacy and rewarding it. By 1874 the whole of the wage-paid staff of the London & South Western company had to be able to write with 'reasonable facility' – new applicants for jobs being tested by examination.[124]

What contribution did the railways themselves make to the advance of literacy among those they employed? This is a corner of a larger subject, which will not be treated here: the part the railways took in the development of education, particularly through the schools they established, or helped to support.[125] They were for the children of the companies' servants; but the companies also paid some heed to the education of those servants themselves.

That was not designed to promote literacy in the first place, for it was initiated chiefly by railwaymen who could already read and wanted libraries of books and newspapers, adapted to their own interests. The directors of the Grand Junction company considered a plan to provide a reading-room for the men employed in its new works at Crewe in 1843, and a year later a library and news-room was established, with a capital of £25 provided by the board. This arrangement ran into some awkward difficulties at once and had to be modified in 1845 into the form of the Crewe Mechanics' Institution. With the support of the Grand Junction company and its successor the London & North Western (if also very clearly under their paternal control), this new body became a useful centre of adult education, open to all the men employed in the works at a modest annual fee.[126] A group of the Swindon men secured a tiny library, on their own initiative, in September 1843. A Mechanics' Institute followed three months later, which had an easier passage to success than the one at Crewe.[127] The Great Western company showed itself liberal in this matter to its black-coated workers also. In 1852 it voted £105 towards the expense of setting up a circulating library, with a room of its own, at Paddington. It even agreed to give £21 towards the establishment of the Marylebone Free Library.[128]

Similar institutions developed in most other railway towns. It is impossible to say how far they helped the men who were illiterate, those who are chiefly spoken of here. The main task of the institutes was to cater for those who could read. But at least in their earlier days they must have afforded some instruction and help of this more elementary kind. At Wolverton, another railway town on the London & North Western, there was a 'weekly evening school for adults' in 1847.[129] One of its main purposes was surely to teach the three R's to those who felt they needed to learn them.

For the rest, railwaymen who desired education, whether elementary or more advanced, sought it wherever it was to be had. A teacher of adults at Leicester recorded in 1851 that railwaymen were attending his men's class on Monday evenings. 'One of the stokers', he wrote, 'came expressly to have the use of figures, that he might find how many revolutions the wheel of his engine would make in a mile, with a view to estimate the consumption of his coke.'[130] Even Brunel might have applauded such a use of literacy as that.

So the railway companies offered their men the means of educating themselves if they wished to do so; and they put a good deal of thought and money into this kind of self-improvement. Towards the end of the nineteenth century, when technical education began to be systematically developed in Britain, some of the companies both assisted and took advantage of it. But here they wore two hats. The companies were at once employers and substantial ratepayers, at a time when all local rates were rising; and that might cause them to change their policies, to further this work at one time and disfavour it at another.[131]

The Language of Place

Railways helped to fix the spelling of place-names, and here and there to alter their pronunciation. They might even invent them.

Before the Victorian age the spelling of many of these names was variable. Railway companies wanted consistency: in their printed literature, timetables, notices, tickets, labels. If there were alternative spellings of the name of the place at which a station was to be opened, the company would select one and usually maintain it thereafter, playing its part (together with other bodies, such as the Post Office and the Ordnance Survey) in standardizing the form that had been adopted. In Cheshire 'Altrincham' and 'Altringham' were ancient alternative spellings, though the second alone rendered the ordinary pronunciation of the place-name. Though *Paterson's Roads* spelt the village with a 'g' in 1829, the Manchester South Junction & Altrincham Railway chose the 'c' in 1845, and there it was in accord with the Ordnance Survey. Together they must have done much to determine the spelling thereafter. But the pronunciation never changed.

The railways and the Ordnance Survey did not always agree. When the junction of the North British lines to Hexham and Morpeth was established in 1862 it was at an unnamed place, and the station took its name from Redesmouth House, the nearest dwelling. For some reason the railway company insisted on calling it 'Reedsmouth'. The Ordnance Survey never noticed this ignorant error. A little settlement grew up there, dependent on the railway. It was always marked 'Redesmouth' on the map, and continues to be so marked still, when the station and the line have both gone.

The railways certainly had their influence on the pronunciation of some place-names. In Norfolk the opening of the line to Hunstanton in 1862 led to a change in that matter affecting four places lying in a row. 'Place-names began to be pronounced as they were spelt, not "Darsingham, Snetsham, Hitcham, and Hunston" as formerly, but "Dersingham, Snet-ti-sham, Heacham, and Hun-stan-ton" as more and more holiday-makers used the railway'.[132] The change was not due to holiday-makers alone. The spellings adopted by the railways in all their notices must gradually have had their effect on the increasing number of passengers who were literate. Contemporaries sometimes overstated the railways' influence in producing such changes as these.[133] Porters may have called out 'Carlísle' on the station platforms, when it was more usual in the city itself to accent the first syllable of the name. But both forms had been in use locally for centuries past;[134] the most the railways can have done was to give a wider currency to one form. Here and there, it is true, the porters habitually called out station names wrong: Balham in south London thus became 'Balámm' and in Scotland, we are told, they rendered Dalmeny as 'Dálmeny'.[135] But neither of these oddities did anything to change the normal pronunciation.

Redesmouth was not the only place where a railway company established a station on an almost uninhabited site. A name might then have to be invented. When a station was required in 1868 at the meeting-point of the Aylesbury & Buckingham Railway with the London & North Western lines from Bletchley to Banbury and Oxford, it was at a lonely place. Though it lay within the parish of Middle Claydon, there was already a Claydon station on the Oxford line. The nearest village was Addington, but the North Western had a station at Adlington in Lancashire, and such confusions were always avoided if possible. So the station became Verney Junction, Sir Harry Verney of Claydon being the landowner and deputy-chairman of the Aylesbury & Buckingham company. No village ever appeared there: only an inn and a few railwaymen's cottages. A similar difficulty arose for the Great Central company in 1899, also on the Verney estates. Its London extension line crossed them, and a station was wanted (by whom?) at the point where it intersected the by-road that meandered from the Claydons towards Bicester. This place too was uninhabited, so the station was called Calvert, the original surname of the then Sir Harry Verney, which he had changed on his succession to Claydon.[136]

One other curious case may be mentioned, from Scotland. On its line from Hamilton to Lesmahagow, the Caledonian company included a station named Tillietudlem. There was no settlement there, and the name was drawn from a novel: *Old Mortality*. Scott had invented it to designate Craignethan Castle near by. The station was used mainly by tourists visiting the romantic scene described in the eleventh chapter of the book.

Railways offered the traveller the means of reaching some stations with names that must have sounded very queer to him indeed: Legacy, Ponkey, Upper Boat, Trouble House, Triangle, Skares. The companies often used strange names for places important in their working: Jumble Lane signal-box at Barnsley, innumerable junctions – Throstle Nest in a grimy quarter of Manchester, Dowlais Zig Zag lines (graphically expressive), Bo Peep, Pye

Wipe, North Pole. And did anyone ever venture to tell Queen Victoria that on her customary journeys between Windsor and Balmoral her train took her through Satan's Den?[137]

The construction of the lines themselves left its mark on the map. Railroad Heath is still to be found near Fleet in Hampshire, a legacy of the London & Southampton Railway from the 1830s. Spoilbank Wood is near the southern end of the tunnel at Potter's Bar, on the main line out of King's Cross. The spoil from that tunnel and the adjacent cuttings formed the bank; the wood was perhaps planted to hide its nakedness.

And finally, in towns the railways set their mark on streets. There were countless Railway Streets and Station Streets; always grubby, never handsome main thoroughfares, as they often were on the Continent. Some of the larger companies got more impressive names adopted. The Midland secured Midland Roads at Bedford and Wellingborough. The Great Central, coming in late, was especially insistent on having its stations called 'Central' (even when, as at Rugby, that term was entirely misleading), and at Leicester it got a Great Central Street. 'Great Eastern Street' was a sound advertisement for the railway of that name in London, applied to a busy new road to and from the docks.

Railways came to be much associated with inns. Some changed their names, on the advent of the railway: the New Inn at Malvern, for instance, which re-christened itself the Railway Inn.[138] In Midland Road, Bedford, the Express and the Engine and Tender stood within a few yards of each other; and near the second station in the town, St John's, there used to be an inn bearing the name of a very rare bird, the Railway Swan.[139] The Railway Telegraph survives at Forest Hill in south London: happily, for those words, standing together, commemorate an early example of a union of two devices that grew very important in conjunction in Victorian Britain.[140]

The Language of Speed

The greatest achievement of the railways was to move passengers and freight on a quite new scale, and at an unprecedented speed. Victorians seem to have attached more importance to the second part of that achievement than to the first. The quantity of movement, and the consequences it led to, were a matter of calculation, proper to political economy; whereas the new speed the railways brought was irresistibly dramatic, a wonder that called out for language to express it. The other aspect of the railways' work, the power they showed to shift the heaviest loads efficiently, was more profoundly important to the society as a whole. But it did not stir the layman's imagination, as speed did.

That bustle came to be reflected in the English language. 'Journey speed' emerged as a unit of computation in the 1880s.[141] Very early in the twentieth century there came to be 'high-speed trains',[142] and 'inter-city trains' too.[143] When, on the other hand, a service was slowed down (whether to reduce cost or to achieve greater punctuality), that too was a matter of public comment.

After the exciting races to Scotland in 1895 a new word was coined to describe this policy. It was said that the trains had been 'decelerated', the word usually carrying an undertone of complaint.[144]

So the English language, eternally supple, continued to admit extensions, in recognition of new practices followed by the railways and new ideas arising from them.

The Welsh Language

Although railways appeared early in Wales and were developed there energetically by local enterprise, they did not produce much of a vocabulary of their own in Welsh. The language of railwaymen in Wales, even of Welsh speakers, was almost wholly English, unaltered or slightly adapted in translation. Thus 'train' became *tren* in North Wales but remained *train* in the South, pronounced 'trine'; 'porter' was reproduced exactly in the South, but in the North was *portar*. 'Station' was *steshon* everywhere – though *gorsaf*, the literary word, was also used in speech. In the same way a sleeper became a *sliper*, a signal-box a *bocs signals*; just as the traveller in Wales today will find notices on some stations containing the words *tacsi* and *traffig*.

On the other hand, Welsh seems to be the only western European language that never assimilated the word 'locomotive' from English. In North Wales the machine was represented by *injan dren* (i.e. train engine), in the South by *endjin*; though *locoshed* appears to have crept into Welsh railway language, as an alternative to *shed yr injans*.

This was the language of ordinary people. Literary Welsh recognized some made-up forms. 'Railway' appeared there as *cledr ffordd*: a plain translation, *cledr* meaning 'rail', as used in fencing, and *ffordd* meaning 'way'. *Fforddoliwr* (literally 'road man') is to be found on gravestones, denoting 'platelayer'.[145]

It was a long time before railway companies took any note of the plain fact that a good many people in Wales understood Welsh, and Welsh only. The census of 1901 showed that they amounted to 15% of the population of the whole country (including Monmouthshire). In four counties – Anglesey, Carnarvon, Cardigan, and Merioneth – barely half the population understood English.

No railway made any attempt to address the people of North Wales in Welsh until the 1880s. The London & North Western company, which by then owned nearly all the system there, found it necessary to strengthen its provisions for preventing trespass on its lines by means of an Additional Powers Act in 1883, and it then recognized that if it warned trespassers of the penalties for this offence through notices worded only in English, the courts would be likely to accept pleas of ignorance of the language from those who understood only Welsh. So at all stations and level crossings west of Mold Junction (outside Chester) it put up cast-iron notice-plates worded in Welsh, mounted below those carrying an identical message in English. Both sets were dated 'Euston Station. London. December 1883'.[146]

[193]

Although it was doubtless the lawyers who emphasized that not all Welshmen were bilingual, the company was soon afterwards made aware of other, more serious grievances of this kind. Allegations that it was discriminating against Welsh-speaking employees began to be heard. They were seized on by politicians (the young Lloyd George among them) and gave the company some trouble in 1890–5.[147] That presently died down, and thereafter no special effort seems to have been made to interpret the railway to Welshmen in their own language for another eighty years until – in a very different political climate – British Rail adopted a general policy of making its notices bilingual throughout Wales.

8
LITERATURE

*Early Railway Verse · Dickens · Mid-Victorian Novelists ·
A New Generation · The Theatre · Satire · Detective
Stories · The Railways' Own Literature · A Glance Abroad*

Early Railway Verse

The success of the first steam railways evoked little interest from English imaginative writers. In London, to which most literary men looked, the first steam-hauled trains were not running until 1836. By that time the doings of the pioneer provincial railways had been reported frequently in the national newspapers. So railways did not burst on London with the same force as they had on Liverpool and Manchester in 1830. The curiosity and interest they aroused when they arrived in the English capital were already muted. Nor were the small railways of the Monklands coalfield noticed by the intelligentsia of Edinburgh.

Only two distinguished poets paid attention to railways in the 1830s: the elderly Wordsworth and the young Tennyson.

Wordsworth's sonnet 'Steamboats, Viaducts, and Railways' was one of a group of poems written in 1833. In August of that year he visited Wetheral, east of Carlisle. There he saw the viaduct by which the Newcastle & Carlisle Railway crossed the River Eden; then brand new in its rich red sandstone, *Ill. 7* the arches closed only in the previous April. He had travelled by steamboat extensively during a tour he had just made in Scotland. Now he looked at what he recognized as a 'magnificent' bridge for a railway, and it projected his mind forward to consider what railways might do when they were fully at work and widely extended. He seized at once on the threat they presented to the peace and beauty of the landscape. But the conclusion he drew at this stage, expressed in the last six lines of his sonnet, was philosophical, even optimistic:

> In spite of all that beauty may disown
> In your harsh features, Nature doth embrace
> Her lawful offspring in Man's art; and Time,
> Pleased with your triumphs o'er his brother Space,
> Accepts from your bold hands the proffered crown
> Of hope, and smiles on you with cheer sublime.

The poet modified these views later, but he never entirely changed them.

Tennyson was a young man of twenty-one when the Liverpool & Manchester Railway was opened, and he saw it at work very soon afterwards.[1] He incorporated an impression of it into a line in his poem 'Locksley Hall', probably written in 1837–8, which became famous:

Let the great world spin for ever down the ringing grooves of change.

Later he came to realize that this description of the railway was mistaken (though he never altered it in any subsequent edition of his works), explaining that he saw the train only on a dark night, among a great crowd, which permitted him to suppose that the rails were grooved. The error was unimportant. He was the first considerable poet of his generation to take any notice of the new achievements of the steam engine, on land and sea. He had already proclaimed himself 'Mechanophilus' (a friend of machines) in a poem written four or five years before 'Locksley Hall', 'in the time of the first railways', as its sub-title declared:

> ... Dash back that ocean with a pier,
>   Strow yonder mountain flat,
> A railway here, a tunnel there,
>   Mix me this Zone with that! ...
>
> As we surpass our fathers' skill,
>   Our sons will shame our own;
> A thousand things are hidden still
>   And not a hundred known. ...

But the excitement these lines showed soon died down. Chagrined by the critics' harsh reception of the *Poems* of 1833, he put away what he wrote. 'Mechanophilus' was not printed until 1892, after his death.[2]

The other well-known poets of the time made almost no reference to railways. Moore does not, I think, mention them anywhere in verse, though he wrote appreciatively of their services to him twice in his journal.[3] Hood's treatment of railways is comprised in 'John Jones: a Pathetic Ballad' (1837), about a builder's clerk who turns railway engineer, takes to drink, and hangs himself.[4]

Small versifiers in the provinces attempted to celebrate the amazing contrivance when it was new. 'Iron Wonders: a New Song' is a crude, jolly little piece written about the competition of locomotives at Rainhill in 1829.[5] Joseph Hardaker, who lived at Haworth in Yorkshire, saluted the Liverpool & Manchester Railway in the 315 lines of his *Aeropteron: or Steam-Carriage* (1830).[6] It has no literary merit, descending here and there to bathos; but it deserves remembrance as the first long poem devoted entirely to the railway. When the Sheffield & Rotherham Railway was opened in 1838, Ebenezer Elliott wrote some bad stanzas to say that railways would destroy tyrants and promote international amity.[7]

That grew to be a favourite theme, particularly in the later 1840s, when several 'tyrants' were toppled, at least for a moment, and the idea of international socialism took a step forward. Charles Mackay – a good man, though no considerable poet – expressed it thus in 1846:

> ... Lay down your rails, ye nations, near and far –
> Yoke your full trains to Steam's triumphal car;
> Link town to town; unite in iron bands
> The long-estranged and oft-embattled lands.[8]

It soon became apparent that such hopes as these were illusory. The Crimean War was followed in the 1860s by the American Civil War and the Prussian wars against Denmark, Austria, and France, none of which had been prevented by any international goodwill created by railways. On the contrary, in them railways became instruments of military action, part of the very machinery of war itself. The idealism of men like Mackay burnt itself out or turned to pessimism or to some form of political agitation.

Dickens

The novelists' response to railways was stronger than the poets'; stronger in Dickens than in any other English imaginative writer in the Victorian age.

Dickens never loved railways. He often came near to hating them. Travelling by them alarmed him; he detested boards of directors and the financial chicanery involved in railway promotion; he criticized the facilities the companies offered, their refreshment rooms above all; here and there, as at Rochester, he saw them sweeping away the relics of a past he loved.[9]

And yet, with his unsleeping curiosity and his interest in the oddities of human arrangement, he could never take his eye off the railways. The sights, the sounds, the human life associated with them, fascinated him; he commented on them to the end.

The word 'railways' appears momentarily in *Pickwick Papers* (1836–7). In the second of 'The Mudfog Papers' (1837) Dickens hints at the notion of an underground railway and tilts at speculation in railway shares.[10] He is not known to have travelled by train himself until 8 November 1838 when, anxious about the proofs of *Oliver Twist*, he went that way from Liverpool to London, apparently without commenting on the experience.[11]

His first descriptions of railway travelling relate to America. They are in letters he wrote to his friends from there in 1842, in *American Notes*, and in *Martin Chuzzlewit*, comparing what he found across the Atlantic with what people were getting accustomed to in England. The comparison did not favour the Americans. The dangers of accident on their light, unfenced track, the noise and heat of the trains, with the incessant and unquenchable spitting there ('I can bear anything but filth', he wrote), made his American journeys disgusting to him.[12]

At home, Dickens was quick to seize on the comic potentialities of the railway: in old Mr Weller's journey from London to Birmingham 'locked up in a close carriage with a living widder' and in Mrs Gamp's indignation at the noise made by the Ingeins, inducing premature births.[13] In 1844 he entertained an audience at Birmingham with his account of an old gentleman who had come down with him from London in the train and denounced it for displacing the stage-coaches, while yet demanding that it should travel faster.[14] Though Dickens himself romanticized the stage-coach, in *Pickwick* and elsewhere, he had already come to terms with the railway and he did not encourage his companion's praise of the former way of travelling.

In 1845–6, when he was involved in the launching of the *Daily News*, he went down to Chatsworth to meet Joseph Paxton and George Hudson. On this occasion, he even agreed to invoking Hudson's help. But he came to feel

> a burning disgust against Mister Hudson. His position seems to me to be such a monstrous one, and so illustrative of the breeches pocket side of the English character, that I can't bear it. There are some dogs who can't endure one particular note on the Piano. In like manner I feel disposed to throw up my head, and howl, whenever I hear Mr Hudson mentioned. He is my rock ahead in life.[15]

Hudson later became for him 'the Great Humbug of England'.[16] Dickens was no financial speculator. But he was deeply interested in money – both in the acquisition of it for himself and as a theme in moral history. He had already drawn characters who were obsessed by money – Ralph Nickleby, Jonas Chuzzlewit. Now, in 1846, he decided to place a London business man in the centre of a novel. He began to write it in June and released the title at the end of August: *Dealings with the Firm of Dombey and Son*.[17] In this book there are four railway scenes: two set in Camden Town, depicting the upheaval when the London & Birmingham line intersected it (see pp. 14, 122–3); Mr Dombey's journey from London to Birmingham; and Carker's death.[18]

The third of these scenes describes the sensations, physical and mental, felt in travelling, with the flow of the words matched to the rhythm of the wheels. The constantly repeated phrases ('away with a shriek, and a roar, and a rattle'), the four successive paragraphs that end with the analogy between the inexorable progress of the train and of the 'monster Death' – these are a mechanism of words arising from the noise made by the train itself.[19] Dickens's account of the journey is no confused phantasmagoria. It is quite precise, showing the passage of the train 'through the chalk, through the mould, through the clay, through the rock'. And it concludes with the entry into the great town, the glimpses afforded from the line of hideous slums, 'deformity of brick and mortar penning up deformity of mind and body'; with the true remark that the railway 'has let the light of day in on these things: not made or caused them'.[20]

Carker's death under a train is carefully set on the railway, with the thunder of approaching expresses and Carker's fascinated horror as he sees an engine taking water, 'watching its heavy wheels and brazen front'. In *Dombey and Son* Dickens depicted the glitter and thrill of the railway, its irresistible strength.

He often reverted to railways, in passing, from this time onwards. In 1851 he wrote a brilliant sketch of a journey to Paris, 'A Flight', more than half of it devoted to the South Eastern Railway; the language telegraphic, keeping pace with the express train and with the telegraph itself, running beside the line.[21] He describes a train journey through the Black Country in snow[22] and discusses a strike.[23] He puts a paragraph into *Bleak House* about the building of a railway through open country.[24] In *Hard Times* he has sixty words (no more: they suffice) showing the arrival and departure of a train at a wayside station in a thunderstorm. That novel also includes an indictment of a callous Parliamentary debate about railway accidents.[25] Then in 1857, in 'The Lazy Tour of Two Idle Apprentices', he picks up some of the themes he played with in *Dombey and Son*, carrying the treatment of them further.

The 'Lazy Tour' was a Christmas story written in collaboration with Wilkie Collins, an account of a walking-tour in Cumberland.[26] A single paragraph in the first chapter describes a journey from London to Carlisle, even more impressionistically than Mr Dombey's but without its continual repetition of phrases. The two tourists idle away some hours at a station – evidently Carlisle – where Lethargy alternates with Madness. A high signal-box there at night becomes 'an enterprising chemist's established in business on one of the boughs of Jack's beanstalk'. Again the observation is sharp, but it is all translated into picturesque and comic metaphor.

In the following year Dickens embarked on what became a gruelling round of public readings from his works, in Europe and America: a performance amazing in its energy and endurance, which railways alone made possible. The holidays he took from it were short. On his way back from one of them, in Paris in 1865, the boat train in which he was travelling was derailed at Staplehurst, and ten passengers were killed.[27] Though he himself escaped physical damage and behaved with admirable calmness in helping the injured, it was a hideous experience, from which he never fully recovered. For some time afterwards he used slow trains in preference to expresses. Then his exacting schedules (and no doubt his own impatience) put an end to that practice, but he repeatedly complained of the exhaustion that fast trains induced in him: on a Midland express from Leicester in 1867,[28] next year on the East Coast day-time train from London to Edinburgh, a journey that he reckoned imposed 'something more than thirty thousand shocks to the nerves'.[29]

His view of railway management now sank even lower than before. Speculation was building up again, rising to a climax with a vast new crop of Bills in Parliament in the autumn of 1865: 'a muddle of railways', he justly called it, 'in all directions possible and impossible, with no general public scheme, no general public supervision, enormous waste of money, no fixable responsibility'.[30] This led to the financial crash of May 1866, which Dickens must have watched with grim relish, holding the views he did about speculation. Yet he returned now to railways, to write the most extensive description of them and their work that he ever produced.

It arose out of a chance happening. That April he was travelling from

London to Liverpool, and when the train stopped at Rugby his carriage was found to be on fire. While another one was being attached instead, he went into the refreshment room for a cup of coffee, where he was treated rudely by the female presiding there, to the infinite merriment of an attendant page-boy. The comic value of the episode struck him, and he worked it into a full account of one of the railway refreshment rooms he had so long detested. It formed part of the next Christmas number of *All the Year Round*.

Under the title *Mugby Junction* that number contained eight chapters, little related to one another, of which Dickens wrote the first four.[31] The third, 'The Boy at Mugby', comprises an indictment of English railway refreshment rooms, compared with those in France. The first chapter includes two passages in which Dickens addresses himself again to describing the sights and sounds of the railway. One of these is the most poetical account of them he ever wrote:

> A place replete with shadowy shapes, this Mugby Junction in the black hours of the four-and-twenty. Mysterious goods trains, covered with palls and gliding on like vast weird funerals, conveying themselves guiltily away from the presence of the few lighted lamps, as if their freight had come to a secret and unlawful end. Half-miles of coal pursuing in a Detective manner, following when they lead, stopping when they stop, backing when they back. Red-hot embers showering out upon the ground, down this dark avenue and down the other, as if torturing fires were being raked clear; concurrently, shrieks and groans and grinds invading the ear, as if the tortured were at the height of their suffering. Iron-barred cages full of cattle jangling by midway, the drooping beasts with horns entangled, eyes frozen with terror, and mouths too: at least they have long icicles (or what seem so) hanging from their lips. Unknown languages in the air, conspiring in red, green, and white characters. An earthquake, accompanied with thunder and lightning, going up express to London. Now, all quiet, all rusty, wind and rain in possession, lamps extinguished, Mugby Junction dead and indistinct, with its robe drawn over its head, like Caesar.

Dickens's attack on refreshment rooms here aroused a little resentment.[32] However the companies' managers asked him to preside at the next annual festival of the Railway Benevolent Institution. He agreed and made an excellent speech there,[33] underlining the dangers that railwaymen faced and concluding with a fine tribute to the service they rendered to passengers in all the ordinary business of life. He often criticized railway management. But his heart was with the men, at their normal work.

In 1867–8, on his second visit to America, he took handsome note of some improvements in his train journeys there. The frightful accident to the Irish Mail at Abergele in 1868 brought back all his old fears of railway travelling.[34] Next year he took a characteristic farewell of refreshment rooms with a description of a pair of tea-urns from Stafford station under repair, 'honey-combed within in all directions', having supplied for years 'decomposed lead, copper, and a few other deadly poisons' to those who drank the fluid from them.[35] He died, at fifty-eight, on 9 June 1870: the fifth anniversary of the Staplehurst accident.

Mid-Victorian Novelists

Dickens used the railways' services much more frequently and demandingly than any other great English writer of his time. His temperamental dislike of management in any form made him always (sometimes excessively) sensitive to the grievances that passengers might feel against the companies, stimulating his pugnacity. So he had special cause to write about railways, publicly and in private.

Still, most of the other leading Victorian novelists had something to say about them, and a number of the lesser ones too. Though Thackeray's chief novels were set in the past, and he never wrote anything extensive about railways (apart from the exasperatingly facetious 'Letters of Jeames', the footman),[36] he had a grasp of their significance, of their emergence in his own lifetime, that arose from his acute sense of history and lay outside the scope of Dickens's imagination. We come on it suddenly, without any preparatory warning, in 'De Juventute', a paper he contributed to the *Cornhill* in 1860, near the end of his life:[37]

> We who lived before railways, and survive out of the ancient world, are like Father Noah and his family out of the Ark. The children will gather round and say to us patriarchs, 'Tell us, grandpapa, about the old world'. And we shall mumble our old stories, and we shall drop off one by one; and there will be fewer and fewer of us, and these very old and feeble. There will be but ten pre-railroadites left: then three – then two – then one – then O!

Railways did not begin to make any strong showing in English fiction until the 1850s. Albert Smith included a brief journey on one in his most popular novel, *The Adventures of Mr Ledbury* (1843). The Mania was not entirely ignored by novelists (it enters into Robert Bell's *Ladder of Gold*, for example, published in 1850), though anybody who thought of founding a character on George Hudson had to attend to the laws of libel. Dickens did not base the character of Merdle in *Little Dorrit* on him, but on the Irish swindler John Sadleir, who killed himself while the novel was being written, in 1856. New fraudulent operators continued to appear, whose fortunes arose in part from railways, crashing with a loud noise in 1857 and 1866. In the end they evoked one powerful figure, and one only: from Trollope.

Trollope was, among Victorian novelists, the one who came closest to Dickens in the frequency and extent of his railway journeying, as a servant of the Post Office and as a hunting man in pursuit of his sport. Railways began to appear in his novels in 1857–8. *Barchester Towers* and *The Three Clerks* were both written then – largely in trains, with the aid of a simple device he fashioned for the purpose.[38] Though railways themselves play only a very minor part in them, they form a leading element in the background of the next novel, *Dr Thorne* (1858), with Roger Scatcherd, the former 'drunken stonemason' of Barchester who rises to wealth and greatness as a contractor, till he comes to 'the making of whole lines of railway'. Among these lines is one particularly needed by the government, built by him under difficult conditions in half the normal time; and as a reward for that service he is made a baronet. But he remains a brutal boor, killing himself off with libations of brandy.[39]

Trollope continued to use the railway freely in his novels as it suited him, putting scenes on it into *Orley Farm*, in the waiting-room at Taunton and the Great Northern Hotel at King's Cross into *The Belton Estate*, and staging a suicide at Willesden Junction (carefully described) in *The Prime Minister* (1875–6).[40] But in *The Way We Live Now* (1874–5) he went further: not in any direct treatment of railways, which figured there very little, but as a commentary on many of the changes they had helped to bring about.

In this book he turned on his contemporaries fiercely and delivered the most formidable and comprehensive indictment of Victorian society that anyone ever wrote in the Queen's lifetime. The dominant figure is a great financial manipulator, Augustus Melmotte: a foreigner of unknown origin, brazen and utterly dishonest. He is into every form of fraudulent promotion across the world: notably a South Central Pacific & Mexican Railway, planned to run for not much less than 2000 miles from Salt Lake City to Veracruz. It is of course a swindle, but Melmotte uses it for his own purposes, as a lure, a bribe, a threat, and a smokescreen. He manipulates everyone in the book, becomes MP for Westminster, finds himself obliged to forge signatures, and in the end takes poison. It is Trollope's ultimate irony that such a disreputable ruffian should show in his own way more courage than any of the English people around him, from duke to yokel.[41]

This long book – grim, strange, and powerful – has something important to offer to the understanding of Victorian railways. In the 1860s and 1870s they came to be fiercely attacked for their misdoings. Every institution, every practice and belief was now being called into question, and the railways had to take their share of this public criticism. Of that mood and attitude *The Way We Live Now* is a sombre memorial.[42]

Like Trollope, the other Mid-Victorian novelists used the railway as part of the furniture of their stories. In George Eliot it penetrates her language too. For her the railway was a constant source of ideas and recollections. Born in 1819, she had grown up with it in the English Midlands and recalled the irruption of the London & Birmingham Railway into Warwickshire in her teens.[43] She drew on her memories of that in *Middlemarch* (1872).[44] In an essay written in 1856 she chose the railway to illustrate 'the images that are habitually associated with abstract or collective terms – what may be called the picture-writing of the mind'.[45] Her last novel *Daniel Deronda* (1876) includes one set piece at a country station;[46] but the railway also left its mark on the general vocabulary of the book. We hear of 'the broadening of gauge in crinolines'; Gwendolen Harleth sees herself as 'slighted, elbowed, jostled – treated like a passenger with a third-class ticket'.[47] The same kind of thing is to be found in Meredith: 'you were an engine shot along a line of rails'; 'a wild regret, like the crossing of two express trains along the rails in Sir Willoughby's head'.[48] Railways play their part in the vague political notions of Nevil Beauchamp.[49] The peppery old Dr Middleton – drawn from Meredith's father-in-law Thomas Love Peacock, who delighted in abusing them – pours scorn on 'the esoteric fashion of spending a honeymoon on a railway: apt image, exposition and perpetuation of the state of mind conducting to the institution'.[50]

So the railway made its way into these writers' habits of thinking. But it had still entered only rather indirectly into English verse and fiction before 1880.[51]

A New Generation

A new generation of writers began to emerge in the 1870s, markedly different in their style, in their outlook and interests, from the earlier Victorian masters. These younger men and women did not at first turn directly to iconoclasm, or to any satire as fierce as Trollope's in his later years. But their independence of mind led them to consider which of the values and assumptions of the age they should accept or reject. They looked at the railways, as they looked at much of the world in which they lived, afresh. They had grown up with railways as a normal part of their world. That made them not less interesting, but more; for these writers chose to deal in ordinary things rather than in the lurid and the wild.

Thomas Hardy exemplifies all this clearly. He was born in 1840. The railway began to penetrate his quiet part of Dorset when he was seven years old; and presently he heard tales of a wonderful excursion train that went up to London for the Great Exhibition in 1851. It figured later in his story 'The Fiddler of the Reels'. A railway journey could provide him with the setting for an episode; a bizarre one at the end of *A Pair of Blue Eyes* (1873). Once, and only once, he set himself to demonstrate the railway's physical power, when in *A Laodicean* (1881) the young architect George Somerset scrambles down a deep wooded cutting to stand in a tunnel and backs into a recess as a train approaches and runs by him. 'The popular commonplace that science, steam and travel must always be unromantic and hideous', he says, 'was not proven at this spot.' And when the train has thundered past, Somerset stands still, 'mentally balancing science against art, the grandeur of this fine piece against that of the castle' – the castle belonging to the woman he was falling in love with.[52]

But the most remarkable use that Hardy made of the railway arose from his observation of what happened there to passengers, his view of it as part of the framework of ordinary life. Nine of his poems are set in trains or on stations.[53] They all record what in an expressive phrase he called 'moments of vision': a single vision, as in the touching poem 'At the Railway Station, Upway', or a more complex one, with a criss-cross of emotions ('In a Waiting Room'); his one description in verse of a railway journey, in 'After a Romantic Day'; what is perhaps the most memorable of them all, the steady view of the sleeping boy in 'Midnight on the Great Western'.[54] In these poems Hardy reveals to us the intimate part the railway had come to take in the casual encounters of human beings.

The writers who were a little younger than Hardy had been born fully into the world of railways and used images and ideas from them instinctively, without any thought of literary effect. The young Robert Louis Stevenson, going through a difficult passage at home in Edinburgh in 1873, writes to a friend: 'the whole world looks to me as if it were lit with gas and life a sort of metropolitan railway'.[55] But Stevenson also described railways more specifically: in his poem 'From a Railway Carriage', as well as in some of his American writings, like *Across the Plains*; and – most especially – in his delectable comedy *The Wrong Box*, written jointly with his stepson Lloyd Osbourne in America and published in 1889. No other considerable Victorian novel owes so much to the railway. Without it the grotesque adventures it recounts would not have been possible. Nor is it *any* railway – the Great Smashem or some imaginary one. Everything happens on the London & South Western, which Stevenson had known when he lived at Bournemouth in 1884–7. The accident in the New Forest occurs to an up London express running 'a little behind time, but not much for the South Western'. The atmosphere of a railway station was never better portrayed by any English novelist than that of the old Waterloo, in the deadly hush of a Sunday afternoon, in chapter 14. These things are Stevenson's entirely: his collaborator had never been in England.

Henry James (Stevenson's beloved friend) is full of the railways.[56] His descriptions of them are few and short. First, a word of admiration for the underground railway in London, which he encountered in 1869 when it was still a novelty.[57] Ten years later he comments on 'the influence of the detestable little railway' on the Isle of Wight.[58] Then in 1888 comes a rich paragraph on the great London stations, which always interested him.[59] He went on to open a novel in one of them, *The Sacred Fount*, at Paddington in 1901.

He enjoyed travelling by train: particularly down on Saturdays to the country-house parties he appreciated so much.[60] In London, as he looked at 'the tremendous piers' of the railways' bridges over the Thames – Charing Cross, Blackfriars, Cannon Street – he felt they were 'the very pillars of the Empire';[61] though the Empire has gone, those pillars endure, and we can see what he meant still.

Railway images occur in his writings again and again, down to his last three great novels.[62] Of a powerful American lady, rich and eternally busy, he wrote: 'She is not a woman, she is a locomotive – with a Pullman car attached'.[63] Much later, in 1899, travelling up from Brighton to London in the autumn twilight, the train brought him an image of a group of Americans, 'hurried by their fate...in search of, in flight from, something or other'. He jotted it down and incorporated, not the image itself but part of the idea it suggested, into a novel that he never finished, *The Sense of the Past*.[64]

The impression the railway made on Rudyard Kipling was not oblique: it was powerful and direct. He delighted in machinery. He wrote splendidly of steamships ('McAndrew's Hymn') and joyously, in his later life, of motor-cars ('A Song of French Roads'). His finest accounts of railways relate to India ('The Bridge-Builders', for example, in *The Day's Work*) and the United States – though his American poem 'The King' concludes with a comment applicable across the world:

> ...'Confound Romance!' And all unseen
> Romance brought up the nine-fifteen.

But the tale 'My Sunday at Home' (also in *The Day's Work*) shows the care with which he observed English railways too. 'On Sunday all things are possible to the London & South Western'; walking down the platform of the country station 'they drifted under the great twelve-inch pinned timbers of the footbridge'. Kipling always knew every detail of an appliance of any kind that he described, and got it right.

The railway enters into the work of other well-known writers at the turn of the century. Like Stevenson, Jerome K. Jerome sported with Waterloo station. In *Three Men in a Boat* (1889) he guyed the hopeless confusion of its arrangements. It must have added to his impish amusement to be pulling the London & South Western company's leg, for he himself had started out in life as a clerk on the London & *North* Western, and though he did not stay there long he thought affectionately of Euston, and of the men he had worked with there, in later years.[65] The station at Stoke-on-Trent, with its arriving and departing trains, popped in and out of Arnold Bennett's stories,[66] and he depicted the construction of the Loop Line through the Potteries, as an event in past history, in the sixth chapter of *The Old Wives' Tale*. The railway figures in several stories by Q, including the delightful 'Cuckoo Valley Railway' (1898) and 'Pipes in Arcady' (1913), and in Saki's brief tale 'The Mouse' (1910). But it must surely be allowed that among short stories set in railway journeys the first prize should go to Ireland: for 'Poisson d'Avril' (1908), in which Edith Œnone Somerville and Martin Ross recount 'the inveterate supremacy...of the personal element' in their country on the railways they knew well.[67]

Two minor poets of these years stand out in the present context, for different reasons: Alexander Anderson and John Davidson.

Anderson is the only one of all these authors who was himself a railwayman.[68] He worked for eighteen years as a platelayer on the Glasgow & South Western Railway, enlarging his scanty education in literature by teaching himself, and writing a number of poems published in four small volumes in 1873-9 under the pseudonym 'Surfaceman' (i.e. platelayer). They attracted attention in

Scotland, and in 1880 he was appointed an assistant librarian in the University of Edinburgh. There he passed the rest of his life in contentment. But his poetic gift died when he left the railway.

Though his inspiration was not powerful, it was authentic. What moved him most were the things he saw and heard in the course of his life as a platelayer: especially the tales of horror and tragedy in which engine-drivers were involved. Some of them he recounted direct, without even altering names. 'Nottman', for example, the driver depicted as saving the life of a child on the line who turns out to be his own son,[69] was indeed Jimmy Nottman, to whom that really happened.[70] 'Jim Dalley' is a convincing tale, in a similar vein.[71] Anderson's range of inspiration was narrow, and when he moved outside it he soon fell into bathos, or became mawkish. But within it he was able to display the endurance and courage of the footplate men with a force that can move one still.

Davidson never loved railways, or romanticized them. But as he looked at the life of poor people in London, like himself, he came to see them in very broad social terms, broader perhaps than any other English poet except Hardy.

He forsook school-teaching in Scotland for London in 1890, determined to make his mark in literature, and published a series of small books of verse in 1891–9. He had a dismal struggle to live, relieved only a little by a civil list pension in 1906. Ill and almost hopeless, he left London for Penzance in 1908, and there a few months later he drowned himself.

What Davidson had to say about railways in his poems was not altogether melancholy. He recognized the chance they offered to Londoners to find relief in the country – on an October day in Epping Forest, for instance, beautifully realized.[72] He could even set himself to depict the motion of travelling, in his 'Song of a Train',[73] and made good fun of the jumble of London Bridge station.[74] But the railway was usually for him a malign presence, with the wretched creatures who clustered about it: the 'station-loafers' and the 'gutter-merchants' whose lives he wrote of with a dreadful insight; the commuters travelling miserably in and out 'a-scheming how to count ten bob a pound'.[75]

A number of other Late Victorian poets took a fresh interest in railways, and the Georgians responded to them too. Like the Camden Town painters at the same time they seemed almost to be rediscovering them. Horatio Brown wrote a happy little poem in 1891 'To a Great Western Broad-gauge Engine and its Stoker'.[76] W. E. Henley produced another quite good description of a journey by train, 'We flash across the level', though he was more excited by the motor-car, to which he devoted his lengthy 'Song of Speed'.[77] Just before the War, and at the very beginning of it, three poems were written, in different moods, which close the sequence fitly: 'The Night Journey' by Rupert Brooke,[78] Edward Thomas's 'Adlestrop', and Siegfried Sassoon's 'Morning Express'.[79] Thomas's is well remembered, and deserves to be. Sassoon's is a faithful evocation of the steam railway:[80]

...The train steams in, volleying resplendent clouds
Of sun-blown vapour. Hither and about,
Scared people hurry, storming the doors in crowds.
The officials seem to awaken with a shout,
Resolved to hoist and plunder; some to the vans
Leap; others rumble the milk in gleaming cans.
Boys, indolent-eyed, from baskets leaning back
Question each face; a man with a hammer steals
Stooping from coach to coach; with clang and clack
Touches and tests, and listens to the wheels.
Guard sounds a warning whistle, points to the clock
With brandished flag, and on his folded flock
Claps the last door: the monster grunts: 'Enough!'
Tightening his load of links with pant and puff....

The Theatre

The railway's machines and trains did not lend themselves readily to the Victorian stage. That is not the sole explanation, however, of the slight attention it received there. The drama was, at least until the 1870s, a generally poor affair, the London theatre dealing chiefly in sensationalism, in pantomime at Christmas, and over the rest of the year in almost mindless farce. The novelties of thought, the new capabilities of action, arising from the railway could not make much appeal to its audiences.

An early Victorian play's title and sub-title composed an advertisement. Anything out of the way that might strike an audience would be included in one or the other. The railways and their doings furnished the kind of novelty that might have been thought attractive. It is therefore surprising to find that they make no great mark on the stage. Between 1830 and 1914 less than sixty plays, identifiable in this way, were licensed for performance in Great Britain.[81]

The first English railway drama seems to be *The Lucky Hit or Railroads for Ever!* by Edward Stirling,[82] written in 1836 and springing directly from the financial speculation of that year. Stirling evidently had an eye for this theme (perhaps he did some speculating himself?), for he returned to it in 1845 with *The Railway King*, acted that October.[83] This was not a satire on George Hudson but a mildly amorous little farce that touched on the business very lightly.

The first attempt to use any part of a railway as the setting for a play seems to be a one-act farce *The Railroad Station*, written in 1840 by T. E. Wilks.[84] The action takes place in the waiting-room of the station at Birmingham. One of the characters comments on the grandeur of the room's appointments, and the stage directions lay it down that 'the whistle of the engine is heard, the noise of the carriages, and the train is seen to pass swiftly by the window'. The opening of W. T. Moncrieff's play *The Scamps of London* (1843) is set at

Waterloo station.[85] Financial speculation figures prominently in only two of the plays of 1845: *Railway Mania or the Irish Stockbroker*, an anonymous farce,[86] and J. S. Coyne's *Railway Bubbles*,[87] in which an Irish gentleman appears who happens to be called George Hudson and whose name is employed to gull investors into taking shares in ludicrous enterprises.

Perhaps the most interesting of these pieces written in 1845 are two pantomimes. *Old Nick the Railway King*[88] looks forward boldly:

> 'Tis certain by the Atmospheric soon
> A ten-hour train will take us to the Moon.

At the close of the first scene the background 'changes to a grand central station. He and attendants mount, train starts' – on a one-hour journey to China. Another pantomime of the same month contrives to work in the theme of speculation. *Harlequin Pervonte and the Steam King or the Woodman's Wishes and the Fairy Fog*[89] opens in a 'Grand Hall of Science. In the clouds of steam, engines and other machinery at work when the curtain rises. From one in centre rises a continuation of bubbles labelled "Railway Scrip"'. A little later 'a railway whistle is heard and Science seated on a locomotive preceded by two imp engineers enters, dismounts, and is received with respect by attendants'. But the fun soon changes its direction, and the railway then disappears from sight. Indeed, it seems never to have made any figure in London pantomime again.

The underground Metropolitan Railway, opened in 1863, afforded a setting quite novel in the theatre. Dion Boucicault's melodrama *After Dark* (1868)[90] begins outside Victoria station and ends with a macabre scene on the underground railway that involves putting a train on stage. The same railway had also been treated in 1866 by M. du Terreaux in his *Waiting for the Underground*. Here the whole action occurs in the Metropolitan station at King's Cross, accompanied frequently by bells and whistles as trains depart.[91] There is genuine station business also in Thomas J. Williams's farce *A Tourist's Ticket* (1872).[92] It is a farce indeed, peopled with stock stage characters; but the station is drawn quite fully, with its refreshment room invaded by passengers from a Parliamentary train.

The railway now seems to vanish almost entirely from the English stage. But in the 1890s it comes back again, in a new and much more realistic form. The third scene of *The Night Express* by Gerald Holcroft (1890)[93] is played in silence as the villain climbs along the footboard of a carriage in a train in France to enter the compartment occupied by the heroine; they then struggle together, and she pitches him out on to the line. *The Swiss Express* (1891), an adaptation from the French, though described as 'a Pantomimic Absurdity', presents the first scene in any of these plays that is convincingly set inside a railway train.[94] And in 1899 part of the action in the anonymous play *The Iron Road* takes place in a signal-box near Rugby, the details observed with some care.[95]

Railways flit gently, almost unconsciously, through Oscar Wilde's plays.

The clever Mrs Erlynne, cornered and apparently defeated, announces she is taking the Club Train to Paris.[96] In *The Importance of Being Earnest* (1895) Lady Bracknell obliges herself to pursue her errant nephew into Hertfordshire by a 'luggage train', and the cloakroom at Victoria (the Brighton line) cuts an important figure in the *dénouement*.

The number of plays for which railways at least form a setting increases markedly in the early years of the twentieth century. How far was this change due to the influence of the cinema, a new rival that could offer exciting effects that lay beyond the capacity of the stage? At least fifteen railway plays appeared in 1908–14. Two of them were called *The Stationmaster*,[97] two *The Level Crossing*,[98] which indicates how the pieces were set. Two others deserve a moment's attention, both written in 1913: an American drama entitled *A Mile a Minute*, including a race between a motor-car and an express train,[99] and *Sixty Miles an Hour* by Harold Simpson, an Englishman, which is concerned chiefly with cars but ends with a reference to 'The Lightning Express', described as 'the fastest train in the world'.[100] Here, as in other branches of literature, speed showed itself a compelling attraction.

But railways never conquered the Victorian stage. No play wholly set on one of them enjoyed any commercial success in London until Arnold Ridley's thriller *The Ghost Train* appeared in 1925. Railways did however afford two services to the theatre that were of great importance to it. They much enlarged its audiences by carrying playgoers in from the suburbs of great towns and out again at night. In London they ran a number of extra trains for this purpose.[101] At the same time it is to be noted that they silently came to influence the length of the evening's entertainment: a play must be over in time to allow for the catching of the last trains. The railways also carried theatrical companies on Sundays, when they were on tour in the provinces: often in special trains of their own, which might need to make extensive provision for the conveyance of scenery and stage props. These journeys became a familiar element in actors' lives. Henry Brookfield wrote a few notes about one of them in 1879.[102] Henry James made at least two, in 1891 and 1908.[103] They were part of the tedious, fixed routine of theatrical life. A circus could trudge about slowly by road, behind a showman's lumbering steam-engine; but a theatre company had to be acting in one town on Saturday night and to open at another on Monday. It was 220 miles from Manchester to Edinburgh. Under these conditions, only a train could provide such transport. Here was a quiet, unseen, essential service afforded by the railways: part of the assumptions on which the Victorian theatre rested in the small island of Great Britain.[104]

Satire

Railways were a sitting target for critics and jokers. Pamphlets and newspaper articles rushed out in the 1830s and 1840s, written or commissioned by opponents of the new means of transport.

In the early days, while railways were a cause of wonder and admiration, some people were not to be awed by their achievements, and one of them stood out: Sydney Smith, who was among the least easily awed men of his time. He was not at all opposed to travelling by them. On the contrary, from his very first journey by train in 1841 they delighted him. But one feature of their management came to alarm him greatly in 1842. The horror of the accident outside Paris in that year had been compounded by the French railway's practice of locking the doors of the compartments in the carriages, which condemned many of the passengers to be burnt alive. The Great Western Railway, by which Sydney Smith normally travelled, did the same thing; and he protested against it in three letters to the *Morning Chronicle* published within a month of the disaster.[105] They command a battery of derision:

> In all other positions of life there is egress where there is ingress. Man is universally the master of his own body, except he chooses to go from Paddington to Bridgwater: there only the Habeas Corpus is refused.

> The first person of rank who is killed will put everything in order, and produce a code of the most careful rules. I hope it will not be one of the bench of bishops; but should it be so destined, let the burnt bishop – the unwilling Latimer – remember that however painful gradual concoction by fire may be, his death will produce unspeakable benefit to the public. Even Sodor and Man will be better than nothing.

Less than a week after the first of these letters was published, the Board of Trade issued a circular to the railways, enjoining them to lock only one door in each compartment. Although the Great Western (the only large company that insisted on locking both) countered with a tedious letter of self-justification, it grudgingly accepted the Board's policy. How much of the victory over what Sydney Smith called the Great Western's 'affectionate nonsense' was due to his letters cannot of course be determined; but his incisive ridicule must certainly have contributed to it.

In 1844–50 the Mania and its consequences afforded many rich invitations to satire. At least three of those produced then had some literary merit. Basil Montagu, a well-known lawyer, published anonymously an elegant little set of *Railroad Eclogues* in 1846.[106] Angus Reach's *Comic Bradshaw or, Bubbles from the Boiler* is still amusing today, for its commentary on travelling and its pictures (by H. G. Hine) alike. But the finest of these efforts came from Scotland, from a satirist of merit, who wrote as well as any of the comic draughtsmen drew: William Edmondstoune Aytoun.

He was a young Edinburgh lawyer, and he published three pieces on railway speculation in *Blackwood's Magazine* in 1845. The last of them, 'How we got up the Glenmutchkin Railway and how we got out of it', is the best. Aytoun wrote with the serious desire to expose the speculation and discourage his countrymen from embarking in it. His method was that of Juvenal and Pope:

he started with a firm moral purpose, and disguised it in a comic dress. The writing is terse and clean, including some good-tempered but also effective sport at the expense of a Sabbatarian undertaker. This squib was reissued three times, on merit alone, long after the Mania was past, in 1858–1907. Aytoun used often to think of friends, less circumspect than he was himself, who had been as he said 'out in the "45"'. But he soon turned to literature, involving himself little in public questions any more.[107]

The commentary on railways in *Punch* (founded in 1841) was generally more effective in pictures than in words. It enjoyed itself hugely with the Mania, which it treated as rollicking farce, larded with occasional moral strictures; inventing bubble schemes (the 'Eel-Pie Island Railway, with a Branch to the Chelsea Bun-house', the 'Grand Antipodean and Hemispherical Junction Railway between Glasgow and Sydney'),[108] seeing speculation everywhere, even in the most august and concealed corners of society – 'Tell me', exclaims the Queen, 'oh tell me, dearest Albert, have *you* any railway shares?'[109]

Though always a comic paper, *Punch* soon came to display notions and prejudices of its own on public matters; especially on the unscrupulousness of railway directors and officers. *Punch* was an organ of the middle classes in their lower reaches, always touchy about any kind of authoritarian control. Its views of the relations between the public and the companies were presented as a struggle of Us against Them. The directors and managers were always Them: dictatorial, irresponsible, greedy, heartless, a sinister force in society. All this is exemplified, for example, in the view *Punch* took of the railways' vandalism; of the companies' carelessness (real or apparent), as a cause of railway accidents; of their harsh, even inhuman treatment of their servants. *Punch* never welcomed the benefits offered by railways; there was not much fun to be had out of that. But then satirists are advocates, not judges.

Blackwood and *Punch* were national journals. Satirical talent might show itself anywhere, however. In 1849–62 the Eastern Counties company encountered more trouble than any other in Britain, partly from misfortune but more from incompetence and from quarrelling among its directors and shareholders. A number of people went into print to attack it or (occasionally) defend it.[110] This pamphleteering makes tedious perusal now. It is however irradiated by the work of one delightful joker, G. Wilson Ancell, who ridiculed the company ferociously and yet with imperturbable good humour in 1856. He put out a tale that a Bethnal Green costermonger, whom he called George Hoy, had wagered that he and his donkey would beat an Eastern Counties train in speed, and that the company had declined his challenge. This quip, published as a leaflet and distributed to passengers on the company's trains, was followed by fifteen others, commenting on its misdoings as far out of London as Sudbury in Suffolk.[111] The text, and the drawings that accompany it, are crude; the fun is implacable. Though of course the satirist exaggerated, the handbills offer fair comment on the lax management of some railways at the time, particularly of those that had little competition to meet from others.

In the later Victorian age this kind of satire dies down. The railways' doings and misdoings were now treated with a much heavier seriousness. They seemed to need reforming, perhaps even reconstituting under some new national management. Those were matters suited to earnest debate rather than to flysheets and comedy.

Detective Stories

Railways made some figure in one new branch of popular fiction that developed in Britain from 1860 onwards: stories of mystery and detection. Here they offered special opportunities to writers. The intricate techniques of railway work were invaluable to them in weaving their plots, and a crime committed in a train limited the number of suspects and their chances of escape.

Conan Doyle made constant use of railways in his Sherlock Holmes stories – indeed their mechanism of detection would have been unworkable without them, for the motor-car scarcely enters them until 'His Last Bow' in 1914. The great detective is aware of every device to serve his ends in travelling on them. 'Silver Blaze' begins and ends in trains; Professor Moriarty is thwarted by a dodge on the Chatham company's station at Canterbury. One tale, 'The Adventure of the Bruce-Partington Plans' (1908), reflected some observation on Conan Doyle's part of the way in which the underground railways were worked, in steam days; it is among the most ingenious of them all. Had he perhaps been led to think of the possibilities of that railway as a setting for one of his tales by Baroness Orczy's 'Mysterious Death on the Underground Railway' (1901)? And may the idea then have crossed the Atlantic to inspire H. S. Harrison's brilliant story 'Miss Hinch', set on the New York Subway and published in *McClure's Magazine* in 1911?[112]

At least one writer specialized in railway stories of this kind before 1914: Victor L. Whitechurch, who contributed a number of them to the *Railway Magazine* and collected some into a book, *Thrilling Stories of the Railway*, in 1912. He was to be much outshone in merit later by Freeman Wills Crofts, a retired engineer from the Belfast & Northern Counties Railway, one of whose stories, 'The Mystery of the Sleeping-Car Express', shows his thorough knowledge of detail on a journey from Preston to Carlisle in 1909.[113]

These are good tales. They excel in accurate description of the mechanism of railways. Few of them attempt to evoke an atmosphere, the tense atmosphere of travelling, enclosed within a railway train in some known conditions of danger. That does not come until 1934 in Agatha Christie's *Murder on the Orient Express*, followed two years later by the American Ethel Lina White's masterpiece of taut narrative, *The Wheel Spins*.

The Railways' own Literature

The Victorian railways called forth a large literature of their own. The character and quality of the technical railway press are discussed on pp. 243–5.

Here it is appropriate to pay attention to some of the general writing on railways that was addressed to the common reader.

The task of describing them, their appliances and their organization, in language intelligible to people who knew nothing of these things was not an easy one. The two best accounts of the Liverpool & Manchester Railway, Booth's[114] and Walker's,[115] attained that end successfully. These little books provided necessary information about the railway, but their modes of addressing the reader were different.

Booth was the secretary of the company, and his work was designed to set out what it had done, and why. He had been continuously at the heart of its affairs since 1822, when it was first promoted, and that gave him absolute command of his subject. Here is a sample of his matter and his manner. It comes from the concluding chapter of his book, in which he looks forward to what he supposed would be the consequences of the development of railways. His words are interesting as an address to the world when the railway was brand new, and as the earliest statement of his prophecy that railways would alter men's perception of time:

> Perhaps the most striking result produced by the completion of this railway is the sudden and marvellous change which has been effected in our ideas of time and space. Notions which we have received from our ancestors, and verified by our own experience, are overthrown in a day, and a new standard erected, by which to form our ideas for the future. Speed – dispatch – distance – are still relative terms, but their meaning has been totally changed within a few months: what was quick is now slow; what was distant is now near; and this change in our ideas will not be limited to the environs of Liverpool and Manchester – it will pervade society at large. Our notions of expedition, though at first having reference to locomotion, will influence, more or less, the whole tenor and business of life.[116]

Walker had no connection with the company; he was an outside observer of what it had done. He called his book an *Accurate Description*. Though its accuracy was not complete, he attained a high degree of it; and it is truly a description, concentrating on the work itself as it appeared to the visitor and the passenger. Walker was a competent journalist, his writing vivid, occasionally touched with imagination.

When the first trunk lines came to be opened, they called forth some interesting books of their own. Many of these were guides; directions to the traveller to help him arrange his journey and point out to him what might be worth seeing in its course, following the example first set by the road-books of the eighteenth century. Most of the early guides were the work of anonymous authors. Among the publishers James Wyld appears to have written his own. He was an intelligent and cultivated man, who had some things of interest to say about railways. Only one professional writer, already experienced in producing guide-books, was drawn into this work: Francis Coghlan, who had published at least nine such guides before his *Iron Road Book and Railway Companion; or a Journey from London to Birmingham* appeared in 1838. A few writers were more ambitious in the 1830s, particularly Peter Lecount: the first engineer who attempted a technical sketch of railways and a popular description of them together, and succeeded in both. He produced a *Practical Treatise on Railways* (justifying its title) and a *History of the Railway connecting London and Birmingham* in 1839. Both are of lasting value.

The railways generated their own technical literature: the manuals and presently the large books required for reference. Some of them established themselves as standard works, and went through numerous editions over the years. Brees's *Railway Practice*, published in 1838, was quickly reproduced in translation in Belgium and France. Simms's *Practical Tunnelling*, which first appeared in 1844, reached its fourth edition (much enlarged and amended) in 1896.

Among general treatises on railway management, one stands out: Lardner's *Railway Economy*. It represents a serious effort to consider the business as a whole, making use of information copiously supplied by a railway manager, Mark Huish, and of the statistical data then available, drawing useful comparisons between the practices of railways in Britain and those adopted on the Continent and in the United States. Lardner was a successful popularizer of scientific ideas and methods. Here he applied that skill to explaining the conduct of railway business in a form intelligible to any educated person. He was a theorist, led away occasionally into absurdities.[117] But his book was – and still is – esteemed by those who treat it fairly.[118] It is a good English example of what the French call high vulgarization.

Lardner had few successors, however, in Britain. Though the literature became rich in guides to the methods and techniques of building and operating railways, which embodied the country's long experience of making them work, it remained weak in the systematic discussion of their management, and of the public policy that regulated it. An Englishman, looking for a sound exposition of these matters as they developed in Britain itself, was obliged to turn to France and Germany, to Charles de Franqueville's elegant and perceptive treatise *Du Régime des travaux publics en Angleterre* and to Gustav Cohn's solid *Untersuchungen über die englische Eisenbahnpolitik*, both published in 1874–5. In North America, too, the general study of railways was pursued much more broadly than it was in Great Britain. A. T. Hadley's *Railroad Transportation* (1885) took a comprehensive view of its subject in America and Europe. No one attempted to write a history of British railways in the Victorian age comparable in any way with Alfred Picard's massive work on the railways of France. The first studies of any part of British railway history that were true works of scholarship appeared in 1915–16: Edward Cleveland-Stevens's *English Railways; their Development and their Relation to the State* and the Canadian W. T. Jackman's *Transportation in Modern England*.

If there was a notable absence in Britain of such works, the deficiency was, at least in part, made up for by the energetic and lively writing produced at the same time to interpret railways to the general reader. This literature began to appear, at a high level, in 1884 with E. E. Foxwell's *English Express Trains: Two Papers*, the first attempt to discuss the effects that fast travelling might produce in the community at large. In 1887 J. S. Jeans published his *Railway Problems*, a full and clear examination of the management of British railways, with some straight warnings of dangers ahead. Two years later Foxwell produced, with T. C. Farrer, a study of *Express Trains: English and Foreign*, and a young economist, W. M. Acworth, came out with *The Railways of England*, which has remained a classic ever since. Acworth's clear thinking and common sense are displayed on almost every page of that book. Here is his account of the Midland line from Skipton to Ilkley in Yorkshire, then newly opened:

> Short and unimportant as the line is, it is a perfect microcosm of railway construction. Let anyone walk along the line – the trains are not as yet over-numerous – and see how in one place the cutting is carried through the most obdurate of all obstacles, the boulder-clay; how, a little further on, the peat has been dug away to afford a solid foundation; how, in a third place, the embankment has been floated on brushwood, as Stephenson floated his famous road across Chat Moss. Let him notice the elaborate drainage, lest water should lodge anywhere to undermine the security of the permanent way; notice too the substantial stone bridges, in some instances not more than 200 yards apart, built for the convenience of a few sheep or an occasional farm cart, because even this is cheaper than the price that must otherwise be paid as compensation for severance;[119] and then he will have observed at least one reason why English railways are beyond all comparison dearer than those of our Continental neighbours. Then let him reflect that the working expenses of the traffic that is to be will swallow up half the gross receipts, and that therefore the railway manager, if he is to earn 5% on the new capital, must succeed in creating new traffic worth £2000 a mile, or £40 per mile a week, and he will hardly go away without feelings both of admiration and sympathy for the men who grapple, and grapple successfully, with tasks like these.[120]

Some of Acworth's best talents are shown there: his firm grasp of the way in which the railway had to be made, of the price paid for that, of the revenue that must be earned to justify paying the price, and of the responsibilities borne by the men who were charged with earning it. The union of those talents with the capacity to express what he has to say in lucid English makes him still, a hundred years later, the most intelligent and rewarding of all British writers on railways.

Railway men rarely set themselves to address the public about their own work. Not many of them indeed could have managed anything like that satisfactorily. Yet a few, when they decided to venture into print, showed up well. Some of the contributions they made to the proceedings of professional bodies were extremely capable expositions of technology and of the reasoning that lay behind it: the papers given to the Civil Engineers, for example by Benjamin Baker and John Wolfe Barry on the completion of the Inner Circle line in London, immediately followed by Stroudley's classic account of the construction and working of the Brighton company's locomotives;[121] William Langdon's on the lighting of trains in 1891.[122] The considerations that determined the fixing of railway rates were set out clearly by James Grierson, general manager of the Great Western Railway, in his book *Railway Rates English and Foreign* (1887), a good statement of the case for the defence. But the best of all such books – yet another publication of the year 1889 – was *The Working and Management of an English Railway*, by the general manager of the London & North Western company: a masterly account of a very complex subject in simple and attractive language.

Acworth's and Findlay's publications both ran through five editions in less than a dozen years. Railways could still command careful attention when their work was explained to the public by men who understood it thoroughly, and knew how to write.

A Glance Abroad

The literature of the Victorian age was enormous in bulk, and it includes much that has worn well; like most Victorian things, it was made to last. Why is it that the imaginative writers gave so comparatively little attention to the railway?

Bagehot had something valuable to say on this matter. 'We live among the marvels of science', he remarked in 1857, 'but we know how little they change us. The essentials of life are what they were. We go by the train, and we are not improved at our journey's end. We have railways, and canals, and manufactures – excellent things, no doubt, but they do not touch the soul. Somehow they seem to make life more superficial.'[123] He was far from a dreamy *littérateur* – a man fully conversant with the business world of his time, soon to become editor of the *Economist*. He wrote those words at the close of a long essay, in the course of which he recalled the delight that many people had taken earlier in the century in the manifestations of the power of science, and their belief in the need to spread the knowledge of it; contrasting that with the disillusionment and boredom that, for many younger people, had succeeded when the facile optimism of Brougham and his collaborators had had its day.

Railways, he said, did not 'touch the soul'. The idea of them might be inspiring, at first; but closer acquaintance did not often increase admiration. The imaginative response to them soon became dulled. That that happened so early in Britain was due in large measure to the immense success the railways had there, promoted by private enterprise. The system became denser, travelling by it grew commoner. The appearance of a train soon ceased to provoke surprise or reflection, indeed to excite any remark.

All this stands out more clearly if we glance abroad. I am not acquainted with any lyric poem about a railway written in Britain in the nineteenth century that has the direct and simple charm of one by the Swiss poet Gottfried Keller. In his 'Zeitlandschaft' he reflects on the passage of a railway through a quiet valley, with an aqueduct crossing it carrying a canal boat with sails. He was moved to write it in 1858, possibly by looking at an English print of 1841.[124]

Again, the fall of the Tay bridge in 1879 was a terrifying disaster: an entire train drowned with everyone in it, through the collapse of the central spans of the brige, blown down in a hurricane. It was of course described (though no one could watch it, in the night), and discussed all over the country. Much breath and ink were expended in pointing out that it occurred on a Sunday, and in drawing conclusions from that about the thinking of Almighty God. Presently its technical causes were examined. But this catastrophe – one of the most spectacular single events in the whole reign of Queen Victoria – drew forth no comment from any leading literary man in the country.[125]

One distinguished writer did however notice it, in Germany: Theodor Fontane, who immediately composed a poem on the subject.[126] Its five central stanzas are concerned with a child who is coming home to keep Christmastide with his parents at the north end of the bridge and plunges down into the river with the train. His story is prefixed and followed by a grim conversation between the three witches from *Macbeth*, forgathering to witness the disaster and then gloating over it with the repeated chant:

> Nick-nacks and playthings
> Are the creations of man.

It is the same in fiction as in poetry. There is no English novel of any importance in which the railway takes a central place. Perhaps the best is *The Iron Horse*, by R. M. Ballantyne, and that is an unimpressive book for boys. In Germany the fall of the Tay bridge was treated well, twenty years after it occurred, by Max Eyth in his novel *Die Brücke über die Ennobucht*.[127] At a higher level, in French there is *La Bête humaine*. That is not, it is true, a book *about* the railway. Zola found himself obliged to combine here several themes, which he originally meant to treat separately. The novel is a study of a murderer, a lust-killer, and at the same time of the corruption of French justice. But its whole setting is on and within the Chemin de fer de l'Ouest, which Zola knew intimately and had observed with meticulous, affectionate attention. The railway becomes more than the setting of the book. It is as much a part of its essence as the sordid and terrible characters who figure there.

Whatever may be felt about the novel as a whole – the melodrama and the imperfect realization of some of the protagonists in it – the rendering of the railway is faultless. Not simply because it is accurate in matters of factual detail (and that is something that laymen, writing about railways from the outside, have seldom achieved), but also because accuracy goes beyond the photographic and transcends it. Zola's appreciation of Impressionism in painting appears in his treatment of the railway. At the opening it grips us as we look down on the tracks approaching the Gare St Lazare in Paris, and it grips us again later, at night around the terminus at the other end of the line, Le Havre.[128] There is nothing in English to touch the sustained power of the depiction of a railway, as a mechanical organization worked by men, in *La Bête humaine*. Nor – looking a little beyond 1914 – has any English writer ever come to treat the railway with the intimate poetic affection bestowed on it by Proust, to convey his 'love of enchanted journeys by train'.[129]

Why should this have been so?[130] When the first trunk railways appeared in Britain they were hailed as the most wonderful achievement of the kind seen anywhere since the building of the Pyramids. That was at the opening of one of the great ages of English literature, as great an age as it was in the literature of France. There was certainly no dearth of talent to do justice to this extraordinary national enterprise: yet, with the exception of Dickens, the writers scarcely noticed it when it was new. What was it that made the French – slower to build railways, and travelling less on them when they had been opened – so much more ready to celebrate them in literature?

Their quick imaginative response to the railway was partly a matter of temperament. It was a commonplace for other peoples to remark, with disapproval, on their passion for novelty, and some clever French writers quickly exemplified that, treating railways in prose and verse – Stendhal, De Musset, Victor Hugo. Then the railway startled France with the terrible accident outside Paris in 1842. If this disaster aroused intense antagonism to railways, it also served to heighten the drama of the railway itself.[131]

In Britain it was a mere commercial instrument. The ceremonies inaugurating most of the great lines were very modest affairs – usually a train trip and a meal for the directors and their friends. On the first long-distance railway opened anywhere in Europe, the Grand Junction, the trains departed from Birmingham, Liverpool, and Manchester on the opening day without any ceremony at all.[132] In France, on the other hand, two of the King's sons were dispatched to Orleans and Rouen to grace the inauguration of the lines from there to Paris.

The British railways took their place beside collieries and textile mills, ironworks and shipyards, as instruments of a powerful, thrusting commercial economy. The French railways presented themselves as a new arm of the public service. There was plenty to arouse dispute in Britain among promoters, entrepreneurs, and shareholders, occasionally coming to touch the fringes of politics; much less to stir the minds of literary men than there was in France.

9

MAILS AND TELECOMMUNICATIONS

*Mail Services in the 1830s · The Transference of Mails to
the Railways · The Post Office and the Railway Companies ·
The Electric Telegraph · The Telephone · The Carriage
of Parcels · A New Collaboration · Benefits Conferred*

Mail Services in the 1830s

In the 1830s Great Britain already enjoyed a good postal service. Since
1784–6 mail-coaches had been running from London along the chief main
roads, operated by contractors bound to the Post Office by strictly-drawn
agreements. They enjoyed some important privileges, denied to the stage-
coaches: in England and Wales (though not in Scotland) they were free of
tolls on turnpike roads,[1] and the keepers of the gates were required to open
them in advance of their arrival; they took precedence over all other traffic;
they carried an armed guard. At first they took only four passengers inside,
none outside. But that rule was found to make the coaches too expensive to
operate, and in 1803–4 the carriage of outside passengers was allowed. Three
was the usual number (against eleven or twelve on stage-coaches), four on
some Scottish services. These were not the fastest coaches on the road, but
with the special protections they enjoyed they were the safest. And owing to
their contracts with the Post Office they were, as a rule, admirably punctual.

Off every one of these services cross-posts operated, carrying letters to the
smaller post towns. They also extended to Dover for the conveyance of mails
to the Continent, to Liverpool and Falmouth for those going overseas.

Of the twenty-eight mail-coaches leaving London daily in 1837, three ran
to Scotland and two to Wales; of those five, three made connections to Ireland.[2]
The average speed at which they all ran (including stops) was slightly under
10 mph.

The established means of handling the mail had by then clearly reached
the limits of its development. The coaches had been steadily improved in their
design, and a virtually new fleet of them was put to work, built to a higher
specification, in 1836.[3] The roads on which the coaches ran had been greatly
improved, and they were well maintained. All further development was
stopped by one thing alone: the limited physical power of the horse. No finer
animals could be produced than those that worked the coach services. Great
exploits were recorded on particular runs made by stage-coaches. One of them

is said to have gone from Liverpool to Manchester at 14 mph, in 1826;[4] on 24 June 1835 the 'Wonder' claimed to have made the journey from London to Shrewsbury (158 miles) at a speed of $12\frac{3}{4}$ mph, inclusive of stops, $14\frac{1}{2}$ excluding them.[5] But no regular services, able to meet the Post Office's exacting requirements of punctuality, could be run at such high speeds as those.

The Post Office was handling 76 million letters a year in 1839, at a cost to itself of just under $2\frac{1}{2}$d each.[6] To the public, the charge made for the service was enormously higher: 8d for the lightest letter from London to Brighton, 11d to Liverpool, 1s 3d to Aberdeen.[7] The Post Office then dealt in letters and newspapers alone, handling no parcels. This national service was held in great respect, save only by eager reformers like Robert Wallace and Rowland Hill, who thought they could suggest ways of enlarging and improving it. They were impatient to secure a cheapening of rates and other new advantages. But the civil servants were not the idle sleepy-heads that their critics made them out to be. They were willing to change methods and practices, when they saw reason to believe, taking into account all the complicated conditions under which they worked, that changes would produce improvement.

The Transference of Mails to the Railways

The idea that the railway might be used for the conveyance of mails reaches back to 1827. The London financier Thomas Richardson, one of the Quakers who supported the Stockton & Darlington company, wrote then to Francis Freeling, secretary of the Post Office, trying to interest him in the new enterprise. On the railway, he claimed, 'coaches were going as fast as any mail in the Kingdom, with one horse and fifty passengers, and much safer than any coach that leaves town'.[8] His letter ended with a suggestion that Freeling might dispatch his son to observe the line at work. That invitation was apparently not taken up. But Freeling was not blind to the possible importance of the new development, and within a month of the opening of the Liverpool & Manchester Railway he was in touch with the postmasters of those two large towns, considering the service it might render in the carriage of mails. He sent one of his staff to discuss the matter with them and with the railway company. The reports that resulted are brisk, observant, and clear. After some sharp bargaining, a treaty with the railway was arranged, and the mails were conveyed by it for the first time on 11 November. Reporting these matters to the Postmaster-General, the Duke of Richmond, four days later, Freeling paid him a courtly compliment, directed of course really to himself: 'The towns of Liverpool and Manchester ought to be thankful for your Grace's having so promptly availed yourself of this facility'.[9]

There was some cause for congratulation. Given the usual deliberate pace of Post Office procedure, Freeling had acted like lightning. He was under pressure. Coaches were already being discontinued, in the face of the railway's competition.[10] 'The Post Office seems to be bound to keep pace with the wonderful improvements with which the present age abounds', he wrote in the same letter to the Duke. '... We seem to have no alternative if we desire to preserve our revenue from injury, and also to meet the public expectation.' Expectation was indeed alert. A writer in the *Quarterly Review* had already prophesied that the mails would soon be travelling at 25 mph, with the result that 'an event, happening in London, would be known in Edinburgh the same day'.[11]

Some postal services continued to be maintained by horse-drawn coaches, but as the railway system developed they fell away and very soon, wherever it extended, the mails came to be entrusted to the 'posts by steam'. The Post Office tried at first to get them conveyed free of charge. When the Bills for the Grand Junction and London & Birmingham Railways were before Parliament in 1833 it framed a clause to that effect, for insertion into them.[12] The railway promoters put up a successful resistance, however, and it was left for the Post Office to negotiate a separate agreement with each company as a new line opened: often a protracted business, generating acrimony and requiring the services of arbitrators.[13] The value of the business that was at stake soon became considerable. In 1837–8 the Post Office paid the railways a total of £1313 for work done during that year. Ten years later the sum had risen to £82,260; by 1852–3 to £194,000.[14]

If it did not get the new arrangements on its own terms, the Post Office could still rejoice in them. George Louis, the Superintendent of Mail Coaches, having travelled up by coach from London to Birmingham and thence by the inaugural train on the Grand Junction Railway on 4 July 1837, wrote triumphantly from Liverpool: 'This is the first time in Europe so long a journey was performed in so short a time.... At 8 last evening was I in London and this letter will reach there tomorrow morning, ... thus performing a distance of 412 miles in $31\frac{1}{2}$ hours'.[15] The service involved the use of the mail-coach and the railway in conjunction, the mails being trans-shipped at Birmingham. When the London & Birmingham Railway got as far as Denbigh Hall, just north of Bletchley, in April 1838, the mail coaches themselves came to be placed on flat trucks in London, to be run on to the road at that temporary terminus and then back on to the railway at Birmingham.[16] This was a device that became common for a time as the railway system grew.

Two bigger innovations were now at hand. The first was the construction of a carriage designed to allow letters to be sorted while the train was on its way – something quite unattainable, on any large scale, in mail coaches, though a similar contrivance had been worked out for them.[17] At the same time the Post Office and the railways were considering the means by which mail could be collected and delivered from a moving train, using apparatus erected beside the line. Nathaniel Worsdell of the Grand Junction patented a mechanism for this purpose in January 1838, but the Post Office refused to pay him the royalties he demanded for it and worked out its own. This went into service on the London & Birmingham Railway in the following June.[18]

Something of the great potential of the railway for the acceleration and improvement of the mail services appeared very early. But the new development brought difficulties with it. As the coaches dropped off the roads, many important intermediate places on the old routes were affected. The coach-masters who had contracts for the mail-coach service between London and Woodside (Birkenhead), for example, informed the Post Office on 27 March 1838 that they proposed to withdraw it, giving no more than the bare fortnight's notice required. What was to be done then to serve all the places that lay off the railway (though on the coaches' route) between Northampton and Lichfield? This problem was solved for the moment by making use of the Holyhead mail through Daventry and Birmingham;[19] but it was a plain warning of what was to come in succeeding years. The officials were often hard put to it to adjust their intricate system to the railways, and to the coaches' shifting and declining business.

The Post Office now needed to place its relationship with the railways on to a statutory basis, and in 1838 an Act was passed 'to provide for the conveyance of the mails by railways'.[20] It obliged railway companies to carry mails on twenty-eight days' notice, at times to be fixed by the Post Office and on terms reached by agreement or arbitration. Section 3 of the Act required any company, on request, to provide a separate mail carriage 'fitted up as the Postmaster-General...shall direct, for the purpose of sorting letters therein'. (What other technical innovation of any kind has ever made its way to figure in a British statute within nine months of its first appearance?) This Act, extended from time to time but very little altered, remained the charter of the relations between the Post Office and the railways throughout the Victorian age.

So the system came to be established, serving the Penny Post, introduced on Rowland Hill's plan in 1840.[21] Its rapid development is well epitomized in the time-bill of the day and night mails between London and Preston in that year. The service was now performed by railway throughout, except between the General Post Office and Euston at one end and between the station and Post Office at Preston at the other. Fourteen stops were appointed *en route*, besides twelve more places where mail bags were 'delivered by means of the apparatus'. The quickest service was the down day mail, which from office to office took 10 hr 46 min., running at an average speed on the railway of 20.5 mph. Four years earlier the fastest mail-coach had taken exactly twenty-four hours on the same run.[22] So here the railway had already more than doubled the speed of postal transmission.

Similar arrangements spread rapidly to all the great trunk lines, though the pattern of services was not identical. New demands were made for their extension and improvement, both by the Post Office and by the public. The railways did not always seem to be meeting them as satisfactorily as they might, and in 1854 a House of Commons Committee investigated complaints. The mails had been behind time on average forty minutes a day at Newcastle; much the same at Edinburgh and Holyhead.[23] Naturally, the Post Office and the railways blamed each other – though Mark Huish of the London & North Western allowed that the late delivery of the mails to his railway in London, which had been a standing grievance, had been largely remedied.[24] The Post Office had had to try to adapt itself to the changes wrought by the railways with bewildering rapidity, and it had not always succeeded. For instance, although the Great Northern line had been open from King's Cross since 1852 the Newcastle mail was still sent from Euston: a route thirty miles longer and involving serious delays at Tamworth, where 'a system of centralization of letters' had been set up at the crossing of the Trent Valley line with the main one from west to north.[25] The adoption of the Great Northern route would have meant a reduction of an hour and a half in the time taken by the mails between London and Newcastle.[26]

One consequence of this inquiry was the establishment by the Great Western Railway of a night mail train between London and Bristol, exclusively for the use of the Post Office, starting on 1 February 1855: the first true postal train anywhere. It comprised no more than two sorting carriages and a van, and it made the journey at a speed (including the seven stops) of 31.7 mph. Having run thus for fourteen years, the train received the addition of one first-class carriage for passengers between London, Bath, and Bristol, the Post Office insisting that in no circumstances whatever were any more carriages to be attached. The train then became in railway language a Limited Mail, of a type that was already established elsewhere.[27]

One railway company, and one service, stood in a class by itself: the Chester & Holyhead, which was built above all for the purpose of conveying the main Irish mail.[28] Nobody contended that its domestic business would be large. The towns it touched along the coast of North Wales were very small, or hardly yet born; there was little industrial traffic except that in slate, which could be handled adequately by sea; the agriculture was poor. The company was authorized at the outset in 1844 to raise £2,800,000, and that proved insufficient. The only valuable revenue it could look for, as a commercial enterprise, was from the carriage of mails and passengers to and from Ireland. The line took six years to complete (including the great Britannia bridge over the Menai Strait), and meanwhile the company wrangled with the Post Office and the Government about the terms on which the mail should be conveyed. It was certain to secure the contract on land. But it hoped for more. In 1848 it secured powers – seldom granted to railways at that time – to own steamships and work them; and then, in March 1850, it saw the contract for carrying the mails across the Irish Sea awarded to the City of Dublin Steam Packet Company.[29]

Several forces were at work here; particularly the pressure that Irish interests exerted on the Government, to put this business into Irish hands. The arrangement made in 1850 was never rescinded, enduring as long as the Union with Ireland. It was one of the rare cases in which the Westminster Parliament favoured an Irish interest in a piece of United Kingdom business; and that – especially in view of the horrors of the Famine, then still unfolding themselves – may appear a small piece of compensating justice. Still, the Chester & Holyhead company got hard measure. It always had to rely heavily on support from the London & North Western, which brought its business into Chester. Shorn of one of its main sources of revenue, it proved an unprofitable concern. All it could do was to accept absorption into the larger company, which came into effect in 1859.

This was the one major British railway enterprise that was undertaken chiefly for the development of postal business; and the revenue from that became very important indeed to it. In the last year of its independent operation (1857) the subsidy it received from the Post Office amounted to over £30,000, 19.3% of its receipts from all passenger traffic.[30] The original proprietors, who got the railway going with so much difficulty, had to be content with little or no financial reward. In the days of the coach, when the Holyhead road had been improved under Telford for just the same purpose, the work had been carried out largely at the expense of government. No government money at all – nothing even from the Exchequer Loan Commissioners – went into the Chester & Holyhead Railway.

The Post Office and the Railway Companies

The relations between the Post Office and the railways were never easy. Neither party fully appreciated the problems and difficulties of the other. In the Early Victorian age the Post Office was being dragged through a series of thorough-going reforms. Moreover, a number of its chief officials were distinguished by their talent for vituperation. Rowland Hill and his brother Frederic are the outstanding examples, and their language became more intemperate as they grew more powerful. Rowland's notion of his own importance may be judged from the remark, made in official correspondence in 1861, that 'the Postmaster-General has again interfered with my Department'.[31] All this lent a special sharpness to the tone of any controversy in which the Post Office engaged.

One particular instance deserves mention here. Finding itself under a fire of public criticism in the 1850s, the Post Office and its apologists devoted considerable ingenuity to developing a thesis that the new Penny Post could have been handled quite well as far as letters were concerned (excluding newspapers and other printed matter) without railways at all.[32] They complained that the railways demanded large payments for postal services, whereas the coachmasters had undertaken them for much less, or for nothing, or had even paid the Post Office for the privilege of being allowed to handle them. Robert Stephenson – who often acted as an arbitrator in disputes about payments to be made by the Post Office to the railways[33] – twice devoted his attention to the controversy; and his second analysis seems to have silenced even the Post Office.[34]

The unreality of the argument is what must strike us most about it now. Had the Post Office's case been proved, that could have been of no more than theoretical interest, for the railways were there, transmitting the penny letters, and they had come to stay. Even the Post Office did not venture to suggest that it should return for its main letter services to the horse-drawn coach. Could anyone suppose that, with trains running at 20–30 mph, the public would remain content if the Post Office sent the mails over any long distances by coaches running at 10? The Post Office deliberately ignored here the whole revolution in speed that the railways had brought – for which of course a price had to be paid; and that was unattainable by any other means.

This is perhaps the first example of the application of counterfactual argument to the history of railways; an academic exercise that enjoyed some vogue in the 1960s. Based on the supposition that railways had not been built, the argument really constituted an unintended tribute to the magnitude of what they had achieved.

It is of course true that the Post Office made large payments to the railway companies for the services they afforded. It had to negotiate terms for the carriage of mails separately with each company. The rates differed in early days greatly. In 1848–9, for example, the North Union company was receiving a rate of 3s 1d a mile for its services, when the York Newcastle & Berwick got 10¼d the Manchester & Leeds 5½d, and two important companies, the London & Brighton and the Manchester & Sheffield, 2d or less.[35] Those figures, varying so greatly, reflect the endless battles the Post Office had to wage, and it was fighting, as we must in fairness recognize, from an essentially weak position. The railways alone could offer the service that was essential to it if it was to meet public demand; and each company could devote time and energy to the details of negotiation, whereas the Post Office, with no more than a small staff of senior officials, had to argue every one of the cases that arose itself.[36] The business was often settled very slowly. In 1855 the Post Office needed to negotiate a large and important contract with the South Wales Railway, for the transmission of the mails over the 155 miles from Grange Court (outside Gloucester) to Haverfordwest. No terms being agreed, the case was put to an umpire, C. S. Whitmore, QC, and he took five months to make his award. When it came, it was a compromise, though in this instance it leant noticeably nearer to the Post Office's demands than to the railway's.[37]

On occasion the Post Office removed the mails from the railway. In 1849, for example, on Rowland Hill's recommendation the night mail to Oxford was conveyed by cart from the Great Western main line instead of on the branch line from Didcot.[38] The slower speed was immaterial in this case, for the mails would not be delivered until the next morning. Years later the Post Office, troubled by the railways' charges for the carriage of parcels, revived the night mail coach: first to Brighton in 1887 and then to Liverpool, Manchester, and Oxford. The coach went at no more than 8 mph; but that was adequate for the long night journey.[39]

Again, when a railway company held out for a heavy payment for its services, the Post Office was sometimes able to send the mails over a different route, for which some other company was prepared to charge less. So the mail from London to Hereford, instead of going the shortest way through Gloucester, travelled round by Shrewsbury at a lower price.[40] Throughout his years at the Post Office, Rowland Hill tried repeatedly to get these troublesome charges fixed by Act of Parliament instead of leaving them to arbitration. He did not succeed.

The railways derived a steady revenue from the carriage of mails, but it never became crucial to their income, as it did to some steamship companies, and to airlines later.[41] In 1856 it represented 2.7% of their receipts from passenger traffic. Four years later that figure had risen to 3.4%. Then it fell back, standing from the 1870s onwards, year after year, at about 2%. At £911,000, it amounted to 1.9% of passenger receipts in 1913.[42]

There were however some companies, operating long lines away from large towns, that derived a really significant part of the revenue afforded by their passenger traffic from the payments they received from the Post Office. It was largest of all on the Highland Railway, where it reached 21.4% in 1890.[43] That company enjoyed abundant business from tourists and sportsmen from June to September; but in the other eight months of the year 'the Highland mail ... probably takes half as many passengers *per diem* as in August it takes carriages, and would not be run as an express at all except for the very heavy Post Office subsidy'.[44] That train offered accommodation to travellers who had started from London and might be going on to Wick, a distance of 755 miles done in just under 22 hours, i.e. at 34.8 mph. The Overland Mail, travelling from Calais to Brindisi, a light train backed by a huge subsidy from the British Post Office, made that journey at 26 mph.[45] So the fishermen and shopkeepers of Caithness, and the islanders of Orkney and Shetland beyond, did much better, in terms of railway communication, than the Governor-General of India. The Post Office and the railways were providing here, between them, a remarkable social service.[46]

The Electric Telegraph

At whatever expense of time and temper, the Post Office and the railways generally established a fair working relationship. Twice, however, in the second half of the nineteenth century the Post Office extended the scope of its responsibilities in a way that brought it and the railways into collision. The first concerned the electric telegraph.

Its invention and its early development by the railways have already been recounted. An Electric Telegraph Company was established by Act of Parliament in 1846 for the general use of the apparatus. Others soon followed, competing with it. In France, Prussia, and Austria it was a State monopoly from the beginning.

The new device had proved itself first in the operation of railways. But its value soon came to be appreciated for other purposes too. In 1845 (in conjunction with a railway) it brought about the arrest of a murderer. It was already helping in the apprehension of other criminals.[47] The Government made use of it in 1848 to foil the threat it had to meet from the Chartists. The telegraph helped to spread Greenwich time throughout the provinces and quickened the dissemination of news. It began to play its part in commercial life: at Norwich for instance in 1846, when London market prices were flashed in by telegraph, established along the Norfolk Railway.[48]

Neither the Government nor the railways had an exclusive call on the services of the telegraph. Private persons were allowed by section 14 of the Regulation Act of 1844 to send their messages by it 'without favour or preference'. Everyone turned to it in emergency. When in 1853 the parish church of Doncaster caught fire, the mayor got a locomotive to run by the South Yorkshire Railway to Swinton, where the telegraph was established on the North Midland line, so that a message could be sent to ask for help from Sheffield:[49] a good illustration of the service that the telegraph-cum-railway could offer and of the weakness of a community that lacked it.[50]

As early as 1854 the Government was being urged to assume control of the telegraph system through the Post Office. 'Is not telegraphic communication as much a function of government as the conveyance of letters?' demanded the *Quarterly Review*.[51] Other people came round to the same opinion, including J. L. Ricardo, chairman of the Electric Telegraph Company, who was also chairman of the North Staffordshire Railway. The Post Office was at first nervous of becoming involved in the business. There was a widespread uneasiness in the country at the idea of increasing the direct participation of the State in its economic life, largely on account of the additional patronage such an extension would place in the hands of ministers. As with the railways, so with the telegraph, the natural course in Britain seemed to be to make the State a regulator, responsible for the protection of private and public interests, at times an umpire in quarrels, but neither a promoter nor a manager of economic enterprise; still less a monopolist.

In exact accordance with this outlook, Palmerston's administration passed a Telegraph Act in 1863,[52] imposing a certain measure of general regulation on the companies and giving the Board of Trade powers analogous to those it exercised in respect of the railways. There the matter might have rested if the companies had not decided to increase certain charges for using the service in 1865. This was most unwise. They were acting in concert, which proclaimed that, as a group, they could exert a monopolistic power when they chose. Their new scale of rates brought the simmering discontent with their charges to the boil. The protests were naturally supported by the newspapers, now dependent on the telegraph; for them whatever rate might be levied would be too high. The Postmaster-General then instituted an inquiry into the acquisition of the companies by his department. A Bill authorizing this measure was introduced in 1868. Against a good deal of opposition from the telegraph companies and the railways, it became law on 31 July.[53]

It did not give the Post Office a monopoly in the provision of telegraph service (though that came about in the following year),[54] merely empowering it to buy up telegraph undertakings, on fixed terms, and obliging it to do so at any company's request. The South Eastern and the Taff Vale possessed telegraphs that were open to the public. The others had systems for their own use and a variety of arrangements with the telegraph companies, which had been permitted to lay their wires alongside railway lines. The Act provided for the full continuance of the service necessary to the railways in their working, and for buying out their interest in the transmission of messages by the public.

Some railway officers became uneasy lest, as one of them put it, this should become 'a stepping-stone to further encroachments'. What such men wanted above all was 'to keep the government officials off their lines'.[55] That cry came from the North Eastern Railway, and the opposition to the Bill was led by George Leeman, MP for York and deputy-chairman of that company.

In the original calculations on which the Bill had been based, nothing was included for compensating the railways. This was a mistake, admitted by the Government and retrieved by conceding them twenty years' purchase of their net profit on telegraphic business. The railways' attitude then changed at once. Leeman himself came near to allowing that they had held the Government to ransom and secured much too high a price from it, remarking in one of the Parliamentary debates that 'anything more improvident that the arrangement come to by the Government with the railway and telegraph companies could not be conceived'.[56] By the time those words were uttered (21 July 1868) the railway interest had abandoned its opposition to the Bill, and all the leading companies except three had come to terms with the Government.[57] The total sum paid to the railways seems never to have been finally published. Claims put forward by them amounting to £2 million were still unsettled in 1876.[58]

In 1868 there were about 3400 points in the United Kingdom at which telegrams could be sent by the public. Just over a third of these (1226) were provided at railway stations.[59] The railways had taken a great part here in initiating a public service. They kept the control of the telegraph as a necessary instrument for their business. In financial terms, they were supposed to have profited handsomely from the transaction. Too handsomely, some people believed; but nobody adduced any convincing proof of that assertion.

Here was the first piece of 'nationalization' in British history, in the sense in which that word is commonly used now, to mean the purchase of private

TABLE 3

NUMBER OF TELEGRAMS SENT IN
GREAT BRITAIN 1870–1913

	000	*% increase or (decrease)*
1870–1	9244	—
1880–1	27675	199.4
1890–1	62735	90.1
1900–1	84674	35.0
1908–13	81626	(3.5)

Source: PP 1913 xxxviii. 401.

undertakings by the State and the subsequent conduct of their business under the aegis of the State itself. The new arrangements were soon seen to work smoothly. The number of telegrams sent trebled in the 1870s and more than doubled again in the 1880s, in the service of all kinds of business, and of private persons. The well-to-do came to use telegrams largely in place of letters. Oscar Wilde's lavish outpouring of them, worded with dexterity and care, gave much enjoyment to his friends; Ada Leverson even thought of compiling a book of his *Collected Telegrams*.[60] Henry James wrote in 1898 of 'the class that wired everything, even their expensive feelings'.[61] The enormous increase in telegraph business gave support to those who thought it was time to consider nationalizing the railways too. J. S. Jeans put it like this in 1887: 'If the postal and telegraph systems were properly taken under Government control, there seems much more reason why the railway system should be, since railways are not only used by all, but exercise a power and influence on our social and our business relations that no other single element can claim to do'.[62] Jeans was not advocating the State purchase of the railways; merely saying that the successful purchase of the telegraphs strengthened the practical case for the application of the same policy to the railways at some time in the future.

The Telephone

A new form of rapid communication was now being developed, which was eventually brought under the control of the Post Office too: the telephone.

Although primitive devices for speaking at long range had been experimented with in the 1850s and 1860s,[63] the telephone as it is used today dates from the patents of Alexander Graham Bell, taken out in 1876. In 1878 the first commercial telephone undertaking was established at Chislehurst, and an experiment with long-distance communication between London and Norwich was successful. The first British telephone exchange followed in 1879.[64] As early as 1883 it was noted that subscribers living in the London suburbs were finding that the telephone allowed them to reduce their travelling by train to and from the City.[65]

The first installation of the telephone by a railway company seems to have been made in 1879. F. W. Webb's office was connected then by this means to those of a few of his colleagues at Crewe; but it was some time before the appliance was extended to the Crewe general offices as a whole.[66] Much more important, the Great Northern company began experiments with the telephone in operating the line between King's Cross and Finchley in October 1879, extending it to Edgware in 1881.[67] The Manchester Sheffield & Lincolnshire Railway was among the earliest subscribers to the telephone in Hull and Sheffield in 1880–1.[68]

The railway companies did not, however, adopt the new device eagerly at first. Nottingham traders had to band together to press the railways in the town to connect themselves with the telephone in 1886.[69] The London &

South Western began to order telephone instruments in 1885, installing them in signal-boxes, but not in the traffic departments until the middle of the next decade.[70] By 1889 telephone circuits were installed in the huge North Western marshalling yard at Liverpool.[71] The Sheffield company was then steadily extending its use.[72] In 1892 Harry Pollitt, its works manager at Gorton, said that in Britain the telephone had 'practically superseded the single-needle instruments in signal-boxes', and added that on the North Eastern system, if at any time the block instruments for working trains were out of order, they could be signalled verbally instead.[73] Pollitt was then reporting to an international audience, and he somewhat exaggerated the extent to which the telephone had been adopted on British railways. In 1893 there were not more than half-a-dozen instruments in use anywhere on the largest system in the country, the Great Western.[74]

Although cautious experiment still continued,[75] it cannot be said that British railways were pioneers in the early development of this form of telecommunication. Unlike the telegraph, the telephone owed no debt to them, except in so far as their use of it may have persuaded other people to adopt it for purposes of their own work.

The volume of its general business, in the country as a whole, began to grow rapidly at the end of the nineteenth century, largely at the expense of the telegraphs. Railway companies observed a steep decline in the revenue they drew from the commission on telegrams sent at their stations.[76] The telephones in turn were nationalized (though with a few exceptions) in 1912.

The Carriage of Parcels

The railways and the Post Office came into serious collision over the conveyance of parcels.

Rowland Hill had put forward plans to extend the principles of the reform of the letter post to the carriage of small parcels. They were defeated for a time by the railways, which saw them as an encroachment on a preserve of their own. However, the Post Office successfully introduced a book post in 1848.[77] It was supposed to be limited strictly to books, which could be sent in open-ended parcels at the rate of 6d a pound. The railways and their supporters saw this as the thin end of a thick wedge. ('If the Post Office can convey over railways a parcel of books, maps, etc.', *Herapath* exclaimed,[78] 'why may they not a load of hay or a hundred head of cattle?') They asserted that many other things besides books were sent at this cheap rate; and indeed the service was much abused. But the new facility proved popular and the Post Office prevailed.

The only means by which parcels other than books could be legally transmitted was by railway or by road carrier. Discussion now arose over small parcels – 'smalls', as they were termed. Large ones, by general consent, must continue to go in the established way. The railways' charges on smalls were high and the carriers tried to circumvent them by sending a large number in one unit by train, packed into a single hamper. The response of the railways was to prosecute the carriers, not to learn the lesson their practice suggested. After much argument a majority of the companies were persuaded, through the Railway Clearing House, to accept a scale of charges based on weight and distance applicable to the whole railway system. This was in force by 1860.[79] The Post Office was emboldened to establish a 'sample post' in 1863; but this, declared to be limited to samples and patterns, was abused as the book post had been. The railways then countered by lowering their charges. Those charges remained complex, however, whereas the Post Office system, ignoring distance and calculating a fee on weight alone, was simple.

There was now evident competition between the railways and the Post Office. In terms of business transacted the Post Office was winning; but the misuse of the sample post was too notorious to be allowed to continue, and the facility was withdrawn in 1871.[80] Meanwhile there was strong pressure on the railways to lower their charges further and simplify them. The Royal Commission on Railways declared in 1867 that 'the time has arrived when railway companies should combine to devise some rapid and efficient system for the delivery of parcels'.[81] A few senior officials tried to secure the abandonment of charging by distance and the introduction of a simple system of prepayment by adhesive stamps. Attempts were made from 1871 onwards to get the Post Office to collaborate in a joint scheme, but they failed.[82]

In 1878 arrangements were set on foot for a conference in Paris to establish an international parcel post. This time the Post Office approached the railways, seeking some agreement over all parcels business, and in the end that was achieved; but the Office had to pay a price for it that seemed unreasonably high, and again the companies stood exposed to a charge of extortion. Whereas on the Continent the rate usually paid by the postal authorities to the railways for the conveyance of parcels was about 40% of the receipts, in Britain the companies obtained 55%.[83] On these terms a Parcels Act was carried in 1882, taking effect on 1 August 1883.[84]

This measure gave the Post Office no monopoly. The railways and the carriers were left free to go on conveying parcels. Inevitably they now lost part of their business in smalls, which the general public found it easier to hand in at Post Offices, though some companies organized the free collection of such parcels from offices and warehouses.[85] Nevertheless the lowering of charges, forced upon the railways by the new postal rates, brought them increased business and raised their total receipts from parcels traffic. It was a plain demonstration of their short-sighted folly in refusing to adopt a cheaper and more rational scheme. They incurred a good deal of odium in these years, from one cause and another, not always justly. Here was a case in which it was well deserved. As for the Post Office, it had made a dear bargain. But, driven forward by the need to make a bargain of some kind, urgently demanded by public opinion, it probably did the best it could.

A New Collaboration

The Post Office and the railways were linked in a partnership that seemed indissoluble and was now starting to grow somewhat easier.[86] Towards the close of the nineteenth century it was extended in some directions. Though the Post Office had a jealously-guarded monopoly of the right to transmit letters, it recognized the special need of the railways for an internal postal service of their own, and agreed to its introduction in 1891.[87] A new night postal train from Euston to Aberdeen was instituted, on the initiative of the Post Office, on 1 July 1885; a train carrying no passengers, given up entirely to the mails as the pioneer venture of the Great Western had been thirty years before. Unlike its predecessor, however, it did not subsequently admit passengers. When it left Euston, the 'West Coast Postal' remained a mail train and nothing else.[88] The handling of the overseas mails at the ports grew steadily quicker. At Plymouth after 1890 there was strong competition between two railways, the Great Western and the London & South Western. Even after they had agreed to divide the traffic, the Great Western taking the mails and its rival the passengers, there was still a race, until it was ended by the shortening of the Great Western route and the destruction of a South Western boat express at Salisbury, which occurred simultaneously on 1 July 1906.[89]

One of the difficulties that had been inseparable from the transfer of the mails from the road to the railway lay in the siting of the stations. They were seldom placed at a town's centre.[90] Sometimes, as at Cambridge and Derby, the station was a mile or more from the Head Post Office. The railway passed by many small towns at a considerable distance. Whereas in the past they had been served by mail-coaches delivering their bags at or close to the Post Office, now they might stand on branch lines, like Dunstable and Haddington, or off the railway altogether, like Chudleigh. Accordingly, in some places of importance sorting offices had to be built, adjoining the railway stations. One of the first was at Crewe, established in 1854. Others followed, as for instance at Shrewsbury, Leicester, and Plymouth. But no English town achieved quite the degree of integration displayed in Scotland at Paisley, where the General Post Office of 1893 adjoined one of the two chief stations.[91] The nearest English approach to that perhaps came at Leeds. A new General Post Office (the fifth to be commissioned in eighty years) was erected there in 1896,[92] close to the three main stations though separate from them all.

At the beginning of the twentieth century a fresh possibility opened up for the Post Office, for the carriage of mails in suitable cases by road motor vehicles. Acting through contractors, it was soon experimenting with them. Some services were at work in 1906: one from Saffron Walden through Bishop's Stortford to Epping, covering a route no railway served,[93] another from London to Slough. These trials were held to have been successful, and the use of motor vehicles soon went further. By 1913 over 150 'services or sets of services' were being performed by motor mail-vans; and in that year they were extended to run from London to Bournemouth, Liverpool, and Derby.[94]

They strengthened the position of the Post Office in bargaining with the railway companies over rates. Nevertheless, for the bulk carriage of mails, both letters and parcels, the old-established arrangements with the railways endured, little disturbed until long after the first World War.

If, in this new sense, the Post Office was beginning by 1914 to make a little less use of railways than it had done in the past, in another way it had determined to use them more. It now secured powers to build a railway of its own. From 1863 to 1866, and again for ten months in 1874, the Pneumatic Despatch Company had operated an underground tube railway in London, which at its greatest extent ran from Euston to Cheapside. Since the tube was only 4 ft 6 in wide and 4 ft high, the railway through it was not suited to the conveyance of passengers. Mails were carried by it to and from Euston station, but the Post Office found it saved very little time. Dissatisfied with the railway's performance, it allowed it to die without protest.[95] In the 1890s, inspired by the example of the City & South London Railway, a number of projects were brought forward either for resuscitating this derelict tube line and working it by electricity or for building a new one for the service of the Post Office. None of them proved acceptable until 1913, when the Post Office secured powers[96] to build an electrically-operated tube linking its headquarters in St Martin's-le-Grand with a number of district offices and railway stations. The outbreak of the war interrupted its construction, and it was not finished, to run from Whitechapel to Paddington, until 1927. Then, at long last, the Post Office was able to make use of a railway on its own terms.[97]

Benefits Conferred

As soon as the railways got into their stride in the 1840s, it became clear that they had the supremacy over all carriers by road in speed, in their capacity to handle loads in bulk, and in regularity of service. By 1850 the whole postal system had come to be based on the railways, as far as they then reached. Thirty years later railways extended into all but the most scantily populated parts of the island. They retained those three advantages, almost unimpaired, down to 1914.

Their higher speed was obvious. When the Great Western Railway was opened throughout from London to Bristol in 1841, the night mail train made the journey nearly three times as fast as the mail coach. That allowed later collection and earlier delivery, the sorting of the mail in the train *en route* producing a further economy of time. By 1883 the London & North Western company was able to put on a mail train leaving Euston station at 1.30 pm, which afforded deliveries of letters from London to Liverpool, Manchester, and Chester the same evening.[98] No road vehicle of any kind could have considered such a schedule, in regular service, before the 1950s.

The quantity of mail the railways conveyed was equally impressive. In 1840 there were 132 million deliveries in Great Britain. Over the next seventy-three years that number rose uninterruptedly, though the rate of increase was slowed down by the impact on the habits of letter-writing first of the telegraph and then of the telephone. Remembering that not all the mails were conveyed by railway (none of those passing within central London, for example), we can get an idea of the growth from these figures:

TABLE 4

DELIVERIES OF LETTERS IN GREAT BRITAIN 1840–1913

Years	Average number per year 000	Increase %
1840–9	231	—
1850–9	399	72.7
1860–9	641	60.7
1870–6	860	34.2
1878–89	1213	41.0
1890–9	1730	42.6
1900–9	2456	42.9
1910–13	2940	19.7

Source: B. L. Mitchell and H. G. Jones, *Second Abstract of British Historical Statistics* (1971), 109–10

The population during that time rather more than doubled. The postal deliveries multiplied nearly thirteen times over.

The mechanism for handling this enormous business grew steadily more complex. Anyone accustomed to the shrunken postal services afforded now must find the provision made for the Victorians scarcely credible. In central London by 1908 there were twelve deliveries a day, from 7 am to 8.50 pm. In Birmingham there were three deliveries in the 1850s, six by 1903. By the 1890s letters posted at the Gare du Nord in Paris before 11.35 am would be delivered to their recipients in London on the evening of the same day.[99] More letters were posted in the United Kingdom in 1900, per head of the population, than in any Continental country (44% more than in Germany, 69% more than in France). Only the American total exceeded the British, and that by the narrow margin of 7%.[100] The Post Office and the railways had achieved an integrated scheme of transmission by 1865. It had then only one great deficiency, in the inadequate train service provided to the emptier tracts of the island, where few or no railways ran – north Norfolk and north Yorkshire, central Wales, Scotland west and north of Inverness. By 1880 the railways had stretched their tentacles out there too, and the Post Office had laid down its lines of communication, based on them and on services provided by road and sea, to serve the people who lived in them. Then they too came to appreciate the benefits they had received: pre-eminently perhaps in rural Scotland. There the great emigration, already in progress for a century, still continued, and the post could now, with speed and a high degree of certainty, link those who were left with their relatives and friends who had gone. By the end of the century almost every house in Great Britain, no matter how far from a post office, had a delivery of its own, arriving dependably at least two or three times a week.[101]

What chiefly threatened that reliability – again most of all in Scotland – were the storms in winter; and the railways were better equipped to battle with them than any other form of transport. Their engines and vehicles were much stronger than horses and coaches, at least as strong as steamships; and they were far better protected than coaches or ships by the devices they had come to use for their own security, their snowploughs, their signalling and telegraphs. There *were* interruptions, but they were not many, and in 1880, when one of the biggest storms was at its worst, the telegraph kept going. The trains might be late, but – most of all, by the tenacity of the enginemen – they arrived.

The Victorians set great store by regularity, and the postal service became one of the elements in the system of their daily lives that they prized most. In the eighty-five years considered here the postal service was interrupted only twice, and then very briefly: in 1850, when Sabbatarians caused deliveries to cease on eight successive Sundays; and in the national railway strike of 1911, which lasted hardly more than two days.

10

THE PRESS
AND THE BOOK TRADE

Railways and Newspapers · Newspapers and Railways ·
The Handling of Newspapers · The Railway Press ·
Station Bookstalls · Advertising Contracts

Railways and Newspapers

The earliest railways had little to do with the press. They were constructed to serve private businesses, coal-mines above all, and they were privately financed. Their need to communicate with the public began to appear only when they sought to become statutory bodies. Many questions arose then in which the public might well be interested: the exercise of powers of compulsory purchase, for example, in the building of railways; the rates and fares they were to charge; the services they offered; problems arising from the use of locomotives. On all such matters as these railway companies might have to address their local communities, and they usually did that by means of advertisements in newspapers.[1]

With the opening of the first steam-worked public lines, railways themselves began to become 'news' for newspapers and their correspondents to record and comment on. At first, the comment nearly all came from the locality, though an article or paragraph appearing in a local newspaper might be copied by one published in London. *The Times* began to show a serious interest in steam-worked railways in 1824, when it made some sensible remarks on the first prospectus issued by the Liverpool & Manchester promoters,[2] and it went on to give attention to the progress of their Bills through Parliament. The struggle waged over them was truly national news, for it involved large issues: the rights of landowners, the needs of manufacturers, the interests of canal companies and turnpike trusts. When the struggle had ended with the victory of the railway, the national newspapers took little notice of it until the trial of locomotives at Rainhill in 1829 aroused their attention again. Here was an event that was exciting both as an experiment with new machinery, conducted in public, and as a competition in speed that attracted bets like a horse-race. So the London newspapers reported it, no less than those in Lancashire. There was even a marked stirring of interest in it outside the island. Across the Atlantic the *Advertiser* carried reports of the contest day by day in Boston, and they were seen to stimulate an immediate interest in the promotion of railways in Massachusetts. When the railway was opened in September 1830, the press of the whole Western world recorded and commented on the event.[3]

It was treated as a single event, however, not more. As the Liverpool & Manchester and other railways settled down to their ordinary business they receded into the background of the news except when they ran into misfortune or gave rise to scandal. No railway company seems to have maintained any close relationship with a newspaper proprietor or editor, though managers sometimes gave facilities to inquirers anxious to investigate the working of their lines. If the result of the investigation was presently described in print, that might lead to useful publicity.

The Mania of 1836–7 greatly enlarged the general interest taken in railways as investments. New periodicals sprang up, devoted entirely to them. It was at this time – not in 1830 – that the railways and their doings became a matter of continuous interest to the national press. The speculative excitement had hardly died down before the first long-distance lines were brought into use, demonstrating the meaning of 'railway speed' to London, and widely across England.

The first leading man in the railway world who appreciated the potential value of newspapers as a means of representing its interests was George Hudson. In the autumn of 1845 he helped to encourage the establishment of a new paper in London, the *Daily News*. This gave much space to the railways' activities. Although Hudson does not seem to have invested in the paper, he is said to have supplied it with information about railways. He certainly procured it the services of a locomotive from the Eastern Counties company to bring up to London, at high speed, the news of an Anti-Corn Law meeting at Norwich in January 1846.[4]

Hudson's decision to become involved with the *Daily News* lost him the support of *The Times*,[5] which might well have been valuable to him in the years to come. On the other hand this gesture offered an example to other directors and managers of railways. It made clear how much importance Hudson attached to establishing some relationship with the newspaper world. And in that he showed wisdom.

That the Victorian railways were private enterprises, not managed by the government, brought them gain and loss, compared with those on the mainland of Europe. One of the gains was that they were not – as they are now – a football kicked back and forth by political parties; British newspapers seldom treated them according to their own political allegiance. Although in the 1840s *The Times* came to take a leading part in attacking railway speculation and exposing the malpractices involved in it, it did so as a matter of choice on the part of its editor Delane, fortified by the ammunition he needed, which was furnished by a financial expert, Henry Scrivenor. The line it took here represented the opinion of no organized group of public men. The railways were often to be attacked in the press. Whatever the merits of the contentions put forward by the newspapers might be, however, they did not spring from any political doctrine, at least until the issue of nationalization began to become a serious one at the beginning of the twentieth century. The railways on the Continent that were worked under the direct supervision of governments were always exposed to attackers in newspapers who assailed them merely because they wished to assail the government then in power. That kind of assault could seldom find a foothold in Britain.

One other element in the relations between the railways and the newspapers may also be mentioned here. It happened that Fleet Street and its neighbourhood, on which the metropolitan press came to be firmly based in the late Victorian age, was worse served by railways than almost any other part of central London. The Metropolitan and District companies had their nearest stations at Farringdon Street and Blackfriars; the nearest tube stations were Strand (now Aldwych) and Covent Garden; the nearest station of any sort was Ludgate Hill, on the London Chatham & Dover line. All these stations were shut down for some five hours in the night, when many newspaper men were at work and wanted their services to take them home. Journalists continually besought the Chatham company to run trains for them in the small hours, but it was not until 1910 that five were put on, to leave Ludgate Hill between 2 and 5 am and run out as far as Clapham, Beckenham, and Bromley. The Great Eastern company had instituted a half-hourly service throughout the night to Walthamstow in 1897, and that was used by some compositors and other newspaper men;[6] but it started from Liverpool Street, which was nearly a mile away. A. A. Jackson has suggested that 'the anti-railway complex that has long been prevalent among London newspapermen' may have originated in the discomforts they were subjected to by the poor facilities the railways afforded them for getting to and from their work.[7] He is probably right.

The relations between railway directors and newspaper proprietors never became close. Hudson's sensible example was not attended to. Edward Watkin was one of the three founders of the *Manchester Examiner* in 1845, but that was before he held any power in the railway world. At the turn of the century Sam Fay had dealings with Alfred Harmsworth, as we shall see shortly. They related, however, only to one special arrangement. The railways often acted as if they constituted a separate world within the United Kingdom. In some respects that aloofness might represent a prudent form of self-defence. Here, surely, it was not. The companies came, after 1870, to need all the help and sympathy they could muster. That they made so small an effort to secure those things from the press shows how imperfectly, as yet, they appreciated the value of good public relations.

Newspapers and Railways

When railways were attacked by newspapers, they were by no means defenceless. Newspapers had to make use of the trunk lines for distribution outside the towns in which they were produced. As time went on, they came to owe more to railways than railways ever owed to them.

All papers sent away from London demanded speed in reaching their subscribers, the local distributors and the offices of country journals, which could then incorporate items of news from London with their own. For national news in 1830 'the local papers remained late echoes of the London press'.[8] Before railways arrived, the London papers were distributed by means of the mail-coaches (which after 1825 conveyed them free of charge) and the privately-owned stage-coaches. Since the mail-coaches nearly all ran by night, a morning paper sent in that way could not begin its journey for at least twelve hours after it appeared in London. Only over a short distance, as to Brighton or Oxford, was it possible to put a London morning paper on sale by the afternoon of publication.

By about 1825 a number of new and fast stage-coaches were running out from London early in the morning. Enterprising newspaper distributors took advantage of them. The most enterprising, the first W. H. Smith,* employed their public services freely, supplemented, on occasions of particular urgency, by 'special expresses', which he chartered.

Smith was quick to see the advantages that railways offered, as they came to be built over long distances out of London. He opened negotiations with the Grand Junction company for the transmission of newspapers from Birmingham to Manchester and Liverpool in 1838. In the 1840s his firm *Ill. 58* continued to use coaches as well as railways, where both were available, but the railways soon won. In 1845 he had 'nine special express engines to Liverpool, Manchester, and Birmingham [running] every day this week'.[9] How, one might ask, did the company manage to spare them?

The acceleration the railways offered was displayed nowhere more startlingly than in the distribution of newspapers. In 1846 a German visitor, arriving at Bakewell in Derbyshire (itself a place at some distance from a railway station) was astounded to find that '*The Times* of this morning, just arrived', gave a full account of some events at Hatfield, at which he had himself been present, on the previous day.[10] By 1851 the London morning papers were in Bristol by 11 o'clock. At 11.30 they were to be had in the Isle of Wight.[11]

The railways soon became involved here in a complicated tangle of relationships, immediately with the distributors, who undertook most of the business of getting the copies of the papers into the hands of their readers,[12] but behind them with the newspapers themselves, whose proprietors and managers watched every stage of the performance of transporting the papers up and down the country. Presently the railways put on trains specially for the conveyance of newspapers, leaving London in the early morning. In 1875 *The Times* tried to get the London & North Western company to provide one to carry copies of that paper and no other. It was to leave Euston an hour earlier than the established newspaper train, giving *The Times* a head start over all its London rivals. However the *Standard* got wind of this negotiation

---

*There were two W. H. Smiths, father and son. The first, mentioned at this point, lived from 1792 to 1865. The second (1825–91) joined the business in 1845, became a partner in it in 1846 and its head in 1857.

and protested at it so vehemently that the plan was abandoned in favour of making the train run earlier, for the use of all newspapers alike. It was now to leave Euston at 5.15 and to reach Manchester by 10 o'clock instead of 11.45.[13] At the same time the Great Western also instituted a special newspaper train for the West Country, leaving Paddington at 5.30. The service to South Wales, however, remained extraordinarily slow, taking over ten hours from Paddington to Swansea. The London & North Western company at length stepped in to convey the newspapers to that town (by a route 62 miles longer), and the Great Western was forced to speed up its own train, to bring the newspapers into Swansea by 1.30 pm instead of 4.15.[14]

All this was for the benefit of the London press. But the railways were not unaware of the needs of the provincial papers too. Smith's initiative in chartering trains to take the London papers up and down the country represented, at the outset, a grave potential danger to all the dailies published in the provinces. It was just at this time that the first express trains were beginning to run – not specially chartered, but in ordinary service. If that acceleration were maintained, the distribution that Smith's offered might get the London papers to the largest cities in northern England early enough to be on sale at the same time as their own dailies.[15] 'As long as news could only travel at the same speed as newspapers London had a decided advantage over the provinces because London was the source of the most important news. Its advantage was the time that it took to set the news in type after its arrival in a provincial newspaper office.' Copies could now be printed by machines at a speed undreamt of in 1800.

The increase in the speed of trains, however, though it continued, did so at a slower pace. In 1847 Smith's, for all their energy, were selling no more than 1500 copies of London papers in Manchester each day when the sale of the *Manchester Guardian* had reached 9000 (more than that of any London daily except *The Times* and the *Daily News*). The price that the Manchester reader had to pay for *The Times* was higher, and it naturally did not give him the Lancashire news, which was one of the things he principally wanted.

Another mechanical change was now approaching, which could place the provincial papers, if they managed their business with enterprise, on almost exactly the same footing as those in London. This came from the electric telegraph, which was already extending both along railway lines and through the independent efforts of the telegraph companies. By 1848 there were some 3500 miles of telegraph in the country, half of it associated with railways. Twenty years later those 3500 miles had become 22,000.[16] The news could then reach the papers in London, Manchester, and Glasgow almost simultaneously. This great change saved the provincial daily press from grave injury at the hands of the papers in London.

The railways' rapid distribution of London papers continued nevertheless. Throughout the Victorian age *The Times* remained unquestionably the leading British newspaper; many people in the provinces insisted that they must have it, and have it early. The great provincial dailies came to benefit from the same method of distribution. Two newspaper trains were running nightly from Manchester at the end of the century, one to Wigan for the North, another to Leeds for Yorkshire.[17]

The Handling of Newspapers

The most important of the services the railways came to provide for the production and conveyance of newspapers related to the rapid and reliable carriage of newsprint to the printing works and of the copies of the papers to distributors and so to readers.

Most of the national papers got their newsprint then from Lancashire or from northern Ireland. It was carried almost entirely by one railway, the London & North Western, and the warehouses at Broad Street station always held a stock of it large enough to last a fortnight. The handling of this paper, in huge rolls, in such a way as to avoid even a slight irregularity that might cause a blockage in the machines, was technically difficult and perfected only after long experience.[18]

When the papers were printed and ready for distribution, the railways took up their other special part in the business. The final printing was always deferred to the last possible minute, in order to allow important fresh matter to be inserted. (A foreman compositor on one of them was portrayed[19] as 'a man grey with just catching newspaper trains'.) The vans that were to carry the papers to the railway through the streets always made the swiftest possible dash through the traffic. At the stations the papers were sorted according to their destinations on the railway system, though some of that task was undertaken in the train *en route*. The railways demanded that the trains should leave punctually, in order to connect with other trains at junctions throughout the system; but they often complained to them of the papers' late delivery.

The hours of departure of these trains from London were altered from time to time, to suit varying conditions of production and sale. At the turn of the century some of them came to be dispatched a good deal earlier than before. In 1899 the Great Central put on one leaving Marylebone for the north at 2.30 am. Its rival the Midland then did likewise at St Pancras. The two lines served almost the same large towns – Leicester, Nottingham, Sheffield, and Manchester – and there was not enough business for both. Presently a sensible division emerged, the Marylebone train serving Leicester, Nottingham, and Sheffield whilst Manchester fell to its rival.

In this business the railways had to try to avoid favouring one newspaper at the expense of others. They were carriers for them all on the same terms. To that rule there were two exceptions. The 2.30 Great Central train was originally commissioned by the *Daily Mail* for its own use, to carry the earliest news of the war in South Africa. A second train followed, at the conventional hour of 5.15, open to all its competitors.[20] So this brash new paper achieved the arrangement that had been denied to *The Times* in 1875. No doubt the company's general manager Sam Fay enjoyed negotiating with the newspaper's proprietor Alfred Harmsworth; they spoke the same sort of language. The *Daily Mail* could now boast that it was on sale simultaneously at Brighton and Newcastle. Before long some of its printing was being undertaken in Manchester, and in 1902 it opened offices there on Deansgate.[21]

The other special arrangement favouring one paper was established much earlier and lasted longer. Copies of *The Times*, and of *The Times* alone, were sent direct to Euston for the 5.15 express in the newspaper's own vans. The London & North Western company addressed an unending stream of complaints to *The Times* concerning their delivery. That the company was prepared to let the train go without waiting for them seems apparent from Acworth's account of a journey he himself made by the train from Euston in 1888. He then observed one of these late arrivals. At 5.15 *The Times* vans had not appeared: whereupon the whistle blew and the train began to move. At the same moment the noise of their approach was heard. The train was stopped, every man and boy hurled himself on their contents, and a second start was made at 5.17. Had the vans been half a minute later still, the train would have gone. Acworth had been fortunate enough on that Tuesday morning to witness 'a sight that, so at least the officials declared, had never before been seen'.[22] If they were to be believed, this was the first time the train had ever been held.

He shows us the business of sorting the 30,000–40,000 copies of the papers that was undertaken in the train between Euston and Stafford; the difference in the loading according to the days of the week, taking the publication of periodicals into account; the rigid refusal of the London & North Western company to allow any bundles of papers to be thrown out of the train at stations it did not call at – a dangerous practice some other companies condoned. He ends with a demonstration of the complexity involved in re-marshalling the train during its twenty-minute stop at Wigan, with vehicles starting from London, Crewe, Liverpool, and Manchester for four different terminal points.

This traffic was in some important respects very welcome to the railways. 'Because of the regularity, certainty, and economy of packing, newspapers represented "the commodity *par excellence*" for the railway companies.'[23] They demanded no special equipment whatever, nothing like the postal lineside apparatus. Nor did they call for any specially-built rolling stock, like mail vans, which could be used for only one purpose. The papers were conveyed in the ordinary vans used in passenger traffic; when sorting was undertaken in the train it was on wooden trestle tables erected at the beginning of the journey. The companies were therefore able to agree on low rates of carriage. Among the arguments that arose from time to time between the newspapers and the railway companies, rates never assumed any prominent place.

The rapid and generally reliable handling of newspapers that emerged from the collaboration of the railways with the publishers and distributors has a parallel, in the part they came to play in the production of books. In the course of the Victorian age the whole of that business underwent great changes, one of which was directly attributable to railways. In 1830 nearly all books published in London (very much the largest publishing centre in the Kingdom) were also printed there. By 1914 the work of printing for the London publishers had come to be spread all over England, and even as far as Edinburgh and Glasgow, 400 miles away. Copy and proofs now passed between publishers and printers overnight, with almost unfailing regularity: so there was no loss of speed, compared with the days when printers and publishers worked within a mile of one another in London. The railways alone made this practice possible.[24]

The Railway Press

A special branch of the press started to emerge very early, comprising periodicals published weekly or monthly, devoted almost entirely to railway affairs. None of the journals of this sort was, so far as we know, financed by the companies or by railway men. The main characteristic, at least of the better ones, was independence: sturdy as a rule, but sometimes ill-tempered and here and there silly. They set themselves to comment just as their proprietors and editors chose on the doings both of the companies and of the government. These periodicals were addressed primarily to shareholders. There they performed a valuable service as regular and usually reliable chroniclers of the railways' doings. But when they chose to discuss public issues their judgement, though sometimes shrewd, was always prejudiced, and it was often unsound.

The first journal in Britain concerned predominantly with railways seems to have been the *Railway Gazette*, a fortnightly paper that ran through a few issues in 1835. In the same year the *Railway Magazine and Annals of Science* began to appear, and it achieved a long life, under a different title. Reshaped as the *Railway Journal* in 1839 under the control of one of the proprietors, John Herapath, it became known simply by his uncommon surname. A former teacher of mathematics, he had written on that subject and revelled in controversies concerning it. When the *Journal* first appeared he was already fifty-nine. He was an able man, but his age told and intense irritability sharpened his pen. On every matter of policy disputed in the railway world he instantly took up a position – hating excursion and express trains, for instance – and then never ceased belabouring those who differed from him. He invested in railways substantially and shouted at shareholders' meetings;[25] but he never kept his private interests out of his pronouncements as an editor. Herapath did more than any other man to determine the tone of railway journalism in early days. When he relinquished the day-to-day control of the journal to his son Edwin in 1847, its language grew noticeably quieter. The chief rival of *Herapath* was the *Railway Times*, which first appeared in 1837; long noted particularly for its fierce opposition to any form of interference by government in the management of railways.[26]

More journals like these sprang up in 1844–5: the *Railway Record* and *Railway*

Bell, for instance; the *Railway World*, which announced that it would concern itself 'in a special manner with the advocacy of direct lines';[27] and the *Railway Chronicle*. The last of these was launched by the proprietor of a literary journal, the *Athenaeum*: C. W. Dilke. He secured as his editor the rising engineer John Scott Russell, and Russell brought in Henry Cole, who was later to play an important part in the Great Exhibition.[28] The *Chronicle* showed a closer interest than the other journals in the railways' social and intellectual effects. The series of fifteen *Travelling Charts* produced as supplements to the paper in 1846[29] were designed to interest the passenger in what he might see on his journey.

By October 1845 at least sixteen railway periodicals were being published, fourteen of them in England and two in Scotland. One of these, the *Iron Times*, appeared daily; nearly all the rest were weeklies. Only *Herapath*, the *Railway Times*, the *Railway Record*, and the second *Railway Gazette* (published twice a week) lasted beyond 1849. Even in their short lives, however, some of the transient papers may have yielded profit to their owners from the advertisements of railway projects that they carried. Yet that did not save the proprietors of the *Iron Times* from bankruptcy.[30]

The journals that lived on past the excitement settled down to a steadier life. They published traffic returns and reports of shareholders' meetings, with the companies' accounts, recorded the opening of new lines, and took note of accidents as they occurred; any of these matters being spiced by the editor's comments when they caught his eye.

A few more specialized journals also appeared later: the *Railway Engineer*, for instance (1860–1935); several organs of the trade unions as their membership increased late in the nineteenth century. House journals were published, circulating among the employees of railway companies. They were not usually financed by the companies themselves, but senior officers gave them their support and encouragement. Sam Fay and two of his colleagues got the *South Western Gazette* going in 1881. The *Great Western Railway Magazine* was started by the railway company's Temperance Society in 1888 and taken over by the company itself in 1904. Under the direction of the young Felix Pole, its circulation rose from 3000 copies of each issue, to stand for a time as high as 65,000.[31] By 1914 most of the leading English companies had journals of the kind, though there were none like them in Scotland.

Popular interest in railways, stimulated by some excellent books from the 1880s onwards, gradually grew large enough to justify monthly magazines devoted to them. Two came to be produced: *Moore's Monthly Magazine* (subsequently known as the *Locomotive*) in 1896, and *The Railway Magazine* in 1897. Both of them became established securely. The *Railway Magazine* was edited by G. A. Sekon, a bright journalist determined to popularize his subject. Like his spiritual ancestor John Herapath, he was opinionated (his opinions often founded on no more than ignorant prejudice) and unceasingly disputatious. Though that for a time made the magazine lively, and many of the articles it carried from its considerable range of contributors were valuable, the editorial sections were soon rendered tedious by Sekon's relentless grinding of axes. He quarrelled with the proprietors and left, founding a new magazine in 1910 that did not have a long life.[32] In strong contrast, when the *Locomotive* got into its stride it settled for a serious tone as a sound chronicler of technical development.

Fourteen railway periodicals were still being published in Britain in 1914, but only two of them were of the kind initiated by Herapath.[33]

Station Bookstalls

The railways' share in the distribution of printed literature was not limited to the conveyance of newspapers and periodicals. Besides carrying them in their trains the companies took an indirect part in the business of selling them, and many other kinds of literature too, by allowing bookstalls to be set up at their stations.

Newspapers were sold to passengers on the Liverpool & Manchester Railway. By 1839 two men and four children were engaged in the business at Lime Street station, Liverpool.[34] These vendors, moving up and down the platforms (no space was reserved for them), supplied a service appreciated by many railway travellers. Reading in stage-coaches was difficult, whether in the crowd perched outside on the roof or in the very cramped quarters inside. The train offered much better facilities, at least to first and second-class passengers travelling in closed carriages. There was an opportunity here for selling more reading matter than newspapers – indeed, for selling other articles that travellers wanted too. What was called for was some kind of shop on the platform. The chance of supplying one was seized – apparently for the first time in Britain – by William Marshall in 1841.

He entered then into a contract with the London & Blackwall Railway to open a bookstall on its Fenchurch Street station.[35] Other bookstalls soon followed; a number of them on the London & North Western Railway, beginning with the one at Euston, for which the contractor was named Gibbs. He and his son were presently found to be making a much more than handsome profit out of their work, at the rate of over £1200 a year against a rental of £60. The company then decided to terminate the contract and to let it out by public tender instead. The successful applicant was W. H. Smith, with an offer to pay the company £1500 a year for the exclusive right to sell books and newspapers on its stations.[36] Gibbs was evicted (by police action, followed by a lawsuit, which he lost), and Smith began trading in his place on 1 November 1848.[37] Within ten years he had secured similar contracts with eleven other railway companies, and the aggregate rental he was paying came to over £11,000 a year.[38]

Other firms were by then in the business too. Horace Brooks Marshall (son of the pioneer at Fenchurch Street) established a series of bookstalls on stations in the West Midlands and South Wales. There he was allowed to sell, in addition to books and newspapers, confectionery, sandwiches, and bottled beer. This enterprise passed into Smith's hands in 1863. Smith did not create a monopoly in the business, however. It was some time before he acquired the franchise of the North Eastern company, and as early as 1857 he withdrew entirely from Scotland, yielding up the only contracts he held there, with the North British company at Edinburgh, to Thomas Murray.[39] In the same year the Edinburgh bookseller John Menzies entered the business, securing contracts with the Scottish Central Railway to run bookstalls at Perth, Stirling, and Bridge of Allan. Before the end of 1858 he had the lease of every bookstall on the railways between Edinburgh and Aberdeen. In 1862 he took over the Edinburgh station business from Murray. His firm went on to become a total monopolist of all the railway bookstalls in Scotland.[40]

As soon as he entered on this new branch of his work Smith set himself, with characteristic energy, to raise the character of all that the railway bookstalls sold. That had been generally low. Newspapers, timetables, and guidebooks were well enough, but most of the other literature they purveyed was trash and a good deal was complained of as subversive, in religion or politics, or salacious. For this there was one prime explanation. Many bookstalls were kept by former servants of the companies (some of them physically disabled) or by their widows; the railways were commendably anxious, wherever they could, to find small jobs for those who had suffered in their service. Such people could not possibly maintain any standards here. They of course put on sale what they were asked for. The arrival of Smith's, and the rapid growth of their empire, represented the supplanting of ignorant amateurs by educated professionals.

The changes the firm now introduced were naturally resented by those who were displaced and by those who found themselves deprived of reading they liked. As pornographic literature was excluded from his bookstalls Smith himself came to be called a prude, and was laughed at as 'Old Morality'.[41] The general tone of what was offered on these bookstalls did not change quickly. A contrast was noted in 1851 between the bookstall at Euston and those for which Smith's were not responsible; but this may well have been drawn too sharply.[42] Four years later Trollope discussed the goods purveyed by railway bookstalls, and though as a frequent traveller he welcomed them he was disgusted by the rubbishy novels they offered – native English, translations from the French, imports from America: 'the very worst that can be culled from our huge receptacles of such wares'.[43]

Some publishers had begun to go into the business of producing cheap paper-covered editions of good books (or at least of better books than those that Trollope spoke of), specially intended for sale on railway bookstalls. 'Routledge's Railway Library' initiated this business in 1848. Then in 1851 three more publishers came in, with other series: 'Bentley's Railroad Library' (which lasted only three years), 'Murray's Railway Reading', and 'Longman's Travellers' Library'. The last two of these series did not include novels at all. Routledge's, which concentrated on them, did best. Their 'Railway Library' was maintained for exactly fifty years. When it came to an end it had included nearly 1300 titles.[44]

Here it could be said that the railways were making some mark on English literature, not only – not chiefly – on account of the 'Railway Library' and 'Railway Reading', but in a broader sense. The range of books sold at stations was considerable, extending even to poetry: Matthew Arnold was astonished to find his *Empedocles* offered on the Derby bookstall in 1854. Hardly less surprising, the third and fourth volumes of Macaulay's *History of England*, when they were new and cost thirty-six shillings, 'were cried up and down the platform at York like a second edition of *The Times*.'[45] As for the cheap reprints, Smith's were steadily selling 200 copies a month of the Waverley Novels. 'Twenty years ago a novel of any kind was an expensive luxury – at the present day it costs only twice as much as a pot of beer.' The same observer noted that station bookstalls offered popular scientific manuals too, and that their customers included some of the companies' servants, in pursuit of self-improvement.[46]

The railways were certainly doing their best, by the acceptance of bookstalls on to their stations and by the facilities they provided for reading in their trains (at least by daylight), to enlarge the publishers' market. A modern analyst of the reading habits of the age remarks that 'perhaps no other single element in the evolving pattern of Victorian life was so responsible [as the railways] for the spread of reading'; and the spread, he adds, was due largely to the station bookstalls, from their 'placing of books in the main-travelled roads of Victorian life'.[47] Railways certainly helped to make reading a more common study or pastime among travellers than it had ever been before.

Smith's business went on growing. In 1851 the firm had thirty-five bookstalls on railway stations; by 1880 there were 450; by 1902 their number was 777, besides 463 'sub-stalls'.[48] They were served by large warehouses, opened in one provincial town after another from 1857 onwards.[49] But these figures do not reflect a corresponding growth in profitability. Seven companies received a total of £10,110 from Smith's, for bookstall and advertising contracts together, in 1855. Fifty years later Smith's were paying ten companies nineteen times as much. There seem to be no figures of profits to set beside those for rents paid in that period. All that can be said is that the firm's turnover on its station bookstalls multiplied by less than a factor of five in 1867–1905.[50]

By the 1880s some railway companies felt that the rentals they received from Smith's, though steadily increasing, were not large enough. Whenever a fresh contract had to be made, both parties came to the meetings armed with piles of figures to support their case, the companies demanding that the rental should be increased, Smith's arguing that their profits were less than it was reasonable to expect. These exercises had become customary; they have been well described as 'strange ritual dances'.[51] In the end both sides would make concessions, and agreement would be reached. But in 1885 the London & North Western company showed itself very intransigent.[52] The contracts covered both bookstalls and the management of advertising. The disagreement between the company and Smith's now went so deep that the two had to be separated. A new contract was reached, with difficulty, for the bookstalls; the one for advertising was postponed, to be settled later.[53] The contracts ran for ten years. In 1895 the going was again very stiff, and the negotiations with the Great Western company were only a little easier.[54] In 1905 no agreement at all could be reached, and these two companies placed their contracts for both bookstalls and advertising in other hands.

The reasons for this breach were numerous. While the railway companies' expenditure on their business as a whole had doubled since 1886, their net receipts had risen by only a third. The demands of the trade unions were worrying them all; so were the continuing rises in local rates; their services of competitive express trains were expensive to provide. They were therefore intent on cutting their costs in all directions. Though the rents paid had increased, the companies had had to accept less than they asked, and to make other concessions besides. The two biggest now called a halt to this movement.

But Smith's had arguments to adduce on their side, and one ace up their sleeve. If the railways' wage bill was rising, theirs was too; the rentals they paid, in respect of both bookstalls and advertising, had increased continually; they were paying the companies more for the carriage of newspapers.[55] But their most powerful argument was that they performed services that no other firm, backed with an organization that was in any way comparable with theirs, could pretend to offer. In this kind of bookselling, and to a large extent in advertising, their skill and experience were unique. How little money were the railway companies prepared to accept, to allow this service to continue at the same level? How much would Smith's pay to retain the business – still profitable, even if at a diminishing rate?

The confrontation had not arisen suddenly. It began with the Lancashire & Yorkshire company in 1902 and dragged on all through that year. By December John Aspinall, its general manager, was saying that the rentals Smith's offered 'could not be entertained', to be met with their reply that the minds of the partners in the firm were *absolutely made up*'. Since it did not seem that the deadlock could be resolved, Smith's began to prepare for the termination of their contracts. In August 1903 they threw down a challenge that was quite new: they indicated that they were already surveying Lancashire towns, to find out what property might be available in them to accommodate bookshops of their own, in place of the station bookstalls. That December Smith's bought a shop at Southport.[56]

The London & North Western, under the guidance of its powerful manager Frederick Harrison, was now concluding that it should turn to other contractors. So was the Great Western. These two companies accounted for one-third of Smith's bookstall business between them. They decided that Smith's had become too strong. Acting in unison in October 1905, they announced that Smith's agreements with them would not be renewed.[57] The two companies were turning to Wyman & Co. as contractors for the bookstalls on their stations instead.

Wyman's were the Great Western's printers. They had no experience of bookselling and had secured these contracts entirely because they offered to pay higher rentals than Smith's. The Great Western directors understood that quite well, noting that 'the London & North Western company admitted that the sum was more than they deserve, and it would appear that they have accepted the tender simply to show an increase in the present payment regardless of the consideration as to whether the contractor fails or not'.[58] Wyman's were soon in danger of failing. By 1908 the North Western company had to reduce their carriage charges. In 1916 they were obliged to admit that their bookstalls were being run at a heavy loss, and the two companies both lowered their rents. Further requests for assistance followed in 1917–18.[59]

Smith's kept their contracts with the other railway companies – even, in the end, with the Lancashire & Yorkshire. Had they given in to the North Western and Great Western, they would clearly have had to face more refusals to accept their tenders. They now set themselves resolutely to transfer their business from station bookstalls to shops in every town where that appeared to be worth while. The exercise was carried through with most impressive energy. The bookstalls to be closed down numbered 250. The railways had been inexcusably dilatory in reaching their decisions,[60] and that left Smith's less than eleven weeks to carry through the operation before the old contracts ran out at the end of 1905. But in those eleven weeks they succeeded in opening 144 new shops.[61] Smith's did not become high-street booksellers because they lost these contracts; they had taken the first steps in that direction before the dispute became serious. But those steps had been tentative and small. Suddenly the firm deployed its whole power and turned itself into a national business, a chain to which there was no parallel in British bookselling. Books and newspapers were now sold by Wyman's on many station platforms; they were sold also by a new team of booksellers in the centres of towns.

The action of the two big railway companies here may or may not have been justified in strictly commercial terms. Provided *some* bookstalls were maintained in their stations, how much did it matter if their stock and service now came to be less satisfactory? In a larger sense however this decision and its execution may be said to have impaired one of the long-valued amenities *Ill. 59* of railway travelling.

Advertising Contracts

Most of the firms that contracted for the right to sell books on stations undertook also to deal with the advertising business that came to the railway companies: requests to rent space for the display of advertisements on their premises, at their stations and inside their carriages. Like bookselling, this was a trade the railways knew nothing about, and realized that they were not competent to handle themselves.

The business is said to have begun with the advertising inside carriages, extending to open display on stations only under the stimulus of the Great Exhibition in 1851.[62] Carriage advertising must have been a very amateur affair, with written or printed signs that were soon defaced or scribbled on until the making of advertisement plaques from embossed metal began in the 1860s.[63] Once advertising had spread to the walls of stations its scale grew rapidly. Very few other buildings of any sort were then to be found on which space to this extent was available for advertising; hoardings in streets were as a rule only temporary erections. The railways might choose to employ some of the space inside stations for crying their own wares, but they soon let out as much of it as they could.

All this expressed itself in the advertising side of Smith's business. From 1870 to 1892 the profits from it showed a rise (though not a regular one) from £26,000 a year to £54,000. They then fell, much more sharply, to £11,000 in 1915–16. Not all that decline represented loss of revenue to the firm, however; its Railway Department had grown into a Railway and Tramway Department, showing that a good deal of the business it handled had now been diverted to trams and buses.

Here and there Smith's had absorbed smaller firms, like Cross & Co. of Plymouth, who handled the modest railway business of Cornwall until 1863.[64] Thomas Gray, who had 'Railway Advertising Offices' in Newcastle, was a bigger man and evidently tougher. In 1887 he held contracts with all the main Scottish companies, except the Highland, and with the North Eastern.[65] James Willing secured the advertising and bookstall contract with the Metropolitan Railway at its opening in 1863 and held it with success until the company began to lose confidence in the firm about 1907. Part of its business then passed to Smith's, which had held the contracts on the District Railway since 1875 and was seizing on the new opportunities opened up by the fast-multiplying tube lines.[66]

Advertising grew to be more and more prominent, an accepted part of life, in the later Victorian age, in every shape and form. Two illustrations may summarize that growth. A commercial traveller, reflecting on its development in 1885, observed that 'a few years ago a good wholesale firm would have considered it as *infra dig.* to send out a circular as a first-class retail concern would to ticket their goods in their windows. Now, the former spends hundreds of pounds per annum in printing, and the latter tickets so much that you fail to see the goods'.[67]

The erection of large hoardings to carry advertisements, placed in open fields beside railways, became a common practice towards the end of the nineteenth century; affording, so it was said, a useful revenue to some landowners suffering from the agricultural troubles of the time. This advertising, especially of patent medicines, aroused a good deal of irritation.[68] Carter's were sufficiently disturbed by public criticism to offer to withdraw advertisements for their Little Liver Pills that faced railways wherever there was any clear expression of public dislike for them.[69] In this matter the railway companies had no power at all, for the land was not theirs to control. Yet it was the passage of their trains that caused the hoardings to be put up. Here the railway was the immediate occasion of what we should now call damage to the environment.

The same nuisance became still more offensive in towns. There the railways were among the culprits themselves, through their own advertisements. Many of the sites on which the hoardings went up were theirs, and they freely allowed advertising contractors to use the external walls of their own buildings. As early as 1859 there was strong complaint about such practices in Leicester.[70] It seemed always to be 'in and about the railway stations and their approach roads that the poster plague was at its most virulent'.[71] So here too the railways attracted the chief odium to themselves.

There were then no public controls over advertising, other than those provided by the courts when an advertisement was adjudged libellous or obscene. There were no planning authorities, with power to forbid advertisements that disfigured the streets in towns or the open country outside them. That railways were totally careless about the defacement their advertising produced, seemed to be confirmed when anyone went into a station and looked around him on its platforms. Here the posters were plastered along the walls, edge to edge, each trying to scream its message louder than its neighbours. There may be some over-statement in the well-known drawing of a London station that forms the frontispiece to Sampson's *History of Advertising* (1874). But the author would not have given the picture such prominence unless it reflected a reality familiar to his readers. Besides being hideous, this practice caused many passengers inconvenience: for they could not pick out the names of the stations, embedded in such an expanse of advertisement. English people were prone to blame the excesses of advertisers on American example. Yet here is what an intelligent American had to say about English stations in 1885: 'As station advertising is carried to a great extent throughout England, it is very difficult to recognise the station sign from the hundreds of advertisements, equally conspicuous, of 'Pears' Soap', 'Lorne Whiskey', 'Colman's Mustard', etc., surrounding the name of the station'.[72]

All these criticisms, of the railways' treatment of their own buildings and the encouragement they gave to others to abuse the landscape, came in the end to influence some of the companies. Serious attempts were made to tidy up the internal walls of stations, and to rationalize the display there. The pioneer in this matter seems to have been E. M. Horsley of the North Eastern.[73] A new practice was adopted on the tube railways in London, with striking effect, under the direction of Frank Pick (who had himself come from that main-line railway). A policy moving further in the same direction was followed by the Caledonian company inside its splendidly-reconstructed Central station in Glasgow. There all advertising was forbidden except the company's own, which could be displayed entirely at the management's discretion. The result, so an enthusiastic contemporary assures us, was that 'the artistic posters...make the station look like a picture gallery'.[74]

It was not often that such a thought would have occurred to anybody who entered a Victorian railway station. Controls like these were applied timidly, and the advertisements that were displayed could seldom be described as artistic. They may be supposed nevertheless to have been effective, at least in the eyes of the advertisers, who went on paying steadily for the space occupied by them. Their purpose was attained largely by the repetition of simple phrases.[75] Until far into the twentieth century, as one ascended to St Pancras station in London or St Enoch in Glasgow, there were metal plates on the risers of the steps, adjuring one to buy Stephens' Inks and the Pickwick, the Owl, and the Waverley Pen. E. S. Turner observed quite truly of such advertisements as those: 'It is wrong to say that no one reads them; they are not there to be read, but to be absorbed, just as a capsule is not meant to be tasted, but to be swallowed'.[76] Therein lay the essential purpose of much of the advertising that appeared on Victorian railways, addressed to all the passers-by.

Yet that is not quite an end of the matter. Some of the railways' advertising gave genuine pleasure: Norman Wilkinson's posters depicting ships, for example. The casual sight of an advertisement on a journey might always start an idea in a receptive mind. The seed of *The Yeomen of the Guard* was planted in W. S. Gilbert by a poster he happened to notice while he was waiting on Uxbridge station in 1887.[77]

11
PUBLICITY
AND PUBLIC RELATIONS

*The Railways' Publicity · The Railways and their Passengers ·
Competition and Monopoly · The Railways in Politics ·
A New Art*

'Publicity' and 'Public Relations' are expressions that have now come to denote different things, linked but separate. 'Publicity' is a convenient word to embrace all the devices that a person or a group of people – a trading company, a manufacturing firm, a political party – may use to present themselves or their services to the public, employing any form of advertisement and extending to printed statements like electoral addresses. The scope of 'public relations' is much broader, standing for the means that such people may adopt to put themselves on continuously satisfactory terms with the public. Publicity will be treated here first, and the successes and shortcomings of the railway companies in handling it will then appear as an element in their public relations, their total effort to address first their customers, then the nation at large.

The Victorians would not have understood the meaning of either of these expressions. To them, 'publicity' stood merely for the presentation of anything in the open; it was the antithesis of secrecy. The notion that there might be a whole battery of devices for bringing something to public notice, that to employ that battery could be a craft or even an art of its own, demanding imagination and special skills, had scarcely come to be accepted in Britain before the end of the nineteenth century, and the word 'publicity' does not seem to have been used there in its modern sense until the twentieth. One of the first to adopt it was a railway company, the Great Central. The expression 'public relations' did not appear in Britain until after the first World War. Then it was introduced from America.* The thing itself existed; it was understood and practised well by some Victorians. But it did not acquire a name in that age.

---

*The young John Elliot was appointed Public Relations Assistant to the General Manager of the Southern Railway, Sir Herbert Walker, in 1925. Walker approved the title on the ground that 'no one will understand what it means and none of my railway officers will be upset': Sir John Elliot, *On and Off the Rails* (1982), 19.

The Railways' Publicity

The earliest advertisements of the railways were colourless notices, giving factual information. They had to face the rivalry of other forms of transport, but they left colour to their opponents. A mere statement of the services the railways offered was, as a rule, enough to show that they were preferable, almost always quicker and usually cheaper. They left it to their competitors to be strident. It was a different matter when railways began to compete with one another.

The first railway ever to be built with the clear purpose of competing with one already at work was the Clarence, launched in 1827 as a rival to the Stockton & Darlington in the business of carrying coal from the Auckland coalfield to the Tees; and what we might fairly call the first competitive railway advertisement was the open letter addressed by one of its leading promoters, Christopher Tennant, to the people of Durham and Cleveland, published in the *Durham County Advertiser* on 19 January 1828.[1] In it he set out the merits of the plan, stated that he had wished the line to be worked in collaboration with the Stockton & Darlington but that his overtures had been received 'uncourteously' by it, and went on to demonstrate that if his line were built independently it would reduce the distance to be traversed between the coalfield and the mouth of the Tees by a third. Tennant's communication is the archetype of thousands of similar announcements that newspapers printed in later years, in the shape of letters or statements issued by railways as plain advertisements. They often became vituperative, and there were scarcely any limits to the assertions that might be made in them.

During the frantic promotion of railways in 1835–7 and again ten years later the total volume of advertising concerned with them, in one form and another, grew exceedingly large. The revenue to be drawn from handling it grew large too. It was estimated that, at the height of the Mania in 1845, the leading London papers derived £12–14,000 a week from the advertisements of railway companies. A single one might cost as much as £750.[2] Some astute men of business made a good profit here as dealers in advertising. The young Martin Henry Colnaghi, after his father's bankruptcy in 1843, was able to build up a lucrative connection in this work in the years that followed, particularly with business arising from railways. He then sold out to W. H. Smith, and that allowed him by 1860 to turn to the more congenial task of dealing in pictures in which he became well known.[3]

No such frenzy of competitive advertising on behalf of railway projects was ever seen again in Britain. At other times of intense promotion, in 1856–7 and 1864–6, though advertisements multiplied (and were cheaper, for the tax on them was abolished in 1853), their tone changed. The joyous excitement arising from a feeling of complete irresponsibility had gone. But, in a wider sense, railway advertising had come to stay, and in the 1850s and 1860s it grew, in support of the new competitive services offered by one company in rivalry with another.

The first advertising of this sort arose from the facilities offered for excursions up to London for the Great Exhibition in 1851. Here the rivalry was direct, between the new Great Northern company and its competitors the London & North Western and the Midland. In 1852–60 regular services from London to Scotland and to several English provincial cities became competitive. The rivalry in the Sheffield and Manchester services grew for a time intense, with reductions of fares to absurdly low levels, until the uneconomic conflict was brought under control in 1859.[4]

Many advertisements were now put out to announce new services that were faster than existing ones, or cheaper, or claimed to be more convenient; but it was not usual to bring a rival company into direct comparison in the advertisement itself. However, the Manchester Sheffield & Lincolnshire issued one attacking the London & North Western in respect of services between Manchester and Liverpool in 1865, and the Metropolitan proclaimed boldly in 1886 that it took its passengers more quickly to certain destinations than its rival the District.[5]

The rules that governed the printing of advertisements in newspapers limited their size, and so affected their visual impact. They were seldom allowed to run to a breadth of more than two columns, and large type was forbidden. Some gimmicks appeared, like elaborate arrangements of small type to form an object, such as a hat; well characterized as 'gruesome feats of typographical topiary'.[6] The pictorial element in the railways' newspaper advertisements was for many years confined to purely conventional representations of railway trains, from little blocks kept standing by until they were ludicrously out of date. Other devices were already available. An elaborate poster had been produced by the South Eastern company about 1845 to proclaim that it offered services to France via both Folkestone and Dover. It seems to be the first British railway poster in which several colours were used, as an element in a pictorial design; the first also to include railway scenes that were not the printers' reach-me-downs but tried to be realistic. It was, however, a special effort, designed to attract unusually valuable business. The general run of the railways' publicity continued to be timid and conventional for at least another thirty years. In 1878, Neele noted, 'the novelty of pictorial posters came into vogue'. His company the London & North Western was shown the design of one prepared for a competing railway, but the directors 'contented themselves with a modest cartoon of the North Wales coast from Rhyl to Snowdon'.[7]

Ill. 53

Those companies that were more adventurous in this matter did not exploit their advantage to much purpose. The quality of their new coloured posters was poor, both in design and in execution. They were badly composed, garish, typographically coarse. Their main purpose was to convey information, in words and figures; they were hardly more than time-bills and fare-sheets, tricked out with perfunctory ornament. Very few of them are to be seen today.[8] One of the survivors may serve as a favourable specimen: the poster produced by the Midland Railway about 1890 to advertise Blackpool.[9] The main picture shows a large spread of brick houses, with a pleasure steamer just leaving the

North Pier and another approaching it. The tints are limp and flat, but at least the arrangement is clean-cut.

The British railways did not begin to make use of good artists for their own posters until the beginning of the twentieth century. Then it was the London & North Western that took the lead. In 1905 the company's printers, McCorquodale's, suggested that it should commission a poster from a young painter, Norman Wilkinson, to advertise its service from Holyhead to Dublin; and he then persuaded the company to agree to the work being done in a quite new way.[10] He concentrated, as he said himself, 'on a really fine day in the Irish Channel, blue sea and a gentle breeze'. The painting was spacious and carried its message admirably, with no letterpress at all except the company's name and a brief title.[11] Before the year was out he produced a

Ill. 54   companion piece, showing a North Western ship crossing Dublin Bay at dusk.[12] On this foundation Wilkinson went on to win lasting recognition for his railway work. His greatest love was always for ships and the sea, but presently he portrayed the North Western main line in a broad, sweeping poster, to which the company attached the phrase 'the best permanent way in the world'.[13]

Ill. 55   Unlike most advertisers' boasts, that one was well justified.

Other companies also saw the value that landscape paintings could offer in advertising the attractions afforded by their systems to tourists. But the artists they commissioned were less happily inspired. Frank Mason's paintings, for example, used frequently by the North Eastern Railway, are crude beside Wilkinson's work. He also produced a pleasant series of etchings of historic scenes and buildings in the company's territory – of Rievaulx and Fountains and Lindisfarne; but though they had the delicacy of that medium, their monochrome and light lines made them much less compelling as posters.[14] The Great Central company employed an immigrant Italian, Fortunino Matania, a good deal; but he was not a landscape painter. He had a marked taste for the lush female form, exemplified in some strong and bold posters. Just how strong they were can be seen if they are compared with the simpering vapidity depicted in the 'Blackpool' produced for the same company.[15]

One of the railway posters of these years achieved immediate fame: John Hassall's 'Skegness is *so* Bracing' for the Great Northern Railway, issued in 1908. His fisherman capering on the sands, rubicund and high-booted, has kept a well-deserved place in popular art ever since.[16] Here the company insisted on including a quantity of letterpress: the poster was designed to advertise not only the resort but also the excursions the company was running to it by special express trains from King's Cross, 263 miles out and back for three shillings return. The place was not yet well known in London, so anyone prompted by the picture to go there needed to be told how easy the journey was, and how cheap. The letterpress was placed quite clear of the picture. The old tradition lived on, however. In the same year the Great Western put out a series of six pictorial posters, of which four exemplified the wildest confusions of design – one of them, advertising Newquay in Cardiganshire, in their worst form.[17]

Hassall also produced another admirable comic poster in 1908, 'No Need *Ill. 56*
to ask a P'liceman', for the underground railways in London. He was among
the first artists commissioned at the behest of Frank Pick when that young
man was given charge of the group's publicity. Pick had to lure the public
into the stations, and safely down to the trains; to get Londoners used to their
new electric underground railways. 'No Need' presented a broad reassurance
to those who were afraid of getting lost in subterranean passages. It was a
persuasive and delightful entertainment. This and 'Skegness' were the first
comic railway posters seen in Britain. Hassall at once set a standard in them
that has rarely been approached since. He followed up this London poster
with another ('When in Doubt', 1913); and an unknown artist produced one
admirably contrived to show that when the streets were blocked with road-
works the underground trains ran clear – 'Our Road's Our Own'.

In the underground group's posters the picture was always dominant,
uncluttered. That must have helped Pick to draw in artists who could know
that their work, if it was accepted, would be well handled. He soon began to
commission posters from a range of able men – Hartrick, Sharland, Brangwyn, *Ill. 57*
Fred Taylor.[18] Years later Hartrick said that Pick 'had a more sympathetic
intelligence in using art and artists effectively for his business than any other
man I have known'.[19]

The poster was not the only form of pictorial advertising adopted by
railways. They came to make much use of the picture postcard too.

The plain postcard established itself rapidly in Britain from 1870 onwards.[20]
The pictorial postcard was slower to make its way. It was not until 1894 that
the regulations of the British Post Office were amended to allow the commercial
publication of picture postcards and their transmission through the mail
service. A few picture postcards came to be produced in Britain then, some
showing the activities of railways, and their sale was encouraged by the use
of vending machines at stations. A number of new firms appeared in the
business in 1902–3.[21] Some of them collaborated with the companies to produce
'official' postcards, and several companies issued their own. The official cards
were designed to promote passenger traffic, to advertise amenities of all kinds,
new or special services, tourist routes throughout the United Kingdom and
across to the Continent. Some companies chose to put the interiors of their
dining-cars on to postcards, which were usually given to the diners free; when
written, one of the attendants would post them at the next stopping station.
The scenic attractions depicted by railways on postcards were apt to be
marred, as on the posters, by intrusive advertising placed on or beside them.[22]
For the rest, the cards showed the companies' trains and engines, stations and
hotels and steamers.

Most of the railways' advertising literature was ephemeral; but some
companies put out carefully-prepared booklets, even substantial volumes,
offered for sale at low prices and aimed particularly at those who wished to
plan their journeys ahead. The Great Western did this job thoroughly, with
a series of short books on different districts the company served, initiated with

The Cornish Riviera in 1904. They were followed by the company's own general guide to the system, listing all the facilities in most popular demand. This, called *Holiday Haunts*, began to be issued as an annual in 1906. The company had not misjudged the market. Over a quarter of a million copies of *The Cornish Riviera* were sold in a single year; nearly 100,000 of *Holiday Haunts* were consumed annually in 1909–14.[23] These productions had nothing to do with fine art, but they represented efficient and successful publicity.

Any study of advertising must be unsatisfactory because it is scarcely ever possible to demonstrate in precise terms the effects that advertising brings about. It is said that nearly 12 million postcards of the London & North Western Railway were produced in 1904–14, either by the company itself or by others with its permission.[24] What return accrued from the expenditure involved here, in printing, in the salaries and wages of its servants? What proof is there that anybody was led by one of the cards to choose Rhyl for his holiday rather than Cleethorpes?

The clear purpose underlying most of the effort demanded by this vast production of literature, of postcards and lantern slides and motion pictures and posters, was to encourage an increase of traffic: a larger number of passengers to and from Rhyl, a larger quantity of goods to be carried there to meet the needs of its shops and boarding-houses. That required heavier and more numerous trains, which called for more tracks; and early in the twentieth century thirty-three of the first thirty-seven miles of line along the coast of North Wales from Chester onwards through Rhyl had to be quadrupled. Most of the heavy cost involved was attributable to the enormous holiday traffic that line carried, for hardly more than a quarter of the year. If the railway's guesswork had been right, and its advertising had helped to engender this traffic, was that expense justified?

Taken as a whole, the main-line British railways' efforts at advertising were not impressive. Thomas Russell, a cool critic knowledgeable in the business, remarked in 1919 that such efforts were 'still in their infancy'. To him a good deal of the railways' advertising had been misconceived. What, he asked, was the point of putting a locomotive on to a poster, or a picture of Euston station? Moreover, the work had been wrongly directed; almost wholly to the passenger side of the railways' business, paying very little attention to freight. The development of freight traffic was left largely to the personal activities of canvassers. Russell thought that the best opportunities for advertising lay there. Substantial new revenue could, he believed, be generated if that business came to be accorded serious treatment, with research and intelligence behind it. Hardly anything had been done in that way at the time he wrote.[25]

The Railways and their Passengers

A few early railway companies made a positive effort to communicate with the public: the Newcastle & Carlisle, for example. Even before it was built, the promoters had the good sense to put out a plan and section of its intended line at the Newcastle Guildhall, for examination by anyone who was interested. Its later advertisements of new services and practices were numerous and sensibly worded.[26] When some other railways had to communicate with their passengers in early days, however, their language was apt to be peremptory. James Wyld remarked on this matter in 1839. He commended the regulations the Great Western company imposed on its passengers and implied that they were sensibly carried out: but those on some other lines were 'apparently modelled on French or Russian police ordinances'.[27] He went on to give awful examples of the consequences of losing one's ticket.

Railway companies were permitted to make by-laws applicable to their passengers. For various offences they prescribed fines, of sums from forty shillings to five pounds. Much of this was bluff, called successfully in the courts.[28] But the exhibition of such threatening notices was often the sole communication the companies made to passengers arriving at their stations, and it afforded them a dour welcome.

Little money was spent on any adornment to lure the traveller into a British railway station, or to cheer the time he had to spend there. 'Station very dreary, being a station', Dickens remarked in Staffordshire in 1854.[29] Nothing appeared anywhere in the island that resembled the beguiling decoration bestowed on the first terminus at Florence, and still to be seen on the one at Toledo.[30] The drabness of railway waiting-rooms was notorious. Did anyone ever commend one of them as cheerful, in all these eighty-four years? The companies provided shelter, and space in which to wait for the purpose of taking tickets. On the platforms, to which access was as a rule given only by payment, there might be a bookstall and a refreshment room (of sorts). There too there would be water-closets and urinals. But nothing more. Essentially the stations were machines for handling passengers and receiving money. Travellers were compelled to use them if they wished to use the trains. The railways knew that, and treated them accordingly.

No marked difference in this matter appeared as a result of the growth of competition. Most stations went unchanged when, from the 1870s onwards, some companies began to provide carriages that were seen to be better than their rivals', better upholstered, better lighted and heated, better decorated. That was a way of persuading them to use one line rather than another. The decision of the Midland Railway to take the press for a trip from London to Bedford and back on 21 March 1874 in the new Pullman cars the company was introducing, and to serve them with lunch on the way, was unprecedented in Britain. It was a plain effort to attract some of the wealthier business traffic from London to Lancashire and Yorkshire, which these cars were to convey, at the expense of the Midland's rivals; a good quiet exercise in public relations. The Midland was also engaged in making a very bold bid for third-class passengers. The splendid vehicles it built, to convey them as well as others paying higher fares (see p. 84), were a strong form of advertising, addressed to that section of the public, which was now becoming more important year by year (see pp. 267, 321).

Under the stimulus of this example, and of decisions taken by other companies equally alert in the competitive business, the facilities offered to passengers, once they had got into the trains and were travelling, grew better. But the stations, the first meeting-points between railways and travellers, underwent little comparable improvement. Although most companies tried to see that they were kept clean and tidy, the cycle of painting revolved slowly, and the colours used were durable rather than cheerful.

A special effort was made, however, by some railways to encourage the creation and tending of gardens on the station platforms by means of prizes awarded annually. The practice can be traced back at least to the 1880s:[31] to the Cornwall Railway in 1884 and the Great Western three years later. The Cambrian was doing the same in the 1890s.[32] In 1906 the Great Western spent £250 a year in this way; and the Great Eastern maintained a small nursery of its own, one of its purposes being to supply shrubs and trees for planting at stations, under the supervision of the company's own forester.[33]

The stations thus agreeably treated were mainly rural; a few were suburban; hardly any within towns.[34] But one other form of horticultural adornment did grace some stations: the hanging flower-basket. No prizes were ever offered here for competition between the companies. If they had been, they would usually have gone to Scotland. These baskets delightfully punctuated the glass and metal roofs of the stations at Perth and Aberdeen, and the trim little masterpiece the Caledonian company built for itself at Wemyss Bay.

But the travellers whom the railways pleased in this fashion formed only a minute fraction of the millions they carried. Every year a much greater number must have wished that their surroundings on the railway – especially during their long waits at junctions – had been less dismal. Some stations were very bitterly complained about.[35] A good many of the larger ones were rebuilt, chiefly from the necessity of accommodating an increased traffic, but even in important towns it was rare for the companies to invite any criticisms or suggestions that might come from their users. The Midland, for instance, ignored everything said to it by the Town Council of Sheffield when it was planning a new main station there from 1890 onwards.[36] Nobody had the power to oblige the companies to make any changes against their will, except in matters concerning safety. Consultation would have cost them nothing but a little time and trouble, yet the companies refused to spend it. Here are two striking cases, in which that disregard of their customers' feelings was very plainly exhibited.

In 1894 the Borough Council of Devonport considered its station on the Great Western Railway so bad that it agreed to establish a committee with the town's Mercantile Association to press the company for improvements. The committee explained that the station's defects needed to be demonstrated on the spot, to be told merely that it was uncertain when any of the directors would next be in the neighbourhood. Two years later the same committee interested itself in improvements at Keyham station (also within the borough). When it asked if it could see the plans the reply from Paddington was that the company 'did not submit their plans for the inspection of public bodies' and that to meet the committee's request would set an undesirable precedent. The same letter – it is almost incredible – then went on to a bland inquiry whether the committee would assist the company with the 'somewhat heavy expense' entailed by the purchase of the land and the engineering works that were required.[37] This egregious document did not come from some underling but from J. L. Wilkinson, then acting as general manager of the Great Western Railway and about to become the substantive holder of the post. Devonport was a place of 60,000 people. The company exercised no monopoly there. Far from it: the London & South Western had opened a highly competitive line leading to London, as recently as 1890. Wilkinson was not an aged dug-out but an able railwayman in the prime of life. Clearly he saw no need for his company to take the smallest trouble to be civil to these townspeople, even when he was at the same time wishing to extract money from them.

The other example comes from Glasgow. The Caledonian company had two terminal stations there. In 1890 its services to the south and along the Clyde coast were concentrated into Central station, a respectable structure that soon became overcrowded until it was magnificently enlarged in 1901–6. The northern services to Perth, Aberdeen, and the Highlands were handled at the station on Buchanan Street; and that was as scrubby as the other was splendid. A journalist wrote this of it in 1897: 'The luckless men who are compelled to spend their days and nights within its precincts have my heartfelt sympathy. A sad-faced, melancholy band they are; they never smile; they die young; and more sad-faced melancholy men come along to fill their places in this living sepulchre'.[38] The Caledonian company did not care a straw. Nothing was done to improve this disgraceful wooden shanty until the 1930s, when the London Midland & Scottish company gave it a stingy face-lift.

What sort of 'public relations' were these?

Competition and Monopoly

While railways were new, still battling with coaches and canals for their traffic, they needed some public support. When those battles were over, they had the mastery of the transport system. The business of the companies was now to order and control, not to persuade. When competition between them grew lively, the talents it called for from their managers were aggressive. They had to be sharp, alert, ingenious, at every point fighters. Here is the explanation, and the real significance, of the well-worn tales of passengers who were bullyragged at Chester and Manchester; of lines blocked and rails removed, to frustrate the efforts of rival companies, at Methley and Wolverhampton and Nottingham.[39] These were clear signs of the companies' determination to secure their ends, whatever inconvenience that might cause to their customers.

But the public could be worse served where there were no squabbles of this kind, because there was no competition; worst of all perhaps in the north-east of the island. There the Great North of Scotland Railway treated everyone who dealt with it, passengers and traders alike, with off-handed arrogance for twenty-five years on end. No alternative services were available by land. The company ignored connections due to be made at Aberdeen from the south, shut the doors of the station in the face of advancing passengers, refused to quote through goods rates to other lines.[40] It gradually moved up towards Inverness, expecting to collect the whole traffic from the far north and north-west of Scotland. But in 1861 the Inverness & Perth Junction line was authorized, to cross the Grampians by a more or less direct route to the south; and one reason for the success of that scheme, in the face of formidable engineering difficulties, was the wide fame won by the bad service the Great North company afforded at Aberdeen. Still it learnt no lesson from that defeat, dragging its way on – financially feeble, physically dilapidated – until at last its firm and effective reform began, with a change of chairman and senior officers, in 1879–80.[41]

In theory the public had a remedy against such malpractices. In 1854 Cardwell's Railway and Canal Traffic Act had required railway companies to 'afford all reasonable facilities for the receiving and forwarding and delivering of traffic', and obliged two companies that had stations near each other to afford those facilities 'without any unreasonable delay'.[42] The Great North's original Aberdeen terminus was $1\frac{1}{2}$ miles from that of the railway coming up from the south; but in 1856 its line was extended to a new station, which lessened the gap between the two to half a mile. The company could not possibly claim then that it was offering 'all reasonable facilities' for the interchange of traffic at Aberdeen. Why then was it not taken to court?

The answer is that the Act did not provide complainants with easy remedies. The procedure it laid down for securing redress from the companies, through the old Court of Common Pleas in England and the Court of Session in Scotland, was cumbrous and expensive, and the Act was little invoked for this purpose; not at all by the critics of this very ill-conducted company. In 1873 Parliament transferred such cases to a new court, the Railway Commission. The proceedings there, though they were somewhat cheaper, remained slow, and this court was in turn superseded by the Railway and Canal Commission of 1888, which provided a generally effective instrument in the hands of those who had just grievances against railway companies. The establishment of these two new courts in succession is itself a comment on the railway companies' public relations, and that appeared in the cases that came before them.

Consider a group of actions brought before the Railway and Canal Commission in 1890, all of them by local boards or town councils. Three concerned the 'reasonable facilities' that should be afforded to passengers. At Beckenham (a junction, where they often had to wait for connections) the South Eastern and the Chatham companies were taken to court for failing to provide adequate accommodation, even 'sufficient covering for protection from rain'. These two companies were also complained of by the town council of Maidstone for their refusal to offer through bookings and other facilities between their separate lines at Ashford. At Winsford the Cheshire Lines

Committee had withdrawn its passenger service altogether.[43] The Great Northern company was prosecuted by the town council of Louth, complaining of some of the charges it made for the carriage of freight.[44] All four of these cases went against the railway companies. In the first two they were ordered by the court to put right what was criticized. The Winsford branch had to be re-opened. In the last case, when the company had agreed to amend its rates and to pay the applicants' costs, further proceedings were stayed.

The root of all these grievances was the same: a refusal of the companies to pay due attention to the interests of their customers. That they had to be taken to court, at quite substantial expense to the ratepayers,[45] shows the strength of feeling against the railways; a clear proof of the failure of their public relations.

Every railway was a target for complaints about its services: the poor provision of them, their bad planning or their unpunctual operation. The better companies made some effort to reply to them politely, either apologizing or seeking to show the complainant how the fault had occurred. If the complaints were pressed by influential customers, the management might consent to receive a deputation to discuss what was being criticized. Where no redress was forthcoming in this way, an appeal could be taken to the President of the Board of Trade, though he had no power to force a company to put right what was evidently wrong.[46] The courts could seldom afford any remedy for unpunctuality, or its consequences.[47] There was however another way of attacking that form of misconduct, by bringing it to public attention in the newspapers.

In 1888 and 1895 the companies carrying the traffic between London and Scotland indulged for a time in 'Races to the North'. In the month after the second series of those contests ended a number of travellers, eternally inconvenienced by the unpunctuality of the suburban services of the South Eastern and London Brighton & South Coast Railways, took part in a *Times* correspondence under the appropriate heading 'The Crawl to the South'. The paper itself entered fully into the fun, with a leader contrasting the invigorating performances of the northern lines with those regularly offered by the two southern companies. They had 'chosen frankly a very different form of distinction, and the struggle between them now is which of them can claim to have established the slowest, the most unpunctual, and the most inconvenient services of trains. . . . It is difficult to say with certainty which of the two has the better right to call itself absolutely the worst line in the country'.[48]

The statements made on behalf of the two companies in reply were fatuous. Watkin, as chairman of the South Eastern, had already rested his case on a lie, ascribing nearly all the trouble to the Brighton company (with which his own shared the line between Croydon and Redhill). The Brighton officials treated complainants to courteous letters that merely declared their inability to do anything. In that case their company should not have been offering the services it pretended to offer. A year before this row broke out it had already taken powers to provide two additional tracks of its own through the bottleneck.

Yet no spokesman of the Brighton company seems to have said anything at all on that matter.

Not every railway manager behaved towards his customers with such grotesque ineptitude. At Southampton, when there was a special rancour towards the London & South Western Railway (it entered repeatedly into Parliamentary elections) a cordial partnership came to be established between the town and its railway company from 1892 onwards. The main reason for this was the South Western's decision to purchase the docks, with a guarantee that it would invest very substantially in their modernization and enlargement, called for imperatively if the port was to retain the international trade that was ebbing away from it. There were obvious risks to the town in committing its port to the company, whose past record was a poor one. Not even the lure of money would have sufficed to silence the objections and produce agreement. But the *volte-face* of opinion at Southampton had other causes as well: among them the skilful, unfaltering conduct of the business by the South Western's general manager, Charles Scotter, as what we should now call an exercise in public relations. For that he had a real talent, showing itself in small things as well as in great.[49] Here was a chief officer of one of the big railway companies who was a natural communicator; a man whose easy intercourse, in his office or across a table or from a platform, displayed an imaginative sense of the feelings of the people he was dealing with. Other senior railway men were also capable of communicating well, and saw the need for it. Two of them, James Grierson and George Findlay, wrote important books specifically designed to interpret the railways to the public.

But those officers were highly exceptional men. Most Victorian railway managers continued to think it was their function to provide whatever service they deemed best, which their passengers must take or leave as they chose. That was not an attitude that other commercial men – manufacturers, in particular – could take up, unless they were purveyors of some unique article, produced on a small scale and much sought after, like Burgess's Fish Sauce.

The railways' shortcomings that have just been referred to were being aired when they had already lost much urban and suburban traffic to horse trams and buses and when their managers could discern, if they had any eye to the future, that they stood to lose much more whenever electric power came to be applied to transport on a large scale. And moreover, for nearly thirty years they had been fighting a fierce and unsuccessful battle in defence of their privileges in a national forum, in Parliament.

The Railways in Politics

There had been a number of stiff Parliamentary struggles in 1838–68 between the railways and their opponents. The government had established its regulation of them, through the Board of Trade; but the railways had never been totally worsted. The restrictions they had been obliged to submit to seemed to represent prices well worth paying, in order to be free of obligations they wished to avoid.

In strong contrast, from 1870 onwards at least seven important issues concerning railways engaged a large amount of Parliamentary time and brought the companies into the full limelight of fierce criticism; perhaps we should say, into the dock. They were: (1) accidents to passengers (already a cause of increasing alarm before 1870); (2) amalgamation; (3) passenger duty on railway fares; (4) employers' liability, as applied to railways; (5) rates for the carriage of freight traffic; (6) the hours worked by the railway companies' servants and (7) the special dangers of their employment. On the first, second, fourth, and fifth of these matters the railways were plainly defeated. On the third they came off with a compromise, not favouring them. The last two stimulated an increasing antagonism between them and their employees that helped to determine the attitude of organized labour towards railway management in the twentieth century.

Although the railway companies headed off the worst of the earlier attacks, they paid highly for doing so. They had to abandon all their larger schemes of amalgamation and to accept the establishment of the new court in 1873. Accidents continued to be frequent, and a Royal Commission was appointed in 1874 to look into the causes of them. The inspectors argued forcibly that their incidence could be diminished by the adoption of safety precautions that most of the railways resisted. When continuous automatic brakes were on offer, none of them seemed to show a clear superiority over its competitors. The comparative merits of the different systems would surely be demonstrable under test, and the Commission asked for trials of them to be arranged. They were held at Newark in 1875.[50] The railway companies' willingness to accept the idea of these tests has been seen as an effort in public relations: the trials 'formed the only continuous piece of propaganda which the railways undertook at any time before 1914'. If there is some truth in that observation, it is important to remember that the companies did not themselves come forward to offer to make these tests. The initiative came from the Commission, and they complied with it.[51]

The railways' defence against the attacks made on them after 1868 did not go quite by default. They brought forward their case in Parliament through directors who sat there. At least from 1847 onwards a substantial body of MPs were railway directors. It is reckoned that their number was then eighty; in 1865 it reached 165 – one in four of the entire membership of the House of Commons. However, that was less important than it looked, for a majority of them sat on the boards of small and feeble companies.[52] These MPs, when taken together with peers who were directors, were commonly said to form 'the railway interest' in Parliament.[53] That phrase, and the thinking behind it, came to imply that they composed a special interest engaged in manipulating government in the railways' favour. *Punch* went on worrying away at this matter in its own peculiar fashion. As general elections approached, it plugged the theme strongly. In 1868: 'Are you a railway director? Yes. Then you shan't have my vote. This should be the way of dealing with a candidate'. In 1873: 'The candidate not to vote for on any account is a railway chairman, director, official of any kind'.[54]

The railways formed a defensive body, the Railway Companies Association, in 1868–70,[55] to represent their interest and their shareholders', and it soon became their spokesman. After a fumbling start, the Association achieved some success in defending the companies in the early stages of the controversy over rates in 1881–2, and in 1891 it encouraged Acworth to write his short study of the argument, *The Railways and the Traders*. But when the companies incurred their greatest unpopularity with the commercial world by raising their rates, as a tactical move, in 1892–3 the Association proved quite unable to retrieve that blunder, or to keep them in step with one another.[56] It was not the Association but the Railway Clearing House that persuaded the companies to bring some of their differing policies into line and so to reduce the friction between them.[57]

That friction sometimes revealed itself with stark clarity. The chairmen of the North Eastern and South Eastern companies, both Liberal MPs, had disagreed sharply in public on the value of competition between railway companies, in 1872.[58] The North Eastern board's decision to invoke arbitration in a dispute with some of the company's servants in 1897 cut it off for a time from all the other large railways and withdrew it from whatever common policies were proposed.[59]

The railway interest now laboured under two defects, of exactly opposite sorts. It was coming to be seen as a phalanx, solid and sinister: yet in truth the interest was deeply divided and was sometimes unable to speak convincingly with one voice. Such a delicate situation required most careful handling by the body they had created to represent them. The Railway Companies Association had neither the authority nor the resources to allow it to perform that task effectively. It was only in 1900 that it acquired permanent offices of its own and a full-time paid secretary. A highly efficient young barrister, Guy Granet, was appointed to that post. But the Association remained a voluntary body, without power to coerce the companies.

The reform of the Association was carried through just three months after the railways' unremitting struggle to keep control of their working in their own hands – the basis on which they had defended themselves most strongly in the previous sixty years – had been finally lost. The Railway Employment (Prevention of Accidents) Act had gone into force on 30 July 1900, giving the Board of Trade the power of requiring the companies to adopt any rules it thought fit to impose in order to protect railway workers from danger.

The railways had now nailed their colours to the mast. In the years that followed they continued their journey to the right, hurried along that path by such implacable diehards as Lord Claud Hamilton and Sir Frederick Banbury, attending little to wise mediators like Sir Gilbert Claughton. Seen in relation to the political tone and temper of the country, this was a stumbling movement into the wilderness. It did much to deprive the total railway interest – that is to say companies, shareholders, and employees, the entire railway industry together – of the public sympathy and support it might otherwise have commanded in the severer struggles that were to come after the First World War.

A New Art

In the years before 1914 some railway managements accepted the need to address the public in new ways.

The public itself had changed. In the late Victorian age the preponderance of third-class railway passengers had come to be overwhelming. In 1874 their journeys constituted 77% of the total of all that were made in Great Britain; by 1900 that percentage had become 91%; by 1913, 96%. The proportion of the revenue accruing from third-class passengers had increased no less strikingly than their numbers: from 58% of the total in 1874 to 74% in 1900 and 85% in 1913.[60] In commercial terms third-class traffic was growing steadily more valuable to the companies. Over the same years the electorate increased substantially, in accordance with the changes made in it by the legislation of 1868 and 1884-5, and a very large majority of the voters added then were of the social classes that, when they travelled by train, travelled third. The companies had to find effective means of communicating with their new passengers.

The leader among them in this matter was the Great Central. In 1899 it opened its London extension, and that launched it on a continuous competitive struggle for traffic with the old-established companies whose lines ran parallel with its own, the London & North Western, the Midland, and the Great Northern. Its first task was to inform prospective customers of its existence as a new trunk line between London and the North. For this railway, in this situation, publicity was not a routine matter of reminding people of the services it offered. It was a necessity.

The company soon acquired a new general manager, Sam Fay, who saw what had to be done here and did it quickly. He took up his appointment on 1 April 1902. Before that year was out he had set up a publicity department and given its manager, W. J. Stuart, a double task: to deal with all branches of advertising and also to handle editorial communication with the press.[61] Here was the dawn of the British railways' concept of public relations. The publicity department was placed within the general manager's office; that is, at the central seat of power. When a question of policy arose, calling for a statement to the press, Stuart took instructions from Fay himself, not through any intermediary or underling.

No other main-line company followed the Great Central's example. The Lancashire & Yorkshire established an advertising department in 1906; the London & North Western a publicity department three years later, the London & South Western in 1913.[62] There are few other formal signs that any special attention was being paid to publicity, still less to public relations.[63]

Though that is true of the main-line railway companies, public relations soon came to be attended to closely on the tube railways in London. For that four men deserve credit: George Gibb and Albert Stanley, who had the same talent as Fay for perceiving what needed to be done; and two subordinate officers, Walter Gott and Frank Pick. Gott came from the Great Northern company to work for the underground railways; Pick had been brought down from the North Eastern by Gibb, to whom he had been a personal assistant. Under-employed at first, he took to criticizing the tube railways' publicity, until Stanley put him to the test of demonstrating how it could be improved. In 1909 he was transferred from the position of critic to the executive headship of a traffic development and advertising department, being called traffic officer. Gott left soon afterwards to become assistant manager of Partington's, a large advertising agency, and Pick had the field to himself.

One of the first things he did was to re-order the display of advertising on the underground stations, devising an acceptable relationship between it and the station signs. Great care was now taken with the level at which the signs were placed, to make them easily visible. Pick was looking here at a commercial matter, but in the context of the railways' relations with their customers. His brief had been drawn up by Stanley in a very broad way. He was not made responsible for advertising in isolation: he was to handle it as an instrument for the direct promotion of traffic. He knew that the advertisements must be easily visible to the passengers, or the revenue they produced would be likely to fall, and the underground railways were in no position to forgo revenue of any kind.[64]

Although none of the main-line companies approached the management of their public relations so carefully, the larger ones – and one or two of the smaller, like the Furness, as well – developed a fresh zeal in advertising their services. Their efforts were now directed largely to addressing their third-class public. Seaside resorts and the pleasures they could offer to children figured prominently on their posters and in their advertising literature. They turned their attention to football matches and other sporting events. The editor of the new *Railway Magazine*, G. A. Sekon, took an interest in the expansion of this branch of the railways' work, and his paper reflects it, with numerous reproductions of posters from 1902 onwards. Cautious though he generally was in offending the managers' susceptibilities, he allowed one of his contributors to characterize an unnamed railway that failed to foster its own publicity as 'The London and Behind-the-Times Railway Company'.[65]

We have very little means of telling what this business cost the railways. Advertising never appears as a distinct item in their accounts; presumably it was comprehended within 'traffic expenses' or 'general charges'. What did the Great Western spend each year on its big guide, *Holiday Haunts*? It was sold to the public at a penny in 1906–7; then, when it was enlarged to 588 pages, at threepence; in 1911 the price rose to sixpence. It appears that the main sale was through the book trade, to which copies must have been supplied at a discount. Some money would have come in from displayed advertising, paid by hotels and boarding houses; but allowing for that and for a revenue from sales, the editing, printing, and distribution of the book must have cost the company a substantial amount. It began to bring in a small net income only in the late 1930s.[66]

For the rest, we have occasional hints. The Lancashire & Yorkshire Railway let it be known in 1902 that its expenditure on advertising was £7000 a year.[67] In February 1906 the London & North Western chairman thought it desirable to defend what the company was spending in this way, though he did not state the sum.[68] There were critics at hand, ready to argue heatedly that it was time and money scandalously wasted.[69]

Looking back over it now, from a world in which publicity of all kinds has become a familiar condition of daily life, we should probably allow that substantial expenditure of this kind, in addressing a very wide public, had become a necessity before 1914. At the same time we may well share Russell's doubts whether all that expenditure was wisely directed.

'The railway managers, as railway managers do, explained that the peculiar nature of their business made it inevitable that they should act as they did.' We owe that epitome of their attitudes to an observant railway man himself.[70]

Those attitudes were not merely insensitive and self-satisfied. Compulsions *were* placed on the companies and their managers, by the legal system within which they had to work and by the technical limits of the instruments they used. Some of these were so complex that any effort to explain them in language that an impatient public would attend to may have seemed a mere waste of time. But was it really that? In a number of the large arguments that have been mentioned here the railways had a strong case, which they put forward feebly or hardly put forward at all. When they turned out to be in the wrong – as they can fairly be said to have been over continuous brakes and interlocking and, at many points, in the debates about hours of work – they made no change until it was forced upon them; the worst policy possible in the circumstances, since it left the credit for the adoption of improved practices to their critics. Nothing but obstinacy seemed to govern them: an obstinate rejection of superior devices; an obstinate pursuit of economy that was dangerous.

At the turn of the century a certain new affection for railways began to show itself. But the general public did not love them, and left them with alacrity when better and cheaper means of transport were afforded by electric trams and motor buses and commercial road services. It was only then, with the loss of their old monopolies, that they began to consider seriously the methods they might adopt to explain themselves to their customers, to those they were in danger of losing and to those who remained. They had hardly begun to measure this task before the First World War. Their public relations were still amateurish, imperfectly thought out, and seldom well aimed. But then in that the railway companies were far from unique, among business corporations in the Britain of 1914.

12

LEISURE (I):
THE EXCURSION TRAIN AND
THE RAILWAY SUNDAY

*Before Railways · The Railways Move In · The Great
Exhibition · Excursion Trains: Growth, Profit, and Risk ·
The Railway Sunday*

Before Railways

The changes that railways occasioned in the use of leisure came to be
perceived quickly. The wilder comments, made both by contemporaries
and by some writers since, might suggest that leisure was something previously
unknown in Britain, associated only with dancing round maypoles in a distant
Merrie England. That is far from true. Every important form of leisure activity
that we observe in the Victorian age and may suppose to have been introduced
by the railways had already been thought of in earlier years, from sea-bathing
to spectator sports, from the day trip to the extended tour in Scotland or on
the Continent.

Railways came to make a larger and a far more varied contribution to the
use of leisure in the Victorian age than any other agency at all. The business
grew to be important to the companies, though it was never shown separately
in their accounts. The present chapter concerns two special forms of this
provision: the excursion train and the changes in Sunday observance and
family behaviour that emerged in Britain in the Victorian age, which railways
did a good deal to quicken and extend. In the next chapter these special
practices will be considered in relation to the growth of tourism, and finally
in the broad context of the use of leisure, in many different forms, all of which
the railways advanced.

The holiday began as a holy day. It descended from the Jewish Sabbath
(kept by Christians not on Saturday but on Sunday), a day when the Fourth
Commandment decreed that no work should be done. To this weekly holiday
there came to be added a multitude of saints' days, which were similarly
observed in Britain until the Reformation; and some of these were still kept
as holidays at the beginning of the nineteenth century. At the Bank of England
there were forty-four such holidays (including some that were not religious in
origin) in 1808. But the number was soon reduced, until by 1839 all but four
had gone.[1] Elsewhere however there was a new movement to be perceived in

the opposite direction. In many factories holidays were declared, at the will of the owners, as a device for saving wages when business was slack. Such holidays – without pay – were naturally apt to be considered, by those obliged to take them, not as a benefit but as a grievance.

Brief and irregular holidays could seldom have meant much more than a cessation of work; welcome enough to those whose ordinary tasks were heavy, for a good many others a rather pointless interlude in the normal routine of the week. The majority of the people in the island spent part of Sunday in attendance at church or chapel. In the warmer months of the year those who were not rigid Sabbatarians could enjoy walking out into the country, which still lay within easy reach of most town-dwellers; perhaps, as an annual treat, borrowing or hiring a donkey cart to convey the whole family out – from London for instance to Blackheath or Epping Forest. Plenty of sports were available to take part in or to watch: angling, pigeon-shooting, coursing, cricket, horse-races, curling. For the rest, there were the inns and ale-houses.

People of moderate means might occupy their holidays in travelling, with or without their families. But that was an uncommon event, scarcely to be thought of every year. In the six completed novels of Jane Austen holidays involving any extensive travel are mentioned only three times: a picturesque tour into Derbyshire; a visit to Southend, to aid the recovery of a sick child; and a short frolic to Lyme Regis.[2] However, at the time of her death in 1817 she was writing a novel about a new watering-place on the Sussex coast, 'Sanditon', in which she gave some prominence to travelling from London:[3] a sign that journeys to such places were occupying public attention. The movement was still very small in scale. The total number of visitors to Brighton in 1794 was reckoned at 4300; by 1818 it had become 11,000.[4]

Coaches and other public road services were now conveying holiday-makers all over the island, though in what numbers we seldom know.[5] There was already a regular traffic, based largely on them, to North Wales and the English Lakes. Wealthier travellers moved about as they chose in their private carriages; or they might ride their own horses, as John Byng usually did in his spirited explorations of England and Wales in the last twenty years of the eighteenth century.[6] Others walked. The pedestrian ramble was already a recognizable product of romantic feeling: a German published an account of a *Fussreise* he had made through the British Isles in 1797; *A Pedestrian Tour of Thirteen Hundred and Forty-seven Miles through Wales and England* appeared in 1836.[7]

These holiday-makers were all moving by land. But others came to be conveyed by water, and in much larger numbers. Margate claimed to have received 17,000 visitors by sailing ships in 1812–13. Then from 1815 onwards steamboats entered the business, and quickly gave it dimensions that no one had ever contemplated before. In 1820–1 the visitors arriving at Margate by sea (mainly from London) had leapt up to 44,000; the average was 85,000 a year by the 1830s.[8] The same kind of traffic was impressive on the Clyde. By 1816 it was credibly reported that steamers going down the estuary of that river were fast superseding coaches, and that they were carrying a larger number of passengers.[9] Steamboats were soon busy on other estuaries too – of the Tyne, the Humber, and the Mersey.

This traffic was seasonal, occurring mainly in the summer months, and its character was essentially local. The steamboats did not provide a national service, as the coaches did, in winter and summer alike. Nevertheless their rapid early development was of much greater importance than has usually been recognized. They carried their passengers by hundreds at a time, instead of tens. They first demonstrated the meaning of mass transport, its capabilities for the future. They, not the railways.

The Railways Move In

The Liverpool & Manchester Railway quickly adopted the notion of carrying passengers along its short line on special cheap trips, at low prices. On 1 October 1830, less than a fortnight after it was opened to public traffic, it took sightseers out from Liverpool as far as the Sankey viaduct in 'the Duke's train of carriages' for five shillings return, instead of the eight shillings they would normally have paid. A few days later the same train was used to convey visitors from Manchester to the Liverpool Charity Festival and back again. These trips were arranged by the company itself. In May 1831 it agreed with a private promoter to take 150 members of the Bennett Street Sunday School from Manchester to Liverpool and back in a special train at one-third of the ordinary fare.[10] Here we have the first appearance of what came to be called 'excursion trains', using that phrase in its strict sense: that is, special trains provided by a railway company – either on its own initiative or by arrangement with other people – to carry passengers on a return journey, normally made within one day, at a fare below the standard rate.

The company then went on to make more provisions of this kind. In the same year it offered special trains, at reduced fares, to the race-meetings at Newton-le-Willows and Liverpool. Other railways took to providing excursions too, led in Scotland by the Garnkirk & Glasgow in 1834.[11] In 1836 the Bodmin & Wadebridge ran a cheap train for those who wished to see a public execution.[12] Three years later the Whitby & Pickering Railway offered cheap trips, by additional trains, to Grosmont for a church bazaar.[13] The idea was taken up by the Mechanics' Institutes. The Manchester one organized a trip by train to Liverpool in 1833.[14] The Leeds Institute arranged an excursion to York in June 1840 for which half-price tickets were issued – first, second, and third class, including tea. Then on Sunday 9 August a special train was run from Leeds to Hull and back, forty carriages being required for it, to convey more than 1250 passengers.[15] This seems to have been the first of the 'monster trains' that did much to publicize the idea of the railway excursion. The same practices were also adopted at Nottingham and Leicester. A train was chartered there that was even bigger than the one at Leeds, with four engines dragging sixty-seven carriages behind them. As the cortège approached Leicester, it 'appeared like a moving street, the houses of which were filled with human beings'.[16]

Another promoter in that locality soon went further. Thomas Cook, a small business man then living at Market Harborough, arranged with the Midland Counties Railway for a special train to take people from Leicester to a temperance fête at Loughborough and back again, and 570 of them went on 5 July 1841, at a fare of a halfpenny a mile for the double journey. The experiment succeeded. It was the beginning of what grew into a great international enterprise.

One of the early London railways offered facilities to holiday-makers, not by means of excursions but in the normal course of its business. The London & Greenwich, opened in 1836–8, was the first in the country to be devoted to the carriage of passengers alone. It had to fight for them against steamboats and horse-drawn buses; but the traffic down the Thames at holiday times was large enough to offer all the contestants a chance of a living. In 1836–40 the railway carried passengers at the rate of over $1\frac{1}{4}$ million a year.[17] Holiday-makers must have formed a significant proportion of this total.

Among the trunk railways, the first to aid the pursuit of leisure was the London & South Western. In 1841–2 it put on several long-distance excursions, taking passengers to Southampton, round the Isle of Wight by steamer, and then back again. It also showed an interest in race-goers and carried them in large numbers to Surbiton, for Epsom on Derby Day, and to Woking for Ascot. The Great Western paid attention to Ascot too, by carrying passengers to Slough and by subscribing to the stakes;[18] but the South Western won this competition outright when it provided a railway through to Ascot in 1856.

The first trunk line that showed a strong positive interest in the promotion of leisure traffic was the London & Brighton. In 1844 it became the chief pioneer of excursion trains in southern England. The first one ran on Easter Monday (8 April), largely at the instance of Rowland Hill, who was one of the directors of the company. He was later given the whole credit for the introduction of excursion trains;[19] but that ignored all that had been done in the provinces over the previous fourteen years. In the following week it was reported that similar trains were being run into London as well as out of it by the Brighton, the Eastern Counties, and the South Eastern Railways.[20] By 1 June the new *Railway Chronicle*, which looked on the whole business with great favour (Herapath's *Railway Journal* did not), was remarking that railway excursions were 'becoming our chief national amusement'.

In the north of England the provision was now extending fast. On one day the whole line between Manchester and Wakefield was thrown open to schoolchildren, with permission to travel between any two stations for sixpence each.[21] The monster excursions continued, one trip from Leeds to Hull on 12 September carrying 6600 passengers in 240 carriages, hauled by nine locomotives.[22]

These trains were often mismanaged. The first excursion from Oxford to London travelled so slowly that it reached London at 4 pm and had to return immediately.[23] One from Leicester to York took nine hours on the outward journey. The engines used were of insufficient power to haul over sixty carriages. North of Chesterfield some passengers could walk as fast as the train; when it stopped for an hour some got out and went nutting in a wood nearby. Other excursions going to York on the same day seem to have fared little better. Asserting that the excursions from Leicester to Nottingham were also mishandled, the *Leicester Chronicle* observed portentously that the Midland directors 'either do not or will not understand the Philosophy of Special Trains'.[24]

The Board of Trade now felt the need to address the companies with a formal caution on the dangers these trains incurred. But its President, the young Gladstone, saw that it must act carefully here lest it might 'touch the purses of the companies and . . . also seem to restrain the enjoyments of the people'.[25] His warning was heeded. When, in October 1844, the Board did address the companies on the matter, it was careful to say that it 'did not wish to suppress excursions of this character', being aware of 'their useful influence on the portions of the community who profit by them'.[26] It did however spell out the dangers involved in running additional trains, not provided for in the normal timetables, and its warnings were treated with some respect.[27] But the trains still ran.

Some companies sought to promote all forms of holiday business alike: notably the Manchester & Leeds and its successor the Lancashire & Yorkshire. Others wished to develop holiday travel in forms more attractive to middle-class passengers than the boisterous and crowded excursion trains. The London & Birmingham and the Grand Junction, for example, introduced first and second-class day return tickets in 1844–5.[28]

The amalgamations that produced the Midland and the London & North Western combines in 1844–6 encouraged the new managements to promote holiday traffic. The enlargement of their systems gave greater scope for it, and greater bargaining power with neighbouring companies that might collaborate in assisting travellers to make extensive journeys. By 1849–50 the London & North Western was offering, with various partners, through bookings to North Wales and Scotland, and to Ireland as far west as Killarney.[29] At the instigation of its quick-witted general manager Mark Huish, it also threw itself into providing excursion trains to the Great Exhibition, held in London in 1851.

The Great Exhibition

The plan for a very large 'exhibition of manufactures' was put forward by the Society of Arts in 1849. It envisaged that foreign countries should be invited to contribute, side by side with the United Kingdom; an important innovation, for no previous trade exhibition held anywhere had been international. A Royal Commission was appointed to be responsible for the project, with Prince Albert as its chairman.

It soon turned its attention to the problems involved in bringing visitors to the Exhibition. Much complaint had been heard about holding it in London.[30] Good and cheap railway facilities for travelling up from the provinces would do something to meet criticisms of that kind. Lengthy negotiations followed, one series with the government, to secure that excursion trains run to convey visitors to the Exhibition would be exempted from passenger duty;[31] the other between the companies themselves. Their senior officers met to discuss the business at the Clearing House on 22 March 1851.[32] That meeting failed to reach agreement; but presently the managers consented to recommend the companies to run excursion trains from 1 July onwards. Joseph Paxton persuaded them to advance the date to 2 June.

Meanwhile the Queen had opened the Exhibition, on 1 May. The total number of paying visitors in the end reached just over six million. The average daily attendance was about 43,000; the fullest day was Tuesday 7 October, when 110,000 people arrived.[33] The Exhibition closed on the 15th.

The railways did little towards bringing up these visitors for the first month. Then the business began to take off, with special trips from country districts. In Maldon and Braintree, for example, all the shops closed for one day to allow as many people to travel as possible. Exhibition clubs were formed to organize these excursions.[34] They began to run from the West Riding of Yorkshire by the Midland and London & North Western Railways and, in keen rivalry with them, by the Great Northern. The companies lowered their fares to undercut one another until the Great Northern excursion agent at Leeds announced that, whatever fare the other companies might fix, his would carry its third-class passengers for sixpence less.[35] Soon after the Exhibition closed, the railways came up with their traffic figures for the period during which it had been open, compared with those for 1850. The increases were largest on the Great Western (by 38.3%); then came the London & South Western (29.9%), the London & Blackwall (28.5), the South Eastern (23.8), and the London & North Western (22.6). On the Brighton Railway they were just under 10%, on the Eastern Counties 4.6.[36]

These figures were of all kinds of traffic, taken together: so the increases were not attributable wholly to passenger business, or to traffic arising from the Exhibition. Nevertheless excursions clearly accounted for a significant part of them. On Whit Monday, 9 June, immediately after they began, twenty London & North Western excursions ran into Euston.[37] In the autumn Mark Huish stated that his company had conveyed 775,000 people into and out of London while the Exhibition was open, its agent adding that 90,000 of them had travelled in 145 excursion trains.[38] Its total was probably bigger than that of any other railway, for it included the whole traffic from Birmingham, the Black Country, and Lancashire, as well as a share of that from Yorkshire and the East Midlands, which the Midland company transferred to it at Rugby. The Great Western also applied itself to the business strenuously, with the additional inducement provided by the Royal Agricultural Society's Show at Windsor in July.[39] On the other hand Laing, the Brighton chairman, merely thought his company's summer business had been reduced, so 'we lost as much by the Exhibition in one way as we gained by it in the other'.[40] Provincial railways reported no net gain in traffic arising from the Exhibition, or actual loss: the South Devon, for example, the Eastern Union, the North Staffordshire, and the Leeds Northern.[41]

The number of visitors coming from abroad was not large. The South Eastern company attributed the meagre volume of business to the high fares it was obliged to levy, under the compulsion of its alliance with the Nord company in France, as compared with 'the rates charged by other inferior means of transit'. The 'inferior means' were indeed more highly appreciated. The South Western was bringing in an average of 1000 passengers a week from France that summer, through Le Havre and Southampton.[42] The striking increase in the Blackwall company's traffic must have been due largely to the carriage of passengers arriving by coastal steamers from Scotland and the Continent.

Very long hours had been worked; the London & South Western board voted a special gratuity to the whole of its staff.[43] But the companies had not relied solely on their own servants. Much of the organization was handled for them by agents. The London & North Western engaged Henry Marcus of Liverpool. The Midland entered into a treaty with Thomas Cook. In later life he stated that he and his son had brought up 150,000 people to London for the Exhibition.[44] He even offered an excursion in the opposite direction, out of London, to send 'citizens and visitors of all nations' to Chatsworth.[45] But his energies failed to secure the financial reward they deserved. The Great Northern competition forced fares down, and his own share in the profits disappeared. Still, the experience and the reputation he had gained proved valuable to him in the development of his business.

Everyone accepted that without the railways the Exhibition could not have matched up to the imaginative ambitions of those who had planned it. In the end, those ambitions were surpassed. Historians, seeking to put the Exhibition into its context, have been in no doubt that the total impression it made was due in large measure to the railways' work. 'Without them', says Francis Sheppard, looking at London, 'the project . . . would have been inconceivable'.[46] Here is a modern French historian's verdict: 'the railways and technical improvements meant that crowds of people could come together in a way that had never been seen before. In this respect the Great Exhibition was a huge popular festival'.[47]

As such it lived on in popular memory, to be translated into literature by one who valued that memory, and understood it. More than forty years later Thomas Hardy conjured up an excursion train – 'an absolutely new departure in the history of travel' – run to the Exhibition from Dorchester. The end of the journey takes a wry twist, with the passengers in their open carriages drawing into Waterloo, soaked by the streaming rain.[48]

Excursion Trains: Growth, Profit, and Risk

When the Exhibition closed, railways stood higher in general estimation than they had done before. Their system was now revealed as a working unit, able to concentrate attention and energy from all the most populous parts of the island at once on to a single object in London. The follies and crimes of the Mania – still a very recent memory – might now appear to have been purged by the railways' achievements. The achievements that came later were never again hailed with the same widespread delight.

The share of excursions in producing this admiration was perhaps exaggerated. We must say 'perhaps', for we cannot know how large that share actually was. Many of those who went to the Crystal Palace by rail had clearly travelled there by scheduled services; and a very large proportion of the total number of visitors – surely much more than half? – had used no railway to get to the Exhibition, for they lived in London.

The running of these trains quickly came to be accepted by all the railway companies having any substantial passenger business. There were other special events, when their services were again in demand: the Manchester Art Treasures Exhibition of 1857, the second International Exhibition in London five years later, the big exhibitions in Glasgow in 1888 and 1901. The seaside traffic grew, along with the holiday resorts to which it was directed.[49] Excursions carried race-goers into the suburbs of the great towns, and far beyond; balanced in later years by those bringing passengers into the towns to see football and cricket matches.

It is impossible to compute the growth of this excursion traffic precisely. Neither the government nor the companies paid it any special attention. Excursion traffic was more volatile than any other part of the railways' business: influenced by the weather, by the state of trade and the size of pay packets. Now and then a chairman or officer might say something on one of these matters relating to his own railway, but we have no continuous information about any of them. No special investigation into excursion business was ever called for by Parliament; no company maintained a separate department to deal with it.[50]

Excursion traffic seems to have figured only once in Victorian government inquiries. The Royal Commission on Railways of 1865–7 made no more than the briefest reference to the matter in its report;[51] but in examining the managers this was one branch of their work that the Commissioners took some trouble to probe. James Smithells, traffic manager of the Lancashire & Yorkshire Railway, said that excursion business 'answers our purpose very well. We have an immense traffic'.[52] William Cawkwell, general manager of the London & North Western, on the other hand, was 'not favourable to low excursion fares', preferring to run these trains 'at very moderate fares at proper times, at holiday times'. He considered them unprofitable unless they ran out and back within one day, which avoided the return working of empty rolling stock. The trains continued to be provided, he thought, because 'it has become the custom amongst railway companies'.[53] Grierson, the Great Western general manager, echoed that remark.[54] Nevertheless, here were representatives of the two largest companies – among the least enthusiastic supporters of excursion traffic – acknowledging that that traffic now formed a permanent part of their business.

The Royal Commission also included questions about excursion trains among the inquiries it circulated to the railways. The Great Western, the South Western, and the Brighton companies ignored those relating to such trains; so did all those in Scotland. However, a little useful information was disclosed. The Midland stated that in 1865 it had carried 391,000 excursion passengers in 559 trains run within its own system – i.e. excluding those taken on to other companies' lines.[55] On the North Eastern the corresponding number was 220,000.[56] The Lancashire & Yorkshire traffic was put at 530,000; but that may be a serious understatement.[57] These figures, together with those supplied on a more limited basis by four other companies (the London & North Western, Great Northern, North Staffordshire, and Maryport & Carlisle) show an average number of 569 passengers carried in each excursion train.

Only one company said anything about the receipts from this business. The little Maryport & Carlisle stated that it ran twenty excursions a year, each carrying some 500 passengers, which produced a revenue of about £600; £30 each, or $14\frac{1}{2}$ d per head.[58] None of the other companies referred to its takings. One or two cats were occasionally let out of bags, but the creatures were few and small.

The inspector William Yolland discovered in 1860 that five train-loads of excursionists from Colne to Manchester brought the Lancashire & Yorkshire company a 'clear profit' of nearly £50 each, or 21d a head.[59] Such a revenue as that was well worth having, provided the trains incurred no accidents, which might involve compensation for injury.

The figure of profit here is much higher than that indicated by the Maryport company. If its trains brought in £30 each, can they have made a *profit* of more than £20, even though they were simple to operate and ran over short distances? The Lancashire & Yorkshire's profit may have been high because it provided exceptionally poor trains at this time.[60] Perhaps then we should split these two figures of profit evenly, to make the rate £35, or – assuming the trains took about 550 passengers each – some 15d a head. But what was the number of those heads? The Midland, North Western, and Lancashire & Yorkshire companies stated that they carried 1,141,000 excursion passengers between them in 1865. A conservative estimate suggests that the total for England and Wales may have come to $3\frac{1}{2}$ million, which would represent about 1.5% of all the passenger journeys made.[61] The profit on them would then have amounted to some 3% of the profits on all passenger traffic. If this was a small proportion of the whole, yet the companies could not afford to neglect it.

There were numerous accidents to excursion trains in these years. The staid

Annual Register spoke of them as 'perpetual occasions of disarrangement and disaster'.[62] They not only brought death and injury. Accidents of all kinds caused the companies financial losses that might be serious, both from the destruction of their equipment and from the compensation payable to the sufferers and their families. Ever since the passing of Lord Campbell's Act in 1846[63] the cost of that compensation had been steadily rising.[64] The spectre of it haunted some railway managers.[65] And no wonder: in 1867–71 the railway companies of the United Kingdom paid out an annual average of £324,474 in compensation for death and injury in accidents, nearly 1.8% of their revenue from passenger traffic.[66] Some companies had recourse to insurance. Through that device the Edinburgh & Glasgow succeeded in reducing its liability for the payment of compensation to one-third of the sum that would otherwise have been required.[67] The chairman of the Brighton company, Samuel Laing, stated in 1870 that two accidents to excursion trains had together cost it nearly £100,000 in compensation. In the second of them the passengers' injuries were minimal – not even one limb was broken: yet 360 of the 600 excursionists put in claims. Laing contended stoutly that the excursions run by his company had 'afforded the means of recreation and health to millions', but he now doubted if they had paid their way.[68]

Some people connected with railways heartily wished that this traffic could be abandoned. Richard Moon, chairman of the London & North Western company, always greatly disapproved of it. No doubt he chuckled sardonically when he read Laing's words and said to himself 'I told you so'. But chuckling can have been his only joy. The railways had released a genie that they seemed unable to control.

The first serious accident to an excursion train occurred at Burnley in 1852. The Lancashire & Yorkshire company had arranged to run two excursions for schoolchildren, to York and Goole. One train comprised forty-five carriages, the other thirty-five. The station had one platform, able to take six carriages only: so they were dealt with in the goods sidings. On returning at night, the second train was diverted by mistake into the station. In the ensuing crash three children and a teacher were killed and many other passengers injured. The entire staff available to handle these enormous trains at the station numbered two, aided by a calico-printer and a blacksmith whom they had called in to help them.[69]

Six years went by before another excursion train met with any comparable disaster. Then, at Round Oak, it was much worse. Again the sufferers were largely schoolchildren, on a day excursion from Wolverhampton to Worcester. The train comprised forty-four vehicles. On the return journey it was divided into two. The first part split, and seventeen of its carriages ran backwards downhill into the second train. Fourteen passengers died; 220 more were injured, fifty of them seriously. In 1860 came another similar accident, at Helmshore on the Lancashire & Yorkshire Railway. Then in the following year two more befell excursion trains, only eight days apart – in the Clayton tunnel, outside Brighton, and at Kentish Town in north London. The first of these was the worst accident that had ever occurred to a train of any kind in Britain, the second only a little less horrible, the passengers being pitched down an embankment rather than burnt to death in a tunnel.[70]

Let us look at two excursion trains of the 1870s, one of each of the main sorts: a long-distance train, carrying passengers of all three classes, and a popular one to the seaside. Both were involved in accidents, and the inspectors' reports supply copious information about the arrangements for running them.

The first befell a Great Northern excursion from Yorkshire to London in June 1870. The trip started out from Leeds at 1.25 am, allowed twelve hours in London, and was to get back at 4.20 next morning. In returning, the train collided near Newark with a wagon that had become detached from a goods train and broken an axle. The driver and fireman died, together with sixteen passengers; forty more passengers and one of the guards were injured.

The excursion train was made up of four portions, from Leeds, Bradford, Halifax, and York, comprising twenty-three vehicles altogether. It was hauled by a brand-new engine and was timed to make the return journey from London to Leeds at 26.5 mph, including stops. The inspector found no fault either with the train itself or with its unfortunate footplate crew. This accident might just as easily have happened to an East Coast express on its way to Scotland.[71]

The other one involved excursion trains alone. It displays the burden placed on the railways' management by sudden demands for accommodation for a much larger number of passengers than had been expected. A temperance excursion was announced to run from London to Southend on Monday 20 September 1875, four trains being booked with the London Tilbury & Southend Railway to convey 3000 passengers. Late in the previous evening the organizers disclosed that the number of those who would be travelling was 4200, and the company arranged to borrow two additional trains from the North London Railway. On the return journey the fourth of the six trains ran into the back of the third at Barking. One passenger was killed, and more than sixty were injured. The company had to pay out £20,000 in compensation.

The driver of the fourth train, who was chiefly responsible for the accident from running too fast up to Barking, was said by one passenger to have smelt strongly of drink. He himself stated that he had had a pint of beer at mid-day with his dinner and nothing else, and a senior railway official confirmed that he was perfectly sober. But one of the guards who should have been with the first train was quite drunk, put into the brake van of the fourth train, where he rolled about the floor helplessly. It was usual for the trippers to give the engine crews and guards 'dinner money'. That this was a temperance excursion made no difference, and the inspector pointed out the result: 'the servants of the excursion trains have to pass long hours of idleness at the seat of the excursion and must, with the help of the dinner money which is allowed them by the excursionists, have many temptations to drink far more than is good for them'. The trains were most inadequately provided with brakes, the signals were unsatisfactory, the line was not worked on the block system. The inspector commented temperately on the danger of running large excursions on a railway so ill equipped.[72]

The worst accidents to excursion trains in the later Victorian age were at Radstock in 1876 and at Hexthorpe in 1887. The first was due to the hopeless demoralization of the Somerset & Dorset company's servants,[73] the second to the carelessness of the engine crew of an ordinary passenger train, which ran into the excursion from behind. It happened immediately outside Doncaster station on St Leger day.[74] Only a few of the really bad accidents to excursion trains in these years occurred because the trains *were* excursions. Two of them arose from the shunting of an excursion into a siding to let an express go by;[75] a well-recognized cause of delay and danger to all trains of this sort.

How dangerous were these trains? The only way to answer that question is to analyse the inspectors' reports, distinguishing between those accidents that would have befallen any ordinary train in the circumstances and those that were attributable to them because they were excursions, carelessly or parsimoniously managed as such. Here is an attempt to make that analysis, stretching over the years 1855 to 1889, when the accident to an excursion train at Armagh in Ireland determined the government to require the provision of adequate safety precautions on all railways carrying passenger traffic.

TABLE 5

ACCIDENTS TO EXCURSION TRAINS IN GREAT BRITAIN, 1855–89

	1 Total number of accidents, to trains of all kinds, reported on (*average per year*)	2 Number of accidents to excursion trains (*average per year*)	3 Number arising from special dangers attributable to those trains (*average per year*)	4 2 as % of 1	5 3 as % of 1
1855–9	71	8.5	5.6	12.0	7.9
1860–4	53	9.1	4.9	17.2	9.2
1865–9	79	6.6	3.5	8.4	4.4
1870–4	145	4.7	1.9	3.2	1.3
1875–9	117	4.1	2.2	3.5	1.9
1880–4	94	5.7	2.3	6.1	2.4
1885–9	47	6.0	1.7	12.8	3.6

Source: Accident reports in PP.

The table shows the steady growth during the 1850s and 1860s in the number of accidents occurring in Great Britain; then the formidable total in the 1870s, reduced in the early years of the next decade and brought down markedly in 1885–9. The number of accidents to excursion trains was highest, in proportion to the whole, in the 1860s but substantially lower in the following years when the total of all accidents was largest. And the number of accidents that could be attributed specifically to excursion trains as such declined greatly at the worst time, to stand at about 2%. Though it rose again in the 1880s, it was still a small fraction of the whole. In subsequent years only two serious accidents have ever befallen excursion trains: at Welshampton on the Cambrian system in 1897 and at Eltham Well Hall on British Railways (Southern Region) in 1972.

The Railway Sunday

When excursion trains first appeared, it was a common practice to run them on Sundays. Those who worked for six days in the week could dispose of their own time on the seventh as it suited them. That did not however mean that they all turned to taking excursions whenever they were offered. On Sunday 20 March 1851 half the population of Great Britain attended at least one service at church or chapel.[76] For many heads of families it would have been unthinkable to break into this routine of life, to carry themselves and their wives and children off on a pleasure trip.

Sunday observance affected the provision of railway services from the start. The Liverpool & Manchester company decided in 1830 that none of its trains should run on that day between 10 am and 4 pm, thus pioneering the 'church interval' that became a well-known feature of the service on many railways in later years. Though few of the trunk lines tried to follow the same practice, they all provided a Sunday service much less frequent than the one they offered on weekdays.

The Sunday timetable, as the system developed in the 1840s and 1850s, came to differ widely from one railway to another. Two generalizations can however be made about it. In the first place, the Post Office was empowered to compel the railways to carry the mails at any time it appointed; and since it had both to deliver and to collect letters on Sundays it insisted on the provision of a good many Sunday mail trains. The railway companies considered it uneconomic to run such trains for the carriage of mails alone, so nearly all mail trains conveyed passengers too. And secondly, on all British railways the Sunday service was very much less liberal than that offered on weekdays. In this matter they differed entirely from those on the mainland of Europe. There the Sunday timetable was virtually the same as the weekday one.[77]

There were many British lines on which no Sunday trains of any kind ran in the Victorian age. In the late 1880s the whole system of the Great North of Scotland Railway (316 miles long) was closed; so were the Somerset & Dorset Joint Railway (103 miles long) and the Central Wales line from Swansea to Craven Arms (96 miles).[78] In Scotland the provision was curbed much more tightly. The suburban system in Glasgow, for instance, was almost wholly shut down. The establishment and maintenance of this unique practice arose from the Fourth Commandment. But the strict regulation of Sunday in Britain was not a passive acceptance of ancient thinking. The Lord's Day Observance Act, which governed public conduct in this matter, had been passed as recently as 1781. Foreign visitors, whether Catholic or Protestant, were startled and dismayed by the strength of that observance. 'The English Sunday is sad for everybody!' noted one of them in 1825.[79]

Though travelling on Sunday was not absolutely forbidden, it was impeded by statute[80] and frowned on by custom. In Jane Austen's last novel *Persuasion*, written in 1815–16, the first thing that opens the eyes of the heroine to the bad character of her cousin Mr Elliot is that with him 'Sunday-travelling had been a common thing'.[81] The view she took of this matter was that of many intelligent English people.

Scotsmen settled these matters after their own fashion. Sabbatarianism was at its most intense among them. No stage-coaches ran in Scotland on Sundays.[82] Only the mail-coaches: and even they came under threat when in 1835 the Sabbatarians' political leader Sir Andrew Agnew persuaded the Post Office to agree not to run one of them, serving his own constituency of Wigtownshire, on Sundays.[83] However, it remained the only mail service in the United Kingdom regulated like that.

Agnew had been chairman of a Commons Committee on the Observance of the Lord's Day in 1832.[84] He made four attempts in Parliament to prohibit all Sunday labour in 1834–7. The third of them was too much for the young Charles Dickens, who attacked it as an 'egregious specimen of legislative folly' in a spirited pamphlet *Sunday under Three Heads*.[85] Agnew lost his seat at the next election, and nobody took up his efforts in Parliament again. When the Scottish Society for the Due Observance of the Lord's Day was established in 1839 he became its chairman. His first speech in that capacity called for resistance to 'the threatened invasion of Sabbath-breaking customs from England by the railway'; an invasion fortified by the large injection of English capital into Scottish railway development.[86]

In England and Wales the policy of providing Sunday trains was often criticized, sometimes strongly opposed. Where Sabbatarian shareholders were lacking or silent, the directors came under external pressure. The clergy of the diocese of Winchester complained that their congregations were much reduced in summer-time 'by the absence of many who, until this temptation allured them, were accustomed to attend their respective churches', whereupon the board cut back the Sunday service; and it adopted a church interval on the line to Richmond and Windsor in 1848.[87] Francis Close, the Evangelical parson who tyrannized over Cheltenham for thirty years, worked himself into a paroxysm of windy rhetoric in 1846 when Sunday trains began serving the town. 'Another page of Godless legislation', he cried, 'another national sin invokes the displeasure of the Almighty.'[88] Ignoring this claptrap, the trains continued to run.

Not all the clergy were as heavy-handed as those of Winchester or ranted like Close. As the railway approached Ipswich in 1846 the clergy and gentry sent a memorial to the directors of the Eastern Union company, quietly expressed and including one argument worth stating: 'At the present time no public conveyance of any description leaves Ipswich for London on Sundays, excepting the mails; and we submit ... that this is a plain proof that the public convenience does not require Sunday trains upon the Eastern Union line'.[89] Nevertheless two trains, in addition to the mails, were provided when the railway opened that June.

The case against running these trains was sometimes stated with cogent temperance,[90] and at least one effort was made to display argument and counter-argument together in a single account.[91] Out of this welter of disputation a general policy emerged in England and Wales of providing some Sunday trains on most main lines, as well as on a number of branches. In 1847 Parliament called for a return of the Sunday trains running throughout the Kingdom. Of the forty English and Welsh companies that replied, thirty-six provided some service; in Scotland, on the other hand, they were run by only three companies out of seventeen.[92]

The Sabbatarians treated Sunday both as a day of observance and as a day of rest. The majority of them gave nearly all their attention to the first element, using the second only as a makeweight.[93] Some secularly-minded Englishmen argued, however, that what was being fought out here was really a battle of classes. The Sabbatarians seemed to them to be denying to the poor what would remain accessible to the rich, who kept their own carriages and could travel as they chose. A modern writer has remarked that Agnew's Sunday Observance Bills represented 'the most rigorous piece of moral – and, indeed, class – legislation since the Long Parliament'.[94] Ought not railways, as an instrument of social mobility, to be made available to everyone? The Duke of Wellington thought so. During the discussion of the Regulation Bill in 1844, while the Committee was considering whether the provision of compulsory cheap trains should or should not apply on Sundays, he took the trouble (at seventy-five) to write to Gladstone to urge that it should, arguing that 'it would be scarcely fair to prevent the travelling of the third-class trains. The people conveyed by them, the poorest, would be stopped on their journey, obliged to incur a day's expense, which would probably amount to more than the whole cost of the journey'.[95] Wellington sometimes showed a more imaginative perception of the interests of ordinary people than the professed humanitarians.

By the 1850s excursion trains were frequently provided on weekdays. In the fifteen years 1857–71 the inspectors investigated eighty accidents to excursion trains in England and Wales. Fewer of these occurred on Sundays than on any other day of the week: only five, against twenty-one on Mondays and sixteen on Saturdays. It is true that traffic was lighter on Sundays, and on that account the chances of accident were less; but on the other hand the frequent use of dilapidated rolling stock and the employment of inexperienced staff[96] made them more dangerous. These figures offer a good random sample of the companies' practice as it had developed by the 1860s.

Of the two most dreadful accidents that befell excursion trains in these years, at Round Oak in 1858 and in the Clayton tunnel three years later,[97] the second happened on a Sunday. Here, some preachers said, was a judgment of God on the sin of providing Sunday excursion trains. But 111 years went by before another bad accident occurred to an excursion train running on a Sunday.

There were now signs of support for increased railway facilities on Sundays. The companies might be asked for more trains rather than for less or for none at all.[98] Popular novelists were beginning to say what they thought on the matter, and it seldom flattered the Sabbatarians. The exchange between Mr Slope and Archdeacon Grantly on this subject must have delighted many readers of Trollope's *Barchester Towers* in 1858.[99] Ten years later: 'The established Sunday tyranny, which is one of the institutions of this free country, so times the trains as to make it impossible to ask anybody to travel to us from London'. It is Wilkie Collins, speaking in *The Moonstone*.[100]

The tyranny seemed at that time to be growing stronger. When in 1856 an effort was made to get the chief London museums and galleries opened on Sunday afternoons, it was turned down in Parliament by an eight-to-one majority.[101] However, when the same proposal was made in 1869, the House of Commons was counted out; an indication that it was growing tired of this argument.[102] Some Sabbatarians were by now growing uneasy. In 1863 one of them argued that they should change their ground. He admitted the case in favour of Sunday excursion trains, in the interest of the health of working people, and turned to attacking the use of the railways on Sundays to carry goods traffic. Only the proprietors benefited from that, he said, 'and this at the expense of robbing their servants of their rightful holiday'.[103]

The report on the Clayton tunnel accident disclosed that the signalman, James Killick, whose errors had contributed to producing it, was just beginning a spell of twenty-four hours' continuous duty over a Sunday. Although he had made this arrangement himself in order to obtain, by exchange, an additional period of rest, he clearly ought not to have been obliged to secure it in this way. In 1868 it appeared that a lad of eighteen had been employed by the Blyth & Tyne Railway as a signalman for fifteen hours seven days a week, 'with a holiday once a month, or oftener if asked for'.[104] The company was then paying a dividend of 10%. There is no evidence that Sunday work attracted extra wages. The payment of overtime was becoming a widespread practice on railways, but the earliest recognition of any entitlement to it for Sunday work so far noted is on the Great Western in 1871.[105]

A distinct change now appears in the attitude of railway managers towards Sunday services; they were beginning to consider not so much their expediency as their profitability. From the 1860s onwards the railway system was being steadily extended into rural districts, some of them very sparsely populated. In 1864 Parliament called for another return of the railway lines on which passenger trains did not run on Sundays.[106] Their aggregate length appeared to amount to some 10% of the whole system. The practice of Sunday closing was then increasing more rapidly in England and Wales than at any other time before 1914.

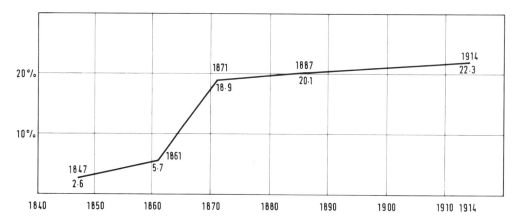

Percentage of the Railway System of England and Wales closed on Sundays to Timetabled Passenger Services, 1847–1914.

The North Eastern stood out as the company most determined in its refusal to run Sunday trains. Of the total mileage shown as closed in England and Wales in 1864, 41% comes from that railway alone. But the other great company of northern England, the Lancashire & Yorkshire, pursued an exactly opposite policy, keeping open the whole of its system to Sunday trains without exception.[107] True, it linked closely-spaced towns and had no long rural lines; still, the contrast is striking.

The operation of Sunday trains had now ceased to be, to any important extent, a matter concerning religious observance. It might be opposed on quite other grounds: at Thurnby in Leicestershire, for example, where on the opening of the railway in 1883 some inhabitants petitioned against the stopping of trains on Sundays, from fear that they would encourage the rowdyism of Leicester roughs, which had already afflicted them.[108] In 1888, when the London & South Western Railway completed its direct line to Bournemouth, the Improvement Commissioners there protested against the running of Sunday excursion trains. The exchange between the railway and the town was conducted throughout in wholly secular language.[109] Things were still ordered differently in Scotland, however, where in 1883 rioting at Strome Ferry, caused by the railway company's employment of men to handle fish traffic on Sundays, was quelled only by the presence of troops sent up from Edinburgh.[110]

A new element in the business was now growing in importance. The railway system carried a traffic that increased year by year almost without interruption. This required relaying of track and the provision of additional lines. Little such work could be carried out satisfactorily at night. Daylight hours were available, in long continuous stretches, only on Sunday.

Wherever an engineering work demanded the closing of a line, or could be cheapened by adopting that expedient, it came to be undertaken on that day. Most of the conversion of the gauge on the Great Western Railway was carried out at week-ends.[111] Acworth commented on this practice in his *Railways of England* in 1889.[112] For his frontispiece he chose a photograph showing the relaying of track on the Midland Railway in Gloucestershire, with the caption 'The Railway Man's Sunday'.

Sunday work and its remuneration had now come under frequent criticism by the new trade unions. It never grew into a really burning issue, however. In 1893 the Board of Trade was required to investigate any complaint made by railwaymen concerning their hours of duty and their periods of rest and relief when they worked on Sundays. Over the next three years the Board examined 325 cases. Only eleven of them were concerned, even in a minor way, with Sunday duty.[113] Satisfactory payments for that duty figured in the 'all-grades programme' accepted in 1896 by the North Eastern company, which conceded 'time-and-a-quarter' rates for Sunday work to goods and mineral guards and to signalmen. Time-and-a-quarter was granted to all grades by the three other largest companies in 1908; the Great Northern and its men went to arbitration next year, and that too resulted in considerable improvements in Sunday pay.[114]

The railways' Sunday business had never been large.[115] It now had to be carried on at a substantially higher cost than the business on weekdays, and that was a strong argument for keeping it down. Most of the new branches the Great Western company opened after 1871 were closed on Sundays from the start – those to Cardigan, Alcester, and Bromyard, for example. The Sunday passenger service was withdrawn from the older Faringdon branch in 1875. On the other hand Witney secured one, for the first time, on its line to Oxford in 1899, and by 1914 there were two.[116] Not many of the new lines opened after 1900 by any company carried regular Sunday services. There were none for instance on those from Kirkstead to Firsby in Lincolnshire, none on the branches to Lyme Regis, Aberayron, or Thaxted.

By 1914 a total of about 3700 miles of the system in England and Wales were closed on Sundays, a little over 22% of the whole. The larger companies' policies are revealed in Table 6. The practice in Scotland continued to be markedly different. There the proportion of lines closed reached almost 60%.

Had the companies decided to cut these services back more drastically, they would have found an unexpected ally: for Sabbatarianism, which had sunk to a quiet murmur in England and Wales, began to revive at the turn of the century. The Anti-Sunday-Travelling Union launched a new periodical, *Our Heritage*, in 1895, fomenting criticism of all the railways' Sunday services. Protesters soon began to bother the managements and to disturb shareholders' meetings once more.[117] Files of these protests have survived from at least three companies.[118] They may have been preserved in case the movement should gather strength – perhaps, in that event, to help managers to cut back the traffic. But none of them had any effect. The doctrine they represented was now entirely opposed to the prevalent thinking of the time.

The successful body in these years was on the other side: the National Sunday League, which had been founded in 1855 to support the Sunday opening of museums and parks. It extended its attention to other activities promoting the rational enjoyment of the day, among them railway excursions.

TABLE 6

SUNDAY CLOSING BY THE ELEVEN PRINCIPAL RAILWAYS
IN ENGLAND AND WALES, JULY 1914

Company*	Miles closed	Percentage of system
Great Central	76	10.8
Great Eastern	193	16.3
Great Northern	141	15.2
Great Western	845	30.1
Lancashire & Yorkshire	49	8.2
London & North Western	468	23.5
London & South Western	129	14.5
London Brighton & South Coast	6	1.3
Midland	462	25.8
North Eastern	610	35.2
South Eastern & Chatham	8	1.3

*The table takes account of joint lines, apportioning
the shares held by the owning companies between them.

Source: Bradshaw, July 1914

In 1876 – a chilly summer – its excursions conveyed about 6000 people to the seaside; it organized twenty-two in 1889, carrying over 20,000. In the year 1913–14 the number had grown to a total of 540, running not in the summer only but all the year round.[119]

The League did its largest business with the Brighton company, whose excursion traffic, of all kinds, continued to grow almost uninterruptedly.[120] That railway paid attention to the rich as well as to the poor. In 1881 it introduced a 'Pullman Limited Express' between London and Brighton on every day of the week. Ill patronized on Sundays (and nicknamed 'The Sabbath-Breaker'), it was discontinued next month, while continuing to run on weekdays. In 1898 a new 'Sunday Pullman Limited' was introduced, with prompt and complete success. The failure of the first Sabbath-Breaker and the smooth triumph of the second epitomize the changing attitude towards Sunday pleasure travelling among the well-to-do in Late-Victorian England.

And what about the Sunday goods traffic? The massive conveyance of coal on the great lines was entirely stopped.[121] Only one business of this kind grew. London and the other great cities had become almost wholly dependent on the railways for their supply of fresh milk. In 1914 there were five Sunday milk trains on the Great Western from Wiltshire to London (carrying no passengers), two on the London & South Western from Somerset and Dorset.[122] The policy urged by that Sabbatarian in 1863 had prevailed. Sunday freight traffic remained insignificant.

Railways had begun by offering an emancipation: opportunities to travel over substantial distances on Sunday, where there had been few in the past, or none. In doing so they violated the old Protestant Sunday in Britain. Its essence had been a quiet, unvaried routine, with observances peculiar to the day, the opportunity to reflect on moral and spiritual matters. The effect of all this was grave, often gloomy: yet as the pace of life quickened and the pursuit of material profit became more insistent, there was something to be said for a fixed break in the cycle of the week: 'a temperate day marked off from other days by an atmosphere of serenity and quiet relaxation'.[123] In 1867 Bagehot remarked that 'the great mass of moderate Englishmen are ... agreed that it is expedient to set apart Sunday as a day of rest from regular toil', but he went on to say that they were 'indisposed to interfere with individual consciences or habits or ways of thinking'.[124] That was exactly right. The railways' intervention enlarged the choice open to those individual consciences.

The people who disliked Sunday trains alleged that passengers by them merely demoralized themselves and everyone they met, attributing chiefly to them the drunkenness that disgraced the streets of Blackpool and Brighton.[125] Their defenders said the opposite, that excursions took working men away from the pubs in London and the great towns; and indeed many of the excursionists brought their own food and drink with them.[126] The railway afforded an alternative to the taproom. In the towns, Bagehot remarked, 'one place is open [on Sundays], the public house; one recreation is allowed, that of drinking with the half-drunk.... There is no form of amusement now allowed on a weekday which would not be less demoralising than the only one now legal on a Sunday'.[127] Here is additional comment, carrying much weight, in support of Brian Harrison's opinion that 'the railway probably did more for temperance in the nineteenth century ... than either the temperance movement or the Vice Society'.[128]

The railways' slow Sunday service became notorious for its tedium. 'It is a dreadful day, a Sunday, to travel a long journey', wrote Daniel Gooch in 1869 – no disgruntled passenger but chairman of the Great Western Railway, on which he had just spent eight hours in getting from Weymouth to Windsor.[129] The railways had indeed established a 'Sunday tyranny' of their own. They monopolized the provision of long-distance travel from 1850 to 1914, and of the facilities for most other journeys too, except in and around great cities. Their timetables were more absolute than Acts of Parliament. Never debated, they had the flat finality of edicts; and even the timetables came to be set aside in favour of 'engineering works'.

So in the end the railways, though they offered a new liberation, widely welcomed, also imposed a strict rigidity of their own. Their policy was made up of very diverse ingredients: anxiety to avoid offending Sabbatarian susceptibilities; the requirement to carry the mails; popular response to the cheap facilities they offered; the demands of railwaymen for additional pay on account of Sunday labour; considerations arising from the working of the system. All these elements went to form a new code of social custom, which came to be accepted by the Victorians and, with all its inconvenience, is endured in Great Britain still in 1990: the Railway Sunday.

13

LEISURE (II): TOURISM AND FAMILY HOLIDAYS

British Practices · The Week-End · Tourism ·
Varieties of Enjoyment

British Practices

The Victorian excursion system was unique. That was noticed at the time. Samuel Morton Peto remarked in 1865, from first-hand observation, that in the United States there were 'no such things as excursions, or at any rate they are very rare'.[1] He did not mean that they were casualties of the Civil War, then just ending, but that they had scarcely been known there at all. The Royal Commission on Railways observed in 1867 that excursion trains ran more frequently in Britain than on the mainland of Europe and then passed on, treating the matter as unimportant.[2] 'Excursion tickets' were to be found in France in the 1880s, but they were only return tickets valid for a fortnight or a month by ordinary services, at a reduced price.[3] When the British government inquired into the management and practices of railways in Europe in 1909–10, the investigators reported that the provision of excursions was negligible there. On the German railways, for example, 'reduced fare excursion trains are put on solely at the discretion of the administration and only run at the principal holiday times, when one or two special trains may be run to the sea coast or mountain districts'. From Belgium, France, Italy, and Austria the reports were similar.[4] Nowhere was there anything in the least like what Foxwell had noted in 1888: 'the volley of "cheap seaside" trains fired off by the Brighton company (in summer)... trains [that] are practically express, and charge one-third of the ordinary third-class fares.'[5]

There are several explanations of this difference. The smallness of the island was itself an invitation to provide the kind of service, out and back in a day, that the true excursion trains represented. The provision of a frequent and quick service to the seaside was a more attractive proposition than it could be in large countries like France and Germany, where most of the thickly-populated districts lay well inland. With few exceptions these districts were also a long way from the other goals of popular holidays, the Alps and the Pyrenees. Then again, in all Continental countries the systems were largely or wholly controlled by the State, in one way or another. There was little room here for the enterprising agent, whose living depended mainly on tourist and excursion traffic.

It might be supposed that competition between the British companies, uncontrolled by the State, had a good deal to do with the matter. But in the excursion business there was not much direct competition between rival companies running services to the same destinations, with the exception – it is important – of the services running up to London. Only four of the chief English seaside resorts, Southport, Southend, Hastings, and Southsea, were served by two competing companies. All the rest were in the hands of railway monopolies, of one company or of two working in conjunction.[6] The excursion traffic is perhaps the division of the English railways' passenger business in which competition counted for least.

It counted for a great deal in one district of Scotland, however: on the Firth of Clyde, where the competition of railways and steamboats, running in conjunction, was intense. But here the regular service, every day, was so frequent in summer as to limit the possibility of fitting in some of the additional excursion services that might have been desired.

The contrast between the policies of the British and Continental railways in these matters reflected other, more profound differences in social habits and attitudes. The higher wages paid in Britain, the shortening of hours of work there and the emergence of the idea of holidays with pay all had their influence on British practices of holiday-making. In the late nineteenth century the average of wages had shown a large general increase. Over the years 1860–1913 they rose in Britain by 72%. That was a substantial amount, but the increase was on rates that were already in 1860 much higher than elsewhere. The Continental and American rates now moved upwards more rapidly, chasing those in Britain. In France they rose by 86% in these years, in Germany by 160%, in Sweden by 217%; in the United States by 113%.[7] But even with these increases the British rates remained substantially higher than those prevailing on the Continent. In 1905 the average earnings of French workmen (mainly in industry) were reckoned to be no more than two-thirds of those in Britain; those of Germans about three-quarters.[8]

The rates are misleading, however, if looked at on their own: for they do not compare like with like. They represent the pay given for working weeks of different duration. The reduction of hours in Britain went back to the Early Victorian age. It was carried further and made more general in 1871–4.[9] By 1905 a 54-hour week was usual there. In the building industry in Germany it was five hours longer; in France ten hours.[10]

There was a further difference here too. In Britain the practice of granting holidays, over and above the usual public ones, had been progressing steadily. By 1860, moreover, some groups of employed people were getting the much greater advantage of holidays on full pay. That was already conceded by at least four English railway companies, joined by a fifth, the Great Northern, in 1861.[11] The period allowed was very short, and the concession was in most cases limited to guards. Very soon the practice was being applied to at least one group of workers less well-paid than these: the letter-carriers of the Post Office, who were getting a fortnight's holiday with pay by 1867.[12] The idea came to be accepted slowly and irregularly. When Wills's in Bristol granted a week's holiday with pay to all their workmen in 1891[13] they went well beyond most other employers. Nevertheless, the idea was firmly established.

Taking all these changes into account, we can say with certainty that most Victorian working men had more money to spend, and more leisure time in which to spend it, than those in France and Germany.

That on the Continent the State controlled the railways and that its bureaucrats did not favour excursions was a matter of much less importance. Those bureaucrats were public servants, who were accountable to politicians; and politicians could be persuaded to change their minds under public pressure. In France, for example, one of the means adopted in 1871 for increasing the national revenue in order to pay off the enormous liabilities arising from the war with Prussia had been a tax imposed on the supplementary fares charged for travelling by express trains. That helped to keep those fares exceedingly high. In Britain the very supplements had come to be almost entirely abandoned, except in south-eastern England, by 1882. The charges in France were much complained of, and in 1892 the complainants forced the government to abandon the tax.[14] Had there been any comparable body of opinion dissatisfied with the provision of excursion trains, and faced by a refusal to provide them, the same remedy would have been open to it. But the French Deputies and their constituents cared more about other things. The social interests represented most strongly in the Chamber were different from those in the British Parliament. It is true that Parliament also ignored the excursion business, but that was because it was the affair of the railway companies, and theirs alone, to determine when and where these trains should run. The inaction of the British government left the way open for a continually increasing provision of excursions, to match public demand. On the Continent, where the demand was much weaker, government inaction restricted these facilities and kept them static.

The Week-End

The provision of excursion trains was not the only practice in the use of leisure fostered by the British railways to a degree not to be found anywhere in Continental Europe. They also encouraged, most deliberately, the habit of taking short holidays over the week-end.

It did not begin with them. The novelist Peacock, employed at the India House, went out to his cottage at Halliford on the Thames each Friday in the 1820s, returning to work in London on Monday; Dickens shows us Mr Spenlow doing the same in *David Copperfield*, driving his phaeton down from Doctors' Commons to his villa at Norwood. The London & South Western seems to have been the first railway to encourage such behaviour when in 1842 it offered tickets at reduced fares from London to Southampton and Gosport, available on Saturday for return either on the same day or on Sunday or Monday.[15] In 1844 the South Eastern company ran six excursions to Dover, with the facility of extending the journey to France for the week-end.[16] Other companies presently adopted the South Western's practice: the North Western and the Great Northern in 1851.[17] The notion may have been stimulated by the policy of closing commercial houses and public offices at noon on Saturdays, which began to appear in Manchester and London at the same time.[18]

A different consideration weighed with the North Western's general manager, Mark Huish. He favoured excursion trains and did much to extend the provision of them.[19] He wholly disapproved of running them on Sundays, however, partly no doubt from his own personal beliefs (he was a firm Dissenter) but also for another reason, which he himself stated in 1862, after he had left the company's service. During his time, he said, no excursion trains ever ran on the North Western system on Sundays. He believed that 'no company ultimately benefits by working its system to the extent of seven days a week, and that by a well-arranged system of Saturday trains returning on a Monday an equal pecuniary return at much less cost is produced'.[20] For him therefore what we should call a week-end ticket provided a substitute for a Sunday excursion. Of course it did not: for it obliged its holder to spend two nights away from home, which put this kind of holiday beyond the means of most day trippers. Here we can see the furtherance of the week-end as a railway manager's device.

Had it been that and nothing more, the idea would hardly have caught on, as it now did quite steadily. Even for very short distances: by 1860 Carlisle business men were being coaxed into going down to the sea-coast at Silloth (23 miles off) from Saturday to Monday.[21] 'Saturday to Monday in Brighton' cried an advertisement in *The Times* on 25 February 1860. By 1863 an express was running from Manchester to Blackpool at 1.15 on Saturdays, returning from Blackpool at 8.15 on Monday mornings.[22]

The Saturday–Monday holiday does not seem to have acquired a name of its own until the following decade. The *Oxford English Dictionary* traces 'week-end', in this sense, back to 1870, with a bunch of references from the succeeding years, including one to a new creature, a 'week-ender'. By the later 1880s the habit had evidently grown. Bradshaw then shows early morning trains running up to London on Mondays only from Eastbourne, Hastings, Ramsgate, and Yarmouth, as well as from Llandudno to Liverpool, Manchester, and Birmingham.[23] It had grown further by 1914, when there were ten such trains altogether. There seem never to have been any in Scotland. The week-enders now ranged over greater distances. Leaving Charing Cross at 4.30 on Friday afternoon they could get to Etaples (the station for Le Touquet, with its two casinos) that night, have two full days there, and be back again in London at noon on Monday.[24]

No similar train services were to be found anywhere on the mainland of Europe.[25] But the French had at least taken note of the social habit it revealed.

They made it plain that the habit was English. The imported expression *le weekend* and their own subtle phrase to indicate the Saturday holiday, *la semaine anglaise* (the English week), had both just made their appearance by 1914.[26]

Here in the Victorian age the British railways did much towards the establishment of a practice that came to be widely taken up in Europe later in the twentieth century. It is adopted today with outstanding energy in France.

Tourism

The history of Victorian tourism has not been studied much. The obstacles in the way of any full investigation of it seem insurmountable.

It was never a matter that concerned the British government; never gave rise to any Parliamentary inquiry, or to official statistics. The census returns do nothing to help, for the enumerations were normally carried out in April, when few tourists were on the move. We do not know with any certainty the numbers of passengers passing through the Channel ports. Some statements of them were compiled, but they are not strictly comparable with one another. They can only reveal tendencies.[27] Even if one set could be shown to be more careful and accurate than the rest, it would be of limited value for this purpose, since no such inquiry could distinguish between British travellers, going out or coming in, and those from foreign countries. Passports were not required for admission to the United Kingdom before 1914, nor was there any general registration of foreigners with the British police.

As tourist traffic grew, in extent and complexity, many of the British railway companies put part of it into the hands of agents. This was the largest division of their passenger business that was managed, in any important respect, by outside firms. Some companies were uneasy at deputing it in this way. Predictably Richard Moon, chairman of the London & North Western Railway, 'expressed the strongest objection to the practice'.[28] Sam Fay, when he came to manage the Great Central, disliked the agencies too and persuaded his company to buy out Dean & Dawson's in 1904.[29] Nevertheless, the expertise required here – much of the business having to be conducted in foreign languages – obliged all British railways with any Continental connections to rely on agents at least to some degree.[30]

Here again was a British practice, differing from that elsewhere. No large private firm emerged in any Continental country that was at all comparable, in the range and extent of its dealings, with Cook's.[31] There were stirrings towards the establishment of such agencies in Germany, and one with ambitious intentions was set up in 1911, but it was overtaken by war.[32] The tourist wishing to come to Britain had to rely mainly on Thomas Cook's numerous offices – there were fifty-two of them on the mainland of Europe in 1914, and thirty-eight in other continents[33] – and on those maintained by British railway companies, mostly in capital cities. The Americans had pursued their own path. Their big agencies tended to be offshoots of the express companies for forwarding parcels. The only travel organization that rivals the one still bearing Cook's name today is called American Express.

The surviving evidence of the work of these British agents is almost entirely external, much of it comprising advertisements and promotional literature. So far as I am aware, no records of any commercial agent are extant save those of Cook and Dean & Dawson.[34] Dean & Dawson's are meagre and disappointing.[35] A student of this business is therefore obliged to lean heavily on Cook's, which have survived in considerable abundance, though in very limited categories.[36] Until the 1920s the firm remained a family business; the management was not responsible to shareholders, and none of its accounts are preserved.

The growth of the tourist industry is therefore difficult to treat. Here is an attempt to draw an outline of the business on a small scale, as far as railways were involved in it.

An 'excursion' was normally an affair of a single day, or perhaps a week-end, and directed to a single place. If it lasted longer, moving on from one place to another, it became a 'tour'. A tour might extend to any length, in time or distance, as the tourist chose. But whereas the specially-arranged day excursion was almost entirely the creation of the passenger-carrying railways, the tour had already a long history before they were thought of.

The word came to be used in England, to describe a journey of pleasure and observation, in the seventeenth century; 'tourists' and 'tourism' appear in the eighteenth. Guide-books and road-books were produced to assist them, and at least sixty accounts of such journeys in Britain were published in 1700–1830 – ten of them by Frenchmen and another ten by Germans.[37] These tourists travelled privately, alone or in family parties, in carriages, on horseback, or on foot.

After 1815 the scale of such travel began to change, as steamboats got to work, able to carry passengers in much larger numbers: to and from the Continent, round the coasts of Britain and on some of its picturesque rivers. By 1824 steamboats were plying on the east coast from London to Leith, the port of Edinburgh; one was named *The Tourist*.[38] These vessels, carrying a hundred passengers or more, accustomed people to the idea of travelling together in large numbers. But their proprietors do not seem to have hired them out for the use of privately-organized parties, still less to have agreed to convey such parties themselves, as the railways did with their excursions. The passengers who used them for journeys of pleasure all made their own arrangements. Those could be troublesome, particularly when they involved moving from one steamer to another on the way to remote places, in Scotland or abroad. In 1845 two men, appreciating what the railways and the steamers could now do in conjunction, came forward with offers to arrange this kind of travel, guaranteeing accommodation on trains and ships in return for a single payment.

Joseph Crisp of Liverpool, who was spoken of as having already 'given the Liverpool public many pleasant railway excursions', now went on to offer his fellow-citizens 'a fortnight in London, or twenty days in Paris'[39] – the first such facility I know of that extended to a journey abroad. Crisp evidently persisted for some time, for we have an account of one of his excursions to Paris in 1849.[40]

These foreign holidays were not tours but excursions. In the same year 1845 Thomas Cook offered two tours by train from Leicester to Liverpool and on by a steamboat he himself chartered to North Wales. He then became fired by the idea of organizing a tour to Scotland. In the following summer he realized it. No continuous railway was yet open, so he took his party by train from Leicester to Fleetwood, by steamer to Ardrossan, and then on to Glasgow by train once more. The tour was so successful that it was repeated frequently, and extended by steamboat up the west coast of Scotland: by 1856 Cook was recording 'his eighteenth trip to Staffa and Iona'.[41] He too had his eye on the Continent and at that time was attempting to arrange tours there.[42] They did not succeed, and new rivals springing up in the business did better in it for a time. Henry Gaze, for example, established himself at Southampton and worked closely in the organization of Continental travel with the London & South Western Railway.[43] His expertise was recognized when the London & North Western company dismissed its excursion agent, Henry Marcus of Liverpool, owing to 'some little want of discretion', in 1866,[44] considered replacing him by Cook, decided against that because Cook was already closely associated with its rival the Midland company, and turned to Gaze instead. Gaze then moved to London and established what became a very substantial agency, which flourished for the next thirty years.[45]

Cook never had any monopoly in this business; nor, with his liberal principles, would he have sought one. But his firm remained much the most famous. As early as 1854 the French Nord and Est companies were collaborating to offer circular tours from Paris to Belgium and the Rhine, with an accompanying handbook written by an experienced compiler of such things, Adolphe Joanne:[46] an exact counterpart of Cook's tours but at a somewhat higher social level.

The outstanding quality of Cook's mind was imagination, served by an intense energy and played upon by moral forces. His organization of travel had begun as a by-product of his work in the cause of temperance, and that cause continued dear to him, linked with his religion; he was a staunch, unswerving Baptist. But his mind was not rigid. Another travel agent of the next generation, John Frame, who was a hard-line teetotaller, is said to have refused to issue tickets for his tours except to those who signed the pledge. Cook was too sensible to do any such thing. For him, temperance was not a matter of dogma but of reason. When on one of his Continental tours he saw a number of his party crowding into a station buffet in Italy to buy themselves wine, he cried out 'Gentlemen, do not invest in diarrhoea' – the wisest plea he could have made to those taking a long, hot journey in a train without any lavatories.[47] An even good humour pervades what he wrote and said. His tourists were under his personal care, and he did his best for them. Who but he would ever have thought of announcing that, if he were asked, he would stop one of his chartered trains at Gretna Green long enough to allow a couple to get married there?[48] His *naïveté*, his spontaneity, endear him to us still.

Though he founded a most successful business, he was not himself a good business man. His restlessly active imagination and his support of the causes that appealed to him diffused his interests, and when his work began to grow fast in the early 1860s he could not impose on it the discipline it called for. That seems to have been part of the reason why the firm found the basis of its work in Scotland pulled away from underneath it. In 1862 the railway companies concerned in the Scottish tourist business suddenly decided that they would handle their own tours in future.[49] Promptly and smoothly, they began to issue their own tourist programmes. Cook was stunned by this blow. 'Those who unitedly control the travelling arrangements between England and Scotland', he announced in his *Excursionist* on 24 May, had decided that there should be '*no Excursion Trains to Scotland this season!*' The main explanation for the change is obvious. The railways had determined to do the work themselves, without paying an agent. But Cook appears to have given the companies some grounds for complaint, arising largely from his hasty improvizations and careless accounting.[50]

Some serious reconsideration of the firm's business was evidently required. Thomas's son John Mason Cook had now joined him. In 1865 they moved their headquarters from Leicester to London. The firm had already taken a stronger grip of the business on the Continental mainland in 1863, with a tour to Switzerland and Italy,[51] repeated with many variations down the years. Almost as soon as the Civil War was over in 1865, Thomas went across the Atlantic to prepare for a tour through the United States, armed with recommendations from prominent British Liberals like John Bright and W. E. Forster. The first tour there, led by John Mason, was not a success, but the Cooks held on to their idea and gradually established it during the next decade. In 1872 Thomas went much further, to conduct a party of nine travellers round the world. He recorded the journey himself in descriptions printed periodically in *The Times*.[52] It was not undertaken at any high speed, like the one in *Round the World in Eighty Days*, which Jules Verne was just then publishing serially in Paris. It took nearly three times as long. Throughout the past thirty years Cook had been working to make travel a simple matter. It must have given him special pleasure to say: 'This going round the world is a very easy and almost imperceptible business; there is no difficulty about it'.[53]

By that time the firm had made another great advance in the organization of its tours. Almost from the start it had helped its clients by telling them of hotels and boarding houses that, after inquiry and inspection, it could recommend. In 1868 it began to sell them, before their journey began, coupons to defray the cost of accommodation in hotels on its list. A single payment could now cover both travelling expenses and board and lodging. Here we approach the package tour, the basis of popular travelling today.[54]

The firm was soon reaching out across the world, with offices in European cities, in Cairo and New York. But there was one serious impediment to its expansion. Father and son were two quite different people, and they now drew steadily apart. The younger man was the exact antithesis of the elder: a natural business man, little touched by idealism, his mind concentrated, not dispersed – fixed on his ambition to make the firm great, and at the same time to amass a fortune himself. He grew more and more out of sympathy with his father, edging him away from the control of the business until he forced a breach in their association in 1878.[55] Thereafter Thomas was no more than a pensioner, a cypher in the determination of policy. The struggle produced a total schism within the family. Thomas presently retired to Leicester, and the close of his life there was protracted and sad, in blindness. John Mason made the firm into a great international concern, a commercial empire, of a piece with the imperialism of the age.

Thomas Cook & Son never lost interest in its original business in Great Britain. It came to handle the whole or a large part of the excursion and tourist arrangements of six of the leading English railway companies, together with two in Scotland, and to issue tickets for journeys to be made over nearly all the rest. Gaze maintained his relationship with the North Western and South Western companies; Frame handled the Continental business of the Caledonian;[56] Dean & Dawson worked closely with the Manchester Sheffield & Lincolnshire.

But Cook's remained much the largest firm in the marketing of travel in Britain, and even further ahead of its rivals in the international business. It owned a fleet of steamers on the Nile, which served the British government in attempting to relieve Gordon at Khartoum in 1885, and in the dispatch of Kitchener for the reconquest of the Sudan. It transported pilgrims from India to Mecca every year, safely and regularly where in the past the journeys of all of them had been cruelly dangerous. And in 1890, when the young German Emperor William II decided to visit Jerusalem, it was to Cook's that his government turned. If he was the most dazzling of all Cook's tourists, the experience that went into the smooth arrangement of his complicated journey had been built up, piece by piece, from the practice that had first been established in Leicestershire in 1841.

When Thomas Cook died in 1892, he left £2731. John Mason, seven years later, left £622,534. That is a simple measure of the total change of scale on which the firm's activities had come to be conducted by the younger man, and of his achievement as an entrepreneur.

The success that attended the Cooks' efforts excited some hostility. 'Cook's tourists' were the butt of much ridicule as they made their way, in their groups with their guides, across Britain, then across Europe and into the Near East.
Ill. 45   Though Cruikshank and Doyle had laughed at such people in the 1850s, their fun was good-humoured. When the novelist Charles Lever turned to it, as British vice-consul at Trieste, he gave vent to an explosion of mere spite.[57] It was directed specifically against Cook's, which bore the brunt of a widespread

hostility towards tourism in the 1870s. Here and there that simply reflected the feelings of people who loved quiet, when confronted by the disturbance and noise that tourists of any kind brought with them. Ruskin was at the head of them, his exquisite and genuine susceptibilities affronted by what he saw: 'All my own dear mountain grounds and treasure-cities, Chamouni, Interlachen, Lucerne, Geneva, Venice, are long ago destroyed by the European populace'.[58] In 1872 Trollope referred to Switzerland, the Tyrol, 'and even Italy' as 'all redolent of Mr Cook'.[59] Four years later he remarked that all respectable London shopkeepers were 'either in Switzerland or at their marine villas. The travelling world had divided itself into Cookites and Hookites – those who escaped trouble under the auspices of Mr Cook, and those who boldly combated the extortions of foreign innkeepers and the anti-Anglican tendencies of foreign railway officials "on their own hooks"'. By such people as these the tourist movement was thought of as mere vulgarization.

Both the railways and their agents now applied themselves to encouraging foreigners to travel to Britain, and around the island when they arrived. A large majority of the European tourists who reached Britain must always have gone direct to London and stayed there. Expensive and odd as it was, it was the largest city in the world, and the Exhibition of 1851 had proclaimed many of its merits. The other great focus of foreign interest was Scotland. Scott's poems and novels continued to be read everywhere. He was an eminently visual writer, and his descriptions of the landscape of Scotland drew many people to it. When Joanne set himself to the task of supplying Frenchmen with guidebooks to countries outside France, Scotland was the first he turned to, in 1852, followed by Switzerland two years later. Thomas Cook's instinct had been sure. He had fastened on Scotland as a main goal of tourism in 1846 and developed his work there effectively in the following decade. It was his very success that determined the railways to take the business out of his hands in 1862.

From this point onwards the railways' Scottish tourist system developed, set out clearly in successive issues of the companies' programmes and guides. The Caledonian Railway's book for the summer of 1878 offers more than fifty circular tours, using rail, road, and sea transport, together with coupons, purchasable in advance (following Cook's example) for hotels and for meals on steamers.[60] Further north, the *Handbook to the Highland Railway and the West Coast*, in its twenty-first edition of 1902,[61] sets off with the round statement that 'the scenery traversed by the Highland Railway far surpasses in interest and variety that of any railway route in the United Kingdom'. As usual, the advertisements faithfully reflect the interests and amusements prevailing at the time (the 'ping pong and dark-room for photography' offered at the Birnam Hotel, for instance), and the commercial trends too, exemplified in the American Toilet Saloon at Inverness.

On the west coast the development of tourism was shared between the railways and the steamers, with horse-drawn vehicles playing their part as well. North of the Clyde estuary only three railways reached across, completed in 1880–1901, to Oban, Mallaig, and Kyle of Lochalsh. They all counted heavily on the tourist traffic they hoped to secure in the summer.

In the steamers' early days a great power had been built up by G. & J. Burns. But in 1851 these brothers (principal founders also of what became known as the Cunard Line) divested themselves of their business in the Highlands, which eventually passed into the hands of their nephew David MacBrayne. They retained their services on the Clyde estuary for a time, but the traffic there soon became intensely competitive. The railways also established themselves in the business, covertly and indirectly. (They had no powers to own steamers.) Their competition grew fast. Summer tourism was combined with day excursions from Glasgow and its suburbs. But in addition there was a steady commuter traffic all the year round from Bute and the shores of the river; taken into Greenock and Helensburgh and on into Glasgow by train. The trains' and ships' times were all tightly interlocked. On some services only three minutes were allowed between the arrival of one and the departure of the other. Here was the British frenzy of competition at its height.

But it was taken too far. In the end there was not enough business to justify it, and all the competitors found themselves losing. In 1909–10 the railway companies came together to discuss pooling agreements, and a number of the duplicating services were cut back or taken off.[62]

The tourist arm of this traffic in the Highlands was under MacBrayne's firm dominion. The train and ship services were complementary. The tourist who enjoyed the pleasure of sailing up the coast and out to the islands in the summer was using services that had a permanent purpose all the year round. For the ships also carried the mails and were the life-line of the people in these remote places. Here tourism was grafted on to a social service; becoming, from the revenue it brought in, almost a part of that service itself.

The vulgarization it had produced was undeniable. On the other hand Victorian tourism can also be seen as one sign of an intelligent, advancing democracy; affecting as yet only a small minority of the British people but introducing them to experiences they would never have received in any other way. One of the young men in Henry James's tales remarks in Venice in 1870: 'We shall certainly cease to be here, but we shall never cease to have been here'.[63] Neither he nor James was a Cook's tourist, but a good many of those people over the years, looking back to their first sight of Schiehallion or the Coolins, of Chartres or St Peter's, would have shared his feeling.

Varieties of Enjoyment

The railways' excursion and tourist business, in all its branches, had come to be very substantial indeed before 1914. The discussion here must end with a general survey of its success, and some of its shortcomings, in the provision of pleasure.

In the early years, down to 1851, the pleasure is palpable, alloyed only by the fear and discomfort of travelling by the new trains. Most of those who went about in this way must have been aware that some risks had to be taken. Now and then the mishaps added to the fun, provided a bonus of comic, unlooked-for enjoyment. Improvization was the keynote of it all. The passengers took whatever came to them. The troubles might be beyond joking about. An early 'experimental' attempt at an excursion to the Continent, from London to Rotterdam via Norwich and Yarmouth, was made in July 1846. On the return journey the sailors were drunk, the ship was driven out of its course by a storm, and when the passengers at last came to complete their journey by train, the boiler of the engine burst, so that they had to walk a mile and a half into Ely.[64] That experiment was not repeated. By the 1860s the business had come, as a rule, to be competently managed. The speed of the trains was kept low; the rolling stock used, though it offered little comfort, was tolerable. Excursions were now an accepted part of British railway working.

They became most obvious in the mass-movements on and around the principal public holidays: Easter and Whitsun, the August Bank Holiday instituted in 1871, the special holidays associated with local events, like the Nottingham Goose Fair. The totals of people, carried by regular and excursion trains together, grew to be very large. A count professing to be exact showed that 7797 excursionists travelled by train from Leicester on the August Bank Holiday of 1881 (6.4% of the whole population of the town).[65] Findlay tells us that 21,000 people went in this way on the August Saturday and Monday of 1889 to the medium-sized resort of Llandudno, 100,000 to the much bigger Blackpool.[66] On Whit Monday of the same year Acworth had been one of the 38,000 who travelled out of London to Chingford, on the edge of Epping Forest. He 'returned to the town in the guard's van, and as special instructions had been given to keep it select, the occupants never numbered more than twenty-five, babies included'.[67]

The institution of the August Bank Holiday soon had its effects on the pattern of holiday-making. The Wakes Weeks, which (under that name or some other) were a well-known feature of life in the industrial districts of Lancashire and Yorkshire, were spread between the towns over a period of two months from July to September.[68] But in the 1870s other towns began to adopt the same practice, of closing all or most of their factories for a stated period, and associating it with the new national holiday. A 'Trip Week' appeared for example at Lincoln in that decade. There it was the one that preceded the Bank Holiday. Not many of the townspeople could afford to go away for the whole period; but by 1897 as many as 17,000 railway tickets were being sold during the week, for day excursions and longer journeys, representing more than a third of the whole population.[69]

Such were the great mass movements, the family holidays that the railways offered, year after year. But their trains made other mass movements possible, offering other pleasures, also. They contributed largely to the growth of spectator sports.[70]

First of all, as we have seen, to race-meetings. As early as 1840 over 25,000 passengers were carried in two days to one at Paisley.[71] The Great Northern company may be said to have turned the St Leger meeting at Doncaster from a highly esteemed but rather select affair into a big popular festival. The competition that developed annually, during those four days in September, between the various railways that had powers to run on to the Great Northern lines, grew more and more intense. That one company had control of it all, however, and it exercised its power well. All goods traffic at Doncaster was suspended on St Leger day, the sidings cleared and used to accommodate excursion trains. Nearly 100,000 racegoers were brought in and out in 1888. Yet the whole traffic was conducted – we have the word of the general manager of another company for it – with entire regularity, and hardly any interruption to the main-line services using the great junction.[72]

The volume of race traffic, the precision and speed with which it was handled, were remarkable. In the late 1880s the London & South Western company managed to bring up twenty trains of racegoers from Sandown Park to Waterloo within a space of sixty-two minutes. All these trains had to be fitted in with the normal service, which was far from light.[73]

It was the same with cricket and football. Cricket was already a popular sport, based primarily on county loyalties. They were strong, and there was even one 'Cricket Ground' station in the 1860s, at Old Trafford.[74] But the excitement of cricket did not come to reach out over the whole country until the first Australian team arrived in England in 1878. Its fortunes, in the games it played in London and the provinces, evoked an intense interest. The railways sensed that quickly, and responded with excursion trains to the matches, which did much towards securing the success of the visit and towards establishing the game as a national one thereafter.[75]

The railways' aid in the promotion of football was conspicuous. Local traffic to grounds on the outskirts of large cities grew heavy. After 1885 the rickety little trains on the North Greenwich line staggered under the burden of the crowds attending the Millwall Rovers matches; the Great Eastern put in special wide doors at White Hart Lane station for those going to see Tottenham Hotspur play – up to 10,000 of them for one game, arriving at five-minute intervals. The Hull & Barnsley company strenuously developed services of this kind, conveying spectators to all the big West Riding towns; a long slow journey over the Wolds and then through a series of crowded junctions. Whereas that company's ordinary passenger traffic never paid, its excursion business is said to have been profitable.[76]

The greatest of all these efforts came to be those involved in carrying crowds to the Football Association's Cup Final matches. When the first of them was played at the Oval in 1872, it was watched by 2000 people. By 1901, at the Crystal Palace, the crowd numbered 110,000.[77] The Brighton and the Chatham companies were able to carry 50,000 people from their London termini to their two Crystal Palace stations.[78] But for a great many of those who arrived at the match that was only the last stage of their journey. They had travelled by excursion trains from all over the provinces. Local loyalties here were intense: 'these very masculine hordes... were supporters rather than spectators.

Many of them had watched their local clubs grow up from waste-land play to the heights of success and they felt themselves passionately involved in the fortunes of their team'.[79]

The men from the provinces could not have witnessed their teams' arrival on the heights without the railways that carried them up to London in fast special trains. The fares were indeed low; but to them had to be added the cost of crossing London and travelling down to the Crystal Palace, besides the food and drink consumed on the way. This expenditure was met by working men largely through subscriptions of a few pence or a shilling, paid weekly over a period of months: a business commonly managed at the pubs, whose landlords would arrange for food and drink to be carried up on the journey and might also join together to book accommodation in the excursion trains, or even secure trains of their own.[80]

One other sporting spectacle may be set beside these, to which two railway companies were able to make an important contribution: the University Boat Race. This was a single event, attracting a large crowd of spectators, many of whom simply walked from the western suburbs of London to see it, standing on the banks of the Thames between Putney and Mortlake. No building was erected here to correspond to the racing men's grandstands, but a satisfactory substitute offered itself: the bridge carrying the London & South Western Railway over the river at Barnes. By the 1870s that was in regular use for the purpose, the company making over 1200 tickets available to those who wished to see the race from such a good vantage point.[81] This brought it in a revenue of about £750, on top of a large number of fares: by 1887 it was carrying over 11,000 people down in fifteen special trains, within less than an hour.[82] In 1880 the Metropolitan District Railway had opened its extension to Putney Bridge, which enabled it also to carry large numbers to see the race.[83] Visitors came up for it from all over the country: in 1891 the Manchester Sheffield & Lincolnshire company was offering an excursion for the purpose.[84]

The railways also made numerous arrangements with the proprietors of business undertakings for the conveyance of their employees on excursions by chartered trains. The earliest example of the practice yet noted comes from 1840, when R. & W. Hawthorn, the locomotive builders of Newcastle, hired a train to carry their men and their friends to and from Carlisle at half price, Hawthorn's guaranteeing a given number of passengers. The trip took place on a Sunday; 320 people were conveyed.[85] This idea gradually took on. In 1846 we find Francis Crawshay of the Treforest ironworks inquiring of the Taff Vale Railway about running a train from Merthyr Tydvil to Cardiff, for a steamer to Weston-super-Mare, so 'helping my men to obtain a day's fun'.[86] Other firms were more generous still. W. D. & H. O. Wills, the tobacco manufacturers of Bristol, not only took all their 120 employees to London in 1851, for the Exhibition; the partners gave each of them £1 to spend there.[87]

Some outings of this kind were repeated regularly, on an enormous scale. The most famous were the day excursions provided by Bass, the brewers, for their workpeople from Burton-on-Trent. They began in 1865 and ran every other year until 1883, when they were established annually. By 1889 they had grown so large that only a few towns could accommodate them (like party conferences today), and henceforward the changes were rung on Blackpool, Liverpool, Scarborough, and Yarmouth. As many as fifteen trains might be required, carrying up to 10,000 people in all. The employees of the brewery travelled free, with their full day's pay and a gratuity, as well as the right to buy tickets for members of their families at cost. The trains began to leave Burton in the small hours of the morning, and the last of them was not back until midnight. The resorts provided their own characteristic attractions for these visitors. Those who rode on the Hotchkiss bicycle railway at Yarmouth in 1909 could refresh themselves with thousands of bloaters and a special boiling of Yarmouth rock. Fourteen of these trains ran to Scarborough on 24 July 1914. But they never ran again.[88]

The railway companies themselves did the same thing for their own people. When the Swindon Mechanics' Institution organized a day trip for its members (all of them employed by the Great Western Railway) to Oxford in 1849, the company agreed to carry them free of charge.[89] This soon became an annual occurrence. Almost every railway eventually did something of the same sort: the Hull & Barnsley, for instance;[90] the Midland & South Western Junction, which arranged an outing at specially low fares, including a passage to the Isle of Wight enlivened by the playing of the Cirencester works band.[91] The Swindon 'Trip' of the Great Western came, in its scale, to beat even the efforts made by Bass at Burton: a set of excursions allowing its men to go out with their families for a day or for longer periods as they liked.[92] The number of those leaving on 9 July 1914 was the largest ever recorded: 25,616, half the population of the town.[93]

And finally, in considering these very varied 'trains of pleasure' we must not forget those carrying children. Many of them, though by no means all, were organized by Sunday schools.[94] Here and there railway managers had to take special note of them. At Eastcote in Middlesex the Metropolitan company found it necessary to double the length of the station platforms in 1910 in order to accommodate longer trains, consisting largely of schoolchildren coming out into that then unravished country on summer treats. Further small improvements were made to the station when the directors learnt that ninety-three children's parties had used it in the month of July 1913.[95]

The experience the railways gained from managing these kinds of business was applied to meeting other needs; above all to the movement of troops.[96] In the South African War of 1899–1902 and the War of 1914–18 the conveyance of soldiers to the ports was carried through to general admiration. Some of the skills it called for had accrued to the railways from their experience in organizing movements of passengers bent on pleasure, not on war.

These outings and holidays were arranged for groups of people travelling together. But not all Victorians wished to take their pleasures communally. We can discern a marked increase in the railways' provision of facilities for the enjoyment of leisure that were open to family groups, to couples, and to single travellers on their own. They were meeting here a desire for privacy, partly no doubt a reaction against the hubbub of the jolly excursionists, travelling at the lowest rates, five hundred or more to a train. The railways still catered well for the family holiday: whether for the rich, able to hire saloons for their own exclusive use (with perhaps the convenience of getting theirs transferred from one train to another, to obviate changing),[97] or for families far less well-to-do travelling third-class by ordinary trains, at return fares offering some reduction.[98]

Those who thought of making such long journeys to please themselves, or themselves and their wives alone, had a large choice open to them in the later years of the age. Angling, the pre-eminent solitary sport, was much encouraged by the railways. The two companies serving the Thames above London both offered cheap day tickets for this purpose to their stations on the river.[99] Similar facilities were available from the Great Eastern company for fishing on the Lea and from the Midland to the Welsh Harp reservoir at Hendon.[100] Some people had always taken pleasure in walking out of towns into the country. The railways began to encourage this recreation with cheap tickets or special excursions after 1900. The Great Western company, for instance, offered day excursions for walkers from London to the Vale of the White Horse (60 miles away and more) on Sundays from 1905 onwards.[101] The Board of Trade noticed the practice in 1910: 'people are acquiring the habit of going long distances by railway in order to walk in the country'.[102] We can get a hint of the volume of the business from the Brighton company. It offered cheap day return tickets from London to the North Downs, not by special excursions but by ordinary services. In 1901–5 it sold, on average, 81,994 of these tickets annually. In 1906–11 the number grew to 141,822.[103] In the earlier period this traffic was variable, falling twice; in the second it rose steadily every year.

Not all those who purchased such tickets would have been going into the country to walk. Some of them must certainly have been cyclists. The railways had done substantial business with those who had taken up that pastime from the 1870s onwards. Roads carrying heavy traffic were often repaired very insufficiently in Late-Victorian Britain. In 1905 Baedeker remarked that, on this account, 'the main roads leading out of London are generally rather rough' and advised cyclists to put themselves and their machines on to a train for the first few miles.[104]

Two successful bodies were founded in 1877–8, to protect the interests of cyclists: the National Cyclists' Union, concerned chiefly with cycling as a sport, and the Cyclists' Touring Club, with a different function indicated in its title.[105] Both tried to negotiate with the railway companies, to get them to lower their rates for carrying bicycles. They made slow progress; but the rates the railways fixed did not prevent this traffic from growing very large. In the three summer months of 1898 the Great Eastern company conveyed over 60,000 bicycles into and out of Liverpool Street station.[106] The CTC complained of the clumsy handling of the machines and put forward proposals for a van specially designed to carry them. Some companies replied that they were devising their own, and vehicles specially equipped for this purpose appeared early in the twentieth century.[107] Even on long-distance services: the brand-new Grampian Corridor Express trains turned out by the Caledonian Railway in 1905 had cycle-racks in their luggage vans.[108]

These facilities were provided by the railways to generate important new business. They also afforded others to people who were much fewer in number but were reckoned to be worth cultivating nevertheless. Here are two examples, of interest to people in widely different social classes.

Pigeon-racing was a small-scale sport, which had its constant devotees. In 1912 the London & North Western Railway produced a special book of instructions for handling this traffic in May–August every year from Cumberland and Furness. Special rolling stock was used for it ('large shelved corridor pigeon vans'), and the pigeons released from them were expected to fly as far as Jersey, or even Nantes.[109]

Another kind of bird was of great interest to rich men and generated an important railway traffic: the game birds that were the prey of sportsmen, above all grouse. The service of overnight express trains from London to Scotland was greatly increased in the weeks before 12 August, when grouse-shooting began. In the summer of 1887 the normal provision of trains by the two main routes was five. Four more were now added, three by the West Coast route (among them an Express Horse and Carriage Train) and one by the East; all of them discontinued after the night of 10–11 August. These expresses converged on Perth, whence the Highland Railway took them forward – made up into enormous trains, hauled by two engines and often banked over the Grampians by a third. The passengers using these trains were not all grouse-shooters: the East Coast one was described as a Special Highland Tourist Express. It was inconvenient for the railways that the shooting season occurred within the main period of school holidays, when family travelling was also at its height. But they had to make all this provision, and it was doubtless well worth their while, for a high proportion of the sportsmen must have been travelling first-class.

It is impossible to compute the volume of the railways' holiday and pleasure traffic in the country as a whole, since no statistics of it were compiled. But we can get an idea of its magnitude from some evidence that has survived. Here are two examples.

We have an account of the numbers of excursion passengers carried by the Brighton company and of the revenue arising from them in 1901–11. It includes excursions organized by agents. In 1911, Coronation year, a great many excursions were run for special events, at the Crystal Palace and elsewhere.[110] Both numbers and revenue grew larger every year in this period, without exception, though the increase in the volume of traffic outstripped that in the revenue it brought in.

That is one kind of information, which so far as I know is not available year by year, over such a span of time, for any other railway that interested

TABLE 7

EXCURSION TRAFFIC ON THE LONDON BRIGHTON
& SOUTH COAST RAILWAY 1901–11

	No. of passengers annual average	*Increase %*	*Revenue annual average*	*Increase %*	*Revenue per head*
1901–5	1,637,380		£214,750		2s 7 d
1906–10	2,456,949	50.1	288,954	34.6	2s 4 d
1911	4,244,725	72.8	373,078	29.1	1s 9 d

Source: R414/537, p. 92

itself specially in the development of this traffic. Another, of a different sort, is furnished by the sets of printed working notices that the companies issued to their employees, advising them of the special trains that were to be run in addition to the regular service, together with the alterations in it that were required. Copies of these survive for a number of railways. A good sample is provided by the series produced on the North British: a company with a dense system in Fife and in the industrial districts of the Forth–Clyde basin but also serving the whole of the lightly-populated country south of Edinburgh. Let us look at the 2300-page volume of notices for 1913, the last year of peace.[111]

Excursion trains are provided all the year round, and they show a great diversity of character. Football excursions run throughout the winter, not merely to the big matches in the great cities but to very small towns like Selkirk. Rich men's sports are provided for specially too. One of the chief Glasgow–Edinburgh expresses is directed to call additionally at Linlithgow 'to lift passengers in connection with the hunt'. Excursion facilities are afforded to allow people to go up to Glasgow for the 'drapery and millinery sales', but equally to the hiring fairs, for engaging servants, at small towns like Lauder and Morpeth and Berwick.[112] Special trains or additional carriages are put on frequently, taking emigrants to Canada. On Sundays there is often special accommodation to be provided for theatre companies, some of them making very long journeys, from Dundee to Hull or from Edinburgh to Portsmouth.[113]

In the summer the range of this travelling comes to seem almost unlimited: works outings (500 people from Peter Scott & Co. of Hawick, going down to Whitley Bay on the Northumberland coast); special express trains carrying German tourists from Leith over to the Trossachs and back. For the trains from Glasgow to the sea-coast of Fife at the height of the holiday season many special arrangements have to be made. Those 'conveying families to summer quarters' carry no luggage; all of it goes in a 'special luggage train' leaving for St Andrews at 5 am.[114]

Sunday School trips abounded, in the service of every denomination. On Saturday 28 June the company set out to provide for the carriage of at least 37,000 children and adults on excursions of this sort. Over 100 extra trains were required accordingly.[115]

All this prompts two questions, to which I can offer only very hesitant answers. But they are important questions, and they lie at the root of the whole business that is being discussed here.

First, how did the North British company provide these trains, and how did it haul them? There had to be an adequate number of carriages; open goods wagons might not now be used. Most excursion trains ran slowly, and old, even feeble engines could be assigned to some of them. Still, carriages and engines had to be found. Does this not imply that there was a very large reserve of them, lying idle for most days in the year?

If so, can that policy have been economic, justified by the profits these trains produced? The expenses incurred by running them did not arise only from the provision of engines and rolling stock. Each of these extra trains called for an extra crew, two footplate men and at least one guard. Staff had to be on duty at uncovenanted hours to handle them – not station staff only but signalmen too; and that set up justified demands for overtime pay. When the whole cost had been met, in capital investment and in the running of the trains from their depots out to their destinations and back again, does it seem possible that they can have yielded a profit? If not, were they loss-leaders? They may perhaps have been regarded in that light, especially by the North British company, locked in unending competition with its neighbour and enemy the Caledonian.

Were those questions ever debated seriously? If they were, the answers to them seem to be wrapped in impenetrable silence.

14

MOBILITY

This book and its companion, *The Railway in Town and Country*, have a good deal to say about the freedom of movement the railways brought, whether wholly new or the intensification of an old one: within London, the inner city and the huge conglomeration that came to surround it; in the suburban growth of provincial towns; in the business of rural markets and in movement into and out of the countryside; in holiday-making and many other pleasures; in the stimulus given to the mind, fed by the mail services, the telegraphs, and the rapidly expanding power of the press, which all owed much to the railways. The survey now turns to look back over those changes together, to consider the mobility as a whole and some of the effects it produced in Victorian Britain.

The word 'mobility' is ancient; defined simply by Locke as 'the power of being moved', admitted by Johnson to his *Dictionary*. But the Victorians came to need a word that meant something a little different: not merely the power of being moved but the desire for motion as well. They do not seem to have fastened on 'mobility' to convey that meaning. One attempt at least was made to express it by adopting a different word, already in use by medical men. In 1861 the *Annual Register* referred to the 'locomotivity' of the English people since railways got to work,[1] meaning by that their passion for movement. 'Locomotivity' was a mouthful, and did not establish itself. Neither did 'mobility', within the Victorian age, though the passion was clear enough:

> But our impulsive days are all for moving:
> Sometimes with some ulterior end, but still
> For moving, moving always.[2]

It was compounded of three essential elements: the high speed at which the railways conveyed their traffic; the prices they charged for their service; and the great scale of the business they engendered.

Speed

The speed of travel by the best coaches on the roads had shown a striking increase before the trunk railways were opened. In 1776 there was a 'flying coach' from London to York making the journey in thirty-six hours; in 1836 the fastest scheduled time was down to twenty hours (almost 10 mph). To Shrewsbury (153 miles) the acceleration was even more remarkable: from $3\frac{1}{2}$ days in 1753 to 12 hr 40 min by the famous 'Wonder' coach in 1835 (12.1 mph).[3] The much greater reductions in time that the railways brought may well have made less impression on the people of such towns: for the coaches made their way conspicuously to their very centres and were a familiar sight to everyone in the streets, whereas the stations into which the trains ran were usually set up at first in the suburbs, seen only by those who had business there.[4]

That remoteness was a drawback to railway travel, offsetting the gain in speed of transit by whatever time it took to reach the station from the centre of the town and the corresponding time to be allowed for at the far end of the journey; requiring calculations much like those we have to make today of the time needed for getting to and from airports. On the other hand the railway offered a greater degree of certainty to its passengers than the coach could do. It was nearly always possible to find a place in any train, for that was a unit taking 100 passengers, or many hundreds, at a time; and if it should happen to be full, additional carriages might be added. The coach was an inflexible unit taking some fifteen passengers only. Places could be booked on it in advance from the starting-point of its journey; but the traveller wishing to join a coach somewhere *en route*, or to travel on a suddenly-arising occasion, might find there was no room for him. In 1767 Dr Johnson, wishing to get up from Lichfield to London, had to say to a friend: 'We have here only the chance of a vacancy in the passing carriages, and I have bespoken one that may, if it happens, bring me to town on the fourteenth of this month: but this is not certain'.[5] That defect in coach travel was never removed. In 1829 it drove a pair of sprightly engineers to out-manoeuvre two other would-be passengers on a Leeds–London coach by walking up the road to meet it.[6] So the railway offered reassurance to travellers here, as well as higher speed.

The trunk lines spread the impression of speed very widely in 1837–41. Trains on them travelled at up to 25 mph including stops, nearly three times as fast as the rate of the average coach. For some critical spirits that was their sole virtue: as one put it in 1837, 'the only pleasant part of the performance is the saving of time'.[7] But for many people that virtue was enough by itself. Sydney Smith took to the railway at once, and it was the speed that delighted him. 'Distance is abolished', he cried exultingly in 1842, 'scratch that out of the catalogue of human evils'.[8] There were those who quickly became unconscious addicts of the speed. In 1844 Rowland Hill, having been largely responsible for the Brighton company's establishment of much faster trains to and from London, was disconcerted to be told by a stranger travelling in one of them that it was 'a slow coach, a very slow coach'. When Hill pointed out that the time on its 50-mile journey had been cut from two hours to $1\frac{1}{2}$, the only response he got was 'they can just as well do it in an hour'. Similar demands were soon being expressed, for greater speed over much longer distances. 'Will these *railroads* do nothing for us when they are finished', wrote the poet Thomas Campbell to his sister in 1850, 'so as to enable us to travel to Edinburgh in eight hours!!'[9]

By that time there was a battle between the protagonists of speed and of caution. The first express trains had got to work with success; but they were costly to run, and some were accordingly taken off or slowed down. Economically-minded managers now tried to secure a common policy between the companies, to produce a general reduction in the express trains' speed, but when the Lancashire & Yorkshire Railway approached the Great Western in 1853 with such a proposition, the directors said they thought that would not 'be conducive to the interests of the public or of the company'.[10] They had already returned to faster running under the spur of competition with the London & North Western to Birmingham.

As early as 1848 readers of the staid *Journal of the Statistical Society* were told that 'an English public will always feel an interest in anything like a race, and we accordingly find the different rates of the express trains a common subject of interest'.[11] The competing services to Manchester, Birmingham, and Exeter ran at times in the 1850s and 1860s as if they were indeed designed to be races. In the 1870s the disquiet felt by some railway managers about the speed of trains between London and the North, kept up in keen competition, was revealed at the inquiries into the accidents at Wigan and Arlesey. At the first of these William Cawkwell, general manager of the London & North Western, stated that his company felt obliged to run trains at a higher speed than it liked owing to the pressure of the Great Northern's competition. 'The public require fast trains', he said. ' . . . The East Coast companies have always carried more than the West Coast companies because they go faster.' In reporting on the accident at Arlesey, to one of the highly competitive Manchester expresses of the Great Northern Railway, the inspecting officer, Tyler, showed some sympathy with the driver (who was killed, together with four passengers). 'There is considerable pressure on the engine-drivers of these fast trains to maintain punctuality', he wrote, 'and they cannot do so . . . without keeping up a very high rate of speed'.[12] Yet speed was not reduced. Signs of the competitive spirit appeared plainly all over the country. In 1877 there was a local commotion about the racing – in a literal sense of the word – between Great Western and Midland trains, running on parallel tracks for seven miles southwards from Gloucester.[13] In 1888 and 1895 came the national excitement over the races to Scotland.[14]

The public attention those contests attracted was remarkable. Serious writers were already beginning to analyse the growth of the speed of British express trains, to compare them with those on the Continent of Europe and in America, even to attempt to draw some conclusions about their social effects. The upshot of these studies was to show, beyond dispute, the great superiority of the British express trains, on all counts, compared with those everywhere in Europe. Two good analysts adopted a double standard for the definition of an 'express train' – in Britain and the United States, one running at about 40 mph including stops, on the European continent one running at 29: 'were we, in compiling a list of Continental expresses, to adhere to the English definition of "40 mph, stops included", we should not collect from the whole of Europe as much express mileage as is run by our own small Great Northern company'.[15]

By 1900 Britain's lead in this matter was reduced. But in 1914 she still showed the fastest express trains running between great cities anywhere in Europe (London–Bristol), the fastest *total service* (London–Birmingham), and much the largest number of express trains on her national system.

Even for stopping trains, the general level of speed maintained was higher in Britain than in Europe. The service on country branches was quicker partly because the mixed train, conveying passengers and goods together and stopping to shunt wagons wherever that might be necessary, was little favoured in Britain; almost prohibited there indeed, for the dangers to which it could give rise, after 1889.[16]

Price

The superior service that railways offered to passengers in speed and in other ways was cheaper, from the beginning, than that provided by any other form of land transport.

Comparisons between the charges imposed for travel by coaches and railways in Britain are difficult to frame accurately for three reasons. To begin with, coach fares were highly volatile. The proprietors were free to fix and alter them, exactly as they chose. The fares from London to Brighton, for example, oscillated continually: in 1813–28 between 23s and 12s for a place inside the coach.[17] The railways altered their fares too in early days, according to the strength or weakness of competition. But every railway company had a set of standard maximum charges prescribed for it in the Act that set it up; and in 1844 a single maximum charge was imposed on all of them alike, for passenger travel of the cheapest description. The coaches were subject to no such controls as these. Something much nearer to standard fares emerged at an early stage in the growth of the railway system, calculable and certain.[18]

Secondly, the coach fares did not represent the whole of what the passengers paid. At the end of the journey, and at stages on the way, the coachmen and the guards were customarily tipped; and the aggregate of these 'vails' added something like an average of 15% to the stated fare. Such demands were never made on the railways. Any reckoning of the cost of coach travel must include this surcharge.[19]

And finally, it must be remembered that the coaches' long-distance journeys entailed expense at the inns where they stopped, whereas the superior speed of the train soon allowed almost all journeys within England and Wales to be made (at least by first and second-class passengers) within the compass of a single full day. Here too was another material saving, though it cannot be expressed in any precise figures.

These statements apply to land transport only. The charges made to passengers on canal boats need not be taken into account here, for that form of conveyance was offered at only a few places in Britain, and then over short distances.[20] But the railways had a stiff battle with coastal steamships. Here their fares were undercut. The difference could indeed be very great. From London to Plymouth the third-class railway fare in the 1880s was 18s 8d single. The Irish steamers calling there charged cabin passengers 15s, deck passengers 7s. From London to Hull the comparable rates were 14s by train, 8s and 6s by sea.[21] The time taken by railway to Plymouth in 1887 was $6\frac{1}{2}$–$9\frac{1}{2}$ hours, with six trains admitting third-class passengers every weekday (together with one by night), whereas the steamers ran only once or twice a week. By that time, with the spread of railways, the only coastal services of any importance that still produced competition were those running up the east coast, from London to Leith, Dundee, and Aberdeen. The coastal steamers fought the railways strongly and successfully in the coal trade;[22] but in the carriage of passengers over long distances, in England and Wales, their part had become insignificant.

So the railways established a standard of charging materially less than the coaches, and they soon grew untroubled by the steamers' competition in passenger business. That does not mean, however, that railway travel had become 'cheap' in Britain. By the 1880s it came to be argued that the British passenger paid more for his journeys than one on the Continent. The comparison was difficult to make fairly. In Britain, by this time, supplements for travelling by express trains had almost disappeared, whereas they were levied on nearly all Continental railways, often at stiff rates.[23] Perhaps more important, although the British passenger could take with him a not inconsiderable amount of luggage free, in Belgium, southern Germany, Italy, and Austria every piece of it had to be paid for.

In the 1880s three writers, two English and one American, published analytical accounts of railway passenger services as they were at that time. Two of these studies dealt with those in Britain alone.[24] The American, R. J. Minot, whose work was the earliest, the most laborious, and the most widely valuable of them all, looked at Continental and American services as well;[25] so did the writers of the last book in the series, Foxwell and Farrer, in 1889.[26] Minot made an effort to enumerate the standard fares. In his list, graded from the cheapest to the dearest, Britain stood about half-way – though even he failed to note the advantage British passengers enjoyed in their free allowance of luggage. 'For number of trains and for speed', he declared roundly and generously, 'England leads the world, surpassing entirely Continental Europe and the United States. The most civilized sections of the latter [by which he meant the States east of the Ohio] approach the mother country most nearly, though still far behind.'[27]

It appears from Foxwell and Farrer that the first-class fares in Britain were higher than the average in Europe as a whole by 0.15d a mile, the third-class by 0.09d; the second-class fares were however lower by 0.11d. Judged on this comparison, then, the standard British fares were a little above the average. But then a large proportion of British passengers paid less than the standard fare: the holders of season and workmen's tickets in and about London and the large towns, for example; those who travelled by the very numerous excursions and other cheap trains. Though some concessions of all those kinds were made on the Continent, they were closely restricted, and used by much smaller numbers of passengers.[28]

Moreover the British railways offered their customers what was, in some respects, a much better service than that on the mainland of Europe. Their highly competitive system produced the familiar, picturesque rivalries: of four competitive services from London to Manchester, three to Liverpool, Bradford, Sheffield, Nottingham, Edinburgh and Glasgow, two to Birmingham and Leeds. This required the provision of many more trains, which increased all the expenses of operation. 'If Englishmen will insist on travelling at the rate of 50 mph', wrote J. S. Jeans in 1887, 'and having more express trains than any other country, they must expect to pay somewhat more for the costly facilities thus provided.'[29] He did not approve of this policy. 'There cannot be any question', he wrote, 'that the practice of running a great many only partly full express trains on all our principal lines has little to recommend it beyond public convenience. . . . The financial position and prospects of English railways are going from bad to worse. Our railway boards have not, as yet, adequately realised this great fact, and consequently have . . . done little or nothing to stem the tide of insolvency that threatens to overtake them, unless they mend their ways'.[30]

They did not 'mend their ways'. Two years after Jeans wrote, Edward Watkin began to canvass the possibilities of building a new competitive line linking London with Nottingham, Sheffield, and Manchester. At the first attempt in 1891 Parliament rejected the plan, but next year it caved in and the authorizing Act was passed in 1893. The construction of this new line cost something like £10 million.[31] 'Public convenience' was still paramount in Britain, even when it occasioned a folly like this one. Nemesis began to overtake that great error in the 1920s.

Scale

At the time when this study begins, the public transport of passengers was mainly undertaken by the coaches (together with some wagon and carriers' services) on the main roads, by the short-stage coaches and the first buses in a few large towns, and by the coastal and river steamboats. We have few satisfactory figures for the volume of this business; but here are some indicators from which rough estimates at least may be made.

In 1838 some 1500 long-distance coaches were said to be leaving London daily.[32] These represented the principal services. Adding another third for those running on cross-country routes, we can perhaps say that the total number of these services was about 2000. It was usual to reckon an average of ten passengers per trip by the main coach services;[33] so the number conveyed by all these coaches together may have reached some 20,000 a day. For the wagon and carriers' services we have no means of making any careful estimates at all. The total number of passengers they carried cannot have been large; many such services ran only on market days, once or twice a week. Expressed as a daily total, the number of these passengers might perhaps have been as much as 5000.

The short-stage coaches were scheduled to make 1190 return journeys a day to and from the City of London in 1825.[34] If we assume that, picking up and setting down intermediately, they carried twenty passengers on each trip, the number of passenger journeys will have been some 25,000 in all. Eight years later the total of journeys had risen by 30%, and the first omnibuses had come into use, which almost doubled the number of passengers travelling. To these we must add half as many again for the services terminating in the West End of London.[35] The grand total for London in 1834 seems therefore to come to some 95,000 journeys a day.

Few short-distance services comparable with these in scale were then to be found in any provincial city, though some frequent ones were being provided to and from other towns in the neighbourhood. From Leeds for example they ran to Harrogate (sometimes as many as seven a day), to Halifax and Wakefield.[36] About fifty-five coach services ran in and out of the Leeds inns,[37] carrying perhaps 1000 passengers daily; but many of these were long-distance coaches, of the kinds already included in the reckoning. A quarter of these passengers – it is a mere guess – may have been making use of the coaches for travelling into Leeds from places near by. Calculated by their population, the corresponding figures for the five cities larger than Leeds – Liverpool, Glasgow, Manchester, Edinburgh, and Birmingham – would be some 10,000 a day. Allowing for the greater volume of business in these larger cities, and something for other large towns too, perhaps the final figure ought to be 8000.

For one of these cities, Glasgow, we have some precise figures, published in the *New Statistical Account for Scotland* in 1834. The number of stage-coach passengers given here (about 1300 a day) is not of much use to us. It is only an estimate, and it includes long-distance travellers. One form of passenger transport was used in that city that was not found in any of the others. There canals were carrying 1230 passengers a day. About 340 were travelling by train on the Garnkirk & Glasgow Railway. The Clyde steamboats took 1650. Two years later another compiler, James Cleland, produced figures for the canals and the railway alone, showing a total 55% higher.[38] Though this increase may have been due in part to some different method of reckoning, it is reflected in other statements too.[39]

The number of passengers taken by the steamboats on the river estuaries in Great Britain had probably now become bigger than most people realized at the time. One estimate of it, suggesting a total difficult to reconcile with the one just given for Glasgow, can be deduced from the evidence of Richard Smith, the Assessor of Stage-Coach Duties, to a Parliamentary Committee in 1837.[40] He stated there that if a new duty of a halfpenny for a journey of four miles, and *pro rata* beyond that distance, were imposed on every steamboat passenger in the United Kingdom, it would produce an annual revenue of £150,000–£200,000. Taking the mean of those totals, £175,000, and accepting that the larger part of this revenue would come from passengers paying more than a halfpenny each, since they would be moving over distances greater than four miles (from London to Greenwich, for instance, or to Leith, from Dover to Calais or Glasgow to Greenock), we may suppose him to have believed that at least 30 million journeys were being made by steamboats a year, or perhaps 90,000 a day. That figure is quite out of step with the one just quoted for Glasgow. Yet Smith's position was an important one, and the evidence he gave to the Committee carries weight. It is fortified by some fragments of information that we have about the numbers of passengers on the Thames steamers, which all suggest that in the 1830s and early 1840s they were exceedingly numerous.[41] His figures apply to the whole United Kingdom. Allowing for passengers using the small number of Irish services, the total for Great Britain would perhaps, on this estimate, be 85,000.

The traffic by all these conveyances seems – accepting Smith's figure for the steamboats, treated as it has been here – to have added up like this in the 1830s:

TABLE 8

ESTIMATED NUMBERS OF PASSENGERS CONVEYED DAILY BY PUBLIC TRANSPORT IN GREAT BRITAIN IN THE 1830s

Long-distance coaches	20,000
Local services: London	95,000
provinces	15,000
Minor road services	5,000
Steamboats	85,000
	220,000

That would give an annual total of 80 million journeys: too high a figure, however, for it makes no allowance for the reduced service on Sundays; so perhaps it should be cut back to 75 million. The estimated population of Great Britain for the year 1835 was 17,200,000. On the evidence of these figures, the number of journeys then being undertaken by public transport appears to be rather more than four per year per head of the population. In the next eighty years those four became 120.

What share had the railways in facilitating or producing that enormous change? The mobility they encouraged is suggested, in outline, in Table 9. This information needs to be studied in conjunction with the census, and since reasonably complete figures for the mileage and traffic of the whole system are not available for any year before 1843, there are seven points only at which useful comparisons can be made, the years of the decennial census inquiries. The table shows the growth in the numbers of passenger journeys at those points in time, and relates them to the mileage of line open and the increase of the population. It must be emphasized that the number of passenger

[316]

TABLE 9

NUMBERS OF PASSENGER JOURNEYS BY RAILWAY
IN GREAT BRITAIN 1850–1910

1 Year*	2 Miles of line open	3 Increase	4 Number of passenger journeys† by railway	5 Increase	6 Passenger journeys per mile of line open	7 Increase	8 Population*	9 Passenger journeys per head of population	10 Increase	11 Passenger journeys by tramway
		%	000	%		%	000		%	000
1850	6084	—	67359	—	11072	—	20817	3.2	—	—
1860	9069	49.1	153452	127.8	16920	52.3	23128	6.6	106.3	—
1870	13563	49.6	315680	105.7	23275	37.6	26072	12.1	86.8	—
1880	15563	14.8	586626	85.8	37694	62.0	29710	19.8	63.2	167300
1890	17281	11.0	796331	35.8	46081	22.3	33029	24.1	22.1	494409
1900	18672	8.0	1114627	40.0	59695	29.6	37000	30.1	24.9	992335
1910	19986	7.0	1276003	14.5	63845	7.0	40831	31.3	4.0	2936892

*The figures in col. 1 are for 31 December 1850, 1860, etc. Those in col. 8 are from the decennial censuses for 1851, 1861, etc., taken some three months later.
†Excluding those made by season-ticket holders.

Source: PP: Railway Returns, Census Returns, Tramway Returns

journeys never corresponds to the number of individuals making them – anyone travelling out and back in a day makes two journeys but remains one person; and that, from the 1860s onwards, the total of these journeys is a good deal understated because they exclude season-ticket holders.*

As we should expect, the number of these journeys increased very rapidly in 1850–80, during which time the railway system grew in length by over 150%; much more slowly in 1880–1910, when the corresponding growth was only a little over 25%. Nevertheless the change that comes over the figures at 1880 is startling; the percentage increase in the number of journeys per head of the population drops from 63.2 to 22.1 in 1880–90. A large part of the cause is indicated by a new figure appearing in col. 11. After the passing of the Tramways Act in 1870 street tramways in towns and their suburbs

*It was impossible to reckon precisely the numbers of journeys made by season-ticket holders: for two reasons, both arising from the nature of season tickets themselves. These tickets were not given up at the end of their journeys, so they could not be counted, as ordinary tickets were; and since most season tickets conferred the right to travel as many times as the holders chose, no exact computation can be made of the number of journeys for which they were used in the course of a year. The railways and the Board of Trade, when they wished to indicate an approximate total of season-ticket holders' journeys, credited each of them with 300 double journeys a year: i.e. a year of 365 days, less 57 Sundays and public holidays, together with a week's holiday in the summer. But that multiplier was probably too high, making no allowance for failure to travel owing to illness or for the practice – common among the wealthier holders of these tickets – of using them on less than six days in the week.

multiplied fast. This is the first point in the table where the growth of their traffic can be observed. Already by 1880 the number of passenger journeys made on them was a quarter of that made on railways. By 1890 it was more than half, almost 90% by 1900. These trams were, with few exceptions, horse-drawn. With electrification in the first decade of the new century came the trams' greatest burst of all. By 1910 more than twice as many journeys were being made on them as on the railways, whose system was nearly eight times as large as theirs.

We have unfortunately no comparable figure for the traffic carried by buses, whether horse-drawn or mechanically-operated, for the country as a whole. In London, however, it was estimated in 1907 that they conveyed 330 million passengers, against the trams' 590 million; the underground railways were then carrying 280 million.[42]

Adding all these figures together and adjusting them, partly by guesswork, it appears likely that in 1910 the total number of passenger journeys made in Great Britain by public transport – train, tram, bus, and coastal steamer – approached 5000 million a year; about 120 per head of the population. The railways' share of this traffic, which in the 1850s and 1860s must have been a good deal more than half, was now only just over a quarter.

There will be more to say about these figures presently, when they come to be compared with those for other countries in the world.

The Mobility of Labour

'Whatever improvement in communication will enable the poor man ... to carry his labour, perhaps the only valuable property he possesses, to the best market, and where it is most wanted, must be a decided advantage, not only to him but to the community at large.' That is Peel, speaking at Tamworth in 1835, in support of the plan for the Birmingham & Derby Junction Railway.[43]

Movement of labour was not itself new. The laws of settlement, designed to keep workers within their parishes, had been increasingly disregarded in the eighteenth century.[44] They prevented no one from making use of railways when they arrived; the deterrents lay only in the difficulties of learning about other work and of finding the money for the fare, or else facing the trudge to it on foot.

The early 1840s were years of high unemployment, which provided a strong incentive to the use of any form of cheap transport to places where work might be found. Much was to be had in connection with the railways themselves. By May 1847 there were 264,000 men employed in building and running them in Britain (over 4% of all occupied males).[45] Most of the navvies arrived at their first jobs on foot, and when they moved to others, they tramped again. These men, the makers of the original railway system, were little aided by it themselves. Where the lines were driven through rural districts the navvies were to a large extent agricultural workers, recruited locally and therefore needing no transport.[46]

The railways facilitated the pursuit of alternative work. The usual tendency of migrating labour was to move over short distances, sometimes stage by stage.[47] But the part played by railways here came to be remarked on in later years with some emphasis. In 1893, for example, it was observed that the decrease of population in the rural Midlands had first become apparent in districts close to the London & North Western Railway line.[48] Cecil Torr, reading his grandfather's diaries, found this entry for 25 January 1846: 'Agricultural labourers are very scarce: most of the young and able-bodied are gone on the railways'. That observation was made in south Devon, where wages in agriculture were especially low. Looking back seventy years afterwards, with his experienced historian's eye, Torr added: 'I fancy this displacement of labour had more effect on wages and employment than the change from Protection to Free Trade'.[49] A few years later another historian, looking at migration, made a more sweeping comment: 'From the rapidity with which its effects were felt all over the country the transition to railway transport probably deserves the name of 'revolution' better than any other aspect of economic development in the eighteenth and nineteenth centuries'.[50]

When, in January 1842, the Board of Trade wished to form some estimate of the number of poor people who had moved about by public transport on roads before the arrival of railways, it addressed itself to the Poor Law Commission, asking what use such travellers had made of carts and wagon services – evidently assuming that the poor never travelled by coach. The reply stated that the Commission had not felt the need to inquire into the matter.[51] It undertook to seek for some information, however, and that was printed two years later.[52] We cannot learn much from it; only that the poor used such services where they were available and could be afforded, and that for the rest they walked.

Most of the larger railway companies began by conveying only first and second-class passengers; but several of them soon felt obliged to provide some kind of accommodation at cheaper rates. The Great Western agreed to allow a contractor to convey some 'persons in the lower stations of life' by goods trains in 1839 and started carrying them on its own account in the following year.[53] The London & Birmingham may have been acting similarly as early as 1838, and was doing so without doubt by the beginning of 1841.[54]

The risks of conveying such passengers in low-sided open goods trucks were exemplified in an accident at Sonning on the Great Western line in December 1841, and the Board of Trade then quickly investigated the conditions under which these people were travelling on railways throughout the country. Its findings revealed a great variety of practice. One important generalization emerged, however: that most of the railways in the industrial districts of northern England and Scotland were carrying third-class passengers in large numbers, and considered that profitable. Nearly all the northern lines provided for it, and some (alarmed no doubt by the fall in their traffic during the recession of 1842) saw this new *clientèle* as a useful source of revenue for the future.

Who were these third-class passengers? There was frequent complaint in the 1830s and 1840s that people who could well afford to travel first or second class were travelling third. Whishaw was 'astonished to see several most respectably dressed persons' riding in the open wagons of the London & Blackwall Railway, which were 'intended especially for those who cannot afford better accommodation'.[55] 'The most wealthy and influential merchants of Glasgow' frequently arrived, we are told, at the station in their own carriages and then travelled to Greenock standing up.[56] To counter such deplorable practices, one of the millionaire Crawshay dynasty was said to have suggested to the Great Western company that it should 'hire *sweeps* to travel in their third-class carriages to scare intruders'.[57]

It was impossible to prevent passengers from making their own choice in this matter; and third-class carriages continued to be used for short journeys by all sorts of people. Good sense was talked here by Capt. M. L. Laws, general manager of the Manchester & Leeds Railway. He allowed that in fair weather 'respectable tradespeople, clerks, etc.' travelled third-class, but added that the great majority of third-class passengers were 'strictly the working classes, weavers, masons, bricklayers, carpenters, mechanics, and labourers of every description, some of whom used formerly to travel by carts but the greater number on foot'.[58]

When the House of Commons attempted to frame some general legislation concerning railways early in 1844, the proper management of third-class travel was brought before it. The Liverpool & Manchester Railway had not yet come to provide any such accommodation whatever. At the other extreme, third-class passengers comprised 68.9% of the total number carried by the Manchester & Leeds in the year 1842–3. On the railway system of Great Britain as a whole the proportion of third-class travelling had then risen to 27.4%.[59]

The provisions of the ensuing Regulation Act that were concerned with cheap travel went into force on 1 November 1844. Although they did not bind companies that were already established, almost all found it expedient to provide penny-a-mile trains at once. A strong inducement was given them to do so, through exempting the fares paid by travellers in trains run in accordance with the Act from the 5% passenger tax that had been levied on all railway fares since 1842.[60] This provided the government with a weapon in its hands for coercing the companies: if they ignored the Act, they would lose the benefit of the remission. It has not been recognized that, by forgoing this revenue, the government made a positive contribution, out of public funds, to promoting the growth of cheaper railway travel in Britain.[61]

In the first complete year during which these new arrangements were in force, that ending on 30 June 1846, the returns[62] show that, out of 40 million passenger journeys made in Great Britain, almost 10% were in the new 'Parliamentary' trains. The Act unquestionably stimulated a very large growth of cheap travelling: the 27.4% of third-class journeys made in 1842–3 had become 32.1% in 1845–6, and to them were now to be added 9.8% in respect of the new Parliamentary traffic. That is to say, taking the two categories together, that railway travel at the cheapest rates had increased by half in two years. By 1850 a majority of the passenger journeys in Great Britain were being made at a penny a mile or less.[63] Thereafter the process went on steadily, almost without interruption. By 1875 the proportion of these journeys had grown from half to more than three-quarters (77.9%). In 1913 it was 96%.

If we repeat the question asked before, 'Who *were* these penny-a-mile passengers?' the answers to it must now be somewhat different.

After 1850 we do not hear much about well-to-do persons who travelled by cheap trains. Some economically-minded business men must certainly have gone on putting up with a little discomfort on short journeys in order to save a shilling or two a week. But such men would have been most unlikely to use any of the long-distance Parliamentary trains. Two sixteen-hour journeys from London to Liverpool and back would not have been acceptable to them when each could be made, by travelling second class, in six.

The growth in leisure travel – much of it, though not all, at very cheap rates – continued. Cheap movement of this kind should not, however, be thought of entirely in terms of excursions, or indeed of holiday-making. The arrangements for such travelling must have been made use of in large measure for visiting relatives and transacting family business.

The main cause of the strongly-continued increase in the volume of cheap travel was clearly the movement of labour, arising from normal employment and the quest for new work; from travelling involved by the transfer of work from one place to another; from resettlement and permanent migration.

The daily journey to and from work is so important that it must be treated on its own, in the next section of this chapter. But certain kinds of employment had always been, by their very nature, mobile themselves. Strolling players and musicians moved from one district to another, from inn to inn. Hawkers and pedlars did the same. At a higher level stood the bagmen, the representatives of manufacturers and merchants soliciting orders, who were now spoken of under the grander appellation of 'commercial travellers'. The daily tasks these men performed were profoundly changed by the railway and its comrade the telegraph. The numbers of orders they handled came to be greatly increased, and their own numbers grew in consequence: by the 1880s half-a-dozen of these travellers employed by a single London house might be in one town at the same time.[64] The extension of railways did much to simplify and improve the conditions in which these men worked, oiling the wheels of trade.

The growth in scale of business management often involved the amalgamation of small units into larger ones, with a single headquarters in London or one of the great cities or with 'divisions' based on two or more widely-separated districts. In the later Victorian age a large dispersal of production went forward, sections of it being conducted not in town centres, where property was expensive, but in small towns, in suburbs or rural districts.[65] Sydney

Smith's cry, 'distance is abolished', seemed now to have been amply justified. Multiple stores proliferated, the London banks absorbed others in the provinces, great steel companies could straddle Britain from Glasgow to Birmingham, from South Wales to North Lincolnshire.[66] Without the railway system no such organization as this could have been made to work. With it, the unceasing communication between one unit of a large company and another, and the steady movement of its employees to and fro, became a matter of ordinary arrangement.

The railway companies themselves afforded perhaps the most conspicuous example of this process. They repeatedly transferred large bodies of their employees from one centre of their business to another. It happened first in 1843, when the Grand Junction company removed its main workshops from Edgehill, outside Liverpool, to Crewe, building houses there to accommodate the men and their families – some 800 people in all. Ten years later the Great Northern did the same thing, taking its repair shops and the 900 men employed in them away from Boston to Doncaster.[67] Much the biggest of all these re-arrangements was the Great Western company's concentration of a large part of the building and repair of its locomotives and rolling stock at Swindon from 1874 onwards, with transfers from Saltney outside Chester, from Wolverhampton and Worcester. Its scale was not immediately apparent because the move was carried out by stages; but the census of 1881 revealed that the town's population had increased over the past ten years by 70% and ascribed it specifically to this cause.[68] The North Eastern company's decision to concentrate all its main locomotive work at Darlington, implemented in 1905–10, involved the migration of substantial numbers of men there from Gateshead and York.[69]

Once it had taken a man into its service, a railway company might switch him from one part of its system to another, and the careers of some railway servants involved constant removal. This practice could be the cause of much anguish. Here is Archelaus Hodges, a garrulously articulate clerk on the Taff Vale Railway, pleading against a removal from Cardiff to Merthyr in 1846: 'I have six small and *expensive* children and wife to maintain. The *expense* and *infinite* trouble I have been put to in moving down the line is what I really cannot afford again'. If the decision to remove him is maintained, he says, he will prefer to resign.[70] In the 1860s the transference of stationmasters and clerks to other posts elsewhere became, on some railways, a steadily-maintained practice. In 1862 the London & South Western company, for example, was moving one in five of them every year; later in the same decade the Brighton company was moving clerks at the same rate, though stationmasters only half as frequently.[71] On the Great Western H. A. Simmons held seven posts in succession at different places, as clerk or stationmaster, in 1861–7, and six of these removals had to be made over substantial distances.[72] True, he was an awkward customer, a perpetual complainant; but that can hardly have been the sole or even the main reason for these frequent transfers, for he was then left undisturbed for eight years in the important post of stationmaster at

Windsor. Removal might represent a penalty, a transfer on account of some misdemeanour to another post. But it was often desired, and applied for if it seemed to afford a chance of promotion.

On the other hand there are plenty of records of men who remained for an extremely long time in the same place. William Chadband, for instance, a signalman Acworth conversed with, still at work when he was near eighty, had passed the whole of his service with the London & South Western Railway at Nine Elms and Waterloo.[73] The companies always kept their options open. Where one of their employees was doing his work satisfactorily and showed no desire to move, he might be left in his post for many years. This applied particularly to stationmasters, for a good one, liked and respected in the community his station served, could be a valuable asset to the company. E. D. Chapman, appointed stationmaster at Blackheath on the South Eastern Railway in 1850, stayed there until 1898, retiring then on full pay in token of his employers' appreciation. They had good cause to feel it. The grossly bad services the company provided had been constantly under fire from aggrieved passengers, but they seem never to have directed their wrath against Chapman, who remained the one element in the railway that they trusted. So there could be immobility in the railway service too, and that might show wisdom on the part of those who managed it.[74] It is especially important to remember that here, where railways are treated mainly as disturbers, promoters of movement.

Their efforts of that sort were carefully confined to their own proper interests and to the duties laid upon them by government, above all in the running of workmen's trains around London and the great cities. It was not their business to promote movement as a social service. They might be willing to collaborate in such an activity, however, when asked for their assistance, as they were in east Devon in the 1870s by Canon Girdlestone, set on organizing the migration of the ill-paid and ill-housed labourers in his parish.[75] There were two goals here, alternatives: removal to other districts in northern England, where wages were better; and emigration out of the island altogether. The railways played a part in both movements.

In 1852 the London & South Western company energetically sought to secure a government contract for the conveyance of emigrants to Southampton and won it, providing not only trains but also a depot for accommodating these people in transit in London.[76] In 1859–63, when Brassey and his partners were engaged in the construction of railways in Australia, they organized the transport of 2000 experienced navvies from England and Scotland.[77] The companies' part in the business went on developing throughout the island down to 1914: carrying on the already ancient tradition in the Scottish Highlands,[78] with the decline of the iron-ore industry in Cumberland at the beginning of the new century providing through carriages for emigrants from Whitehaven to Southampton every Friday night.[79]

The emigrants whom the British railways conveyed were by no means wholly British. Many of those leaving Germany, Scandinavia, and Russia for the United States from the 1850s onwards made part of their journey across

England by train from Hull to Liverpool, sometimes to be re-forwarded in another train from Liverpool to Southampton.[80] The traffic grew, and a station was built to handle it at the Alexandra Dock in Hull; special rolling stock was provided for it by the North Eastern Railway in 1907. In the three summer months of 1913 the little Midland & South Western Junction Railway carried nearly 3000 such emigrants to Southampton.[81]

These people were all crossing the Atlantic. Many British emigrants were doing the same; and a large number were on their way to South Africa, to Australia and New Zealand. Their journeys were long, often involving considerable hardship. But there was another, far larger group of British railway passengers whose journeys, little discussed so far, were entirely different: not migrants, still less emigrants; men and women committed not to one long journey but to as many as 600 short ones every year. Let us now turn to look at these people, the commuters.

The Daily Journey to Work

Railways did much to encourage people living in the vicinity of large towns to move daily on the same journey to and from their work, usually from suburbs into the towns' centres though here and there – notably in Glasgow – in the opposite direction.[82] They began to address themselves to this business in the 1830s in Glasgow, London, and Newcastle (in that order).[83]

Most of the early trunk railways ignored or discouraged such traffic, providing stations only at long intervals apart and services that hardly suited the convenience of travellers of this kind. They had been built almost wholly for the purpose of conveying long-distance traffic, which would have been impeded by frequent trains stopping at numerous, closely-spaced stations. Moreover, little traffic of this sort offered itself as yet. There was no substantial settlement, for example, anywhere along the line of the London & Birmingham Railway between Camden Town and Harrow. The first of these companies to move into suburban business deliberately was the London & South Western, which in the 1840s promoted or encouraged branch lines that poured traffic on to it from established outer communities like Richmond.

TABLE 10

PASSENGER TRAFFIC ON THREE SUBURBAN RAILWAYS, 1843–4

	London & Blackwall			London & Greenwich			Newcastle & North Shields		
	Number of passengers carried	Passenger revenue	Pence per head	Passengers	Revenue	Pence	Passengers	Revenue	Pence
		£	d		£	d		£	d
1843	2460550	41160	4	1551048	40993	6.4	805363	15750	4.7
1844	3452288	49136	3.4	2085582	44845	5.2	854922	15944	4.5

Source: Railway Returns

The early development of some suburban business can be glimpsed from the returns made for the years 1843 and 1844[84] by three small independent companies whose business was confined to suburbs; two in London and one on Tyneside.[85] On each line the traffic increased (on the London & Blackwall by 40%) and the revenue per head fell; a growing number of passengers were travelling at the cheapest rates. Not all of them were moving about in connection with their daily work. The Blackwall line conveyed a considerable number to and from ships at the docks. All of them had a large holiday traffic in summer.

Ten years later it becomes possible to observe this growth more clearly, over the whole country, in a different way: through the companies' widespread issue of season tickets, which first figured in any credible form in their returns to the Board of Trade for the year 1853. This device for those who wished to make frequent and regular journeys had been introduced by the London steamboats[86] and was taken up to a small extent by certain railways in the 1830s and 1840s.

We think now of the holders of season tickets as daily travellers to and from their places of employment between suburb and town centre. But these tickets were bought in the Victorian age by different kinds of people too: by commercial travellers over their wide-ranging journeys, for example, and by others who made use of them over long distances.[87] The total number of such people can never have been large, however, nor the aggregate distances of the journeys they made significant as a proportion of all that were undertaken by those who purchased these tickets. We shall not be exaggerating seriously if we consider all season-ticket holders as commuters. But by no means all commuters held season tickets. Many might, for various reasons, pay ordinary fares. Millions used other forms of transport for the purpose, especially the trams after 1870. Other millions walked: 'Victorian towns were predominantly places for walking, not for riding, for legs not for wheels'.[88]

The number of season tickets issued increased in the 1850s very gradually. New suburban railways were now at work – the North London, for instance, the Manchester South Junction & Altrincham, the Liverpool Crosby & Southport. New stations were opened: fourteen were added south of the Thames within eight miles of the London termini.[89] Those additions were small, pointing to a slow growth in the numbers of people who travelled to work by train. There is however some evidence of an increasing public interest in the business. In June 1851 for example the town clerk of Reading wrote to the Great Western Railway asking it to issue season tickets between his town and London. The board replied that it would consider extending them beyond Maidenhead (to which place they were already available) at some later date. The town clerk then wrote again, and got what he wanted in February 1852, when the board agreed to offer first and second-class tickets at annual rates, for the 36-mile journey, of £50 and £36 respectively.[90] This request would hardly have been persisted in without some clear demand from the town itself.

A number of railways now began to encourage the building of new houses along their lines, to be occupied by people who would travel by them to and from their work. Some companies offered to give the householders season tickets for a limited period of time; sprats to catch mackerels. The London & North Western, for example, did that at Alderley, south of Manchester, as early as 1846.[91] The contractors Brassey Peto & Betts, who were closely involved with the London Tilbury & Southend Railway and worked it, arranged that season tickets to London should be 'included in the rent paid by occupiers' of their houses.[92] At Bishops Stortford the Conservative Land Society did a deal with the Great Eastern company, by which it granted such people cheap first-class season tickets for seven years.[93] In Scotland the North British Railway offered a Line Residence Ticket at a favourable rate to anyone building a house near its lines at distances over eight miles from Edinburgh. One of the holders sued the company for £5000 because it changed the traction on the North Berwick branch, which he used for travelling to and from his business in Edinburgh, from steam to horse power. The case went to the Court of Session and was very properly dismissed there, with costs against him, in 1859.[94]

The demand for season tickets grew faster after 1860, not only in and around London but in the provinces too. In 1860–75 the number of them issued on the Manchester South Junction & Altrincham Railway doubled; on the Lancashire & Yorkshire it multiplied six times over, on the North Eastern eight times. But they were seldom offered to third-class passengers.

In these years the journey to work in London made its first appearance in a novel form: the workmen's train, one provided by compulsion, under statute, at specially low fares for travelling early in the morning, to return in the evening.[95] It was designed to afford some compensation to those whom the railways had dispossessed of their homes as their lines were extended towards the centres of cities; to provide an inducement to them to move further out and to travel in to their work at an exceptionally cheap price. When the idea was first carried into effect in 1864–5, it was hailed with relief as a means of solving the grave social problem to which it was directed. But that view was soon shown to be optimistic, even laughed at as simple-minded; and in the end the real value of workmen's trains came to be perhaps too much depreciated.[96]

It was often pointed out that the number of workmen's trains the companies came to run far exceeded that which was statutorily required of them, and the inference was drawn that these trains must pay, or they would not be provided. But the statement is misleading. Although in 1903 the total number of these trains 'required by Special Acts' was twelve, and the actual number run was 1067, those Acts had been virtually superseded by the Cheap Trains Act of 1883, which laid it down that these trains were to run to whatever extent the Board of Trade required, under a fiscal penalty.[97] The companies emphasized that unless the trains were well filled they did not pay. C. H. Parkes, chairman of the Great Eastern Railway, was quite specific, telling its shareholders in 1891 that 'supposing there are 500 passengers in the train, then it pays'.[98] The last words of that statement were sometimes dishonestly quoted without the preceding qualification, in support of those who argued that these trains were in fact profitable.

Just as the railways were beginning to develop this kind of traffic with some success, they found themselves confronted by a new competitor: the horse-worked street tramway, introduced into Britain in 1859–62 and soon working with fair success in Birkenhead, Liverpool, and the Potteries, as well as in London for a year, ending for a time in failure. The tramway was a railway laid along a public street, and the competitor it fought first was the bus. In that conflict it enjoyed two great advantages: in the reduced rolling resistance its iron wheels set up, running on iron rails, compared with those of the bus on stone-paved streets; and in the larger body that those wheels could support. A pair of horses was able to haul a tramcar weighing twice as much as a bus and carrying almost twice as many passengers. On the other hand, the laying-down of lines for the tramway frequently encountered opposition from the local authorities in charge of the streets they traversed.

A general Tramways Act was passed in 1870, allowing local authorities to forbid the construction of tramways absolutely in any or all of their streets and giving them the right to purchase the tramways after twenty-one years. Many people now saw railways as a wastefully expensive form of transport, and the much cheaper tramways found a warm welcome, extended not only from prospective investors but also from prospective customers. Jack Plane may stand as their spokesman, writing to the *Builder* in 1871 to say that he had abandoned workmen's trains in disgust at the effort to get a place in them, walking to work instead, and that he and his friends now looked forward to trams as a great improvement on railways. The editor of the paper, George Godwin, showed sympathy with him.[99]

The trams enjoyed other advantages too. They ran along the public streets and stopped at numerous points to pick up and set down passengers, whereas trains called only at their fixed stations. Moreover, tramways were much cheaper to construct than railways: their equipment was lighter and far less elaborate (they required, for example, no signalling), and they did not have to purchase their own land. Hence they were able to carry their passengers at fares well below the railways'. Five years after the passing of the Act almost as many passenger journeys were being made on the trams in London as on the vehicles of the General bus company,[100] and more than half as many as on the North London and the two underground railways put together.

Though the London tramway system came by 1883 to extend ten miles outwards to the north, east, and west,[101] its cars could not compete with the trains in speed. Nor were the trams allowed to penetrate so close to the centre as the railways with their stations at Cannon Street, Holborn Viaduct, and Charing Cross. In conveying passengers to work over distances greater than seven or eight miles, the railways clearly held their own. So clearly that some of the large companies still made little effort to develop their suburban traffic, either in London or in the great provincial cities.[102]

[327]

We should hesitate before describing such inaction as evidence of a merely complacent attitude, of the companies' feeling that they could wait to develop this business until some time in the future when they could undertake it conveniently. The steady growth of passenger and freight traffic, which continued with few interruptions, meant that, more than ever before, the presence of frequently-stopping suburban trains on trunk lines was unwelcome. The only remedy lay in doubling the tracks from two to four, and that (with new station buildings, sidings, and other equipment) was expensive. This need was met very slowly. It took twenty years (1859–79) to complete the enlargement of the London & North Western line from Camden Town to Bletchley (45 miles); ten (1875–84) to get the Great Western's four tracks over the 23 miles from Paddington to Maidenhead bridge. As for the cost, in 1882–3 the Great Northern had to raise £869,000 for quadrupling the eight miles of line (traversing five tunnels) from Wood Green to Potters Bar. In this case the chairman justified the expenditure primarily on the grounds of the company's 'enormous suburban traffic'.[103] The number of its suburban passengers, he said, had increased in 1867–81 from 1.7 million a year to 12.9 million, the revenue they produced to the company from £39,000 to £195,000.[104]

It would be unwise to lean heavily on such figures as these, produced in order to justify the expenditure of money. But they open up another way of measuring the growth of the business: in terms of the revenue that season tickets brought in. In the last quarter of the nineteenth century it trebled in Great Britain. By 1913 it represented (together with that from workmen's tickets) almost one-seventh of the total receipts from passengers.

TABLE 11

REVENUE FROM SEASON AND WORKMEN'S TICKETS
IN GREAT BRITAIN 1875–1913

	Season or Periodical tickets	*Season tickets*	*Workmen's tickets*	*Total*	*Proportion of total revenue from passengers*
	£000	£000	£000	£000	%
1875	1110	..	..	1110	5.2
1880	1409	..	..	1409	6.2
1890	2259	..	..	2259	8.1
1900	3383	..	..	3383	9.3
1913	..	4773	1665	6438	14.2

Source: Railway Returns

So, however troublesome it might be to some companies to convey passengers on their daily journey to work, that had to be treated seriously for the contribution it made to their income.

The comfort of those who made these journeys came to vary widely, from the opulence of the under-filled trains of the Great Central lines into London[105] to the packed overcrowding on the Great Eastern (to be illustrated later) and the provision made by the South Eastern & Chatham, which was the worst of all.[106] Many of that company's carriages were dilapidated, and crammed far too tightly with passengers. The trains were notorious for their unpunctuality: in strong contrast to those of the Great Eastern, which kept admirable time on their journeys. We have silent evidence of the South Eastern & Chatham's treatment of its commuters in that the number of third-class season tickets it issued was lower, in proportion to the whole, than on any other important line in England. The company's management no doubt rubbed its hands with cynical pleasure; but its suburban services had become a public scandal. The war delayed the passengers' relief until electrification arrived in 1925–8.

Elsewhere we can observe some levelling-up of standards in the years before 1914. Much new rolling stock was now built expressly for suburban services, some of it of high quality. The Midland Railway provided sets of bogie carriages for work around Leeds, Bradford, and Manchester in 1900–2. They afforded seating, all together, for 12,000 passengers.[107] That represented a massive exercise in re-equipment, plainly a response to the current electrification of the tramways in those cities. The Midland had not been among the leaders in the suburban business. Yet its revenue from season and workmen's tickets amounted to 8.1% of all it received from passengers in 1900. By 1911 that figure had become 10.3%; by 1913 – after the purchase of the Tilbury company – it had reached 14.7%.

But the greatest improvement in service arose from the railways' own electrification. It was introduced first in Liverpool and Newcastle in 1903–4, and then arrived in London with the tube railways, and with the conversion of the underground Metropolitan and District Railways in 1905; that of a group of lines on the Brighton and South Western systems followed in 1909–15. None of the daily travellers by train in Glasgow or Birmingham benefited from it, however, none in Manchester until 1916.

The electric trams' business now grew even more spectacularly than the horse trams' had done in the preceding decades. By 1910 over twice as many passenger journeys were being undertaken on them as on the railways. The growth showed itself everywhere in and around the great cities, where the competition between trains and trams was at its fiercest.[108] For the first time since 1830 the railways were now seen clearly to be in retreat; closing down passenger services, in Glasgow for instance and in north-east London, because the trams had rendered them hopelessly unremunerative. Where the trams' pressure was weak or absent, however, the railways could still do excellent business.

One suburban railway flourished in the early years of the twentieth century, the London Tilbury & Southend; and that indeed flourished exceedingly. In 1907–11, the last five years of its independent life, the annual number of passenger journeys made over it averaged 30 million, besides those of 10,000 holders of season tickets (another 6 million, calculated by the usual guesswork), and it was steadily rising.[109] The company's business was principally with the conveyance of suburban passengers from Southend and the other dormitory settlements adjoining it to London. The growth of that is attributable largely to its own astute and energetic management; but also to the absence of any serious competition from electric trams except at the inner end of the line, from Barking westwards. The London Traffic Branch of the Board of Trade rightly seized on that as a principal explanation of its achievement, unique at this time among all the suburban railways in Britain.[110]

Looking back over the railways' efforts to develop and ease the carriage of suburban passengers, we can observe in it three elements of success, partial or complete: in the scale on which they could operate, in their penetration of city centres underground, and in their speed, steadily increasing the distances over which they could handle this traffic effectively.

Steamboats had been doing well before the railways arrived, but only for half the year or less, and only on routes that lay along river estuaries. They were of little interest to Londoners who lived in Islington or Peckham; they had almost nothing to offer to people living in Birmingham or Leeds. Short-stage coaches and the horse-buses were very small units, capable of little enlargement, and the multiplication of them helped to cram the streets, in competition with other traffic. The railways did not have to face the veto of street authorities. They could be made to go wherever they chose; and the streets they forged for themselves with their rails were their own, to be used as they determined. The scale of their work appeared capable of almost infinite enlargement. The railways became in Victorian Britain – what they remain still – unequalled movers of people in large numbers at a good steady speed.

These huge people-movers found the means of thrusting their way very close into the centre of cities, and did so in nearly all the greatest, in London, Birmingham, Liverpool, Edinburgh, and Glasgow. True, their success in Manchester was very incomplete, and they failed entirely in Sheffield.[111] But those were skirmishes lost, to be set against battles that were won. As buses and trams converged on central districts they either stopped short (trams were forbidden to run in the centre of London) or moved at walking pace over the long last stage of their journey. The trains' pace below the streets of London and Glasgow remained the same as in the open suburbs, lowered solely by the number of stations at which they had to stop. They also provided cross-city services – from Clapham Common to Golders Green in London, from Airdrie underneath the centre of Glasgow to Maryhill and Clydebank – that might become important in the future. The through service over the 80 miles between Bedford and Gatwick Airport that British Rail introduced in 1987 made use of an intricate succession of lines, completed in 1839–78. So the railways' urban and suburban services proved almost infinitely extendible, as megalopolis grew.

And finally there was the factor of speed, playing on distance. The maximum length of the journeys that wealthy business men were prepared to take by train – daily, or at least several times a week – greatly increased. Some went to live far beyond the outermost rim of suburbs: merchants from Bradford at Grassington, from Glasgow in the Tinto Hills. There was commuting to

Manchester from Windermere (a journey 80 miles long), to London from Bournemouth (108 miles).[112] H. G. Wells's prophecy of a 100-mile radius from London, made in 1902, now became perfectly credible.[113]

Such services as those concerned only a very small number of commuters, of a special kind. But they showed the differences that the journey to work, now made practicable by railways, had made. Moving down the scale of wealth, we can observe many people who were very far from rich beginning to appreciate that the railways were now opening up to them an entirely new range of choice. Something very different from Brickfield Terrace, Holloway, was now being offered to the next generation of Pooters. Several railway companies saw opportunities here in the early years of the new century, with publicity directed towards showing the houses – many of them quite modest, but all with their own gardens – that were now being built along their lines to attract commuters, associated with season-ticket rates of 4d–6d a day.[114] A number published elaborate magazines given up to describing and advertising them in detail – the Great Central's quarterly *The Homestead*, for example, and the Great Northern's *Where to Live*.

The Metropolitan company went a good deal further, becoming a suburban property developer itself. Alone among British railways it secured the power (through a nominally separate company) to exploit the 'surplus lands' it bought, beyond what were required for working trains. It began to go earnestly into the business at Willesden Green from 1880 onwards. In 1901–12 houses went up on estates it had acquired further out, at Pinner in the foothills of the Chilterns. The foundations had been laid for the company's zealous and profitable development of 'Metroland' in the years between the wars.[115]

In all these activities around London the railways enjoyed one conspicuous advantage over the electric trams: the much higher speed they could attain, running on their own tracks, allowing them to bring people in and out of the city on daily journeys of no unreasonable length at a moderate cost. As the new tramway systems grew, different estimates came to be made of the radius from the centre of London within which their services had the advantage of the railways'. In 1909 the London & North Western company reckoned it at 12 miles and that was accepted by the Board of Trade.[116] In Greater London the radius did not subsequently increase, though it did in Greater Glasgow, where the tramway system was still being extended in the 1930s.

So the railway enlarged megalopolis, both as an accomplished fact and as an agency of development in the future, and offered many city-dwellers the chance of adopting a life they came to like much better than the one they had lived before in close-packed urban streets. But it must, on the other hand, be recognized that the conditions under which very many of these people travelled were horrible. Even in first and second-class carriages the lighting was exiguous, and few of the carriages were heated before 1900. Third-class passengers may hardly have noticed such defects, overwhelmed by another, much more pressing.

A large number of these trains were hideously over-filled. Not all; not those running into Paddington or St Pancras, for example, nor the Metropolitan trains into Baker Street; and not on some of the earliest trains before the main body of travellers had arrived to use them. But on the rest the passengers endured great miseries, both in boarding the trains at intermediate stations, when they were crowded as they came in, and from the tightly-packed company and the atmosphere it engendered when they had succeeded in getting on to them. We have plenty of evidence of these things: evidence of the passengers' daily struggles, evidence of mere numbers. It must be remembered that except on the tubes and on the other underground railways after 1905 every carriage used on these services was divided into compartments. Each held ten or twelve passengers seated and whatever additional number could be accommodated standing (on the Walthamstow line it was accepted that boys travelled in the luggage racks), to make up to thirty occupants in a compartment altogether.[117]

This was not the only new form of mobility developed by the railways that succeeded beyond their calculations, until it grew difficult to control. But the fear of competition led them to obstruct or destroy palliative measures that might have enabled this traffic to be carried better. The Great Eastern company, faced with three projects for tube railways through north-east London in 1901–5, opposed them all fiercely. The first two were rejected by Parliament, and the third failed to find financial support. So tube trains did not come in to ease the journey to work there until 1946–9.[118] The Great Northern, groaning under what it called the 'incubus' of its suburban traffic, showed some favour to plans for extending tube railways into its territory from central London; but it then turned against them and stopped their advance beyond Finsbury Park.[119]

By 1914 the railways had come to afford the dwellers in great cities a considerably enlarged measure of choice, in their work and in the ways in which they fashioned their lives around it. The new suburbs gave many of them opportunities and pleasures they had never dreamt of before.

The railways did less for those who lived nearer the centres, in the suburbs developed during the nineteenth century; less than the trams and buses, though still a good deal. In the eastern districts of London both north and south of the Thames, their business was largest and, given the constricting limits within which it was carried, much the most difficult to handle. The majority of those who came into and out of Liverpool Street by the cheap trains must simply have stuck out the journey with stoicism as a dismal necessity that occupied an hour of every week-day. For some of them, however – the ailing, the ageing, the imaginative – it must have been a constantly-recurring nightmare: taking us to the fringes of the world depicted in the novels of Gissing and Arthur Morrison, in the agonized poems of John Davidson.

The Liberation of Women

In the later Victorian age it began to be observed that railways were helping to produce a change in the lives and habits of women.

The publication of John Stuart Mill's *Subjection of Women* in 1869, with the ridicule and intense antagonism it aroused, brought those lives and habits more than ever before into public discussion. From that time onwards the debate was never silent. It canalized itself partly into the demand for the alteration of the franchise, to allow women to vote at Parliamentary elections, which became prominent in 1908–14. But well before that time, over the last forty years of the nineteenth century, it was generally appreciated that the position of women in British society had undergone great changes, and that they were quickening: through the enlargement of their education, for example, and the widening opportunities for employment that now opened up before them. The effects of these changes were much debated. A good many people attributed the differences they noticed here largely to the development of railways, easing all conditions of travel and offering opportunities to many people – women included – who had never felt able to travel before. That was a simple fact of the times, and sensible people accepted it, whether or not they liked the conclusions to which it pointed.

Before the Victorian age most women were unable to move about when and where they wished, unimpeded by the wills of others. Only the very rich were independent, widows who could take with them what servants they chose, determined wives with large fortunes settled on them at marriage; and the number of such people was very small. No upper-class women travelled alone in any coach. Most went with their husbands or relied on some other male relative to see them through the complications and dangers that might arise on the journey. However kind their escorts might be, they were bound to recognize their own state of dependence. Jane Austen made frequent journeys between Hampshire and Kent in the opening years of the nineteenth century. They had always to be arranged to suit the convenience of at least one other person (usually one of her brothers), and she had to hope 'not to be obliged to be an encumbrance'.[120]

Well-mannered men made as light of this kind of duty as possible, and when railways began to reduce the need for it, some of the elderly still wished to see the practice maintained. Hearing in 1848 that his eldest son was going to allow his wife to make a journey by railway to London and then another on to Windsor by herself, Wellington remarked: 'I do not like to see her treated otherwise than as if she was worth taking care of!'[121] But the voice of progress was already against him. The *Quarterly Review* observed with approval in 1844 that railways had brought about 'the emancipation of the fair sex, and particularly of the middle and higher classes, from the prohibition from travelling in public carriages, which with the majority was a prohibition from travelling at all'.[122]

On American trains there were 'ladies' cars'. Dickens, who approved of little that he observed on his railway journeys there in 1842, commented favourably on the polite behaviour of American male travellers in this respect: 'any lady may travel alone from one end of the United States to the other,' he wrote, 'and be certain of the most courteous and considerate treatment everywhere'.[123] The vehicles used on American railways were open from end to end, which encouraged that kind of conduct. The division of British carriages into small compartments had the opposite effect. By 1845 some companies were marking selected compartments 'Ladies Only'.[124] Presently a demand appeared that such accommodation should be compulsorily provided on all trains.[125] That would have been quite impracticable, however. The companies usually offered ladies' compartments on their long-distance trains, some even on crowded suburban trains too. Moreover, in general they tried to see that the label on the compartment meant what it said.[126] When in 1887 a notorious case of assault drew public attention to this matter, the Board of Trade inquired into the companies' practices in providing such accommodation. Most of them did so, either under a standard rule or on request; but many also said that, when provided, these special compartments were very little used.[127]

The railways had a double problem here, which was insoluble. The dangers from which they tried to protect their women passengers were subtly advertised by each 'Ladies Only' label on the window of a compartment; and the cases of assault in railway trains that appeared before the courts – some of them very dubious – encouraged blackmail. In 1866 *Punch* supported the allocation of 'distinct carriages for unattended females', but only on condition that they should be forbidden to travel in any other: this on account of 'the dangers of extortion to which male passengers singly are exposed'. Many men echoed its sentiments.[128] When there was a crop of further cases in the 1890s, they gave rise to the same reflections.[129]

Nevertheless, such cases were uncommon. They made good salacious news when published, and yet the total number recorded in newspapers seems to be insignificant, looked at against the numbers of journeys women were making in trains by this time. There is clear evidence that those numbers were beginning to grow: from the increasing employment of women in jobs that demanded daily travelling, from pictures, and from written records. At Liverpool Street station, for example, the Great Eastern company made special provision in its waiting rooms for women arriving before 7 am, off the cheapest workmen's trains, and the rector of All Hallows-on-the-Wall opened his church to them too.[130]

There were still not many such travellers. In 1851–81 the number of women clerks returned at the census for the whole country rose from nineteen to 7000. Ten years later it was 22,000; in 1911, 146,000. The great majority of these women must have been employed in offices in the larger towns, above all in London, where many certainly went to and from their work daily by train.

This is only one kind of women's employment that the railways directly assisted. Another example may be taken, as far removed from it in every sense as it well could be. The huge growth of the fishing industry in the later Victorian age, in which the railways played a large part, called for many kinds of specialized labour. Most of it was provided by men and women who lived on the spot, in the ports. But not all: there were seasonal demands, and demands for particular sorts of experience. It was a regular practice for women in eastern Scotland, familiar with the herring business, to take work at the English ports in the gutting and curing of the fish, travelling down and back by train. They went from Buckie, for example, to Lowestoft, the journey lasting nearly twenty-four hours. This annual migration was large and certain enough to justify the Great North of Scotland company in arranging a through fare, at not much above $\frac{1}{2}$d a mile, and in printing special tickets for the journey. So both for the typist travelling six miles every weekday from Walthamstow to London and for the fisher girl going more than 600 from Banffshire to Suffolk once a year, the railway figured essentially in her budget.

The railways also came to be employers of women themselves, though not on any large scale before 1914. The Census Commissioners reckoned that in 1911 the companies had 7170 women in their service, making up 1.3% of their total labour force.[131] Women were to be found in specialist trades within the companies' own shops, particularly in carriage work. Some kept level-crossing gates. The stationmistress was not unknown, though she was rare enough to be pointed to as someone special. Mrs Argyle looked after the whole business of Merrylees station for the Leicester & Swannington and later the Midland Railways (including the signals) most competently from 1832 to 1871.[132] At St Harmons in Radnorshire Kilvert noticed one in 1876; Mrs Huxley had charge of Braceborough Spa station (Lincolnshire).[133]

Female booking clerks are heard of as early as 1858 – three of them, at Edinburgh.[134] By the 1880s the London & North Western company had 130 women in its service in the accounts departments of its larger goods stations.[135] The most widespread employment of them in any business connected with the operation of railways was in telegraph offices, and later at telephone switchboards, where their quickness and manual dexterity were valued, both by the railways and by the telegraph and telephone companies.[136] (They were of course engaged at lower rates of pay than those given to men.) Even in this specialized employment, however, some railways were very slow to take women into their service. The Great Western did not decide to do so until 1908.[137] There were no women clerks engaged at the Railway Clearing House before 1912. The Great Central company had only seventy in 1914.[138]

There were some other divisions of the railways' work in which women always had a place. At passenger stations they were necessary as attendants in ladies' waiting rooms. The Great Western appointed its first woman, Mary Coulsell, to take charge of the one at Paddington ten days before the railway was opened for public traffic in 1838.[139] They were called for in larger numbers for everything to do with the preparation and serving of refreshments. In *what* numbers it is quite impossible to say, for the majority of them were engaged not by the railways but by the contractors who undertook their refreshment business, and they are therefore not entered among the companies' servants but lost in the censuses' broad categories of domestic service. Even the enumerators' books, so far as they are available to be consulted, help us here very little, since the enumerations always took place on a Sunday, the entirely untypical day in all work connected with railways. Here and there we are given an exact figure for the staff employed. Sir Francis Head for instance shows an establishment of twenty-eight in the refreshment room at Wolverton in 1849, sixteen women, twelve men and boys.[140] That was a large staff, as it must have been also at the big junctions, where nearly all kinds of refreshments (including full meals) had to be served in great haste to passengers changing trains or stopping on long journeys to dine, for the regulation twenty or thirty minutes. The same impossibilities of accurate rendering apply to the staff of the railway companies' hotels, of which a substantial proportion – perhaps the greater part – comprised women, employed as clerks, waitresses, and chambermaids, as well as in kitchens and laundries.

Only one general statement can be made with certainty: that railways created a considerable new demand for the employment of women in such branches of domestic service as these and began in the later years of the Victorian age to find work for them elsewhere in their business. But the second of those processes was slow, until it was greatly accelerated by the war of 1914–18.

In a wider sense the railways contributed to lessening the differences that had always been felt between one sex and the other. Apart from the provision of separate waiting rooms for men and women passengers, the one conspicuous attempt they made to discriminate between the sexes – in reserving a small part of the accommodation in their trains for women – was more of a gesture than a useful expedient. In all other respects railways brought men and women together. Trains and stations were convenient places of meeting, by chance or by design, and the two sexes had equal rights on the railway. Among the numerous differences the railway lessened, none was more apparent than this one, more generally taken for granted.

Here is what Foxwell – a strong though never uncritical progressive – meant when he wrote of women in 1888: 'Compare the portentousness of a hundred-miles' journey for a girl last century with the ridiculous ease of travel now, and we see how they cannot bask in the new freedom without tingling to assert their own individuality'.[141] The 'ease of travel' that the railway supplied was an essential element in the claims that many of them were then putting forward; in fact, and no less in idea, a symbol of liberation.

New Movement in Wales

The new opportunity to move that the railways offered was seized on strikingly in Wales. That was remarked on again and again, from different points of view.

Before the Monmouthshire company decided to undertake the reconstruction of its lines in the Western Valleys, to make them fit to carry a regular passenger traffic, the idea had been discussed of establishing services to and from Newport by means of a single horse-drawn coach, which might perhaps have conveyed twenty or thirty people a day. By 1854, when the railway service was fully at work, the number of passengers it was carrying daily up and down those valleys was nearly 1000. 'Standing at the station entrance at the arrival of a train', one writer noted, 'the passengers are so numerous and crushing that the wondering exclamation as they emerge from the train is "Where do they all come from?"' [142] By 1870 that daily average of passengers had trebled.

In 1864 a more sophisticated spectator, Matthew Arnold, wrote after a train journey in North Wales, through the quiet country from Llanrwst to Llandudno: 'the people travelling about in Wales, and their quality, beggar description. It is a social revolution which is taking place, and to observe it may well fill one with reflection'.[143] Since the line had been opened only the year before, it still had the attraction of novelty; and doubtless some of the people travelling were visitors from outside Wales. Nevertheless the traffic was there, as never in the past, and the impression it made was evidently very strong. Similar remarks have been passed continually down to recent times. As he surveyed the passengers at Paddington station, John Betjeman remarked on the 'large contingent of South Welsh, who seem to be always travelling in trains'.[144]

How is this to be explained?

In 1841 the largest town in Wales was Merthyr Tydvil, with a population of 35,000. The next three, Swansea, Newport, and Cardiff (in that order), were not, taken all together, as big as Paisley. When they grew later in the century, it was they alone; there have never been any large towns in Wales north of these. All the towns of the south-east were awkward to reach by road down the narrow, twisting valleys from the coalfields, and the public passenger services on them were insignificant. Along the coast the steamers ran infrequently, except in summer.

The mechanically-operated railways that began to be opened there from 1840 onwards to serve the iron and coal industries came to form a system unlike that anywhere else in Britain, except in some degree around Glasgow, running down the valleys from the coalfields to the sea, and occasionally crossing from one valley to another, in competitive profusion. The district bounded by Blaenrhondda, Brynmawr, Pontypool, and Barry comprised an area approximately 25 miles square, in which there were 500 miles of railway carrying regular passenger services by 1913. H. S. Jevons believed this to be a greater length of line than was to be found in 'any other area of the same size chosen in any part of the world, except possibly London, with its tubes',[145] and he may well have been right.

The business of these lines came to be, above all, the carriage of coal. The passenger service shown in the public timetables was frequent on many of them. But that was by no means the whole service that was offered. Here, to an extent found nowhere else in Britain, the collieries secured trains run for their employees under contract with the railway companies and over their tracks, not open to ordinary passengers.[146] Since these services were never advertised, they could be altered at the coalowners' request. As mines became exhausted, or inconvenient to work, the miners could be transferred to another pit and their conveyance switched accordingly without any need for them to find new houses. When seeking to open up a fresh district, a colliery could often get a train service of this kind provided. If permanent new settlements grew up along the railway line the railway might substitute a regular public service for it. Exactly that pattern of development appeared down the Cynon valley from Aberdare to Mountain Ash and Navigation House (Abercynon today) between 1846 and 1902.[147] This system could also ease the stresses created by great changes of employment. When the iron industry at the head of the valleys began crumbling in the late 1870s in favour of the steel manufacture further south, the iron workers were taken daily by contract trains from their established homes, for instance in Tredegar, to work in collieries down the Sirhowy valley.[148] These Welsh companies showed a lively willingness to discontinue old services and provide new ones in their place; all the greater perhaps because they were small corporations, locally financed and sensitive to local needs, besides being intensely competitive. Here was an enterprising flexibility.

The railways encouraged an exceptional movement of labour in south-east Wales. As time went on the effects of that inevitably extended, in the minds of the men travelling to and from their daily work and of their families too. They could now leave their shut-in mining villages, to take a pleasure excursion for a day, to travel in order to see relatives (family ties in Wales were always particularly close), or to leave home for good.

Wales came to have three trunk lines only, all running east and west. Two were taken along the coasts, promoted under the aegis of English companies seeking to establish connections with Ireland. The third, crossing the middle of the country, remained poor. All the lines that ran north and south were poor too: they traversed a difficult terrain, serving thinly-peopled districts. A modern Welsh historian remarks that railways 'were largely designed to link the various parts of Wales with the markets and urban centres of England, rather than with each other. Progress from north Wales to the far south was almost as laborious still as it had been for George Borrow.... In general, transport and the communications network served to divide the Welsh people still further'.[149] That hardly does the railways justice. Before they arrived, there had been not one stage-coach service from north to south Wales.[150] By the 1880s the railways had made it possible to travel from Bangor to Cardiff, from Wrexham or Newtown to Swansea; slowly, and with changes of train, yet well within the compass of a single day. They provided facilities for movement here that were quite new. Unfortunately we cannot tell how many people took advantage of them.

It was an accident of nature that the most valuable resources of the country, its slate and its minerals, lay close to the north and south coasts, and that four-fifths of its whole area, away from the sea, comprised not very rich farmland that afforded pasture for sheep alone, or no profitable sustenance at all. There was very little economic inducement for railways to traverse the country from north to south, and those that did so – the Mid-Wales, for example, and the line from Carmarthen to Aberystwyth – had a stiff struggle to keep going, until in the end larger companies took them over.

The one trunk railway that crossed the centre of Wales from east to west, the Cambrian, remained an independent corporation until 1922, but much of its business came to it from the English North Western and Great Western companies. On the other hand many of the small country railways, the quiet branches, were entirely Welsh, home-spun; built as a result of great struggles by men of the locality, for the locality.[151] Few of these railways were in any sense by-products of the rivalry of the big companies, as their counterparts were apt to be in Scotland. They came to form part of the very bone of the rural communities they served and were used accordingly. The communities were too small to make them pay. They held on nevertheless, bringing traffic down to the main line from remote places in the hills: the Corris line, the Talyllyn, the Glyn Valley. When they died, worn out with their financial struggles, they might be resurrected – the Van and the Mawddwy Railways for instance in 1896 and 1911. There was still work for them to do, and until the development of motor services after 1918 there was no one else to do it.

The population of rural Wales always remained very sparse. The Cambrian company's three principal lines and the Central Wales line of the London & North Western were each of them 60–80 miles long, with big gaps between market towns. The roads were hilly and poor; there was less scope for carriers' services than there was in England. The extra trains on Tuesdays to Newtown market and on Thursdays to Knighton gave a facility beyond the competition of horse-drawn carts.

Only one of these railways represented a speculation: the Aberystwyth & Welsh Coast, promoted by Thomas Savin of Oswestry, which aimed at the development of resorts along the whole northern shore of Cardigan Bay and was associated with the building of hotels and other ancillary enterprises. But though much of that ambitious scheme collapsed in the financial *débâcle* of 1866, the railway itself was carried through with a spirited tenacity to its completion to Pwllheli in the following year. The first wild dreams (for example, of making Aberdovey 'equal to Portsmouth')[152] vanished, and the building development that ensued was quite modest; but it had a windfall with the injection of capital at Towyn (amassed in England, in the Worcestershire salt industry), and the coast put itself firmly on the map of Late-Victorian holiday-making.

Something similar had already been happening for some time on the coast of North Wales, but there the scale of the business grew to be very much bigger. In this district too the fixed population of the towns did not become great – Llandudno, the largest of them, had less than 10,000 residents in 1901; but the excursionists brought by train along the coast were much more numerous, drawn from the great industrial districts not far away to the east. The Cardigan Bay railway could not have looked at handling the 182 passenger trains taken into and out of Llandudno station on the Saturday and Monday of the August Bank Holiday of 1888, and Barmouth would certainly not have known how to deal with their 21,000 passengers.[153] But then neither would it have wished to do so. On both these coasts the resorts were small, numerous, and highly competitive with one another. They were also different: the northern ones more popular (in both senses of the word), those on Cardigan Bay quieter and cheaper. The trains brought both the larger and the smaller armies of holiday-makers to them annually, to the great economic benefit of that large tract of country, in which coal was hardly to be found west of Denbighshire.

Horse transport had been much less improved in Wales than it had since the seventeenth century in richer – and flatter – England. Suddenly, from 1840 onwards, railways confronted Welshmen with wholly new opportunities to move, never dreamt of in the past and seized on now with enthusiasm. And at the same time the railways also ministered intelligently to the passion for movement that Welshmen discerned in their English neighbours.

Some International Comparisons

Railways on the mainland of Europe developed a little later than in Britain, and more slowly at first. In the 1830s and early 1840s they engaged British engineers and technicians to work for them, and they imported rails and locomotives from Britain in substantial quantity. On the Prussian lines 88% of the rails were British in 1843. Two years later the Dowlais ironworks alone were producing nearly half as much bar-iron as all the Prussian manufacturers together. In 1853 half the firms that had supplied rails in use throughout Germany were British; more specifically, most of them were Welsh.[154] But by that time the Germans were taking over the business themselves. Though they had gone to Britain for locomotives at first, by 1853 the proportion of British machines in service on their railways was under 18%.[155] Much the same happened in Belgium and France. British locomotive manufacturers continued building for Continental railways – notably for the Dutch, down to the 1880s and beyond; but their export business now came to be mainly concerned with countries outside Europe.

In early days a fair number of visitors from the Continent arrived, either on purpose to examine the British railways or at least willing to travel on them and report at home what they had observed. But as their own railways got going their interest in these prototypes decreased. Moreover, theirs were managed differently from those in Britain. Nowhere on the mainland of Europe did a national system of competitive private railways grow up, as it did in Britain and the United States. It became increasingly hard to make useful comparisons between the railway system of Britain and any of those on the Continent. Some French and German writers on technology and on public law turned their attention to them: Perdonnet, Franqueville, and Malézieux; Schwabe and Gustav Cohn. But in all the diligent studies they produced we can observe the underlying consciousness of difference, of the alien character of the British railways and of the thinking that had made them what they were.

The British system was much closer to the American: based on the free play of private enterprise, with the power of government over the railways even weaker in the United States, though – as in Britain – starting to grow stronger in the 1880s. But the development of American and British railways had, from the outset, shown some differences, arising quite as much from physical differences in the countries themselves and in the two societies as from the legal systems under which they were administered. As they looked at British railways, the smallness of everything in the island naturally struck most Americans more than anything else. What possible comparison could there be between their railway system, beginning to reach across the whole continent by 1869, from New York to San Francisco, and one in which the longest possible journey extended over the 900 miles from the little town of Wick to the little town of Penzance? The small scale struck them everywhere: most obviously in the size of the British companies' engines, their ludicrous carriages and the pathetically diminutive wagons that carried their freight traffic. Only a few American observers came to appreciate the merits these railways had to show, even to suggest that here and there they might offer lessons worth learning.

Altogether, the British railways remained a tight enclave – shut in, as it were, by the sea; not observed very much from outside, and appearing to many of those who did look at them antiquated and incomprehensible.

One peculiarity, however, could hardly fail to be noticed by a visitor in the later Victorian age whose eyes and mind were alert: the extraordinary bustle of travelling, of railway business of all sorts, the frequency of the service of trains on the main lines – expresses, little short-distance trains, the unending procession of coal trains. The railways might appear to be strangely managed; but they were obviously carrying a very great deal of traffic. Anyone who chose to inquire would find it was steadily growing, and that substantial sums of money were being spent on the enlargement of existing facilities in order to cope with that growth.

The increase of traffic in early days, when the system was expanding at its fastest, had been very rapid. During the 1850s the numbers of passenger journeys made in the island doubled. The rates of growth then settled down at lower levels. Passenger journeys multiplied by a quarter in the 1880s and well over a third in the 1890s; in 1900–13 – even with the electric trams' competition in full blast – by 28%.[156]

The statistical evidence does not allow a satisfactory comparison to be made, over the whole period 1850–1913, between these increases and those that occurred on the railways in Europe. No entirely reliable figures seem to be available for railways throughout Germany until 1888. But two positive statements can be made.

The first is well known: that whilst the construction of mechanically-worked railways had started sooner in Britain and was carried forward there with much greater energy than in any Continental country in 1830–50, the lead she enjoyed over her neighbours was steadily reduced in the years that followed. When the German Empire was created in 1871, its railway system almost exactly equalled Great Britain's in length; by 1914 it was nearly twice as large. The French system, substantially smaller in 1871, was larger than the British by over 25% in 1914. Everywhere on the mainland of Europe the railways were still then extending on a large scale – except in Belgium, where the system had been laid down, as in Britain, very early.

The second statement, though it was made over 100 years ago, has never received the attention it merits. J. S. Jeans, using figures compiled by 'an international Statistical Commission composed of leading railway and statistical authorities in every country in Continental Europe', came out with the assertion that in 1882–3 the number of passenger journeys on the railways of the United Kingdom was 'in excess of that of all the rest of Europe put together'. On the basis of those figures, he stated the number of journeys made every year per head of the population as 19 in the United Kingdom (23.2 in Great Britain), in Belgium (where the figure was greater than in any other European country) as 9.3, and in the United States as 5.4.[157]

TABLE 12

PASSENGER JOURNEYS MADE ON THE RAILWAYS OF GREAT BRITAIN AND NORTH-WESTERN EUROPE, 1861–1911

The years are those in which the census was taken in each country. The table shows the numbers of journeys made there per head of the population.

	Great Britain	France	Belgium	Netherlands	Germany
1861	7.1	1.7	—	—	—
1866	—	—	2.4	—	—
1871	13.8	—	—	—	—
1872	—	3.1	—	—	—
1879	—	—	—	3.3	—
1880	—	—	10.2	—	—
1881	20.5	4.8	—	—	—
1889	—	—	—	4.3	—
1890	—	—	13.6	—	8.6
1891	24.9	6.7	—	—	—
1899	—	—	—	5.5	—
1900	—	—	20.8	—	15.2
1901	31.0	10.7	—	—	—
1909	—	—	—	7.4	—
1910	—	—	26.0	—	23.7
1911	31.7	12.6	—	—	—

Based on B. R. Mitchell, *European Historical Statistics* (2nd ed., 1981), 30–4, 611–12, 629–34.

These margins of difference are striking. The figures are open to some criticisms.[158] But though not corroborated they are, broadly, endorsed by those that the best modern authority offers us.[159] They are summarized in Table 12. Much could be said about them. Jeans himself pointed out that 'the United Kingdom . . . differs from most other countries in respect of the average distance over which each passenger is carried. There is, however, no standard by which we can test the average length of each passenger journey on British railways, owing to the absence of any record of the passenger mileage'. Still, with all necessary regard to the imperfect and incomplete nature of our information we can be sure that a much larger number of passenger journeys was being made in Victorian Britain than in any other country. The difference was in fact larger still, for these figures all exclude the journeys made by season-ticket holders. When in 1913 it becomes possible for the first time to see in some convincing terms how numerous those journeys were in Britain, it appears that in that year they increased the total by some 25%.

What accounts for this unique intensity of movement?

Some of the main causes of it have appeared here already: the abundant – sometimes over-abundant – provision of services that the competing companies

TABLE 13

LARGE TOWNS IN GREAT BRITAIN AND NORTH-WESTERN EUROPE,
1861–1911

The table refers to towns of 100,000 people and more and shows the percentage of the population of each country that these towns contained.

	Great Britain	France	Belgium	Netherlands	Germany
1861	23.9	7.7	—	—	—
1866	—	—	8.1	—	—
1871	25.7	—	—	—	4.8
1872	—	9.1	—	—	—
1879	—	—	—	14.4	—
1880	—	—	10.6	—	7.2
1881	29.2	10.5	—	—	—
1889	—	—	—	17.0	—
1890	—	—	11.5	—	12.1
1891	31.4	11.5	—	—	—
1899	—	—	—	22.4	—
1900	—	—	11.6	—	16.2
1901	34.9	14.0	—	—	—
1909	—	—	—	23.4	—
1910	—	—	11.0	—	21.3
1911	37.0	14.8	—	—	—

Based on P. Flora and others, *State, Economy, and Society in Western Europe* (1985–7), ii. 66-7, 253–80.

offered; the early decisions of some managers to foster third-class travel (when that policy was to be seen hardly anywhere on the Continent except in Belgium), prevailing over the reluctance of others to become an accepted practice over the whole system by the 1880s; the lavish concession of still cheaper forms of travel. The nature of the island itself stimulated much travelling, to the sea and to the hills, so easily and quickly reached.

Many of the social arrangements that emerged in Victorian Britain made in the same direction too. Its great cities grew to become greater in their aggregate population, and to contain a much larger number of people than in any other country during the nineteenth century. That is illustrated in Table 13, by comparisons with north-western Europe. It is a matter especially important here: for these cities were centres of the railway network, steadily enlarged by competition. Eight of the principal companies converged on London. Of the twelve largest provincial cities, only Newcastle was served by one company alone. Every one of them generated its own suburban traffic, vast in London, but not inconsiderable even in the smallest of the other twelve cities. Sixty such trains ran into Nottingham before 10 o'clock every weekday morning in 1914.

One other factor entered clearly into this exceptional propensity for movement. Travelling cost money and took time. There were rather more of both those commodities in Britain than on the mainland of Europe: a generally higher standard of wages and a shorter working week; by 1914 a growing disposition on the part of employers to concede holidays with pay. These things expressed themselves in the increasing use of railways to service leisure. Holiday-making, in all its varieties, clearly did much to swell the totals of British passenger journeys; a great deal more than it did anywhere else.

These are all elements in the explanation of the mobility generated by the railway in Britain. Taken together, they may not be thought decisive. But the mobility itself, and its peculiar intensity, remain beyond denial. Some of the consequences it led to have been indicated already. Others will be suggested at the conclusion of this book.

15

UNIFORMITY AND DIFFERENCE

Standard Time · The Materials and Design of Buildings ·
Food and Drink · Localities · Class Distinctions ·
The Power of Government

As they looked at the freedom of movement that the railways had brought, reflecting on the changes it had produced in the character of their lives and in the conduct of business, some Victorians laid stress on the increased uniformity that, as they believed, the railway had imposed on them. In 1870 Disraeli made his Lord St Jerome say: 'I used to think when I was a boy that I lived in the prettiest village in the world, but these railroads have so changed everything that Vauxe seems to me only a second town house'.[1] When T. A. Trollope (the novelist's eldest brother) cast his mind back in 1887 to the Brittany he had known in 1840, the judgment he expressed was applicable equally to Brittany and Britain. 'The people and their mode of life', he wrote, 'the country and its specialities, have all been utterly changed by the pleasant, indispensable, abominable railway, which in its merciless irresistible tramp across the world crushes into a dead level of uninteresting uniformity so many varieties of character, manners, and peculiarities.'[2]

Let us consider three ways in which quite new kinds of uniformity were undoubtedly introduced by railways, one as a matter of deliberate choice, the other two less directly and less completely.

Standard Time

Until the 1780s it was accepted without question that time differed as one moved east or west. There was twelve minutes' difference between the time in London and Liverpool; almost half an hour's between that in Yarmouth and Penzance. But these differences were unimportant, for nobody moved fast enough to notice them at all sharply or to be troubled by them. The establishment of the mail-coach services from 1784 onwards first brought them out. The maintenance of punctuality in them was complicated by the differences of time to be found on every route that lay east or west of London. But they appeared then to be unalterable. Local time must still prevail over London time.[3]

[345]

The opening of the trunk railway lines, however, soon effected a change in thinking. The South Western and the Great Western resolved to keep London time at all their stations, announcing their decisions to do so in 1840. The practices of other companies differed. At Rugby the London & North Western observed local time and the Midland, branching out of it to Leeds, had adopted London time. As the railways grew towards forming a national system it became clear that nothing would do for them but one standard of time everywhere. Henry Booth, secretary of the Liverpool & Manchester Railway, was a strong advocate of uniformity. His company petitioned Parliament to establish one standard time in 1845. He himself wrote a pamphlet in support of the change, observing that 'there is sublimity in the idea of a whole nation stirred by one impulse, in every arrangement one common signal regulating the movements of a mighty people!'[4] Dickens alluded to the matter in *his* way, remarking of Camden Town that 'there was even railway time observed in clocks, as if the sun itself had given in'.[5]

The Railway Clearing House now passed a resolution recommending all its member companies to adopt Greenwich time. Local prejudice remained strong, however, here and there. In North Wales for example the Chester & Holyhead company regulated the clocks at its stations by the Craig-y-Don gun ($16\frac{1}{2}$ minutes after Greenwich time); a special absurdity in this case because that railway's prime purpose was to carry traffic to and from Ireland, and the newly-instituted Irish Mail train took its time from Greenwich.

The Royal Observatory soon formed a partnership with the South Eastern Railway for the transmission of time signals by means of a specially-constructed telegraph line from Greenwich to Lewisham station, which was brought into use in 1852. It enabled time signals to be sent from the Observatory along the lines of most of the chief railways, as their telegraph installations came to be completed. A submarine telegraph cable had been successfully laid from Dover to Calais in the autumn of the previous year, and that opened up the possibility of extended communication with the Continent. So Brussels was connected with the Observatory in this way in 1853, and Paris in 1854.

Greenwich time was welcomed by most railway companies, in Scotland as well as in England. It was also accepted by nearly all the principal cities. Some malcontent voices were heard. In 1851 'railway-time aggression' was attacked in *Chambers' Journal* as a 'dangerous innovation';[6] there was some desultory correspondence in *The Times*, for and against, in October of that year. The only determined hostility to its introduction arose in the West Country, and there a spirited battle took place between traditionalists and innovators at Bristol, Exeter, and Plymouth.[7] It reached its conclusion, with the victory of standard time over local, when the Dean of Exeter directed that the cathedral clock should be put on fourteen minutes on 2 November 1852 – the day after the first time-signals had begun to arrive from Greenwich by the recently-completed telegraph, running beside the railway.

That event marks the effective establishment of a single time system for almost the whole of England.[8] The notion grew at once to be a commonplace.

In a trivial farce written for the London stage in 1853 a character speaks of the railway as 'the leviathan regulator of the clockwork of society'.[9] But there had been no legislation in the matter, which left uniformity of time debatable in the courts. A case at Dorchester assizes in 1858 came to turn on the difference between local and Greenwich time, and on appeal it was held that local time must prevail. At length the Statutes (Definition of Time) Act laid it down in 1880 that Greenwich time was to be observed throughout Great Britain.[10]

Apart from the Liverpool & Manchester, the railways did little to demand the adoption of standard time, though it was on an initiative of the Lancashire & Yorkshire company that Manchester Town Council was persuaded to make the change in 1847.[11] As their timetables grew important in ordinary life, so their dictation in this matter came to be accepted.[12] On the South Wales Railway in the 1850s all station clocks were wound up once a week by a clockmaker's assistant, who took each in turn, east of Swansea on Mondays, westwards on Tuesdays.[13] On the Border Counties section of the North British Railway it was laid down in 1861 that this regulation should be undertaken daily by the guard of the first train.[14]

At the same time that company gave instructions for the use of the timepieces it entrusted to its guards. Some railways expected their other servants to provide them at their own expense. Accidents sometimes arose from ignorance of the time. That was a factor in four occurring in 1856, and the companies were then urged to supply their men with clocks and watches. In 1870 the London & North Western was still being criticized for failing to do so.[15] A new market now opened up to the makers of timepieces, to be put into the hands of railwaymen, erected in signal-boxes and at stations. Joyce of Whitchurch in Shropshire, Bell of Lancaster, and others – the makers displayed their names on one platform after another. William Avison of York produced a handsome bracket clock in 1849 bearing on the dial-plate in bold letters the words 'Railway Time'. It finds a place now, quite rightly, in the National Railway Museum.

Some of these clocks were erected by the railway companies outside their stations or on towers above them. There were several on the great stations in London,[16] and they appeared widely in the provinces: at Eastbourne, for example, Leicester, Shrewsbury, Manchester, Sunderland, and Dundee. It was not a mere accident of taste that the erection of a public clock came to be a fashionable civic gesture from about 1850 onwards. What made the idea seem useful but the new consciousness of time that the railways had brought, the need to have it fixed precisely? In the 1830s it had been observed that, owing to them, people were beginning to 'reckon distances by hours and minutes'.[17] Some business men took to using the language of the timetable in ordinary speech: 'train tomorrow morning at 7.25', says Disraeli's Mr Head of Stalybridge, 'get a fly at the station and you will be at Millbank by 8.40'.[18] The railways enforced a new observance of punctuality. Through them the clock came to guide – even to rule – lives as it never had before.

The Materials and Design of Buildings

Railways did much to promote the distribution of building materials that were suited to large-scale production, and that helped to encourage certain kinds of uniformity in buildings for domestic and commercial use.

They evolved standard designs for those they erected themselves. Something similar had already been done, in a small way, by government, central and local, in the construction of barracks, dockyards, prisons, and workhouses, but no commercial organization had ever attempted anything like it on a comparable scale before.* The companies' practice in this matter shows both the imposition of uniformity and the retention – here and there, even the encouragement – of difference.

The early steam-worked railways made use of materials from local sources. The Liverpool & Manchester was fortunate in passing close to Rainhill, where a good sandstone was quarried. Though the Sankey viaduct was originally intended to have been built of stone throughout, the railway company decided to make the piers of brick, cladding them with masonry, and to establish for this purpose brickworks on Newton Common that could also supply bricks for another shorter bridge to the east.[19]

Whishaw frequently mentions the materials that went into bridges and other works, sometimes recording the sources from which they came; seldom at any distance from the railways that used them, though the London & Brighton selected Heddon stone from near Newcastle for dressings on its brick bridges and imported limestone from France for the balustrade and the eight pavilions on the Ouse viaduct.[20] The stones Whishaw refers to, local to the railways themselves, include some that were famous: those from Gatherley, Newbiggin, and Longridge in northern England, from Craigleith and Giffnock in Scotland.[21]

The early trunk line that has been least altered in Britain, the Newcastle & Carlisle, still displays in its bridges and other works a series of the building stones quarried near its route: carboniferous on the eastern side in Northumberland, red sandstone in Cumbria. The change in the stone from buff or grey to red, even rose-pink, shows clearly on the railway very close to the boundary between the two counties.

There were some districts (such as East Anglia) where no suitable building materials were available, or where other materials imported from a distance were less expensive than those to be had on the spot. The railways called for brick nearly everywhere in England and Wales – though it was not always cheaper than stone.[22] One particular variety found a special place in railway work: the blue engineering bricks from south Staffordshire. They made their way at first in the Midlands, as what might be considered a local material: on the Trent Valley line for its bridges; in the low-level station at Wolver-

---

*The cottages provided for gatekeepers by turnpike trusts and for lock-keepers by canal companies were often built to standard designs. But their systems were much less extensive than the railways'.

hampton some years later, blue bricks being used there for the whole structure. In many of the railways' early tunnels the common bricks they were lined with scaled and crumbled under the dripping of water. These blue bricks proved satisfactorily resistant and they were employed to an increasing extent both in the building of new tunnels and in re-lining old ones.

Large concentrations of brickworks grew up beside the railways' lines, near Peterborough and Bedford for example, and at Bletchley. Though there was water transport in the first of those districts, it was inadequate; it was not available in any satisfactory form in either of the others. All the main groups of brickworks here were established before motor vehicles were available on roads.[23] The production developed in them called for massive bulk transport, which railways alone could offer. Where production was on a smaller scale, however, bricks might continue to be manufactured prosperously even when no rail transport was available at all.[24]

The railways often made special use of bricks from these rail-connected works. The reds of the coal measures, of Accrington, Ruabon, and Bristol, were used for stations and other buildings on the lines that traversed their districts, above all those of the Lancashire & Yorkshire and the Great Western. They went extensively into house-building too. Hideous in colour, hard and shiny in their texture, they overpower every place in which they are used. They are among the most repulsive endowments owed by the country to the railways.

One great company manufactured its own bricks: the London & North Western at Crewe. In 1861 John Ramsbottom told his directors that he could make bricks at a price a third less than the company was paying. Production began in the following year. By the 1880s the annual output reached 5 million.[25] These Crewe bricks were carried all over the company's system. Pink or pale red, gritty and rough, often banded with horizontal courses of vermilion, they were always readily distinguishable: in the cottages the North Western built for its employees as well as in stations and signal-boxes across the country from Swansea and Holyhead to Leeds, from London to Carlisle.

There was another building material, not much less important than brick, which the railways played an important part in distributing throughout the Victorian age: slate for roofing, especially that produced in north-west Wales. The demand for it grew rapidly at the end of the eighteenth century in London. Most of the principal slate quarries there lay close to the sea, which made their products easy to transport; easier still as canals were opened taking the traffic, by way of the Mersey, far inland. The biggest groups of quarries commanded ports devoted to the handling of their business, notably Port Penrhyn and Portmadoc. Each of those two came to be served by a narrow-gauge railway from the quarries, the Penrhyn Railway, opened in 1801, and the Festiniog (1836);[26] but from the ports the slates reached their destinations by water.

The railways' breakthrough into the transport of slate over long distances came after the opening of the line along Cardigan Bay in 1867. The traffic by sea dwindled rapidly when standard-gauge railways began to penetrate the quarrying district itself in and around Festiniog in 1879–83. Up to 1867 the whole of the Festiniog slate was sent away from Portmadoc by ship; twenty years later only 72% went that way; by 1907, 46%.[27]

Welsh slate triumphed over all its rivals as an economical material. Visually that was regrettable, for it remained a dull substance: dull in colour (the purplish and grey tints always preponderated); dull because the lightness of slates allowed the pitch of roofs to be flattened;[28] dullest of all in texture because the slates were normally supplied in only one or two sizes, whereas most English slates were graded, the smallest being used at the ridge of the roof, the largest at the bottom. These roofs represented a depressing form of standardization, enormously extended by rail transport. But Welsh slates had sterling virtues in functional terms; they greatly cheapened the cost of adequate housing.[29]

It has sometimes been said that the railways, by their work in distributing mass-produced materials throughout the country, destroyed local vernacular building. But the railways did not begin that business, nor did they carry it through to its completion. The truth in this matter has been admirably expressed in a study of houses in rural Wales:

> Railway and canal did not completely solve the problem of distribution. The most characteristic factory-produced building material of the railway age was the red Ruabon brick, but it is never found very far from the station yard. It was the lorry, carrying its Peterborough brick and the concrete tile to the remotest mountain *cwm*, that by about 1930 had finally destroyed the economic basis of regional materials and ended the last vestiges of real regional architecture.[30]

The buildings the railways erected for their own use in early days exemplified both uniformity and difference. Tite had a real feeling for local materials, and showed it in his passenger stations. He used rich red brick with stone dressings in the Thames Valley, flint in north Hampshire, honey-coloured oolite in Dorset, red sandstone on the North Devon line. But the designs and plans of each set of his country stations had many features that were interchangeable. Mocatta, on the other hand, in his London & Brighton Railway stations, used no local materials at all. They were built of Suffolk brick, rendered, with York stone dressings and Welsh slate roofs. Yet again, Francis Thompson pursued variety as a delightful end in itself, further than any other architect employed by a railway (see p. 33).

The emergence of standardization, and also a slight resistance to it, was apparent on the Leicester–Hitchin line of the Midland Railway, built in 1853–7. Here the stations were closely similar in design, and they included common elements, in their window-framing and in the iron and glass canopies at the larger stations. But the station houses were built of different materials: Desborough in ironstone, Glendon in limestone, the rest in brick of different sorts. On the Midland's Settle & Carlisle line (1876) there was some variation still, but the general patterns were firmly established.[31] Standardization had triumphed.

That became obvious on the last long lines: the West Highland, opened in 1894; the Great Central's line to London and the North Cornwall's to Padstow, both completed in 1899. But the policies adopted by the three managements in this matter were different.

The West Highland Railway, 100 miles long from Craigendoran to Fort William, displayed standardization very thoroughly. In that remote, unpeopled country there were no vernacular buildings that could have influenced the railway's thinking at all. Since part of its purpose was to open up a new tract of the mountainous Highlands to tourism, and since many Victorian tourists associated mountains with Switzerland above all, it was natural to think of giving the buildings here some Swiss character. Charles Forman, the company's engineer, clothed that idea in a very pleasant form, designing eleven of the fifteen stations to a common plan with single island platforms carrying substantial buildings, well protected from the abundant Highland rain. They had the flavour of chalets; the roofs and walls were covered with shingles brought from Switzerland.[32] Here the railway was sensibly addressing itself to a special market.

On the Great Central line the use of standard designs and materials was pressed further than on any other trunk line in Britain. Over the 93 miles of this railway there were twenty-five passenger stations, all except two laid out to one basic plan. The most conspicuous materials used everywhere were Staffordshire blue bricks. Red commons were manufactured close to the line; some facing bricks came from Leicestershire, together with the terracotta used in decoration; but those were all the materials that were local. Cutting its great swath across the Midlands, the railway stood out as an alien, exemplifying standards and ideas evolved in Manchester, Sheffield, and London, scarcely at all in the country it traversed.

On the third of these lines, the North Cornwall running down to Padstow, the station buildings were closely similar to one another, but the materials in them were largely local. They were roofed in the agreeably variegated slate from Delabole, which came from quarries on the railway itself. They were of a piece with the plain, substantial houses that had gone up in the later Victorian age in Launceston and Camelford and the villages the railway served.

Food and Drink

It was frequently remarked by Victorians that railways were abolishing the differences in food and drink that had been found in different districts of Britain in the past. There was some truth in this commonplace, but the conclusions to be drawn from it may not be the same as those it seemed to suggest when they made it.

[351]

Improvements in transport were already lessening these differences before the railways came. Coaches had brought up new, unknown delicacies to tickle the palates of London. Stilton cheese, for example. The cheese had itself little to do with Stilton; most of it was made thirty miles and more away, in east Leicestershire. In the middle of the eighteenth century Cooper Thornhill, landlord of the Bell at Stilton, introduced it to the notice of his guests as they called in their coaches and carriages, travelling along the Great North Road.[33] They liked it, he took to selling it, and it bore the name of his village. So this cheese came to secure a high reputation at a great distance, with the aid of horse transport.

Canals played a more important part than roads in the transference of foodstuffs from one part of the country to another: salt, on a very large scale, from Cheshire and Worcestershire; grain, potatoes, and other root vegetables; butter and cheese, over shorter distances. Though they never took any large share in the provisioning of London, when their network was complete they were able to change the sources of supply of some other important markets, bringing flour from the eastern counties into Manchester, for instance, to displace what had previously come from Ireland.[34] The same sort of trade was being carried on by coastal shipping.

It was with the transport of fish to inland districts that the railways first made a clear mark on the distribution of foodstuffs. Before they got to work, fish was eaten in the large industrial towns by those who could afford to pay for its expensive carriage by coach; the Catholic poor could get it only dried, or in very inferior condition. All this now soon changed. By 1841 a Northern Fishery Company used a still-incomplete chain of railways to carry fish daily from Hartlepool to Leeds and Manchester.[35] In 1846 fish was being sold in Manchester, brought by railway from Hull, at a quarter of the price previously charged or less, and the quantity consumed had grown from three to eighty tons a week. In London the competition between rail and sea-borne fish soon brought prices down so low that the poor treated it as a staple of their diet.[36] In later years all inland towns came to expect large supplies of fish, brought by rail; and there was a clamour if it was not available early in the day.[37]

Railways also made early experiments with the conveyance of milk. Here the Liverpool & Manchester company was the pioneer, in 1832. By 1840 rail-borne milk was well established in both those towns; in 1850 the London & North Western company set up a milk market at Lime Street station in Liverpool.[38] It took longer to make its way in Birmingham, longer still in London. Though it could be brought in from the country faster than before, and over much greater distances, when it arrived it could not be as fresh as the milk supplied from cows kept within the towns themselves; and they were maintained in large numbers in the 1860s until the cattle plague led to an entire re-organization of the trade. There were difficulties in carrying milk by rail. It was often jolted severely *en route*, and time was needed to devise satisfactory cooling apparatus for use in summer. But these problems had been largely solved, and rail-borne milk now grew to be accepted. By 1880 it dominated the market in almost every large town. In 1910, 96% of the liquid milk consumed in London was brought in by rail.[39]

Here the town householder came to consume what was virtually a standard article. Instead of dealing with a milkman who kept perhaps five or ten cows, yielding a milk whose properties were known to him, he was now likely to be in the hands of a large company, pooling milk from many herds together: national concerns (the Express Dairy Company, United Dairies Ltd.), even international (Nestlé). A wholesale depot for the supply of London milk was established on the London & South Western Railway's Exeter line about 1871.[40]

Changes in the distribution of food and drink, arising from new railway services or the improvement of those already existing, sometimes produced startlingly rapid results. The inefficient Somerset & Dorset passed into the control of two big companies, the Midland and London & South Western, late in 1875. Almost at once the beer of Burton-on-Trent came to reach Exeter by this route. The traffic soon grew so large that 'three trains, carrying Burton beer alone, [were] all *stopped*, at one time', on the single line between Evercreech and Bath.[41] One of the new lessees, the Midland, was the leading railway established at Burton. Its canvassers would have lost no time in drawing the brewers' attention to the opportunities afforded for the carriage of traffic down into the West Country, opening it up to products widely recognized elsewhere under a name like Bass or Allsopp or Worthington.

The establishment of such standards was an important consequence of the railways' work, exemplified in most manufactured foods. It was not only a matter of quality and taste. It was also one of price. The railways made their comparisons of that themselves. In 1875 the North Eastern company gave instructions that the price-lists of local tradespeople submitted to its Zetland Hotel at Saltburn should be compared with those of the Civil Service Stores in London.[42]

Comparisons of that sort were soon being made more easily through a trading development, new to Britain, which was just then getting under way: the establishment of chains of retail shops, dealing chiefly in groceries but later in other goods too. The proprietors most conspicuously successful in the nineteenth century all started out with a single shop selling tea. One of them, Arthur Brooke, remained a tea dealer: his firm, Brooke Bond, handled no other commodity. The rest diversified. Thomas Lipton began to multiply his shops in Scotland in 1878, reaching London ten years later. H. E. Kearley and his partner G. A. Tonge established the International Stores about the same time, dealing at first in a wider range of groceries than his rivals; they had 200 branches by 1890. The Home and Colonial Stores, which Julius Drew established with one partner in 1885, were so brilliantly successful that in 1890 Drew was able to retire (a rich man only fifteen years after he had started out in the tea business), devoting much of the abundant energy of his later years to the creation of a great house, Castle Drogo in Devon.[43]

Though some of these enterprises concerned themselves with manufacturing, to a small extent, their main business was one of distribution; and it would have been unthinkable for them to embark on that then, without the service of railways. Their chief rivals here were the local co-operative stores. Those grew to depend in large measure on two great central organizations, the English and Scottish Co-operative Wholesale Societies, founded in 1863 and 1868; and their wholesale supply to the retail shops of the local societies depended vitally on railways too.[44]

When we take into account also the great development of the manufacture of goods known by their brand-names all over the island, like Bovril and Huntley & Palmer's biscuits, all distributed in the same way, we can see the railways underpinning in Late-Victorian Britain an enormous exercise in the standardization of foodstuffs, both in quality and in price.

In one matter concerning food the railways had an opportunity to render a service of their own that they deplorably missed. As soon as trains began to run over long distances they created a need for the provision of refreshments, at least at large stations. Some companies entered into this business energetically at first. Head and Lardner both gave favourable accounts of the refreshment room at Wolverton on the London & North Western Railway in 1849–50, Lardner being delighted that 'the animals of prey, who ... infested the coach taverns' had been replaced by staff controlled directly by the railway, receiving travellers in 'magnificent salons, luxuriously furnished, warmed, and illuminated'.[45] Neither of these writers said a word about the quality of the fare that was provided. Here is the English habit – stoutly maintained today – of noticing the appurtenances of eating but paying no attention to the food.

Other companies also began by making some show with their refreshment rooms. Brunel himself took pains with the planning of the one at Swindon[46] and with its decoration.[47] But he *did* notice what he ate and drank, as he showed in 1842 in his celebrated letter to the refreshment contractor about the 'coffee' he supplied, ending up with words that many passengers all over British railways echo now: 'I avoid taking anything there when I can help it'.[48] The number of these rooms multiplied as long-distance services extended. The expresses between London and Scotland made stops of 20–30 minutes for dining at York, Normanton, and Preston; and this called for large rooms, with a nimble service of meals.

Towards 1860 complaints about the refreshment facilities at stations began to be heard insistently. At the head of the critics stood Dickens. Restlessly active, first as a young journalist and then in later life when he made the tours arranged for his public readings, he needed refreshment at all hours of the day and night. Here he is in 1856 stopping in the small hours at Peterborough: 'The lady in the refreshment room ... gave me a cup of tea, as if I were a hyena and she my cruel keeper with a strong dislike to me. I ... had a petrified bun of enormous antiquity in miserable meekness'.[49] Four years later he wrote an embittered essay, 'Refreshments for Travellers'.[50] Then his loathing for these places exploded in *Mugby Junction*, where he contrasted them with those in France, in which the pleasure of eating well was carefully attended to. Many other people agreed with him. 'The real disgrace of England is the railway sandwich', wrote Trollope in 1869, adding that 'in France one does get food at the railway stations'.[51] Henry James, in his way, said much the same in 1877 when he contrasted the refreshments offered at Folkestone and at Boulogne.[52] The reformer William Galt wrote: 'On many lines it is absolutely a national disgrace; squabs of pork pie offered without the slightest reference to the season, old three-cornered jam puffs, fossil sandwiches'.[53] T. H. S. Escott thought these rooms should be investigated by the Railway Commissioners.[54] Here and there some merit was allowed to the railways' dining rooms, even to the fare afforded in them: by Foxwell, for example, to the one at Preston.[55] Acworth acknowledged in 1890 the excellence of the Tay salmon in the station breakfast at Perth – a pleasure, he thought, to equal the *bouillabaisse* offered at Marseilles; but he felt obliged to remark that when he went on to Aberdeen he found 'a sandwich composed of equal parts of gristle, fat and sawdust'.[56]

The policies of the railways in the running of their refreshment rooms varied. Some kept it in their own hands, others let the business out. One catering firm emerged that took railway contracts seriously. In 1861 Felix Spiers and Christopher Pond, who had had experience of running cafés and a railway refreshment room in Australia, went into the same business in London, with the Metropolitan and the London Chatham & Dover companies.[57] The firm made contracts with other railways too[58] and it kept some of them for a long time.

In general, the companies tended as time went on to take the business into their hands. They must have done so because they considered it profitable. Considering the ease with which food of nearly every kind could be transported and the railways' own control of that process, as well as the great scale on which the large companies operated in the conveyance of food and drink, it is difficult to excuse their shortcomings. Chains of restaurants and cafés were only beginning to emerge and grow strong in Britain at this time. Here were chains ready-made, and what was almost a captive *clientèle*. In this matter the railways might have set a high standard of performance if they had given it a place well up in the scale of their priorities. They certainly imposed a new uniformity here. But, with a few honourable exceptions, it was a uniformity of the fourth rate.

Localities

All railway systems were apt to treat one community they served differently from another. One district offered a more profitable traffic than its next-door neighbour – in central Scotland, for example, in coal or iron rather than in sheep. One might be dominated by great towns, generating large business on their own, whereas in another immediately adjoining it there might be few towns, as appeared everywhere on the fringes of the industrial districts of west Yorkshire. In a commercially-managed system there were always special pressures from some community or interest or trade. And finally, there was the force of competition.

Differences of this kind were much less pronounced in Scotland than in England. The most valuable traffic the railways could look for there was concentrated into the tract between the basins of the Clyde, Forth, and Tay; and, except in the suburbs of Edinburgh and Glasgow, it was nearly all competitive between two companies or three. Acworth saw 'universal and ubiquitous competition' as 'the keynote to the Scottish railway system'.[59] No company in Scotland exercised a monopoly comparable in magnitude and value with the London & South Western's in Hampshire or the North Eastern's in its own large territory.

The neglect, and then the favour, displayed by the South Western company to Southampton has already been discussed. Something similar in its main outlines occurred at the same time at Hull.[60] There the North Eastern company was intensely disliked by many shipowners and by the Corporation. Hull was alleged to be less favourably treated by it than the railway's own port of West Hartlepool. As at Southampton, the provision of docks was inadequate. But in 1893 the North Eastern secured powers to purchase the feeble company responsible for them; implacably opposed by the Corporation but now supported by a number of the chief shipowners. All those who lived in the future, even in the present, saw this as the only way ahead. The Corporation was now living in the past.

The companies did not always modify their relations with such communities in this way. Swansea was unfortunate at the hands of the South Wales Railway and its successor the Great Western.[61] Although the topography of the town and its surrounding district were unusually awkward, the difficulties it presented could have been surmounted. Two other great railways, the London & North Western and the Midland, established themselves there firmly in the 1870s: but the competition they set up made, in this respect, no difference. The richest man associated with the place, H. H. Vivian, took the lead in building a new and costly railway to tap the coal of the Rhondda valley in 1881–95. That made no difference either. The town now came to have six railway stations. The Great Western's, much the most important of them, was perched on a ledge in a hillside, too narrow to accommodate it adequately. It was the terminus of a short branch out of the main line from England to West Wales, and that often obliged travellers to or from the town to change trains. In the course of the Victorian age Swansea lost out to Cardiff steadily, in size and consequence. For that there were many reasons. Its muddled and inferior railway accommodation stood among them. From Dornoch in Sutherland to St Ives in Cornwall, many towns were placed on little branch lines. The practice was not unknown on the mainland of Europe: in western France, for example, at Orleans, Tours, and Biarritz. But Swansea, with 115,000 people by 1911, was a larger town, and commercially far more important, than any of those. Here the difference we are examining seems to amount, on the part of the Great Western Railway, to something much like neglect, paralleled in England perhaps by the North Eastern's neglect of the interests of Gateshead[62] but in Scotland not at all.

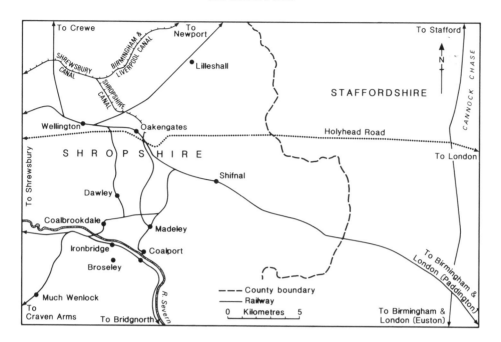

Communications in East Shropshire

The railways' lack of interest in certain localities on their systems was not confined to towns. It included some considerable tracts of country. The industrial district of east Shropshire affords a good example.

In the seventeenth and eighteenth centuries the development of the industries here had been distinguished for energy and inventiveness; shown in the smelting of iron with coke (instead of charcoal) in Coalbrookdale in 1709 and the erection of the Iron Bridge seventy years later.[63] Water power was readily available, from the streams running down to the Severn, which formed a natural highway for the products of the ironworks, though it was impeded by difficulties of navigation. Small wooden railways had been built here very early (one at Broseley by 1606).[64] It was at the Coalbrookdale works that the first iron rails were cast in 1767, and that the first locomotive – or one of the first – was built in 1802.

The district remained unconnected to the national canal system. No such link was made until 1835, when at last a branch was completed from the Birmingham & Liverpool Canal. The improvement of the Holyhead road, which ran across the northern edge of the district, was not finished until 1836. Next year the Grand Junction Railway was opened, connecting Birmingham with Liverpool and Manchester. No branch from it into Shropshire was made until 1849, when a line was taken from Stafford to Wellington and Shrewsbury. Another one soon joined it, coming up from Wolverhampton; by 1852 it had been continued northwards to Birkenhead (for Liverpool) and southwards to Birmingham and London. The ironworking district itself was not penetrated by any branches from this trunk line until 1854, when one went to Madeley. A cluster of other little ones was built, linked to long cross-country routes, in 1861–7; but no more thereafter.

Most of these lines were in the hands of one company, the Great Western. The London & North Western competed for some of the traffic.[65] But before long the competitors came to live together, their rivalries no longer intense. True, the system did not shrink; no lines were closed until the Madeley branch went, in 1915. The railway system simply stood still.

There were other railways in the district besides those owned by the two great companies: the small private lines serving individual works. Most of them were archaic, never modernized, and managed with extreme conservatism. Through running from one of these lines to another was often prevented by diversity of gauge or the lack of necessary facilities. 'A unified system in the coalfield', Barrie Trinder remarks, 'could have provided a tolerably efficient form of transport'. He is right in suggesting that this hotch-potch of railways 'ossified the systems for supplying the ironworks with raw materials'.[66]

Many of these Shropshire industries were already in decline early in the nineteenth century. Broseley became a stagnant place, its miners and ironworkers moving off to the Black Country in Staffordshire and to South Wales.[67] There was no large population to be served: about 50,000 in the whole district in 1851, and steadily falling thereafter. The two great railway companies could have provided, jointly or in competition, a system that would have served it much better. The London & North Western seriously neglected some of the business of the Shropshire Union Railways and Canal Company, which it controlled by lease after 1847, even when complaints were made by the big Lilleshall ironworks.[68] Elsewhere, railways afforded really valuable help in encouraging the development of new industries – in east Northamptonshire, for example, and north Lincolnshire. In Cornwall the railways were able to offer some compensation for the catastrophic decline of tin and copper mining after 1860 by fostering its fisheries and market gardening, besides its new holiday trade.[69] Nothing at all of this kind happened in Shropshire.

The indifference that the railways showed in developing their business here stands out in strong contrast with the energy they gave to it in the districts immediately adjacent on the east, the Black Country and Cannock Chase. In them there was intense competition between the North Western, the Great Western, and the Midland companies, which were opening new links and branches vigorously down to 1883 and continued to improve their lines after that.[70]

This contrast can be accounted for in part easily enough. Even by 1800 the aggregate of industrial enterprise in south Staffordshire was larger than in Shropshire; by 1870, when the development of Cannock was well under way, it was much larger still. Staffordshire had more business to offer than Shropshire, and it was favoured accordingly. Moreover, though the Midland company fought the North Western eagerly in Staffordshire, it never penetrated into Shropshire, so that stimulus to competition was absent there. All in all, the whole district became, in the economic terms of the late nineteenth century, a backwater, and no railway company considered that any special effort to revitalize it would be worth making.

The railways' power to discriminate between communities and districts also appeared in the services they provided in some of the large cities' suburbs. Certain companies came to arrange their services in such a way as to encourage one kind of traveller and discourage another, as at Oxted in Surrey.[71] That kind of policy was taken further by the Great Eastern, which set itself to develop the heaviest traffic it could accommodate in cheap trains from Walthamstow into London but firmly refused to apply the same methods in and around Loughton. Here the railway was making a clear difference between the facilities it chose to afford to one class of its customers and another.[72]

Nevertheless, very few railway companies that adopted a policy in any matter like these stuck to it rigidly thereafter. When circumstances changed, or pressures or opportunities, they all had to be ready to re-examine old practices, to discard old principles. There could be no uniformity in the treatment of all parts of their systems.

Class Distinctions

There has been a good deal of dispute about the extent to which the Victorian railways increased or diminished the distinctions and divisions between classes. It has seldom taken much account of the problems that arose from the nature of railways themselves.

Both on the coaches and on the steamboats two types of accommodation had been provided, charged for at different rates. In one the passenger was enclosed, in the other he travelled in the open, unprotected from the weather. The first type was called 'inside' on the coaches, 'cabin' on the steamers; the second 'outside' and 'deck'. Neither coaches nor steamers used the word 'class'. It quickly became obvious that few people would travel on the roofs of railway trains in the open air, exposed to the engine's cinders and to the dangers presented by overhead bridges and by tunnels. How was the distinction to be made between the best accommodation (the equivalent of the coaches' 'inside') and the next best, covered-in but plain, for which the price charged would be competitive with the coaches' 'outside'? The Liverpool & Manchester company coloured its vehicles differently, yellow for those providing the best accommodation, blue for the others. It first applied the word 'class' not to fares or vehicles but to trains, the 'first-class trains' being quicker.[73] Similar practices were followed by some other railways. By 1835–6 however the Leeds & Selby and the Newcastle & Carlisle were using the words 'first class' and 'second class' in the sense accepted today.[74]

These details deserve attention, for it appears that 'first-class' and 'second-class', as adjectives denoting quality, were first brought into general use by the railways. If that is right they contributed here to making the idea of class division much firmer than it had ever been before. Although the effect was unintentional, it may well have been important.*

Various types of special accommodation were tried out on the early railways, for which higher fares were charged. But the standard types remained two, with another, a 'third class' provided on some of them for passengers travelling in open wagons, with or without seats, at fares lower than those charged for the second class. Then in 1844 another class was added by legislation, generally known as 'Parliamentary' or 'Government'; in the terse language of Bradshaw's timetables 'Parly.' or 'Gov.'.

These class distinctions were all designed to meet the special difficulties of working a railway. A stage-coach had had a fixed quota of passengers, four inside and about a dozen outside. The demand for places on the railway was immediately such that no formula of that kind would do for a train. Yet a train was not indefinitely extendible: the engines' power was limited, brakes and couplings were weak, and slow trains impeded faster ones following them. The railway managers' task was to find the right average accommodation for the number of passengers paying for their travel at different rates. It was a matter of logistics as well as of commercial reckoning.

The companies handled it in different ways. A few, whose lines were short and simple, tried for a time making their accommodation and services uniform, to be paid for at one rate – the Canterbury & Whitstable for example, the Newcastle & North Shields, and the Edinburgh & Dalkeith. At the other end of the scale, most companies charged extra for travelling by mail or express trains. For that practice there were two good reasons. Mail trains were run primarily for the benefit of the Post Office and took a strictly limited number of passengers. With express trains, it was not unreasonable that those who got an exceptionally fast service should pay for it: a principle enunciated in 1844, just as these trains were introduced, when the *Quarterly Review* argued that there should be 'a relation between fares and velocity, between the *value* received and the *price* paid'.[75] The expenses of providing fast trains were high. Five years later, in the light of experience, one railway manager asserted that it cost twice as much to run a train at 30 mph as at 15, and another that 'the immoderate damage to both the road and the stock, from high speed, outweighs...the additional fare received'.[76]

But a further consequence followed; an odd one. Although express trains originated in Britain, and the principle of relating fares with speed was proclaimed there at once, the charging of supplements by these trains quickly showed itself to be irritatingly unpopular, and in 1859–65 four large companies abolished them: the Midland, Great Northern, North Eastern, and (with one exception) London & North Western.[77] By 1882 the charging of express fares was maintained (with the same exception) only by the three small companies

---

*'First class' and 'second class' were already in use to describe orders of merit in university graduates; but that was a highly specialized usage. The OED and its Supplement both accord much more importance to examples taken from railways.

in south-eastern England.[78] On the European mainland, however, they were imposed in almost all countries alike.

Continental railway managers favoured express fares both as a source of revenue and as a regulator of traffic. The British companies never seem to have regarded the receipts from them as important in themselves; but where traffic was particularly dense they might be used in some degree to control it: as for instance on the South Eastern & Chatham, where they were still being charged in 1914 on boat trains, partly in order to deter passengers who were not crossing the Channel from travelling on them. On the Continent, where the service was much less frequent than in Britain, the timetable was arranged with a view to spreading the load as evenly as possible. That objective could be reached partly by encouraging third-class passengers to make their journeys overnight. At the turn of the century the usual practice of the French companies was to provide one day train from Paris taking third-class passengers to each distant city of importance and three overnight – some so slow that they occupied a large slice of the following day as well.[79] And all those companies, right down to 1914, debarred third-class passengers from using the faster trains intermediately over short or moderate distances.

In the great improvement of passenger facilities that began on the British railways in the 1870s, third-class travellers benefited most. When they were first admitted to all trains on some of the great systems Joshua Fielden, the wealthy cotton-spinner of Todmorden, condemned the policy altogether, both on the Midland and on the Lancashire & Yorkshire Railways.[80] It soon came to be fairly generally advocated by managers, who believed that in the long run it would increase revenue – though the intensely conservative G. N. Tyrrell, superintendent of the Great Western, opposed that notion stoutly in a memorandum to his board in 1886.[81] The Midland did not gain from these changes as handsomely as it had hoped. But one company after another came to do as it had done, making the first change quickly under the stress of competition, the second more gradually. In north-eastern England and in the whole of Scotland second class disappeared in 1893; by the beginning of 1912 it had gone on all other British railways save the London & South Western, on some London suburban services, and on boat trains. No practices similar to these were adopted anywhere on the Continent (except to some extent in Scandinavia) before 1914.

The withdrawal of second class was itself a convenience to the railways because it simplified the marshalling of their trains and therefore cheapened their operation. Why then were the two greatest companies, the North Western and the Great Western, among the last to adopt that policy? To answer that question we must turn away from railway working to look at class relationships.

They embodied an assumption that, for most Victorians, had the sanctity of an axiom, that society divided itself into three classes.[82] Matthew Arnold, who did not adopt axioms uncritically, accepted this one and made it the basis of his division of English society into 'Barbarians, Philistines, and Populace', expounded in *Culture and Anarchy* in 1869. Five years later a leader in *The Times* went further. Commenting on the withdrawal of second class by the Midland Railway it observed that 'by universal admission there are, roughly speaking, three classes in all societies, and the existing arrangement of railway carriages appears to correspond very closely with the ordinary habits of life'.[83] This assertion was made by other people too, including some railway managers: Findlay, for example, and Scotter.[84]

There was some force in their contention, but not very much. Looking at the railways' structure of fares closely, we can see that in the Victorian age they came to provide not for three classes but for eight: mail, express, Pullman, first, second, third, Parliamentary, and workmen's. Moreover, if we take that generalization of *The Times* literally, as applicable to 'all societies', why should the fourth class, which dropped out of use in Great Britain,[85] have remained firmly established on most of the railways of Germany? The British railways were not acting in these matters on any sociological principles. They were pragmatists; in their own frequently-heard phrase, 'charging what the traffic would bear'.

In choosing the type of accommodation they would use, most British travellers no doubt thought first in terms of price. Some desired the quickest service they could get, others thought most about the comfort of their accommodation. How many preferred dearer to cheaper travelling from a desire not to occupy compartments side by side with people they considered their social inferiors?

At first, we may suppose, a good many carried over quite simply their earlier habits of travelling 'inside' by coach. Caricaturists added to the stock of public fun by depicting grandees – or persons who thought themselves that – in trains, aloof and self-absorbed. The railway companies wisely made no attempt to interfere in such matters. We very rarely get a hint that the practice of any of them was determined by a purely social distinction. On the London & North Western, it is true, the Irish Mail trains went on taking first and second-class passengers only, at express fares, with the object – the company's secretary said so in 1866 – 'of keeping them select';[86] and both the Great Northern and Great Western continued to exclude third-class passengers from two or three celebrated trains for a time, after all the rest had come to carry them. But the normal policy of all British railway companies was to treat the purchase of a ticket as a financial transaction, nothing more.

It cannot fairly be said that the railways set themselves deliberately, for any reason whatever, to induce snobbery among travellers. That had been very marked on the road: particularly at the inns where the coaches stopped, where even the best-heeled 'inside' passengers might expect to be less well served than they thought was their due if a grander guest was there, travelling in a post-chaise and changing horses. It was soon being remarked that the railways had had exactly the opposite effect. In 1851 Samuel Sidney wrote, with only a little exaggeration: 'The earl or duke, whose dignity formerly compelled him to post in a *coupé* and four, at a cost of some five or six shillings a mile, ... now takes his place unnoticed in a first-class carriage next to a gentleman who travels for a great claret and champagne house, and opposite another going down express to report a railway meeting at Birmingham for a morning paper.... The levelling tendency of the railway system is ... plainly exhibited'.[87] The novelist R. S. Surtees (a Durham squire) made a similar observation, with approval: 'Railways ... have annihilated the prejudice against public conveyances, and abolished the old stiff-necked demarcation between posting and coaching company. They have opened out the world to everyone'.[88]

Railway travelling did certainly induce some new forms of snobbery. Trollope illustrates one of them well in the remarks passed between two commercial travellers and a lawyer going from Leeds to London. Mr Moulder, travelling first-class, 'was a man who despised the second class, and was not slow to say so before other commercials who travelled at a cheaper rate than he did. "Hubbles and Grease", he said, "allowed him respectably, in order that he might go about their business respectable; and he wasn't going to give the firm a bad name by being seen in a second-class carriage, although the difference would go into his own pocket". The other two went up cheerfully together in their second-class carriage, dismissing Moulder as a 'domineering party'.[89] His fear of 'being seen' to travel second was shared by others. It could have curious consequences. Here is a prosperous merchant who saves a little by travelling third-class every day to the City and is surprised to notice one of his clerks going first. When joked with about this, the clerk replies that his employer is well enough known to do as he chooses, but that he himself has a more precarious position to keep up in his neighbourhood. 'Were I to adopt an inferior mode, it would be attributed to some serious falling off of income', and that would at once shake his social position and injure his credit with his tradesmen.[90]

It was largely on this account, as we can now appreciate, that the discontinuance of second class was deplored by some people. The second was the compromise class, between the expensive, ostentatious first and the mean, ignoble third; and that was the ground on which its retention was defended. The difference of price between second and third came to be of little importance. A large and general reduction of long-distance first and second-class fares took place in the closing years of the century.[91] This produced an immediate, temporary increase, here and on the other railways that followed a similar policy, in the receipts from second-class travelling, but it appeared chiefly attributable to a shift of passengers into the second class from the first.[92] There was by this time very little difference between the comfort offered in second and third-class carriages, nor was the second class notably less crowded. It seems probable that the social *cachet* of second class was what counted most.

The final decision to abandon the intermediate class seems to have been due largely to the force of example. Those companies that had discontinued it could not be shown to have lost by doing that, in financial terms. The Great Western, seeing its second-class traffic decline again after 1903, withdrew that class from its trains in 1905–10.[93] It might have gone on the London & North Western had not its chairman, Lord Stalbridge, resolutely opposed the change.

He retired in 1911, and second class disappeared throughout the system (as it also did on the Lancashire & Yorkshire) on 1 January 1912.

It is curious that the British railways, which moved so steadily in the improvement of third-class services, at the expense of the other two, should have been particularly criticized for their treatment of the third-class passenger by a distinguished French scholar, Elie Halévy, in the first and still one of the best histories of the Victorian age.[94] He wrote as if the British railways imposed a uniquely harsh and rigid structure of three classes on their passengers, when in reality the same structure was adopted, with minor variations, in France and in every other European country, and the service offered in Britain to the third-class passenger reached a much higher standard than it did anywhere on the European mainland. We may close this discussion, more justly, by listening to the views of two Englishmen who were, in their very different ways, notable protagonists of liberal thinking.

The first is Thomas Arnold, and his remark has often been quoted. Looking at a train from a bridge on the London & Birmingham Railway, he exclaimed: 'I rejoice to see it, . . . and think that feudality is gone for ever. It is so great a blessing to think that any one evil is extinct'.[95] To Arnold the railway was a destroyer of unjustly-exercised privilege. His remark may well have had a wider application still, indicating that he saw it as a leveller.

Forty years later John Bright asked a question, and answered it: 'Does not the railway, on most of the lines at least, take the third-class passenger at the same speed at which even royalty itself travels? . . . Science as applied to railways has come down to the humblest of the people, and has given them advantages which are far greater than what it gives to the rich because . . . though it has increased the power of the wealthy, it has given to the poor a power which they did not at all possess'.[96]

The Power of Government

There was one other kind of uniformity that was made possible by railways, and to some extent actually imposed in Victorian Britain. The railways and the telegraphs that grew up in conjunction with them added immeasurably to the real power that could be exercised by the central government in London over the whole Kingdom. The law now became uniform, to a much greater extent than it had ever been in the past: not merely on paper but in its immediate enforcement.

In the seventeenth and eighteenth centuries the inhabitants of Britain had been widely regarded as a turbulent, ungovernable people. They had had a civil war, they had cut off their king's head, they had forced another king into exile, bringing about a revolution in 1688. A change of dynasty on the throne had followed, challenged by two military assertions of the displaced dynasty's strength, in 1715 and 1745. Those public disturbances had been accompanied by continual outbreaks of noisy and often violent rioting in protest at the prices of food and drink, at the activities of customs men and the press-gang.

As long as such things continued, it could not truthfully be said that the government's authority was secure.

Similar things – some of them even more alarming to quiet people – happened on the Continent. In France rioting was no less endemic in the eighteenth century, and protest spilt over into full revolution in 1789. But Great Britain was a much smaller country, only two-fifths of the size of France, and its population was already concentrated predominantly in the southern half of England. The inability of the government to prevent rioting was demonstrated at Manchester in 1819, at Bristol and Nottingham in 1831, and at Newport in 1839. Here were plain proofs of the incompleteness of its control.

In the face of these disorders the government could hardly fail to recognize the new power placed in its hands by the construction of the trunk railways. The Melbourne administration was too feeble to seize the opportunity that presented. But Peel's showed an appreciation of it in 1842, by obliging the companies to convey troops or the civil police to its orders; and these provisions were enlarged two years later. The government was also quick to appreciate the value of the electric telegraph, requiring it to be laid down beside any railway at its behest.[97]

The military use of railways had already been under discussion in France and Germany since 1833,[98] but chiefly in relation to international warfare. In Great Britain, protected by the sea, it was considered at first as an extension of the government's power at home. In 1844 the Quartermaster-General, Sir James Willoughby Gordon, gave evidence to the Commons Committee on Railways, showing the extensive and satisfactory use that was already being made of them in troop movements and a clear appreciation of the advantages arising from it. In the two years 1842–3, he said, 118,000 soldiers had been moved within the country by rail, together with 12,000 of their women and children. A battalion of 1000 men could be conveyed by train from London to Manchester in nine hours; marching, the operation took seventeen days.[99] That was a particularly apposite illustration, for the government had sent troops to Manchester to keep order in the Chartist disturbances in 1842.[100] A London political gossip noted down a friend's remark in a letter: 'This extraordinary facility afforded for repressing a dangerous outbreak will perhaps reconcile the Tories to the *enormity* of railroads generally.... Your great man will like well enough to have regiments whirled down to protect his person and property at the rate of forty miles an hour'.[101]

There were no more riots comparable in danger with those of 1839–42 in any British town thereafter. For that there were several reasons. Wages soon began to rise, and working conditions to improve; the local police forces grew bigger and more efficient; protest was diverted into political and trade-union activity, conducted more effectively than the Chartist movement had been. Disturbances might still break out anywhere, at any time; a Riot (Damages) Act was called for in 1886. Troops were brought in by railway now and then, as for instance at Exeter in 1867.[102] The Strome Ferry riots of 1883 necessitated the dispatch of a small contingent of troops over the 200 miles from Edinburgh to Fort George outside Inverness, where their train stood by; but it was not in the end called on to move any further.[103] Two hundred hussars and two companies of infantry were concentrated at Swindon during the miners' strike in the Rhondda in 1910, and the cavalry went to the scene of the disorder.[104]

The part played by railways in strengthening the power of government came out more prominently through the contributions they were seen to make, in the later Victorian age, to the country's defence. Their value for this purpose was not much appreciated at first except by a few military men. In the 1840s Willoughby Gordon, again, and Sir John Burgoyne (inspector-general of fortifications) gave evidence to the Royal Commission on Railway Termini in London, supporting the construction of a circular line round the outskirts of the city, on the ground that it would assist the movement of troops.[105] A number of soldiers and politicians – the Duke of Wellington included – tried to secure the building, by different companies, of a continuous line parallel with the coast between Dover and Plymouth.[106] That consideration was occasionally referred to in the long contest over the building of a second main line to Exeter. Pressure was exerted here by the War Office, but those who were engaged in fighting the railways' battles did not pay it much attention. Their attitude is reflected in a private letter written in 1852 by the chairman of the Bristol & Exeter company to his colleague of the Great Western. Speaking of the projected line from Dorchester through Bridport into Devon, he remarked:

> The whole district till you approach Exeter is thinly inhabited, and surely a single line will carry the farmers and their produce, and in case of invasion by a French army. If Lord Hardinge [the Commander-in-Chief] insists on precautions against that calamity a single line will carry all the troops and guns which he can send by a single narrow [i.e. standard-gauge] line from Portsmouth to Dorchester. The nation is very lukewarm in organizing a militia to defend us, and we are not called upon to expend the funds of our proprietors in guarding against what is I trust a most distant and improbable contingency.[107]

Hardinge, together with a group of four leading politicians headed by Palmerston, testified in favour of this Bill, and it was passed. The line was never made, however. Parliament agreed in 1856 to the substitution of another one further inland, somewhat more attractive commercially but having no military value at all.[108]

Meanwhile the country had been engaged in a war in the Crimea, the first it had fought in Europe since 1815. There a railway was built, some seven miles long, to bring up supplies from the port of Balaklava. It gave good service in 1855–6. In the words of an American military observer: 'For the first time in the art of war…was the railroad resorted to as a means of transport in *presence of an enemy*, and I feel warranted in saying that the English army could not have performed its immense labour without its use'.[109]

In 1859 there was another brief alarm at the possibility of a French invasion of England. Closer attention then began to be paid to the country's southern defences and the part that railways might play in them. The imaginative engineer William Bridges Adams urged the completion of a line parallel with the south coast, coupling with it the suggestion that 'moving forts' should run on it: guns mounted on railway wagons protected by the armour-plating that had now come to be accepted for warships. 'There is', he wrote, 'less difficulty in clothing a railway wagon in plate-armour than a gunboat on water.'[110] Some soldiers perceived the value of this proposal, and armoured trains of different sorts were used on a small scale both in the American Civil War and by the French during the siege of Paris in 1870–1; more thoroughly by the British army in Egypt in 1882–5 and – after experiment at Newhaven in 1894 – in the South African war of 1899–1902.[111]

From the 1870s onwards Britain began to face the prospect that it might have to engage in another general war. A Regulation of the Forces Act (1871) empowered the government, on the declaration of a state of emergency, to take possession of any or all of the railways and their plant, and in 1888 a National Defence Act declared that, in those circumstances, naval and military traffic was to take precedence over traffic of every other kind. An Engineer and Railway Volunteer Staff Corps had been established in 1865, which drew up detailed plans of action at successive stages in such an emergency. This body and the War Office also prepared schemes for the movement of troops at the time of mobilization.

Some of these arrangements were first tested out in 1899, on the outbreak of war in South Africa. The burden of transporting troops to the ships that were to carry them to the seat of war fell principally on one company, the London & South Western, the whole movement being concentrated on to its port of Southampton. In the first fifteen months of the war 235,000 soldiers and 30,000 horses were dispatched through the port, together with stores, guns, and other equipment. Nearly 5000 men left, in five transports, on a single day in 1899.[112] The whole task was carried through with a smooth, calm competence. It was an impressive demonstration of the partnership that had been formed between the military and the railway authorities, of the power the British government commanded to implement the decisions it had taken.

That partnership was now being strengthened and developed in other ways. Ever since the Crimean War the Admiralty and the War Office had been steadily increasing the use they made of railways in the service of their bases. Though there had at first been great resistance to allowing branches to be built into naval dockyards, by 1871 such lines had penetrated those at Chatham, Portsmouth, Devonport, and Pembroke.[113] By the end of the century the government had begun the development of a great new naval base in Scotland at Rosyth, to which the Admiralty built a branch railway running out of the North British main line near the north end of the Forth bridge. There was similar collaboration between the railways and the army, though it did not develop as rapidly as might have been expected. The new depot at Aldershot was inaugurated in 1856 and a town grew up there in consequence with startling speed, but the London & South Western company's line to serve it was not opened until 1870.[114] A much bigger tract of southern England was acquired for military purposes in 1895 on Salisbury Plain, and in the development of that the railways played a substantial part, with branches carrying public traffic and running to Tidworth, Amesbury and Bulford, opened in 1901–4.[115]

So the railways did a good deal to assist the government to maintain public order and to defend the realm. All this represented a very large extension of the power it exercised, effective and dependable. In any emergency it would now have an internal transport system under its entire control. That was then a system based almost wholly on railways. In 1913 there were only 254,000 mechanized road vehicles in the island, two-thirds of them private cars and motor-cycles; and the number of mechanized goods vehicles was no more than 64,000.[116]

Such was the great instrument now at the disposal of the State if war came. But it was also there in reserve in any kind of emergency whatever. The strikes of 1910–12 were a threat to internal security. The grave troubles in Ireland were mounting. Reluctant though a Liberal administration might be to increase its power, Asquith's had to accept that necessity. The settlement of the national railway strike of 1911 in two days was influenced by a realistic appreciation of the country's dependence on that industry as the dangers lying ahead of it grew more imminent.

From all these causes, national and international, the power at the government's disposal had grown far greater in 1914 than it had been in 1830. 'Equality before the law', though it might be unthinkingly accepted as a principle, was a matter brought daily into dispute, in one connection and another, in the courts. Equality before the State was a concept nearer to the truth. Here was a uniformity among the British people that increased steadily over these years, and a diminishing difference: a change produced at least as much by new techniques placed in the hands of government as by new theories of the ways in which it should act. Among these techniques those in the speed and regularity of communication stood out, for anyone to see: the railway, the tramway (a railway too, though it ran along public streets); the telegraph, allied closely with the railway at first, and by the beginning of the new century its young cousin the telephone. They enabled the government not merely to ordain but to verify almost at once that its ordinances had been carried out, no matter who might oppose or try to thwart them; not only in quelling disorder and repressing crime but with a beneficence too, more obvious to people in their daily lives. The General Board of Health in London was able to instruct its medical inspectors by telegraph during the cholera epidemic of 1848. The railway and the telegraph could quicken action drastically on the outbreak of fire, ease communication in snow or fog.[117] They brought with them a degree of security unknown before; a security depending not on the power of individual persons (Arnold's 'feudality') but on the strength of the government, exercised over the whole island from London.

[368]

16
LOSS AND GAIN

It has been a principal aim of this book to present railways as the Victorians saw them, warts and all. When they were new they were fiercely attacked: by many landowners, by all coachmasters and canal proprietors whose traffic they threatened to take away. Presently they had to meet other enemies, who were dissatisfied with their services or their financial performance, who disliked their physical presence or feared the power they exercised in the life of the island.

This opposition was political, commercial, social in the broadest sense; intellectual and emotional. It was strengthened by mistakes and wrong-doing on the part of the railways themselves. The companies found few good defenders, and most of them were linked in some way with the railway interest. No well-informed observer, uncommitted either to that interest or to its critics, thought it worth while to sum up the gains that had accrued to Britain from the invention and development of railways and to set them against the losses, the disadvantages, the unhappiness that could be ascribed to them too.

That attempt was never made, in any careful or systematic fashion, until 1916, when the Canadian scholar W. T. Jackman produced his analysis, with reference to the British railways' early history – chiefly their economic history – down to about 1850.[1] Methodical, learned, calmly judicious, it allows twice as much space to the drawbacks arising from the railways' work as to the benefits they conferred, which Jackman no doubt thought obvious. He broke off his enumeration of them with the comment: 'the history of the remainder of the nineteenth century is the record, in part, of the achievement of the railway'. The present book turns at its close to a brief consideration of losses and gains, taking up where Jackman left off: not in any sense a full balance sheet – that analysis is a subject for a book on its own – but a retrospective view of some of the topics that have been discussed here, looking at the advantages the railways brought and the prices that had to be paid for them.

The contrast between loss and gain seldom presents itself in terms of black and white. In many matters the two might appear to be evenly balanced. Hunting men, for example, began with denunciations of railways for cutting up their country,[2] and some never departed from that point of view.[3] Before long, however, many were contending that the sport had benefited by more than it had lost, through the ease of movement that railways had introduced, for men and horses alike. By 1860 the sporting novelist Surtees had come to extol their services as 'a great boon' to hunting.[4]

Some of the losses, the disturbances and miseries the railways brought with them, were undeniable: the physical and social damage they wrought by their passage into towns, for instance, the shabbiness and squalor they created or intensified. The pollution they produced has been referred to here more than once, in various forms. Nothing has been said, however, of the noise their operations set up. That was incessant, and vehemently complained of, particularly in north London down the years. A local association was formed in 1860, of people living near Primrose Hill, to try to get their whistling quietened.[5] In 1871 it was stated that though the North London Railway permitted no trains to run during the church interval on Sundays, cattle trains ran then, whose engine-drivers made 'such an infernal tumult with their shrieking whistles as to cause the service of the church to stop'.[6] A resident on the same line wrote to the company in 1903 to say that he and several of his neighbours had 'been driven insane by that devilish screech and only wait an opportunity to shoot either the driver or the engine'.[7]

Railways certainly might impose themselves brutally enough on the senses of people who lived near them, on their noses, their ears, and their eyes. They also effected another intrusion, widespread and subtle. They made life more public, reducing intimacy. We smile today when we read of well-to-do people who insisted on travelling in their own carriages, mounted on flat trucks in trains. But they had never been accustomed to travelling in the company of strangers. Why should they begin now? When the railway established itself, it offered no equivalent to the carriage holding two or three people only, the chaise, the chariot, or the curricle. Such vehicles almost passed out of use, as a means of long-distance travel, until a new version of them, in the form of motor-cars, appeared after 1900. More broadly the railway, in alliance with the telegraph, did much to impair privacy; a genuine and usually innocent pleasure of life. It exposed everyone more to the curiosity, the impertinences of other people. It helped to make the private life public.

Railways might damage public life as well as private. Sometimes literally, as when one of them was carried straight across the middle of a village splitting it in two – Snodland in Kent, for example,[8] Littlehempston in Devon[9] – or a town, like Shifnal, Knaresborough, or Cullen. Frequently their effect was one of erosion, through the removal of the villagers they facilitated. Within villages, as also in towns, they could weaken smaller social units by easing or even encouraging withdrawal from them. That is part of the objection that many church and chapel people felt to the development of Sunday excursions and the extension of holidays.

They also appeared dangerous to society as an agency of crime; and not merely to timid folk, liable to take such a view of any innovation. Here is the Hammersmith coroner in 1858, sitting at an inquest on two murdered babies: 'If there had been a railway in the parish, I should not have been so much surprised'.[10] To him, a man occupying a responsible public office, it was already a commonplace that crime was rail-borne.

The enclosed compartments of trains certainly offered convenient facilities for murders[11] and sexual assaults. Railways also aided criminal behaviour by carrying large crowds of people to a single spot, bent on mischief. Their readiness to do that to prize-fights, for example, became notorious, and they had to be forbidden by law to convey such traffic in 1868.[12] Rowdyism and brawling were to be looked for from time to time – it might be expected – on trains returning from race-meetings, and they were apt to appear at any stage of railway excursions. Sylvia Pankhurst always remembered the hideous scenes of drunken disorder she observed as a child at Clacton in the 1880s.[13] Escott went on to generalize his experience of such behaviour in trains of all kinds: 'Rowdyism is, of its essence, gregarious. It has an ineradicable tendency to gravitate to a special part or parts of that street which a train may be regarded as being. There is a kind of Alsatia in every steam locomotive bound on a long journey'.[14] There the train is seen to be, from its very nature, a potential seat of violence.

In Britain, however, the railway was not a source of violence itself. Though strikes among its aggrieved servants did occasionally produce some disorder, that was trivial compared to the explosions that occurred in the American railway strike of 1877 (at Pittsburgh above all) and on the Nord railway in France in 1910.

Trains also provided other invitations to crime. They travelled fast, and while in motion they were enclosed units. That made them an invaluable new aid in robberies and in the flight of criminals of all sorts. The railways themselves suffered from the use of trains for such purposes. The up and down mail trains were both robbed in one night at Bridgwater in 1849.[15] A famous bullion robbery was carried through by means of the night mail train to Dover in 1855.[16]

Railway companies might be said themselves to have facilitated crime, in a different way. In their earlier days at least, the accounting practices of many of them were sketchy, and as money poured into them they offered almost an invitation to their employees to cook their books.[17] One of the chief revelations of the Mania of the 1840s, as its history came to be exposed, was the ease with which Hudson and other unscrupulous promoters had been able to advantage themselves, owing to the lack of effective controls over the investment in their companies and over their expenditure. A quiet young man who had absorbed this lesson was soon working away in the share registration department of the Great Northern company, creating bogus stock that brought him in more than $£\frac{1}{4}$ million before he was detected in 1856 and sentenced to transportation for life. Leopold Redpath was a strange and interesting person, a real artist in fraud.[18]

But though railways became a focus of crime, they seldom set out to promote it. Their misdeeds arose much more from carelessness, to which most accidents were attributable.[19] The carelessness might be outrageous: at Headsnook, east of Carlisle, for example in 1881;[20] at Hoylake seven years later, when the accident entailed a six-months' prison sentence for a stationmaster.[21] Such derelictions of duty as these, publicly proclaimed, gave point to allegations of the railways' cynical disregard of safety, repeated in *Punch* and elsewhere down the years.

Railway companies became enormous corporations, whose business was all regulated by complex rules for dealing with their customers. Although a trader submitting a grievance to a goods agent or a stationmaster could expect that it would be handled civilly, the official would usually point to the company's regulation, which he had no power to alter. Still, he might have to interpret it, and many cases arose in the courts concerning special conditions imposed and accepted in the handling of goods.[22] Equally, what was to be considered ordinary 'passenger's luggage' – a rocking-horse, a cello?[23] The case might go to the House of Lords (most of the larger companies could afford that if they chose) before it was settled.

In one sense this was quite fair: there was a dispute, and it was decided in due course of law. But the notorious multiplication of such cases, and the stolid unwillingness of the companies to re-examine their codes, gave them the air of tyrants fighting rearguard actions, not at all of commercial enterprises anxious to please their customers.

By the turn of the century some of their shrewder critics on the left were beginning to make a reproach even of their triumphs. 'Our rage for fast trains, so far as long-distance travel is concerned, is largely a passion to end the extreme discomfort involved': there is H. G. Wells in 1902. He could have enjoyed his journeys on them if they had been 'neither rackety, cramped, nor tedious'. As it was, he was already prepared to contemplate, and welcome, 'a world without railways' in the future.[24] Another commentator, little known but not negligible, published a small book in 1909 under the significant title *The Fallacy of Speed*, remarking that 'we have looked on distance as an enemy to be conquered, but whether the well-being of the world is on the whole advanced by its improved travelling facilities may be reasonably questioned'.[25] His main attack was directed against the great city, for the growth of which he held the railways largely responsible.

To many Victorians the railway companies came to represent a power over their daily lives that was more immediately oppressive than the government's. The power – embodied in rule-books and by-laws, its irregular exercise demonstrated in accidents – might well have appeared to some of them a malignant creation of their age. Or perhaps all these things were a necessary price to be paid for the gains the railways had brought? How are those gains to be measured?

Here are two round summaries of them. The first is of 1856:

> We would have the public...somewhat more mindful of the benefits they have already derived from railways; it would improve their patience under evils for the time unavoidable.... They save the public two-thirds of their time in transit, and two-thirds in fares and tolls; they have given us the penny post, which could not have existed without them; they have intersected the country with telegraph wires employing 3000 persons, stretching a distance of 86,000 miles, and flashing a million of messages a year, many of them to and from places hundreds of miles apart; they

have reduced the cost of many articles of general consumption, and rendered others common where nature had seemed to plant an interdict against them... In 1854 they transported 111,000,000 passengers... in such safety that in the first half of the year but one accident happened to every 7,195,341 passengers. In these journeys, each passenger gains an hour in time, amounting in all to 38,000 years of working life at eight hours a day. Supposing the day's labour to be worth three shillings, these deplorable railways save the nation £2,000,000 a year in the item of time alone.[26]

The second summary is packed into one sentence. Railways, says a distinguished historian of our own time, 'created new business, reduced transport costs, standardised trade routes, made people more mobile and brought new recreations and opportunities to large masses of the people who had never previously had them'.[27] He allows that some modern economic historians would adopt 'a more cautious approach' to these statements: yet all of them have been exemplified in the treatment, mainly of passengers and passenger services, in this book. The new business that railways created was evident; so was the reduction in cost, comparing like with like. The traffic of some main lines soon grew large enough to justify development: the London & South Western company's extension to its Waterloo terminus, opened in 1848, carried four tracks from the start; the approach to London Bridge station was widened to accommodate six in 1850. Each of the trunk lines, the great 'trade routes' of the country, required similar enlargements over the years, down to 1914. The new mobility the railways afforded, and their services to recreation, have been treated in chapters 12–14. All these efforts produced great gains, in speed, ease, and cheapness of movement.

The gains were not unaccompanied by loss, and they were achieved at a high cost. How far that cost was justifiable, what profits the railways really brought in, and what national savings they effected: economic historians have done much in recent years towards elucidating those questions and have extensively debated the answers given to them.[28] This book has been mainly concerned with inquiry into other aspects of Victorian life, few of which have yet benefited from any comparable investigation. Few of them, moreover, are suited to discussion in the same precise terms of volume and cost.

Let us look first at one of the gains that is among the hardest to quantify. It came to be suggested very early that railways were contributing to the improvement of health.

The mobility they offered extended to the medical profession. As soon as the trunk railways settled down into regular working, the consultant medical men in London began discussing a revision of the fees they charged for attending patients in the provinces. These had been calculated in the past at the rate of a guinea (21s) a mile. Now these practitioners considered charging not by distance but by time. A fee of five guineas an hour would evidently benefit both them and their patients. At the old rate a specialist called down from London to Southampton would expect 78 guineas. His fee now would not much exceed 40 guineas (allowing for the drive to and from the London terminus); but he would gain a whole working day without any of the fatigue of travel, a day in which he could see other patients and earn their fees in his London consulting room. The lowering of the charges would increase the number of patients who could afford to pay them; and, following the honourable practice of their profession, some of these specialists would be willing to undertake such journeys in particular cases for a lower payment or none. They could now afford sacrifices of this kind more easily. Reporting the discussion, a newspaper pertinently went on to ask: 'Cannot lawyers consider imitating this example?'[29]

The railways themselves were already providing a new amenity very important to public health. The water-closets and urinals that they included in many of their stations soon attracted notice. In 1846 the public parks committee of the Manchester Borough Council recommended the immediate provision of 'the requisite conveniences for persons frequenting the parks, which have been so judiciously provided by railway companies'.[30]

Railways were also able to afford direct service to medical institutions. The big Three Counties Asylum at Arlesey in Bedfordshire (opened in 1866) was served by a station and a siding for its freight traffic on the Great Northern main line. A number of branches were taken into hospitals in later years, at Netley (Hampshire) for example and at Hellingly (Sussex).[31]

To these useful services another may be added, which might have been more important than it proved to be in practice. The burial of the dead presented an urgent, serious problem in the health of large towns, and in 1852 a London Necropolis & National Mausoleum Company was established by private Act, which acquired an estate of 2000 acres a little west of Woking in Surrey. It adjoined the London & South Western Railway, so that a train service could be taken right into it, starting from a station built for the Necropolis Company's sole use at Waterloo. The funeral trains began to run in 1854 and did so daily until 1900, thereafter on weekdays only.[32] But the enterprise never realized the hopes that lay behind it. Only one-fifth of the original estate was developed as a cemetery, and that has never been filled. Although the railway performed its part in the business competently, the cost of such interments, including a sixty-mile journey out and back, put them beyond most Londoners' reach. Smaller (though still extensive) public cemeteries were set apart instead; much closer to town centres and presently engulfed in some of them.

The benefits the railways brought, in matters concerned with health, seldom caught the eye of the public, except in some special circumstances: as for instance in a typhoid epidemic at Lincoln in 1905, when the railways conveyed large supplies of pure water from Newark and east Lincolnshire into the city, quickly and free of charge.[33] More noise was made by those who singled out diseases they were alleged to produce or to foster. The *Lancet* assailed them in 1862 in a pamphlet entitled *The Influence of Railway Travelling on Public Health*, criticizing the 'inelasticity' of the railway carriage, which it likened to 'a worn-out horse…, a framework of bones without muscles'. It also drew attention to the extreme fatigue induced by commuting. The effects of railway accidents on those who survived them, both physical and psychological, were naturally much discussed. But the leading medical authority who devoted particular attention to them in Britain was careful to point out that 'there is in reality nothing special in railway injuries, except in the severity of the accident by which they are occasioned',[34] and he put his discussion of accidents on railways in a proper perspective by citing others that produced similar results but were not due to railways at all.

That travelling by train did not itself aid health but could injure it was true enough. These drawbacks were, however, much less important than the contribution the railways quietly made – in the carriage of the sick, the supply of hospitals, the meeting of emergencies of every sort – to the improvement of health in the whole community.

It was often remarked in the Victorian age that railways had served to bring people in Britain closer together. That loose statement was applied again and again, to many different aspects of their work. Railways, said Cobden in 1845, 'are drawing us more together; they are teaching the landowner to feel for the manufacturer, and placing the manufacturer upon better terms with the landowner'.[35] If he was a politician, with axes of his own to grind, he knew something of what he was talking about here, for he was a farmer's son who had become a successful calico-printer. Railways also helped, in some ways, to draw Englishmen and Scotsmen closer. Though the railway systems in the two countries grew up, to a large extent, independently and there was never any extensive penetration of English companies' lines into Scotland or vice versa, each of the three trunk routes that came to cross the border represented a partnership in working between a Scottish company and one or more in England, and – except at times on the East Coast route, when there was friction between the North British and the North Eastern[36] – these arrangements worked smoothly enough. The services provided on them incidentally gave the Lowlands benefits they would scarcely have enjoyed without them: neither Dunbar nor Hawick nor Moffat nor Dumfries would have generated enough traffic to justify the provision made for them if it had not been a place lying on or close to one of the main trunk routes to and from the south. In early days English capital was freely invested in Scottish railways. Although that produced some divisions of interest that were serious, the earliest trunk lines in Scotland could hardly have been built without it, except at the price of long delay. More than three-quarters of the original subscriptions to the Caledonian company came from England; its links with the Grand Junction and the Lancaster & Carlisle were 'clearly essential to its very existence'.[37] It has been said that these trunk railways between England and Scotland 'represented the greatest step towards economic integration since 1707', and the leading historian of the Scottish railways endorses that opinion.[38]

Above all, the railways were an instrument of liberation, a breaking of the customary bonds of the past. Any station could represent that. The historian of a quiet parish in the Vale of the White Horse – a plain, sensible writer who did not deal in rhetoric – remarked in 1900 that at Wantage Road 'the would-be traveller is placed in direct communication with the whole world'.[39] In 1830 such a trope would have been applicable only to Liverpool or Dover. The railway had come to personify an almost infinite release.

Changes of this kind are often accompanied by other changes that work in the opposite direction. In one very important respect at least that was not true of this change, as it came to be realized in Britain. The minimum cost of travelling there was lowered, in real terms, as the Victorian age advanced: less by any general reduction in standard fares than by the multitude of concessions the British railways offered, in competition with one another, to travellers by particular trains, or on certain days of the week. Taking all these things into account, they can be said to have provided a service in 1914 that was, by European standards, notably fast, cheap, and frequent.

All these benefits and facilities could of course be misused. A leading general manager, Wiliam Cawkwell of the London & North Western, said in 1866 that railways afforded 'an inducement for a great many people to take advantage of them and take long journeys, which they can very badly afford to do; the labouring classes spend a great deal of money sometimes which could be better spent at home'.[40] But then he disliked excursion trains as such, on many grounds, and most of his directors did too: so he was making use of all the arguments he could, on a public platform, to discourage their extension. Other people shared his opinion. It lay near the root of a comment made by Henry James on Victorian Britain as a whole (all classes included) in 1899. He saw it then as 'a community mainly devoted to travelling and shooting, to pushing trade and playing football'.[41] He had his own reasons for taking a despondent view of the country at that time. At the close of his life he came to modify it. Every one of the activities he referred to was promoted by railways, or even depended on them. So did the smooth working of much else in the whole society, less apparent on the surface but of more fundamental importance.

Railways were indeed, in Harold Perkin's good phrase, 'the great connecter'.[42] Having formed their connections they came to penetrate into every corner of the Victorian world.

NOTES

Abbreviations used in the Notes

Acworth RE	W. M. Acworth, *The Railways of England* (1889 and subsequent eds.)
Acworth RS	W. M. Acworth, *The Railways of Scotland* (1890)
AG	Art Gallery
Ahrons BSRL	E. L. Ahrons, *The British Steam Railway Locomotive* [1927]
Ahrons LTW	E. L. Ahrons, *Locomotive and Train Working in the Latter Part of the Nineteenth Century* (1951–4)
Bagehot, *Works*	W. Bagehot, *Collected Works*, ed. N. St-J. Stevas (1965–86)
Bagwell RCH	P. S. Bagwell, *The Railway Clearing House* (1968)
Barclay-Harvey	Sir M. Barclay-Harvey, *History of the Great North of Scotland Railway* (2nd ed., 1949)
Barry	J. W. Barry, *Railway Appliances* (4th ed., 1884)
BE	Sir N. Pevsner and others, *The Buildings of England* (1951–74)
Biddle GRS	G. Biddle, *Great Railway Stations of Britain* (1986)
Biddle VS	G. Biddle, *Victorian Stations* (1973)
Boase	F. Boase, *Modern English Biography* (1965 ed.)
BR	T. C. Barker and M. Robbins, *History of London Transport* (1975–6 ed.)
Bradshaw	*Bradshaw's Railway Guide*
Brooke, *Navvy*	D. Brooke, *The Railway Navvy* (1983)
BRSM	*Bradshaw's Railway Manual, Shareholder's Guide, etc.*
Brunel	I. Brunel, *Life of Isambard Kingdom Brunel* (1870)
Chaloner, *Crewe*	W. H. Chaloner, *Social and Economic Development of Crewe* (1950)
Clark, *Bidder*	E. F. Clark, *George Parker Bidder* (1983)
CMCR	R. Christiansen and R. W. Miller, *The Cambrian Railways* (1967–8)
CMNS	R. Christiansen and R. W. Miller, *The North Staffordshire Railway* (1971)
Conder	F. R. Conder, *The Men who built Railways* (1983); originally published as *Personal Recollections of English Engineers* (1868)
DBB	*Dictionary of Business Biography*
Dickens	References are to the *New Oxford Illustrated Dickens*
DNB	*Dictionary of National Biography*
Dow GC	G. Dow, *Great Central* (1959–65)
FF	E. Foxwell and T. C. Farrer, *Express Trains English and Foreign* (1889)
Findlay	Sir G. Findlay, *The Working and Management of an English Railway* (1889 and subsequent eds.)
Francis	J. Francis, *History of the English Railway* (1851)
Gourvish, *Huish*	T. R. Gourvish, *Mark Huish and the London & North Western Railway* (1972)
Grinling	C. H. Grinling, *History of the Great Northern Railway* (1966 ed.)
Hansard	Hansard's Parliamentary Debates (House of Commons)
Head SP	Sir F. Head, *Stokers and Pokers* (2nd ed. 1849)
Herapath	*Herapath's Railway Magazine*
Heritage	G. Biddle and O. S. Nock, *The Railway Heritage of Britain* (1983)
HLRO	House of Lords Record Office
ICE	Institution of Civil Engineers
IGM	Ironbridge Gorge Museum, Telford, Shropshire
Irving	R. J. Irving, *The North Eastern Railway Company, 1870–1914* (1976)
Jackman	W. T. Jackman, *Transportation in Modern England* (1916)
JLLR	A. A. Jackson, *London's Local Railways* (1978)
JMet R	A. A. Jackson, *London's Metropolitan Railway* (1986)
JLT	A. A. Jackson, *London's Termini* (1972 ed.)
JTH	*Journal of Transport History*
Kellett	J. R. Kellett, *The Impact of Railways on Victorian Cities* (1969)
Lee PCD	C. E. Lee, *Passenger Class Distinctions* (1946)
Lefèvre & Cerbelaud	P. Lefèvre & G. Cerbelaud, *Les Chemins de Fer* (1888)
Lewis	M. J. T. Lewis, *Early Wooden Railways* (1974 ed.)
Lowe BSLB	J. W. Lowe, *British Steam Locomotive Builders* (1975)
LPA	Local and Personal Acts of Parliament
MacDermot	E. T. MacDermot, *History of the Great Western Railway* (1964 ed.)
Marshall 1830	C. F. D. Marshall, *History of British Railways down to the Year 1830* (1971 ed.)
Marshall LMR	C. F. D. Marshall, *Centenary History of the Liverpool & Manchester Railway* (1830)
Marshall LYR	J. Marshall, *The Lancashire & Yorkshire Railway* (1969–72)
Mitchell and Deane	B. R. Mitchell and P. Deane, *Abstract of British Historical Statistics* (1962)
Neele	G. P. Neele, *Railway Reminiscences* (1904)
NRM	National Railway Museum

OED	*Oxford English Dictionary* (1971 ed., with Supplement)	RTC	J. Simmons, *The Railway in Town and Country, 1830–1914* (1986)
Ottley	G. Ottley, *Bibliography of British Railway History* (1966, with Supplement, 1988)	Ruskin, *Works*	J. Ruskin, *Works*, ed. E. T. Cook and A. Wedderburn (1903–12)
Parris	H. Parris, *Government and the Railways in Nineteenth-Century Britain* (1965)	RYB	*Railway Year Book*
		SB	Signalling Study Group, *The Signal Box* (1986)
Perdonnet	A. Perdonnet, *Traité élémentaire des chemins de fer* (1865 ed.)	SM	The Science Museum, London
PGA	Public General Acts of Parliament	SRO	Scottish Record Office, Edinburgh
PL	Public Library (the Central Reference Library of the town concerned)	SPS	J. Simmons, *St Pancras Station* (1968)
PP	*Parliamentary Papers*. The pagination given is that of the set in BL. All are House of Commons papers, except those indicated as 'PP (HL)'	*Stationmaster*	[*H. A. Simmons,*] *Memoirs of a Stationmaster* (1974: new ed. of *Ernest Struggles*, 1879). The author's initials are wrongly given on the title-page as 'E. J.'
		Thomas LFR	R. H. G. Thomas, *London's First Railway* (1972)
PRO	Public Record Office, Kew	Thomas LMR	R. H. G. Thomas, *The Liverpool & Manchester Railway* (1980)
Profile	*Locomotives in Profile*, ed. B. Reed (1971–4)	Thorne LSS	[R. Thorne,] *Liverpool Street Station* (1978)
R	The group 'RAIL' at the PRO	Tomlinson	W. W. Tomlinson, *The North Eastern Railway* [1915]
RB3	J. Simmons, *The Railways of Britain* (3rd ed., 1986)	Turner LBSCR	J. H. Turner, *The London Brighton & South Coast Railway* (1977–9)
RCHM	Royal Commission on Historical Monuments: Reports	*VCH*	*Victoria History of the Counties of England*
Reed, *Crewe*	B. Reed, *Crewe Locomotive Works and its Men* (1982)	*Victorian City*	*The Victorian City*, ed. H. J. Dyos and M. Wolff (1973)
Reg. Hist.	*A Regional History of the Railways of Great Britain*, ed. D. St. J. Thomas and others (1960–89)	Whishaw RGB	F. Whishaw, *The Railways of Great Britain and Ireland* (2nd ed., 1842)
Repr.	Reproduced in...	Williams LSWR	R. A. Williams, *The London & South Western Railway* (1968–73)
REW	J. Simmons, *The Railway in England and Wales, 1830–1914* (1978)	Wrottesley GNR	J. Wrottesley, *The Great Northern Railway* (1979–81)
RM	*Railway Magazine*	WTT	Working Timetables
RO	Record Office (Archives Office in some places)	*Zug der Zeit*	*Zug der Zeit – Zeit der Züge: Deutsche Eisenbahn 1835–1985* (pub. Siedler, Berlin, 1985)
Robertson	C. J. A. Robertson, *The Origins of the Scottish Railway System, 1722–1844* (1983)		

Chapter 1

1 2 *Fortnightly Review* (1867) 518, reprinted in the opening paragraph of his *Physics and Politics* (1872).
2 *Anticipations* (1902), 4.
3 A description of a journey over the line made in October 1830 was written for the *Village Magazine* of Wath-upon-Dearne, Yorkshire. See 126 RM (1980) 407–9.
4 *Journals*, ed. A.R. Ferguson, iv (1964), 226.
5 F. Kemble, *Record of a Girlhood* (1878), ii. 159–64.
6 Abbé J.A. Dubois to J. Menzies, 25 April 1831: SRO, GD237/117/6.
7 Chaps. 5 and 16.
8 *Middlemarch*, chap. 56.
9 Conder, 9–10.
10 See A. Burton, *The Canal Builders*

(1972), 133; for landowners' objections to canal building, Jackman, 396–7.
11 Consider the mild skirmishes between the surveyors for the Wey & Avon Canal and landowners and farmers in 1811–12: P. A. L. Vine, *London's Lost Route to the Sea* (1965), 52.
12 Morritt to J. G. Lockhart, 4 June 1838: National Library of Scotland, MS. 935, letter 19.
13 *Public Addresses* (1879), 414.
14 J. C. Young, *Memoir of Charles Mayne Young* (2nd ed., 1871), 296–7. The cutting is probably the one north of Lyneham, near the edge of the steep Wootton Bassett incline, rising eastwards; but the incline continues more gently for another five

miles. Did they see two trains, the other tearing westwards down the bank?
15 Somerset RO, DD/X/SFF C/1722; *Stationmaster*, 94–7.
16 As on the timber viaducts in Cornwall: MacDermot, ii. 146–7.
17 Attempts to illuminate railway tunnels did not succeed: Turner LBSCR, i.141.
18 A. R. Bennett, *London and Londoners in the Eighteen-Fifties and Sixties* (1924), 242.
19 Lady C. B. Noble, *The Brunels Father and Son* (1938), 149–51; 93 RM (1947) 246.
20 PP 1839 ix. 386.
21 See G. Hardy, *The Londonderry Railway* (1973), 12–15, 19.
22 Earl Stanhope, *Conversations with*

the *Duke of Wellington* (World's Classics ed.), 124.

23 RTC, 308.

24 *Wellington and his Friends*, ed. 7th Duke of Wellington (1965), 244, 266–7.

25 See *Gryll Grange: Novels*, ed. D. Garnett (1948), 808, 877.

26 In 1840–1912 boiler explosions are stated to have caused eighty-three deaths among railwaymen in the United Kingdom, and nine more among bystanders; none to a passenger in a train. Reckoning from C. H. Hewitson, *Locomotive Boiler Explosions* (1983).

27 All these horrors were exemplified within two months in 1864. See *Annual Register*, 1864, Chronicle, 117–18; *The Times*, 20 July 1864, 12.

28 See L. T. C. Rolt, *Red for Danger* (4th ed., 1982), 181.

29 At Hawes Junction, Ditton Junction, and Ais Gill: *ibid.*, 173, 200, 233.

30 Arnold Bennett was in one in France, at Mantes on 7 July 1911: *Letters*, ii (1968), 285–6.

31 A. Ponsonby, *Henry Ponsonby* (1942), 312–13.

32 Francis, ii. 59, 60.

33 *Railway Jubilee at Darlington*, ed. J. S. Jeans (1875), 35.

34 As in the fierce winter of 1891: WIR, 427–36. The storm of March 1886 in the country south of Sunderland is graphically described in Hardy, *The Londonderry Railway*, 76–82. For snowstorms in the north of Scotland see H. A. Vallance, *The Highland Railway* (4th ed., 1985), 113–18.

35 J. Pendleton, *Our Railways* (1896), ii. 507.

36 See 8 RM (1901) 462–7.

37 The Queen was only once in serious danger on her railway journeys to and from Scotland, at Forfar in 1863 (Neele, 483); though the driver of her train was killed in 1898 (RB3, 210). Her eldest son had a narrow escape in 1869, travelling on the Caledonian Railway. The engine was then derailed in passing over Drumlithie viaduct. See PP 1870 lix. 135–7. A good idea of the elaborate arrangements adopted for the journeys of royal trains can be got from the papers in R1014/9–12 and, for some made in Scotland, from SRO, BR/HRPS/3/1–24, 43. Special security precautions had to be taken in 1880–3 and in 1891 (Findlay, 6th ed., 1899, 27, 222; HRPS/3/8). In 1896 the journey of the Tsar and Tsarina of Russia from Leith to Ballater (for Balmoral) and

afterwards to Portsmouth was especially complicated to manage (*ibid.*, 3/11).

38 True perfection must include the ability to rectify errors or unforeseen misfortunes. Queen Victoria's funeral train was delayed at Fareham, leaving there nine minutes late, but the crew of the London Brighton & South Coast locomotive *Empress* made up all that time, to arrive at Victoria station two minutes early; pleasing Edward VII, who was meeting it and detested unpunctuality, and delighting the German Emperor William II, who was a passenger and had probably never travelled as fast before, or would again. See 86 RM (1940) 136–40.

39 Quoted in Brooke, *Navvy*, 106.

40 R. Smiles, *Memoir of the late Henry Booth* (1869), 113.

Chapter 2

1 Lewis, 157; *Reg. Hist.*, xii. 33, 88.

2 Marshall 1830, 117–19.

3 The Surrey Iron Railway and the Kilmarnock & Troon were however laid out as double lines at the beginning.

4 BL Add. MS. 35071, f. 117; Tomlinson, 254–5.

5 L. T. C. Rolt, *Thomas Telford* (1958), 112, 115; J. Copeland, *Roads and their Traffic* (1960), 57.

6 See RB3, 108; RTC, 307.

7 Reckoning from those for four railways, given in Whishaw RGB, 22–3, 53, 189, 327; for the most expensive see 271, 22, 316.

8 PP 1844 xli. 171.

9 Brooke, *Navvy*, 69–70.

10 19 RM (1906) 182.

11 See D. Brooke, 'The Advent of the Steel Rail, 1857–1914': 7 JTH (3rd series, 1986) 18–31.

12 Reed, *Crewe*, 78

13 Dates in J. Gough, *The Midland Railway: a Chronology* (1986), 12, 21. The engineer of both structures was J. Underwood.

14 For tunnelling on canals see A. Burton, *The Canal Builders* (1972), 195–9.

15 30 *Trans. Leicestershire Archaeological Society* (1954) 63–7, 79.

16 His sketches for some of these works are in Bristol University Library: e.g. Brunel Misc. Sketchbook 1, f. 56; Sketchbook 1836, f. 18.

17 PP 1846 xiii. See also Dow GC, i. 60–8; Brooke, *Navvy*, 155–6.

18 J. Devey, *Life of Joseph Locke* (1862), 120.

19 *Strictures on a Pamphlet* (1846); full title in Ottley, 4002.

20 Marshall LYR, i. 43–4, 74–5, 182, 190, 197–8.

21 T. A. Walker, *The Severn Tunnel: its Construction and Difficulties* (1888).

22 *Ibid.*, 46–51.

23 *Ibid.*, 110–16, 131–4.

24 For reasons arising from the law of property: see BR, i.100.

25 *Ibid.*, plates 39–42.

26 For conditions imposed on the District Railway see LPA, 27 & 28 Vict. cap. cccxxii, sects. 34, 55.

27 Such a device had been used by Marc Brunel in his Thames Tunnel.

28 For the line in its early days see 4 RM (1899) 52–9.

29 RE, 471.

30 L. Troske, *Die Londoner Untergrundbahnen* (1892, reprinted in 1986, with introduction by R. M. Robbins); G. Kemmann, *Der Verkehr Londons* (1892).

31 Engineers of course appreciated them. See for instance the discussion of the tunnels driven under the Thames for the Bakerloo tube in 150 *Proc. ICE.* (1902) 25–54.

32 *Heritage*, 168.

33 See the admirable section on Scotland in *Heritage*, 120–73.

34 Whishaw RGB, 73.

35 J. C. Bourne, *History of the Great Western Railway* (1845), 40.

36 Francis, i. 190.

37 See L. G. Booth's excellent chapter 6 in *The Works of Isambard Kingdom Brunel*, ed. Sir A. Pugsley (1980).

38 *Brunel*, 192.

39 MacDermot, ii. 146–7, 149, 161.

40 Details in *ibid.*, ii. 146–7.

41 Marshall 1830, 123; B. Morgan, *Civil Engineering: Railways* (1971), 17, 162.

42 D. Walters, *British Railway Bridges* [1963], 19, 21.

43 While it was being built, Stephenson's reputation had suffered a damaging blow from the collapse of his Dee bridge at Chester in 1847.

44 The crossing of navigable water could be made at a lower level if the bridge opened for the passage of ships by sliding, revolving or lifting. There were sliding bridges on the London & Birmingham Railway (1838) and near Arundel (1846). The first revolving bridge for a railway in Britain, at Trowse outside Norwich, was designed by G. P. Bidder (1845). Others followed, on the same principle: in Scotland for example at Clachnaharry outside Inverness (1862) and at Alloa on the Forth (1885). The first lifting bridges in Britain seem to have been Robert Stephenson's at Leicester (1834) and Brunel's at Carmarthen

(1854); the most sophisticated was at Keadby on the Great Central Railway, built to an American design in 1912–16.

45 There is a good account of this work in P. S. A. Berridge, *The Girder Bridge* (1969), chap. 4.

46 See Mitchell and Deane, 493.

47 Berridge, 47–8.

48 In the Crumlin viaduct this was replaced by iron plates in 1868; the other two retained their timber decking to the end.

49 Tomlinson, 695; *Reg. Hist.*, iv. 26, 69.

50 See the final verdict of the Commissioner of Wrecks, W. H. Rothery, a member of the Court of Inquiry into the accident: PP 1880 xxxix. 41.

51 For these accidents see Berridge, chaps. 6 and 7.

52 151 *Proc. ICE.* (1903) 397.

53 Berridge, 74.

54 A most valuable series of 472 photographs showing the site and the bridge under construction (1883–90) is in SRO, BR/FOR/4/34.

55 C. E. Lee, *Metropolitan District Railway* (1956), 6–7. The bridge stood for only about four years.

56 Illustrated in *Heritage*, 87.

57 E. Clark, *The Britannia and Conway Tubular Bridges* (1850), 533–4. The original design forms the frontispiece to the second volume of this work.

58 R. Taylor, *George Washington Wilson* (1981), 86, 90.

59 T. Mackay, *Life of Sir John Fowler* (1900), 314, 316.

60 Tomlinson 123, 130.

61 Thomas LMR, 128.

62 *Ibid.*, 108, 119, 123, 225; R. S. Fitzgerald, *Liverpool Road Station, Manchester* (1980), 57–8.

63 K. H. Vignoles, *Charles Blacker Vignoles* (1982), 175.

64 R. Wood, *West Hartlepool* (1967), 20.

65 Sir N. Pevsner, *History of Building Types* (1976), 227.

66 The separation of responsibilities between Tite and Turner is set out by Tite, as he saw it, in a letter to Henry Booth of the London & North Western Railway, 13 April 1849: R1008/96 (R204).

67 Dobson signed on his own some at least of the payments to builders for work done: R527/79.

68 Bristol Univ. Library: Brunel Large Sketchbook 3, ff. 5, 10, 32, 37.

69 L. T. C. Rolt, *Isambard Kingdom Brunel* (paperback ed.), 301.

70 Biddle discusses this matter admirably: GRS, 111–13.

71 A water-colour drawing of it by John O'Connor is at Dunster Castle, Somerset.

72 Managing committee reports, BL 08235, f. 97.

73 See Biddle VS, 62–7, for a summary of his English railway practice.

74 See D. Cole's paper on these stations in 3 JTH (1957–8) 149–57; C. Barman, *Introduction to Railway Architecture* (1950), 46, 64–5.

75 Brunel wrote to him on 10 Jan. 1842, asking him to send in his account for work done on the refreshment room at Swindon and saying he would be glad to have his assistance with the design of some 'cottages at Swindon of a totally monumental description' (Bristol Univ. Library, Brunel Private letter-book 26, f. 249). Thompson's reply does not appear to have survived.

76 7 JTH (1955–6) 10.

77 Assuming that he is the Francis Thompson of 15 St Mary Abbot's Terrace, Kensington (formerly of 11 Conduit Street, Hanover Square), whose will, dated 6 July 1871, was proved on 27 December following, the estate being sworn at under £12,000.

78 See M. J. Minett's article in 7 JTH (1965–6) 44–53.

79 See his name in the index to *BE York and E. Riding*.

80 By G. Beale: *British Railway Journal*, no. 8 (1985).

81 30 *Proc. ICE.* (1869–70) 78–105.

82 Holborn Viaduct was not so served, but all trains running into it stopped at St Paul's, which offered a connection with the underground railway.

83 33 *Builder* (1875) 315.

84 *Railway Appliances* (4th ed., 1884), 199.

85 See the photograph in 2 RM (1898) 484.

86 Birmingham Snow Hill was rebuilt at platform level, but the old buildings above were retained.

87 C. Johnston and J. R. Hume, *Glasgow Stations* (1979), 41.

88 A good account of the station is given by Johnston and Hume. See also Matheson's own brief account of it in 21 RM (1907) 196–9; O. S. Nock, *Caledonian Railway* (1973 ed.), 112–16, 119–21; Biddle GRS, 129, 163–4.

89 O. Green, *The London Underground* (1987), 31.

90 Mins. of shareholders of hotel company, 1 September 1840: R384/98.

91 See my *Victorian Hotel* (1984), 4–5, and RTC, 56, with references given there.

92 Many years later some of them secured these powers: the Bristol & Exeter in 1874, the Caledonian, Cambrian, and Midland in 1891–2, and then fifteen more companies in 1897–1905: PP 1911 xxix. 925–33.

93 The Crewe Arms was at first no more than an inn, built by Lord Crewe.

94 J. B. Radford, *Derby Works and Midland Locomotives* (1971), 14.

95 G. Measom, *Guide to the Great Western Railway* (1852), 42–3; PP 1852–3 xxxvii. 516–17, 611. For the one at Normanton see *Reg. Hist.*, viii. 110.

96 R770/32.

97 *VCH City of York*, 477, 480–1. *Murray's Handbook for Yorkshire* (1882 ed.) called it 'tolerably good'; it was still listed in the edition of 1904.

98 Wrottesley GNR, i. 81.

99 *Report of a Special Committee on Great Western Affairs* (1856), 13.

100 H.-R. Hitchcock, *Early Victorian Architecture in Britain* (1954), 212–13; *Victorian City*, 324.

101 See prospectus in BL, 1881 b. 23.

102 See SPS, 93.

103 For other examples see *Victorian City*, 309 (note 113).

104 SPS, 49.

105 *Ibid.*, 78–81.

106 Arnold Bennett in *The Grand Babylon Hotel* (Penguin ed.), 41.

107 Thorne LPS, 38–40.

108 Dow GC, iii. 5–7.

109 For the gang see J. Thomas, *The North British Railway* (1969–75), ii. 148–50; and for comment on the building – judicious and restrained, just and deadly – *Buildings of Scotland, Edinburgh*, 285.

110 See RTC, 257.

111 *Ibid.*, 259.

112 Sir M. Barclay-Harvey, *History of the Great North of Scotland Railway* (1949 ed.), 112–13.

113 *Reg. Hist.*, xiv. 100, 124.

114 P. E. Baughan, *Chester & Holyhead Railway* (1972), 255–7.

115 Papers relating to this hotel are in R253/24–6; 266/45, 109; 267/45.

116 PP 1914–16 lx. 735–41, 792–4.

117 R236/193, pp. 275, 293, 310, 344.

118 GWR statistics, sect. vii (R266/109).

119 T. Woodman, *The Railways to Hayes* (1982), 31–2.

120 CMCR, ii. 55, 58.

121 R405/34, p. 32.

122 1910 ed., 25.

123 *Liverpool Road Station, Manchester* (1980), 29–49. The building survives, now forming part of the Greater Manchester Museum of Science and Industry.

124 Thomas LMR, 131–3.

125 See the description in Head SP, 69–75.

126 The station is meticulously depicted in three large water-colour drawings at the NRM.

127 See RTC, 42–3.

128 See plans of those at King's Cross and Paddington in Perdonnet, ii. 311–12.

129 This process was already under way at Nine Elms by 1862: *Stanford's Map of London* (1862), plate 14.

130 See Kellett, 320; RTC, 49–50; 6 RM (1900) 315.

131 *Ibid.*, 313–14, 318–19.

132 See Acworth RE, 114–19, and Findlay (6th ed., 1899), 240–52.

133 Dow GC, i. 73; Acworth RE, 11–13.

134 PP 1881 xiii. 681.

135 Sir C. Reilly, *Some Manchester Streets and their Buildings* (1924), 80–1.

136 *Heritage*, 99; P. J. G. Ransom, *Archaeology of Railways* (1981), 252.

137 *Some Liverpool Streets and Buildings in 1921* (1921), 48–9.

138 See the plan of the site in Dow GC, ii. 409.

139 The Great Central was primarily a carrier of freight. In 1913 freight traffic accounted for nearly three-quarters of the company's total receipts.

140 Findlay (1st ed., 1889), 202.

141 A. S. Peck, *The Great Western at Swindon Works* (1983), plate 62.

142 Repr. Peck, pl. 17.

143 See *ibid.*, 129–35; J. B. Radford, *Derby Works and Midland Locomotives* (1971), pls. 61–5, 68–9.

144 Peck, 15, 19.

145 S. C. Brees, *Railway Practice*, 4th series (1847), pl. 63; Radford, 15; Whishaw RGB, 320, 375; Marshall LYR, i. 44.

146 7 JTH (1965–6) 158–9.

147 *Remarks on Secular and Domestic Architecture* (1857), 218.

148 Plan in Dow GC, i. 212.

149 *Railway Practice* (3rd ed., 1847), 243, plates 51–6.

150 Perdonnet, ii. 297 (with plan).

151 See the report of Barton Wright, the Lancashire & Yorkshire locomotive superintendent, to his directors in 1885, summarized in Marshall LYR, iii. 97–8.

152 D. L. Bradley, *Locomotive History of the South Eastern Railway* (1985 ed.), 224.

153 The numbers of signal-boxes are taken from SB.

154 See the diagram in R. D. Foster, *Pictorial History of LNWR Signalling* (1982), 254.

155 SB, 26.

156 *Ibid.*, 8–9, 33; plates 13, 16.

157 *Ibid.*, plate 275.

158 *Ibid.*, plates 158, 172, 260.

159 SB, plates 62–4, 163, 166, 247; A. Vaughan, *Pictorial Record of Great Western Signalling* (1984 ed.), plate 110.

160 SB, 197.

161 *Ibid.*, 136–46.

162 See for example the big box at Bradford: *ibid.*, plate 212.

163 *Ibid.*, plate 91.

164 Foster, 14–16.

165 A good idea of the scale of the machinery is given in *ibid.*, plate 11.8.

166 SB, plate 40.

167 *Ibid.*, 54–5, 112–13 and plates 272, 274.

168 A. A. Maclean, *Pictorial Survey of LNER Constituent Signalling* (1983), 192, 181.

169 SB, 197, plate 298.

170 For a general discussion of railway towns see RTC, chap. 6.

171 Chaloner, *Crewe*, 44–5; Head SP, 82.

172 R250/2, pp. 158–61, 176.

173 J. Orbach, *Victorian Architecture in Britain* (1987), 447.

174 See Peck, 49–51 and plate 11; *Heritage*, 226; K. Hudson in 1 *Transport History* (1968), 130–52.

175 Chaloner, 49, 50–1, 197–8.

176 RTC, 190–2.

177 Barclay-Harvey, 141–2. See photographs in SRO, BR/GNS/4/44.

178 *The Glasgow & South Western Railway* (Stephenson Locomotive Society, 1950), 19; 28 RM (1911) 286.

179 R220/35.

180 R44/6.

181 As at Malton, Yorks.: 7 JTH (1965–6) 46.

182 Penkridge, Staffs., is an example: Biddle VS, 24.

183 3 JTH (1957–8), 154.

184 *Stationmaster*, 90.

185 *Trans. Soc. for Promotion of Social Science*, 1874, 617.

186 It may have been due to Watkin that another company (of which he was also chairman), the South Eastern, took powers in 1872 to erect houses for its servants (LPA 35 & 36 Vict., cap 53, sect. 50) and that a third, the Metropolitan, built houses for its men from 1882 onwards. In the last case, however, the rents charged were much more than economic, representing a $6\frac{1}{2}\%$ return on the capital invested. See JMetR, 82–3.

187 *Railway Appliances* (1884 ed.), 190–1.

188 Findlay (1st ed., 1889), 167.

189 SRO, BR/COB/4/25A.

190 J. H. Proud, *Stockton & Darlington House Number Plaques* (North Eastern Railway Association, 1974): copy in NRM library. Specimens of the London & Birmingham plates are at the NRM.

191 Findlay, 168; 41 *Builder* (1881) 406. Figures from annual reports for 1914: R1116/150.

192 Chaloner, *Crewe*, 65.

193 6 RM (1900) 392–3.

194 Photograph in NRM: Horwich F 736.

195 See Kellett, 337–46, and RTC, 32–5, with references given in both.

Chapter 3

1 Reckoning from annual reports in R1116/150.

2 Thomas LMR, 172–7.

3 Neele, 145.

4 John H. White jr., *American Locomotives* (1968), 5. On this subject more generally see J. Jewkes, D. Sawers, and R. Stillerman, *The Sources of Invention* (1960).

5 The railways' development is admirably set in its context in A. Briggs, *The Power of Steam* (1982).

6 *Profile*, i. 99–100.

7 J. G. H. Warren, *A Century of Locomotive Building* (1923), 93–4, 96; chap. 23, esp. 309, note 3.

8 Lowe BSLB, 179–80, 553.

9 Disregarding firms known to have built only one or two locomotives. See E. Craven in 9 *Locomotion* (1938) 7, 24; Lowe BSLB.

10 D. L. Bradley, *Locomotive History of the South Eastern Railway* (1985 ed.), 23; C. J. Allen, *Great Eastern Railway* (1975 ed.), 86.

11 PP 1839 x. 302, 375.

12 P. Lecount, *Practical Treatise on Railways* (1839), 198.

13 For these machines see MacDermot, i. 372–97; papers relating to them are in R1008/37–47.

14 MacDermot, i. 466.

15 A file of inventors' submissions to the company is at R1008/57.

16 C. Babbage, *Passages from the Life of a Philosopher* (1864), 323–5.

17 MacDermot, i. 412.

18 PP 1846 xvi. 694–726.

19 Ahrons BSRL, 69–70. See also H. C. B. Rogers, *G. J. Churchward* (1975), 22–3, 116.

20 For the history of this form of traction see C. Hadfield, *Atmospheric Railways* (2nd ed., 1985).

21 Hadfield, 39, 196–200.

22 The Edinburgh & Glasgow

(1844), London & Birmingham and Glasgow Paisley Kilmarnock & Ayr (1845), Glasgow Paisley & Greenock and Great Western (1846), and Lancashire & Yorkshire (1847) – disregarding companies that built one or two engines only. See entries in Lowe BSLB.

23 White, 19.

24 Thomas LMR, 166.

25 B. Poole, *The Economy of Railways* (1856), 15. Lardner, however, merely commended the practice, considering that it had been forced on the companies by the manufacturers' inability to supply their needs satisfactorily: *Railway Economy* (1850), 107–8.

26 Except the three machines built in France in 1903–5: see p. 91.

27 MacDermot, ii. 284; Reed, *Crewe*, 142.

28 Radford, 67, 69, 89.

29 Reckoning from appendices of locomotives built, published in each volume of Dow GC.

30 Ahrons BSRL, 24–5.

31 See S. C. Brees, *Railway Practice* (4th ed., 1847), lxxvi, plate 11.

32 As on the Lancashire & Yorkshire Railway: Marshall LYR, iii. 101.

33 See Bagwell RCH, 37–8, 42–3, 49–50.

34 Flagmen signalled the whole line from New York to Albany as late as 1870: *Appleton's Handbook of American Travel. Northern and Eastern Tours* [1870], 50.

35 This section owes much to J. Kieve, *The Electric Telegraph* (1973).

36 See G. Wilson, *The Old Telegraphs* (1976).

37 T. Baines, *Liverpool in 1859* (1859), part ii, 58–60.

38 B. Bowers, *Sir Charles Wheatstone* (1975), 15, 100–2.

39 Williams LSWR, i. 243. The agreements successively concluded between the Electric Telegraph Company and the London & South Western Railway are in R411/348-59, 362.

40 Dow GC, i. 63; MacDermot i. 320.

41 Calculation from PP 1861 lvii. 207.

42 Ahrons BSRL, 163.

43 White, 32.

44 In America some engineers were preferring it still in 1904: *ibid*.

45 The account of British practice here is based chiefly on Ahrons BSRL, 103–6, 206–7, 284.

46 H. Ellis, *Railway Carriages in the British Isles* (1965), 52–5.

47 F. A. S. Brown, *Great Northern Locomotive Engineers* (1966), 91–2;

MacDermot, ii. 303.

48 A 'railway reading lamp' is advertised in G. Measom, *South Western Railway Guide* [1856], advts., p. 6.

49 M. Robbins, *North London Railway* (1953 ed.), 24; JMetR, 28.

50 Findlay (1891 ed.), 126; *British Railway Journal*, no. 13 (1986), 164.

51 *Railway Economy*, 85.

52 Wilkie Collins observed them, travelling from Boulogne to Paris in 1855: K. Robinson, *Wilkie Collins* (1951), 88.

53 MacDermot, i. 371; Williams LSWR, i. 236.

54 Marshall LYR, iii. 103.

55 R250/6, p. 416.

56 PP 1865 i. 17–29.

57 PGA 31 & 32 Vict. cap. 119, sect. 22.

58 R. D. Foster, *Pictorial Record of LNWR Signalling* (1984), 4–6.

59 *Ibid.*, 8.

60 L. T. C. Rolt, *Red for Danger* (4th ed., 1982), 54–5.

61 PGA 3–4 Vict. cap. 7, sect. 5; PGA 6 Vict. cap. 55, sect. 6.

62 Parris, 91; T. Coates, *Railways and the Board of Trade again discussed* (1864), 16.

63 PP 1862 liii. 171; 1873 lvii 553–4.

64 PP 1866 lxiii. 119, 220.

65 PP 1871 lx. 277.

66 PP 1854–5 xlviii. 468, 483; 1856 liv. 403, 405.

67 L. T. C. Rolt, *Isambard Kingdom Brunel* (1957). 217.

68 See 37 *Proc. ICE* (1874) 240.

69 PP 1875 lxiv. 331. The Board's brief and dignified answers were admirable.

70 PP 1873 lvii. 420.

71 The Nord company shareholders, for example, for many years received 13% a year. The highest dividend ever paid over a long continuous period by any large railway in Great Britain after 1847 was the North Eastern's average of 7.95% over the years 1871–83.

72 Lefèvre & Cerbelaud, 296.

73 PP 1844 xi. 375.

74 *Ibid.*, 615–16.

75 *Railway Property: its Condition and Prospects* (1849), 57.

76 Hansard, 3rd series 72 (1844), col. 252.

77 See board mins. 1211, 1223, 1241, 1252, R635/36.

78 Findlay (3rd ed., 1900), 158; (6th ed., 1899), 313.

79 See plan of the original train (it was soon altered) in Neele, 411. The corridor was not intended to allow passengers 'the opportunity of promenading the whole length of the train', however: see K. Hudson,

Working to Rule (1970), 14.

80 The price of the smaller of the two standard Midland types was £1700 in 1908: R. E. Lacy and G. Dow, *Midland Railway Carriages* (1984–6), 220.

81 Calculation from D. Jenkinson, *Illustrated History of LNWR Coaches* (1978), 27, 34, 168, and from D. Jenkinson and B. Essery, *Midland Carriages* (1984), 60, 62.

82 R491/173, min. 6956. See also Lacy and Dow, 28–9.

83 For what follows see *ibid.*, chap. 3, where the details of the company's new vehicles are set out admirably and related to its recorded policies.

84 Lacy and Dow, 79.

85 Wrottesley GNR, ii. 184.

86 Marshall LYR, iii. 110–11; H. Ellis, *South Western Railway* (1956), 126.

87 MacDermot, ii. 302; Jenkinson, *LNWR Coaches*, 4, 8.

88 O. S. Nock, *Caledonian Railway* (1973 ed.), 108; Stephenson Locomotive Society, *Glasgow & South Western Railway* (1950), 44; Barclay-Harvey, 212.

89 Some of them are well explained in H. Ellis, *Railway Carriages in the British Isles* (1965), 207–9. For the difficulties experienced in France see Perdonnet, iii. 576, iv. 336.

90 Dow GC, i. 218; Williams LSWR i. 236; Marshall LYR, iii. 103.

91 Acworth RS, 179.

92 Lacy and Dow, 439; Dow GC, ii. 264.

93 Lacy and Dow, 258.

94 G. Behrend, *Pullman in Europe* (1962), 37–8.

95 Lacy and Dow, 58, 95, 101, 120, 175, 452.

96 H. D. Welch, *London Tilbury & Southend Railway* (1951), 31; CMNS, 241; Barclay-Harvey, 211.

97 Findlay (1st ed., 1889), 139–40.

98 The North British board received a suggestion that 'certain conveniences should be placed in passenger carriages' in 1862, which it disregarded (SRO, BR/NBR/1/10. 16 April 1862). Various 'conveniences for travelling' were offered by surgical manufacturers. See advertisements in Bradshaw, June 1861, xvii, and Eyre Bros. (pub.), *Watering Places of the South of England* (1877), advts., p. 155a.

99 See Perdonnet, iv. 75; RB3, 176.

100 Brown, *Great Northern Locomotive Engineers*, 226–7; Lacy and Dow, 91. For the technology see Ellis, 214–17.

101 E. Foxwell, *The Best Trains* (1888), 25; Acworth RE (1st ed.),

183.

102 Reckoning from Jenkinson, *LNWR Coaches*, 169–73.

103 Orders were placed by the Great Central company for 218 passenger vehicles in 1902–5 at an average price of £1883 each: Dow GC, iii. 143–4.

104 Reckoning from Lacy and Dow, 55, 59. Writers about rolling stock often fail to supply information about prices and weights of vehicles, or to indicate their capacity. If these essential figures are not available in the records, that should surely be stated. Jenkinson observes however (*LNWR Coaches*, 110) that, in that railway's suburban carriages, increase of size brought a reduction in the weight per passenger seat.

105 PP 1914-16 lx. 787, 789.

106 *Ibid.*

107 The Caledonian company seems by this time to have been using 30-ton wagons for 'general goods' traffic: 21 RM (1907) 205.

108 E. B. Dorsey, *English and American Railroads compared* (2nd ed., 1887), 10, 115.

109 J. Grierson, *Railway Rates English and Foreign* (1886), 119–21.

110 See 22 RM (1908) 445–6.

111 PP 1874 lviii. 435.

112 See Acworth's comments: RS, 187–8.

113 Bagwell RCH, 198.

114 See J. B. Snell, *Mechanical Engineering: Railways* (1971), 127–8.

115 Admirably set out in Bagwell RCH, 198–210.

116 C. I. Savage, *History of the Second World War: Inland Transport* (1957), 68; T. R. Gourvish, *British Railways 1948–73* (1986), 86.

117 R. J. Essery, *Midland Wagons* (1980), i. 157.

118 See RTC, 47, and references given there.

119 Marshall LYR, iii. 122.

120 G. Paish, *The British Railway Position* (1902), 51.

121 For the North Eastern company's policies (much influenced by American example) see Irving, 221–4, 250–3. The Board of Trade's chief inspector, Arthur Yorke, went to America to report on this matter, and his recommendation firmly favoured the 20-ton wagon: PP 1903 lx. 851.

122 A good sample of prices – mainly of locomotives built by the company itself, usually about 10% lower than those charged by manufacturers – is given for the Caledonian 4-4-0s in *Profile*, iv. 222.

123 BSRL, 204.

124 See the excellent study of them by Brian Reed in *Profile*, i. 221–44.

125 PP 1914–16 lx. 982–6.

126 The London, Midland & Scottish company built 195 more of them in 1924–32.

127 See W. A. Tuplin, *Midland Steam* (1973), 92–9, and *The Steam Locomotive* (1974), chap. 5.

128 See H. C. B. Rogers, *G. J. Churchward* (1975), 84.

129 Rogers, 113.

130 For the evolution of the type see *Profile*, i. 49–62.

131 B. Reed in *ibid.*, ii. 195.

132 Reckoning from the returns. Their basis changed in 1913.

133 See Irving, 242; for the Great Western company, H. Holcroft, *Outline of Great Western Locomotive Practice* (1971 ed.), 108.

134 WTT, R968/32 (1888), 67 (1912).

135 Irving, 85.

136 See A. F. Anderson, 'Robert Davidson – Father of the Electric Locomotive' (History of Electrical Engineering Conference 1975, Group 57), and in *New Scientist*, 11 June 1981.

137 R635/110.

138 *Herapath* (1852) 38.

139 The best account of it is by C. S. Lascelles: *The City & South London Railway* (1955).

140 For a full account of this development see BR, vol. ii, chaps. 3–5, 7.

141 Papers in R227/356–7. For its bold experiment with a steam locomotive that achieved the same rate of acceleration as could be got from electricity, see REW, 187.

142 The report is in R491/631.

143 Irving, 257–60.

144 PP 1913–14 lx. 842.

145 PP 1905 xxx. 630.

146 *History of Inland Transport and Communication* (1912), 495.

147 M. Robbins, *The North London Railway* (4th ed., 1953), 24.

148 Marshall LYR, iii. 55–6, 102–3.

149 Neele, 168–9; JMetR, 33.

150 PP 1877 xlviii. 97–121.

151 See the simple tables in Barry, 289–90.

152 He is said, on a well-supported tradition, to have offered Webb £20,000 if he persuaded the London & North Western company to adopt his brake, whereupon Webb curtly broke off negotiations with him: 47 *Railway World* (1986) 543.

153 Deuchars to Conacher, 17 May, 7 October 1897: SRO, BR/NBR/8/1395.

154 PP 1898 lxxxii.

155 MacDermot, ii. 306.

156 MacDermot, ii. 97; Dow GC, ii. 26–8.

157 See for example Barry, 168.

158 PP 1881 lxxx. 27.

159 Neele, 303.

160 This struggle is well treated in Parris, 189–97.

161 PP 1873 lvii. 347–8.

162 SB, 34.

163 *Ibid.* 16, 79, 89, 97–9, 101, 105, 107.

164 PP 1873 lvii. 409.

165 Tyler printed the petition and commended the men for their action: PP 1874 lviii. 359.

166 Grinling, 314; Wrottesley GNR, ii. 44–5.

167 JLT, 85; 25 RM (1909) 346; Vaughan, 21; Foster, 158.

168 C. E. Box, *The Liverpool Overhead Railway* (1984 ed.), 20, 22.

169 C. E. Lee, *The District Line* (1973), 23–4.

170 For the one at Crewe see Foster, 200–6.

171 The instruments are described in Vaughan, 142–3.

172 The reduction in the number of signalmen cannot be calculated from the companies' returns or reports, since signalmen did not form a category of their own there.

173 The typewriter began to be employed in the London & North Western offices about 1890, judging by the reports to the board in 1888–91 (R410/68). For its arrival on the Great Western see *Felix Pole his Book* (1968 ed.), 26.

Chapter 4

1 L. T. C. Rolt, *Thomas Telford* (1958), 39–40.

2 Telford, *Life* (1838), 34.

3 The OED's first example of the use of 'mechanical engineer' is however of 1881 (under 'mechanical' 8b).

4 *Proc. ICE.* (1841) 88–90.

5 Colvin, *Biographical Dictionary of British Architects* (1978) 122; A. F. Sealey and D. Walters, 'The First Railway Architect': 135 *Architectural Review* (1964) 364.

6 See Rolt, *Telford*, 155–61.

7 *Autobiography* (1875), 294.

8 Thomas LMR, 17, 19, 34, 37, 44, 54.

9 Marshall LYR, ii. 18, 29.

10 Robertson, 191–6.

11 This largely explains the unchanging hostility of the Liverpool Quaker James Cropper towards the Stephensons. See L. T. C. Rolt, *George and Robert Stephenson* (1960), 176, 232–3.

12 L. T. C. Rolt, *Isambard Kingdom*

Brunel (1957), 63.

13 G. P. Bidder's surviving diaries do not cover the years in which he was most engaged in railway work (see Clark, *Bidder*, xxv); Daniel Gooch's do not begin until 1868 (Gooch, xvii). The diaries of Henry Robertson for 1845–54 are in the National Library of Wales. They form part of a voluminous archive, including a great many working papers and specifications for the lines Robertson laid down (chiefly in Wales), and they deserve careful study. A useful brief introduction to his work is provided in G. G. Lerry, *Henry Robertson* (1949).

14 Now in the Goldsmiths' Library, University of London.

15 See N. W. Webster, *Britain's First Trunk Line* (1972), 23–5.

16 Marshall LMR, 160–88.

17 By O. J. Vignoles (1889) and K. J. Vignoles (1982). The original diaries are in BL, Add. MSS. 34528–36, 35071.

18 BL, Add. MS. 34528.

19 *Ibid.*, f. 40.

20 *Ibid.*, ff. 154v–76.

21 *Ibid.*, f. 70.

22 From 3 October and 10 November 1838 onwards: Add. MS. 34529.

23 Brian Reed comments on this very unfavourably, in relation to the North Union Railway: *Crewe to Carlisle* (1969), 42–5.

24 Add. MS. 34529 (25 January–14 February 1839).

25 Now at the Institution of Civil Engineers. See M. Robbins in 56 *Trans. Newcomen Society* (1984–5).

26 *Ibid.*, p. 63.

27 By Henry Parris in 6 JTH (1963–4) 14–23. The original diaries for this part of Pasley's life are in BL, Add. MSS. 41989–92.

28 He delighted in speed when riding on the engine's footplate: 6 JTH 19.

29 See for example Conder, 142–4, 154–5.

30 9 *Punch* (1845) 107.

31 Parris, 113.

32 R770/41.

33 See Robertson, 196.

34 J. S. Maclean, *Newcastle & Carlisle Railway* (1948), 49; Williams LSWR, i. 27–9. Giles never ceased taking on too many engagements: R. Pike, *Railway Adventures and Anecdotes* (1884), 127–8.

35 Tomlinson, 351.

36 Boase, iii. 1305.

37 They are bitingly characterized by Conder, and his criticisms are borne out in evidence about the construction of the Waterford &

Kilkenny, his one railway in Ireland. See Conder, v–vi.

38 Thomas LMR, 136, 174–7.

39 See *Profile*, i. 108–9, 113.

40 Evidence from Joy's diaries: 22 RM (1908) 476.

41 See Ahrons BSRL, 42, 49, 76; J. G. H. Warren, *A Century of Locomotive Building* (1923), 365, 368; J. Marshall, *Biographical Dictionary of Railway Engineers* (1978), 97–8; J. P. White, jr., *American Locomotives* (1968), 192.

42 J. Thomas, *North British Railway*, i (1969), 71–9, 155–6, 178.

43 Clark, *Bidder*, 292–3.

44 Bristol University Library: Brunel Letter-book 1, 43–4, 79. See also *Brunel*, 476–7.

45 *Post Office Railway Directory for 1847*, 17, 27, 57, 60, 106, 109.

46 See 197 *Proc. ICE.* (1914) 328–9.

47 6 JTH (1965–6) 113.

48 *Reminiscences of my Life in the Highlands* (1884), ii. 155–6.

49 Diary of Edward Ryde, 29 March 1858: Surrey RO (Guildford), 1262/15. For Ryde see F. M. L. Thompson, *Chartered Surveyors* (1968), 129, 140, 370.

50 Tomlinson, 515–18, 525–6, 549.

51 MacDermot, i. 391–5. For Brunel's consultation with Harrison see *ibid.*, i. 377, and Brunel Letter-book (Bristol University) i. 414–5. Harrison's sketchbooks, are in R1021/87.

52 Obituary: 94 *Proc. ICE.* (1888) 301–13.

53 Thomas NBR, i, chaps. 4–6; Dow GC, ii. 176; RTC, 232.

54 Diary, 19 January 1858, 2 December 1863.

55 Reed, *Crewe*, 236; Rogers, *Churchward*, 125, 156–7.

56 C. P. Atkins, *The Scottish 4-6-0 Classes* (1976), 23–7. A similar case arose on the London Tilbury & Southend Railway in 1911, though there it was involved in inter-company politics. See *Profile*, iii. 68.

57 See W. H. Bailey's paper on Stannard's work in *Trans. Manchester Association of Engineers*, 1889; Thomas LMR, 46–9; M. Robbins, *George and Robert Stephenson* (1966), 32.

58 Sir A. Helps, *Life and Labours of Mr Brassey* (1870), 119–25.

59 Grinling, 15, 17, 21, 23; Wrottesley GNR, i. 15.

60 They are judiciously appraised in Brooke, *Navvy*, chap. 4.

61 MacDermot, i. 50–1, 55; *Brunel*, 477–8. For other examples see Robertson, 201–2, and Richard Hattersley's doings on the Andover & Redbridge Railway in 1861 (Williams LSWR, i. 189).

62 *Reg. Hist.*, v. 134.

63 *Brunel*, 478.

64 See obituary in 104 *Proc. ICE.* (1891) 288–91.

65 Sir Charles Fox was an assistant to Robert Stephenson on the London & Birmingham Railway; then a partner in Fox Henderson & Co., the builders of the Crystal Palace and Paddington station; then a civil engineer again, with a practice extending across the world. T. R. Crampton and Sir Daniel Gooch were both much involved in contracting, side by side with railway engineering. Among lesser men F. R. Conder, James Scott, and Thomas Marr Johnson may be adduced as examples of contracting engineers. For Scott see 155 *Proc. ICE* (1903–4) 441; for Johnson, BR, i. 117.

66 The most important of their biographies known to me are those of Arrol, Brassey, Falshaw, Firbank, McAlpine, and Shelford (all listed in Ottley).

67 See 2 RM (1898) 599.

68 R598/10–11.

69 Brooke, *Navvy*, 74–5.

70 Some bought small farms in the Fylde: J. Caird, *English Agriculture, 1850–1* (1851), 281–2.

71 BE West Kent, 141.

72 *The New Zealander* (1972), 17.

73 *Works*, x. 452.

74 Without their investment in railways (often a condition of the award of contracts) many lines might not have been built. See H. Pollins's admirable discussion of the contractors' part in railway finance in 3 JTH (1957–8), especially 46, 103–5; Barclay-Harvey, 12; Kellett, 75–8; RTC, 315.

75 *Autobiography* (1904), i.

76 That of Henry Swinburne (1841–3: Northumberland RO, ZSW 539/2–4) reflects the miscellaneous work to which young men might be required to apply themselves, in this case under Robert Stephenson and G. P. Bidder. So do the reminiscences of John Brunton, published in *John Brunton's Book* (1939).

77 M. Robbins, 'From R. B. Dockray's Diary': 7 JTH (1965–6) 1–13, 109–19, 149–59.

78 SRO, BR/GPK/4/7; 28 May 1838.

79 Extracts in 22–3 RM (1908).

80 I have discussed some brief diaries kept by engine-drivers in 2 *Back Track* (1988) 66–8.

81 SRO, BR/NBR/4/192.

82 See PP 1847 lxiii. 303–20; Thomas NBR, i. 32–3.

83 R343/722.
84 See *Stationmaster*.
85 An attempt was made to establish a Railway Society in 1839, with the support of Glyn and other railway chairmen. A plan for a Railway Exchange Club House and Chambers was put forward in 1845 (prospectuses in BL, 1890 e. 1, nos. 81–2). A Railway Club was founded in Manchester in 1855, with Watkin as president (Dow GC, i. 160; rules in R1014/17).
86 D. L. Munby, *Inland Transport Statistics*, i. (1978), 47.
87 For what follows see W. D. Rubinstein, 'British Millionaires, 1809–1949': *Bulletin of Institute of Historical Research* (1974).
88 Peto's baronetcy recognized his services in constructing the Balaklava Railway during the Crimean War. A baronetcy was conferred on Gooch on the completion of the Atlantic cable; Watkin's, in 1880, had political inflections.

Chapter 5

1 Repr. Lewis, plates 43, 56.
2 *Ibid.*, plate 61.
3 Repr. Marshall 1830, fig. 53.
4 Repr. F. D. Klingender, *Art and the Industrial Revolution*, ed. Sir A. Elton (1968), plate 11.
5 The earliest is in SM (repr. *Rail 150*, ed. J. Simmons (1975), 22.
6 These series are well discussed in Klingender, 129–33.
7 No doubt it was lighter when fresh from the quarry; but even when new it is characterized by Alec Clifton-Taylor as 'a somewhat sombre pink': BE *South Lancs.*, 58.
8 This fault became grotesque in Edward Calvert's drawing of an engine at Newton station, from which an aquatint was made by Robert Havell: copy in IGM, AE185.817.
9 See Marshall LMR, plates X and XVI.
10 The prints in *The Railway Companion . . . By a Tourist* (1833) deserve attention for the homely detail they afford. They were engraved by E. Colyer.
11 See especially the plates at pp. 52, 54, and 56.
12 For a description of his life see Sir A. Elton, 'The Piranesi of the Age of Steam' (*Country Life Annual*, 1965), and Klingender, 153–9.
13 At NRM and IGM.
14 Sketches of them, and of scenes later worked up into finished drawings are in IGM, AE 185.128–40.
15 NRM 317/68.

16 Other drawings of the railways' earthworks include John Absolom's of the Weybridge cutting on the London & Southampton Railway (NRM); George Childs's of the eastern approach to the Box tunnel on the Great Western (SM); and others, by an unknown hand, of works on the Brighton-Shoreham line (Brighton AG).
17 Owing to dissension between the two publishers concerned. See Ottley, *Supplement*, 5930*.
18 The attribution of the authorship to him was made in the DNB, based it seems on information supplied by Clark's family. It may I think be accepted, and assumed that the notes on the plates are his also.
19 All at IGM.
20 K. H. Vignoles, *Charles Blacker Vignoles* (1982), 118, 128, 142, 164.
21 Repr. *ibid.*, plate 45.
22 Repr. *ibid.*, plate 90.
23 Repr. Klingender (in black and white), fig. 93.
24 Dawson described himself as 'civil engineer and surveyor' on the title-page of *Landslips in East Devon* (1840), produced jointly with W. D. Conybeare.
25 See Brees's drawing of the mouth of the Northchurch tunnel on the London & Birmingham Railway, forming the frontispiece to his *Railway Practice* (1st series, 1837), and Humber's of the Digswell viaduct on the Great Northern (repr. J. Simmons, *Transport*, 1962, pl. 130).
26 After his death his father bound up the finished drawings into an album, prefixed by a portrait. It is now, together with his sketchbooks, in SM. I am grateful to a member of his family, Mrs D. Dupré, for some information about him.
27 A very fine example by John Elmslie is reproduced in Klingender, pl. II.
28 Repr. RB3, 17. The painting (artist unknown) is now at Young & Co.'s brewery, Wandsworth.
29 First published in 1889; see Ruskin, *Works*, xxxv. 598–601.
30 John Gage, in his interesting study of the painting (*Turner: Rain Steam and Speed*, 1972, 85), dismisses it on the ground that the railway was opened only on 1 May 1844, two days before the picture was exhibited. But Lady Simon carefully indicated that her journey on the train with Turner began over the line between Beam Bridge, near Wellington, and Bristol, and that section was opened on 1 May 1843: MacDermot, ii. 74. Another version of the story – I think less convinc-

ing – is recorded in A. M. W. Stirling, *The Richmond Papers* (1926), 55.
31 M. Butlin and E. Joll, *The Paintings of J. M. W. Turner* (1984 ed.) 256–7.
32 Gage, 19. See also L. Herrmann, *Turner* (1975), 53.
33 Klingender, 102.
34 *Ibid.*, 154; Gage, 76.
35 Besides the one reproduced here there is another in the possession of Sir Claud Hagart-Alexander, repr. S. Stevenson, *David Octavius Hill and Robert Adamson* (1981), pl. 25.
36 IGM.
37 Birmingham AG.
38 N. Usherwood in *Country Life* (1983) 911.
39 NRM.
40 Birmingham AG.
41 See *Train Spotting* (Nottingham Castle Museum Exhibition, 1985), 10–11, 23. The original 'First Class' is at the National Gallery of Canada, Ottawa; the other two paintings are at the NRM.
42 NRM.
43 IGM, AE185.146.
44 There is an interesting file devoted to the picture at the PRO: R1005/56.
45 The original painting is at Royal Holloway and Bedford College, Egham, Surrey.
46 W. P. Frith, *My Autobiography* (8th ed., 1890), 320–1.
47 Institution of Mechanical Engineers.
48 It forms the frontispiece to Jeaffreson's biography.
49 NRM.
50 National Portrait Gallery.
51 NRM.
52 MacDermot i. 163–4.
53 H. Murray, *Servants of Business* [1984].
54 The artist was either Henry Heath or Hugh Hughes: see *Art and the Industrial Revolution* (Manchester City AG, 1968) 60.
55 See 'Effects of the Railroad on the Brute Creation': repr. Marshall LMR, 157–8.
56 Great Western Museum, Swindon. The initials are 'C.A.S.' Can they possibly stand for Charles Alexander Saunders, the secretary of the Great Western company? I do not know of any evidence that he drew.
57 When? Hudson believed that Sydney Smith devised it: R. S. Lambert, *The Railway King* (1934), 90. As an undergraduate at Oxford, his son was known as the Prince of Rails: G. V. Cox, *Recollections of Oxford* (1868), 334.
58 9 *Punch* (1845) 234.

59 Doyle had already sketched little scenes on the Great Western Railway in a diary he kept at the age of fifteen. See *Richard Doyle's Journal 1840*, ed. C. Wheeler (1980), 45–7.
60 DNB.
61 55 *Punch* (1868) 70–1.
62 *Ibid.*, 101 (1891) 55. The reference is to the Norwood Junction accident on the previous 1 May. Tenniel's original sketch is in IGM, AE185.62. He depicts cracks in the sides of the bridge, but the accident was due to the failure of the girders underneath the track: P. S. A. Berridge, *The Girder Bridge* (1969), 36–9.
63 Among others see 63 *Punch* (1872) 161 (an 'overworked pointsman'; a comment on the Kirtlebridge accident on the Caledonian Railway); 67 (1874) 79 (excursion train).
64 Linley Sambourne's comment in his cartoon on the Races to Scotland in 1888 is milder than Tenniel's. It is on the theme 'More haste, less dividend': 95 *Punch* (1888) 86–7.
65 S. Stevenson, *David Octavius Hill and Robert Adamson* (1981), 210 (Landscape 9).
66 Parts of the model were made by Joseph Clements, who died in 1844: A. Platt, *Life and Times of Sir Daniel Gooch* (1987), 62. By February 1846 Gooch was building a much larger engine, *Great Western*, and for such a portrait as this he would surely have wished to show his newest creation. The daguerreotype is in the Science Museum.
67 *Art Union*, 1 October 1847, 362. I owe this reference to Roger Taylor.
68 K. J. Vignoles, *Charles Blacker Vignoles* (1982), 164.
69 Albums of them are at the Guildhall Library and the ICE.
70 R. L. Hills and D. Patrick, *Beyer Peacock* (1982), 26, 43. The surviving photographs are now in the Museum of Science and Industry at Manchester.
71 See pictures in K. Montague, *Private Owner Wagons from the Gloucester Railway Carriage and Wagon Co. Ltd.* (1981).
72 Reed, *Crewe*, 7.
73 J. B. Radford, *Derby Works and Midland Locomotives* (1971), 73. The earliest photographs I know of the wreckage of railway accidents were taken at Hereford and Tottenham in 1858 and 1860: repr. A. Trevena, *Trains in Trouble* (1980). A photographic dealer of Wellingborough, Leonard Brightwell, took a number of photographs of the accident that occurred there in 1898. See J.

Thompson, 'L. Brightwell and the Manchester Express': *British Journal of Photography* (1986) 275–6.
74 2 RM (1898) 150; the writer here, S. Damant, was on the staff of the company's general manager.
75 Marshall LYR, iii. 105.
76 Radford, 74.
77 6 RM (1900) 425.
78 They are in R1014/19. Malan was not alone in photographing broad-gauge express trains in motion. Roger Langdon, the stationmaster at Silverton, east of Exeter (who became known as a student of astronomy) did the same, from the early 1880s onwards: *Life* [1909], 83.
79 Albums of pictures of the first two of these lines are at ICE and at SRO, BR/WEH/4/3.
80 Pictures at NRM.
81 *Train Spotting*, 43; the album is still at the Institution.
82 For his work see M. Hiley, *Frank Sutcliffe* (1974).
83 L. T. C. Rolt gives a good appreciation of Newton's work in his introduction to *The Making of a Railway* (1971), which reproduces 290 of Newton's photographs. The negatives are at Leicester, in the RO and the Museum of Technology.
84 Admirably illustrated, for example, in Rolt, 95, 104, 154. For one not used by Rolt see RB3, 7.
85 See J. Huntley, *Railways in the Cinema* (1969), 7–9, together with a still reproduced on a following unnumbered page.
86 *Ibid.*, 11–13.
87 R. B. Wilson, *Go Great Western* (1987 ed.), 124.
88 JMetR, 239.
89 Huntley, 21.
90 Nine of these paintings are reproduced in *The Impressionists in London* (Arts Council exhibition catalogue, 1973), plates 4–12.
91 Now at the Courtauld Institute, London. The station may perhaps be Lordship Lane.
92 *Railway Art* (1977), 95. To these French expatriates we may add the novelist Zola, who lived in England briefly in 1898–9 in retreat from a prosecution at home. He was a good photographer and always attentive to trains; he took some pictures of railways in and near the Crystal Palace. See *Zola Photographe* (1979).
93 Repr. Ellis, 84–5.
94 The Willesden painting is in the Dunedin Art Gallery, New Zealand, the other is reproduced in *Train Spotting*, 17.
95 Now in the Museum of London.
96 Repr. *Image of the Train*

(National Museum of Photography, Bradford, 1985), 4.
97 Atkinson AG, Southport.
98 'From a Canal Bridge' (1913): York AG. Repr. *Train Spotting*, 31.
99 NRM.
100 See his photographs 'The Hand of Man' (1902) and 'In the New York Central Yards' (1903), repr. D. Bry, *Alfred Stieglitz: Photographer* (1965), pl. 7, and *Image of the Train*, 2.
101 H. Bauenhauer, *Hermann Plauer, der schwäbischer Impressionist* (1964).
102 See the print repr. W. Schivelbusch, *The Railway Journey* (1980), 32.
103 As in the theatre bill, 'Les Trains de plaisir': copy in IGM, AE185.542.

Chapter 6

1 This chapter is based on a paper I gave to the Society of Antiquaries of London in 1978 and benefits from the discussion that followed its delivery there.
2 M. J. H. Liversidge, *The Bristol High Cross* (1978), 2.
3 Tomlinson, 195–8, 264–5.
4 J. C. Bruce, *The Roman Wall* (1851), 275.
5 LPA, 3 Will. IV, cap. 36, sects. 98–9.
6 *RCHM Hertfordshire*, 97; Sir C. Peers, *Berkhamsted Castle* (1948, unpaginated).
7 *RCHM Buckinghamshire*, ii. 82.
8 *RCHM Middlesex*, xxiv.
9 PP 1839 x. 158.
10 LPA, 7 & 8 Vict. cap. 58 sects. 10–15; Robertson, 128–33; D. Robertson, *The Princes Street Proprietors* (1935), 31–46.
11 *RCHM City of Edinburgh*, 36–7.
12 *Murray's Handbook for Northants and Rutland* (1901 ed.), 10; R. M. Serjeantson, *The Castle of Northampton* (1908), 54–5; R410/1041.
13 *The Study of Urban History*, ed. H. J. Dyos (1968), 236.
14 Comparable examples from Switzerland are cited in W. Stutz, *Bahnhöfe der Schweiz* (1983), 9.
15 *RCHM City of York*, i. 53–4, 76–92, 130–5.
16 York City Council mins. (York RO), ii. 230, 242 (1840), iii. 162–3, 209–10.
17 LPA 7 & 8 Vict., cap. 65, sect. 257.
18 *Ibid.*, sects. 282, 284.
19 J. C. Jeaffreson, *Life of Robert Stephenson* (1864), ii. 111–12.
20 A. J. Taylor, *Conway Castle and Town Walls* (1956), 43.

21 *BE Shropshire*, 249, 270.

22 See P. Marsh in *Victorian Shrewsbury*, ed. B. Trinder (1984), 107–8, 111.

23 G. Hart, *History of Cheltenham* (1965), 2.

24 *RCHM Westmorland*, 206.

25 *BE Dorset*, 395.

26 MacDermot, i. 54.

27 C. Nicholson, *Annals of Kendal* (1861 ed.), 392.

28 *Murray's Handbook for Yorkshire* (1882 ed.), 481.

29 G. Measom, *Guide to the South Eastern Railway* (1853), 195.

30 *VCH Rutland*, ii. 22; E. Jervoise, *Ancient Bridges of the South of England* (1930), 118.

31 *Murray's Handbook for Lincolnshire* (1890), 97.

32 M. Robbins, *Middlesex* (1953), 250; *VCH Middlesex*, v. 212.

33 W. M. Bowman, *England in Ashton-under-Lyne* (1960) 247; T. B. Peacock, *Great Western London Suburban Services* (1970 ed.), 16.

34 *Herapath* (1845) 238–9; *Journal of Gideon Mantell*, ed. E. C. Curwen (1940), 197–200.

35 *VCH Sussex*, vii. 46, 49; 3 *Sussex Archaeological Collections* (1850) 185.

36 N. Hawthorne, *English Notebooks*, ed. R. Stewart (1941), 157; Ruskin, *Works*, xxxiv. 513–16.

37 *Murray's Handbook for Wilts and Dorset* (1899 ed.), 524.

38 LPA, 9 & 10 Vict., cap. 313, sect. 16. See also J. G. Cox, *Castleman's Corkscrew* (1975), 31.

39 See R. Fothergill, *The Inches of Perth* (?1980), 26–9.

40 *Collected Works*, ed. J. M. Robson vi (1982), 328.

41 *Works*, vol. xxxiv, pp. xxx–xxxi.

42 RTC, 272.

43 Cox, *Castleman's Corkscrew*, 16–18; PRO, F24, 25.

44 See Mitchell's *Reminiscences of my Life in the Highlands* (1884), ii. 190–5, and photograph of Killiecrankie viaduct in R. Taylor, *George Washington Wilson* (1981), pl. 179.

45 *RCHM Roman London*, 83.

46 See REW, 116-18.

47 *City Press*, 7 January 1860.

48 *Ibid.*, 11 August 1860.

49 J. M. Wilson, *The Imperial Gazetteer of England and Wales* [?1869], ii. 167.

50 Sir W. P. Treloar, *Ludgate Hill Past and Present* (1892 ed.), 131.

51 *RCHM Roman London*, 112–13.

52 PP 1863 viii. 149.

53 See the comments in D. Hudson, *Munby, Man of Two Worlds* (1972), 174–5.

54 PP 1863 viii. 88, 106, 154.

55 IGM: AE185.414.

56 LPA 27 & 28 Vict., cap. cccxxii, sects. 34, 55.

57 *RCHM Roman London*, 83, 99–100.

58 See REW, 121.

59 44 *Punch* (1863) 184; see also 45 (1863) 146.

60 *Ibid.*, 46 (1864) 149.

61 *Ibid.*, 44 (1865) 96–7. On this plan see MacDermot, ii. 16; RTC, 165–7.

62 See REW, 242–3.

63 See J. M. Dunn, *The Wrexham, Mold & Connah's Quay Railway* (1957), 9; and Dow GC, iii. 65; for the ill effects on Wrexham, *Buildings of Wales: Clwyd*, 298, 306, where the two lines are confused.

64 They begin with one in Dublin: 34 *Builder* (1876) 1202.

65 See HLRO, evidence on the Eastern & Midlands Railway Bill, 1883; Norfolk RO, N/TC/49/3; A. J. Wrottesley, *The Midland & Great Northern Railway* (1970), 48, 55.

66 HLRO, Bristol & London & South Western Junction Railway Bill, 1883. The Wiltshire Archaeological Society and the Society of Antiquaries of London protested. See *Wiltshire Archaeological Society, 1853–1953* (1953), 27.

67 46 *Builder* (1884) 188.

68 Dow GC, iii. 153.

69 This account is based largely on J. Thomas, *The West Highland Railway* (3rd ed., 1984), 67–8.

70 69 *Builder* (1890) 324.

71 See *Victorian City*, i. 304, and references given there.

72 LPA 56 Vict., cap. i, sect. 29 (17).

73 LPA 54 & 55 Vict., cap. 196, sect. 69.

74 See correspondence with the London & North Western company in PRO, R410/2042.

75 *BE North Yorkshire*, 328; *Reg. Hist.*, iv. 80.

76 JLT, 29–30. See Biddle GRS, 141.

77 R410/111, min. 43891 (appointment of committee); R410/63, nos. 239–40 (reports). Surviving plans (incomplete) in R410/1021.

78 For the origins of the preservation movement, in its international context, see D. Lowenthal, *The Past is a Foreign Country* (1985), 389–95.

79 On the other hand at Moissac the French government, on the initiative of Prosper Mérimée, stopped the demolition of the abbey cloister by the railway from Bordeaux to Sète: a direct intervention by the State to which there is no parallel in nineteenth-century Britain.

80 See M. Berger, *Historische Bahnhofsbauten*, ii. (1987), 98.

Chapter 7

1 Lewis, 90.

2 'Waggon' was the spelling generally used by writers on horse-powered railways; 'wagon' came to prevail after 1830.

3 Lewis, 236, 256.

4 R. C. Overton, *Gulf to Rockies* (1970 ed.), 19.

5 *Works*, xxxiv. 604.

6 C. E. Lee, *The Evolution of Railways* (2nd ed., 1943), 20–1, 69.

7 Glamorgan RO, D/DG 1835(1), f. 1109v.

8 Tomlinson 130: K. Hoole in *Rail 150*, ed. J. Simmons (1975), 26. On the early use of the word see M. Robbins in 1 *London Journal*.

9 Thomas LMR, 83.

10 30 *Trans. Leics. Arch. Soc.* (1954), 78.

11 H. Belcher, *Whitby & Pickering Railway* (1836), 89.

12 F. Whishaw, *Analysis of Railways* (1837), 286.

13 *The Grand Junction, and the Liverpool & Manchester Railway Companion* (pub. J. Cornish, 1837), 12. 'Road stations' were also used in Scotland, on the Edinburgh & Northern Railway for example, in 1847: SRO, RB(S)1/60, p. 59.

14 OED 'train' 16 (examples of 1824 and 1830).

15 It was so used in the *Annual Register* for 1830, four times (Chronicle, 205).

16 OED 'train' 16; *Letters of Charles Dickens* (Pilgrim ed.), i. 449.

17 LPA 7 Geo. IV cap. 95, sect. 103.

18 Warren 123.

19 J. C. Jeaffreson, *Life of Robert Stephenson* (1864), i. 121; J. G. H. Warren, *A Century of Locomotive Building* (1923), 74.

20 As in an estimate furnished to the Bolton & Leigh Railway in 1827: Lancs. RO, DD 6/19.

21 *The Creevey Papers*, ed. Sir H. Maxwell (1912), 545, 555.

22 See for example Head SP, 65, 83; D. Lardner, *Railway Economy* (1850), 241, 425, 527; S. Sidney, *Rides on Railways* (1851), 53, 55.

23 PGA 1 & 2 Geo. V cap. 34.

24 PP 1850 xxxi. 149.

25 Francis, i. 292.

26 J. G. Lockhart, *Memoirs of the Life of Sir Walter Scott* (2nd ed., 1839), iii. 87.

27 42 *Quarterly Review* (1830), 377–404.

28 *Works* (1869 ed.), 790.
29 S. C. Brees, *Glossary of Civil Engineering* (1841), deals freely in railway terms. For some other glossaries see J. A. Sewell, *Complete Set of Rules and Regulations for the practical Management of a Locomotive Engine* (1848); R. Bond, *Murray & Co.'s Book of Information for Railway Travellers* (1865); E. B. Ivatts, *Railway Management at Stations* (1885).
30 *Chambers' Edinburgh Journal*, n.s. 6(1846) 193–4.
31 Edward Fitzgerald was using this expression, without any kind of emphasis, in 1847: *Letters* (1894 ed.), i. 224.
32 *Works*, xiii. 654.
33 K. Hudson, *Working to Rule* (1970), 13.
34 This is based mainly on the *Lexique Général des termes ferroviaires* produced by the International Union of Railways, abridged in the *Glossary of Railway Terms* published by Elsevir in Amsterdam in 1960.
35 *La Formation du vocabulaire des chemins de fer en France, 1778–1842* (1955).
36 See Wexler's most interesting paper on 'The Naming of the Vehicle Brake' in 5 *Cahiers de Lexicologie* (1964) 69–83.
37 Lewis, 264.
38 Wexler, *Formation*, 26, 40, 53.
39 *Ibid.*, 105.
40 Lefèvre & Cerbelaud, 30, 56, 67, 137, 230.
41 *Railway Economy*, 326. See also OED.
42 OED.
43 'The travelling buffet has also become an institution' (J. Pendleton, *Our Railways*, 1896, ii. 139).
44 Lewis, 7–8.
45 'Engineer' was used with the same meaning in England, though the OED gives no example of it. See for example *Annual Register* 1830, Chronicle, 205; PP 1839 x. 33–4; Lardner, 69–70; Conder, 161. There were Americans who felt this use of 'engineer' was absurd: 'The engine-driver on our railroads is thus magniloquently designated' (J. R. Bartlett, *Dictionary of Americanisms*, 4th ed., 1877, 201).
46 e.g. 'Chaddesden deals mainly with goods traffic; Toton is concerned almost wholly with minerals': Acworth RE (1889 ed.), 172.
47 The distinction is clearly made in J. S. Jeans, *Railway Problems* (1887), 272, and in Bartlett, 512.
48 *The British Railway Position*, 54.
49 See examples dating from 1923 to 1931 in Ottley, 3818, 3822–3. The OED Supplement has no example

from Britain earlier than 1955.
50 This word has a long history, meaning a beam or 'dormant timber'; something 'dormant' being fixed or stationary. See OED 'dormant' A3, 'sleeper' 18B.
51 E. B. Dorsey, *English and American Railroads compared* (2nd ed., 1887), 10. A set of equivalents for eighteen English and American railway words is given in Bartlett, 512.
52 See examples in OED.
53 A. H. Neve, *The Tonbridge of Yesterday* (1933), 125.
54 'Labourers', 'artificers', 'miners and quarrymen' employed on railways under construction on 1 May 1847 totalled 210,413: PP 1847 lxiii. 101. But the figures are not reliable: see Brooke, *Navvy*, 53.
55 *British Railway History, 1830–76* (1954), 53.
56 For boatmen's language see L. T. C. Rolt, *Narrow Boat* (1944), 201–8, and H. Henson, *The Canal Boatmen* (1975), 169, 173.
57 J. Dunstan, *The Origins of the Sheffield & Chesterfield Railway* (1970), 18.
58 For a good account of the Railway Missions and their work see Brooke, *Navvy*, chap. 7.
59 T. Coleman, *The Railway Navvies* (1965), 140.
60 67 *Trans. Devonshire Association* (1935) 389.
61 P. W. Kingsford (*Victorian Railwaymen*, 1970, 103) gives some examples of the payment of overtime by railway companies that reach back as far as 1835, but these seem to have been isolated practices. The contractors must have had to pursue some common policy on such a matter as this in the 1840s and 1850s if they were to retain their men.
62 W. G. Hoskins, *Devon* (1954), 99.
63 D. W. Barrett, *Life and Work among the Navvies* (3rd ed., 1883), 41; Coleman, 138–9.
64 WIR, 141; Coleman, 137.
65 See OED.
66 Barrett, 51.
67 T. Fayers, *Labour among the Navvies* [1862], 5.
68 J. Steel, *Guide to the Lancaster & Carlisle Railway* [1846], 24.
69 Fayers, 9.
70 Barrett, 44.
71 *London & Birmingham Railway: Table of Fares and Rates* [1838], 8. Copy in BL, T 968* (4).
72 The Great Western was using it by 1840 (MacDermot, i. 337); the Great North of England preferred the coaches' Time Bill in 1841 (Tomlinson, 431).

73 Thomas LMR, 191.
74 D. L. Franks, *The South Yorkshire Railway* (1971), 22.
75 See Ottley, 7909, 7911, 7913, 7923, 7931. The *ABC Railway Guide* (published continuously since 1853, and appearing still) was constructed on a different principle from Bradshaw's and gave less information. *Murray's Diary*, covering the railways in Scotland, was published from 1842 to 1952.
76 Ottley, 7950.
77 *Reprinted Pieces*, 552.
78 *Letters*, ed. R. B. Booth (1951), 253.
79 'Bradshaw' found no place in the original OED in 1888, but was recorded in the Supplement of 1933. 'Chaix' is likewise a one-word synonym for the national railway timetable in France, published by Napoléon Chaix in 1846 and continued ever since.
80 Advertisement in IGM, AE185.519.
81 See also, from the same year 1911, Arnold Bennett, *Hilda Lessways*, 385–9.
82 Henry James, *The Golden Bowl* (Penguin ed., 271).
83 It even came to be used as a school textbook: see DNB, art. George Edmondson.
84 The evolving usage of the word is set out with beautiful clarity in OED.
85 Attention has been paid mainly so far to the language of the twentieth century. See F. McKenna, *A Glossary of Railwaymen's Talk* (1970), concerned chiefly with that talk since 1946. Here is a valuable start. Might not somebody compile another glossary for the nineteenth century?
86 Lewis, 366.
87 F. Whishaw, *Analysis of Railways* (1837), 267.
88 Lewis, 360, 362.
89 *Ibid.*, 359.
90 See rules of the Glasgow Paisley Kilmarnock & Ayr Railway (1846), p. 50 (SRO, BR/RB(S)/1/59), and Edinburgh & Northern Railway (1847), p. 65 (*ibid.*, 1/60).
91 *Ibid.*, 2/75.
92 But in 1848 the presiding officer at Queen Street station in Glasgow was a 'stationmaster': *ibid.*, 1/49, p. 77.
93 D. L. Smith, *Tales of the Glasgow & South Western Railway* (1970 ed.), 72, 73, 90, 92.
94 In October 1988 a new Scotticism was introduced into the national timetable, which laid it down (pp. 1468, 1474) that the

Royal Highlander express was to make two stops to 'uplift' passengers for stations in England.

95 Acworth RE (1900 ed.), 60.

96 OED, 'tube'; letter from Charles Lee to Michael Robbins, 18 March 1974.

97 Letter from Charles Royce, 10 May 1841: Manchester PL (Archives Dept.), M70/1/2/4.

98 WIR, 264.

99 *Notes and Queries*, 6th series, 2 (1880) 84.

100 Bradshaw, April 1910, 364.

101 JLLR, 238.

102 C. G. Maggs, *The Midland & South Western Junction Railway* (1967), 130.

103 E. Mason, *The Lancashire & Yorkshire Railway in the Twentieth Century* (1975 ed.), 181.

104 C. Highet, *Scottish Locomotive History* (1970), 89.

105 MacDermot, ii. 248–9.

106 Turner LBSCR, iii. 76.

107 65 *English Historical Review* (1960) 333–51.

108 R1014/3/32–3.

109 PP 1839 x. 384.

110 Turner LBSCR, i. 168.

111 PP 1841 xxv. 207.

112 PP 1841 viii. 67–8.

113 PP 1843 xlvii. 36–7, 44, 50. The use of a mark in place of a signature may not be satisfactory proof of an inability to write (see R. D. Altick, *The English Common Reader*, 1957, 169–70). Here, however, I think it can be accepted as adequate.

114 PP 1857 xxxvii. 145, 164. See also 2 *Back Track* (1988) 66–8. Illiterate drivers continue to be heard of much later in the century: Smith, *Tales*, 29.

115 PP 1839 x. 117.

116 Neele, 80.

117 Occasionally a known illiterate had himself to give written instructions. On the Great Western Brunel stated that a foreman at Reading had had his illiteracy supplied by the addition of a clerk, to write his letters for him: PP 1841 viii. 68.

118 Thomas LMR, 142.

119 e.g. on the Edinburgh & Northern Railway in 1847 and the Edinburgh & Glasgow in 1848: SRO, BR/RB(S)/1/60, p. 65; 1/75, p. 60.

120 Copy of rule book in Bristol PL, Bristol Collection 3467 (Rule 58).

121 K. Hudson, *Working to Rule* (1970), 35, 113.

122 J. G. Cox, *Castleman's Corkscrew* (1975), 24.

123 Now in R414/767.

124 Kingsford, *Railwaymen*, 10.

125 A list of schools established by railways in 1840–59 is given in Kingsford, 73; but additions can be made to it. For example, two were set up by the Stockton & Darlington company: at Shildon, certainly in existence by 1847 (see Hudson, *Working to Rule*, 20), and in the remote railway village of Waskerley in 1849 (papers in R667/498). The matter is well discussed in Chaloner, *Crewe*, 61–4 and chap. 8.

126 *Ibid.*, 233–8.

127 A. S. Peck, *The Great Western at Swindon Works* (1983) 53–4, 57–9.

128 R250/5, p. 363; R250/6, p. 226.

129 G. Lipscomb, *History and Antiquities of the County of Buckingham* (1847), iv. 419.

130 *Leicester Domestic Mission; 9th Report* (1851–2); copy in Leicester PL. The writer was Joseph Dare.

131 The unhappy relationship of the London & North Western company with the Board of Education and with local authorities is touched on in Chaloner, *Crewe*, 245–8, and in J. Simmons, *Rugby Junction* (1969), 19–20. For a brief general summary of the railways' activities in this field see H. Pollins, *Britain's Railways: an Industrial History* (1971), 105–6.

132 V. Berry, *The Rolfe Papers* (1979), 39.

133 See the discussion in *Notes and Queries*, 10th series, 1 (1904) 371, 471.

134 It is pronounced in both ways in the Border ballads: see 'The Lochmaben Harper', stanzas 4 and 16.

135 Private information; *Notes and Queries*, 10th series, 2 (1904) 36.

136 Dow GC, ii. 322.

137 Barclay-Harvey, 55. This was a deep cutting about 25 miles west of Aberdeen. The name is not on the Ordnance map, but the author's word can be trusted, for he was himself a landowner near by.

138 B. S. Smith, *History of Malvern* (1964), 203.

139 J. Hamson, *Bedford Town and Townsmen* (1896), 46.

140 Forest Hill station was built by the London & Croydon Railway, worked on the atmospheric principle, which required the telegraph.

141 See for example FF, 9.

142 OED (under 'speed', sb. 2, 5c; example of 1904).

143 In 1906 the North British company introduced 'Inter-City Expresses' between Edinburgh and Aberdeen: *Reg. Hist.*, vi. 252.

144 For this word see SPS, 72n.

145 I am much indebted to V. H. Phillips of the Welsh Folk Museum, St Fagans, for his help here.

146 J. M. Dunn, *Chester & Holyhead Railway* (1948), 53.

147 See file of papers in R410/2503.

Chapter 8

1 He was mistaken in saying that he travelled 'by the first train from Liverpool to Manchester', for that ran in the day-time.

2 For 'Locksley Hall' and 'Mechanophilus' see *The Poems of Tennyson*, ed. C. Ricks (2nd ed., 1987), ii. 118, i. 534. Some doubt has been expressed about Tennyson's intentions in 'Mechanophilus'. Were they perhaps satirical? A careful reader must surely conclude that his words are serious, beneath the buoyant, light-hearted phrasing. As an old man, moreover, in 1884 he wrote out the last four lines quoted here and gave them to Sir Henry Parkes, Prime Minister of New South Wales. Tennyson was not the man to choose these lines for such a purpose as that if he had written them as a joke.

3 *Memoirs, Journal, and Correspondence*, ed. Lord John Russell, vii (1856), 231–2, 350–1.

4 *Poetical Works*, ed. W. Jerrold (1935), 485–6.

5 Thomas LMR, 74.

6 There is a copy in Keighley PL.

7 J. Guest, *Historic Notices of Rotherham* (1879), 549–50.

8 *Poetical Works* [1876], 214. For Mackay's other aspirations of the same kind see the conclusion of 'The Arriving Train' (1844). I cannot find this poem in any of the editions of Mackay's work that I have examined, but it is printed in Kenneth Hopkin's anthology *The Poetry of Railways* (1966), 118.

9 See the opening of 'Dullborough Town' in *The Uncommercial Traveller*, 116–17. Dullborough is Rochester.

10 *Pickwick Papers*, 96; *Sketches by Boz*, 642–3.

11 *Letters of Charles Dickens* (Pilgrim ed., 1965–), i. 449–50.

12 *Ibid.*, iii. 100–1, 109–10, 119; *American Notes*, chaps. 4 and 10; *Martin Chuzzlewit*, 341–2.

13 *Master Humphrey's Clock*, 79–80; *Martin Chuzzlewit*, 626.

14 *Speeches*, ed. K. J. Fielding (1960), 62.

15 *Letters* (Pilgrim ed.), iv. 410–11, 598.

16 *Ibid.*, v. 65, 350.

17 J. Butt and K. Tillotson, *Dickens at Work* (1957), 91–2.

18 *Dombey and Son*, 62–4, 217–19, 277–82, 774–9.

19 H. House, *Dickens World* 141.

20 Dickens transferred these slums to Birmingham from elsewhere. He had been by train to Birmingham three times (*Letters*, Pilgrim ed., ii. 50, iii. 6, iv. 56), when the railways all terminated on the eastern outskirts of the town: see Guest's map of 1840 (copy in Birmingham PL). The Birmingham slums were not to be seen from the train.

21 *Reprinted Pieces*, 474–84.

22 *Miscellaneous Papers*, ed. B. W. Matz (1914), 417–19.

23 *Ibid.*, 89–95.

24 *Bleak House*, 745. This line is the one from Rugby to Peterborough, which Dickens himself saw under construction when visiting the Watsons at Rockingham Castle in 1847–51.

25 *Hard Times*, 213, 124.

26 *Christmas Stories*, 661–758.

27 See *Letters*, ed. W. Dexter (1938), iii. 423–8. The inspector's report on the accident is in PP 1865 xlix. 207–10.

28 F. G. Cockman, *The Railway Age in Bedfordshire* (1974), 83–5. Dickens did however allow that travelling by the London & North Western was 'admirable', much better than on the Midland: *Letters*, ed. Dexter, iii. 509.

29 *Ibid.*, iii. 680. He had a second narrow escape in an accident on an Irish railway in January 1869, travelling in an express between Belfast and Dublin: C. Dolby, *Charles Dickens as I knew him* (1885), 366–8.

30 *Letters*, ed. Dexter, iii. 445–6.

31 *Christmas Stories*, 474–536.

32 See my *Rugby Junction* (1969), 14–15.

33 *Speeches*, 361–6.

34 *Letters*, ed. Dexter, iii. 665–6.

35 *Ibid.*, iii. 746.

36 *Works* (1911 ed.), viii.

37 *Roundabout Papers* (Everyman, ed.), 87.

38 *Autobiography* (1883), i. 137.

39 Samuel Morton Peto, having taken a leading part in the construction of the Balaklava Railway for the Government during the Crimean War, became a baronet in 1855, but no one would have drawn any parallel in character between Peto, the careful, calculating Baptist, and the rough and drunken Scatcherd. One work on Trollope identifies Scatcherd with Paxton (J. Pope Hennessy, *Anthony Trollope*, paperback ed., 267), an even greater absurdity.

40 Tolstoy read this novel with admiration while he was writing *Anna Karenina*, published in 1877. It seems likely that the idea of Anna's suicide under a train was at least influenced by Trollope's example. See A. N. Wilson, *Tolstoy* (1988), 274.

41 Melmotte owes only one thing to Hudson: the memory of the great balls Hudson used to give at his house in Princes Gate (the French embassy today). But he would have been widely recognized for the likeness he bore to Baron Albert Grant (*né* Gottheimer), a fully-fledged 'international' financier of a type that emerged in the 1850s. For Grant's career see DBB.

42 Trollope's novel had its counterpart in the United States in *The Gilded Age* (1873), by Mark Twain and Charles Dudley Warner, an exposure of the greed and swindling there under the Grant administration.

43 G. S. Haight, *George Eliot: a Biography* (1968), 25.

44 Chap. 56 (Penguin ed., 597–600).

45 *Essays*, ed. T. Pinney (1963), 267–8.

46 Chap. 21 (Penguin ed., 269).

47 Chap. 8 (Penguin ed., 122), chap. 23 (Penguin ed., 306).

48 *The Egoist* (1879), chap. 14 (Mickleham ed., 161); *Beauchamp's Career* (1876), chap. 14 (161).

49 *Ibid.*, chap. 22 (234).

50 *The Egoist*, chap. 19 (213).

51 A sample of the writing of numerous novelists about railways – some of them very obscure – is to be found in M. Brightfield, *Victorian England in its Novels* (1968), iii. 188–212.

42 *A Laodicean* (New Wessex ed.), 120, 122. The tunnel is almost certainly the one at Bincombe between Dorchester and Weymouth.

53 Nothing fixes precisely the time to which any of them relate. In 'Midnight on the Great Western' (published in 1917), 'the roof-lamp's oily flame' suggests the nineteenth century rather than the twentieth, when the lighting on such a train would have been by gas.

54 *Collected Poems*, ed. S. Gibson (1978 ed.), 607, 518, 641, 514.

55 *Letters* (Skerryvore ed., 1926), i. 84. Stevenson may well have travelled on the Metropolitan Railway (whose carriages were lighted by gas) as he passed through London in 1872, on his way to Frankfurt.

56 Henry James was, of course, an American by birth. But most of his writing about railways dates from after 1876, when he settled in England.

57 *Letters*, ed. L. Edel, i (1974), 90–1.

58 *English Hours* (1941 ed.), 142.

59 *Ibid.*, 21–3.

60 See for example *ibid.*, 23; 'The Lesson of the Master' (*Collected Tales*, ed. L. Edel, vii. 244).

61 *English Hours*, 95.

62 *The Ambassadors* (Penguin ed.), 215; *The Wings of the Dove* (Penguin ed.), 104; *The Golden Bowl* (Penguin ed.), 79, 346.

63 L. Edel, *Henry James* (1953–72), ii. 383.

64 *Ibid.*, iv. 311–12.

65 See Neele, 216–17.

66 As in 'The Death of Simon Fuge' (*The Grim Smile of the Five Towns*) and 'Catching the Train' (*The Matador of the Five Towns*).

67 *Further Experiences of an Irish RM* (1908), 56–76.

68 He was not the only railwayman who wrote verse. John Ceiriog Hughes (1832–87: see *Dictionary of Welsh Biography*) was manager of the Van Railway in Mid-Wales. But his poetic interest lay chiefly in the traditions of Welsh song and in nursery rhymes; it seems that 'he never once in his poetry made the slightest reference to railways of any kind': *Railways of Wales* (National Museum of Wales, 1981), 43.

69 *Songs of the Rail* (1878), 110–13.

70 D. L. Smith, *Tales of the Glasgow & South Western Railway* (1970), 46.

71 *Songs of the Rail*, 141–5.

72 *Fleet Street and other Poems* (1909), 46–53.

73 *Ballads and Songs* (1894), 103–6.

74 *Fleet Street*, 44, 54.

75 *Ibid.*, 92.

76 *Drift* (1900), 3–4.

77 *Works* (1908), i. 145, ii. 169–94.

78 Written in 1913. *Poems*, ed. G. Keynes (1952), 120–1.

79 Written on 8 January 1915: *Collected Poems*, ed. R. G. Thomas (1978), 70.

80 First published in *The Old Huntsman* (1917); *Collected Poems* (1961), 44–5.

81 Plays had to be licensed by the Lord Chamberlain before they could be legally performed in public. The texts of all those submitted are now in BL, Dept. of MSS, though prior notice is required for their production for readers. Three series cover the years 1830–1914: Add. MSS. 42899–43308 (1830–51) and 52929–53701 (1852–99). Thereafter they are classified simply under the heading 'Lord Chamberlain's Plays'. The plays that were subsequently published are cited here in the printed collections in BL; those that appear not to have been printed bear the MS. references.

82 BL, Add. MS. 42935, f. 644.

83 *Duncombe's British Theatre*, no. 431.

84 *Ibid.*, no. 42.

85 *Lacy's Acting Edition of Plays*, vol. 81.

86 Add. MS. 42990, f. 403.

87 Add. MS. 42989, f. 898.

88 Add. MS. 42990, f. 346.

89 Add. MS. 42990, f. 586.

90 Add. MS. 5307M.

91 Add. MS. 53052Q.

92 *Lacy's Acting Edition*, vol. 96.

93 Add. MS. 53459C.

94 Add. MS. 53487D.

95 Add. MS. 53686V. *An Hour at Rugby Junction* (1873, by Frank Harvey: Add.MS. 53123D) was set in a waiting-room there.

96 *Lady Windermere's Fan*, Act 4. These trains ran only in 1891–3: G. Behrend, *Pullman in Europe* (1962), 48–9.

97 Lord Chamberlain's Plays, 1912, vols. 12 and 21.

98 *Ibid.*, 1911. vol. 6; 1914, vol. 18.

99 Lord Chamberlain's Plays, 1913, vol. 20.

100 *Ibid.*, 1913, vol. 27.

101 RTC, 54.

102 *Random Reminiscences* (1902), 96–7.

103 Edel, *Henry James*, iii. 227, v. 377.

104 There is a survey of this business in 3 RM (1898) 555–61.

105 Text in *Works* (1869), 789–95.

106 The attribution to Montagu is made in the British Library catalogue.

107 He published one more paper on railways, 'The Champions of the Rail', in *Blackwood* (December 1851). See (Sir) T. Martin, *Memoir of William Edmondstoune Aytoun* (1867), 104–17.

108 9 *Punch* (1845) 125; 8 (1845) 170.

109 9 *Punch* (1845) 183.

110 The literature is listed in Ottley, 5811–35.

111 See *ibid.*, 5829, for a list of the leaflets and comment. Ancell was careful to send copies of them to the British Museum for preservation; in no. 9 he proudly printed the letter of acknowledgement he had received from Panizzi, the librarian.

112 These stories have all been reprinted: in *The Penguin Complete Sherlock Holmes* (1981) – the scene at Canterbury is on p. 476; the last two are in *Rivals of Sherlock Holmes*, ed. H. Greene (Penguin ed., 1971) and *A Century of Detective Stories*, intro. G. K. Chesterton (n.d.).

113 This story can be found in *Tales of Detection*, ed. D. L. Sayers (1936).

114 H. Booth, *Account of the Liverpool & Manchester Railway* [1830].

115 J. S. Walker, *Accurate Description of the Liverpool & Manchester Railway* (1830).

116 *Account* (2nd ed., 1831), 90–1.

117 *Railway Economy* (1850), 118.

118 See G. R. Hawke, *Railways and Economic Growth in England, 1840–70* (1970), 93–9.

119 For the meaning of this term see RTC, 304.

120 Acworth RE (1st ed., 1889), 150–1.

121 81 *Proc. ICE* (1885) 1–165.

122 *Ibid.*, 106 (1891) 127–77.

123 *Works*, iii. 191.

124 S. Russell's lithograph of Bull Bridge, on the North Midland Railway in Derbyshire, matches it almost exactly. I am grateful to Alfred Heinimann for drawing Keller's poem to my attention.

125 The only literary comment in English that is remembered is the preposterous poem by poor William McGonagall (*Poetic Gems*, 1934 ed., 42–3), and that is solely on account of its bathos.

126 'Die Brück 'am Tay', published in *Die Gegenwart* (Berlin) only a fortnight after the accident, on 10 January 1880. I am grateful to David Jeffreys and Alfred Heinimann for helping me to understand Fontane's meaning. His poem and Keller's, just referred to, are both printed in W. Minaty's good anthology *Die Eisenbahn* (1984), 85, 95.

127 Translated into English as *The Bridge Builder* in 1937.

128 An admirable translation of the novel, with a good introduction by L. Tancock, is published by Penguin Books. Zola was the son of an engineer, who had laid out the first railway in Austria. See F. W. J. Hemmings, 'Le Père d'Emile Zola': *Cahiers Naturalistes*, no. 55, 1981.

129 *Remembrance of Things Past* (1983 ed.), ii. 1038. For 'the little train', which he specially loved, see i. 926, ii. 812, 1147; G. D. Painter, *Marcel Proust* (1977 ed.), i. 227, ii. 82.

130 I am not thinking here only of Zola and Proust. For a good general survey see M. Baroli, *Le Train dans la littérature française* (1963).

131 For the impact of that on French literature see chap. 3 of Baroli's book.

132 N. W. Webster, *Britain's First Trunk Line* (1972), 95–6.

Chapter 9

1 H. Robinson, *The British Post Office* (1948), 158. Chap. 17 of this book provides the best succinct account of the system.

2 *Ibid.*, 235.

3 *Ibid.*, 231.

4 Jackman, 699.

5 J. Randall, *Shifnal and its Surroundings* [1879], [2].

6 M. J. Daunton, *Royal Mail: the Post Office since 1840*, 23: an excellent study to which I am much indebted.

7 *Ibid.*, 6.

8 T. Richardson to Sir F. Freeling, 11 April 1827: Post Office Records, Post 11/16, File 1.

9 *Ibid*, File 2.

10 See Thomas LMR, 186.

11 42 *Quarterly Review* (1830) 402.

12 Draft in Post Office Records: 1545/1833.

13 The feeling that the railways should be required to carry the mails for nothing, in return for the privileges Parliament conferred on them, persisted. That arrangement was recommended by a Commons Committee in 1845. PP 1846 xiv. 26.

14 PP 1852–3 xcv. 3. The total payments, including the arrears payable for work done earlier, were substantially larger: £1744, £121,860, £329,964.

15 Louis to Col. Maberly: Post Office Records, Post 11/16, File 6.

16 See the report by Louis, *ibid.*, File 11.

17 Robinson, 333.

18 Descriptions of the travelling post offices and the lineside apparatus will be found in Whishaw RGB, 246; Head, *Stokers and Pokers*, 96–9; J. Hollingshead, *Odd Journeys in and out of London* (1860), 256–66; *Graphic*, 21 December 1889; Acworth RE, 95–101. See also J. E. Hosegood, *Great Western Railway Travelling Post Offices* (1983), iii, 14, 16.

19 Post Office Records: Post 11/16, File 10.

20 PGA, 1 & 2 Vict. cap. 98.

21 See Daunton, chap. 1.

22 Post Office Records: Post 11/17; A. A. Bates, *Directory of Stage Coach Services* (1969), 75.

23 PP 1854 xi. 4, 8–10.

24 *Ibid.*, 292–3.

25 *Ibid.*, 6–7. For the Tamworth arrangements in the later Victorian Age see Ahrons LTW, ii. 112–13.

26 This was the only Parliamentary investigation found necessary by defects in the railways' mail service down to 1914, with one very minor exception: PP 1866 xxv. 309–11.

27 Its history as an independent undertaking is well recounted in MacDermot, i. 344–5.

28 P. E. Baughan, *Chester & Holyhead Railway*, i (1972), 40–1.

29 The history of the mail services via Holyhead is summarized in PP 1898 xxxiv. 301–4.

30 PP 1857–8 li. 569, 597.

31 Daunton, 97.

32 For this controversy see Daunton, 124–5. See also F. E. Baines, *On the Track of the Mail Coach* (1895), 312–14.

33 PP 1846 xiv. 228.

34 The documents are printed in Sir C. P. Roney, *Rambles on Railways* (1868), 83–5, 439–81.

35 PP 1851 li. 8–11.

36 It could, at need, call upon the advice and help of the Railway Department of the Board of Trade: Parris, 141.

37 Papers in R253/66.

38 Sir R. and G. B. Hill, *Life of Sir Rowland Hill* (1880), ii. 181.

39 Robinson, 412–13.

40 Hill, *Life of Sir Rowland Hill*, ii. 277–8.

41 See Daunton, chap. 5.

42 PP 1914–16 lx. 748.

43 PP 1890–1 lxxv. 381.

44 Acworth RS, 59, 137.

45 FF, 96.

46 By 1913 the Post Office subsidy to the Highland Railway remained almost exactly the same; but, the passenger business having substantially increased, the proportion had dropped to 15.1%, still the highest in Britain.

47 The murderer was John Tawell: see MacDermot, i. 327. Thieves were then being caught by the agency of the Great Western Railway and the telegraph: see 45 *Quarterly Review* (1854) 129.

48 *Reg. Hist.*, v. 163.

49 Dow GC, i. 253.

50 The range of telegraph business in 1849 is indicated by Head (SP, 118–23). The business was not always well managed at railway stations, from the point of view of the public, since the railway's needs came first and the telegraph was often left unattended. F. E. Baines, *Forty Years at the Post Office* (1895), i. 301.

51 95 *Quarterly Review* (1854) 150–1.

52 PGA, 26 & 27 Vict. cap. 112.

53 PGA, 31 & 32 Vict. cap. 110.

54 PGA, 32 & 33 Vict. cap. 73.

55 A. A. Walker to T. MacNay, 17 April 1868: R667/1137.

56 Hansard, 3rd series, 193, col. 1546.

57 PP 1867–8 xi. 1–9.

58 Kieve, 175. On this arbitration see E. B. and C. Bright, *Life Story of . . . Sir Charles Tilston Bright* (n.d.), ii. 317–21.

59 Kieve, 72. The figure given in PP 1867–8 xli. 734 is slightly lower: 1174 (904 at stations in England and Wales, 270 in Scotland)

60 O. Sitwell, *Noble Essences* (1950), 138.

61 'In the Cage': *Complete Tales*, ed. L. Edel, x (1964), 150.

62 J. S. Jeans, *Railway Problems* (1887), 457.

63 'Speaking or conversation telegraphs' were referred to by one of the Board of Trade inspectors in 1858: PP 1857–8; lv. 355. In 1859 one such was installed by W. D. & H. O. Wills at Bristol: R. C. Tombs, *The Bristol Royal Mail* [1899], 199–200.

64 *History of Technology*, ed. C. Singer and others, v (1958), 77.

65 *Remarks upon a Letter by 'A Large Shareholder' of the Great Eastern Railway* (1883), 7: copy in R227/346. Before long the London cabmen were saying much the same: BR, i. 261.

66 Chaloner, *Crewe*, 74; Reed, *Crewe*, 122.

67 Wrottesley GNR, ii. 32.

68 Dow GC, ii. 185.

69 R236/722/13.

70 Williams LSWR, ii. 305.

71 Acworth RE (1889 ed.), 113.

72 Dow GC, ii. 207.

73 International Railway Congress, St. Petersburg, 1892: *Compte rendu général* iii (1893), XVIIB, 194–203.

74 *Felix Pole his Book* (1968 ed.), 15.

75 e.g. in 1910–11 with systems providing telephonic communication between moving trains and fixed points like signal-boxes. See Turner LBSCR, iii. 169; J. M. Dunn, *Stratford-upon-Avon & Midland Junction Railway* (1952) 9.

76 On the London Brighton & South Coast system it fell by a third in 1898–1907: R414/537, p. 90.

77 Daunton, 55.

78 14 *Herapath* (1852) 357.

79 The part played in this business by the Clearing House is recounted in Bagwell RCH, chap. 5.

80 Daunton, 55–7.

81 PP 1867 xxxviii (1). 63.

82 Neele, 183.

83 It must be remembered that the British railway companies' financial position differed essentially from that of railways on the Continent: see pp. 81–2.

84 PGA 45 & 46 Vict. cap. 74.

85 Neele, 245, 280.

86 Baines, ii. 192–3.

87 See H. T. Jackson, *Railway Letter Posts of Great Britain* (2nd ed., 1970).

88 Neele, 305–6. It admitted passengers on a strictly limited basis from Holytown northwards in Scotland.

89 The Great Western mail services from Plymouth are recorded in Hosegood, chap. 3.

90 RTC, 142–4.

91 For Crewe, see Chaloner, *Crewe*, 97. For Paisley, see picture in *Rail 150*, ed. J. Simmons (1975), 102.

92 Information from Head Postmaster, Leeds.

93 P. Paye, *The Saffron Walden Branch* (1981), 41.

94 Postmaster-General's Report for 1913: PP 1913 xxxviii. 337.

95 C. Hadfield, *Atmospheric Railways* (1967), 96–9.

96 LPA 3 & 4 Geo. V cap. 116.

97 See D. A. Bayliss, *The Post Office Railway, London* (1978).

98 Neele, 278.

99 *Guide Joanne: Gascogne* (1894 ed.), advts. 30.

100 Daunton, 44, 47–8, 81.

101 Daunton, 44.

Chapter 10

1 A good idea of those relating to the Stockton & Darlington Railway in 1825–31 is given by the extracts printed in *The Stockton & Darlington Railway: the Foundation of Middlesbrough*, ed. N. Moorsom [1975], 25–42, 60–70.

2 *The Times*, 20 Nov. 1824.

3 C. F. Adams, *Railroads: their Origins and Problems* (1886 ed.), 55–6; 1 JTH 3rd series (1980–1) 5–6.

4 Dickens, *Letters* (Pilgrim ed.), iv. 410, 472.

5 R. S. Lambert, *The Railway King* (1934), 182.

6 JLLR, 40.

7 JLT, 25.

8 C. Wilson, *First with the News. The History of W. H. Smith 1792–1972* (1985). What follows here owes much to this admirable book.

9 *Ibid.*, 79; Neele, 77–8.

10 Dr Carus, *The King of Saxony's Journey* (1846), 156.

11 Wilson, 47.

12 The London & Brighton Railway undertook in 1844 to convey a daily paper to any part of its line at a charge of £1 1s. a year (R386/21, p. 293). Similar practices were followed elsewhere: W. Vincent, *Seen from the Railway Platform* (1919), 85. This unpretentious little book supplies an informative and amusing

account of a Victorian railway bookseller's life.

13 Neele, 205; Wilson, 168.

14 MacDermot, ii. 247; Vincent, 73–4.

15 What follows owes much to D. Ayerst, *Guardian* (1971), 93–6.

16 J. Kieve, *The Electric Telegraph* (1973), 48, 73–5.

17 Ayerst, 292.

18 Acworth RE, 118.

19 C. E. Montague, *A Hind Let Loose* (Phoenix ed.), 110.

20 Dow GC, ii. 340.

21 R. Pound and G. Harmsworth, *Northcliffe* (1959), 260.

22 Acworth RE (1st ed., 1889), 81.

23 Bagwell RCH, 118.

24 See RTC, 278–9.

25 See for instance 15 *Railway Times* (1852) 562–3, 631–2.

26 C. Mitchell, *Newspaper Press Directory* (1854 ed.), 25.

27 *Railway World*, no. 1, 13 Sept. 1845.

28 G. S. Emmerson, *John Scott Russell* (1977), 27–34. This group of men came to include Joseph Paxton.

29 They are listed in Ottley, 7914.

30 D. M. Evans, *The Commercial Crisis 1847–8* (2nd ed., 1849), 10.

31 *Felix Pole his Book* (1968 ed.), 16–17.

32 This was the *Railway and Travel Monthly*, published in 1910–22. Seron's real name was Nores.

33 *Willing's Press Guide*, 1914, 124, 169.

34 Thomas LMR, 195.

35 Vincent, 13. There is no record of this agreement in the directors' minutes: R385/2.

36 The tenders are in R410/873. Marshall offered £650 for Euston station alone.

37 Wilson, 102–4.

38 Details in *ibid.*, 99.

39 *Ibid.*, 145.

40 *The House of Menzies* (1958), 38–9.

41 This jest is said to have been made by *Punch*. If it was, when?

42 Samuel Phillips wrote an article in *The Times* (9 August 1851) that virtually condemned all the station bookstalls in London except Smith's. But he was a staff reviewer for that paper and a personal friend of the younger W. H. Smith himself. Other complaints were also being made about station bookstalls (not Smith's): of the high prices demanded for *The Times* and *Punch* at Paddington, for example (*The Times*, 28 July 1855).

43 A. Trollope, *The New Zealander*, ed. N. J. Hall (1972), 183–4; written in 1855 (xi–xii).

44 F. A. Munby, *The House of Routledge* (1934), 141.

45 Arnold, *Letters* (1895), i. 32; 3 *Saturday Review* (1857) 100–2. This article was based on information supplied by Smith's.

46 *Ibid.*

47 R. D. Altick, *The English Common Reader* (1957), 89, 305.

48 Wilson, 182. For sub-stalls see Vincent, 27, 71–2.

49 Wilson, 144, 214.

50 *Ibid.*, 182–3.

51 *Ibid.*, 148.

52 In 1881 there was said to have been some question of Smith himself becoming chairman of the London & North Western Railway: Sir H. Maxwell, *Life and Times of W. H. Smith* (1893), i. 44.

53 Wilson, 180.

54 *Ibid.*, 194–5.

55 Figures in Wilson, 210.

56 *Ibid.*, 207–8, 214–15. The firm had already bought shops in the south, at Clacton and Gosport, in 1901–2.

57 There was no reason why they should not try to concert their policies by private discussion. But at one critical point it appears (Wilson, 239–40) that Harrison disclosed information about the volume of Smith's business to the Great Western company that had been given to him by Smith's in strict confidence, and that was unforgivable.

58 Wilson, 238.

59 *Ibid.*, 240–1.

60 *Ibid.*, 238.

61 The operation is described in *ibid.*, 242–5; and some amusing sidelights on it (especially at Llandrindod Wells) are cast on it by Vincent (153–8).

62 Wilson, 100. '1861' here seems plainly to be a mistake for 1851.

63 James Willing is said to have introduced the practice on to railways: T. Russell, *Commercial Advertising* (1919), 268.

64 Wilson, 121.

65 See letter from him, 12 March 1887, to the Callander & Oban company: SRO, BR/COB/4/16.

66 BR, i. 69, 82–3, 120–1; JMetR, 26; Wilson, 258–9.

67 A. P. Allen, *The Ambassadors of Commerce* (1885), 106.

68 A. D. Godley expressed it neatly in his poem 'Urbs in Rure': *Reliquiae* (1926), i. 355.

69 E. S. Turner, *The Shocking History of Advertising* (Penguin ed.), 110.

70 Wilson, 116–17.

71 C. Barman, *The Man who Built London Transport* (1979), 29.

72 E. B. Dorsey, *English and American*

Railroads compared (2nd ed., 1887), 16.

73 R. Bell, *Twenty-five Years of the North Eastern Railway* [1951], 31.

74 20 RM (1907) 6–7.

75 Anybody who supposes, however, that Victorian advertising lacked variety should look at P. Hadley's brilliant *History of Bovril Advertising* (1972).

76 Turner, 84.

77 *Savoy Operas* (World's Classics, ed.), ii. 134.

Chapter 11

1 Text in *The Stockton & Darlington Railway: the Foundation of Middlesbrough*, ed. N. Moorsom [1975], 171–3.

2 D. M. Evans, *The Commercial Crisis 1847–8* (2nd ed., 1849), 10.

3 Obituary in *The Times*, 29 June 1908.

4 See advertisements reproduced in Dow GC, i. 181 189.

5 *Ibid.*, ii. 24; M. Robbins, *The Railway Age* (1962 ed.), pl. 9.

6 E. S. Turner, *The Shocking History of Advertising* (Penguin ed.), 81.

7 Neele, 215.

8 Two, of 1889 and 1897, are mentioned in R. B. Wilson, *Go Great Western* (1987 ed.), 66.

9 Copy in NRM. The Tower (built in 1891–4) does not figure in it. The Midland company never got to Blackpool, or ran any through carriages there. Moreover, it had strong interests in Morecambe, further up the same coast. That it should have commissioned this poster is a silent testimony to the value of the Blackpool traffic.

10 See N. Wilkinson, *A Brush with Life* (1969), 19.

11 This excellent formula was applied to many of the company's posters thereafter: see an example of 1909, depicting Llandudno, in 25 RM (1909) 208.

12 These original paintings and copies of the posters made from them are in NRM.

13 Copy in NRM.

14 The NRM has a large sample of Mason's railway work.

15 Matania's posters were reproduced freely in the RM; the Blackpool one is at the NRM.

16 Hassall produced a companion piece in 1914, showing a jolly lady cutting similar capers (repr. 9 *Railway and Travel Monthly*, 1914, 8). But it is much less effective.

17 Repr. Wilson, 18. J. T. Shackleton, *Golden Age of the Railway Poster* (1976), pls. 86–7, 92, 107.

18 Fourteen of the posters produced before the war of 1914 are reproduced in *London Transport Posters*, ed. H. F. Hutchison (1963).

19 A. S. Hartrick, *A Painter's Pilgrimage* (1939), 220.

20 M. J. Daunton, *Royal Mail* (1985), 72.

21 See A. Byatt, *Picture Postcards and their Publishers* (1978); M. I. Bray, *Railway Picture Postcards* (1986); and a contemporary survey in 18 RM (1906) 137–43.

22 See for instance Bray, pls. 8, 20, 202.

23 Wilson 84, 112. Copies of most of the early editions of these books are in R268–9.

24 Bray, 47.

25 T. B. Russell, *Commercial Advertising* (1919), 270–4. The Great Central company's *Per Rail*, advertising its freight services, stands out: a cloth-bound book of more than 200 pages, issued in 1913. See Dow GC, iii. 258.

26 Announcement and handbills at NRM.

27 *Great Western Railway Guide* (pub. J. Wyld, 1839), 1–2.

28 See G. B. Lissenden, *The Railway Passenger's Handbook* [1906], 5–11; H. W. Disney, *Law of Carriage by Railway* (6th ed., 1923), chap. 13.

29 *Miscellaneous Papers*, ed. B. W. Matz (1914), 422.

30 See *All Stations* (1981), pls. XI (6), XXV (7).

31 Wilson (*Go Great Western*, 157) said that such competitions originated on the Bristol & Exeter Railway in 1865, but without quoting evidence.

32 R134/41; R267/140; R92/67, f. 285.

33 18 RM (1906) 314.

34 Of the chief Great Western prizes awarded in 1905, ten went to country stations; two – surely well earned – to stations in suburbs, of Bristol and Birmingham: *ibid*., 296.

35 For some examples see RTC, 297; also R. Jackson, *History of the Town . . . of Barnsley* (1858), 138.

36 RTC, 105.

37 Devon RO (Plymouth) D3/X3, ff. 85, 296.

38 *St Mungo*, 23 April 1897; see scrap-book in SRO, BR/HRP(S)/51.

39 Dow GC, i. 187–8; C. E. Stretton, *History of the Midland Railway* (1901), 141–3, 150–1; MacDermot, i. 188, 193–4.

40 Barclay-Harvey, 70–4.

41 The ensuing reform is a most creditable story: *ibid*., 89–107.

42 PGA 17 & 18 Vict. cap. 31, sect. 2.

43 See RTC 296, and note.

44 PP 1890–1 xxvi. 617–18.

45 Expenditure of this kind might be questioned by councillors and ratepayers, as at Folkestone for instance in 1861, 1875, and 1884: Kent RO (Folkestone), AM2/4, p. 184; AM2/5, pp. 193, 204.

46 Lord Middleton headed a deputation to the President, C. T. Ritchie, in 1899, which complained that the London & South Western suburban services were so unpunctual that it was becoming impossible to keep appointments in London. Ritchie, who lived on the line himself, could only undertake to convey the deputation's criticisms to the company. See Williams LSWR, ii. 311–12.

47 Disney, 221–5.

48 See Ahrons LTW, v. 63–6.

49 See A. T. Patterson, *History of Southampton*, iii (1975), 66–70, 95–7, 119–24; RTC, 155–6, 158, 211–13; Williams LSWR, ii. 199; 1 RM (1897) 397–8.

50 The official account of the trials is in PP 1877 xlviii. 97–121.

51 G. Alderman, *The Railway Interest* (1973), 53. My work is much indebted to this valuable study.

52 Alderman points out (28) that in 1888 the President of the Board of Trade, Sir Michael Hicks-Beach, showed himself most unsympathetic to the railway companies, and that in the House of Lords at the same time the attack on their rates was led by Lord Henniker; both these politicians being themselves directors of railway companies – the East Gloucestershire and the Mellis & Eye respectively. Of course: for these were little companies, dependent on big ones and often grumbling at them. Both men were therefore interested in assailing the large companies.

53 Alderman (230) speaks of the directors of national companies as forming the 'efficient interest'.

54 55 *Punch* (1868) 98; 65 (1873) 195.

55 Alderman, 20.

56 *Ibid*., 33, 99–101, 146–51.

57 See for example Bagwell RCH, chap. 11, for the important part played by the Clearing House in the development of pooling agreements and rates conferences.

58 Alderman, 34.

59 *Ibid*., 165, 168, 176, 189; Irving, 54–64.

60 These figures all exclude season-ticket holders.

61 Dow GC, iii, 32, 35. See also L. T. C. Rolt, *The Making of a Railway*

(1971), 139–40.

62 Marshall LYR, ii. 253; RYB 1910, 13, 189; 1914, 12, 216; JMetR, 238.

63 Even within the Great Central company the power of the publicity department waned. Stuart was transferred to another post in 1909. His successor, F. W. D. Smith, was receiving a salary of only £220 in 1919, and his department had been moved to the office of the superintendent of the line. Dow GC, iii. 102, 338.

64 Pick's early work is summarized in C. Barman, *The Man who built London Transport* (1979), 26–34.

65 10 RM (1902) 540.

66 Wilson, *Go Great Western*, chap. 5.

67 10 RM (1902) 536.

68 Report of meeting in R410/10.

69 Labour MPs, for example, in 1913: 47 *Hansard* (1913), 1589, 1632.

70 M. Robbins, *The Isle of Wight Railways* (1953), 1.

Chapter 12

1 PP 1937–8 xii. 279.

2 *Pride and Prejudice* (1813), chap. 42; *Emma* (1816), chap. 12; *Persuasion* (1818), chap. 11.

3 *Works*, ed. R. W. Chapman, vi (1954), 363–427.

4 E. W. Gilbert, *Brighton* (1954), 92.

5 But see J. A. R. Pimlott, *The Englishman's Holiday* (1947), 76.

6 See *The Torrington Diaries*, ed. C. B. Andrews (1934–8).

7 J. P. Anderson, *Book of British Topography* (1881), 42, 44.

8 PP 1850 xiv. 677.

9 R. Buchanan, *Practical Treatise on Propelling Vessels by Steam* (1816), 13.

10 Thomas LMR, 195.

11 Lee PCD, 9.

12 MacDermot, i. 353.

13 Tomlinson, 372.

14 M. Tylecote, *Mechanics' Institutes of Lancashire and Yorkshire before 1851* (1957), 173.

15 Tomlinson, 372–3.

16 *The Times*, 26 August 1840.

17 Thomas LFR, 77.

18 R250/4, p. 40 (1850).

19 In DNB (1891): an extension of his own more modest claim in the matter (Sir R. and G. B. Hill, *Life of Sir Rowland Hill*, ii. 21). The directors sanctioned only one of these trains in 1844 (R386/7, pp. 262, 345). They were not discussed either by the traffic committee or by the shareholders.

20 *The Times*, 13 April 1844.

21 PP 1846 xxxix. 58.

22 *Leeds Mercury*, 14 September 1844. The excursions did not travel as a single unit, however, but in several separate trains.

23 [S. Quelch,] *Early Recollections of Oxford. By an Old Freeman* (1900), 12.

24 *Leicester Chronicle*, 28 September, 5 October 1844.

25 Gladstone to Dalhousie, 16 September 1844: SRO, GD 45/7/14 (4).

26 PP 1846 xxxix. 26–7.

27 The Midland drew up most explicit regulations for the working of excursion trains, on the lines recommended by the Board: R491/13, min. 244.

28 Gourvish, *Huish*, 76.

29 *Ibid.* 121, 125–6.

30 C. R. Fay, *Palace of Industry* (1951), 137.

31 See for example the Great Western negotiations: R250/4, pp. 6, 21–6, 210, 239, 258–9, 426; 250/5, p. 28.

32 Bagwell RCH, 56–7.

33 C. H. Gibbs-Smith, *The Great Exhibition: a Commemorative Album* (1950), 33–4.

34 14 *Railway Times* (1851) 600, 646, 673, 697. A proof copy of regulations for such clubs drawn up by the South Devon Railway is in R631/25.

35 14 *Railway Times* (1851) 745; Grinling, 163.

36 14 *Railway Times* (1851) 1057. The Great Northern company's startling increase, of 178.4%, arose because its line had been opened only on 7 August 1850.

37 9 *Builder* (1851) 408, 453.

38 Gourish, *Huish*, 187. It has been mistakenly said that the company carried 775,000 *excursionists*; but Huish was referring to passengers of all kinds. The agent's figure for the excursionists is likely to have been approximately right.

39 15 *Railway Times* (1852) 142.

40 *Ibid.*, 73.

41 *Ibid.*, 210, 211, 70, 243, 247.

42 *Ibid.*, 259–60, 145.

43 *Ibid.*, 145–6.

44 *Temperance Jubilee Celebrations at Leicester and Market Harborough* (1886), 56.

45 Fay, 93–4.

46 *London 1808–70*, 135.

47 F. Bédarida, *History of England, 1850–75* (1979), 7–8. For a fuller treatment of this whole subject, written from a somewhat different standpoint from mine, see A. B. Rae's valuable M. Phil. thesis, 'Visitors by Railway to the Great Exhibition of 1851' (Open University, 1987).

48 'The Fiddler of the Reels': *Life's Little Ironies* (pocket ed.), 179–81.

49 See RTC, 244–68.

50 An 'excursion department' is referred to in a railway manual written by three Great Central men and a 'section dealing with excursion arrangements', but the business was mainly in the hands of the 'district excursion clerks', at monthly meetings: C. Travis, D. R. Lamb, and J. A. Jenkinson, *Practical Railway Working* (1915), 72, 159, 165.

51 PP 1867 xxxvii (1). 58.

52 *Ibid.*, 739.

53 *Ibid.*, 639–40.

54 *Ibid.*, 745.

55 PP 1867 xxxvii (2). 622.

56 *Ibid.*, 668.

57 Smithells asserted that the company had carried 653,000 passengers in Whitsun week alone: *ibid.*, xxxviii (1). 739.

58 *Ibid.*, xxxvi (2). 1025.

59 PP 1861 lvii. 66.

60 Marshall LYR, i. 258.

61 Scotland is omitted here, since no information about excursion traffic was furnished to the Commission by the Scottish companies.

62 *Annual Register*, 1861, Chronicle, 181. See also *ibid.*, 1875, Chronicle, 77–8.

63 PGA 9 & 10 Vict. cap. 93.

64 See the *Annual Register* again: 1857, Chronicle, 131; 1858, 129–30; 1861, 1–2.

65 See for instance Grinling, 137.

66 PP (HL) 1873 xviii. 475.

67 PP 1861 lvii. 181.

68 33 *Railway Times* (1870) 123.

69 L. T. C. Rolt, *Red for Danger* (1982 ed.), 44–6.

70 *Ibid.*, 178–81, 51–8.

71 PP 1870 lix. 247.

72 PP 1875 lxvi. 224.

73 See Rolt, 147–53, and report of Court of Inquiry: PP 1877 lxxii. 469.

74 Report, PP 1888 lxxxviii. 156.

75 At Crosby Garrett, Westmorland (1888), and Colwyn Bay (1889): PP 1888 lxxxviii. 460, 1890 lxv. 149.

76 A special inquiry was made then into this matter at the decennial census. It was never repeated. See G. F. A. Best, *Mid-Victorian Britain* (1971), 176–81, 194.

77 I know of only one line on the Continent that carried no Sunday service, the Yverdon & Ste Croix in Switzerland, in accordance with a landowner's stipulation: *Murray's Handbook for Switzerland* (19th ed., 1904), 70; *Bradshaw's Continental Guide*, August 1914, 263a.

78 Bradshaw, August 1887.

79 A Pichot, *Voyage...en Angleterre et en Ecosse* (1825), i. 60. See also F. de la Rochefoucauld, *A Frenchman in England* (1933), 79–80; and W. O. Henderson, *John Conrad Fischer and his Diary* (1966), 164.

80 Some turnpike trusts were required to charge double tolls on Sundays: S. & B. Webb, *The Story of the King's Highway* (1963 ed.), 137, 158.

81 *Persuasion*, chap. 17.

82 Sir A. Agnew, *The Observance of the Lord's Day* (1841), 9.

83 T. McCrie, *Memoirs of Sir Andrew Agnew* (1850), 206–7.

84 PP 1831–2 vii.

85 Text in *The Uncommercial Traveller*, 636–63. Dickens also refers to Agnew as 'the Lord's Day Bill Baronet', in *Sketches by Boz*, 161.

86 Robertson, 152, 156, 159–60, 334. See the same author's admirable article 'Early Scottish Railways and the Observance of the Sabbath': 57 *Scottish Historical Review* (1978) 143–67.

87 S. Fay, *A Royal Road* (1882), 34–6; Williams LSWR, i. 224–5.

88 J. Goding, *Norman's History of Cheltenham* (1863 ed.), 570–1, 600.

89 Suffolk RO, 50/1/1, box 14.

90 For example by I. C. Wright in his *Letter to the Directors and Proprietors of the Midland Counties Railway* (1839): a copy in Nottingham PL.

91 As in *Hear Both Sides! The Question of Cheap Sunday Excursion Trains* (1850): Bristol PL, Bristol Collection 1408.

92 PP 1847 lxiii. 87–91.

93 Wright was among the few who stressed the second element more strongly.

94 G. M. Young in *Early Victorian England* (1934), ii. 456.

95 Letter of 29 July 1844: BL, Add. MS. 44361, f. 201.

96 As at Doncaster in 1868: PP 1868–9 liv. 98.

97 See Rolt, *Red for Danger*, 178–81, 51–7.

98 See petition to the Great Northern Board from Barnet in 1854–7: R236/726/6.

99 *Barchester Towers*, chap. 5.

100 Fourth Narrative (Penguin ed., 461).

101 See Greville's comments: *The Greville Memoirs*, ed. L. Strachey and R. Fulford (1938), vii. 203.

102 W. L. Burn, *The Age of Equipoise* (1964), 280.

103 26 *Railway Times* (1863) 136.

104 PP 1868–9 liv. 87.

105 P. W. Kingsford, *Victorian Railwaymen* (1970), 103–4, 120.

106 PP 1864 liii. 917.

107 The company made no return, but Bradshaw discloses its practice.
108 R236/721/10.
109 L. Popplewell, *Bournemouth Railway History* (1973), 150–1.
110 J. Thomas, *The Skye Railway* (1977), 85–9. There was similar rioting, due to Sabbatarians, at Newlyn in Cornwall in 1896, though there the railway was not directly involved. See L. Luck, *South Cornish Harbours* (1988), 16–17.
111 MacDermot, ii. 37, 197; C. R. Clinker, *New Light on the Gauge Conversion* (1978) 15. For another example of a large engineering work performed on a Sunday at this time, the replacement of the bridge south of Peterborough, see Wrottesley GNR, iii. 18.
112 Acworth RE (1889 ed.), 244–5.
113 Annual reports in PP.
114 Wrottesley GNR, iii. 112.
115 On some urban railways the volume of Sunday traffic was not negligible. On the Cheshire Lines, for example, a census of October 1911 showed that the number of Sunday travellers leaving its termini in Manchester and Liverpool constituted respectively 24.4 and 19.2% of those on weekdays: R110/180.
116 A. Vaughan, *History of the Faringdon Branch* (1979) 60; S. C. Jenkins, *The Witney & East Gloucestershire Railway* (1975), 12.
117 Like the crazy Mr Lloyd Davies, who addressed a telegram to the Great Western Railway from Pembrokeshire, ten pages long, warning it of the 'woes' to come from the running of Sunday trains (R1014/8/20): a showpiece from the wilder shores of this strange literature.
118 R226/410, 256/80, 527/1700.
119 An incomplete set of the Council's reports is in BL, 4355 bb. 35.
120 R414/537, p. 16.
121 On the Midland line to London in 1914 two general goods trains ran up during the day, but no coal train: WTT, R936/105.
122 WTT, R937/114, 948/60.
123 K. Chorley, *Manchester Made Them* (1950), 170. See also the Claphams in *Early Victorian England*, i. 243.
124 *Works*, vii. 305.
125 J. K. Walton, *The Blackpool Landlady* (1978), 18: E. W. Gilbert, *Brighton* (1954), 205–6.
126 *Ibid.*, 206–7.
127 *Works*, vii. 306–7.
128 *Drink and the Victorians* (1971), 336.
129 *Sir Daniel Gooch: Memoirs and Diary* ed. R. B. Wilson (1972), 190.

Chapter 13

1 *Resources and Prospects of America* (1866), 290.
2 PP 1867 xxxvii (1). 58.
3 Lefèvre & Cerbelaud, 284.
4 PP 1909 lxxvii. 394, 1910 lvii. 65, 168, 416.
5 FF, 52.
6 To Yarmouth and Lowestoft there was some competition from the Midlands but none for the more valuable traffic from London.
7 E. H. P. Brown and M. H. Browne, *A Century of Pay* (1968), 67.
8 *Ibid.*, 46.
9 M. D. Bienefeld, *Working Hours in British Industry* (1972), 109, 142.
10 Brown and Browne, 55–6.
11 See the detailed statements in R236/725/2.
12 L. Levi, *Wages and Earnings of the Working Classes* (1867), 19.
13 R. Till, *Wills of Bristol* (n.d.), 42.
14 Lefèvre & Cerbelaud, 284; *Hommes et choses du PLM* (1979 ed.), 147.
15 Williams LSWR, i. 223.
16 1 *Railway Chronicle* (1844) 516–17, 700.
17 R236/16, pp. 223–4.
18 RTC, 86, 133.
19 Gourvish, *Huish*, 186–7.
20 F. G. Cockman in *The Railway Age in Bedfordshire* (1974), 109.
21 See J. K. Walton in 15 *Northern History* (1979), 204–5.
22 PP 1864 liii. 692.
23 Bradshaw, August 1887, 84, 92, 110, 132, 216.
24 *Bradshaw's Continental Guide*, August 1914, 18a, 19.
25 There were two trains from Brussels to the coast at Blankenberghe on Saturdays only, though no extra back on Mondays; one Monday train from Dives-Cabourg and Trouville to Paris was announced to run in September (*ibid.*, 102, 178).
26 *Le petit Robert* dates them respectively to 1906 and 1914.
27 I summarized the most useful series I have found, compiled for the South Eastern & Chatham company and now in R633/425, in RTC 231. This set was a little extended, to include some other services, in another table: R779/94.
28 Neele, 140.
29 Dow GC, iii. 39, 41–5.
30 Some agencies sprang out of educational and religious work: the London Polytechnic's from 1886 onwards, for instance, Henry Lunn's from 1892. See E. M. Wood, *The Polytechnic and its Founders* (1932 ed.), 152–3: Sir H. Lunn, *Nearing Harbour*

(1934), chap. 6.
31 J. Pécheux, *L'Age d'or du rail européen* (1975), 173.
32 *Zug der Zeit*, 753–4.
33 Cook's *Traveller's Gazette*, 18 July 1914.
34 I understand that some records of John Frame's business have been preserved but I was refused permission to look at them.
35 They are in R226/123.
36 Now in the company's offices in Berkeley Street, London. I am much indebted to Edmund Swinglehurst for his assistance here.
37 J. P. Anderson, *Book of British Topography* (1881), 41–4.
38 *The London and Leith Smack and Steam Packet Guide* (1824), xi, 225.
39 Advertisements in *Liverpool Mail and Post*, 12 July 1845.
40 J[ohn Bell], *The English Party's Excursion to Paris in Easter Week 1849* (1850). Copy in Lancashire RO.
41 *The Excursionist*, called the *Traveller's Gazette* from 1903 onwards (file of both papers in Cook's archives), 1 July 1856.
42 *Ibid.*, 20 August 1855, 1 July 1856.
43 Obituary, *The Times*, 4 May 1894.
44 Neele, 140–1.
45 There is a collection of the firm's tourist programmes in BL, 2500 v.
46 Pécheux, 172.
47 J. Pudney, *The Thomas Cook Story* (1953), 43.
48 E. Swinglehurst, *The Romantic Journey*, 31.
49 Cook's fully matured system of tours in Scotland is set out in his guide to it for the year 1861: copy in BL.
50 E. Swinglehurst, *Cook's Tours* (1982), 29.
51 It is delightfully recorded in a simple diary kept by Jemima Morrell, who was one of the party: see *Romantic Journey*, chap. 5.
52 Published in book form as *Letters from the Sea and from Foreign Lands* (1873).
53 *Ibid.*, 23.
54 Announcement in *Excursionist*, 1 July 1868, see W. F. Rae, *The Business of Travel* (1891), 94–8.
55 Six years earlier Thomas told his wife that their son did 'not like mixing missions with business' (letter, 24 March 1872: Cook's archives). In January 1878 John Mason wrote a defensive memorandum concerning his treatment of his father (Guard-book Folio, no. 13, pp. 296–306).
56 20 RM (1907) 513.
57 Rae, 150–8.

58 In 1876: *Works*, xxxiv. 138.

59 *The Eustace Diamonds* (Penguin ed.), 329; *The Prime Minister* (World's Classics ed.), ii, 303

60 SRO, BR/LIB (S)/18/62.

61 *Ibid.*, 18/35.

62 An agreement was arrived at between the Caledonian and Glasgow & South Western companies in 1910, but the North British declined to join it: SRO, BR/GSW/9.

63 'Travelling Companions': *Complete Tales*, ed. L. Edel, ii (1965), 194.

64 C. Mackie, *Norfolk Annals* (1901), 457.

65 *Leicester Daily Post*, 3 August 1881.

66 Findlay (6th ed., 1899), 356–7.

67 Acworth RE, (1889), 405–6.

68 See the good account of Oldham's by R. Poole in *Leisure in Britain*, ed. J. K. Walton and J. Walvin (1983), 71–98.

69 Sir F. Hill, *Victorian Lincoln* (1974), 305.

70 See also RTC, 88–90, 134–5.

71 Robertson, 245.

72 Findlay (4th ed., 1891), 300–2.

73 Acworth RE (1st ed., 1889), 324; Williams LSWR, ii. 79. For the traffic at Aintree on Grand National day, 1905, see 18 RM (1906) 237–8.

74 Dow GC, i. 129.

75 See G. F. A. Best, *Mid-Victorian Britain* (1971), 248.

76 JLLR, 172, 35; *The Hull & Barnsley Railway*, ed. K. Hoole and B. Hinchliffe (1972–80), ii. 61.

77 J. Arlott in *Edwardian England*, ed. S. Nowell-Smith (1964), 470.

78 JLLR, 108.

79 *Edwardian England*, 471.

80 All this is set out in a useful article by H. Macfarlane in 22 RM (1908) 201–7.

81 Williams LSWR, ii. 47–8.

82 Acworth RE (1st ed., 1889), 323.

83 JLLR, 351.

84 See J. T. Shackleton, *Golden Age of the Railway Poster* (1976), 134.

85 Tomlinson, 372.

86 R1008/120: F. Crawshay to Walter Coffin, 8 September 1846.

87 R. Till, *Wills of Bristol* (n.d.), 18.

88 D. Stuart, *County Borough*, part i (1975), 43–7.

89 A. S. Peck, *The Great Western at Swindon Works* (1983), 61.

90 Hoole and Hinchliffe, ii. 62.

91 C. G. Maggs, *The Midland & South Western Junction Railway* (1967), 116.

92 Peck, 108–10.

93 26 *Great Western Railway Magazine* (1914) 231.

94 For an example of their early organization see the *Sixteenth Report to the Ministry of the Poor* (1850), 47: copy in Manchester PL.

95 JLLR, 225.

96 Findlay (6th ed., 1899), 360.

97 See for example Sir O. Sitwell, *Tales my Father taught Me* (1962), 122–4.

98 One such journey is well described in M. V. Hughes, *A London Family* (1946), 85–91.

99 *Dickens's Dictionary of the Thames*, 77, 110.

100 *Dickens's Dictionary of London* (1879), 9, 25; for 'holiday trips' for this purpose see *Ward & Lock's Pictorial Guide to the Environs of London* [1879], 120–4.

101 A. Vaughan, *History of the Faringdon Branch* (1979), 115.

102 PP 1911 xxxiv. 74.

103 R414/537, pp 45, 268.

104 K. Baedeker, *London* (14th ed., 1905), 76.

105 See the Earl of Albemarle and G. L. Hillier, *Cycling* (1895 ed.), chaps. x and xi.

106 3 RM (1898) 498.

107 J. T. Lightwood, *The Cyclists' Touring Club* (1928), 29, 76. See 7 RM (1900) 26, 16 (1905) 68.

108 *Ibid.*, 406.

109 R946/17.

110 For example the Festival of Empire: see RTC, 54.

111 SRO, BR/NBR/30/30.

112 pp. 141; 119; 1733; 83, 117, 123.

113 pp. 244, 308, 902; 44, 2185.

114 pp. 896; 1454; 911–13.

115 pp. 888–918.

Chapter 14

1 *Annual Register*, 1861, Chronicle, 160.

2 T. L. Peacock, *Gryll Grange: Works*, ed. D. Garnett (1948), 934.

3 Jackman, 335–7. Other comparisons are made by H. W. Hart in 4 JTH (1959–60) 147–9.

4 See RTC, 285.

5 *Boswell's Life of Johnson*, ed. G. B. Hill and L. F. Powell (1934–50), ii. 45.

6 Journal of Hekekyan Bey: BL, Add. MS. 37448, f. 80v.

7 Mrs Fawcett, *Life of . . . Sir William Molesworth* (1901), 132–3.

8 *Letters of Sydney Smith*, ed. N. C. Smith (1953), 774.

9 Sir R. Hill and G. B. Hill, *Life of Sir Rowland Hill* (1880), ii. 21; W. Beattie, *Life and Letters of Thomas Campbell* (1850), iii. 114.

10 R250/6, p. 423.

11 11 *Journal of the Statistical Society* (1848) 333 n.

12 PP 1874 lviii. 783.

13 PP 1877 lxxii. 390.

14 See O. S. Nock, *The Railway Race to the North* [1959].

15 FF, 93.

16 Random samples of trains in Britain and France, taken from Bradshaw's British and Continental timetables for January 1901, show that most British stopping trains on country branch lines (not light railways) averaged over 20 mph, whereas many in France ran at 15, a few even at less than 10.

17 See H. W. Hart in 4 JTH (1959–60) 151–2 and W. C. A. Blew, *Brighton and its Coaches* (1894), especially pp. 151, 189.

18 The variations in maxima appear in a Parliamentary return of 1879: PP (HL) 1879 xii. 373.

19 Jackman (346) estimates vails at $16\frac{1}{2}\%$ of the fare. That seems a little too high, certainly for inside passengers, in the light of notes made by the engineer C. B. Vignoles in his diary. On two sets of journeys, nineteen in all, made between London or St Albans and Warwick, Birmingham, Liverpool, Warrington, Manchester, and Lowestoft, he spent £42 7s in coach fares and gave £6 12s in vails: so his vails amounted to 15.6% of the fares. (Diary, 5 March–19 May 1830, 8 February–27 March 1831; BL, Add. MS. 35071). These are the notes made by one man, not by a number of diarists or letter-writers, and Vignoles was a seasoned traveller, well able to assess what he ought to pay. The notes were made to allow him to reckon up his professional expenses. I believe 15% to be about the right average.

20 C. Hadfield, *British Canals* (6th ed., 1979), 185–94; L. A. Williams, *Road Transport in Cumbria* (1975), 139–40.

21 Railway fares from London can be ascertained from the *ABC Railway Guide*; the steamer fares and services listed above are in Bradshaw, August 1887.

22 See RTC, 42–4.

23 In the 1880s they could be as high as 25% above the first-class fare in Belgium and Germany: Lefèvre & Cerbelaud, 285. They averaged well over 30% in Austria in 1914: *Bradshaw's Continental Guide*, August 1914, 237b.

24 E. Foxwell, 'English Express Trains in 1883' (96 *Journal of the Statistical Society*, 1883, 517–74), and *English Express Trains* (1884).

25 R. J. Minot, *Railway Travel in*

Europe and America (Boston, 1882).
26 FF.
27 Minot, 14.
28 For excursion tickets see p. 290. The issue of workmen's tickets in Continental countries is set out in PP 1909 lxxvii. 265, 388; 1910 lvii. 211, 314, 416.
29 *Railway Problems* (1887), 267.
30 *Ibid.*, 372.
31 For the genesis of this plan see H. Pollins in 4 JTH (1959–60) 85–95; Dow GC, ii. 236–43.
32 J. Copeland, *Roads and their Traffic* (1968), 101, quoting *Essex Standard*, 1 June 1838.
33 So Benjamin Horne said, a leading coach proprietor: PP 1837 xx. 298.
34 BR, i. 26.
35 *Ibid.*
36 See G. C. Dickinson in 4 JTH (1959–60) 6–7.
37 Reckoning from T. Bradley, *Old Coaching Days in Yorkshire* (1889), 209–37.
38 These figures are tabulated by J. R. Hume in his valuable paper 'Transport and Towns in Victorian Scotland': *Scottish Urban History*, ed. G. Gordon and B. Dicks (1983), 198.
39 See e.g. Robertson, 88, 261.
40 PP 1837 xx. 323.
41 BR, i. 42–3.
42 BR, ii. 134. No figures can be given for the numbers of passengers carried by other railways within London.
43 *Staffordshire Advertiser*, 19 December 1835.
44 T. S. Ashton, *An Economic History of England: the Eighteenth Century* (1955), 14–15.
45 PP 1847 lxiii. 162–75.
46 Brooke, *Navvy*, 19–21.
47 A. Redford, *Labour Migration in England* (1926), 164, 190–1.
48 Joseph Ashby and Bolton King in 3 *Economic Journal* (1893) 195–7. The movements in individual parishes, commented on in the census returns, often reflect this process. See for instance those collected in *VCH Wiltshire*, iv. 318–25, where substantial migration is noted in 1841, the Great Western line having entered the county in 1840. A large majority of the parishes in which migration or emigration are recorded down to 1871 lay on or close to railways.
49 *Small Talk at Wreyland*, i (1918), 45.
50 Redford, 162. The scale of internal migration within Victorian England is demonstrated in Sir A. Cairncross, *Home and Foreign Invest-*

ment (1953), chap. iv.
51 PRO, MT/1/6/28.
52 PP 1844 xi. 640–59.
53 MacDermot, i. 50, 333.
54 Alfred Russel Wallace describes a journey in an open goods vehicle from Berkhamsted to London, which he dates to 1838: *My Life* (1905), i. 135. C. R. Clinker *(Birmingham & Derby Junction Railway*, 1982 ed., 14) says that the London & Birmingham introduced third-class accommodation on 5 October 1840, without quoting any authority. Third class is stated to be available on that line in the January 1841 issue of Bradshaw's *Railway Companion*.
55 Whishaw RGB, 267; also 311 (Manchester & Bolton company).
56 Robertson, 384.
57 74 *Quarterly Review* (1844) 263.
58 PP 1844 xi. 96.
59 *Ibid.*, 158.
60 Admirably elucidated in Robertson, 246–52.
61 Moreover Parris (93–9) pays a well-merited tribute to the labour of the civil servants in supervising the new system as it went into operation.
62 PP 1847 lxiii. 177.
63 The percentage was 55.2. For the figures see PP 1851 li. 238, 252.
64 A. P. Allen, *The Ambassadors of Commerce* (1885), 104–7.
65 The diffusion of book-printing from London illustrates this process clearly: see RTC, 278–9.
66 J. C. Carr and W. Taplin, *History of the British Steel Industry* (1962) chap. 26 gives a useful short account of such amalgamations in that industry.
67 Wrottesley GNR, i. 84–5.
68 *VCH Wiltshire*, iv. 325, 358.
69 Irving, 110–11; Lowe BSLB, 518, 525.
70 Hodges to G. Fisher, 17 December 1846: R1008/120.
71 P. W. Kingsford, *Victorian Railwaymen* (1970), 56–7.
72 *Stationmaster*, v.
73 Acworth RE (1889 ed.), 309–12.
74 N. Rhind, *Blackheath Village*, i (1978), 124–5. Similar examples of long service are given in P. Paye, *The Buntingford Branch* (1980), 118–19, and A. Vaughan, *History of the Faringdon Branch* (1979), 76–7. For a Victorian appreciation of a stationmaster's work see WIR, 300–5; for a modern one, D. St. J. Thomas, *The Country Railway* (1979 ed.), 68–79.
75 See W. G. Hoskins, *Devon* (1954), 99–101; RTC, 332.
76 A. T. Patterson, *History of Sou-*

thampton (1966–75) ii. 104–5.
77 A. Helps, *Life and Labours of Mr Brassey* (1872), 235–9.
78 See Acworth's touching account of the departure of one of the emigrants' trains from Aberlour in 1889: RS, 134–6.
79 *Reg. Hist.*, xiv. 185, 227.
80 The earliest trace of this traffic I have found is an entry in the diary of a Lancashire & Yorkshire officer for 16 September 1851, which records the printing of a special notice of instruction for emigrants in German: R343/722.
81 C. G. Maggs, *Midland & South Western Junction Railway* (1967), 111–12; *VCH East Riding of Yorkshire*, i. 396; R. Bell, *Twenty-five Years of the North Eastern Railway* [1951], 36.
82 For Glasgow see Kellett, 93, 255; for other examples, on a smaller scale, see RTC, 122–3.
83 Robertson, 240–1; RTC, 61–2, 112.
84 The series cannot be extended because the figures given for 1842 are defective and from the beginning of 1845 the London & Greenwich was leased to the South Eastern company, with which its returns were merged.
85 No railway in Scotland can be satisfactorily compared with them. The promising passenger business of the Garnkirk & Glasgow company fell off; the Glasgow Paisley & Greenock was something more than a suburban railway; the Edinburgh & Dalkeith was worked by horses (Robertson, 239–45).
86 See the concluding sentence of Dickens's paper 'The River': *Sketches by Boz*, 103.
87 The North Eastern Railway issued 1000-mile first-class contract tickets: Irving, 43. The London & South Western offered 'passes' to visitors from abroad stopping over at Southampton and wishing to run up and down freely to London. [T. C. Haliburton,] *The Season Ticket* (1860) gives an account of the use made of one.
88 T. C. Barker in *Transport in Victorian Britain*, ed. M. J. Freeman and D. H. Aldcroft (1988), 135.
89 R. H. Clark, *A Southern Region Record* (1964), List 5.
90 R250/5, pp. 55, 330, 345.
91 RTC, 113. The London & Birmingham company had already been urged to issue such tickets, following the steamboats' example, as early as 1838: *Railroadiana. First Series* (1838), 211.
92 *Where Shall We Go?* (pub. Black, 4th ed., 1866), 162.

93 G. Measom, *Guide to the Great Eastern Railway, Cambridge Line* [1865], 89.

94 Thomas NBR, i. 113–15.

95 See H. J. Dyos's pioneering article 'Workmen's Fares in South London, 1860–1914' (1 JTH, 1953–4, 3–19); also Lee PCD, chap. 7.

96 Dyos in 1 JTH 15, 18; 2 JTH (1955–6) 93–4.

97 PGA 46 & 47 Vict. cap. 34, sect. 3.

98 59 *Railway Times* (1891) 109.

99 29 *Builder* (1871) 16–17.

100 BR, i. 196.

101 See map in *ibid.*, i, 258–9.

102 Kellett, 63–4.

103 Grinling, 355.

104 For comment on the Great Northern company's policies here see 3rd series JTH (1985–6) 71–8.

105 Dow GC, iii. 314, 317.

106 The bad services provided by the companies making up this combine were already an old song. See *The Rise of Suburbia*, ed. F. M. L. Thompson (1982), 75–7; Ahrons LTW, v. 3–5.

107 R. E. Lacy and G. Dow, *Midland Railway Carriages* (1986), 269–71, 471.

108 RTC, 114–18.

109 *Ibid.*, 75.

110 PP 1911 xxxiv. 89, 289.

111 See RTC, 111–12, 105.

112 See RTC, 119–20; O. S. Nock, *The Caledonian Railway* (paperback ed.), 141.

113 *Anticipations* (1902), 46.

114 For an example see 18 RM (1906) 430.

115 The history of the Metropolitan company's dealings in land down to 1914 is clearly recounted in JMetR, 134–42, 238–40, 256.

116 PP 1910 xxxviii. 47.

117 C. C. Pond, *The Chingford Line* (1975), 12.

118 C. J. Allen, *Great Eastern Railway* (1975 ed.), 71–2, 117–18, 123.

119 BR ii. 47–50, 251–2; 3rd series 6 JTH (1985) 75–6.

120 *Letters*, ed. R. W. Chapman (2nd ed., 1952), 188–9.

121 *Wellington and his Friends*, ed. 7th Duke of Wellington (1965), 268. For another illustration of the persistence of the old idea see Miss Stanbury's observations in Trollope's novel *He Knew He Was Right* (1868), chap. 8.

122 74 *Quarterly Review* (1844) 250.

123 *American Notes*, 62–3.

124 *The Times*, 10 November 1845, à propos an 'outrage on the Norfolk Railway'; *The Glasgow & South Western Railway* (Stephenson Locomotive Society, 1950), 7.

125 45 *Illustrated London News* (1864) 126.

126 G. B. Lissenden, *Railway Passenger's Handbook* [1906], 23–5.

127 PP 1888 lxxix. 97.

128 51 *Punch* (1866) 70; K. Robinson, *Wilkie Collins* (1951), 211; *The Hardman Papers*, ed. S. M. Ellis (1930), 153–4.

129 For a few of these cases, beginning with the famous one of Col. Valentine Baker in 1875, see J. Pendleton, *Our Railways* (1896), ii. 22–7. Prostitutes operated regularly in some urban trains over very short distances: JLT, 177; G. W. Parkin, *Mersey Railway* (n.d.), 15.

130 Thorne LSS, 47.

131 Census of 1911: *Report*, x. 110.

132 C. E. Stretton, *History of the Midland Railway* (1901), 31.

133 *Kilvert's Diary*, ed. W. Plomer (1938–40), iii. 288; 25 RM (1909) 349.

134 *The Times*, 16 December 1858.

135 Findlay (1890 ed.), 25.

136 *Ibid.* G. P. Bidder seems to have had a hand in persuading the Electric Telegraph Company (of which he was a director) to employ women in this capacity, from 1850 onwards: Clark, *Bidder*, 272–3, 456.

137 R258/343, Traffic Committee mins., 5 November 1908.

138 Bagwell RCH il. 53.

139 Dow GC, iii. 296.

140 Head SP, 85.

141 FF, 73.

142 A. Byles, *History of the Monmouthshire Railway & Canal Company* (1982), 54–5.

143 *Letters* (1895), i. 236.

144 *First and Last Loves* (1952) 89. See also his *London's Historic Railway Stations* (1972), 108.

145 *The British Coal Trade* (1915), 59.

146 See the useful account of them in P. N. Jones, 'Workmen's Trains in the South Wales Coalfield, 1870–1926': 3 *Transport History* (1970) 21–35.

147 *Ibid.*, 26.

148 *Ibid.*, 29–30.

149 K. O. Morgan, *Rebirth of a Nation* (1981), 8.

150 See N. Coltman's *New Map of all the Coach Roads of England and Wales* (1826).

151 See RTC, 315–17.

152 CMCR, i. 67.

153 Findlay (4th ed., 1890) 298.

154 *Zug der Zeit*, 127.

155 *Ibid.*, 122–3.

156 These figures are from Mitchell and Deane, 225–6; for 1913 the journeys are reckoned here on the old, not the revised, basis of calculation.

157 J. S. Jeans, *Railway Problems* (1887), xxviii, 230–4.

158 For example, Jeans's statement purports to relate to the years 1882–3, but the number of passenger journeys in the United Kingdom he records is that for 1885, not 1882.

159 The authority, as stated below the table, is B. R. Mitchell; and everyone who tries to study the British railways in their wider context must be indebted to his work. It is frequently referred to throughout this book, and I am glad to express my gratitude to him.

Chapter 15

1 *Lothair*, ed. V. Bogdanov (1975), 45.

2 *What I Remember* (1887), ii. 20.

3 Williams LSWR, i. 43; MacDermot, i. 337; D. Howse, *Greenwich Time* (1980), 87. This section owes much to Howse's excellent book.

4 R. Smiles, *Memoir of … Henry Booth* (1869), 67.

5 *Dombey and Son*, 218.

6 15 *Chambers' Journal* (1851) 392–5.

7 Amusingly recounted by Howse, 109–13.

8 It was not accepted in Cornwall until 1859, when the line was connected to the national system. Penzance town council then adopted Greenwich time: P. A. S. Pool, *History of … Penzance* (1974), 153. In Mid-Wales the Cambrian company accepted it in 1867: CMCR, i. 129.

9 BL, Add. MS. 52943 P, f. 2.

10 Howse, 111–13.

11 Kellett, 173–4.

12 In Scotland the North British company made a laconic announcement in its timetables: 'Time taken from the Railway Clocks' (SRO, BR/TT (S)/53/8).

13 W. Vincent, *Seen from the Station Platform* (1919), 23.

14 Copy of notice in Northumberland RO: NRO 306/55, box 1.

15 PP 1870 lx. 235.

16 The earliest at Bricklayer's Arms in 1844.

17 Francis, i. 292.

18 *Coningsby* (World's Classics ed.), 156. The novel was written in 1844.

19 Thomas LMR, 44–5.

20 Whishaw, RGB 273; Turner LBSCR, i. 124; R. Brunskill and A. Clifton-Taylor, *English Brickwork* (1977), 51.

21 Whishaw, 92, 108, 136, 338, 393.

22 Conder, 128.

23 *East Midlands Geographer*, 1 (1953) 44.

24 As at Nettlebed: *VCH Oxfordshire*, ii. 274.

25 Chaloner, *Crewe*, 96; Reed, *Crewe*, 60–1.

26 C. E. Lee, *Narrow-Gauge Railways in North Wales* (1945), 8–12, 14–16, 25.

27 F. J. North, *The Slates of Wales* (1946 ed.), 95.

28 E. Hull, *Building and Ornamental Stone* (1872), 289.

29 See A. Clifton-Taylor and A. S. Ireson, *English Stone Building* (1983), 229; Clifton-Taylor, *Pattern of English Building* (1987 ed.), 170.

30 P. Smith, *Houses of the Welsh Countryside* (1975), 324–5.

31 See D. Jenkinson, *Rails in the Fells* (1973), chap. 7.

32 J. Thomas, *The West Highland Railway* (3rd ed. 1984), 64; *Heritage*, 172.

33 *VCH Hunts.*, iii. 222.

34 F. C. Mather, *After the Canal Duke* (1970), 310.

35 R. Wood, *West Hartlepool* (1967), 20.

36 D. Alexander, *Retailing in England during the Industrial Revolution* (1970), 17; G. Dodd, *The Food of London* (1856), 105.

37 As at Burslem in the 1880s: PP 1890 xxxviii. 201. See also RTC, 47–8, 129.

38 8 *Builder* (1850) 19.

39 See RTC, 50–1, 128–9, and references given there, especially to the work of P. J. Atkins.

40 *VCH Derbyshire*, ii. 320; J. H. Bettey, *Rural Life in Wessex* (1977), 86; *VCH Wilts.*, iv. 227.

41 L. H. Ruegg, *The Salisbury & Yeovil Railway* (1878), 58.

42 R667/102, minutes of 12 July 1875.

43 Biographies of these men are to be found in DBB.

44 The English CWS, however, established in Manchester, backed the Ship Canal in the 1880s, from dissatisfaction with the railways' services and rates: D. A. Farnie, *The Manchester Ship Canal* (1980), 50–1.

45 Sir F. Head, *Stokers and Pokers* (2nd ed. 1849), 85–9; D. Lardner, *Railway Economy* (1850), 147.

46 See M. Girouard, *Victorian Pubs* (1975), 57.

47 Bristol University Library: Brunel Collection, GWR Sketchbook 11, pp. 28–9.

48 MacDermot, i. 75.

49 *Letters* (1893 ed.), 390.

50 *The Uncommercial Traveller*, 53–60.

51 *He Knew He Was Right* (World's Classics ed.) 1. 351–2.

52 In his essay 'Occasional Paris';

reprinted in *The American* (Bantam Books ed., 1971), 398.

53 *Railway Reform* (1865), 183.

54 *England, its People, Polity, and Pursuits* (1885 ed.), 264.

55 *Pall Mall Gazette*, Extra Number 42 (1888), 29.

56 Acworth RS, 65.

57 BR, i. 121; C. E. Lee in 110 RM (1964) 873.

58 See for instance Williams LSWR, ii. 319; Cambrian Railways timetable, October 1914, p. 71 (copy in R923/41).

59 Acworth RS, 3. He neglected Fife. There and in the adjacent county of Kinross the North British had a complete monopoly.

60 RTC, 204–7.

61 *Ibid.*, 162, 206.

62 RTC, 181.

63 In what follows I am indebted to Barrie Trinder's full study *The Industrial Revolution in Shropshire* (1973).

64 Lewis, 95.

65 Neele, 66.

66 Trinder, 249, 253, 256, 259.

67 *Ibid.* 248.

68 C. Hadfield, *Canals of the West Midlands* (1966), 234–7.

69 9 (n.s.) *Journal of the Royal Institution of Cornwall* (1982) 18–22.

70 The growth of the system here is recounted in *VCH Staffordshire*, ii. 314–24. The North Western began quadrupling its tracks in this district, to accommodate increasing traffic in 1881: Neele, 536.

71 RTC, 93.

72 *Ibid.*, 72.

73 See timetable (February 1831) in Marshall LMR, 69–70.

74 E. Parsons, *The Tourist's Companion* (1835), 242: Tomlinson, 419.

75 74 *Quarterly Review* (1844) 263.

76 S. Smiles, *Railway Property* [1849], 33; Gourvish, *Huish*, 152.

77 *Ibid*, 199; Tomlinson, 621; PP 1867 xxxviii (1). 818.

78 Lee PCD, 43, 48.

79 The services to Bordeaux, Lyons, and Belfort exemplify this arrangement: *Bradshaw's Continental Guide*, January 1901, 34, 48–49a, 68.

80 SPS, 72; Marshall LYR ii. 233.

81 R267/132.

82 See H. Perkin, *The Origins of Modern English Society* (1969), 251.

83 *The Times*, 12 October 1874.

84 Findlay (ed. 1889), 125; 28 RM (1911) 455.

85 See Lee PCD, 23, 27; H. Ellis, *Railway Carriages in the British Isles* (1965), 38–41.

86 PP 1867 xxxviii. 818.

87 S. Sidney, *Rides on Railways* (1851), 12.

88 R. S. Surtees, *Town and Country Papers*, ed. E. D. Cuming (1929), 229.

89 *Orley Farm* (1862; World's Classics ed.), i. 154–5).

90 *Railway Traveller's Handy Book* (1971 ed.), 50.

91 See Acworth RE (5th ed., 1899), 456–60.

92 See G. Paish, *The British Railway Position* (1902), 154, 201, 285.

93 See MacDermot, ii. 235–6.

94 *History of the English People*, iii (1950 ed.), 276.

95 A. P. Stanley, *Life of Thomas Arnold* (4th ed., 1845), ii. 403.

96 *Public Addresses*, ed. J. E. T. Rogers (1879), 419.

97 PGA 5 & 6 Vict., cap. 55, sect. 20; 7 & 8 Vict., cap. 85, sects. 12–14.

98 See E. A. Pratt, *The Rise of Rail Power in War and Conquest* (1915), 2–8.

99 PP 1844 xi. 187–93.

100 See F. C. Mather, *Public Order in the Age of the Chartists* (1966 ed.), 161–3.

101 T. Raikes, *Journal* (1856–7), iv. 222.

102 R. Newton, *Victorian Exeter* (1968), 154.

103 J. Thomas, *The Skye Railway* (1977) 85–8.

104 *Annual Register*, 1910, 223–4.

105 PP 1846 xvii. 255–7.

106 J. G. Cox, *Castleman's Corkscrew* (1975), 9.

107 Devon RO, 2065M.SS 1/8: J. W. Buller to C. Russell, 8 August 1852.

108 MacDermot, i. 149–51.

109 Col. R. Delafield in 1860, quoted in M. Robbins, *Points and Signals* (1967), 180.

110 *Roads and Rails* (1862), 352–3.

111 Pratt, *Rise of Rail Power*, chap. 7.

112 8 RM (1901) 435–6.

113 See RTC, 222–6; *Reg. Hist.*, xii. 239.

114 Williams LSWR, ii. 63–7.

115 *VCH Wilts.*, iv. 290–1.

116 For these figures see Mitchell and Deane, 230.

117 J. Kieve, *The Electric Telegraph* (1973), 49, 56, 59, 65.

Chapter 16

1 *Transportation in Modern England* (1916), 589–601.

2 See for example *VCH Gloucestershire*, ii. 290; J. K. Fowler, *Recollections of old Country Life* (1894), 125–6.

3 E. Pennell Elmhirst, *Foxhound, Forest, and Prairie* (1892), 269–70;

T. F. Dale, *Foxhunting in the Shires* (1903), 102.
4 *Plain or Ringlets?* (1951 ed.), 309-10. For a balanced view of the matter see W. C. A. Blew, *The Quorn Hunt* (1894), 234, and Sir R. Carr, *English Foxhunting* (1976), 106-10.
5 R410/1510: memorial, November 1860.
6 29 *Builder* (1871) 291.
7 R529/113: letter of 20 September 1903.
8 E. Course, *Railways of Southern England: Secondary Lines* (1974), 133.
9 Ordnance Survey map, 1st ed. (David & Charles reprint, sheet 91).
10 *History of Hammersmith*, ed. P. D. Whitting (1965), 228.
11 There were at least five celebrated cases of this kind in these years (Boase, iv. 587; M. Robbins, *The North London Railway*, 1953 ed., 28).
12 See RTC, 89.
13 S. Pankhurst, *The Suffragette Movement* (Virago ed.), 110.
14 *England: its People, Polity, and Pursuits* (1885 ed.), 256.
15 R. C. Tombs, *The Bristol Royal Mail* [1899], 53-5.
16 M. Robbins, *Points and Signals* (1967), 143-7.
17 Among the cases of malversation that came to light in these years four more may be instanced: those of Charles Thomson on the Sheffield Ashton & Manchester Railway in 1841 (Dow GC, i. 33); G. H. Sale, Maryport & Carlisle, 1850 (papers in Cumbria RO, D/Sen); C. Stovin, London & South Western, 1852 (Williams LSWR, i. 219-20); and J. W. Stable, Manchester Sheffield

& Lincolnshire, 1853 (Dow GC, i. 154).
18 Robbins, *Points and Signals*, 139-43; Boase, iii. 76-7.
19 This statement is based on a sample of three substantial series of accidents in random years, 1849, 1871, and 1913.
20 PP 1881 lxxx. 566.
21 C. Highet, *The Wirral Railway* (1961), 3-5.
22 For examples see H. W. Disney, *Law of Carriage by Railway* (6th ed., 1923), 39-44.
23 *Ibid.*, 131-6.
24 *Anticipations* (1902), 20-1, 37.
25 T. F. Taylor, *The Fallacy of Speed* (1907), 7, 9, 21.
26 5 *Chambers' Journal* (1856) 227.
27 C. Wilson, *First with the News* (1985), 47.
28 See for example H. J. Dyos and D. H. Aldcroft, *British Transport* (1969); G. R. Hawke, *Railways and Economic Growth in England and Wales, 1840-70* (1970); T. C. Barker and C. I. Savage, *An Economic History of Transport in Britain* (3rd ed., 1974); P. S. Bagwell, *The Transport Revolution* (1974); M. C. Reed, *Investment in Railways in Britain, 1820-44* (1975); R. J. Irving, 'The Profitability and Performance of British Railways, 1870-1914', 31 *Economic History Review* (1978), 46-66; T. R. Gourvish, *Railways and the British Economy, 1830-1914* (1980).
29 *Leicester Chronicle*, 24 April 1841, based on report in the *Globe*.
30 A. Redford, *History of Local Government in Manchester*, ii (1940), 219. West Ham Corporation tried, unsuccessfully, to get the Railway

and Canal Commission to oblige the Great Eastern Railway to provide free lavatories at all its stations within the borough: PP 1896 xxv. 767.
31 W. Hames, *Arlesey* (1978), 30, 40; Wrottesley GNR, i. 176; E. Course, *Railways of Southern England: Independent and Light Railways* (1976), 126, 129.
32 See J. M. Clarke, *The Brookwood Necropolis Railway* (1983). A similar effort, made at East Barnet, lasted only from 1861 to 1867: Wrottesley GNR, i. 129-30.
33 Sir F. Hill, *Victorian Lincoln* (1974), 235; Lincs. Archives Committee, *18th Archivists' Report* (1967), 9.
34 J. E. Erichsen, *On Railway and other Injuries of the Nervous System* (1866), 46.
35 *Speeches*, ed. J. Bright and J. E. T. Rogers (1880), 161-2.
36 See for example J. Thomas, *North British Railway* (1969-75), ii, chap. 5.
37 Robertson, 334-5.
38 R. H. Campbell, quoted in Robertson, 315. Although English investment in Scottish railways grew much less important after 1850, it is worth pointing out that two-thirds of the capital required for building the Forth bridge in 1882-90 came from three English companies.
39 W. H. Hallam, *History of the Parish of East Lockinge* (1900), 111.
40 PP 1867 xxviii. (2), 639.
41 *Selected Literary Criticism*, ed. N. Shapira (1968 ed.), 224.
42 *The Age of the Railway* (1970), 101.

PHOTOGRAPHIC ACKNOWLEDGMENTS

Aberdeen University Library (George Washington Wilson Collection), 11–13, 20
Bristol University, 34
British Library, London, 14
British Museum, London, 35, 41
British Rail, 36
Crystal Palace Foundation (per R.C. Riley), 59
Glasgow Museum of Transport, 9
Ironbridge Gorge Museum (Elton Collection), 3, 4, 15, 22, 40, 45
Leicestershire County Council: Museums, Arts and Records Service, 40, 52
London Transport Museum, 56–7
National Gallery, London, 37
National Railway Museum, York, 1, 2, 5–8, 16, 18, 19, 21, 25, 26, 28 (F. Burtt), 29, 31, 32, 38, 42, 50, 51, 53–5, 60
Perth Art Gallery, 17
Public Record Office, London, 48
Science Museum, London, 24, 27
Scottish National Portrait Gallery, Edinburgh, 47
Jack Simmons, 49
D. C. Treffry, 10

INDEX

References given in the notes are not indexed. Entries in the index covering additional material printed in them appear in the form '379 (1/26)'. meaning page 379, chapter 1, note 26. References to pictures are in italics. Abbreviations: archt = architect; co = company; cont = contractor; eng = engineer.